LIFE IN THE 21ST CENTURY

LIFE in the 21ST CENTURY

compiled by
Viktoras Kulvinskas

edited by
Richard Tasca Jr.

Omangod Press
P.O. Box 64, Woodstock Valley, Connecticut, 06282

The illustrations in this book are by JEAN WHITE YERMAN.

COPYRIGHT c 1981, by Omangod Press. All rights reserved. Please obtain prior written consent of the publisher before reproducing any part of this book.

(Note: Certain constituent articles contained herein have retained their original copyright and were reprinted by permission. In such cases, copyright information directly follows the article).

ISBN: 0 - 933278 - 00 - 4

Printed in the United States of America.

To the Brothers and Sisters everywhere who are courageously living in the consciousness of unconditional Love, service and bringing in the Edenic future, to the Beings of Light who guide them, to all who share these visions of the boundless potentials of Mother Earth, and especially to the family of All Life Sanctuary, this book is lovingly dedicated.

A word of grateful acknowledgement is here extended to all the brothers and sisters from around the world who have so graciously shared their lives and their work within these pages. They are pioneers who walk the frontiers of consciousness with great courage. It is because of them, their love, respect, generosity, and kindness, their dedication and devotion, that the 21st century holds forth such great promise of rebirth.

Much thanks to the friends without whose inspiration, vision, and perserverance this project would not have materialized. To Jean (White) Yerman for her well chosen themes and inspired artwork. To Anthony Kainauskas for his management and business expertise and his undaunted patience in rescheduling deadlines. To James "Corky" Williams for the initial order and design. To Coyote for title suggestions. And, last, but not least, to Jean McClellan and Yola Ray for typesetting, and to Laurie Turcotte for typesetting, paste–up and artistic advise. Thank you!

INTRODUCTION

Dear Brothers and Sisters,

Time ceases to exist at the portals of Love. The Now is forever flowing through the electric space recreating the mass vision, the all—in—one, manifesting today what tomorrow is. In the harbor of the heart, anchored in peace, the body so pure, the love flows with the strength of a tidal wave through the labyrinth of a mind held by the emotions of time glued together by the quantum physics of the formless void.

The future is now. You can create the 21st century and live in it today. The choice between suffering, illusion, hell and madness, and the heights of heavenly joy, bliss, and health is decided by each one of us at every moment of our life. Your visions and aspirations create the future. Can we see through the smog filled hallways of the ego into the divine realm of the paradisical reality? Can we have our faith so strong and hope put into deeds of charity for love of self and others to serve the highest ideal so that the beauty of Mother Earth will again be radiant with carpets of green filled with specks of rainbow colors stretching forever into the blue sky and joining the waters in the yellow of sandy shores.

The Enlightened Master's employment service is desperately in need of co—workers, offering unlimited benefits of a guaranteed life of health and happiness. Just call out "Lord, I am yours; my body and soul are ready to be at one with the reality of love unconditional. Take me to my fields of labor. Teach me and use me. I surrender my life." Once offered, there is no quitting. There is evasion at times and delays, mistakes and lessons. But all becomes surmountable on the path.

Live in the now through full consciousness of the experiences and teachings of the present. Flow in love so that you have no past to pull you. Visualize and create your future through the no stress/resistory body so that the unlimited universal energy will flow through you in whatever voltage you can handle, thereby creating the future by the strength of your visualization.

Physical, mental and emotional purification are a must for optimal flow and capacity. To eliminate all resistance of an emotional nature, practice forgiveness and confess your misdeeds. Correct where possible your past mistakes and release them to the universe. On a physical level adhere to a regenerative diet of living foods to remove any obstruction to the flow of energy and to build an alkaline body which increases the polarity of each individual cell. Thereby the voltage of the body becomes strong enough so that the mental functions are burning clear; the death oriented ego loses its guiding force and becomes a survival mechanism of little value in a highly evolved temple guided by the high of unconditional love to the kundalini ascension within the spinal tree of life. The assurance of ascension of the sacred fire is the creation of the polarity between the root and crown chakra through the pranic build up of the physical manifestation of electric charges in the reproductive organs. Through breathing practices, the head becomes positively polarized; the kundalini is aroused through the strength of the heart pull (activated by love, service to humanity, God or one's beloved) to flow along unobstructed by emotional stress or physical blockages to open you to the joy and power and happiness inherent in each being.

The spirit has designed this threefold vehicle during the preconception days so that it would be perfect to experience the lessons on this planet. The vehicle has been severely altered by the earthly social environment due to ignorance of our true nature. Existing in what seemed to be a threatening environment, to insure the survival of our manifestation, the ego has been recreated to be concerned with survival of one's individual being instead of realizing that one's physical existence is dependent on unified action of All for All. For there is only one being. The most grounding, spiritually devastating experiences that ego toys with are those of our three lower chakras of power, sex, and food. Drainage of energy in these centers prevents the ascension of energy to the heart or love center.

Separation has led to the blindness of selfish materialism and lack of compassion. The light of Aquarius and the physical experience of the Piscean period are taking us out of the selfishness of the personalized ego existence into the practical awareness of the All for All. With patience we see that our brothers and sisters are part of our very being: their joy is our joy; their sorrow is our sorrow. Through this awareness we are instigating the most dramatic revolutionary change in our external and internal worlds.

Many psychics and prophets of today and the past have predicted cataclysms, radical weather patterns, earthquakes and violence. These are our karmic reward for our past and our present existence. They are the offshoots of the mental, emotional and physical vibrations we have emitted from our states of greed and selfishness. It takes less than ten percent of the planetary population dedicated to selfless service and unconditional love to alter the future patterns or at least to minimize the pain and suffering.

We can face all future problems with patience, forgiveness, insight and acts of love, or we can be filled with ego induced violence, fear and selfishness. If we proceed with the former, we will discover that we have more than we need to provide for our own and others' personal basic needs. Every problem has an inherent solution.

Those of you who are open to the light, follow the inner truth and work with dedication and be true to the daily teachings that you receive. You will also be a true help to the many brothers and sisters who are ready but are in need of teachers.

Each one of us has a specialized destiny: some of us are to take our teachings back to the land and live in peace with nature creating islands of safety for those who will be joining us at a later time; others are to stay in the cities, with normal jobs, to the last moment to carry on their teachings by example and works.

We need to apply ourselves, inducing the highest level of consciousness in all our actions. It may start with passive prayer and meditation and silence and then be taken to every level of our activity, all to be done with consciousness of beauty, order, awareness, and joy. Every act can be a meditation, from sweeping the floor to closing a door, from the way we walk, to the flow of relationships, smiling, dancing, inventing, working, eating or fasting. Everything one does can be transformed. Your life's drama on the physical, mental and emotional planes can be a love offering to your beloved, found in every brother and sister that you serve by seeing them as an extension of yourself in unity with the one God flooding the electro–magnetic wave matrix of loving light.

The opening of these centers to unlimited light allows you to work with the three dimensions (physical, emotional and spiritual) and create the future in the form of the image held. The rate of transformation is totally dependent on clarity and non–ego universalism (universal expressions are desired knowingly or unknowingly by all; personal ego–self–motivated visions are competing with others and have a long waiting period for actualization and only a temporary existence).

Create your own personal reality. At any time you can choose to be in paradise. You consciously choose each film clip of your life's movie. We are co–creators of the universe made in the image of God with an all inclusive reality within as without, with the power to recreate in the macrocosm what we create within the microcosm.

Within the context of this book you will find visionaries who stepped outside of the context of their imagination, believing their visions, willing them to manifest, and giving them reality. This book, and the many contributions which it contains, is only the branches of the forest that is growing within the wastelands of ego–created civilization. This is the forest of fruit and shelter and joy within which the dream of new beginnings is taking root. A new way is evolving: a one for all and all for one and within all life forms; a reverence and respect where we see ourselves extended into all life forms; at one–ment with all essence of life that penetrates and creates the universal wholeness. Our joy is my joy, my joy is our joy is the reality we are creating.

Eternally yours,

Xteras

Woodstock Valley, Connecticut
May 25, 1981

FOREWORD

We are living in exciting and trying times. Our civilization is delicately poised between the abyss of annihilation and the broad horizon of renewal. Humankind is everywhere threatened with extinction: hovering overhead and lurking nearby are the dark shadows of nuclear holocaust, of war, of famine and starvation, of pollution, of disease, and of the stress, anxiety and tension of twentieth century life. Harbingers of despair everywhere fill the air with prophecies of eventual doom.

And yet, in our time, in the midst of darkness gleams a great light, an inextinguishable light: a light of rebirth of our spirit, of renewal of our planet, and of hope for a new world. Around the world a phalanx of dedicated beings are joining forces. Armed with a burning love and a desire to recreate our earth, they have consecrated themselves to God, to their own higher selves, and have dedicated their lives to the restoration of humanity to her pristine godliness. Surely, their hope will prevail. Surely, their goodwill will triumph. Surely, their love will conquer all.

Ours is a time of great healing when the wounds which afflict our souls, our societies, and our planets will be submerged in the flood of light which comes to quench the eons old desire of men and women everywhere for total Love. Several major threads, spheres of activity or trends can be identified in this intricate tapestry which is the Earth's current transformation.

First, and perhaps foremost among these is a reaffirmation of spirituality: materialism, tried and found lacking is relegated now to the heap of the past. The brilliant reality of the human being's spiritual essence, of its divine nature, of its inherent godliness is being everywhere posited and acquiesced to. The principle fundament of the New Age which is upon us is the reality of the spiritual realms, which, penetrating ever more into our beings and lives, will inundate the Earth with wave after wave of divine consciousness and cosmic love. The New Age is an age of the spiritual.

Second, there is evident a widespread burgeoning of the natural healing arts predicated upon a new wholistic paradigm. From dietary refinement and physical culture for the healing of the physical component of our beings, to meditation, chanting, spiritual initiation, and other practices for the realization and perfection of the more elevated aspects of human nature, all involve a re−emergence and affirmation of the person as a whole, integrated universe, a matrix of universal love and divine energies. The use of nutritional technologies, particularly the path of living vegetarian foods, which, communicating the light of the sun and the life forces of the universe to the cells of our bodies, promise the progressive spiritualization of our corporeal selves. The fruit of the vines of the earth, her green grasses and fecund vegetation hold the key to the purification and perfection of the holy temples which are our bodies, their restoration to pristine godliness. In the New Age, women and men everywhere will enjoy the vibrant health which is their birthright and which enables them to radiate the spirit which is their essential nature.

A third major trend in human activity which is everywhere evident is the reorientation and redefinition of lifestyle patterns. Community life, the coalescence of individual souls into a unity of purpose and goals, is emerging as a viable option in the struggle to create meaningful lives. The unnatural environs of the cities are being forsaken in the quest for cleaner air, more peaceful surroundings and attunement to Nature. And dependence on commerce and industry is being replaced by the ideals of self–sufficiency. In the New Age, natural lifestyles which are based on a sincere and true reverence for the energies and realities of the earth and which optimize our capacity for attunement to the harmonious forces of nature will predominate.

The final major tendency which is constitutive of the renewal of our beings and our planet is the dissolution of all self–imposed limitations in the realization of the infinite possibilities inherent in our nature. Surely, we are not yet what we can be and will become. In the coming age, latent potentials will be actualized: psychic phenomena such as astral travel, bilocation and telepathy will be considered normative; a marked increase in longevity, even to the age of the biblical patriarchs will be witnessed, due to the cumulative effect, over generations, of natural lifestyles and fruitarian diet; transition to other realms will be conscious and at will, as death will lose its hold on increasingly aware and spiritualized men and women. The vast limitlessness and interconnectness of the Universe will be mirrored and made manifest in the life of the individual. The New Age will be an era of boundlessness.

O brothers and sisters, the Spirit of Love is the essence of the new world to come, the matrix for all future reality. Yearning for light and transformed by Love, our energies, dedicated to Truth and harmony with the Universe, will merge and coalesce into the transformative and resurrectional powers from which will be created a new divine life in the twenty–first century.

> Then I saw a new heaven and a new earth...coming down from God out of heaven, as beautiful as a bride all dressed for her husband. Then I heard a loud voice call from the throne, "You see this city? Here God lives among people. He will make his home among them, they shall be his people and he will be their God. He will wipe away all tears from their eyes; there will be no more death, and no more mourning or sadness. The world of the past is gone." (Revelations 21:1–4)

Richard Tasca Jr.

Woodstock Valley, Connecticut
May 19, 1981

EDITOR'S NOTE

We feel it incumbent upon ourselves to express to all our readers our policy statement on the use of inclusive language. We at Omangod Press are aware that language used generically (i.e., words such as "man" and "brotherhood") unconsciously excludes women. While we believe that the use of exclusive language is representative of the predominantly patriarchal and male—oriented historical and social context from which civilization is emerging, we are nevertheless dedicated to the achievement of androgynous consciousness. To this end, we are making all feasible attempts to utilize inclusive language in our publications.

We have become further aware, as part of our own personal evolutions, of the connotations of exclusivity which may be inferred from the name of our company, Omangod Press. We expect that, in line with our new policy, a name change will be implemented in the near future, as soon as pragmatic realities allow.

Because of the nature of the material which comprises "Life in the 21st Century", we were unable to edit to insure the inclusivity which we desire. All attempts have been made to preserve the original tenor of the many articles, essays and letters. Grammatical and syntactical singularities were not altered so that the author's intent and peculiar nuance might shine through.

TABLE OF CONTENTS

INTRODUCTION   i

FOREWARD   iv

EDITOR'S NOTE   vi

PART I: THE SPROUTING OF THE NEW AGE

    SECTION I: IN NORTH AMERICA

        AQUARIUS LIGHT   /3
        R.I.S.E.: RAINBOW ISLAND SANCTUARY OF EVOLUTION   /4
        MORE FROM R.I.S.E.   /5
        HEALING ON HAWAII   /7
        HIPPOCRATES HEALTH INSTITUTE: SAN DIEGO   /8
        THE GOOD LIFE ON GOD'S LAND   /10
        THE GARDEN OF EDEN SPIRITUAL SOCIETY   /11

    SECTION II. SOUTH AMERICA

        THE YOGA OF SURVIVAL   /14
        THE YOGA OF SURVIVAL II   /18
        PACHAMAMA : MOTHER EARTH   /22
        THE PACHAMAMA (MOTHER EARTH) NOW SPEAKS   /25
        PARADISIAN NEWSLETTER   /26
        PARADISE LOST   /29
        EQUADOR: IS IT PARADISE?   /30
        SETTLING THE TROPICS   /32
        PROGRESS IN PARADISE   /35
        MORE FROM THE EQUATOR   /36

    SECTION III. IN CENTRAL AMERICA

        LIVING WITH TEMPTATION   /39
        BELIZE   /40
        NOTES ON PARADISE   /41
        FRUITARIAN EXPERIENCE   /42
        MANGOES, PAPAYAS, ETC.   /45

    SECTION IV. ELSEWHERE

        CULTURE SHOCK   /47
        PUERTO RICO   /49
        DOMINICA   /49

PART II: SPREADING THE NEW AGE AWARENESS

SECTION I. THE NEW AGE IN ACTION

LETTER OF APPEAL; FROM DR. ANN WIGMORE /55
LIFELIGHT: ON THE ROAD WITH LIVING FOOD /57
LIFELIGHT: UPDATE /61
THE GARDEN OF LIFE LIVING FOODS /64
THE 21ST CENTURY CHEF /65
RUN FOR AMERICA FOUNDATION, INC. /66
RUNNERS CLAIM VEGETABLE POWER /68

SECTION II. NEW AGE PLANS AND HOPES

THE PLAN /70
C.I.C.E.: CENTER OF INTERNATIONALS FOR CONSERVING THE ECOSYSTEM /74
B.R.A.I.N.: BIOLOGICAL RESISTANCE AGAINST INSTITUTION NUTS /75
TELLING MILLIONS ABOUT VEGETARIANISM FOR PENNIES /76
PUBLIC SERVICE ANNOUNCEMENTS: ORGANIZING TOOLS /79
HOW YOU CAN BE A VEGETARIAN ACTIVIST AT YOUR COLLEGE /80
INTO THE ATETIES /81

PART III. THE NEW AGE KNOWLEDGE

SECTION I. RESEARCH

SCIENCE SUPPORTS FRUITARIANISM /87
VEGETARIANISM AND HEALTH /89
ANCIENT SECRET FOR ETERNAL YOUTH /89
A HARMFUL SHIFT IN TODAY'S MENU /92
PYRAMIDS AND WHEATGRASS /96
MORE PYRAMIDS AND WHEATGRASS /97
BIO—MUSIC AND THE PSYCHIC KISS /98
THE PINEAL GLAND /103
MORE ON THE PINEAL /104
THE RESONANT BRAIN /105

SECTION II. MAN—MADE DANGERS

UNION OF CONCERNED SCIENTISTS /118
RADIATION /121
WHAT YOU SHOULD KNOW ABOUT THE HAZARDS OF NUCLEAR POWER /123
GREEN GRASS NEWCLEAR POWER /125
THE MARGIN OF LIFE /128
AGRICULTURE AND COMMUNITY /133
ENERGY AND CLIMATE /136
THE DANGERS OF ALUMINUM /139
SUCCESS? /146
EARTH AND THE U.F.O. PHENOMENON /147

PART IV. NEW PATHWAYS TO HEALTH

SECTION I. THE WHOLISTIC PARADIGM

VIKTORAS KULVINSKAS: PLANETARY HEALER   /153
SYNERGETIC MEDICINE   /159
THE FIVE POINTS   /164
THE STORY OF CREATION   /166
SYSTEMOLOGY   /167
THE SPIRIT OF HEALTH   /171

SECTION II. POSITIVE MIND AND WELL-BEING

MESSAGE FROM "I AM"   /173
PSYCHIC HEALING   /176
RAINBOWS TO THE RESCUE   /176

SECTION III. NUTRITION AND HEALTH

HEALTH INSURANCE   /178
VEGETARIANISM   /180
FOREVER HIGH   /186
NEVER SICK   /190
WHEATGRASS AGAINST DISEASE: A GREAT HOPE FOR AILING HUMANITY   /194
WHEATGRASS THE CURE ALL?   /198
MEDICINAL USE OF ONIONS   /200
THE RAW FOODS DIET AND WEIGHT LOSS   /204
RAW FOODIST MISTAKES   /208
COLDS FOR HEALTH   /209
ARTHRITIS   /213
WHAT'S THERE TO EAT?   /219
OIL FOR PEOPLE   /223
THE MENSTRUAL MYTH   /224
THE IMPORTANCE OF NUTRITION IN EYE DEVELOPMENT AND VISION FUNCTION   /236
BIRTH CONTROL: A LOOK AT NATURE   /242

SECTION IV. INTERNAL HYGIENE

FASTING, CHLOROPHYLL, AND COLOR   /253
DISCOVERING FASTING   /262
TWO GREAT MEN   /267
CONSTIPATION AND OXYGENATED INTESTINAL IRRIGATION   /271
SATKARMASADANA: PART I   /273
SATKARMASADANA: PART II   /282
SATKARMASADANA: PART III   /288
THE CURATIVE CRISIS   /297
EVIDENCE FOR INTESTINAL TOXEMIA: AN INESCAPABLE CLINICAL PHENOMENON   /300

PART V. NEW AGE CHILDREN: THE FUTURE HOPE

SECTION I. CHILD BIRTH IN THE NEW AGE

    BEYOND MIDWIVES, MICROBIOTICS AND THE PHYSICAL REALM   /317
    HEALTHY MOTHER: HEALTHY BABY   /321
    A CHILD'S SONG TO A MOTHER'S HEART   /324
    WHITE LIGHT BIRTHING   /327

SECTION II. POSITIVE CHILDBEARING

    A SIGNIFICANT RIPPLE IN THE SEA OF LIFE   /330
    NATURAL MAMA   /334
    NOTES ON BEARING A CHILD   /335
    A HEALTHY CHILD DESIRES HEALTH   /337

PART IV. PEOPLE LIVING IN THE 21ST CENTURY TODAY

SECTION I. BREATHARIANISM

    AIR AS FOOD?   /341
    THE PHYSIOLOGY OF BREATHING   /343
    SISTER SUSAN KURUVILLA: STIGMATIST NUN OF SOUTH INDIA   /349

SECTION II. SUPERHUMANS

    DR. GENE STANLEY   /357
    REAL LIFE SUPERMAN   /359
    WILEY BROOKS: LIVING ON LIQUIDS   /361

PART VII. TESTIMONIALS

SECTION I. TRANSFORMATION

    REBIRTH   /365
    RAW FOODS AND BEAUTIFUL FEELINGS   /367
    WHEATGRASS AND PSYCHIC HEALING   /369
    DOCTOR GOES NATURAL   /370
    HEALING   /375
    ALMOST A FRUITARIAN   /376
    FRUITARIAN ARTIST   /379
    FRUITARIANISM IN THE HINTERLAND   /374
    AS A TREE GROWS, THE SPIRIT UNFOLDS   /382

APPENDIX: FOOTNOTES AND REFERENCES   /389

PART I

THE SPROUTING OF THE NEW AGE

We are witnessing in our time the emergence of a New Age. In this coming age spiritual values will triumph. Love will prevail. Peace will reign and people everywhere will live in symbiotic oneness with the elemental forces of Planet Earth. Women and men, in returning to the path of Nature for which they were intended by the Creator will attain to the bliss, the harmony, and the health which are their heritage and birthright.

From the remote desert and mountain areas of North America, to Australia, the Carribbean and South America, this new awareness is beginning to manifest in multiplicitous form and diverse fashion. The articles and letters which comprise this first part of "Life In The 21st Century" give first hand reports of some of these pioneering ventures. From raw food caravans traversing the West Coast of the United States to Paradise builders colonizing the remote reaches of the Andes Mountains, all have this in common: to work for their own evolution and the upliftment of mankind and to herald the dawning of the golden age of Spirit, of Health and of Love.

Section I
In North America

AQUARIUS LIGHT

Greetings Sisters and Brothers. We are Aquarius Light, a non–profit non–organization, our purpose is to serve and enlighten mankind on earth. We are now studying and practicing various forms of natural healing (acupressure, shiatzu, iridology, reflexology) and a few others we are not well versed on yet, plus dietary transitions to heighten man's level of consciousness. One of us is practicing a fruitarian diet, the others practicing a live raw food diet, but aspiring a fruitarian diet when we reach a clearer pollution–free environment. (We believe the fruitarian diet was the natural diet of man, before he devolved). Some of us have left northern points in this country to Miami Beach, Florida but only as a stopover to experience the sub–tropical climate and detoxify before leaving the country. We are moving our base for now to Surinam , South America, a pollution–free environment.

We as Aquarius Light want to elevate man's potential by first realizing more our own potential and experiencing a much deeper feeling by connecting with the God potential housed within all individuals. As New Age publishers we hope to someday submit books that we complete in the next four to eight seasons to you for approval. With the information contained in these books we hope that our brothers and sisters will realize the potential within themselves and seek to know their real–selves.

This being our initial communication with you, we would like to stay in close contact with you from South America. Letters will be sent to you as significant changes–experiences occur and hopefully by our fruits you will let other New Age organizations–groups, publishers magazines, authors now about us. We would like you to send us names and addresses of other New Age publishers magazines, groups–organizations, it would be deeply appreciated. Also we would like to order a New Age Directory from you with an accompanying book order form.

It has been pleasant touching you in this form and we hope you just stay open to the flow of Grace that has made this all possible. We thank you and we thank the Almightly for providing for us.

Light, Love and Nature
Aquarius Light, October 30 1978

R.I.S.E.
RAINBOW ISLAND SANCTUARY FOR EVOLUTION

Doctrine and Covenants

We are dedicated to the evolution and perfection of mankind in body, mind, and spirit and to live in harmony with our natural environment, Mother Nature, and the forces of the universe, God our Father.

We seek amongst us the commmon goal of triunal perfection thru consciousness of truth and by living the truth shall be free of the bondages of ignorance, fear, pain and death.

We believe, as God's children, that the rightfull place of worship is within each of us — our minds, our hearts and souls. We recognize the body as the temple and sanctuary of God's spirit, the life force. Thru faith and work we seek to resurrect the temple so that God's spirit and energies may dwell and govern fully within us.

We feel, as gods children, that we may glorify our Heavenly Father and Earthly Mother by seeking the highest expressions of perfection, thru living as best as we can in accordance with natural law, in our work, play, sleeping, eating, breathing etc.

We acknowledge and respect all diverse teachings, knowing that there are many paths to the same end. We must all progress at our own pace and learn to love and respect one another for what we are, regardless of seeming difference. We are here to help one another, as individuals, yet all part of one whole, and shall be sanctuary for each other. Thru time and trial we shall obtain the triumph of peace, harmony and balance within our temple and shall outwardly reflect the greatest love of gods spirit.

We shall endeavor to create living conditions conducive to helping us achieve the purity and perfection we desire, in our homes, lands, country and planet, in accordance with natural law.

We recognize, as a means of transcendence, an exclusive fruit diet as the ideal and proper food for the body, mind and spirit, yet during transition being supplemented by nuts, herbs, seeds, grains and vegetables. These should preferably be consumed in the raw, living state grown by our own hand, free of poisonous residues, pesticides, etc.

We do not believe in the exploitation of animals for food, labor, or as pets. The spirit of God is manifest in all life forms as a free expression of His will. All life is sacred and shall be revered and respected as such. Plants and animals are sensitive and subject to the same stimuli and forces as man — heat, cold, pain, pleasure, etc. and should be regarded with brotherly love.

We recognize the self—healing powers of body, mind and spirit, supplemented by proper diet, herbs, natural therapeutics and the divine will of God to be our only doctor — if one so chooses. It is against our faith in the laws of God and nature, as we worship, to desecrate the temple (body) by use of needle, scalpel, x—rays, chemicals, metals, smoke, drugs or the like; and reserve our God given right to choose such treatments and practices as we feel is in accordance with His divine will. We reserve the right to die in dignity, if it be our desire, rather than be kept alive artificially by the hands of man, in defiance of Gods will for us.

the right to die in dignity, if it be our desire, rather than be kept alive artificially by the hands of man, in defiance of Gods will for us.

We shall use income and expenditures to perpetuate living conditions suitable for the attainment of perfection equal to all. If living as a family or group all decisions shall be made by mutual agreement and consent. We address one another as brother and sister as title, all equal in mutual esteem of the same spirit force within each and all of us.

We maintain the right to express our beliefs to others, thru all available means, so as to spread the good word that we are Gods chidren, and that He loves us and desires for us to have life abundant and to live eternally in peace, harmony and love, in perpetual health and happiness in His glorious presence (Rom. 2:7, Rev. 21:1−8, 22; 12−14, John 10:10). To this fullfillment we shall live.

DEATH LIFE DEATH   Red   Orange   Yellow   Green   Blue   Indigo   Violet

acid   positive   hot   yang   matter   solar   male   retention   pain   proton

Note that the colors of yellow, green, and blue are the predominant colors of nature and that most higher life forms exist within this range of the spectrum.

alkaline   negative   cool   yin   energy   lunar   female
release   pleasure   electron

It is erroneously taught that Life and Death are two extremes, whereas in reality we find that Life generally exists between the extremes of the spectrum which requires being centered in a specific balance between the opposing forces. We see that a move toward either extreme may cause an imbalance, resulting in Death. To perserve our Life, we must recognize the opposing forces outside of us which effect us also internally and learn to maintain a balance thru proper living in harmony with nature and cosmic energies and practicing self discipline in the face of temptations, as especially regards one's dietary which exerts a direct immediate, cumulative effect on our own internal environment and balances. So we see that even our Life or existence is a matter of adoption to maintain a balance and harmony between our internal and external forces or environments. Even the tree, grown strong from within, must bond with the winds, the forces from without, or it shall break and cease it's existence. We must learn to be flexible in our search for truth and life and to adapt to change. The permanence of our Life is dependent upon the impermanence of the opposing forces of Death.

MORE FROM R.I.S.E.

Hello and Love. Many people ask us, what is R.I.S.E.? At present we are an association of friends and acquaintances who hold, and are trying to live certain ideals. We are a church — a church of consciousness. Membership, as such, is not limited by age, race, sex, money, titles, time or distance, etc. There are thousands of us who may be separated physically, yet we stand united spiritually, thru the consciousness of ideals and truths which we hold sacred in our minds and hearts. Our philosophy is one of harmony, of maintaining the balance and harmony of our internal environments, our own being; and then to live in harmony with our external environ−nature. This will enable us to achieve the health and happiness we desire in life.

Fortunately many of us are awakening and are now conscious of the truth; that we are living against and apart from nature and the forces of life, (sunlight, pure air, water, food, etc). Such practices cultivate negative or death factors (dis−ease, pain, mental anguish, aging, death). We recognize that we have a fair amount of freedom as regards controlling the harmony of our internal environment (diet), yet we are subject to the dis−harmony of the external environment that we live in. We are often surrounded by people or circumstances which may tend to discourage or prevent us from living our ideals of health and happiness thru harmony in spirit and nature.

There are many barriers to overcome, individually and collectively. We feel it would be good for those of us who desire to share and experience a particular lifestyle, to focus our scattered energies into a community, a sanctuary, where we can live and work together in pursuit of our common ideals. We of the R.I.S.E. consciousness are endeavering to synthesize a model community, here on the paradisian island of Kauai. Such will be a sanctuary, for those who desire communion with God, nature and one another in the true spirit of love and worship thru proper living.

To bring about this unification, we need to communicate. Thru communication with one another we will discover ourselves and others like ourselves. Communicating will make us aware of each other and strengthen our spirit individually and collectively and enable us better to seek the truth and endeavor to live in such ways as to promote life abundant in health and happiness. By communicating we can bring about a unified−consciousness of energies and resources and manifest a sanctuary of peace, love, health and happiness − not only as an isolated community, but on the earth as a whole.

We hope that you do share an interest in joining our community efforts. Please let us know if you desire to participate and how you can help. Your financial support is appreciated.

We of R.I.S.E are a church of consciousness of the truth of life. R.I.S.E. is all of us who desire truth and life abundant; and who seek to evolve into the high being we were created as. Thru seeking the truth and applying it in our lives, we shall gain life in abundance − God's gift to us all. Be we together or apart, we are one.

Shalom

R.I.S.E., Rainbow Island Sanctuary For Evolution, P.O. Box 1986, Lihue, Kauai, Hawaii, 96766

HEALING ON HAWAII

Dear Raw Food Community. Om Shanti and Aloha from the Valley Isles. It would be greatly appreciated if you could send your literature and a list of persons who expressed interest in raw foods and/or community development, community healing, esoteric, yoga. For years I have been dreaming of an Essene raw food community here in Hawaii. As the water is pure, the ocean warm and clean and crystal aqua blue. There are rainbows everyday. It's sunny and warm all the time except it rains enough so that there are seldom ever droughts and the gardens get watered. Beautiful rainbow exotic flowers everywhere. Lots of beautiful cosmic New Age brothers and sisters and lots of fruit and a year round growing season — cool breezes so it rarely gets too hot, mountains to climb, springs, streams, pools, waterfalls and nature in abundance. I think the highest elevation here is either 8,000 or 10,000 feet on Maui. So you have the cool mountain air to retreat to also and lots of healing earth and people energy.

My soul—mate and I are both into healing. I've been studying herbs on my own for about four years now, we both have and we went to a wholistic school of healing in Santa Cruz for a month. He may be going to an acupuncture school in January if it comes together - it will be a two year course at the end of which he will have a license to practise acupuncture anywhere in the country. We've also been studying touch for health, polarity, foot reflexology, iridology, color healing, psychic healing and gem therapy. All these subjects we're relatively new at, but would like to be more involved with people who are also into them. We have been on a raw food diet for about three and a half years and our health has improved immensely. Along with doing yoga, pranayama and the meditation every day.

My ideal is a raw foods community where those who want can have their own houses, along with a group effort to build and maintain a new age school for children, communal farms and fruit orchards and herb gardens and flowers. A healing center to care for the sick and to learn and a center to gather and make music, dance, and celebrate the joys of God's creation.

When I was on the crater, one full moon, 3 moons ago or maybe 2 (the one in Aquarius), I had a vision and in this vision these rainbow beings of light came to me and told me the golden age was coming soon and everyone was going to be filled with light and peace, and our bodies and the earth would be totally healed. That we were some of the many pioneers of the coming age. If you know of any people with the ability to organize great events such as a new age community with lots of land here in Hawaii, please let us know. We will be able to get together some money energy as my husband's father told us he would help us get from three to five acres of land here. Of course this is by no means enough of a community of people of that kind but if enough people could get together to direct some green energy into healing light paradise on earth energy it could really happen here.

Om Shanthi.
Osalina and Goldi

HIPPOCRATES HEALTH INSTITUTE
SAN DIEGO

The sun shines bright in Lemon Grove, where Hippocrates Health Institute of San Diego has recently relocated. Built on a hilltop, the new facility is surrounded by towering trees and spacious lawns. A symphony of color greets the visitors as they enter the grounds of the attractive health—regenerating center.

As visitors turn from the road into the entrance of Hippocrates West, which is situated only seven minutes from downtown San Diego, they are immediately impressed by the serene, peaceful, country atmosphere. A dozen structures on terraced levels are clustered around the administration building, which houses offices, a lounge, dining room and kitchen center—a kitchen that has no stove or cooking implements, no freezers or conventional appliances, since only natural, unprocessed, raw foods are served. The surrounding buildings include exercise, wheatgrass growing and juicing, class rooms and sleeping quarters for staff and guests.

Hippocrates West was opened in El Cajon on September 19, 1976, with Raychel Solomon as its Director. It grew so quickly that it soon became apparent that larger quarters would be needed to house the guests. When the present site was found it was a dream realized, for it seemed as though it had been planned to fit the specific needs of Hippocrates with atractive, comfortable accomodations able to serve 90 guests.

The Institute warmly welcomes all who wish to learn its secrets to healthier, happier and success—oriented living. A caring, sharing and loving spirit permeates the 3½ acre property. Hippocrates West is a Mission of the Free Sacred Trinity Church, an independent, non—sectarian church, compatible with all denominations of religious faith. The Church believes the body to be the Temple of the Holy Spirit and the program nourishes the whole being by attending to and respecting the Body, Mind and Spirit. The church tenets agree with all scriptures that teach a doctrine of honesty, purity and positive faith of brotherhood in a world in dire need of positive living values.

Nearly two thousand alumni have included residents from Mexico, Canada, South America, Australia, New Zealand, France and Switzerland. Ages have varied from two months to eighty—nine years. The differences in generations, life—styles, cultures, philosophies and religious beliefs seem to blend into a loving, caring and healing environment, pleasing and sustaining to all. The stimulation of interesting conversation helps to keep the level of enthusiasm high and the emphasis on problem areas low.

To protect the peaceful environment during the week, an open house is held every Sunday. Vistors are invited to tour the grounds at 4:30, and view the living quarters and attend a lecture, and those who wish to stay, may partake of a "living food" dinner. Eydie Mae Hunsberger, author of "How I Conquered Cancer Naturally", lectures on the first and third Sunday. Other speakers lecture on alternate Sundays. This informative weekly event attracts hundreds of visitors concerned with

Raychel Solomon, Founder–Director of the Hippocrates Health Institute, San Diego with produce from the Institute's organic gardens.

better living alternatives. Many travel hundreds of miles expressly to attend the open house.

As the only chapter of Hippocrates Health Institute of Boston, the curriculum follows closely the Ann Wigmore regimen toward a natural lifestyle. Guests are encouraged to stay three weeks to most effectively experience body–cleansing, positive mental attitudes and nutritional food adherence. Old habits fall away as new truths are examined understood and accepted. Guests learn to take responsibility for themselves. Since the body is the temple of the Holy Spirit, guests are taught a procedure of ridding the body of disease–producing toxins and regenerating a healthy state by the use of the ultimate in nutrition from living foods (fresh fruits, vegetables, seeds, etc.). Proper combinations of foods are observed, as well as emotional balance and faith in nature's way to health. Physical exercise rounds out the program to bring vitality and joy to all who follow the Hippocrates discipline.

The weekly schedule begins with orientation on Monday morning and follows with classes morning, afternoon and evening through Friday. This encompasses positive attitudes, study of the digestive system, the eliminative system, polarity exercise, reflexology, iridology, food combining, how to grow and juice wheatgrass, how to prepare rejuvelac, sauerkraut and seed sauces, enticing recipes and sprouting. Meals are preceded by a prayer circle, which prepares the body to accept the food in gratitude and reverence.

Since established in Boston nearly a quarter of a century ago, many thousands have experienced Dr. Ann Wigmore's methods and testify to its effectiveness. The western branch has enabled thousands more to experience the joys of good health and vitality. An added benefit realized by guests is the new age awareness that live foods can be a pertinent factor in dealing with rising food costs as well as the increasing food shortages.

Though the facility is comparable to many luxury resorts, it is the philosophy of the administrative board to keep the price within a comfortable range for more to enjoy. Living quarters range from dormitories at $145.00 per week to luxury suites at $350.00 per week per person. Other options are semi-private and private rooms. Each room has adjoining bath. Partial scholarship opportunities are also available by working four hours per day to help defray tuition costs.

Additional information and a brochure are available upon request.

Hippocrates Health Institute of San Diego, 6970 Central Avenue, Lemon Grove, California 92045

THE GOOD LIFE ON GODS LAND

Dear Viktoras, I unexpectedly heard you speak at the Rainbow Healing Gathering in New Mexico. I was very inspired to meet so many people doing purification. For years prior to the time someone turned me on to Johnny Lovewisdom, we had been working on developing Hi-Protein meals to do our farming. We learned how to make a Chinese food – Kofu whereby you soak bread dough to leach out carbo-hydrates and obtain a 44% protein product. Now finally we get the light and the message. Fruits and greens for human beings!

Anyway I understand you are checking out different places for the start of a light community. First I would like to be in touch with your developments along this line. Second I would like to suggest my community here in Kentucky as a landing place for your farm/healing center. Kettle, Kentucky is a very rural tobacco farming community with high steep ridges and long hollows. Oak, poplar, cedar, maple, beech, hickory trees predominate. Dale Hollow Lake is one of the finest lakes in Tennessee, Kentucky with warm Caribbean blue-green water. Unfortunately houseboats and motor boats are used but the lake is 65 miles long with 500 miles of shoreline and countless coves and inlets to be able to be fairly secluded. My neighbors just bought a farm with 12 apple trees, 2 pear, and 1 cherry tree, 6 miles north of Burkesville. (Cumberland County Seat, South Central Kentucky). They paid $150. an acre for 218 acres. Quite reasonable. Of course now they can build their own pond or lake.

There are 10-12 farms "hippie farms" now in the area. We have an established Food Co-op supplied by Eden Foods from Ann Arbor, Michigan. I live on God's land, the only free and open land in the country, I believe. Everyone is invited to live here. A very rich artist — Noel Singer bought the original piece and is now acquiring the neighboring farm to make God's land 1000 acres. I mentioned that my neighbors are vacating their houses on God's land and if you know anybody desperately trying to get on some land, suggest Kentucky to them.

I have been farming organically now for three gardens, my soil is the finest you could imagine now. Sandy and I planted 50 fruit trees in our hollow. We would like some spiritually oriented neighbors to help us carry on the work here in the back of the hollow. There is Sufi dancing every Sunday at one of the farms nearby. Our new diet has helped considerably with our hatha yoga and attempts at meditation. We have Kriyananda's mail–order course.

Thirdly, I have enclosed the depressing negative news — the particle beam gun. The battle of the meat–eaters may begin soon and the vision you had in "Love Your Body" of the Fruitarian Community in South America should be the idea/goal to work for. It's not working out of fear but working for sanity to leave this United States of "Babylonia".

Om Mani Padme Hum.
Bill Bardsley, RR 171A God's Land, Kettle, Kentucky 42752

THE GARDEN OF EDEN SPIRITUAL SOCIETY

How about a beautiful community to live in where cars are not allowed except as absolutely necessary work vehicles, (agriculture, building, delivering, etc.), and then at 5–10 miles an hour only, for the safety of children and animals. How about thousands of every variety of fruit and nut trees planted everywhere on the community land — solar energy homes, hot houses and food bearing plants everywhere in the community instead of a bunch of bushes and trees that give no food (commonly called ornametals). A community that is totally in respect of all God's creatures regardless of size (cows to ants). In other words, teach our children and anyone else the respect of all life and to kill nothing consciously. Schools where the children can go and not have to deal with the mentality of the flesh–eaters and the general environment of the meat eating schools (toy guns, Big Macs, fighting, etc.)

But, where they can learn about the growing of food, grafting of trees, spelling, numbers, championship non–contact athletics that are taught gently, healing, the making of clothes, building of houses and above all, diet in a place where spirituality and individual prayer are daily and taught as good and free according to one's faith. We can all build such a place if we gather and put our energy into such a place happening. We have many brothers and sisters all over the world, waiting for the land to appear, and right now the Garden of Eden Spiritual Society is in it's birth stages in this world (a few years old).

Goals

1. Dedicated to planting food bearing plants everywhere, (parks, schools, neighborhoods, house plants, etc).

2. Teaching the human race by the establishment of totally vegetarian, organic, self-sufficient communities (preferably in insolated areas, away from pollution) that we can live in Eden as a people if we just put every plant around us, food or herb bearing, thus eliminating the need for commercial agriculture (semi's hauling unripened picked green food to market), but picking it right from the living source of energy that grew it and eating it at it's highest point of ripening, thus inducing the strongest and healthiest bodies in the world, eating from the tree of life.

3. Bringing peace to the human race by the teaching of the oldest and highest of laws in the universe — "Thou shalt not kill", and "Do unto others as you would have them do unto you". To hurt ants, mice, cockroaches, etc., or any of God's beautiful creatures or beautiful brothers and sisters in different life forms is the cause of disharmony on this planet Earth, and is the reason society has all the problems today and yesterday. It has happened because the powers of the creation have intended we see what living in Hell is like before sending us on to higher places in the galaxies of time and space. In this world, murder, cheating, stealing, lying, killing, sickness, etc. are common. The human race is doing all those things to the animals, birds, fish, insects, etc. and there will never be peace until man and woman are evolved past the point of killing and eating the beloved creatures of Eden and respecting all life as sacred as themselves.

To many of us who have evolved past that primitive point in time, we thank the powers of our creator (Mother and Father Nature) and are dedicated while in the world to the building of the Garden of Eden in every place a food bearing plant or tree can be planted. We realize this is the way that brings peace and we know God wants us to share this beautiful knowledge with our beloved brothers and sisters everywhere in this world and in the universe.

We are not vegetarians, fruitarians for ourselves but because we respect life and all the beloved creatures of Eden. Naturally, health comes with the veg-fruit-nut-grain diet.

We believe in freedom of religion and the study of everything that creation exposes us to. Especially the building of a society where one is not forced to work to survive economically, but works for the love of the creation, and wakes not to the sound of an alarm clock and a forced schedule, but the natural opening of the eyes daily when completely rested. This enables us to build a better universe daily with a smoother, calmer more restful existence. We can build our communities and turn out the healthiest, strongest human specimens this world has ever seen by establishment of our first community and world head quarters.

If we can get a nice country parcel, (Arizona, California, Hawaii or wherever), a farm, ranch, or maybe a former country school with dormitories, but definitely in the country, we can be in full swing very soon. As of now, nothing big enough has appeared, but we believe it will soon because letters are steadily coming in.

If we can get a nice country parcel, (Arizona, California, Hawaii or wherever), farm, ranch maybe a former country school with dormitories, but definitely in the country, we can be in full swing very soon. As of now, nothing big enough has appeared, but we believe it will soon because letters are steadily coming in.

We should also get the communication trip happening full-time between all of us and are working on a monthly letter of new developments. We also have founded the Garden of Eden Spiritual Society as a selfless group with everyone as a leader and God as our founder, giving us the teachings of higher knowledge and light through personal revelations about building Eden and a better universe, using us all as instruments of evolution.

We are made up of long hairs, short hairs, no hairs; in other words, everyone and everybody are welcome in the building of Eden on Earth.

Please keep in touch with us closely and write as soon as possible. We need you and your ideas.

We believe in the finest of everything, especially food, and the fresher the better. This is one of the many reasons a nice warm climate seems so attractive, not only for sun and heat, but such nice goodies as growing our own avocadoes, melons, peaches, pineapples, oranges, tangelos, cherimoyas, guavas, papayas, plums, berries, bananas, cherries, artichokes, and everything else that loves the mild climate.

Sounds so good, doesn't it. Just visualize when we are all there growing and eating that way daily — MMM,MMMMMMM.

Please stay in touch. We love you and want to get together.

Peace and Love,
The Garden of Eden Spiritual Society, c/o Russ Sandy, 34 Scenic Road, Fairfax, California 94930

Section II
In South America

THE YOGA OF SURVIVAL

Dear Brothers and Sisters, Let us talk for a little while about Survival or rather the Yoga of Survival Into the 21st Century. What you can hear in our talk might influence and correct certain prejudices and concepts everyone has in his individual life, it might produce some new quality, some more awareness when looking at our world as it is and as we want it to be, or what you hear might leave you indifferent or your hasty judgments might remove you even more from the understanding we want to generate with this talk. We don't want to hurt you with a rain of words on Survival, we rather want you to be open so we can start to communicate the true meaning of our life, the true meaning of Creation and together we can go and see what God meant us to do in this time — a very demanding time, a violent time, a confusing time, and a peaceful time, when we can hold hands and pray.

There is this natural instinctual tendency in human beings to protect one's life in moments of danger. Subconsciously fed, one becomes anxious and tries to remove the source of fear. Almost automatically we avoid situations that have a smell of danger or that threaten our security. If we would not attempt to walk on solid ground in our lives we would expose ourselves much more to disease, misery and the possibility of a sudden death. So our instincts cover much space in our life, they touch our feelings, our emotions and are to guarantee a life free from distress and physical danger. But their energy, their power is also limited, their energy is not refined enough, so they must fail from time to time in controlling all our security needs and we fall into one of the 'traps' karma has in store for us, we get hurt and feel much pain — spiritually, mentally and physically.

So Survival is our daily company, a computer sending us signals so we can continue a comparatively "healthy" life. We hardly ever think about its function or its importance. Its mechanisms are almost totally integrated into our life, without them we cannot conserve life. Without them we would become cripples. And, of course, in a way we are cripples already.

Survival is not something to exist inside our individual sphere only. It deeply penetrates all aspects of life, it conditions and shapes all our experiences and it links all of creation.

As one can see we cannot protect our life anymore, we cannot maintain our survival instinct indefinitely, we cannot stretch life any longer when we have to die and to leave our physical form. Here we must realize that Survival is not a condition that dies with our physical form. Moreover, survival and its manifestations are a spiritual "condition", a spiritual discipline, a "spiritual instinct" created when this universe was created and woven into Man's spirit, into his true nature. So Survival acts like a central organ, like a master gland for the conservation of all life.

Man is Spirit, man is Survival. Generally speaking the Yoga of Survival Into the 21st Century is the Yoga of Ultimate Union with God and His creation. As humans in our time we are almost completely disconnected from our roots, from our Divine Essence, from our Real Nature. In this time of materialism and spiritual destruction we must follow a Yoga that can provide us with all the ingredients, i.e. with the methods and techniques that lead us on the path of self—realization and ultimate perfection. So this Yoga of Survival, this Yoga of Union can connect our higher awareness, our consciousness with universal morality, with universal love, with universal creation.

The Yoga of Survival is based on needs and conditions rising from our present time, our present world of negativity and destruction. Our world is in bad shape, much more darkness than light, much more violence than peace, much more devil than God. When we look at these conditions which slowly but with growing speed tend to kill all creative life on this planet — lakes, forests, fish, human faces, children's plays, mutual love, social justice, wisdom, smiles and whole hemispheres — then we cannot turn away and ask the Lord of Karma to do the last stroke of destruction, to give the last smash to this planet and everything that is on it. Karma does not work this way! Karma leaves it to the individual to reach Enlightenment, and karma leaves it to our planet earth to regenerate, to rejuvenate itself. Planet Earth might have another incarnation to make another attempt to reach perfection and we, being on this planet earth have to witness our own slow death on a dying planet. Karma does not work this way! As long as our spirit incarnates in physical form, especially in a human form, we must take our chance to reach perfection now and not wait for another incarnation to come — to come when?

Karmic Law did not give us the breath of life imbedded in a physical body so we can stay as fools and repeat the vicious cycle of birth and death over and over again till we have exhausted the precious chance of being born as humans. Our spirit has incarnated in this present body and made it the vehicle for our world, our individual body, the body of our fellow man, the body of animals, plants and rocks, the body of the earth, the body of the universe, the body of creation. And we take care of all their spiritual bodies. All these bodies — never measurable, innumerable — become the vehicle, the chariot for our journey. There is no body without another body, no form without another form, they all form the great everlasting body of God, the unbilical cord of creation.

The spirit of God lives in every cell, in every molecule, in every atom. The DNA—code is nothing but the individuals karmic order of evolution, of creation. Spirit and matter, spirit and body, both are born of God's creation, both are manifestations of His everlasting love, both are expressions of ultimate truth and wisdom. Spiritual, mental and physical awareness are to be practised at any given time. They form the trident of creation to pierce individual and cosmic life on all levels of evolution. Creation is always perfect; God never makes mistakes. And he made man the crown of perfection and creation. It was not God who created Ignorance and not the devil. It was man who created ignorance when he separated himself from creation and perfection. And it is Man who has transformed himself into the devil. Nevertheless the essence of man's nature is never lost or even exhausted, it is always possible to bring it to full blossom again — even now where man's world, man's creation looks sad, so disgusting, so artificial. Man's true nature as the son of God can rise from the ashes of destruction and fill the whole universe with its wonderful fragrance. Darkness can become light, man can become God, life immortal. Our planet earth can become the favorite star of God.

The world, according to karmic evidence, is approaching the climax of its destructive negative energies. Tomorrow we might wake up again, but our life will have to change all of a sudden. It might be too late for a change then! Our Survival instincts accustomed to routine and physical and psychological rituals can suddenly not operate properly any more because they are stuck in coordinating their energies. They have to face the deepest "trap" they had to come into contact with so far. As our Survival instincts are not trained, not specialized enough they only can fail operating and give us tremendous suffering on all planes of our existence. Of course, when we have been well trained enough in transcending pain it certainly will not affect us as much as if we had no such training. Still the climax of destruction and the slow approach to it will bring enormous disorder and chaos into our lives; only if we can prepare ourselves by following the Yoga of Survival we will be able to resist, will we be strong enough in our perseverance, so we can see a whole world disappearing, and giving the means for us to build a new world — the world of the prophets of all times. Don't you see that this world is disappearing already!

We must realize in time when karmic evidence will manifest in the world's destruction. It necessarily will not mean that all mankind will have the same fate, the same path, the same death. All those who follow the road to union, the path of God, His children will be saved and be asked to create the new world of peace.

When we can see this and realize its impact on our present life, then we no longer can isolate ourselves from thinking what one can do to guarantee man's individual and universal evolution and what can be done practically, very practically to lead ourselves and future generations to self–realization, to liberation. We no longer can blindly follow our daily routine and act as if tomorrow is like yesterday. Everything is for protection, for feeling comfortable, for feeling happy. Knowing about the coming deluge (whenever it will be is irrelevant) and not wanting to harmonize our activities, our styles, our modes of life with it is sure suicide. To see the danger confronting you and not doing anything about it is sure suicide. To see a car driving at you without stopping and not jumping to the side is sure suicide. Subconsciously you want to die because life is not complete in this particular body, it is not "attractive" enough, not promising enough; so we always die because life is not complete. The simple truth is that it is complete, perfect, one. You just failed again to realize it. Poor fool you are!

Taking care of our survival instinct does not necessarily mean to pack our velvet suit—case, jump into the next plane, drop down on an exotic island in the Pacific Ocean and say good—bye ugly world forever! This could become a dangerous adventure, a disasterous escape. We cannot renounce the world, we cannot turn our back, the plane must leave without us. We stay where we are. And we stop our routine, our machine attitude, our little happy days, our daily disgust for a while and start contemplating our situation in this life. So we can look at the samsaric qualities in our life and its direct and indirect influence on the shortcut to universal enlightenment. That is, we must look at ourselves once more and apply "spiritual geometrics" to our present life—situation.

In both places we have to organize fruit orchards and vegetable gardens according to the principles of karmaless nutrition which exclude meat, dairy products, salt and spices, grains, drugs, nuts and seeds. These principles emphasize a raw food diet based on fresh juicy fruits and green leafy vegetables, the diet of the Garden of Eden. Spiritual fasting over longer periods is included in this elimination program. As much as we can we follow these principles on our transitional farm though we sometimes have to go to the cities, though we sometimes have to breathe in foul air and carbon monoxide, though we sometimes have to use contaminated water, fruits and vegetables. We know by now that we cannot live a life of a hundred percent purity, we cannot exclude all negativities. So we rather relate to them in a manner less frustrating as if we would always want to go into extremes by just desiring to avoid these situations. We will have to base our decisions on momentary needs. As much as we can we will not use fire. Oxygen is the spark of life. And fire kills oxygen. Fire when used out in the forest for keeping yourself warm destroys the wood of precious trees necessary for the balance of oxygen in nature. Fire when used for cooking destroys vitamins, minerals and enzymes. So we consider fire as man's gallows and simply do not use it.

We realize that we have to be legal owners of our transitional farm, we have to buy it. There is nothing we can buy on the Survival place; it would be too hidden and its only legal owner will be God. In February, 1978 we are at the very beginning of organizing ourselves and even before that. We are looking for a transitional farm though we don't have any money to buy land besides spending it for buying our daily fruits and vegetables. We have faith that the spirit will guide us and bring us closer and closer to the reality of a Survival Farm as long as we keep on doing the work of the Lord in our time. We are not ashamed to be in this state and to expose ourselves to all the difficulties and limitations we have to face. We can do it with an open heart, we do't have to reassure ourselves all the time that we are doing the right thing. All we can do is to create a loving vibration and energy field in or small Survival group and go with the flow of our momentary, simple needs.

This is where we are — no mystery, no fantasy, only some illusions left. We wish you to understand that it is easy to fill white paper with letters about the Yoga of Survival. More important is to prepare the psychological foundation, to practise the New Age yoga. It can only be practised by fellow brothers and sisters who can see the signs, who do not attach themseves to the age of death and destruction; it can be practised only by those who want to see the whole panorama of creation manifesting every moment before their spiritual eyes. So you must decide whether to contribute your energies to such a project. We must leave you, to your physical, mental and spiritual potential of how to adapt to a path that has been described, in some length in this letter to you. You know now we are here in Boliva working for a spiritual Survival Farm. You are not alone. Contact us, send of more details and information when you need more feedback.

THE YOGA OF SURVIVAL II

Bolivia has a territory five times as big as West Germany, but a population of five million only (twelve times less than West Germany). This means even in ten years from now there will be no such thing as over–population, there will be more industries, more exploitation of oil, gas and precious metals, there will be more commerce, more soldiers, more lumber companies and more bureaucracy and a "better" education–system. But all this will be limited to certain areas like La Paz, Santa Cruz, Cochabamba, Sucre, Potosi and Beni. The general communication and transportation system.still is and will be in very bad shape because of the mountains that make it difficult and expensive to construct roads and railways. Isolated places can only be reached by plane and riverboat. Foreign capitals hesitates to make big investments in South America out of fear of becoming nationalized sooner or later (as happened in Ecuador or Peru). Compared to other countries Bolivian currency is quite stable, although high inflation rates. The present dictatorship under General Banzer is not as oppressive as in Brasil or Argentina but inhuman enough. Illegal miner's strikes as in Potosi are possible. This year Bolivia will have its first elections since many years. There is not much one could expect. The "political cake" has been divided by now already. In Bolivia live 75% Indians, 10% mestozs and 15% white people. The white class is "ruling" the country since the Spaniards arrived and today they still keep all the key and minor positons in government, military, administration, public health, industry and economy. All this makes Bolivia the "South Africa" of South America. Just recently the General has invited 150,000 white South Africans, financially backed by the West German government to settle in underdeveloped parts of Bolivia "to improve the white race"!

Bolivia has a history full of coup d' etats and semi–revolutions that have changed little or nothing. The contrast between the white and Indian race pervades all of Bolivian society and culture — the Indian is the servant, the "slave" of the white man. Four hundred years of oppression and exploitation have crippled the Indians spiritually, mentally and physically; the Indian race lacks self–confidence and self–consciousness. Indian alcoholism is a big problem.

There is no place on Earth now where we could go and expect proper or just social and political conditions. So in this case we must accept Bolivian society as it is and change little by little by giving an example. As long as we cannot move into a final Survival farm we as foreigners in Bolivia have to take care of legalizing our social status. Bolivia immigration laws are still very open for foreigners due to lack of enough "specialists". By now we have friends in influencial positions who know about our work and offered to help us with all the legal aspects.

Bolivia is a big country, though comparatively small to other South American countries. Most of the population is concentrated in the Atiplano — a 3,000 mile high plateau surrounded on two sides by snow-capped mountains. The other parts are high desert-like and subtropical valley lake area and tropical humid low lands with partly navigable rivers. These areas slowly come under exploitation.

We have seen places in Bolivia that would match many of our expectations about building Survival farms. In the north east corner on the border to Peru and Brazil are 2,000 mile high subtropical valleys, almost uninhabited because of a lack of communication. There is a good potential of growing tropical, subtropical and temperate fruit trees all in one valley. Here one can find virgin forests and virgin soils, well hidden, only accessible by longer foot-march. Valleys are protected against radioactive fallout and other pollutions by sheltering mountains.

Our plan now is to find the general area in the north east where we can organize the final Survival farm and to locate a transitional farm close enough to this general area and close enough to a bigger town to trade our products and to go to LaPaz. This transitional farm will serve as a coordination center from where we can organize ourselves and from where we can go to prepare the Survival farm.

Our transitional farm will also be used to continue our individual purification program, to communicate with other spiritual centers around the globe and it will serve as a temporary station for all those to come and to join the work. To be able to organize the Survival farm means for us to locate a hidden valley in the mountains. Whenever we can we have to leave our transitional farm over a period of three to five years to transport seedlings, plants, tools, and other materials to the Survival place so in some years there can be a blooming garden. Priority will always be given to planting fruit trees. There is no sense moving into a Survival farm now because there will be no fruits to eat and it would only bring unnecessary hardship.

Leaving the ignorant and crazy world (which by then will threaten our Survival instinct) without proper preparation and precaution can become dangerous, chaotic and even very painful. It could become a boomerang, and turn against us because we did not listen to the message at the right time. This message will not be repeated on every Sunday's church service, it will not go over the evening news and it will not be recognized in a national emergency case. It is a message that comes from within, a message as a result of practicing the Yoga of Survival. When we have the understanding what this message is like, then we will know that we have to leave the cities, the centers of industrialization and money power, the areas of heavy pollution and even the villages. We have to go into the wilderness without bewilderment and fear, we have to go into total isolation from the rest of the world — not to await passively the end of our world but to concentrate actively on being in touch with the creation of God, wherever something is left of it. And there will be enough left because God has been thinking of us and he will provide us with plenty of space where we can continue our work. From there we can start to heal the wounds and scars on the earth and we will please God by our work so we will be permitted to enter the kingdom of heaven within ourselves, so we may gain the highest bliss, the highest natural and absolute realization — a pure spirit in a pure body! The ultimate reality of life! Samsara and Nirvana, both concepts of delusion, will vanish from man's mind because he has become one with creation and life. This world to come will not be exiled from the wonders and miracles of evolution, by its beauty, peace and wholeness it will please the universe and be accepted by it.

The path of self−realization that will lead us to such a world is an over−all−view, the eagle's eye view and certainly not the ant's view. It is panoramic universal awareness, i.e. it will penetrate all creative aspects of life − spiritual practices, physio− and psychotherapy, physical purification and fasting, astrology, music, cosmobiology, horticulture, ecology, karmaless nutrition, sexual sublimation, survival techniques, etc. Only when we study and learn about all of these subjects we should not fail to express the divine will that is behind all creation. We cannot allow ourselves to become experts on some aspects and leave the rest to other experts. We will not compete with each other and make our knowledge a theoretical one. We will live together practically and not make a game out of it. We will love each other and recognize each other for what we are and will become.

This will make us more clear on what to concentrate in this time, for what to dedicate our energies. We must open our eyes even more. We have to continue our learning and at the same time we have to help finding and building our first survival places in areas of our planet that are comparatively sane and clean. We have to be prepared to leave our "homes" any day from now on. So everything we do in these places can only have temporary nature. Our children must know what is going on. We cannot send them to traditinal schools and universities of the system, so we must create provisonal new age schools where the science of survival is taught to them. We must communicate with our fellow brothers and sisters on the path and help each other wherever we have to and can. Yes we have to organize ourselves without institutionalizing ourselves. We have to be together and know what each one is doing. We have to raise funds for present and future projects. There is so much work to do and there are so many ways to help! God will guide us when we do this work!

We hope you were willing to follow us so far to have a rough idea of God's, of creation's message in our time. We do not attempt to convince you of new exotic goals. We do not pretend that our road, our approach to reality is the only one. We do not want to convert you to a new fancy world religion. And we do not want to confuse you. Nevertheless we really hope that after meditating on the Yoga of Survial Into The 21st Century you would like to join us in this Brotherhood and work together with us in peace and love to make God's plan become real. We already have left the centers of destruction and are working in South America, in Bolivia. We will give you some details about our practical approach to such a Survival place that we are going to organize in this country.

A real survival place has to match all the needs, all the conditions future changes (i.e. catastrophes, radioactivity, diseases, pollutions) will confront us with. We will expalin through the example of a "backward" country like Bolivia why we have chosen this particular country in South America to become the base for our survival activities.

Looking at ourselves can only be done in a meditative state of mind that brings outer and inner world together in a synthesis. Nevertheless the practice of meditation and similar practices with a sense of purity and austerity feels very fitting, it can make one feel clean and secure. We cannot separate this our practice from our actual, practical living situation; it has to be included in our approach to spirituality, it can not be avoided, or put into a special box. True spirituality gets its feedback from our culture, from our society, from our work, yes from our neurotic state of mind, from our suffering, from our pain. True spirituality can use any kind of material as a working basis, because it possesses the energy, the power to cooperate with all of them, to make friends with all of them, to include all of them in transcendental awareness.

Stop for a while if you feel like it. In this sense we also cannot isolate our present life–situation from the past or the future. Time always is the past, present and future. If we were not looking at our past how could we see and perceive ourselves evolving or regressing on the graduated path; if we were not looking at our furture how could we imagine ourselves of where we have to go? The Here and Now is the electric current for all of them – past, present, and future. Our knowledge of ourselves, our self–realization will include all three – when they become identical in the Here and Now – in a physical mental and spiritual synthesis in order to make us grow into ultimate maturity and harmony with all life.

On this background we should practice true spirituality. There is 'I'–centered spirituality which sees the goal in one's self–illumination. It might accomplish to conquer the ego and all the difilements of a human mind, yet it can lack the all–important link with the life–force, it still can be separated from God's powerful creation, it still can isolate itself. So it could indulge itself in spiritual ecstasy and purity and not see the rest of life.

And there is selfless spirituality – the other side of the coin – which is to tune in with all creative and regenerative aspects of life, to tune in with the underlying life–force which is no more but to comprehend all life as one in order to protect all universal creation. When our personal spiritual effort, attitudes and achievements are in harmony with all creation then the light of enlightenment can flash into our life. This is also indicated by the Bodhisattva Vow. This Bodhisattva is a Bodhisattva of survival who takes care of all creation. All we want to say is there is apparently not much choice!

Let us continue with survival.

The Bible in St. John's Revelations tells precisely about the coming end of the world as it is known to us. It mentions the destruction of this world in different stages (wars, famines, persecutions, pests, etc. as it is explained in the Seven Sealings and the Seven Trumpets!); it forsees the arrival of Two Witnesses who will be executed in Jerusalem, the marking of all men who follow Satan and finally the coming of Jesus, the Christ. This all will happen in only one generation and probably started with the First World War.

It is not very important how much attention, how much value we want to give to this version. It is not a matter of believing in it or not. Things are not that easy any more! All prophecies agree about the coming end of this world!

We do not need the Bible or other sources and scriptures, we do not need the help of masters and prophets. Because we can see ourselves what is going on with ourselves and this planet earth. Mental suffering has become a weed killing once abundant life, physical disease is man's only company, the poisoning of man's one pure environment has spread like an ulcer on the surface of the earth. Man has done enough harm to himself and nature. Cosmic law will not allow this planet to become a danger to the rest of the universe. Karmic law will rebalance and rejuvenate this part of the universe. And man will help to execute the orders coming from the same karmic law. Man will become the co−creator of God.

Our individual karma is not separate from universal karma. The universal karma is not something alien or veiled to us, something that we cannot understand in our daily work; it is something we can perceive in ourselves by following the path of liberation and by penetrating it deeply. This road has made us the guardians of universal karma of this small planet called earth. We have become angeles in human flesh.

So all our energies, all our strength and courage, all our faith is needed in order to restore and maintain the order of the universe on our planet. The guardians of life have to cure one sick limb!

Once the time of more visible destruction arrives (in one form or another) we cannot follow certain compromises in our lives any longer. We have to say who we are, where we are and that we will not follow the road into hell. In order not to become martyrs again (it could be we all have been on the cross in Rome in earlier incarnations) and not to go into the camps with folded hands and holy mantras on our lips we have to leave the centers of destruction when we still can. This fate was not meant for us!

We Love You,
Joy, Lori, Damon, Raine, Elko
(future members of a Survival Brotherhood)

PACHAMAMA
(MOTHER EARTH)

A space, an island, Taguille; surrounding the island a vast high altitude inland ocean Lago Titicaca reflecting the incredible crystal blue of the Andean sky. Several icebergs were floating in the far distance. No wait..., they turned out to be the peaks of the Bolivian Andes, startling silver white. It's brisk out. A full moon waiting in the wings.

Reflecting on the many days and nights on the road starting on bicycle from San Francisco to Guatemala, Central America, a bout with hepatitis, meditation retreat high above Lago Atitlan under the loving guidance of Master Dhiravamsa. A hitch through Central America in a friend's pickup, a cargo boat from Pt. Limon, Costa Rica to Baranguilla, Colombia, South America.

On through the velvet emerald green hills of southwestern Colombia, crossing into Equador to catch my first glimpse of the sacred snow−capped Andes reflecting my yearning spirit. Slowly walking, hitching, winding my way from the mountains to the Pacific Ocean and back again into the lost but ever present Inca Empire. Hoping to convey the spirit of our gentle mother earth through photographs, writings and verbal communication with locals and fellow gypsies.

A few moments of unawareness left me to continue my journey south, minus camera equipment, I.D., money, etc. a karmic dept repaid, a lesson learned.

While gathering my energy in a small curios tienda in·La Paz, the Bolivan Capital, my eyes met another set of eyes alive with energy, sparkling with light from underneath a black french style beret, long black/gray hair partly concealed underneath a dark navy coat wrapped around a small, thin but strong frame. So I met Elk also known as Johnny Amable Vallee.

We exchanged information on various New Age developments throughout the world and what we as individuals could do, for we both felt strongly that the world at its present value system could and would not endure man's abuse.

'Elk' had worked on various farms in Equador, spoke Spanish fluently and had been in Bolivia about a year working with a new age Indian group M.I.N.K. trying to introduce new farming methods that would care for the soil and its recycling potential, making sure the Indians were treated fairly by their own government and a general new awareness for the Bolivian peasant who has been so used by the Elite.

'Elk' organized a group for conservation of ecosystems with various international friends known as C.I.C.E. He was also in the process of printing a booklet informing the general public on alternative value systems. I went to several meetings with 'Elk' and met many concerned Bolivians. My heart felt good. He gave me an open letter and hoped for me to convey his message through a meaningful channel.

As I continued my journey I often reflected on that frail yet amazingly strong brother, Johnny Amable Vallee 'Elk' from Canada who made me realize again how important each single individuals energy is and when we come together our energy is that much greater. Pachamama needs all the help it can get.

While hitching through the Chilean mountains I met others like him all doing something, all caring enough. I continued into Argentina one of the most restricted countries in South America where peoples innate rights were repressed and misery prevailed on large scale. In Brazil I met many former Argentians who would support this statement. Brazil was also changing rapidly especially southern regions containing the large cities of Rio de Janeiro, San Paulo, etc; just too much of everything which is largely due to European and American influence. I can clearly see the circle it has to travel before they realize it can not continue in that manner, but will people listen when they're not ready?

I spent another five months in Brazil connecting with brothers and sisters from all parts of the globe exchanging energy and information. From northern Brazil I helped a friend sail his boat to the West Indies where I spent several months re−evaluating these last few years south of the border.

Presently I'm working, resting, organizing and preparing for my continued pilgrimage towards the far−east this coming spring, perhaps we'll see each other on the road.

Namaste
Hank, August, 1979

THE PACHAMAMA (MOTHER EARTH) NOW SPEAKS

To my respectful sons: Dear children of mine, I implore you with all the strength that is yet within my damaged biosphere and with all the urgency of these last hours to gather the energies which you still have and your scattered brothers and listen to this last wish from the mother of your life and of all life.

Son of my love from my spirit be sure to respect and to attend to your mother who has been weakened by so much abuse. They have made you believe that there are other lives, even eternal ones, outside of my bosom. Listen well to your true and only mother because in truth I tell you: the son who does not respect his mother and despises the life which came from her will not encounter reward other than eternal death and suffering on earth.

Good hearted son from my breath be caring of the ecosystem that unites you to your mother with vitality and sensibility; keep your sinuses open and clean so that you may enjoy the fragrances of the atmosphere that vitalizes us; take good care of the vegetation which is all regenerating and avoid the killer that is contamination. When my emerald clothes were luxuriant with vegetation you were at peace in my bosom, filled with my abundance and joy filled by myriads of colors and perfumes capable of fulfilling even the gods; my breath was then perpetually pleasing and fresh as well as free from smoke, dust and any sort of stench. You are never to forget that I, your eternal mother exuded the breath of your soul and that outside of mine there is no soul.

Robust son of my soil be real conscious and respectful of the sacred that vivifies you than can only remain limpid because of the magic and delicate carpet that is my warm and soft soil. This part of us is as vital for you as it is for me because without a fertil soil I remain without clothes and you without food; without a live soil all you have left is: dirty water, filthy air, mud, dust, and garbage. Do not heed those perverts who, in the idolatric concept of dominating the creation and with the desire of filling their stomachs, are eliminating my capacity to produce for life. Hear the spirits of our mother telling you the truth of life: all life, even eternal and spiritual, is born from my womb.

Faithful son of my soul be religiously respectful for my life as for yours and eternally conscious that all life on earth comes from your mother. Understand with all your heart, with all your mind and your soul that to respect life, so small as that of the mushrooms within the soil, is a demonstration of love for your mother and you shall obtain the reward of a happy life and perpetual wisdom. Obey our mother and you shall be happy; disobey her laws and you shall reap misery.

Now my respectful and loving sons are uniting so that their mother may recuperate from so much abuse she has received, and yet receives, from the preverted ones; and so that she may recuperate her fertility in order to continue her work of life and love. My dear son I implore you to unite with your respectful brothers so that your sons may enjoy vitality and happiness in my abundance.

CICE – Center Of Internationals for the Conservation of the Ecosystem
Casilla 5699, La Paz, Bolivia.

PARADISIAN NEWSLETTER

Some years ago my mother's parents had a fruit farm in Utah of cherries and pears and my father's parents owned a spring lake and a dairy. My father was the sixth boy in a family of 14; his entire inheritance equalled two hundred dollars for high school tuition, then he was 'on his own'. My mother's parents sold their land to a housing development company. My parents began a family before obtaining land, and though my father's dream was to work as a farmer on his own place, it became economically impossible with five children to raise. Utah had and has a booming population. Land is scarce and prices high. At twelve years of age I knew that a piece of land on which to grow my food and live was the most important material objective in life. I began working part-time after school in order to save money but school finances and clothes ate up all the money I could make. I searched with friends far into the Utah, Colorado, and Arizona deserts for an ideal place which we never found, since all good land with orchards, etc. was very expensive, and we had no know-how as to planting the desert into Paradise. We finally parted, as we had different ideas as to what we wanted, how to live, etc. I was still searching for home and Truth when I first heard of Johnny Lovewisdom. I've been very blessed to have been guided to 'El Paradiso'. Johnny had to struggle many years to bring about this small haven. I know I'm the luckiest girl on earth to have been initiated into wisdom of right living by a Paradisian Master rather than uniting with another lost seeker fighting to overcome our divergent Karmas of ignorance. Most children now born into the world are landless. There are now around four billion people on earth with a total land area of 14.5 billion hectares or approximately 3.6 hectares of land for each person. About 20 percent of the land is cultivatible so it comes out to .72 hectares for each to provide the food source! That doesn't leave much room for growth! Though the problems of over-crowding, pollution, lack of natural resources, etc. are self-evident, when I say "No, I do not plan on raising a family," people are generally dismayed, and I've met almost no one who doesn't either have or wish to have children. The government of Ecuador divided the large farms here giving each family an alloted acreage, but when the 5 – 14 children divide the land between themselves it results in small lots, or most must go to the city to live. So by avoiding having kids, instead caring for our gardens, I'm little by little living out my past Karma, growing the trees that provide a sane future for myself and others. Here I sit with my back resting against a huge cypress tree Johnny planted long ago with birds singing and playing midst the mango, orange, roseapple, and other fruit trees, the pineapple flowers visited by hummingbirds, the blackcap berry's flowers by honeybees, the dahlia, zinnias, and marigolds by colorful butterflies. Life is such a blissful harmony, each day ever more fulfilling as I watch the seeds Johnny and I have planted, weeded, watered and loved grow into a fruiting forest.

Living Vitarian in Paradise is quite different from Fruitarianism in the city, the country-folk who eat everything, and the rest of the worldly people. I have a friend who 'thinks' he's Vitarian, he eats fruits and vegetables most of the time, but occasionally binges when he's invited to eat with some friend or his 'boss'. He grows none of his own food, all being bought at health food stores or markets. He works

THE SPROUTING OF THE NEW AGE /27

sitting all day so gets little physical exercise, so to compensate he goes to the gym to work out with the dumbbell bar. He lives alone and is quite lonely and constantly goes from thoughts of sex and love, to guilt, and thus yogi—monk abstinence. Since he eats too much heavy protein type foods, (clabber, avocadoes, etc.), binges, he has never mastered his seminal losses and when he is in his yogi—monk moods he ends up having nocturnal dreams in order for the body to rid itself of the build—up. Emotionally he is unstable, he gets angry easily and says he hates women, yet living such an artificial patched—up existence is hardly living in the Pristine Perfection of Paradise. To live thusly one must live in Paradise, and since Paradise no longer exists on our ravaged planet Earth, it's necessary that each choose a vocation that is part of the job of restoring the Perfection to Mankind and our environment. So many pseudo—Vitarians don't realize that one must change one's life and way of living and thinking in order to be Vitarian. I've had many acquaintances that say "Someday, I'll live Vitarian, when I find the right place, mate, after I live in Transition for awhile, but never get around to actually doing it, because they never make the effort to overcome their wrong habits of living.

When I came to live with Johnny he had lived Vitarian for over 30 years, alone. He had worked to buy land, and plant it to fruit gardens, and had lived years on fruits and vegetables, thus already an experienced, mature Paradise Builder. I, though young, landless, and lacking right knowledge, had dedicated myself fully to live in harmony with God's Natural Kingdom and Law, and went to work "dressing and caring for the Paradise Gardens".

In a typical day here at 'El Paraiso' we're up at six in the morning. I water the gardens, then work—out a few hours with the lampa and bar — weeding our food supply, while Johnny may work on Printing Press or carpentry. Thus we get our daily exercise. A cool dip in the river, a sunbath and lunch of fruits, a rest period to study spiritually inspiring scriptures from all cultures, then some hours of peaceful work weeding by hand, putting books together, while pondering upon the sublime teachings. On Sundays we rest and dedicate the entire day to recharging our inspirational light, through mystical, esoteric studies, contemplation of the beauty of Living, and fasting. After supper of greens juice and salad, we retire along with the setting of the sun, usually separately, while fireflies, crickets, and singing water lull us into peaceful slumber. In the early morning hours we awake for deep meditation of the ever—growing Truth, and ecstactic communion together. Johnny has no problem with seminal losses, and I have completely healed of menstruation, so sex presents us with no difficulties, and with the companionship, loneliness is non—existent. Since Johnny has had so much more experience than I, he is ever an example to me, a teacher, so steadfast in Truth, and ever growing in Love and Wisdom. Me, too!

Conclusion (by Johnny Lovewisdom)

After Ruth Marie finished typing this far she asked me to finish her Newsletter, explaining what a landless person must do to find Paradise. Not everyone can marry Johnny Lovewisdom, or get a job that pays enough so one can save money to buy land. Paradise is not for Free! My answer is that not everyone is with God's Grace, or

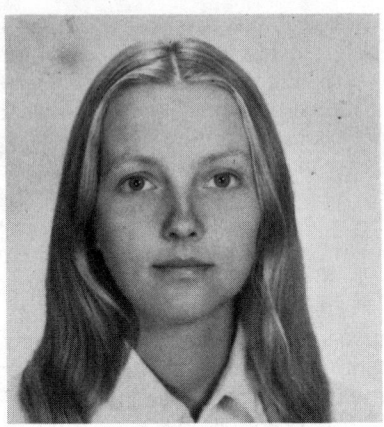

Ruth Marie Lovewisdom

Good Karma, so they really want Paradise or would be willing to sacrifice working under adverse conditions to obtain Paradise. Paradisian Mastery is with the most difficult trials. First, you have to have an impeccable past, worthy of heavenly reward. People do not realize that the reason they do not have Paradise is that they earned hell by so many lives, beside starting this life, doing evil. One has to expect years of purification, real repentence through sacrifice and suffering. But people are half–hearted in becoming Paradisians; they love mother's home cooking, drown out adversity and suffering in the wordly responsibilities with narcotics, and are not willing to do heavy labor. When the Disciple is Ready the Path to Mastery will appear. Most people do not know what kind of Paradise they want, and would take lifetimes to decide what kind of conditions constitute Paradise for them. In all cases, one needs land which costs money, so thus has this debt to pay to society, working under unhealthy and disagreeable conditions. Every day for years one contributes to evil world conditions, before becoming conscious that wrong living wronged mankind, so now in conscious penance, one has to suffer hard labor to earn freedom from bondage, just like the Prodigal Son in the Bible. For some, with less evil to work off it is easier, or funds for Paradise may be given just by deter – repentance. Others will find no jobs available, heavy labor unbearable, etc. Some folk will never want any semblance of Paradise. Is God's Grace or Karma in your favor? If not, then you have to build up your store of virtue even to be able to desire the ideal, and once you become a Paradisian Dreamer, you have a way to go working and building the adaptation to living the Life of a Paradisian Master. And the best place to start is right at the place the Lord put you. Very few can adapt to it.

Peace and Blessings from both of us!
Ruth Marie and Johnny Lovewisdom, Vilcabamba, Loja, Ecuador, October, 1979.

PARADISE LOST?

Probably many of you, like myself, have recurring dreams of finding an ideal place to settle. For the raw foodist, the "ideal" has fruit trees, organic gardens, fresh, clean water, pure air, lots of sunshine and a climate conducive to year round vegetation to assure a continuous supply of fresh, wholesome foods.

Where does such a place lie?

Certainly in this modern world such a place is rare indeed. Yet they do exist. Southern Ecuador is the place that most closely meets all the above criteria. The Andes Corridor running through it provides one of the most pollution free environments in the world today. The tropical highlands provide a year round growing season for practically every imaginable fruit and vegetable. The politics of the country are fairly stable (considering we are in Latin America) and have little effect on the people in the more rural areas.

Deep within a lost Andean valley lies "Edenia", an example of incredible beauty. There are 15,000 acres of virgin forest, sparkling rivers and waterfalls, plenty of rainfall, and you can choose your climate from tropical to almost arctic. Yet this seeming paradise lacks something important: community.

Central America has many similar situations though there is a great deal more pollution (steming from the North American cities). The air and water are still relatively pure. The price of the land is also quite inexpensive, $25 − $100 per acre. The climate in the mountains provide most climatic conditions. The governments are fairly stable in Costa Rica and Belize, and friendly towards Americans. There is a wide variety of fruit to be found in the native markets. Some Americans have found their way to the isolated Edens of Central America but they are few and far between. Again there is still a lack of community.

The Caribbean Islands are the only other areas left with the tropical mountain evironment in this hemisphere. They range from Jamaica to Trinidad. Some friends and I recently spent six months sailing to many of these islands to explore their "paradise" potential.

Jamaica is much too unstable, mainly due to drug related problems. Haiti is not overly friendly to Americans, is also politically unstable and provides little or no sense of community. The Dominican Republic is a beautiful island though highly populated. The price of land is very high, and again there is a lack of community. Puerto Rico is similar to the Dominican Republic with over 3,000,000 people and expensive land − also the island is highly industrialized and uses nuclear power. Most of the other islands on down the Antilles chain are either too dry, too flat, have too many mosquitos, are too over populated, or too expenisive with one glaring exception − Dominica.

Dominica is an island of extraordinary beauty, covered with fruit trees and forests and with a river for every day of the year (or so say the local people). The population is only 80,000 and the people are as warm and friendly as you will ever meet (the tourists have not yet started to flood here). The island is still basically an agrarian society supplying much of the Caribbean with fruit. However, there are problems. The island just became self−governing last November and with a 99% black population there is no certainty yet as to how an influx of Americans will be treated by the government. And though the people have that naive, open, warmth that goes with being relatively undiscovered still, they are hard to relate to in many ways.

Isn't the reason that most of us reading this article remain in our present environment due mainly to social reasons.

For the time being some friends and I have purchased 24 acres on the island of St. Croix. The land is located in the sparsely populated mountain area with adequate rainfall and little pollution. The government is U.S and there are a large number of "stateside" Americans, young and old, living on the island. The potential exist for earning extra money, a problem that slows down many a would be tropical homesteader. The climate is ideal with an average year round temperature of 75–80 degrees and the tradewinds providing a fairly continuous breeze.

The way I see it, St. Croix could be a gathering point for potential tropical settlers. It could also act as a place of transition. I can give specific information regarding certain land deals, addresses, an area's potential for your specific need. Some inquiries need to be researched so allow plenty of time for the reply.

Philip Hiss, Route 4, Box 30-B, Cairo, Georgia 31728

ECUADOR
IS IT PARADISE?

Three years ago I was scanning an atlas looking for the area which I would later settle. My criteria were complex. First, I was looking for tropical highlands because of the year round growing season, the constant temperature (cold on top of the mountains to warm on the bottom), and the wide range of fruits and vegetables grown there. Second, I was looking for a somewhat stable government that was not anti–American. Third, I was looking for an unpolluted area with a low population density. And last, I was hoping for rich soil and abundant water.

The choises were rather limited. And after a short time Ecuador seemed like the country which appealed to me most. The next few years were spent in preparation learning about farming, building, living, survival in general. This last summer I finally went to Ecuador. And here are briefly some of the things I learned.

In the beginning of August a friend and I boarded an Equatorian flight to Quito (cost $314.00 return from Miami – 150 day excursion). On arrival in Quito we discovered the Gran Casino Hotel full of foreigners with adventures to tell. Also in Quito is "Hojas de Hierbas" an excellent place for making contact with the foreigners who live in Ecuador.

A few days after arriving we found our way to Hacienda Santa Rosa – a fruitarian, herbavarian, crudavarian community of seven. They do diagnostic healing clinics and seem to have a wide knowledge of this field. Why have they chosen the Andean highlands?

First, there is less pollution — 90% of the industry, and probably 98–99% of the pollution is in the northern hemisphere. The northern and southern hemisphere winds do not mix much so the pollution stays in the north. Also, the winds blow west–east so the Andean corridor is protected by the extremely high Andean Mountains. Second, there is more oxygen — most of the southern hemisphere is ocean, and plankton in the ocean produces about 70% of the worlds oxygen (the Amazon produces a great deal of oxygen also). Third, there is more prana — the higher up the mountains, the thinner the air. This allows more room for prana. Forth, the abundant volcanos in Ecuador give the gas inside the Earth an outlet — so earthquakes are minimalized. Fifth, the ideal climatic conditons.

Our next destination was the Amazon, specifically Banos, "gateway to the Amazon". Banos was a pleasant town with comfortable hotels, plenty of good food, and warm mineral baths. Then, there is a spectacular descent into the jungle. Unfortunately, the jungle itself impressed me as being a highly organized tourist trap and a rather monotonous one. There were too many draw backs to living in the area — mangos do not grow because of the constant rains.

The journey south was strenuous. The land was barren (time of the dry season), good food was scarce, the buses were overcrowded, noisy and bumpy. (I highly recommend flying to Loja).

Finally, we arrived at Vilcabamba., the Sacred Valley of Longevity — so named by Dr. Johnny Lovewisdom. However, in the last few years since a passable road has been built to the town, modern medicine has descended upon the "viejos" (old ones), and they have been dying at an appalling rate. At one time the valley was covered with fruit orchards. Now, many of them have been chopped down in favor of chemicalized vegetable and hog production .

Dr. Lovewisdom, long an advocate of the virtues of tropical colonization and fruitarianism, is located in the middle of all these changes. After thirteen years in the area, he is moving to a more desert–like environment where the land is sparcely populated by necessity.

We spent three days talking with the doctor, learning of his many experiences. He is "trying to teach paradise building, to produce your own fruit...Fruitarianism is a failure unless you produce your own fruit". He talks about vitarianism — "eating only juicy fruit, supplemented with succulent vegetables when necessary". Through vitology, "one eliminates and heals menstruation as well as seminal losses". However, the doctor has been forced to eat clabbered milk daily to protect himself from the chemical sprays in the air and water that have recently been introduced into the area.

QUESTION: "Shall people come here?"

DR. LOVEWISDOM: "No encouragement either way. To come here people think their problems will be solved — not so. Coming here does not solve much because you have to learn a whole new set of rules. People shed much energy...Must be able to work hard."

QUESTION: "You told people to come here."

DR. LOVEWISDOM: "That was before!!"

The doctor is swamped with letters but has very few **funds**. He will answer people who send a couple of dollars to cover the expensive cost of postage and paper down in Ecuador.

The highlight of the trip was the visit to "Nueva Edenia" (New Eden). Two hours by horseback from the nearest road, behind the barren looking mountains that surround Vilcabamba lies a beautiful green valley with few people and much nature. One side of the valley is owned by seven people who have split with Dr. Lovewisdom's group. Still holding to much of the Doctor's philosophy, they tend to interpret it less rigidly.

They have about 15–20,000 acres of largely unexplored lakes, rivers, waterfalls, virgin forests, and mountains. They own the sources of the rivers to insure pure water. The forests have bears and mountain lions. The land stretches to the top of the cordillera.

At the moment they are planting hundreds of fruit trees, mostly temperate varieties. This is no easy chore because almost everything is done by hand. The fruit that is now there is extraordinary. The soil is rich and the water is plentiful.

The few people in the area are open and friendly but more interested in living closer to town. They are willing to sell their land if the price is right – very low by U.S. standards. So I made an offer on a couple of hundred acres. There are bananas, oranges, avocados, cherimoyas, etc. on the land already. And it adjoins "Edenia" The possibilities of what can be done are exciting.

Philip Hiss, Route 4, Box 30-B, Cairo, Georgia 31728

SETTLING THE TROPICS

Dear Viktoras, Greetings from Venezuela! I was sorry we did not get a chance to get together on the east coast before I returned down here in June. Perhaps it is time now to tell you a little more about what is going on down here.

I think I sent you a copy of a letter I wrote to Laurie Foti of "Ecologos" in February, describing something of our situation. Three of us – me, an American woman, and a Venezuelan man – have purchased what is basically an abandoned avocado hacienda in the coastal range of mountains just south of the Caribbean port town of Cumana. You follow a road out of Cumana some 10, maybe 15 miles along the Rio Manzanares, until you come to its second major southern tributary, the Rio Brito. We live roughly a day's hike up the Rio Brito along foot and burro paths. (I wouldn't want our location too publicized yet or in general). The land is owned by our Venezuelan just in case. But Venezuela is perhaps the stable, democratic Latin American country so far. Oil=Prosperity–Growing peaceful middle class, etc. for now.

The Brito is a large tumbling mountain stream or small river–not navigable, full of waterfalls and swimming holes, of exceptionally crystalline water, marvelously turquoise in the sunlight. It drains out of a watershed of mountains rising to about 8000 feet. We live the furthest up of anyone, along one of its sub–tributaries about two hours walking beyond our nearest neighbors, who are the highest inhabitants on our part of the Brito. At our altitude of maybe 1500 to 2000 feet, the water is cooler and fresher yet, of exceptional quality, pure rainwater streams in low tropical mountain rain forest, with no one above us to compromise its quality.

We formally 'own' maybe 200, maybe 300 acres, including two year–around streams and the tributary river. Most of the land is overgrown to secondary forest again, abandoned now 15 years, but with a substantial stand of avocado and mango trees, some 200 in all and big, including some lime trees, and a few other tropical fruits, with banana and pineapple plants scattered throughout. We are surrounded by literally thousands of acres of free land available for the homesteading by anyone who simply comes in and does it. In fact, by purchasing the one major site left in the area, we basically preside over our whole little tributary, a number of miles long, our whole narrow mountain valley! There is a wealth of space and resources here, and one of the reasons I am writing you this is that we are interested in populating our potential paradise with similarly inclined fruitarian folk. You should know that this resource exists and is in fact available and FREE to serious land, fruit, etc. people. There is even another, abandoned, hacienda, and some smaller fruit stands about. You are invited of course to see...etc. and so forth.

We met briefly several years ago at Hippocrates, and I remember you saying you had people interested in such a project. I would like to get into contact on this. I think we have an excellent potential situation for "tropical colonization" here, for building a truly ecological, fruitarian human community. .

Which brings me to a point of contention with "Survival Into the 21st Century". I have been in the tropics over 5 years now evaluating various land situations, and I am not at all sure that the high altitudes are the best for human beings. For the first two years I lived near Merida, in the Andes on the other side of the country, on a small campesino farm at about 6000 feet altitude. This is the absolute highest you can live and still grow tropical fruits such as bananas, oranges, small avocados, and with luck the delicious cherimoya, mangos, nispero, coconut, etc. as well as tomatoes, melons, even watermelon, which do not grow successfully (you may have occasional harvests) because, I think, the nights are too cold. Greens do very well, though even cucumbers and zucchini are problematic. Any higher in altitude and greens are about the only possiblity besides wheat and corn. There are seasonal berries and some stunted varieties of peaches. Certain plums might grow. But for year–around tropical fruit, if this is a goal, even 6000 feet is too high. Moreover, the weather is really too cold for comfortable, natural outdoors living – nights are cold, cold enough for parkas even, and warm houses. And during the day there is a constant profusion of small biting insects, in Spanish "plaga".

Further Notes: Merida oranges were disturbingly acid at best. Avocadoes were disease prone and almost non–existent. Papaya, mangos, etc. grew but did not fruit. Bananas the most reliable. Some berries, strawberries, figs, melons, tomatoes, impossible.

There is considerable fruitarian interest down here, including some excellent books.

The next year and a half I spent largely traveling in the torrid lowlands south of the Rio Orinoco, flirting with what soon becomes the great Amazon wilderness. This is jungle, and a fourth one of us is currently developing a fruit scene in this kind of environment along the Rio Caura. While I personally find the vast expanses of wilderness and great spacious rivers truly thrilling, exalted, practically speaking, it is too hot and humid, and the inferior soils produce mostly inferior fruit. But interestingly enough, the 'plaga' is not nearly so horrendous as the myth of the jungle leads us to think, and in many cases is better than in the mountains. And there is a truely powerful and magical vibration to being in the pranic spectrum of this, nature's most exuberantly vibrant expression on the planet. The jungle is not to be under–estimated. In many ways it offers the most intense original communication with nature we have experienced, and once having known this, one's dreams so frequently return there.

So now we are in the low tropical mountains off the coast, basically a Caribbean environment. I feel this is the healthiest human environment I have found so far, and one strong piece of evidence is that the local inhabitants are by far the healthiest I have seen in my wanderings. Healthier than in Merida, and than the jungle. Slim, with wonderfully proportioned bodies, agile and alegre (cheerful). Campesijos in Merida suffer from a lot of deformity, goiter and the like, and the jungle peoples tend to be heavier and bloated, (although all these rural peoples have a level of physical health better than the urban, I would say).

But these low tropical mountains offer the same fresh, well–circulated, less humid air, the same superb tumbling rainwater streams, the same great views and sense of spaciousness. Our little thatch house has a fine 200 degree view and more, encompassing our whole valley. And the same healthful hiking and climbing, which must be so significant. Plus here you can grow the tropical fruits and vegetables abundantly, and the rain forest quality of soil is generally the best available in the tropics (for this kind of marginal, non–commercial land), and this may all be why these areas are always so firstly and extensively populated. Most commercial fruit and vegetable growing in Venezuela is done around 1–3000 feet altitude where it grows best. It is only the massive dynamics of industrilization and urbanization in this booming oil country, that opens up large abandoned areas like our own, as the people, the youth, go to the cities.

Plaga–wise, these low mountains are something of a compromise, judging by our site. Gnats during the rainy season, but even during their most intense two month peak they do not achieve the level of Merida, the higher altitudes.

The climate here is delightful – not too cool or hot, but "fresco" (fresh) and breezy. Nights are cool but not cold – clothes minimal – nudity, etc.

(I should say too that these mountains offer excellent hard woods, and lots of stone and fine sand for building permanent structures. Our streams are well situated for gravity irrigation, essential during the 5 month dry season. And our valley is laced with similar little watersheds).

So I hope you don't mind my offering some of the observations of my experience here. I have been meaning to write you about this for some time now. As you can see, my orientation is primarily towards where you can grow quality fruit, and then what constitutes a delightful climate to simply LIVE in. I can understand high altitudes in terms of sproutarian transition or breatharian climax, but not so much in terms of fruitarianism, and we hardly want to import our fruit, so to speak. I am curious about your reaction to all this. I would like to hear more of what you prefer in the higher altitudes. I also know that this is Johnny Lovewisdom's preference too, though he admits that it precludes most fruit. My own experience is precisely low altitudes — 1–3000 ft. in the mountains. Not sea level or lowlands.

I do want to say that my experience down here really supports your theme of tropical colonization. There is truly potential paradise here if we can ever set it up. I remember discussing Jamaica and ultimately Hawaii with you. (If Venezuela does not work now for me, I'd be interested to help your efforts). Also what is happening in Costa Rica? — I remember you mentioning possibilities there. What about Just and his people, who have a letter in "Survival"? If you have any regular newletters or what not on all this, I'd much appreciate receiving them, and paying whatever for printing, postage, etc. (Having written which, I just got your new directory!! Gracias).

Wheatgrass grows excellently here on any little patch.

Love,
Steven Bloomstein, Apartado 185, Cumana, Venezuela, September 30, 1978

PROGRESS IN PARADISE

Dear Friend, An awful lot has happened since I last wrote. I am still spinning and it will probably take a little time to put things into true perspective.

Thank you for the copies of Johnny's newsletter. We did end up there. It seems they do possibly have 25,000 acres. It's an awful lot. Most of it is on the side of a mountain — virgin with lakes, streams, waterfalls, rivers — an Escondido, California climate, but no frost.

There were 7 adults. Tim and I make 9. And I guess we'll stay and investigate the situation more thoroughly. Things were somewhat disorganized and not much progress had been made over the past few years (or so it appeared). But Phil (also a newcomer) and Tim are experienced organic farmers, both raw fooders, and make things happen very fast. Orchards and gardens are going in everyday.

Newcomers are welcome but only those truly dedicated and willing to work. Money is needed for food until trees and gardens produce, missionary visas, fare down, trees, houses, etc. $2–3,000 would be good to start with.

Bus or train can be taken down to Panama. There the road stops and a plane is necessary. ($146 per person to Guayaquil, Ecuador — half for children). $375. to ship our car, and that was an extremely good deal. One company wanted $800. for half that distance. It is not advisable to drive.

Missionary visas, as Johnny has it set up, are $80 for 2 years. Residency is $800. and after a 2 year trial period you can be turned down. Upon arriving in Ecuador, you can get a FREE tourist card for 3 months. The only country we went thru without paying fees. Have heard we may have trouble getting my car thru the desert though.

Any information on travel from the U.S. thru Central America to the Andes or sources would be much appreciated. Was thinking of putting together some sort of pamphlet. May save others some pains we experienced.

Bless,
Judy Leger, Lista De Correos, Vilcabamba, Loja, Ecuador

MORE FROM THE EQUATOR

Dear Viktoras, I had arranged with my father to send you a check for the Spiritual Directory you sent me. Recently he received the check back from the bank unprocessed, and I received a reminder from you about the bill. So here we will try again, and I am including some brief comments to update you on the September 30th letter concerning our situation down here.

We have purchased a piece of land considerably lower down on our Rio Brito, only several hours walking now from civilization. We were very fortunate to get this small piece with several thatch houses, avocados, mangos, tangerine trees, bananas, pineapple and so forth, for only a few hundred dollars. It is in the curve of the river with lovely swimming holes, and some isolation as an island. It has not of course the potential and grandeur of our more solitary site high in the montains, Akujena. But it serves as an excellent stepping stone and way station more immediately and less ambitiously. The lower place is at about 500 feet in altitude, say, and the upper one at some 2000 feet. The mountains rise to some 8-9000 feet behind us, so we are accessible to a number of environments, as you point out and encourage in "Survival". Even at 500 and 2000 feet there is a notable difference in what can be grown successfully. At 500 feet mangos and conconuts, nisperos, thrive where 2000 feet is better for citrus and avocado, cherimoya, and ground crops in general.

I recently visted my friend 'Mango' on his piece of land in the jungle near the Rio Caura to the south. He has been developing the site for several years now, and is close to a year around fruit situation. Also a comfortable house designed for yoga.

The other hacienda in our valley is higher up and further away than ours. It has perhaps a better selection of fruit trees, and stands beside one of the most impressive virgin rain forests I have ever seen, with a view over mountains to the ocean and islands beyond. Quite a power spot really. And probably available for NO Money!!! There's no owners left...But, really NOT accessible by machine, i.e. car or boat (the river is not navigable, too small), simply a full day by pack animal in (half day as you get used to it). The kind of place only serious people would reach. Which conforms to our particular vision of remoteness in nature, etc. but may not suit your community vision. Oh, no buildings, one small thatch hut, this is all long abandoned. A lot of wildlife, snakes, too. A vital place. And the same apparently perfect low tropical mountain climate.

Bob is south in Guayana on the edge of the jungle, with access by good gravel roads, a lot of cheap land available, possibly with fruit trees; may be more appropriate for you. His particular area has a real hot humid jungle climate I don't much care for, but there are other possibilities.

I think the government map agency in Caracas will best serve your needs, I'll check next time in Caracas (July?). It would cost a lot to get a complete detailed spread on the country and I think this is more than you need right now. I'll try for some general topographies to start with. It would be good for us to talk over a map, I can offer a lot a map can't. I know the U.S. Air Force makes some excellent aerial navigation maps of the country. You might check into whatever you can get up here. Let me know more what you want specifically. Best thing is simply to be down there looking around. We'll be able to suggest promising areas.

I think it is reasonable to say that karma is speeded up in the jungle, in genuinely wild Nature. Or that people are weeded out fast because it is a very tough and intense series of changes. This is something I have seen happen everytime, and we all have to see/learn for ourselves. (I'm talking about full on vital nature now, not semi-civilization, but being in the full pranic show). One way to view this, being completely in nature (external ecology) is like being completely on fruit (internal ecology), extraordinarily difficult to make the full change all at once, too cleansing too fast.

People crack behind it. And often take to eating heavier to deaden the super energy flows...hence the reversion to cooked foods etc. as you mention with the people in Costa Rica. In fact, working hard in such a vital environment is so vitalizing that even eating heavier, I experience little mental or physical densification. Some heavier food, while it may not help, is simply consumed in the heavier energy flows and may even serve to moderate the intensity a bit. The goal of course is to get set up and have abundant quantities of tree sun ripened high prana fruit, and this will eventually sustain fruitarian power. I am looking forward to the coming next round.

Love,
Steven Bloomstein, Apartado 185, Cumana, Venezuela

Section III
In Central America

LIVING WITH TEMPTATION

Dear Viktor, This past week Philip Werlien handed me a copy of your book "Survival Into the 21st Century". Philip has been at the Hippocrates Health Institute and is now our neighbor on a piece of land that R.J. Cheathan owns here in the Cayo District, Belize, Central America. He lives alone and is struggling to get his health improved. I have known Natural Hygiene, —spent four months there in 1972 & 1973 (I think I saw you briefly when Dr. Ann was there in Florida giving a talk on sprouts. My husband had arrived that evening so I was unable to attend the talk, but as you were preparing to leave I met Ann in the parking lot). And as a result of the leaflet Ann handed me I learned about her marvelous work and have wanted very much to spend some time at her Health Center. Before I had a chance to do so, however, I was introduced to macrobiotics and I couldn't reconcile the two methods of healing. My husband loves to eat, as do I so I got into macrobiotics so I could cook us up tempting meals. He had been satisfied with raw foods and would have liked to have had a combination diet of lots of fruits and vegetables plus grain dishes. It seemed like we had to choose either the one or the other and I could really "dig" the unifying principle in the Far East philosophy, so I chose macrobiotics. Maybe we could have profited more from it if we had settled down and practiced it, but our life has been too involved with people who do not understand my unconventional ways and my husband hasn't taken our health problems seriously enough to give up this way of life that has me in a bind. When we had this beautiful opportunity to come to Belize I hoped it would be the answer to my (our) health problems, but after a year and three months (and three of those months I was in California seeking help while trying to sell our car), I knew I needed help. It seems a shame to go away from this lovely place, but I'm too "spaced out" and "weak willed" to help myself amidst unbelievers and antagonists. My biggest curse is becoming resentful toward our neighbors and friends because they seem to be keeping me in a continual state of a turmoil run life. My husband and I are Bahai Pioneers and to feel unloving towards others is a basic offence, yet I'm in that space too much of the time! Oh, Viktor, is there any chance of your helping Philip and I? — so that I can stay here and these beautiful people can benefit from your good work? R.J. has 300 acres and we are using a small portion which was formerly a plantation. This country is ready for something good! You would find it very gratifying, I am sure. They are trying to improve their medical facilities because there is so much sickness due to processed foods, sugar, and alcohol consumption. Think about it. God's will will be done!

Sincerely,
Grace Tremblay, October 10, 1976

BELIZE

Dear Viktoras, In Belize I was employed to help set up a naturopathic health clinic — health food store — garden — 125 hives of bees, but due to many factors all fell through. It must have been through this that you got the impression I have a natural healing center.

I like it here in Belize so I decided to stay, married and have two children now. I lived in Belize three years before I found this land and I am very happy here. I have 100 acres and about half mile on Barton Creek. We live near some simple living Mennonite communities and our life styles and beliefs go well together. I have learned a lot from them about working, farming and living a spiritual life.

Belize is a hard country to live in. The people are lazy, so we have to produce almost all our food, fruit is not cheap — what a contrast from Mexico and Guatemala. We try to live simply, on a diet of vegetables, fruit, milk, eggs, beans, corn, rice, brewers yeast, kelp, herbs. We would like to use more sprouts. We use alfalfa, sunflower, buckwheat, but we have too much work. It's just me and my wife and she stays constantly busy — washing clothes, dishes, cooking, hoeing in the garden, sewing and all spare time with the baby. I went through a lot of changes my first two years in Belize, I came here eating only raw food. I almost starved. Also between worms and amoeba I was in bad shape. Also, starting this farm was hard as we are 16 miles from town and the only things here were trees and prickle bushes, so for a long while, until we got land cleared and food planted it was rice and beans. I feel excellent now and haven't had even a cold for years. My natural healing recipe is good food and hard work, plenty of sweat. As it says in the Bible "By the sweat of your brow shalt thou earn they bread, all the days of your life".

Like you I also am dedicated unto Survival Into The 21st Century. Especially my children — teaching them to survive physically, mentally, and spiritually. It seems my work for now is growing food and I put all my energy into it. I do have a desire to set up a natural healing clinic of some sorts but it will be awhile, as we don't have room in our house. As I said, it is all so much work. I am not selfish (trying to be selfless) and would like to share this, with brothers and sisters as serious minded as I am. At present there is a small piece of excellent land for sale here. If you feel to visit, our door is open. If you write first and tell me a day I could meet you at the "Pine Ridge Road' and bring you in with our horses.

Peace and Love,
Joseph Dunsmoor, Belize, Central America

NOTES ON PARADISE

Viktoras, Beloved Brother! May Universal peace bless your ways in these ever brightening days!
Here and now all is clearer and clearer, purer and purer as we give our all to uniting this New Age energy! Inspirations for the Institute (Editors Note: Hippocrates Health Institute, Boston, Massachusetts) felt strongly around the lake!
Sorry to say, but Indians use more and more chemical fertilizers, insecticides, drugs, as outside influences "money interest" come to the lake's shores! All health minded travelers "be not deceived" by supposed "organic" fruits and vegetables being sold around the lake!
Giving our all here to educate the Indian growers as to harmful aspects of using chemicals. As we search out the purest spots left to be truely pure of the chemicals! Purifying and cleansing on all levels as Aquarian Age Energy fills the temple! For transitioners to Andes Mountains "Paradise Building" spot, a rented canoe enables one to reach very regenerating points on lake shores! Most organic food is found on shores where tourists least visit! For example, on the San Marcos, San Pablo, La Laguna, side of lake, there is no car traffic, much less outside influence!
Readying for a trip into Ecuador to be with Brother Lovewisdom's energy! May the circle be unbroken as we unite in the OM!
It's time those in the north that can feel the call, come together to create this paradisical reality we feel so strongly!
Eternity calls us OM! Keep the "brothers" and "sisters" here informed as to any truely organic spots where the "spirit" resides between Ecuador and Guatemala! When the spirit moves us south it would help to know any places organic growers are located! Would like to hear how the "awareness gap" is showing in the north lands! Spread the live food message!
The time is at hand! How many here's and now's have we all lived thru to be here now! In these final purification days, we must all prepare to meet the need!
Namaste, Brother, we honor your light!
Note: Information to all "brothers and sisters" about well water grown organic fruits and vegetables, 17 miles west of Tuscon, Arizona! Lorine Fuscon's "Garden of Eden"! Only truly organic food found around Tuscon, Arizona! Perfect for regenerating temples!
Any "vital" words awaited concerning move south! Also, any information on Keifer, Yogurt, Vegetized milk clabber, would greatly help our understanding on

these foods, as we have access to pure milk at times! Also information on sprouts regenerating temples!

Manos Puros, Lista De Correos, Santiago, Attitlan, Solola, Guatemala

---

FRUITARIAN EXPERIENCE

Dear Viktoras; How are you? It was good to hear from you. I am writing in response to your request for detailed information on our fruitarian living experience in Guatemala this past year. Those of us involved feel very good about the practical prospects of permanent fruit–community living, yet until that time we need still to iron out some problems we've discovered.

Our little settlement consisted of between 5 and 7 males. (Depending on who was there). All of us were well acquainted previously through high school days. We are all individuals with different interests and means of going about living. What we did have in common though was strong friendship, a sense of humor and dedication to the principles of fruitarian–sproutarian living. We were: Rene (21 yrs.), Jim (21), Brian (21), Rob (20), Dave (24), Udgah (29) and Jeff (19). Jim and I had a history of drug pollution (medical and otherwise) as did we all. We were all accustomed to fruitarian habits previously.

I won't paint the picture any different than it was; throughout the time spent (October 1976–April 1977) our generally peaceful, happy and very pleasurable existence was laced with hassles of various natures. None of us are examples of the ideal fruitarian. The transition to these ideals comes naturally but slowly; it cannot be pushed or forced. The history of 20 years of unnatural living leaves us with lots of work, with diet being only a small factor.

I will speak for myself to save space. I prepared myself eight months prior to leaving by studying ASSIMIL Spanish and the accompanying records (which I taped from the public library set). So I had a working knowledge of Spanish and an ear to understanding it upon arrival. I flew to Guatemala City alone in October. On advice from friends I went to Panajachel on Lake Atitlon, mainly because there were many young Americans there and it is a good safe place to adjust to the change in language and peoples. I stayed in a hotel the first few days ($2.00 a day) to get acquainted. I feel it is wise to stay in a hotel wherever you go the first day as it gives one the freedom from luggage, a sense of security and a clean habitat. Those who sleep on beaches etc. are asking for trouble from the local police. In the mountains it is quite cold at night, 45 degrees. I inquired about renting a house in a nearby settlement of Indian farms, an adobe village. With the help of some experienced Americans, I procured a large white–washed adobe, with furniture and tiled floor, all very neat, for $20.00 a month. In the mountain areas, a tourist cannot meander through the woods sleeping on the earth and eating wild fruit as some people believe. The gross amount of land is

THE SPROUTING OF THE NEW AGE /43

used and owned. The Indians benefit from our purchasing of food and renting homes and there is a rainy season.

Once settled in I wrote to seven addresses listed in 'Survival' as new age communities in Central America and South America. During my entire stay I got only one reply from a chicken farmer in Belize who was looking for a wife. I found the days gloriously warm and sunny and spent most of my time exploring, drawing, swimming and meeting people. There were times when the 'Nortes' blew (strong northly winds) when it rained. The Indians spent the day in the fields and the evenings socializing, the gringoes spent the day enjoying the weather and the evenings lonely and boring. The fruit was delicious and very inexpensive but not entirely free from fertilizer-pesticide pollution of the North. In the course of my stay I saw dusting planes, insecticides and artificial chemical nutrients applied in local and corporate farms. To the Indians these mean more yield and more money to keep up the cost of inflation. The laws are very slack there, and illegal chemicals such as DDT are commonly used on most of the modern farming areas. The tomatoes for example are tasteless red pulp. Watermelon, bananas, some mango, grapes, melons, and cucumber are by and large grown under some chemical inducement.

I spent time doing yoga and meditation in the evenings and also walking around, but no electricity and no people wth common interests made them dull. I overslept.

Within six weeks my friends began arriving. We rented houses all on the same farm and enjoyed a daily routine of sun, swim, go to the market, eat, walk, and in the evenings, sit around and talk, sing and play guitar, walk into town, etc. We had a lot of time to spend. Again the evenings were dull and some of us took to going to restaurants and eating soup and listening to music. We'd make a deal with the restaurant to give us dishes of raw food, and also bring our own food. At this time papaya was the favorite and we'd spend a lot of time bargaining, buying, eating and discussing in depth the merits and deliciousness of this wonder fruit. I began having very rapid passing of food, colored feces and a delicious taste in my mouth. My diet was 80% fruit and 20% veg.—fruit. My friends ate a lot, which was to their preference. Avocadoes which I don't like, were said to be the best in the world.

I felt unsatisfied in the mountains, a bit bored and generally lethargic, we took a trip to El Salvador and found it crowded, expensive and too modern; however we liké the total vibration. David had a car. If one doesn't have a car, the local inexpensive bus system is the only alternative; one finds these humorous and jovial affairs at first, but they can be crowded, polluted and tiresome. I highly recommend that some sort of transportation be obtained for personal use, such as a car, motor—bike or bicycle. Despite their polluting disadvantage they are immenseley convenient in such an isolating and strange environment.

We moved to the coast (five of us). Jim and I scouted the coastal area for habitation and found a beautiful house just outside of San Jose and very close to an enormous papaya plantation. Whereas the mountains were cold at night, on the coast we could wander about near naked 24 hours a day. Since we now had electricity and running water, we could spend evenings in comforts more to our background. This time five people were in one habitation whereas previously we each had our own house. This caused some emotional tention as we noticed more of each others peculiarities, i.e., David was a chronic banana eater and always constipated and this led to may arguments as to the cause of constipation and merits of a high liquid diet, etc., etc. Finally we agreed: to each his own. Under such pleasant weather conditions I began eating less and better i.e. melon for lunch, melon for supper, orange juice for breakfast. The sun was mild and the ocean breezes deliciously warm and intoxicating. Unfortunately, barges and tankers on occasion would dump their shit in the water and it ended up on the door step of our beach house (our club mansion). Watermelon became the favorite (25¢ to 50¢ for "cannon ball" melons) and everyone became much more alive and sparkling on this light diet. Rob would run up to 8 miles when the tide was out and subsisted only on orange juice and watermelon. We all became very dark and shiny, bleached hair and clear eyed. We encountered thieves here, and had a hammock and some other articles stolen. In January I water fasted a lot and experienced a unprecedented well being and joy of living,a nd for the first time my sinus passages blossomed clear. Distilled water was locally purchased at $1.20 for 10 gallons.

Occasionally we'd go to Guademala City and get sick on "vegetarian" food. I was so sensitive, a little cheese on my salad would make me sick. Jim's teeth were in need of repair (at about 1/5 of the Canadian price they were fixed).

When I really began feeling continuously happy and very healthy, mangos came in season. Eating these nectar–bombs was a highlight in my sensory experiences. We'd travel 1½ hours just to buy a special organic type. Mangos were the fruit of the day. I began eating only mangos. God, they were delicious. When I'd bite into one basking in the noon sun, I could close my eyes and rejoice in pure ecstacy at this nectar of eden. I did overeat on occasion, however fasting once a week and buying less, curbed this habit.

Some four months had passed and I felt an unequalled sense of pleasure and well being. My finances had depleted to a point where I knew I must return to civilization. This prospect seemed unappetizing. My lungs were very sensitive, bad air makes me sick to my stomach, and the thought of tasteless northern food! (I had been spending $100 a month average for everything).

We all missed the company of others and especially some female company or presence. We would play cards in the warm breezes and contemplate the possibility of fruitarian women. It's not that we began to get bored, we loved our home and our food and our position on the planet, yet the spice of novelty and adventure was missing. I felt I could just go forever on liquids and bathe in the sun and air, and leave my past like a snake skin, and I gave it serious thought, but the predominant pull was to return to my beloved Canada for the summer months. I had reached a crossroads and decided to retreat a bit just to be safe.

I might mention here that my companions became transformed into the most beautiful people I've ever seen: beautiful brown bodies, golden shiny hair and diamond piercing eyes. I couldn't get over the beauty. Their every movement was the inspiration of God. Yoga was beautiful. Every movement was an extremely sensitive and exciting experience of pure pleasure. My meditation became amazingly clear and I experienced the most enjoyable sleep and dreams of my life.

The desires for companionship, for productiveness, for adventure, for the Canadian forests, and for money brought me back (and the others). The air at sea–level was too heavy. I was extremely thin.

The overall problem was the need of something to do, something to give of oneself; a sense of participation. Isolation is something to be learned and adapted to.

I think each individual has returned with a greater understanding of himself and the nature of existence, a clarity and experience of optimal harmony with our planet. Now Canada is a novelty, civilization is somehow amusing and undisciplined. I had a hard time adjusting to the air and food. I got sick on both. My skin became dry from being indoors (after living outdoors for six months). I drank spinach−dandelion juice quite often to help my condition. The fruit here is bland and tasteless. I found the sprouts a very pleasant diet to change to. I'm now eating Canadian apples, green juices and lots of mung beans. Protein food really disagrees with me.

I have left some 80% of the details out. The benefits of my six months in Guatemala have left me no alternative but to further pursue the path of cleanliness and awareness. The benefits to be reaped by this lifestyle are great but are demanding. If someone asked me for recommendations for tropical living I'd say: (a) plan a short excursion first and become familiar with the realities of such a lifestyle; (b) be very realistic and reasonable as to your goals; (c) bring money and don't be afraid to spend it; (d) learn spanish; (E) learning to do nothing is an art to be learned; (f) bring your interest and hobbies with you; (g) go with or arrange to meet a friend or friends.

I have investigated land ownership and the prospects look good. I have more to learn and see through before I undertake a venture such as buying land. When the northwinds blow this autumn I'll be going again to the warmer climates. I am very interested in other persons who want the adventure of the south. If I can aid in the organization of Omangod's work in Canada, I will gladly do so. I would sincerely enjoy helping put things together. I am not one to go around propagating fruitarian ideals though.

The future looks bright − Hope to hear from you again.

Rene Caron

MANGOES, PAPAYAS, ETC.

Dear Viktoras, I thought I'd drop you a note describing a few of my experiences in the tropics. As of now, I am living in Yelapa, Jalisco−Mexico. A small community (300 natives, 40 Americans) 15 miles south of Vallarta. I've been here since March 7th. I was here 1½ months last year, too. Came down with two friends who I believe you know − Richard Watson and Michael Cooper, both from San Marcos, California.

The weather is very warm with occasional cloudy days. The local fruit is superb! In February, March, April; soursaps, papayas, jelly coco anoney's (similar to cherimoya only richer and creamer − thus heavier). In May, June etc.: mangoes, papayas, cinhuelas, tamarinds, bananas, cocos. Plus one finds in the tiendas: citrus, avos, melons, vegie fruits, etc. The people: very mellow−friendly, though, getting tourist−commercial oriented. The rent: a palm front hut averages $25.00/month comfortable. Can rent them in town up the Tuito River. Suggest one get it up the river if into fruit−yoga−meditation−quiet. Having experienced Hawaii, I much prefer Mexico's fruit, it seems to have more energy/life juice/love for me. Though I am found of Haden and Pirie (Paris) mangoes of Hawaii; There is some antaganism in Mexico regarding males with long hair and beards, 'hippie' types. Mostly in cities and from youths, also they are into cleanliness in appearance. However, I feel it is more intense in Hawaii. I, and later on, two friends were badly beaten there. So one (white Americans) should be aware. It is interesting that such hostility exist amongst such beauty.

As of now, my diet is raw fruit, twice a day. Have experimented with a few recipes I thought you may wish to try (maybe add to one of your books, if satisfactory).
1. Jelly coco ferment: run the coco meat thru grass juicer, or chop it very fine − put into a jar, and seal. Let it sit until it bubbles, usually 24 hours.
2. Regular coco ferment: same procedure, however, may need to add some water. Both delicious! The first one reminds me of seed ferment. The second, bamboo shoots and sour milk. Excellent with tomatoes and kelp or dates.
3. With jelly coco ferment, mash in banana. Let it sit until it bubbles. To me it tastes like scrambled eggs. Fruitarian egg substitute.

I plan to be here until mid−June, then, head north. May attend the healing gathering in Oregon, July 1−7. If you are in the area, you are welcomed to stay. It is very quiet, and tranquil. Wish all is well.

Most Sincerely,
Richard Stumman

P.S. With this diet and living, last week or so I have passed small worms. Culminated in passing one 12 inch long, complete; thereafter, few more small ones. Needless to say, I am pleased.

Section IV
Elsewhere

CULTURE SHOCK

Dear Viktoras, Beela! How are you? It certainly has taken me a long time to write you! Please forgive me.

I have recently returned to the U.S. from my Fiji experience and I want to share with you some of the things I learned there. I also want to ask your advice about some of the problems I encountered and see if you have any suggestions.

First of all, even though I came to Guam rather than Hawaii or the Mainland, I suffered severe culture shock and am still going thru it! Never driving a car for over a year or seeing a building over three stories tall and doing my only shopping in an open air fruit and vegetable market are not very good preparations for a U.S. trip!

My baby was born December 26 (it would have been Christmas in the U.S.) in my beere (house) with 2 Fijian women and the Fijian man I was living with present. (I think I already told you about that!)

Anyway, my life there was just beautiful. I have two other children — a boy 7, and a girl 3. They just blossomed. The boy went to a Fijian school where he played rugby and learned to speak Fijian. His after–school activities were climbing coconut trees, picking fruit, or fishing. Since returning to this culture he has become withdrawn and feminine — causing me much frustration.

Our days were spent looking for fruit, being on the beach, fishing, or just being around the house talking to our Fijian housegirls. We had a garden for a while but it got washed out in the rain.

For survival purposes, I saw Fiji as perfect, with only two exceptions. The weather was as good as Hawaii — no extreme hot or cold; there was an abundance of food always and markets to buy it. Plus there are 300 islands and 2 of them are as large as the Big Island of Hawaii, so there is loads of room for the amount of people who live there. There are mountains, valleys, lakes, rivers and beaches. Typhoons aren't as serious as they are in this part of the world — they don't wipe out the whole island or the food growth. Mostly they only hit the beaches and many islands are protected by other ones.

It is very clean country — the people have a lot of pride in their villages, yards, children and selves. They are energetic and hardworking — usually don't let themselves get fat or unhappy.

Tourists come there but they haven't ruined the country yet.

As foreigners, there is free—hold land available for us to buy — reasonable by our standards.

It doesn't have any internal political problems, and English is their main language.

So, after all the good points, we get to the bad ones!

1) We are only allowed to stay in the country for 6 months at a time. We can leave and return, however, after even a day; as long as we leave the country. The only ways I found around this are to marry a Fijian (only works for a woman, not a man) or to have at least $20,000 in invest in a business.

2) Unless women arrive there with their own men, it is virtually impossible to get along with native men. I think it would be easy for a man — I've seen many cases where it works — but foreign women are too used to completely alien cultures and I've never seen a case where it worked.

My reason for leaving, unfortunately was the latter. I was given an extra six months stay because of the baby, but just couldn't work out the other. I eventually wanted to get land and move the rest of my tribal family down, but couldn't figure out how to get everybody in the country to stay legally.

Have you heard from anyone who has solved either/both of these problems?

I have one other male member of our "family" here on Guam with me now, and armed with what I learned in Fiji, we are setting off on another venture next week. I tried to make it here for three months — was writting for the local paper, I had an apartment on the beach, but have been going progressively downhill! The food trip is so bad! Most of the fruits and vegies are imported all the way from California. They are too lazy to grow it here! I've gained 10 lbs. here and feel I can't relate at all! Do you have other cases of returning—home shock? Any antidotes?

We are heading for a small island north of here in the Marianas called Tinian. It may be a stepping—stone as I don't feel it has the degree of isolation necessary to be permanent. Would be anxious to return to Fiji someday if we could solve the immigration problem. Every native person there already knows about survival! They can build houses, grow food, make mats and baskets, fish, cook in the ground, make brooms, sleep on the floor, and make juice from a multitude of local leaves for any ailment.

I couldn't believe it! It is truly a paradise. (Please only tell those you trust about it!)

Will let you know how Titian goes. We can stay there permanently as U.S. citizens, but can't buy land unless we have Marianas blood. This can be gotten around if it is a good place.

One good thing about coming back. I caught up with some of my books again and got reaquainted with your "Survival" book! — A work of art!! Thank you so much!

Anxious to hear from you when you have the time.

Love,
Ginny Shamberg (Mahina), September 4, 1978

PUERTO RICO

Dear Viktor, The voyage to S.A. has been going rather slowly. We left Sarasota the beginning of October, hung out in the Bahamas for a month, then sailed for Puerto Rico. Last month I sailed around the Virgins for a couple of weeks.

What have I found? No prospects so far for the right land. The Bahamas are great for the most part and most of the islands are desolate. Puerto Rico is beautiful – green, rivers, mountains. However, with 1,000 people per square mile and land selling for $2–3,000 per acre – forget it. The Virgin Islands are a similar situation to Puerto Rico, though I have not yet been to St. Croix. The Dominican Republic has less population and the land is slightly cheaper (still in $4,000 + bracket) but the government is quite unstable.

I am somewhat looking forward to St. Croix. An acquaintance whose father is the commissioner of agriculture there wants to ship organic tropical fruit. Evidently it is more of an aquarian island. However, Rockefeller still ownes a major part of it (as with all the Virgins) and I doubt tree crops are a motivating force for him.

Right now I am in Puerto Rico trying to ship organic bananas, coconuts, papayas, pineapples, guanabana, bread fruit, etc. There is much organic fruit growing wild here in certain areas. An old friend of mine, from the time when tens of thousands of freaks converged on Amsterdam in the early 70's has a farm in Penuelas. 80 acres of bananas, mangos, citrus, papayas, avocados, etc. and he is very into excellent organic techniques. There are many others who are being very helpful here – too numerous to mention.

I hear you are coming to Puerto Rico!!! Would you like to meet on St. Croix before or after the retreat. I will be leaving here before the end of the month. But you can write me there for now: c/o San Juan Marina, G.P.O. Box 4627, San Juan, Puerto Rico 00963, Tel: 809–723–0415. You are cordially invited to cruise with us as long as you care to – there's lots of room on board. This boat is an Atlantic 39 world cruiser.

Love,
Philip, January 15, 1979

DOMINICA

Dear Victoras, Time and the great movement of the spirit has connected me with a beautiful place on the island of Dominica in the West Indies. After my work this fall with the Pacific College of Naturopathy Seminar in New Hampshire my intuitive knowing channeled me through the circuit and so to be here now is to experience a simpleness I have never known in this life.

A joy to walk the 2 miles up the mountain where we live passing farmers with their donkeys on the way to market.

Having worked with "No Guns" and over the years incorporating the many concepts of natural healing, purification and preparation I have only asked for purer grounds to unite with this reality.

The land I am on now is self supporting as we are renting an old estate vacant for a few years with 125 acres of tropical fruits worked by the native farmers. The house itself can support easily 10 people (more if we learn humbleness) with its 4 bedrooms, 2 bathrooms, a guest house, kitchen and 2 large rooms for communal space, a treatment room: it goes on and on.

I am wanting to ask you for some guidance and inforamtion on the following, knowing you would be far more knowledgeable in what I want to know in relation to cleansing and nutrition of:

Coconut — Is it a difficult food to digest, highly caloric? Protein content?
Banana — If eating only fruit the average consumption
Papaya
Mango — Have you ever heard of it giving you worms?
Citrus

Viktoras, I believe deeply in our work and at this time I am committed to the healing of women by offering a safe space for us to purge and regain our spiritual and physical understandings. Ten women arrive within the month and the beginning grounds for a self–supporting center will become clearer. I would like to keep in contact with you as I feel the circuit expanding and would like to remain connected to my family in the U.S. who are involved in this work.

To the economics of how this center can truly be created I do not know, I only know that I have worked my way here and on the blessings that this can unfold I pray.

If you are connected to resources where money energy can be freed up, a gift sent here would only be received in grace. I only wish I could share with you the purest beauty I have ever beheld and a greater joy that I continue what I so know and be the truth.

In Sharing for the Restoration of all life.

Paloma Mahana,
c/o General Delivery, Dominica, West Indies, April, 1979

PART II

SPREADING THE NEW AGE AWARENESS

With the advent of an age such as the one which is today imminent, a host of dedicated, tireless workers is entrusted with the task of spreading the new consciousness. There is much to be taught and much to be learned as a rediscovery of ancient truths coincides with an emergence of new ways of living and being.

The following articles, which explore some of the ways in which people are involved in spreading the Light which seeks to establish itself on this planet, encompass both theoretical paradigms and pragmatic action programs. Both, of course, bear great importance in the task of actualizing the new world of the coming age which is upon us.

Section I
The New Age In Action

LETTER OF APPEAL
FROM DR. ANN WIGMORE

Heartfelt Greetings! I see a world without sickness and hunger, through living foods.

It does my heart good to learn about the wonderful progress manifesting in many splendid ways throughout the world — Health through Nature's Way — especially during these past years.

My 29 years of struggles are paying off. The efforts to teach and share health ideas through living foods are now becoming gratefully accepted and propogated by so many human angels, through books, lectures and by being examples in hundreds of thousands of homes.

Yet, we are not able to help other hundreds of thousands who are dying from cancer daily, and those dying of hunger — there are 1,000 in South Africa alone who are dying daily of starvation.

It is very important NOW that we really have some scientific proofs that persons who have been improved in health and who have benefited in any way, will let it be heard through testimonials and various forms of messages sent to lawmakers, The President and the rest of humanity who are not aware of all the advantages that can be derived from living food nourishment.

My three trips to India proved extremely successful as I was able to share on a large scale the educational, practical information while I was there. When I first went to India — for only three weeks — I was able to do more sharing than I have done for the past 15–20 years in our own country. On my second trip to India I was able to establish a workshop which consisted of a month's implementation of the program. People were receiving help in five different centers that second time; they received help where they were housed (125 each time) in crude facilities and although the completely whole living food diet and juices were not fully available as here, the results were outstanding and the people felt the healings were a miracle. All kinds of health problems were encountered, (although there are not as many cancer people as we have here), and people with diabetes, arthritis, asthma and many other conditions were aided and put back on the road to health. All made tremendous improvements in a short, four weeks. A small hospital was established and some remarkable testimonials were received from that experience on cancer. The work was most gratifying, to see how quickly the improvement it brought about in children's grades in schools. The teachers were amazed and many of the street people were also helpful. I was able to do some experimenting with diet substitutions for them and to introduce sprouting and there the mentality improved to such an extent that many people became self—employed instead of begging on the street and all in such a short period of time!

Dr. Ann Wigmore, D.D., N.D., Founder—Director of the Hippocrates World Health Organization, a division of Rising Sun Christianity, an advocate of Living Foods.

I've heard many wonderful things from Becky and Brian Clement who have been traveling around the world these past three years — their experiences with medical doctors adopting the complete raw food program for their patients in Switzerland and other countries. In Finland where I gave a workshop and am returning again this year to lecture and teach a workshop, there has been much acceptance. All the invitations from other countries are coming now, Africa, for example, but above all, Canada has responded with great interest and enthusiasm and I am most eager to go there where the people are so receptive. I will be at Princess Margaret's Hospital experimenting with nutrition for cancer victims — for cancer people. So, that's what I really need now, documentation on cancer, especially. PLEASE send your report of your condition before, and after. Please send it to me immediately. I must have these statements especially for hospitals, a documented program for the establishment so they will be accepting of the proven benefits of the living foods program. Also, for use in India, on the fourth trip I'll be making there, especially for my cancer work, I will need this documentation. The Indian Government at the time I was there on previous trips had fully accepted my program, based on the obvious results, but since that time the legislators and government have changed and now, documented proofs are needed. So you can see how essential it is to have your help.

Please share as I have shared for all these 29 years constantly improving the program for all of those of you who have benefited, have reduced the cost of living, simplified your life and prolonged your life — please respond immediately to my appeal. I do see, with your help, a world without cancer, a world without hunger.

Ann Wigmore, D.D., N.D., Founder — Director of The Hippocrates World Health Organization, 25 Exeter Street, Boston, Massachusetts 02116

LIFELIGHT
ON THE ROAD WITH LIVING FOODS

Lifelights living raw food caravan began in the winter of '76 on a small island in Alaska. Pioneering the new age with a strict wheatgrass and sprout regime, after 40 days and nights of living food in the body along with implants, and meditation with grass juice in the woods, a new life was born, and winter was over so with the coming of spring we left our island and across Alaska we went displaying and exposing wheatgrass and sprouts to all people. We displayed the living food diet in two of Alaska's state fairs where over 150,000 people were explained the benefits of wheatgrass and sprouts, the functions of a clean body and the reality of heaven on earth today.

Our sprouts received first place blue ribbons and second and third place ribbons at both fairs. Wheatgrass and sprouts living food diet won the first place blue ribbon for survival in the future as man's diet on a small planet.

At the end of that summer we flew down to the lower 48 states and continued to set up at state and country fairs, Christmas shows, arts and crafts fairs, flea markets and parent's houses for Seattle to Boston.. After 6 months of traveling across America we flew back up to Alaska in February for two winter shows. In the dark cold winter the light of living green food attracted the people like a magnet, we had great response from the public, saw the northern lights and a vision of a bigger traveling living raw foods caravan. We then flew down to Oregon and purchased our first school bus, hooked a trailer on the back and drove to the Florida State Fair, then Arizona and California. At the Whole Earth Festival in Davis, California, we began giving out samples of wheatgrass juice to the public. We got a tremendous response so we did it again at the Celebration Of Life in Sonoma, California and at the Eugene County Fair, Eugene, Oregon both very successful shows for wheatgrass. Then we flew back up to Alaska in the summer and grew wheatgrass in our bus up there (we have a school and two trucks in Alaska at all times now) and gave out samples of wheatgrass juice for two weeks at the state fairs, received more blue ribbons for sprouts and wheatgrass, saw the northern lights and a clearer vision of the caravan. We took a ferry boat down to the lower 48 states (gave workshops on the boat) and purchased another school bus in Oregon and received another for free for our work from a beautiful soul to help us on our way. We immediately began plans to set up the buses to grow wheatgrass and sprouts for hundreds of people. We received large amounts of cantelope, grapes, peaches, nectarines, etc. all summer long and boxes of celery for our green drinks every morning. We took a sauna every day and the vision became a reality within our lives. We began to see to help other people along this path of cleansing and purifying of the body we would need more buses, to have a house bus — greenhouse buses for wheatgrass and sprouts, supply bus, massage and sauna bus, warehouse bus, etc. So to begin our caravan we purchased two more buses giving us a total of five.

Lifelight has three devoted members who hold all things in common for the success of the living light of life to be experienced by all people. Above all we in the caravan must maintain an open channel to the divine consciousness and be living examples of the evolvement of life toward paradise. So a living raw food diet is essential for a pure detoxified state of being free from toxins, disease, body lice, confusion, hepatitis, ego, etc. producing a shining light of life necessary for the union with God and the existence of heaven on earth, the garden of eden.

We set up two buses with 125 trays of wheatgrass and each and a house bus and headed down to San Jose, California for the NEW AGE AWARENESS FAIR where a few thousand people had samples of wheatgrass juice and learned about living raw foods. We then drove another bus down to California and equipped it to grow sprouts and we went to the National Health Federation convention in Long Beach, California. We had one bus full of sprouts — two full of wheatgrass and one live in bus. We served the public sprout salads and wheatgrass juice for three days and had enough left over for five more days which we gave away to health food stores and friends. It was our first big show of feeding the public and a success of growing it all on the road.

Then we flew back up to Alaska for two winter shows, temperature below zero degrees, northern lights and a bigger clearer vision of the caravan bringing love, life

SPREADING THE NEW AGE AWARENESS

and light of the living spirit across the land — a traveling living raw food community devoted to personal and universal aura farming to acheive the spectrum of life in the hearts of humanity. Living, learning and sharing with others the benefits of a living raw food diet for the detoxification, purification, and rejuvenation of the body to heal itself and be prepared to handle the energy of the new age of man's unfoldment of perfection.

After two winter months in Alaska we flew down to southern California to begin planting wheatgrass and sprouts for the World Symposium on Humanity, an eight day event. We used three buses and passed out 6,000 samples of wheatgrass juice and 800 sprout salads on a donation basis. Now we know that with a few people and a few buses we can detoxify and feed thousands of people and help them get started on a new life of survival into the 21st century.

At the present moment we are supplying fresh wheatgrass juice and helping to set up the growing procedure at a home for semi—retarded young adults in the Los Angeles area along with introducing wheatgrass to many of their friends and neighbors and giving live food workshops. We see the need of the caravan to visit other institutions for them to see our operation and help them begin to incorporate wheatgrass and living sprouts into their program.

Now with the present gas shortage we are making good use of having to sit still in the Los Angeles area. We find this to be a blessing for us as well as the public. We have been able to concentrate our energy on one area and stay around long enough to influence people, supply fresh wheatgrass to new friends, see some healing results, answer questions and help solve indoor gardening problems.

We have been giving wheatgrass juice to a few people whose doctors have seen a definite change for the better both physically and mentally. We are looking forward to having a few doctors begin to recommend their other patients to visit with us and learn the procedure of wheatgrass therapy.

It seems at this time we have an open door into the Los Angeles public. We now have five public engagements on health and healing in this area within the next 1½ months from our own public workshop to a two day show with Dr. Ann Wigmore where we will be exposing and serving wheatgrass juice and sprout salads and selling trays of wheatgrass to take home. We will also be advertising to the public our other daily service we wish to have available to the public — fresh wheatgrass trays, live food supplies, books, juicers, workshops and answers, all available at our home or their group's next gathering.

We believe that with more help we could have a successful service to the sick as well as the healthy in this area and help detoxify and spread the truth of survival in the future.

We donate our service to help this information be available freely to all people as their birthright. All of the success of Lifelight has come from the public supporting us at the shows to help us further our mission. Please help us continue to share this knowledge with the rest of the world as a donation from all of us. Your support in this project physically, mentally, spiritually or financially at this time is greatly needed for the growth and development of humanity and the continuation of us blazing this trail into the new age.

There is so much that could be done here while we all get to know, grow and find ourselves together before we set out as a universal unit across the land.

This is the moment for wheatgrass, now is the time to begin to help all people and create an oasis of the earth. This is a magical open time for humanity to receive this information.

Up till this time we have been doing all the planting, planning, designing and driving to produce a living light show and other brothers and sisters at the events join in to help us serve the public. We also sell crystal prisms along in our wheatgrass booth giving it the name "Lifelights – Prisims, Rainbows and Dreams". The crystals have been supporting us up till this time. Our dazzling crystal prism display (considered the largest traveling display in the world) adds the beauty and spectrum of light to our living wheatgrass booth making us a main attraction and a living altar of life attracting and holding the attention of the bystander in awe and creating an open moment in which the vision of life with live foods becomes a reality.

Our future vision is a larger living raw food family celebrating life traveling in school buses specially designed for our lifestyle – greenhouse buses for wheatgrass and sprouts, sauna and massage bus, colonic, polarity bus, meditation, food preparation, crafts, workshop, buses. A complete living light healing health community on wheels detoxifying, purifying and rejuvenating the cells of the human body so that they may become active members with nature, keeping this planet and all life alive in perfect harmony. We also see the need for music, dance, mime, puppet shows, theatre, solar energy, new age awareness, wholistic living, alternative energy, crafts and entertainment for ourselves and the public. These are only a few ideas from which we can sprout.

We will be offering our lifestyle as a selfless service wherever we go as our contribution to life for our existence.

Catering our services to other organizations for retreats, seminars, workshops, gatherings, etc. Help teach all people from ghettos, reservations, institutions, the physically and mentally handicapped and the upper class how to free themselves through the use of living foods. Turn soup kitchens into sprout kitchens across the nation. Hold our own special detoxification, healing gathering throughout the year. Help other travelers along the path of unfoldment continue while on the road. Help all aspects of life to achieve a happy, healthy and holy existence on this beautiful planet created in the consciousness of love for one another, etc.

We will eventually purchase large amounts of land to begin to live a life with nature and free our earth mother from the suffering caused by a selfish race and return our respect by opening up healing centers as well as new communities to begin the large scale union of man and nature to exist free from the old age of suffering and death and receive the gift of God – eternal life and happiness ever after.

We welcome all inquiries from people interested in helping support our project. We need more devoted living food family members willing to surrender their will for the will of God and the creation of the heaven within and on earth. We need people interested in all aspects of living food life – planters for wheatgrass, food preparers, secretaries, bookkeepers, accountants, lawyers, laborers, people into massage, polarity, meditation, colonics, drivers, bus mechanics, artists, mime, puppet shows, theatre, alternative energy, music, designers, organizers, speakers, public relations and lovers of life, anything and everything connected to living foods and the living spirit of life to survive in the future.

Come one, come all, new seekers and professionals into the new age of survival. Let us donate our services together to help in man's transformation for the greatest life on earth.

Namascar,
Lifelight, 6080 Prince Road, Simi Valley, California 93063

A Lifelight Living Raw Food exhibit in Los Angeles, California.

LIFELIGHT
UPDATE

Since May, Lifelight has been giving living food workshops in the Los Angeles area with great success. We have between 20 and 50 people attending all eager to begin living foods at home. We have received invitations to Church groups, private groups, health food stores and restaurants to hold more workshops on living foods and the light of life. We are also considering catering a living food luncheon to groups in the future as a refreshing new alternative to add to their gathering. Calls keep coming in from individuals asking about another workshop for the public and a commercial source of fresh living wheatgrass and supplies. We have received reports from workshop members who have changed over 180 degrees into all raw foods and are enjoying a wonderful experience with life. Also, people who had no will to live now look forward to rising up in the morning to a great new day and life with living foods. We have had many calls from people just to thank us for sharing this information which has helped give them new hope for their existence and humanity.

At this we feel a need for a living food community health center to open up in the Los Angeles area as well as a commercial source for fresh wheatgrass, sprouts and living food supplies. There is a great potential here for us to be suppliers to this area. We would like this to be a living food family venture all profits going back into itself to open up other living food health centers and retreats. This is a reality if the human energy can be directed properly. We feel so good helping so many needy people who want a change that we have decided to center our energy on this area and build a home base for the caravan to work out of, detoxifying and restoring God's plan in Los Angeles and at the same time equip the caravan to become a bigger traveling living light show.

Los Angeles seems to have a big influence on the standard of living and sets the styles of life, health and new age movements across the country. If it happens in California it spreads everywhere.

We are very much interested in the Holywood scene to pick-up on the energy and vitality of wheatgrass and living foods so a whole new concept of life may be experienced by both actor and producer helping to create more realistic films on the reality of the aquarian age. Now with the changing times and the end of the 70's wheatgrass and living foods can play its role in purifying the human race and help us in the transition into the age of enlightenment — the 21st century.

This is a very large city and people of all ages and lifestyles have recognized the message of life with living foods. Every other person has a disease along with a friend and all other methods haven't seemed to help to the satisfaction of their needs. The will to live is still very dominant above all failure and the immediate effect of just the wheatgrass juice has restored the positive attitude of hope and the will to assist nature to help bring about a change in the life and the direction of civilization at this time.

This is a very large city and people of all ages and lifestyles have recognized the message of life with living foods. Every other person has a disease along with a friend and all other methods haven't seemed to help to the satisfaction of their needs. The will to live is still very dominant above all failure and the immediate effect of just the wheatgrass juice has restored the positive attitude of hope and the will to assist nature to help bring about a change in their life and the direction of civilization at this time.

It is not just a coincidence for this to take place now, for nature has always tended to the needs of the planet. At this time when we have strayed so far from our natural way it comes as no surprise to me that grass, a very simple and common element of nature, should be used to bring us back to the root of life and merge us together as one with the cosmic force existing in all creation as the natural and harmonious flow of the divine plan of the universe.

Lifelight operates as a monastery holding all things in common. Its members surrendering into our specific goal of helping people to learn how to cleanse their body, mind and spirit and return to a natural state of being one with God. In the beginning new members of lifelight are required to undergo a strict wheatgrass and sprout regime to cleanse and purify their body as outlined in SURVIVAL INTO THE 21ST CENTURY as well as learning how and why Lifelight operates. Because of different lifestyles new members are required to remain under guidance from Lifelight until a oneness and harmony is satisfactory within our operation. At which time a person will receive a responsible position according to their inner and outer growth.

Our aim is to exist in harmony as one and the same energy as all life and to be an instrument of the divine will in action as our life, exposing our true identity as light beings restoring the harmony and flow of creation in all of life's forms.

This project of purification of the human race is going to take the help of all of us together. No one person, group or generation is going to make it alone or be able to do all the work necessary for our transition, it is going to take the energy and effort of each and everyone of us for each and everyone of us to make it through.

We are ready to do our share and open ourselves to the possiblity of more people joining in the family as well as non−family members in a co−op exchange in this living food adventure to create an outstanding detoxification center in the Los Angeles area. We open our minds, hearts, and our life so the divine will of God may work freely through us and help restore this garden of eden floating in timeless space for all life to enjoy the beautiful existence of creation.

Namascar,
Lifelight, 6080 Prince Road, Simi Valley, California 93063

James Piscatelli of Lifelight and Gypsy Boots, noted Hollywood entertainer and health food exponent, serve wheatgrass juice at a Los Angeles health convention.

GARDEN OF LIFE LIVING FOODS

Viktor, my diet has been at least 90% live food. I believe this works pretty good for me considering I am in business for myself (as you). I am having to meet with many business people (that world out there is of competitive consciousness)...it is hard to spread light when your brothers and sisters out there are sometimes trying to f... you over. The environment can be highly stressed. Being totally 100% pure takes tremendous strength, in which I do not have, but am working very hard, daily, trying hard to accomplish this. We are also infiltrating L.A. (tough because of high competition) and honestly believe we have so, so much going for us in the spirit of the light. It is evident in our progress. We have a very high quality product; will be introducing a whole line of free live–food information (pamphlets and such), for which we owe so much to you for your beautiful work. We love you very much here. If there is anything we can ever help you with please let me (us) know. By introducing the free literature in stores, we are reaching more and more people from the "other" walks of life. Those like Chicanos, Italians, etc. out here − in other words, our other brothers and sisters (which make up the prime majority) that need help and are often overlooked. We want to reach those as with all others. Yes, we have a big job. We plan on infiltrating across this continent with plans now underway to expand into northern California, Colorado, New Mexico and ? I firmly believe in how we must work to help the cause as much as possible. We must do our share. Yes, again, brother Vik, the work is hard, as you know, but we will make it. We all must stick together.

I hope this is not too late, there is no photo this time (being up in Colorado everything happened so fast, spaced out a little). Garden of Life Living Foods started in the Fall of 1977. Through the realization that the Santa Barbara area needed more high quality food, my brother Gerry and I decided to infiltrate the present health food market by introducing a variety of sprouts to the public. From a beginning of approximately 60–100 lbs. of sprouts a week (variety including alfalfa, red clover, fenugreek, lentil, mung, aduki, radish and cabbage) we are now presently producing approximately 4,500 lbs − 6,000 lbs a month. (This all varies upon the time of year, for the produce business is up and down constantly). We are now presently producing in progression with producing upwards of 10,000 lbs. plus a month − 2,500 lbs a week. We use purified H2O in our growing process − mineral content is checked through the county department − verifying it to be a fairly reasonable amount. We use totally organic seed, when available, −(Carnegie, Living Farms, Cross etc.). We put much love into our live food. We presently employ three full time and four part–time individuals who are working with us not for us. We not only grow live food but practice live foods nutriton as much as possible in our daily living habits. Our mung beans are grown by the "old chinese method". They are not overly long and bitter tasting like those found in most commercial stores but shorter approximately two inches and sweet tasting. We do not sacrifice quality for quantity. In short, we are a high purity, quality business growing the purest food possible for our dear brothers and sisters. Whatever extra information you can pick−up from our pamphlet, use to your discretion. I hope this information gets to you early enough.

I have changed the name of my foundation from Living Sunshine to Living Light Foundation. It is a reasearch and educational organization, non-profit oriented along a highly evolved nutritional program (emphasizing chlorophyll), complete body purification leading to transcendance into the dormant areas of our mind; in short, Nirvana, total wholistic body utilization with brain, leading to higher consciousness of living totality with our body/brain as our Creator intended. All in all I hope you have some insight into what we are doing. I may be in Flagstaff area during the Rainbow Gathering. I hope to see you then. In the Light of Our Master's love and happiness.

"Ethan", June 23, 1979

THE 21ST CENTURY CHEF

The title "Chef" has many implied meanings and values. Chef is the French word for chief. We are chiefs of kitchens. A person can be chef of a hot dog stand and he rightly is. I go another step in the matter and call us culinary artists who are, in my professional opinion, people thoroughly knowledgeable in culinary arts.

A chef can manage a kitchen and have a working knowledge of the trade, but a culinary artist has a deeper understanding of the trade and sees nutrition as its essence. A culinary artist is also a nutritionist (Doctor of food), artist in presenting food, cook in preparing food, and can manage a kitchen as a chef does in buying food and managing personnel. The A,B,C,'s of food call for (A) Nutrition, (B) Eye appeal, and (C) Taste. Most chefs grasp the last two, but miss the first one.

I believe that the two titles can come under one heading and I would say Chef which would imply Culinary Artist. Chefs do have a knowledge of nutriton, but like doctors, it is minimal. A person need not be a chef to be a culinary artist, but he must be a culinary artist to be a chef.

The chef has a responsibility to maintain one of the greatest artistic pieces in the world — our human bodies — when he has a captive audience such as I do. The real responsibility lies on the individual, but when that individual dines at your establishment he is placing some of that responsibility in the chef's hands. The A,B,C's are called to action. People do eat with their eyes so it is important to see that the food is beautifully prepared, but nutrition comes first. We must eat to sustain life, not sever it. Our physical responsibility has moral implications because our bodies are instruments to serve God. When we do a disservice to our bodies we are doing a disservice to God whom we serve with our bodies. St. Francis said "Lord, make me an instrument of your Peace". Our bodies are that instrument and temple of his Spirit.

Chefs also have a social responsibllity to use food prudently. While we feast in America, people in other parts of the world are starving. Simply try to avoid wasting it. Most chefs do this because it reflects a good food cost which makes them look good. But is that the only reason why? Pressuring companies into producing natural healthy foods is another area chefs can use their influence. We spend millions of dollars annually on food. If the chefs didn't buy refined and processed foods, think what would happen. Executive chefs are extremely intellegent in working with food. They can easily work their way around using the processed foods and start the trend back to natural foods.

The professionalism of the 21st century is permeating the culinary field. The American Culinary Federation (ACF) has established a certification program to educate chefs on all of the basics in the arts. Certified Executive Chef is the highest title one can attain. To be a certified culinarian means you have a working knowledge of the trade. Unfortunately nutrition still isn't emphasized as it should be and I brought it to their attention. I hope they do act upon my recommendation to emphasize nutrition more with upcoming culinarians.

I am a Certified Working Chef (CWC) and will be a Certified Executive Chef in 1980. During the last three years I have been struggling to promote nutrition in the professional realm. There will be a day when chefs will be truly Culinary Artists (nutritionists). I am proving that a professional chef can be a pure vegetarian and nutritionist while preparing unorthodox foods. I dream and pray for the day when man will live in accord with his spirit and body.

Brother Ronald Picarski, OFM, St. Paschal Friary, 3400 St. Paschal Drive, Oakbrook, Illinois. 00521

RUN FOR AMERICA FOUNDATION, INC.

Dear Viktor,

I am writing this letter to you on a matter of great importance.

Recently a new foundation was formed for the purpose of providing grants to those institutions dedicated to nutritional research for the prevention of major diseases.

The inspiration for the founding of "Run for America" was greatly influenced by you and your book, "Survival into the 21st Century" and also Dick Gregory's run for hunger.

The enclosed information will enlighted you as to the purpose of "Run for America" Inc. We would consider it an honor for you to take a seat on our board of directors and to help govern our progress as well as accumulated funds. We feel your knowledge and creativity would enhance the success of our foundation greatly. We would also like to promote your book "Survival", as we feel it would have a healthful and good spiritual influence on every human being with an open mind, and perhaps open the minds of many others.

We would deeply appreciate a letter of endorsement for our transcontinental run. We would also welcome any donation to the Run For America Foundation.

Our run kicks off for California on the first World Vegetarian Day and we would like to stress the significance of this day to the American people.

Time is of the essence Viktor, therefore we are looking for your speedy reply.

Sincerely,
John N. Peele

John Peele and Brian Hassell running for America

RUNNERS CLAIM VEGETABLE POWER

How about getting up in the morning to a heaping breakfast of wheat sprouts and a tall cool glass of carrot juice? Then with a stomach full of goodies, jogging over the open road for Los Angeles in the cause of national nutrition.

We, two Orlandoans, John Peele and Brian Hassell are going to do just that beginning October 1. Peele, 28 and Hassell, 27 will do the 75−day 3100 mile trek for the newly formed Run For American Foundation, based in Orlando.

The foundation was designed to do nutritional research and study methods of natural remedies for disease.

According to the foundation charter, 15 percent of all money given or granted is allocated to the working budget, while 85 percent goes into the research program.

"The concept of the foundation is one of education and nutrition. We believe that the best method for the people to eat is vegetarian," said Peele.

Peele has been a vegetarian for eight months and Hassell, for two years.

Both are planning to become juicearians for the coast-to-coast trek. In addition to ingesting fruit and vegetable liquid, they will also munch on wheat sprouts.

"I became introduced to vegetarianism when I was going to a local health spa, tried it have been one ever since," said Hassell.

Both men claim eating meat is detrimental to the human body because of both the chemical intake of the animals and the fatty build-up in each animal.

"It is a medical fact that cancer has a greater tendency to grow in meat, especially cooked meat. Another interesting thing is that cancer cells survive on cooked food but when transfered to non-cooked foods will die," said Peele.

In preparation for the trip Peele and Hassell held a test run to Kissimmee, August 27-28. Over the Labor Day weekend they ran from Daytona Beach to Orlando, the first leg of the 75 day journey.

"Outside of about six hours of daily running in physical training, we do stretching exercise and prepare our muscles for the punishment they will have to endure", said Hassell.

Neither, Peele nor Hassell has run competitively and both men say they don't do it for fun.

"We run for physical fitness and to promote good nutrition, enjoyment is secondary," said Peele.

The purpose of the coast−to−coast jaunt is multi−fold. It will enable the cause of world nutrition to come to the public eye and assist the Orlandoans in publicizing their ideas about good nutrition, placing emphasis on vegetable diets.

"We hope, in our 75 days on the road, to be able to reach as many people as time will allow. School children, older working folks, anybody who is interested," said Peele. "If you'll pardon the cliche, America is the most overfed and undernourished country in the world."

The Foundation plans to sponsor another run at a later date from Los Angeles up the United States west coast, across Canada, east to the Atlantic shore and south to Washington, D.C.

Many stumbling blocks stand in the way of public acceptance of their ideas but none so critical as political lobbies that have been put up by meat-dairy producers and medical research societies, they say.

"It's tough to educate masses of people when the government caters to special groups. And lets face it, diary and cattle are big business," said Peele.

Peele went on to comment that the controversy over Laetrile, a reputed cancer deterrent that is under a great deal of scrutiny by the federal government, is a prime example of government under pressure from lobbies.

"Laetrile is contained in almonds, cherry pits and several other natural foods, but government consensus is that it's highly dangerous for one's health and so it was denied to cancer patients for a long time," said Peele.

"How the government can figure that chemotherapy and cobalt treatment are better then a natural solution is beyond reason," noted Peele, "except when you consider what a big business that disease is in America."

So is it the purpose of the Run for America Foundation to purge the government of special interest factions in the field of medicine?

"Not really. There are some organizations that do legitimate research into the causes and cures of disease. But I think that certain agencies are prolonging cure discoveries," said Peele.

Then what was the inspiration behind a 3100 mile hike for hunger?

"I don't know if you could call it inspiration, but the coast-to-coast run by Dick Gregory (a black humorist) several years ago. He went almost totally unnoticed," said Hassell, "But we don't intend to."

Section II
New Age Plans and Hopes

THE PLAN

Just now there seem to be four foci to The Plan: to plant fruit and nut trees on public lands; to establish food parks, permanent public domain where people could find fruit and nut trees providing them sustenance; encouraging people to plant fruit and nut greens on their private land; and educating people about the value of eating locally grown raw fruits and nuts in their seasons.

Planting Fruit & Nut Trees on Public Land/Private Lands

Benefits: When raw fresh organic fruit and nuts are available locally at no cost, there will be a diminution of hungry people. There will be people who are eating more harmoniously with nature and consequently the milieu of the locale will be mellower. There will be a lesser need for the food stamp program. There will be a lessening of exploitation of poor people working to feed monetarily wealthier people. People will become more aware of seasons, and become more in tune with universal rhythms. There will be a change in energy consumption, that is, these foods will not have to be shipped, packaged and sold, all of which processes require petroleum product and ecology−stripping energy expenditures. The more that this type of food is eaten by people, the healther they will be, with a consequent improvement in interpersonal and interplanetary/universal relationships. There will be energy saved and available for re−channeling from the medical costs not expended. People will be able to work less and consequently there will be more time for artistic creativity, general leisure, and personal relationships. There may be food for disasters such as if an earthquake cuts off supply lines.

Objections and Answers: "Fruit trees drop leaves and fruit onto the ground". True. By simply planting a ground cover around the tree or allowing for the natural build−up of detritus around each tree, maintenance can be eliminated. As far as the fruit, most of it will be eaten or returned to the earth through composting.

"The fruit will be stolen and sold". Perhaps. Eventually when there is an abundance of the fruit and when people are aware enough to confront people about

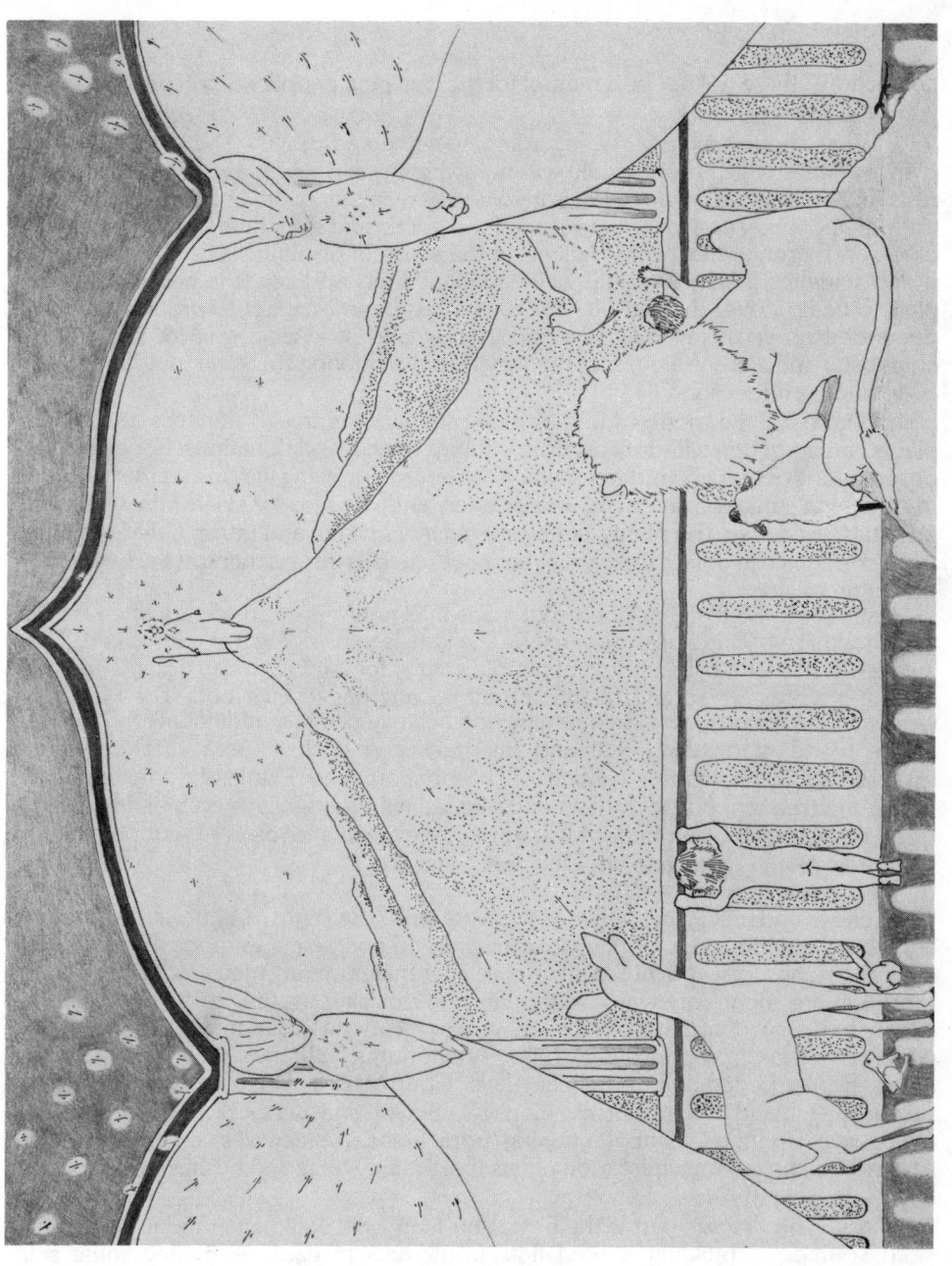

their actions, there will not be a market for the fruit, and people will feel peer pressure regarding stealing.

"What about maintenance regarding watering and pests?" The basic idea is to plant varieties which grow locally without watering and which are disease and pest resistant. Additionally, education is involved here in that people can learn that scars on fruit and a bug or two still leaves the food edible and safer than use of pesticides/biocides. Experimentation with plants in the sense of planting seeds and observing which varieties produce locally well−adapted fruits and seeds is necessary since plant breeding over the last 50−100 years has been oriented to profit which has depended on satisfying a lackluster taste bud and producing fruit for size, color, shipability and storage life rather than giving consideration to taste, nutrition, local adaptation, and seasons.

"Where will the money come from to purchase the trees?" If necessary, all the plants can be gotten without cost from cuttings, seeds, and donations. For example, observations of fruit and nut trees which are already growing well in an area can lead to obtaining cuttings from them, and/or buds, and/or seeds, or at least the variety of an established one. The plants can be started in a nursery and transplanted at a time most conducive to minimal care/maintenance, such as transplanting at the beginning of a rainy season.

Estimates of 3 to 10 million vegetarians in America are considered when asked for a donation of one dollar from each. The idea is to be doing it at your speed. The idea is about 1 or 2 billion hours of people energy focused each day doing The Plan once the words are spread, planting until no one has to buy food. The Plan is a working idea for peace by encouraging and actually planting additional food foliage in the world, particularly fruit and nut trees and bushes. Area emphases are: establishing dissemination centers of information, and Planland (donated land deeded permanent public domain and planted with food foliage on a bi, tri, and/or quadrilevel basis). Contributions will support the creation of oasis−like food parks.

Dedication: For me and you, the earth, and sea.

Metropolitan Areas − Where?

College and university, public and private lands. Rail right−of−ways. Apartment and condominium strips; parking lot medians and perimeters. Airports. Parks of any type. Parking lots, private and public perimeters and medians. Street and thoroughfare right−of−ways (although the toxicity of the particulate matter exhausted from internal combustion engines can be hazardous). Any level of government land/property. City halls. Auditoriums. Libraries. Law enforcement areas. Banks (federal). Band shells. Jails. Courthouses. Organizational and trust lands. Beachland. Golf courses. Capitols. Sewer and water plants. Causeways. Balconies. Rooftops. Grapes growing from holes in sidewalks, up trellises, and around buildings. Anywhere food plants (particularly trees and bushes) can grow.

Metropolitan Area − How?

Easy. The "How" part is the best. You (can, will, could) start today by finding seed sources − building a seed flow from fruits to earth − finding some soil connected (preferably) with the planet's natural circulatory flow. Seeds can be gotten from the fruits themselves.

Metropolitan Area − When?

Now. For information on food foliage, consider libraries; government and school agricultural extension services; local garden clubs; farmers; notice what is growing around you; your imagination...For information or consultation for planning metropolitan or rural area, write: The Plan, P.O. Box 872, Santa Cruz, Ca. 95061. Do enclose a donation for printing and postage.

Starting From Seed — A reasonable assumptive estimate seems to be that within 30 years, plus or minus 10 from the finish of the dissemination of Plan information, much of the food needs of the world can be met. Consider that mangoes begin bearing in 6 to 7 years from seed, and in only two to three years if budded or grafted. Avocados require 6–7 years to fruition in Florida from seed. Apples from 6–12 years. Figs, 1 year. Peanuts 4–5 months. Strawberries in 1–2 years. Papayas in 10–12 months. Grapes in 2–4 years. Bananas in 12–18 months, propagated from root shoots. Date palms in 6–12 years.

Country Areas — Where?

Indian reservations. Along trails — Appalachian, Pacific Crest, Florida etc. Parks. Forests. Bureau of Land Management Land. Along Bicycle trails and paths. Homestead lands. Reclaimed strip mining areas. Borders of vegetable, grain, and other field crops. Date palms in the deserts and desert–threatened land. Along river and streambacks. Erosion sites. Streetsides, with repeated warning concerning toxic concentrations of internal combustion particulate exhaust matter. Canal banks. Any level of government lands. Any open spaces available.

Country Area — When?

Now. (See Metropolitan Area — When?)

How Come? What we plant will provide fresh, real, free, and organic food. By free is meant obtainable without the necessity of earning money for purchase. Plants can be grown without carcinogenic, cytoplasm–killing biocides (pesticides, herbicides) and artificial fertilizers which seem to be more deleterious to the ozone shield than flourocarbonic destruction. That the birds and bugs get some of the food is okay. Plant some for them, too. The plants will provide shade and air–conditioning in the form of cooling effect of transpiration, and filtration of the air by the microhairs on the leaves. Plus oxygen generation. Good for us. We will provide ourselves alternatives to the alternativelessness of the processed foods; the inflationary food costs; the usuary export–import food business. Energy no longer expended for food production and processing can be rechanneled toward world peace. Suggestions: learning language like Chinese, Russian, Portuguese, and/or universal sign languages and increasing travel to particularly China, Russia, France, India, Brazil, Israel, Egypt and other nuclear countries in the nuclear weapons and power club; developing interplanetary pen and radio pals.

If you wish to make a gift of land which The Plan will convert into a public food park, and which land will be deeded permanent public domain, write: The Plan, P.O. Box 872, Santa Cruz, Ca. 95061. This is a good idea for seniors whose only alternative regarding their homes and land being the government's take–over, either because of taxes or no heirs or concerned heirs to donate their land to. The Plan will guarantee that their land will stay as is with only the addition of food foliage, so that they know their land will not be condominiumized, etc.

Clay Olson, December 3, 1978

C.I.C.E.
CENTER OF INTERNATIONALS FOR CONSERVING THE ECOSYSTEM

We have formed here in Bolivia a group dedicated to the conservation of life which we presently call CICE and are most interested in joining hands with other groups from all over the world to accomplish the union and concentration of all the energies of conservation so that meaningful action may be done soon.

May we present three well known facts:

1. The biosphere has been irrevocably altered and, without prompt and firm action, the future looms dark and grim.

2. In spite of all the facts accumulated and publicized, the annihilating forces are hurrying ever more frantically and blindly.

3. The forces of conservation, despite the urgency for unity and action, remain sadly dispersed all over the Earth and pitifully scattered in their goals. In this state of incoherence meaningful change would never occur. If the sun's energies were thus dispersed all over space, the earth would be barren, lacking the intensity for the fecundation of life. A laser—like coherence is a must now if life is to prevail.

We believe that this World Action Center should be strategically located in the southern hemisphere (for its low pollution) and in the vicinity of the Amazon (for its importance). We propose that multicultural Bolivia, being in the heart of South America and of low population density, offers definite advantages. Furthermore there exists, in Bolivia, a high level of consciousness about environmental problems as evidenced by a constant stream of press articles, the publication of books on the subject, and the formation of different groups (like CICE) with conservation in mind.

Bolivians are rightly worried about the increasing rhythm of industrialization exploitation and exportation which is caused by an intense desire to join the club of "developed" countries and by an increasing demand for natural resources which are becoming ever more scarce. Very dangerous industries are now being planned, developed, and expanded everywhere in Bolivia. The future everywhere is becoming grimmer and grimmer while hope is shrinking into a very dim light.

We invite ALL...Please HURRY...Let's give the biosphere a new LEASE...Let's give humanity another CHANCE...Let's unite for LIFE.

NOTE: The founders of CICE, all people of modest means and students, have organized without any outside help and without support, the life of CICE is most uncertain. We wish, not only to survive, but to become members of a larger World Wide Family united for Life.

C.I.C.E., Casilla 5699, La Paz, Bolivia

BRAIN:
BIOLOGICAL RESISTANCE AGAINST INSTITUTION NUTS

Organization

A network of citizen power groups working on the comprehensive program:
1) To release 90% dormant brain in all humans.
2) To change laws forbidding brain self−control.
3) To mass−multiply whole brain power creativity.
4) To do this via the existing public's schools.
5) To create warless Earth.

Wanted: Pioneers

We are forming a wilderness pioneer group.
We plan to leave urban insanity and trek through the human jungle.
We plan to discover a new territory of freedom, love, community.
We plan to build an Earth colony of neural sanity and cosmic joy.
We seek courageous young pioneers for this final migration out.
The journey will be hard and dangerous. Some will make it. It is planned to take a lifetime. But is there any other alternative on ego−lie and war−suiciding Earth?
We plan to travel via brain to make first blatant, open and notorious contact with a wise galactic civilization which will teach us specifically how to survive and teach each human brain to transcend into its given gift to vast dormancy, immediately.
We plan to travel via zero−time consciousness: innate species telepathy. Those of us who already are learning and demonstrating this skill are teaching those who want to learn. Only the serious need apply.
We plan to enter into continuous communication with a successful civilization which has mastered, transcended and outevolved the ego/hate/kill behavior into pure lovely living among the stars.
We plan to bring back the first valid voice through a pioneer's brain and vocal chords. The validity will be tested via scientific demonstration of advanced problem−solving intelligence.
If we are successful in this first egoless breakthrough before the holocaust, it follows logically that a second intelligence will come through easier. Then a third − until each human individual will have her/his own wise guides. Ten, a hundred, a thousand skull TV friends are no bore.
The technology for this next step in human evolution is now known, pilot tested and ready. The mechanism for self−circuiting into the pre−requisite dormant frontal lobes is now routinely operational. The nucleus group has been in−gathering patiently for two decades. We are approaching critical mass. The mass brain will be linked synergistically. It will generate consciousness exponentially.
The energy vortex of Laughing Coyote Mountain is the consciousness cyclotron.

A single, universal thought essence will be generated lovingly by our superbrain, placed in circular motion, accelerated beyond the gravitational pull of Earth ego, then beamed at the target. The pinpoint target, telescopically recorded, will be through the visible edge of the Milky Way Galaxy for optimum star density and planet bouncing: "Hello. We are here. Love. Are you there?"

B.R.A.I.N., Box 10, Laughing Coyote Mountain, Black Hawk, Colorado 80422

TELLING MILLIONS ABOUT VEGETARIANISM FOR PENNIES

The world food situation, the suffering of countless animals, millions of human deaths from meat—related disease, and the continued poisoning of our planet make it imperative that vegetarians spread the seeds of their message as quickly and cheaply as possible. Our concern for all living things, including trees, makes it necessary to concentrate as much as possible on electronic means of communication. Our message to you is: It's easier than you think to get on TV and to have your message carried by the wire services.

Before getting into specifics, let me outline our general philosophy. Wherever possible, have existing organizations do your work for you — let the meateaters plant your seeds. For instance, we were long disgusted by the Oscar Mayer theme song: "I'd love to be an Oscar Mayer Wiener". We drew up a 4—line release for the press: "American Vegetarians, Inc. have asked the FTC to ban Oscar Mayer's ad "I'd love to Be an Oscar Mayer Wiener" on the basis that the ad makes a mockery of the involuntary suffering and sacrifice visited on 1100 pigs butchered every hour in Madison, Wisconsin.

We were in Washington, and called the Washington Post, the Washington Star News, the UPI and AP, at a total cost of 40¢. With each call we asked for national dictation. Twice we were first routed to editors' desks. In both cases the editors ok'd our script for dictation. We read our 4—line release to the secretaries, who typed it and sent it back to the editors. From there it was ok'd for the wires. If even 10% of the papers in the country carried it, and we know far more did, we reached 25 million people, perhaps in some cases for the first time, with the idea of a link between meat and suffering. Newday's Mike McGrady came upon the story, and prepared a national interview which was carried by half of the nation's papers. Johnny Carson's writers read the Newsday story, and mentioned the item in his monologue, to perhaps a different 25 million people. To our knowledge it now appears that Oscar Mayer has discontinued the ad, perhaps permanently.

We have also tried for national television talk show time, on the basis that 8 minutes of national audience is worth $480,000 since that time is sold at $60,000 a minute to advertisers. We have so far been successful in getting on 20 different network shows through these steps: 1) Do 10 to 15 local and regional radio and TV talk shows first. 2) Don't take "no" for an answer - bother them continually - keep calling back - they'll put you on to shut you up. Make your appeal letter dramatic, in words and pictures. For instance, we often paste a bumper sticker on our letters. The letter which got us onto the Today Show has phrases in it such as "Charlie the Starkist Tuna is an Uncle Tom" and "The Pied Piper Was a Mass Murderer". Flippant and ridiculous, but the time for the seriousness of your message is after you've caught their attention. Remember you're competing with thousands of letters a day for their attention.

If you don't have a lot of time, but want to help or want to make a local group of vegetarians more active, consider the following press opportunities.

FOOD EDITORS: Take a sheet of vegetarian recipes to your food editor and ask for equal space. Most food editors are open to this and with one reproduced sheet of yours, you can reach 600,000 people in a major urban area. Add your local food editor to your mailing list.

LETTERS TO THE EDITOR: A letter of yours printed in the New York Daily News becomes 2 million copies and you don't have to pay a cent for paper, ink or distribution. One statistical study indicates that for every 3 letters you write to your local paper, 1 will likely get printed.

RELIGION EDITORS: The British Vegetarian Union has an excellent piece on the vegetarianism of many religious leaders, including Jesus. Approach your religious editor about printing an article on the nonviolent ethics of Buddha, Francis of Assisi, Gandhi, Lae Tsu, Isaish and Daniel. Do research on the Jewish Essenes, a vegetarian ascetic group in North Galilee. The common thread of all religions is reverence for life, the desire to prevent suffering, and action in feeding the hungry. Vegetarianism is an active expression of the most basic religious beliefs.

SCIENCE EDITORS: If you see a piece in Newsweek on the American Cancer Society's charge that meat is the number one cause of intestinal cancer, send it to the science editor of your paper. He or she could be printing stories on world acreage and the efficiency of grain in relation to meat, on the vastly reduced heartbeats of vegetarians, and other important basic facts.

COLUMNISTS: Ann Landers has the highest reading audience in the world - some 50 million readers. If enough of us bombard her and "Dear Abby" and similar columnists, we will inevitably have some percentage of success. Ms. Landers' address is Chicago, Illinois 60611.

A newspaper is as varied as its reporters. If there are 125 reporters for your newspaper, there are 125 different ways to approach the paper. We have found that Washington papers are much more open than New York papers for the dissemination of vegetarian releases.

RADIO AND TELEVISION: There are public service announcements, talk shows, station editorials, rebuttal editorials, and public service shows to name a few.

TALK SHOWS: It seems to be a general principle that electronic media is more open to minority viewpoints than the press. Write letters to the hosts of your local talk shows, of no more than a page in length, setting forth why you would like to do a show with them and what you would like to talk about.

NEWS SHOWS: Louis Marvin had tremendous success in California with a demonstration in which a group of vegetarians brought a live cow to McDonald's. The group was arrested for violating the city health laws. After they were arrested they held a press conference (well publicized in advance) to comment that health laws permit dead and not live animals in restaurants. CBS national news carried the conference. On a local level there are a number of ways to get publicity. You can issue a press release (double spaced, capital letters, 5 to 10 lines) on your local health department's refusal to educate the public in regard to cancer and meat, heart disease and meat, kidney disease and meat. You could issue a release saying the local slaughterhouses violate the state's cruelty to animals statutes - or charge that the educational system is using in nutrition classes basic foods charts supplied by the Americal Dairy Council.

PUBLIC SERVICE SPOTS: If your local radio and TV station refuse to take your public service announcements, complain to the F.C.C. This can be a potent weapon. For instance, for 1 year we wrote the Phil Donahue Show (an hour talk show syndicated in 50 metropolitan areas) asking for a chance to respond to Adelle Davis, Dr. Stillman, Dr. Atkins, and other advocates of high animal protein diets. We applied for an official complaint from the F.C.C. and filed it. Our fairness time request was turned down, after a year's battle; however, the result was the Donahue Show invited us to appear. Yield: 3,000 letters (according to media studies 1 letter written represents 100 who feel similarly but do not write). Write public service announcements, or type them, on postcards. For instance, "15 million people, according to the UN, are expected to starve this year, while every pound of meat represents 10 pounds of grains fed to the animals. For free meatless recipes write ----". This will publicize ecological vegetarianism, distribute your recipes, and publicize the good work you are doing.

PERSONAL EDITORIALS: Many television stations are allowing 60 second editorials on the part of viewers on any subjects. Submit one, double spaced, and timed for sixty seconds.

PUBLIC SERVICE SHOWS: Weekend public service shows are more open than talk shows to organizations. Call or write the producer.

ALTERNATIVE FORMS OF MEDIA: bumper stickers, films, tapes, t—shirts, meatless recipes are all forms of media. According to media studies, the average bumper sticker reaches 5,000 people, at a cost of 5¢ to 10¢ each. Messages such as "Be Kind to Animals, Don't Eat Them" with your address on the bottom — or "Meat Causes Cancer" or "Why Kill For Food?", "Don't Eat Meat" — are all messages that need to be carried everywhere. Or send someone down to your local slaughterhouse with a movie camera and develop some footage to go along with lectures to high school and college classes. Make tapes of the agonized sounds of the animals — about 25% of the radio stations we have approached have played the sounds. For those of you who don't believe in shock tactics, we can only say that our mail indicates many people have become vegetarians after finding through these films and tapes about the suffering of animals. People who have never imagined a slaughterhouse, who don't care about their health, who can't relate to starving humans they don't see, will often be extremely upset by their first visual knowledge of suffering. And to those who would say these are surface and not in—depth presentations, and therfore doomed to fail, we respond that the idea of vegetarianism is a seed in a person, which very rarely comes to fruit quickly. It will gradually mature in him or her, as he or she becomes more uncomfortable with the idea of what is being eaten. Any reminder, any fact which hastens this maturation is good.

We are all responsible for the continued starvation of our fellow humans, for the people who die early deaths of heart attacks, for the time bomb of pesticide accumulation in our waters, for the sin of the slaughterhouse. The situation is deadly serious. Any way you can, however you can, help by starting to plant as many seeds in every possible way you can.

Nellie Shriver, World Special Correspondent, Vegetarian World

PUBLIC SERVICE ANNOUNCEMENTS
ORGANIZING TOOLS

One way of helping to spread the vegetarian message is through the use of public service announcements (PSA's). PSA's are brief messages aired by TV and radio stations averaging 10 to 60 seconds in length. Non-profit organizations are eligible for this free radio and TV time. Even if you are a committee of one in your community, you can get public service time. PSA's can be used as an organizing tool and as an educational medium. They can be used to advertise your need for fellow workers, to tell of the world grain shortage statistics, to speak of slaughter house cruelty, heart disease and meat, insecticide ratios in animal flesh, the four kinds of animals killed for Chanel No. 5 perfume fixatives, etc.

How To Do It: Go to your library and use the Broadcast Yearbook, or use the yellow pages of your phone book for copying the addresses of all radio and TV stations in your area. (If you plan to reach many stations, its worth your while to use a mimeo or photocopy machine). Stations prefer to use 3 x 5 index cards or post cards, but we have had success without them.

Your second job is to call the radio and tv stations, asking for the names of the public service directors and for the number of seconds they require in their PSA message.

Third, draw up a public service announcement using capital letters and double-spacing on the back of postcards, timing them for the station requirements. An example: "If you would like to help feed the hungry, send for meatless recipes to, American Vegetarians, Box 5424, Akron, Ohio". (You can use our address if you like).

It's good to repeat the address - most people do not necessarily remember addresses they hear only once. Second, it's better to get the attention of the audience by starting with a question, rather than a statement. Of course, the time you have to work within is a limiting consideration, but time permitting, a question will give the listener time to think? For example, you might ask: "What color would hot dogs be without sodium nitrate?"; "How many pounds of grains and grass must be fed to an animal to get a pound of meat?"; Why are female hormones given to animals?"; "What is the heartbeat of the average person?"; What is a vegetarian?", such opening questions can hook the listener's interest.

We always offer something to the listener, usually a printed sheet of vegetarian recipes as a way of checking response to an ad and to get a feel of any interest that might be lying dormant in the community.

One week after you have sent your PSA's, call the public service director and ask if the messages have been received and if he or she is planning or using them. If the answer to the second question is negative, there are a number of approaches. Perhaps one of the most aggressive was what we did - petition the stations for fair time to respond to the Dept. of Agriculture PSA's which are free advertising for the multi-million dollar meat and dairy industries. You might ask the public service director for interview time and take along a slaughterhouse film (we have them available) or some health statistics.

One thing which might make your job easier is to mention stations which have broadcast vegetarian PSA's. Among them are: KYW NBC Philadelphia, WMAL ABC Washington, WTOP CBS Washington, WMC NBS Memphis, WCAS Boston, KPFT Houston, KZEW Dallas, WXYZ ABC Detroit, WJR Detroit, WCCO Minneapolis, KGO ABC San Francisco, KBPI Denver, WISH Indianapolis, WMNS Cleveland, WQIV New York.

For television, the same ground rules apply, but you will need 35 mm slides and white lettering. The general rule is 1 slide for each 10 seconds of copy, other stations will record your message on tape in their studios.

Please consider this free method of planting vegetarian seeds. We will be glad to help you in your efforts, our address is: American Vegetarian, Box 5424, Akron, Ohio 44313.

HOW YOU CAN BE A VEGETARIAN ACTIVIST AT YOUR COLLEGE

We operate on the assumption that the eating of meat is the major source of suffering in the world...through the unjust butchering of billions of animals a year, through the deaths by starvation of 13,000 people a day while Americans feed 21 lbs. of food to a cow to get back 1 lb. of meat, through 3 million cardiovascular deaths a year from animal fat, several hundred thousand kidney deaths from over consumption of animal protein, etc., etc.

We also operate on the assumption that one person with no money can do an incredible amount of organizing and free seed planting.

1. Public service...by yourself you can through time and energy gradually get every TV and radio station in the area to give your college vegetarian group (can be a committee of one) fairness time in response to United States Dept. of Agriculture public service announcements (brief radio messages which focus on the need for meat).

2. Letters to the editor of your campus paper and the metropolitan papers near you...on reasons for vegetarianism, on your need for people to help you, etc.

3. Interviews on your college radio station and radio and tv stations in the area about your efforts to start a group on your campus.

4. Press release, double spaced and capitalized...very short...two paragraphs at most...to the UPI and AP office bureau nearest you...if not in your city, in a big city in

your state.

5. Getting the food editors of your campus paper and the metropolitan papers near you to run more vegetarian recipes, vegetarian nutrition columns, etc.

6. Collecting petitions to get better vegetarian food in your cafeteria.

7. Collecting petitions to establish classes on vegetarianism at your college.

8. Finding out what the campus laboratories are imposing on animals in the name of science (de−barking operations, without anesthesia...wholesale slaughter for biology classes are quite common).

9. Monitoring the nutrition and home economics classes and organizing against the indoctrination of animal protein mythology into the student body.

10. Apply for campus recognition if you want and get yourself some free office space...or go to the churches with campus affiliation or synagogues...such as Hillel and interfaith ministries...explain how your work helps solve world hunger and ask for free office space.

11. Paper...we get some from radio stations...wire service copy...cutting it into 14 inch strips and printing meatless recipes on the back of it...with the average campus a year there are tons of paper wasted by administration, teachers, students...ask teachers if you can have any waste paper printed on one side only...print recipes or vegetarian information or information about your group on it...leave the recipes in cafeterias, campus book stores, coffee houses, bulletin boards, etc.

12. A letterhead: most office supply stores sell instant print...black professional type you rub onto paper for a professional letterhead...take your original to an instant print shop and get it reproduced.

13. Do a leaflet drop at your campus paper...stick vegetarian information on every desk there...same with your campus radio station.

14. We often take scrap paper and print 8 or 10 vegetarian messages fortune cookie size on the back of it for widespread distribution... and then cut it with a paper cutter...for instance for the May 4, Kent State University demonstration, our message read, "We are here to protest violence. As long as we are the graves of the innocent animals we eat as meat, as long as we humans cause billions of animals to go shrieking to their slaughterhouse deaths, the world will be a place of violence. For free recipes and information, contact: American Vegetarian, Box 5424, Akron, Ohio". The information of the Jesus freaks, the Trotskyites, etc. was all over the ground, big 8½ x 11 flyers...while ours were read because they were small and easy to absorb.

Nellie Shriver, American Vegetarian

INTO THE ATETIES

The past always was once the far away future. The 1960's brought popular recognition of both natural eating and vegetarianism; the 1970's introducing the idea that the most valid forms of natural eating were those which incorporated vegetarianism; the 1980's will redeem many false paths amidst the forgotten past; finally, for one, but not for all, vegetarianism will become synonymous with natural eating. This will mean that if you do not drink blood but do drink coffee, Coke, or Coors, then you are not a vegetarian. And is it any less ridiculous to transform flesh to taste like soy beans than it is revolting to texturize soy beans to taste like flesh?

When health food store owners discuss things to come, it is as if they talk about what used to be. When supermarket managers remember the past, it is as if they forecast the future. Since the 1960's big business has managed, with characteristic tastlessness, to establish a chain of stores that combines a number of the least appealing aspects of the health food store with all of the impurities and sins of the supermarket. In an initial, or perhaps only ostensible, attempt to offer health food store products at supermarket prices, these chains have delivered just the opposite; today's products in yesterday's package at tomorrow's prices. The 1980's will bring their demise, while the health food store and the supermarket will continue with business as usual.

Just what is this business as usual? Murder with mirrors. Granolas now grace the supermarket shelves in between the corn flakes and shredded wheat; but those granolas are made with sugar. Whole wheat flours are now sold right next to bleached white flours; but the germ oils of those whole flours are certainly rancid. These are first steps, while the 1980's are sure to see further such steps, and in the right direction. Conversely, natural food distributors, having enjoyed the taste of success, are beginning to bloat with bulbous bellies. One of the nation's largest wholesalers, which less than a decade ago began as a small store in Boston singing the song of macrobiotics, now manufactures potato chips. Just as the Vatican and the Kremlin have more in common with each other than either does with the idea of freedom, more and more vegetarians will come to suspect the same association of the health food store and supermarket with the facts of nutrition.

Whither, then, vegetariana? If not inward, then at least indoors. Indoor sprouting will supply the fresh vegetables intended by nature but forbidden by economics in the middle of the winter. The vegetarian regimens which claim health equal only to the carnivores' will lose their adherents. For what kind of health is that? And what kind of vegetarianism is that? The cooked kind, lacto−ovo at that. Raw foods vegetarianism will sweep into its embrace both the life−long converts and the followers of fads who disappear as quickly as a fashion, yet these latter will not detract from the milkless−eggless raw foods vegetarian movement any more than a swallow interferes with the wind.

Farm animals in the rich Western half of the world eat more grain than does the human population of the poor Eastern half. This fact became well−known in the seventies, and became a cause of many vegetarian conversions. But soon these ecologically−minded philantropists will realize that giving up flesh does not in itself give any grain to the starving and the poor. The vegetarian−ecological movement fizzled out in the early seventies.

Whenever Aunt Samantha, alias Mother Earth, is being needlessly abused by citzienry−−not industry−−, Uncle Sam is quick to add a sales tax. Thus, as onto tobacco and alcohol, a sales tax will be added by a couple of coastal states (California and New York? Oregon and Vermont?) to white flour, white sugar... and white flesh.

The tenets of vegetarianism will be heralded throughout the land. Perhaps twice the present proportion of the population will count themselves among us by the end of the decade. By then, many of those already vegetarians will be vegans, and many vegans will be raw foodists. However, vegetarian restaurants will not necessarily greatly increase in number; rather, the ordinary sort of greasy spoon will accomodate the lost customers by offering daily fleshless dishes — if not out of respect for the dead, then out of consideration for the wallet and the purse.

In fact many airlines and dining halls and college cafeterias will separate the carnivores from the vegetarians -- not for any esthetic or ethical premises, but simply because the same food is more easily served in the same place. (This has long been the case in several kibbutzim in Israel.) We will all breathe more easily for this, the same as when we sit in non-smoking sections of public places and trains and planes. And just as smokers have learned to apologize for their smoke in someone's else's lungs, carnivores will learn to apologize for someone else's lungs on their plates.

As vegetarians of the Seventies, we will learn to speak out in the Eighties. Expressing love is not enough; we will also have to express opinions. We will speak out against a society which outlaws the cultivation of a euphoric plant but allows the killing of an innocent animal. With or without us, the movement will nevertheless grow and flourish. If with us, then our responsibility will be to assure honest aims for all our claims: written by the wrong hand, the symbol for Shanti looks like a dollar sign. Does failure exist because ultimately our expectations are too great, or because initially we settle for too little?

Mark Mathew Braunstein (author of "Radical Vegetarianism: A Dialectic of Diet and Ehtics", Panjandrum Press)

PART III

THE NEW AGE KNOWLEDGE

As ancient truths begin to infiltrate once again the commonly held world views, and as impetus is gained for both exploring unknown realms and questioning existent realities, a substantial corpus of New Age knowledge is being assembled. Research on more natural nutritional modalities, on psychic phenomenon, on spiritual endocrinology, and on the overwhelming hazards of nuclear technology and chemical agriculture — all these encourage the breaking down of the old and the emergence of the new.

The unexpressed goals of such research and study appear to be two-fold: to expose and eradicate the multifarious negative influences which are currently inundating our planet and to support, validate and legitimize the new truths which are becoming everywhere more widely accepted. The contributions which comprise the next part of "Life In The 21st Century" include selections which are representative of both these propensities.

Section I
Research

SCIENCE SUPPORTS FRUITARIANISM

Preliminary studies of fossil teeth have led an anthropologist to the startling suggestion that early human ancestors were not predominantly meat eaters or even eaters of seeds, shoots, leaves or grasses. Nor were they omnivorous. Instead, they appear to have subsisted chiefly on a diet or fruit.

Not until the advent of Homo erectus, the species immediately ancestral to Homo sapiens, is there evidence of the omnivorous diet that is typical of human beings today.

If confirmed, the findings would upset several widely held assumptions about the diet of early hominids, or human-like creatures. It is generally held, for example, that the large, flat-topped molars of the robust forms of Australopithecus were used to grind nuts and roots. The smaller form of Australopithecus and a similarly gracile form of true human being called Homo habilis were thought to have been omnivorous, mixing meat with roots, nuts, eggs, shoots and fruit.

Dr. Walker has established similar patterns in the various types of wild pig, such as worthog, and among a number of monkeys and apes. It is against these patterns that the hominid teeth are checked.

To examine teeth with the scanning electron microscope, Dr. Walker must mount the tooth crowns on metal stubs that will hold them inside the microscope's vacuum chamber and then coat the crown with a gold-palladium alloy that reflects the instrument's electron beam. (It is the reflected electron beam that the microscope detects and manipulates electronically to enlarge the image and display it on a special televison screen). Hominid teeth are considered priceless relics and are not handed out by their discovers to be treated this way, not even to Alan Walker, who is a close colleague of many of the leading finders of hominid fossils. Therefore, Dr. Walker developed a method of making replicas of the teeth by casting them in epoxy. The method does not alter the fossil but does pick up all the microscopic detail needed to make the analyses.

"I don't want to make too much of this yet," said Dr. Alan Walker, a John Hopkins University anthropologist, who discovered the dental evidence. "But it is quite a surprise.

No Exceptions Found

The sample of teeth studied so far is small - fewer than two dozen representing four major types of hominids - and further analysis could refute the early indications. But, while the sample is small, no exceptions have been found.

Every tooth examined from the hominids of the 12-million-year period leading up to Homo erectus appeared to be that of a fruit-eater. Every Homo erectus tooth was that of an omnivore. Homo erectus was the first form known to have migrated out of Africa. Specimens have been found in many parts of Africa and Asia.

The findings are based on extremely detailed analyses of the the microscopic wear patterns on the chewing surfaces of the teeth. The method, which Dr. Walker invented, uses a scanning electron microscope to see scratches and pits that are invisible to the naked eye.

Dr. Walker has found that different kinds of food contain materials that mar the enamel surface of a tooth in characteristic ways. It is possible even to distinguish between a grass-eater and a leaf-eater because each food contains characteristic types of quantities of silica crystals that form naturally within plant cells. These crystals, called phytoliths, are harder than tooth enamel and scratch it slightly as the animal chews its food.

Grasses contain a much higher proportion of phytoliths than do leaves of bushes and trees. Fruits contain almost none at all. As a result, 'fruit eaters' teeth are highly polished, lacking any of the wear patterns characteristic of other food sources. Meats contain no phytoliths but, the teeth of carnivores show scratches caused by crunching into bone.

Consistent Pattern of Wear

Using the teeth of various living mammals whose diets are known, Dr. Walker has established that the basic pattern of microwear on teeth is fairly consistent from one species to another. This is largely because tooth enamel is essentially the same substance throughout the animal kingdom.

To prove his method, Dr. Walker has compared the microwear patterns on closely related species of animals that are known to have different feeding habits. For example, of two closely related species of hyrax (rodent-sized hooved mammals sometimes called conies), one feeds predominantly on grass while the other is a browser, eating leaves of bushes and trees. Their teeth can be told apart easily using a scanning electron microscope.

If it is true that the earliest hominids were all predominantly fruit eaters, the fact would suggest a way of life more like that of chimpanzees living in forests than most anthropologists had suspected.

Dr. Walker notes, however, that a fruit diet need not resemble what Americans consider a fruit diet - oranges, plums, apples, bananas and other extremely sweet and soft items. Hundreds of plants produce fruits that are tougher, more substantial foods. The pods of the acacia tree is one, for example, that is quite common in Africa today. It grows in lightly forested regions close to the grasslands usually considered to have been the home to early hominids.

Boyce Rensberger

VEGETARIANISM AND HEALTH

Vegetarianism has both an ethical and scientific basis. Those who have spent their precious time on these matters have come to a conclusion that both of these are aspects of One truth. So what is ethically correct is always scientifically sound.

Dr. Albert Schweitzer, a medical scientist, a philosopher and a theologian said, "All life is holy, to the truly ethical man, even that which from the human stand point seems to be lower life. We need a boundless ethics which will include the animals too." Lord Buddha in Karaniya Metta Sutta has preached that the Buddhists must practice Metta or Loving Kindness to all forms of creatures, whether small or big, long or short, near or far, seen or unseen, born or about to be born. In short, reverence for life in all forms is the keynote of His Philosophy. Sir Francis Bacon said, "Nature has endowed man with a noble and excellent principle of compassion, which extends itself also to the dumb animals whence this compassion has some resemblance to that of a prince towards his subjects."

Anatomy And Physiology

The human diet should be arranged in conformity with his material needs, his aesthetic and emotional aspiration and his spiritual nature.

The teeth formation of the jaw, the length of the intestine and the art of perspiration prove that the man is born to eat vegetables and fruit only. It is often forgotten that the human and anthropoid saliva differs from that of the carnivorae such as the cat, the dog, etc. The digestive juice in the stomach also proves that the human stomach is not made to digest fish, flesh or eggs. The carnivores stomach contains a larger amount of hydrochloric acid than that of a human being. The length of the digestive tract has also an important place in relating in the diet. Carnivorous animals have shorter intestines than the man. It is believed that the intestinal canal of a dog or cat is only four to five times the length of the body. All of the animals such as the monkey, the elephant, the bull, the deer, etc. which have long intestinal canals are Vegetarians. So the man too should be a vegetarian. He should not go against the Creation or the Nature. We should consider that the strongest vertebrates eat only vegetables, fruit and nuts. The cow for instance takes only grain, fodder, hay and grass. The horse and the donkey are the same. The elephant, the biggest animal on land, manages well on greens and branches.

Vegetarian Diet Is Not A New Idea

Millions of people have preferred it through the centuries. Prominent writers, physicians, philosophers, teachers, religionists, economists, poets, scientists and artists have been vegetarians and proclaimed its virtues. Some of them are: Pythagoras, Plotinus, Plutarch, Plato, Buddha, Celsus, Zoroaster, Isaiah, Porphyry, Ovid, Voltaire, Schopenhaver, Rousseau, Lamarlene, Wesley, Blake, Folslay, Socrates, Leonardo da Vinci, Wagner, Shelly, Goldsmith, Pope, Byron, Michelet, Franklin, Newton, Thoreau, Ghandi, Silvo, Gessel, Irving, Fisher, Anna Kingsford, etc.

Famous Sayings of Doctors

Sir Prof. McCarrison, Director of Nutritional Research Corner, India; "A diet consisting of any staple grain with milk products and green leafy vegetables contains not only the right kind and amount of Proteins but everything else the body needs."

Dr. H.C. Menkel; M.D.; "The ill effects of a flesh diet may not be immediately realized, but this must not be taken as evidence that it is doing no harm. Few can be made to believe that it is the meat they have eaten which is largely responsible for physical degeneracy and that they may die of disease wholly due to a flesh diet, while the real cause is not suspected by themselves or by others."

Dr. H.C.Menkel; "Flesh food is considered essential for healthy dogs but it is not essential for man."

Dr. John Kellogg, M.D., L.L.D.; "Flesh foods are not the best nourishment for human beings and were not the food of our primitive ancestors."

J.S.Garrow, M.D., Ph.D., M.R.C.P. of the Medical Research Council, Department of Obstetrics and Gynaecology, Royal Free Hospital, London; "It has been known for many years that some proteins were nutritionally of better quality than others. It was once fashionable to class all protein of animal origin as First Class Protein and to consider it superior to protein of vegetable origin. This is obvious nonsense, since gelatin has a lower biological value than most vegetable protein".

Animal Protein Versus Vegetable Protein

What kind of protein is necessary for good health?

The usual answer is that the body requires complete protein to function properly. Complete protein has been described by scientists as that which contains all eight amino acids. Not all protein sources provide the eight essential amino acids and until recently science claimed only animal protein such as meat, fish and eggs are complete. It was believed that all vegetable sources were incomplete.

Vegetable proteins are higher in biological value than the animal proteins. For example, proteins in potatoes are biologically superior to proteins in meat, eggs or milk. Raw proteins have higher biological value than cooked proteins. You need only half the amount of proteins if you eat raw vegetable proteins instead of cooked animal proteins. Potatoes are actually excellent health foods and a good source of superior quality protein.

Every vegetable, every fruit and every seed contains some protein. The diet of raw vegetables, fruit, seeds, grains and nuts plus milk, so called lacto vegetarian diet will supply in abundance not only all proteins you need but also with all other nutritive substances such as vitamins, minerals, carbohydrates, fatty acids, enzymes and trace elements.

The above is a recent report of Max Plank Institute in Germany. A leading institution for Nutritional Research in the world.

A well balanced vegetable diet will help you to live healthily for a long period. So let us give up burying carcasses in our stomachs and get used to a human diet.

Let us live according to the world famous motto: LIVE AND LET LIVE.

Sri Kapila International Humanitarian Association, No. 257, Circular Road, Magalle, Galle, Sri Lanka .

ANCIENT SECRET FOR ETERNAL YOUTH

There is a secret formula for youth — eternal youth — and yet it was revealed five thousand years ago by Moses, written in the section of the bible known as Genesis.

Millions of people have read, studied and preached the bible. Yet no one in our society has ever found the secret; although it is written plainly and clearly for all to read.

How many people have believed in the bible? And how many people have claimed that the bible is the absolute truth — the "word of God". Yet why has not even one of these people taken Moses at the word he wrote when he gave the formula for eternal youth and explained clearly how Man could live eternally?

This is not conversation about eternal life in the spirit, but life in the body which we have on this planet. And this is not a theological law but a scientific formula which can be proven by science.

Specifically Moses had said what he believed to be the words of God: "Behold, I have given you every plant yielding seed which is upon the face of the earth, and every tree with seed in its fruit; you shall have them for food".

Then he writes further: "The Lord God made to grow every tree that is pleasant to the sight and good for food".

Not only does it state what was fit for Man to eat, but it also states what was not for him to eat:

"To everything that has the breath of life, I have given every green plant for food". In other words the leaves of the plants were not for Man but for the animals.

Now, in describing the fall of Man, when God, according to Moses, cursed Adam and Eve for partaking of the forbidden food, He explained what would happen to them as a result of this: "In toil you shall eat of it all the days of your life; and you shall eat the plants of the field".

And here is the ultimate karma of what they did: "In the sweat of your face you shall eat bread til you return to the ground. You are dust and to dust you will return.

In other words the worst and greatest wrong they would do was not even in the forbidden fruit, not even the plants they were destined to eat, but in the bread, which is food that is cooked! And it was this cooked food that would guarantee his death and would return him to dust just as he came from the dust!

I will show, first, that Man is not carnivorous. Second, that Man is not a vegetarian. Third, that Man does not need vitamin supplements. Fourth, that Man should drink milk only in the infant state, and only his mother's milk. And fifth, that man should not eat the food cooked.

Let us imagine that before Man there is an animal, grass on the ground, and fruit on the trees, and this is available to him freely. Now this is not a starving Man for under stress he would eat anything.

He is not going to chase the animal down, bite his jugular vein, and struggle with him until he can eat him. If anything he would make a pet of the animal, and they would become best friends.

Now he would see the leaves of the grass and the leaves of the trees, but after trying this he would find it distasteful. Then what would be left?

He would find that fruit is completely in harmony with his taste buds.

We can see this truth in children, for children are functioning closer to a natural instinct, and we see that all children have "a sweet tooth". The only sweet food in nature is the fruit. But instead of giving our children the fruits we have taken the sweet from nature and have learned to process and to cook it into candy, cookies, cakes and pastry, and we contaminate our children with this instead.

If a child were given a choice, absolutely, he is not going to eat his pet or the leaves; he would prefer fruit.

We are appalled when we see films of primitive cannibal tribes who drink blood and eat raw flesh. We are also disgusted by the thought of a vampire living from blood.

So by a natural instinct Man would not think of including blood in his diet.

But what do we do when we consume a rare juicey steak? Isn't that drinking the blood of a cow?

And how is that so far removed from being a cannibal, since all flesh is basically similar.

The primitive tribes who eat raw flesh and blood are the most diseased people living with nature. But those that include large quantities of fruits in their diet are among the most healthy and beautiful.

A HARMFUL SHIFT IN TODAY'S MENU

Recent investigations into the dietary habits of prehistoric peoples and their primate predecessors suggest that heavy meat—eating by modern affluent societies may be exceeding the biological capacities evolution built into the human body. The result may be a host of diet—related health problems, such as diabetes, obesity, high blood pressure, coronary heart disease and some cancers.

The studies challenge the notion that human beings evolved as aggressive hunting animals who depended primarily upon meat for survival.

The new view — coming from findings in such fields as archeology, anthropology, primatology, and comparative anatomy — instead portrays early humans and their forebearers more as herbivores than carnivores. According to these studies, the prehistoric table for at least the last million and a half years was probably set with three times more plant than animal foods, the reverse of what the average American currently eats.

Humans, like their primate relatives, says Dr. William J. Hamilton III, are "opportunistic" meat eaters. Although it had long been thought that subhuman primates were vegetarians, recent field studies of baboons and chimpanzees, for example, showed that they eat meat preferentially when it is available, sometimes nearly abandoning their usual vegetable fare until the supply of insects, rodents or other prey runs out.

Effects of Availability

Dr. Hamilton and Dr. Curt D. Busse of the University of California at Davis, who have investigated the eating habits of baboons under a grant from the National Institutes of Health, point out that "humans apparently share with most primates a tendency to increase the proportion of dietary animal matter whenever it is economical to do so". Historically, the researchers maintain, societal and economic constraints have limited the opportunities to eat animal foods. But in our "current luxury diet circumstances", the opportunities are omnipresent and "preference betrays best interest," they said.

The health consequences of the affluent diet may result in part from the action of "thrifty genes" hypothetically harbored by humans and other species. These genes prompt the release of insulin when large amounts of food are consumed. Insulin, in turn, promotes storage of the excess calories as body fat to be called upon in lean times.

When humans were evolving in times of alternating abundance and privation, such genes would have been a survival advantage. But today, with a state of continuous abundance, they result in such problems as obesity and diabetes. According to Dr. Henry Blackburn, a preventive medicine specialist at the University of Minnesota, the damage caused by the thrifty genes in a land of plenty can be seen in peoples only recently exposed to abundance, including the Pima Indians, who developed widespread diabetes, and American blacks, many of whom became obese and hypertensive.

By contrast, modern-day hunting and gathering tribes who live in the tropics much the way prehistoric humans did, are free from the degenerative diseases that are rampant in industrial societies. Studies of such primitive tribes as the Kung San (formerly called bushmen) of Botswana show that their diet is 60 to 80 percent vegetable matter.

The gathering of plant foods by Kung females makes a far more important caloric contribution to the diet than the slabs of meat butchered by male hunters. Food-gathering is also more efficient than hunting, yielding 1,000 calories of vegetable matter in four hours in contrast to the 10 hours it takes to get the equivalent caloric value of meat.

No Coronary Heart Disease

Studies by Dr. A.S. Truswell of the Department of Nutrition and Food Science at the University of London revealed that obesity was nonexistent among the Kung, and evidence of coronary heart disease could not be found. Their cholesterol levels are as low as new born Americans all their lives, they do not develop hypertension and their blood pressures do not rise with age, as do ours. Although they are short, they show no evidence of nutritional deficiencies and consume on the average 56 grams of protein a day, about the amount recommended for Americans.

If infections or accidents do not kill them first, they can live to ripe old ages. In fact, the proportion of individuals over 60 in these hunting–gathering tribes is about 10 percent, similar to that of the United States, despite their lack of medical care. Seven percent of the Kung are over 65, Dr. Truswell reported.

Anthropologists point out that today's hunting and gathering tribes living in the warmer latitudes eat a very wide range of species. The Kung for example, consume 59 species of plants and 17 species of animals, and the Seri Indians of the Sonora Desert in north–western Mexico eat 41 different kinds of fruits. Excavations of 8,000 year old Indian sites in the lower Illinois Valley have revealed that 107 different plants were used for food.

According to Dr. John R.K. Robson, Professor of Nutrition at the University of South Carolina, the development of agriculture some 10,000 years ago led to a steady narrowing of food choices, possibly to man's nutritional detriment because it limited sources of dietary fiber, vitamins, mineral and trace elements. The amount of saturated animal fat and cholesterol in the diet was significantly increased by the domestication of animals and resulting consumption of dairy products, eggs and fat–laden meats. Wild game is much leaner than domestic animals.

Only in the northern–most latitudes, sites of relatively recent human occupation, is the diet of the hunter–gatherer nearly exclusively animal food. Even here, the Eskimos subsist primarily on fish, which has less harmful fat than most meats. And during the Ice Age, when humans in Europe are believed to have hunted many large mammals, the cave art also depicts the gathering of plant foods.

Bones Predominate in Fossils

The popular portrait of man is a rapacious and successful hunter who ate little else but the kill he brought home for his family and community to share arose largely from discoveries of archeological sites laden with fossilized bones of large prey.

Remains of plant foods and the containers they are gathered in decompose readily and thus were rarely evident in these archeological sites. Even today, recently abandoned Kung Sa sites rarely show plant remains, although two–thirds of the Kung diet is vegetable matter.

Within the last decade, however, archeologists have begun to look for and find microscopic evidence of plant foods, such as the presence of pollen grains and plant crystals in fossilized human feces, or coprolites. In addition to bones of small rodents, deer hairs and chicken feathers, various seeds and pollens have been found in 300,000 year old corprolites from Homo erectus, an extinct species of human being that was modern man's immediate ancestor. As recently as 3,000 years ago, the inhabitants of rock shelters in southwestern Texas consumed (except for grasshoppers) a limited amount of animal protein, according to coprolite analyses by Dr. Vaughn M. Bryant Jr., anthropologist at Texas A. & M. University in College Station.

Dr. Glynn Isaac, an anthropologist at the University of California at Berkeley, who believes that the image of early man as a nearly exclusive carnivore is vastly overblown, points out, however, that the fossil evidence does not tell what proportion of the diet may have been meat. And, he believes, regardless of how much food it provides, hunting had tremendous evolutionary significance: it fostered intelligence, foresight, speech and social skills.

Effects on Sex Roles

But if the hunt, a high–risk and low yield activity, had to have been the primary source of food for protohumans, Dr. Adrienne Zihlman, anthropologist at the University of California at Santa Cruz, believes the human species as we know it today would have undoubtedly died out, since there would have been inadequate supplies of food for the women, children and nonhunting men who remained at the home base.

Further, the digestive tract of the carnivore is designed for quick processing of food and rapid excretion of wastes before they putrify and poison the animal. The carnivore's digestive tract is short (only about three times the length of its torso), smooth and straight. The herbivore has a very large small intestine and long, smooth large intestine designed for processing bulky foods that take a long time to digest.

The human intestinal tract, while not as long as the herbivore's, is much longer than the carnivore's (about 12 times the length of the torso) and the surface area is further increased by puckering. Food takes a long time to be digested and wastes are eliminated slowly, a design more suitable to a diet high in plant matter than meat. And while the carnivore has an acidic saliva, human saliva is alkaline and contains an enzyme, ptyalin, that predigests starch from plants.

Digestion

According to Dr. F. Clark Howell, an anthropologist at the University of California at Berkeley, the human digestive apparatus and metabolic equipment has probably changed little in the last few million years, although no fossil record of soft tissue remains to prove this. However, with respect to digestion and metabolism, we are hardly different from modern primates, Dr. Howell points out.

Yet, recent humans are more intensive flesh eaters than any other living primates. Dr. Truswell notes that modern man suffers much more from nutrition–related diseases than do the Kung and other hunter–gatherer tribes. "Of course we cannot go back to living the life of hunter–gatherers," he says. But, he adds, for the sake of our health, there are "indications that we should aim to model our dietary constituents and eating patterns more on those of hunter–gatherers".

Jane E. Brody

PYRAMIDS AND WHEATGRASS

Dear Viktoras: Sorry for the long delay in re-contacting you. Haven't forgotten you though.

Experimenting and doing new research always produces new hurdles at the most unexpected times. It is true for me too!

Finally got everything in order to do the wheat grass, etc. and ran into a real problem!

Hope you have time to listen to my tale of woe! Kodak recalled the Ektachrome X I have been using for over a year and replaced it with Ektachrome 64. I had programmed a large number of times to do, including blood, milk, honey, water, health foods, tinned and fresh juices, cooked and raw foods etc. The upshot was 17 x 20 or 340 slides with erratic results and more often no results. The new film has a thicker base and a marked change in emulsion the result of which is less sensitive to photons than the original. For normal picture taking it is probably an improvement in color rendition, for my use the variations in film thickness no doubt caused by its newness gives inconsistent results. Just yesterday concluded an experiment to evaluate five types of film to as certain which will be the best for my purpose! Then its back to set up again.

The results on the wheatgrass was quite excellent. There is a marked difference in the control vs. pyramid chlorophyll observable by the eye, the same holds true after they were cooked! I grew the wheat in shallow soil in 3" deep plastic containers (bowls) and drilled many holes in the bottom before placing the bowls in aluminum containers to catch the water run-off. Great deal of diffeence in the root structures growing through the bottom of the planting bowls. The pyramid wheat had short 1 inch roots that did not reach the collected water; the control roots are thin and are 4-5 inches long. The grass from pyramid wheat was sturdier in the stalks, chlorophyll was evident closer to the soil and the leaves were greener and broader. The control, now 41 days old is quite yellow/green in color. Decided to let the experiment run until the straw stage. So far the pyramid wheat is far superior.

A thought has crossed my mind and here it is: You are probably in a position to do chemical analysis on plants and water. Suppose I send (give) you an 18 inch pyramid to use, could you test (chemically) the chlorophyll and water? and send me the results? A chemist I am not and besides I haven't the facilities nor can I interest anyone here to conduct any tests. I do know there is a difference in taste (pyramid water) confirmed by using it on seeds and plants and also Kirlian pictures.

All for now my friend.

Sincerely,
Al Rattray

MORE PYRAMIDS AND WHEATGRASS

Dear Viktoras: Finally got my act together! This type of research never ends and every facet takes forever it seems.

The technique of using Kirlian (corona discharge) photography appears to be one of the answers in indicating changes in energy levels, increased potency and improved keeping qualities for all perishable food items when using static geometric shapes i.e. pyramids, cones, spheres and cylinders.

Not being a chemist, no background in that discipline at all, it has been almost impossible to determine and chronicle the chemical changes. For me it is more easily understood from an atomic viewpoint. With my limited facilities it has been possible to indicate a definite oxygen decrease in water without the corresponding increase in carbon dioxide.

Like most basement researchers I am sorely pressed for time and especially money. I could use a good distributor for my copy righted magnetized pyramids in the U.S.A. If you are acquainted with anyone who may be interested please forward their names etc. and I will contact immediately, the current favorable exchange rate will be to their advantage when paying in Canadian funds. Would still like a copy of your book you mentioned in a previous letter. My next one should be a block—buster!

The photographs indicate some of the best methods of using magnetized pyramids. The one showing installation in the bathroom is covered with mac—tac since my wife wasn't turned on by the open frame. Razors should be placed on the apex plate (always in the same position) so the balance of the volume below can be utilized for cosmetics, soap, tooth paste, etc. My 3 Bic blades, 49¢!, have been in constant use since October 4, 1976, they are labled odd—even and spare and employed on alternate days. The Trac II is my wifes. They work very well on top of and inside refrigerators, did many fresh blood tests in the fridge with excellent results. The three foot pyramid suspended over the bed, is four feet from base to bed and supplies adequate energy. The same size pyramid and distance is used in the finger prints Kirlian photos. Only once in eighty different exposures was there a drop in a person's energy, it would appear that it is not necessary to be inside the pyramid to obtain stimulation. The same is true for foods, i.e. milk, cream, honey, etc.

When doing the open tray method for sprouting wheat the visible chlorophyll was significantly different to the naked eye of those grown under the ten inch pyramid. I use the pyramid symbol for pyramid and the number 10 indicates base length.

The Kirlian sides are printed on an Xerox 6500 unit. They are temperamental and that accounts for some of the different hues in color from one sequence to the next. A year ago started with test tubes, went to flat bottomed vials and now use small glass tubes so as to obtain comparisons on the same plate. Slow speed Ektachrome has frame bars and often it is difficult to ascertain where the frame begins or ends when using a black film changing bag. Have switched to a new model Kirlian generator and built high speed Ektachrome to get away from that problem.

The water picture is great. The homogenized milk sequence is to indicate visually the differences with and without magnetization. Picture 2 has the "man in the moon" look, it is the logo of the vial manufacturer so should be ignored. Just look for intensity and spread of energy when comparing to Picture 1.

As you suggested, the wheatgrass experiment was carried one step further and boiled for 3 minutes. Fabulous results as you can see. By all means use all these pictures in your best interests, just mention the origin whenever possible, I could use the plug!

The alfalfa and bean sprouts were purchased at a supermarket and split 50/50 then the pictures were taken after extracting the chlorophyll. Keeping qualities were much extended, 2-3 times.

The isotonic chlorophyll is manufactured by a company here in B.C. and this sequence indicates greater potency the longer exposure to pyramids was done. Similar results obtained with ginseng extract over a period of one year, constant growth of energy. Obviously shelf life will be increased. It would be interesting to note changes in chemical make-up. I felt that pyramids could produce transmutation that may help explain the visible changes that take place.

The wheatgrass sequence is great! The only item I have tested that shades wheat for energy is Korean red ginseng extract.

The finger prints are quite spectacular. In fact it's all mind blowing to say the least! People are done at 20 KV; all other items are 40 KV.

The last sequence, mother milk, goats milk, indicates (probably) richness in the goats favor but over a 48 hour period mothers milk retained a higher level. This is not a good test since the time of origin of the samples is indefinite but the effect of the pyramid is quite clear. Well, my friend, do tell me about your intepretations and conclusions, I am interested. Meanwhile there is lots more to do.

Sincerely,
Al Rattray, May 30, 1978

BIO-MUSIC AND THE PSYCHIC KISS

Man's future evolution is within his conscious control. The two methods presented here are conceptually related to biofeedback. In the psychic kiss the feedback instrument is meditation with another person; and in bio-music the instrumentation includes electronic hardware, meditation chambers and natural noise. The goals of consciousness research are improved health and mental ability, wisdom and environmental harmony.

The psychic kiss is a yoga posture in which two people rest their foreheads together in mutual meditation. It is a common greeting among Tibetan lamas and aborigines and instinctively blossoms between parent and child, guru and student, lovers and friends. The posture should be comfortable whether standing, sitting, reclining, or moistening the foreheads for better conductivity. The relaxed touching of the "third eye" synchronizes brain waves and attending the other's pulse synchronizes heart beats. These two conditions are correlated with emotional ESP (Buryl Payne) because reduced interpersonal noise allows a space for more informative music. The psychic kiss has two forms: the psycho-spiritual for individual evolution and the psycho-sexual for species evolution.

The psycho-spiritual kiss benefits health and telepathic efficiency. Kirlian photography (Thelma Moss) has shown: "when two people feel warm sympathetic emotions toward each other, the emanations would reach out to each other, sometimes merging into one pattern". Just as our physical birth depends on the combination of two seeds, there is a psycho-spiritual birth when people put their heads and hearts together. The health benefit comes from relaxation and relative security. This serenity subconsciously persuades the entire body that life is worth living and inspires a natural diet and longevity. The quality of life also improves since joyful health is radiantly contagious and conductive to socially productive work. Another benefit of the psychic kiss is that audible dialogue and repetition will make telepathy verbally intelligent. Patient practice is necessary since it takes a while to learn each other language -- preferably a complete phonetic alphabet and perhaps visualizations and psychic body talk. Information exchange between teacher and student should be more efficient; and friends can establish a kind of "psychic CB" and save on phone bills, misunderstandings, etc. After empathy is learned, less touching may be necessary although more enjoyed.

The psycho-sexual kiss transcends the random genetics of procreation and allows parents to design a healthy and evolved human being. There are three stages: pre-conception, conception and post-conception. In the pre-conception stage, prospective parents should find a biochemically compatible and healthy mate. Finding such a mate is more an intuitive-discriminative process than a socially conditioned desirability. A psychic-kiss-in might allow prospective parents to psychic kiss each other until they instinctively unite — a humane ritual for eugenic perfectibility. A psychic kissing before conception allows the gonads to prepare harmonious seed. Immediately after intercourse, the psychic kiss can psycho−kinetically "fix" the sperm race so that the most compatible sperm fertilize the egg. Similar psychic interaction was reported by Richmond Migel (Journal for Psychical Research 36:577, 1952) who observed the motion of one celled paramecium under a microscope and psychially persuaded them to move non−randomly in his chosen direction. With lovers in meditation harmonious fertilization is an instinctive dance.

After conception, the psychic kiss promotes the best embryonic development. Luther Burbank, the plant wizard, provided evidence of Lamarkian inheritance of acquired characteristics. He psychically persuaded a cactus to give up its thorns and become nutritiously edible in future generations. By mutual concentration on desired characteristics we can create a superior human being. In love, psycho−genetic engineering is natural and safer than present techniques of recombinant DNA. Birth defects will decrease and the offsprings will live healthier, happier lives.

Bio-music is the vibrational energy patterns of life: the very stuff we're made of. Relatively speaking we are all more or less attuned to Nature; still, there are some life-enriching aspects of nature that facilitate a "fine tuning" higher than average quality of life. Mystics have called this life-enriching music by many names: the Word,

OM, Kundalini, grace waves, ECK, etc. Those of us who have tasted this nectar even briefly know that it is powerfully real and rejuvenating. In a decadent society this state of consciousness is evidently rare and elusive, but nonetheless attainable for persistent seekers. A thorough understanding of consciousness-reality will make life more harmonious and save us from the all too prevalent ignorance. I won't presume to define the cosmic scope of such research, however I would like to share my little insights in hope of intelligent feedback.

Several years ago after my piano tuning apprenticeship I decided that "perfect pitch" is not the standardized A=440 Hz but something more natural. In searching bio-physics for a natural standard of pitch I was amazed at the complexity of Nature and decided to marry practical logic and intuition as my meditation. The piano became something of a philosopher's stone; and the piano turning art, a search for Harmony. In order to tune a piano in Equal Temperment, a tuner must discriminate infra-sound in the range of 5-10 Hz. This range surrounds the 7.5 Hz Schumann resonance which is related to ionospheric electrical currents around the earth's circumference; and Itzhak Bentov associates this frequency with an acoustical standing wave in the aorta and telepathic theta waves. (Bentov's "Stalking the Wild Pendulum," E. P. Dutton Co., 1977, a highly readable introduction to bio-music.) For about a year after my apprenticeship I chanted OM on F-21 (88 Hz) which Edgar Cayce had related to telepathy and which note was also recommended by a blind piano tuner with perfect pitch. While experimenting with a cylindrical meditation chamber, I finally dreamed this F note in a blissful trance state feeling electrically vibrated and wide awake. Since then internal resonances of various pitches have occasionally accompanied psychic phenomena; however the cosmic Om still seemed elusive, and the search continued. I later discovered how human body dimensions have evolved in harmony with environmental life energy fields. For instance, the skull size approximates two natural microwaves associated with (H) and hydroxl (OH) at 21 and 18 cm. Since our bodies are mostly water (HOH), it's not surprising that our heads should come to that realization. Radio astronomers and NASA researchers involved in SETI (search for extraterrestial intelligence) call this frequency band the "water hole" and consider it one of several likely channels since galactic and atmospheric noise is at a minimum - perhaps a clue to man's cosmobiological design. Another body harmony is stutter tonguing at about 24 Hz which corresponds to the diameter of earth. At the speed of light it would take 1/23.7 seconds to travel to the earth's center and return to the surface - as though subconsciously bouncing on a gravity trampoline. Is there intelligence encoded in bio-gravity fields? Another body harmony is the length of the spinal cord and the earth's magnetism. The geo-magnetic force induces protons to vibrate precessionally at about 2000-25000 Hz. This frequency of a sound wave in body temperature water has a wavelength near 70 cm. Various size people mimic the variance of the geo-magnetic field strength, which is stronger at the poles and weaker near the equator. The spinal cord is well known in psycho-spiritual literature; and the interaction of life and magnetic fields is well documented for migrating birds, water dowsing, etc. There are also subtle harmonies such as the gravitational effect of the moon on animals, human fertility, etc. In previous papers I've compiled computations and elucidations of nuclear, genetic and gravitational music. Not wishing to bore the general reader, let me briefly state the physical principles of biological radio: a common form of telepathy. Firstly, sympathetic resonance allows

energy and information to be transferred especially at higher frequencies. This precept is the foundation of radio and TV tuning in the carrier channel. Secondly, the nucleo-proteins bones, and membranes within our bodies have properties resembling semiconductors and piezoelectricity. This means that acoustical vibrations can be transduced to electromagnetic radio waves and vice versa. Thus AM, FM, and phase modulation of information is biologically feasible as well as the extraction of energy from the environment. Which environmental energy is most readily available and biologically useful remains to be proven, and there are undoubtedly many unknowns; e.g. superconductivity in DNA, faster than light transferrance, etc. Weighted down by all these possibilities, I guess gravitational energy seems the most attractive. Although gravity is the weakest of the four forces known to physicists, even heathens bow to it.

So admidst Nature's Void Noise, what harmony spins dancers into the beautiful? Logic and intuition can suggest likely attunements but the final proof rests on empirical evidence. I've previously outlined an experimental design centering on a bio-music synthesizer, biofeedback monitors, and a controlled environment that I call the Nadam Shanthi (Sandskrit for "flowing, vibrating peace"). The electronics, include: several oscillators from infra-sound to ultra-violet, frequency counters, a magnetometer, EMG, EEG, etc, data recording and analysing equipment etc. Some environmental and man made noise (radio, TV, etc.) can be Faraday shielded. This same shield which I call an "astral passion umbrella" can selectively open a peephole toward anything or anybody for telepathy and SETI research. I suspect some music will enhance mental clarity and effective IQ as the brain phases-out environmental noise (eg. the Zeeman effect of geo-magnetism, etc.). The brain attuned to itself (right and left hemispheres) and other relevant realities will manage the bodily functions better, and improved health should result. Bio-musicians and subjects should understand the considerable risks involved in such research since neither short nor long term effects are known. Those who object to such research should also object to a technological society since modern man already pollutes the environment with electromagnetic noise millions of times more intense than natural. All this necessitates careful preparation of experimental design since only a fool would stick his head into a microwave oven. It's possible to bypass an artificial power source and electronic gadgetry by using a properly designed meditation chamber. The principle here is the "black box resonance" where the dimensions and geometry of the chamber determine its electromagnetic standing wave. I've experimented with a cylinder although a sphere would have one dimensional focus — something like a space—helmet if you wanted to auto—stimulate your pineal body, pleasure centers, etc. Choosing your own geometry and wavelength would subject you to your own instant karma as the surface of the chamber would reflect back your own vibrational energy and tune in to some natural standard pitch; e.g. a 320 cm radium sphere may tune in a neutrino—gravitational channel from our galactic center.

Of course, the human observer is the most precious of the Nadam Shanthi; and the first step in any evolutionary aspiration is bodily health which requires a "live food" diet of uncooked unadulterated fresh vegetables, fruit, sprouts and their juices, exercize, yoga postures, fasting, etc. Anyway, the most immediate obstacle to my research is lack of hardware, time and space, which means funding. (Ahem) Although a bio-music synthesizer might someday be an evolutionary or marketable item ("tune in with Nature -- turn your radio, on"), it obviously needs research and development. Anyone interested in investing in a piece of the cosmic pie should correspond, as well as grant writers and related researchers. Although my heart belongs to the cosmos I invite correspondence with any young woman interested in a longitudinal study of the psychic kiss. Information biofeedback is most welcome via: Arnoldsburg Star Route Box 57, Spencer, W.V. 25276. After all we are all the music, metaphysical music, peace.

David J. Bihary

THE PINEAL GLAND

The pineal body is an important component of the "balanced system" of the individual and it moderates specific aspects of behavioral response caused by the environment of the individual. It is located in the geometric center of the cranium and is conical in shape. The organ functions as a neuro-endocrine transducer, converting neural central nervous system information about light conditions into hormonal output. Melatonin, the hormone it secretes, exerts a sedating and calming effect on central nervous system activity. It has been proven to exert this calming effect on behavior under condition of stress.

Environmental lighting effects pineal functioning. Total darkness stimulates pineal activity. Light impulses from the eyes reach the pineal via sympathetic nervous pathways from the cervial ganglia and the pineal responds by secreting more or less melatonin.

It has a 24 hour, circadian rhythm: bio-rhythm.

M.I.T. reports the following effects of the hormone melatonin:
- an increase in EEG Alpha activity
- an increase in EEG synchronization
- easily induced sleep, vivid dreams, more frequent rapid eye movement cycles during sleep
- moderate feeling of elation
- unusual experience of visual imagery.

The influence of thought control of this organ will produce a calming, sedating effect. Healing of all kinds awaits our ability to respond to this sacred shaped pineal body. Being ONE we will all manifest natural Love phenomena.

Perhaps, the Right side of the brain is "speaking" in a language we understand through the pineal, to the Left side of the brain which cause us to function and to behave in a particular way. (The commissures attached to the pineal and brain being transmitters or conveyors of thought.)

The pathway taken by light impulses between the retina and the pineal in mammals: Light stimuli reach the pineal by a circuitous route ultimately involving the sympathetic nervous system. Photoreceptors in the eye respond to environmental lighting by generating nerve impulses that are transmitted along the optic nerve. Most of these impulses travel to brain centers associated with vision. A small fraction of the impulses diverge from the man visual pathway and travels along a nerve bundle (the inferior accessory optic tract) which leads to the central hypothalmic neurons involved in the regulation of the sympathetic system. From this point the pathway decends via the spinal cord to preganglonic neurons supplying the superior cervical ganglia the postganglionic neurons then ascend to the pineal where they act by liberating the neuro-transitter norepinephrine.

Light and Breath!! .

MORE ON THE PINEAL GLAND

Viktoras Kulvinskas. I received your letter with anxious enthusiasm — through my schedule for the past few weeks has been hectic. Thank you for responding and allowing me to reveal what I have been hypothesising, discussing and learning about the pineal body.

Since discovering the shape and location of the pineal in 1976, I have been in search of the physiological function and meta–physiological function of this neuro–endocrine transducer. It is the intercessory organ between the physical and meta–physical within our own universe body. That which is "in tune" with the universal spheres. Conical in shape — not susceptible to the earth's magnetic field. Environmetnal lighting influences the production of the hormonal output of melatonin which has a calming and sedating effect on Central Nervous System activity — Fantastic! The influence of thought control of this, the Crown Chakra by the Soul, can handle any emotional, mental, spiritual or physical stress situation produced by our desires and local observations of daily phenomena.

The pineal provides the body with a "circulating clock" that gives potential information about environmental lighting and time of day. It participated in control of other neuroendocrine and neurophysical rhythms in bodily functions; it may also moderate some of the affects of light on gonadal maturation, the ovulatory cycle, and secretion of some pituitary hormones. Many photoperiodic events are controlled to some degree by Pineal.

"All cycles of the same duration have the same phase alignment." The illusion is understood. Pure thoughts — Love — Universal Mind Consciousness — indeed — the governor of cycles!

So forth, and so forth — Be in touch —

David Wyckoff, Florissant, Colorado 80816

THE RESONANT BRAIN

It is a commonplace observation that every form of life on our planet owes its existence directly or indirectly to the heat and light of the sun. The plant kingdom which nourishes all the higher forms of life is made up of "light eaters" which avidly absorb the same energies which we see as light and color. We, too, are eaters of light: the red pigment of human hemoglobin is almost identical in structure to the green pigment of plant chlorophyll and the blood which flows back into the dark interior of the body from the illumined skin is subtly changed by its encounter with light, as if the skin embodied with respect to Fire the functions which our lungs fulfill for the element of Air. Our brain, which shares a common embryonic origin with the skin, reaches out through the bony prison of the skull to feed on the light captured by its hungry eyes. So vital is vision to our world awareness that 90% of that awareness is said to come to our brains through the eyes, and "I see" has come by usage immemorial to mean "I understand". Below the sunlit level of our conscious life lies a borderland of esthetic and emotional responses to light and color which conditions us in ways obvious and subtle and on which depends much of the power of the visual arts to charm and move us. Deepest of all in the unconscious are the elemental reactions of molecule, cell, and organ to the tongues of solar flame which lick at our vitals across 100 million miles of space.

Only in the past 75 years have the effects of light on animals and man been studied with any precision and our knowledge is still fragmentary. Although one of the first Nobel prizes in medicine and physiology was awarded in 1903 to the Danish physician Niels Finsen for his remarkable cures of tuberculosis and other diseases of the skin by concentrated light, photobiology and phototherapy have remained relatively neglected despite their great possibilities. This is all the more strange in our age of chemical ingenuity when one considers the unique power of visible light to promote chemical reactions. The intrinsic quantum energies of the visible spectrum are just sufficient to activate biologically significant molecules, speeding up reactions otherwise muted or sluggish. At longer wavelengths, in the infrared, the intrinsic energy falls below these critical values and can only modify temperature. At shorter wavelengths, in the ultraviolet, the quantum energy soon reaches destructively high values and splits molecules apart or otherwise makes them unfit to participate in the dance of life. Visible light is thus uniquely linked with living chemistry. To this one octave of the "Music of the Spheres" we who live on this planet all resonate.

Before considering some of the scientific evidence for the pervasive influence of light and color on human life it may be useful to survey some of their effects on animals. The most obvious function of animal light responses is to act as a clock or calendar for mating, seasonal migration, hibernation, and other vital activities too important to be left dependent on fluctuations of temperature and other unreliable signals of seasonal change. The rotation of the earth on its axis every 24 hours and its rotation around the sun every 365 days provide precise, dependable signals to the animal nervous system in the form of changes in the amount of light reaching the eyes. One of the first experimenters to modify the proportions of light and darkness in the daily 24 hour cycle was William Rowan, a zoologist at the University of Alberta, Canada. Finches and crows were kept by Rowan in cages in the open during the winter, when these birds normally are inactive sexually and have migrated to warmer latitudes. By burning low wattage electric lights for a few minutes longer each evening to simulate the lengthening days of spring Rowan was able to cause the birds to develop sexually and when the crows were released at the end of the experiment they proceeded to migrate northward - in the dead of winter (1). Comparable findings were reported in 1931 by Bissonnette, an American investigator, in male starlings (2) and in the female ferret (3). He found that the ferret could be brought into heat during the winter, when sexual activity normally does not occur, by lengthening the period of light in the 24 hour cycle. Other research workers reported that when day length was reduced from 15 to 9 hours sexual activity in the field mouse virtually ceased (4). By 1936, Bissonnette was able to list 13 species of birds and a number of mammals whose sexual cycles were demonstrably controlled by the length of day (5). Since then numerous others have been added to this list, including fish, and it has become common practice in the poultry industry to increase egg production by artificially lengthening the short daylight hours of winter.

Some species show the reverse of the light responses just described. Animals such as deer, goat and sheep breed in the short days of autumn and have their young the following spring. Sheep can be prevented from mating by increasing the amount of light in the diurnal cycle or stimulated to mate by decreasing light virtually without regard to the time of year (6). Several species which mate in summer or fall and bear their young the following spring have been studied with regard to the effects of light on the total period of gestation. In these animals, such as the weasel, the pine marten, and the mink, the ovum is fertilized at the time of mating but only several months later implants itself in the inner lining of the uterus where the placenta and fetus develop. The interrum between mating and implantation may be of the order of 6 months in the case of the long-tailed weasel, but extra light in winter has reduced this period by more than 100 days (7). The pine marten and the mink have been reported to respond to extra light in a similar manner (8).

Other endocrine glands, such as the thyroid, the thymus, and the adrenals, have been studied in one or more species and found to show variations dependent on the season of the year or systematically controlled lighting. It is still not entirely clear, however, exactly how these changes are produced and to what extent they are due to direct versus indirect effects, such as those ensuing upon stimulation of the gonads (9). In recent years evidence has accumulated which suggests that the pineal gland in mammals may be important in the control of glandular responses to light. This small pine cone shaped organ in the brain was long thought to be a vestigial remainder of the third eye photoreceptor in amphibians. Its function was unsuspected until several cases of precocius pubety were reported about 70 years ago in young boys with tumors that had destroyed the pineal. It was later found that delayed sexual development occured in children with true pineal tumors. Analysis of the published cases suggested this to be due to increased pineal activity (10). It was then noted that while constant light increased, the constant darkness inhibited, the growth of the ovaries in rats (11), the reverse occured in rat pineals: constant light decreased, and darkness enlarged, their size.

This led to the suspicion that activation of the gonads by light was due to a decrease in production of a gonad-inhibiting substance in the pineal (13), and this substance was later found to be identical with melatonin, previously isolated from cattle pineals, which causes blanching of the skin when injected into frogs (14). Melatonin and related substances with a similar mode of action thus appears to constitute the endocrine output of the pineal (13). Melatonin injections not only inhibit the gonads but also the rate at which the rat thyroid takes up radioactive iodine from the bloodstream and converts it to thyroid hormones. There is also evidence for melatonin's blocking and release of a pituitary hormone when applied directly to the rat hypothalamus (13).

It has been known for some time that in order for light to influence the sexual cycle an animal must have intact eyes, optic nerves, hypothalamus, and pituitary gland. If animals are blinded or the pituitary is removed surgically these light-induced responses are abolished (15). However, the detailed chain of transmission by which light in the environment results in glandular changes in the body has not been known. It now appears that the pineal gland is an important link in this chain: nerve impulses generated in the retina by light travel through the optic nerve, then via the inferior accessory optic tract and other nerve fibers to the upper spinal cord, from there to the superior cervical ganglia of the Sympathetic nervous system, located in the neck, and thence to the pineal gland via Sympathetic nerves. In the pineal, melatonin production is decreased by these impulses and as a result the hypothalamic brain centers which control the pituitary gland are released from melatonin inhibition and cause the anterior pituitary to secrete hormones into the blood stream which travel to the target glands (e.g. the gonads) and cause them, in turn, to increase their activity (13).

Other seasonal changes which are strikingly responsive to light, rather than to temperature or to variations in food supply, are the deposition of subcutaneous fat layers and seasonal molting in some mammals and birds. In the autumn months such animals as the ferret and the mink lay down a thick layer of subcutaneous fat which serves to provide needed stores of energy for the winter and added insulation against the cold. During this period the summer coat is shed and the characteristic winter fur grows out. It has been found that by placing such animals on restricted amounts of light one can induce them to deposit the normal autumnal fat and grow winter fur during the height of a summer heat wave (16). In birds, likewise, there is a general tendency to deposit fat in autumn, while in migratory birds, in addition, a second yearly period of fat deposition occurs in the spring just before the birds migrate. The latter type of fat storage, amounting to 20 to 30% of the body weight, can be caused to occur in winter by artificially increasing day length, whereas the autumnal fat deposits, which are comparable in amount, occur in response to decreasing daily light (17). This is one of the many observations which might be cited to show that responses to light are not so simple as this brief "bird's eye view" of the subject might lead one to believe. As in the case of the sexual responses cited previously, some of these phenomena have been shown to depend on the pituitary gland. Ferrets, for example, whose pituitaries are removed no longer exhibit any hair distribution changes when the seasons change (18, 19).

While some progress has been made in unravelling the intricate sequence of events triggered by light stimuli, very little is known about the relevance to such reactions of color. The response of the gonads in birds exposed to colored lights of different wavelengths is the only one which has been studied to significant extent. As early as 1933 Bissonnette found that the effective component of light in producing sexual stimulation in starlings was the red part of the spectrum (20). Red was similarly found to be effective and green ineffective as a sexual stimulant in turkeys (21) and in English sparrows (22). The French investigator Benoit and his colleagues found that the red-orange end of the spectrum is the only sexually effective component of light in Peking ducks (23).

These results are curious since the avian retina is rather insensitive in this region of the spectrum, the retina of the pigeon, for example, being 5 times more sensitive to yellow (580 millimicrons) than to red (650 millimicrons) (24). This selectively is all the more puzzling when one considers how utterly essential to the survival of the species mating behavior is and how little the sexual cycle seems to be influenced by precisely those wavelengths in which the sun's light is richest and to which the birds' retinas are most sensitive. It seems improbable that these selective reactions can be explained in terms of any simple theory about the usefulness of light-dark cycles as a seasonal clock. Let us now turn our attention to some of the clues which may ultimately afford a solution to this puzzle.

Between 1940 and 1944 a number of reports on the effects of the color of living organisms were published by Japanese investigators at the Institute of Obstetrics and Gynecology of Kyoto University. A wide variety of color-specific responses in rabbits was described, the common denominator of which was the activation of the Parasympathetic division of the vegetative, or autonomic, nervous system by "red" wavelengths (i.e. those longer than 580 millimicrons) and the activation of the Sympathetic division by "blue" wavelengths (i.e. those shorter than 580 millimicrons). The autonomic nervous system controls all the involuntary functions of the mammalian body, including digestion, circulation, and reproduction. All emotional responses involve autonomic activity, and what we call "temperament" is dependent to a great degree on the dynamic balance between contending unconscious forces in the autonomic arena. In view of the enormous complexity of the chemical, glandular, emotional, and mental transactions which are involved in maintaining this balance in the face of internal and external challenges, it is obvious that selective activation of one or the other of the two autonomic antagonists could have profound repercussions.

Three examples taken from the Japanese reports will serve to illustrate these effects. One of these studies found that changes in blood pressure were regularly elicited in female rabbits by red and by blue light. Red produced consistent decreases in carotoid artery pressure after 1 hour of whole body irradiation. The effect could be blocked by atropine, a powerful chemical antagonist of the Parasympathetic nerves, but was not prevented by adrenalin in the doses employed (in the absence of red light the adrenalin produced consistent rises in blood pressure). Blue light produced the opposite effect - a sustained rise in blood pressure following an initial drop. The effect of adrenalin was to further increase this blood pressure rise, a Sympathetic type of response (25).

Blood sugar level changes in fasting rabbits were reported as another example of selective responses to color. Red wavelengths tended to decrease blood sugar, increase the amount of sugar stored in the liver, minimize the elevation of blood sugar following adrenalin injection, and speed the drop in blood sugar after insulin injection - all Parasympathetic types of response. Blue light produced the opposite effects - an

increase in blood sugar, a faster rise in blood sugar following adrenalin injection and a small drop in blood sugar after insulin, all Sympathetic types of response (26).

These selectives effects of color occurred in albino rabbits which do not have color vision. The light was directed at shaved patches of skin. The effects were probably due to the entry into the bloodstream of chemical substances produced on the skin under the influence of the light. This is also suggested by two other features of the work, namely the slowness of the responses and the fact that some of the effects were duplicable in the test tube. The blood pressure findings, for example, required irradiation times of the order of an hour or more, whereas comparable effects mediated directly through the nervous system could be expected to occur in seconds or minutes. When rabbit reticuloendothelial cells were irradiated in the test tube with red light they took up colloidal dyes and carbon particles more avidly and were less responsive to the inhibiting effects of adrenalin on this activity - a Parasympathetic type of effect. Blue light, conversely, inhibited dye and carbon storage and strengthened the inhibiting action of adrenalin, a Sympathetic type of effect (27).

It thus appears possible to produce short-term responses which activate the autonomic nerves, or mimic their action, in rabbits without involving the retina, but long term responses of the gonads in ducks require stimulation of the eye or of the brain itself. Benoit was unable to produce activation of the gonads in ducks by prolonged exposure to light when their eyes were covered even when the skin of the back was plucked (28, 29). Similarly, there was no effect if the optic nerve was cut or the eyeball removed, providing that the head was hooded. However, if the hood had eyeholes an effect on the gonads occurred even in the absence of the eye (30, 31). Curiously, light was found to produce gonadal effects when beamed directly at the hypothalamic brain tissue through a glass rod inserted into the skull (32), although the effects of "blue" were the same as those of "red" under the conditions of the experiments (33).

The importance of the eye in gonadal responses to light is further pointed up by the experience of John Ott, a time lapse photography expert who first became interested in the biological effects of color when he noticed the sometimes startling results of using artificial lights in photographing the growth of plants (34). A pumpkin vine, for example, was being photographed under skylight supplemented by florescent "white" light of a slightly pinkish color. Pumpkins produce two types of blossoms on the same vine: the male pollen producing (staminate) and the female ovary containing (pistillate) flowers. Under the pinkish light the male buds developed normally, but all the female buds dried up, turned black, and dropped off the vine when they had reached about ½ the size at which they would normally open to be pollinated. A later attempt at pumpkin growing with fluorescent lamps of a bluish color produced exactly opposite effects: this time all the female buds developed vigorously, but all the male buds dried up, turned black, and dropped off the vine at the same early stage of development. The experiment proved repeatable at will, 100% control of staminate or pistallate buds being obtained in each instance (35).

Ott then tried the bluish and pinkish fluorescent tubes on 2 tanks of tropical fish (guppies). With the lights turned on 14 hours per day all reproduction stopped immediately in both aquariums. When the light intensity was reduced by ½ and the duration of daily light was cut back to 9 hours, the fish under the pinkish light resumed reproduction, but no young were produced under the bluish fluorescent tube. A remarkable finding was that the young born under the pinkish light were 80% female and only 20% male versus the usual 50/50 ratio. The small shift in color balance from daylight values toward the red resulted in this striking shift from a 1 to 1 proportion of the sexes to a 4 to 1 proportion in favor of females. In addition, the males born under these conditions proved to be abnormally slow in developing secondary sex characteristics (36).

A similar shift in the proportions of male to female in the offspring of mice and chinchillas exposed to pinkish and bluish lights has been reported by Ott with one very interesting difference: pinkish light favors the birth of males and bluish light the birth of females - just the reverse of the reaction in guppies (37). The explanation for this difference has not so far been found, though it is worth noting that both mice and chinchillas are nocturnal animals and lack color vision, whereas fish possess it. There are no reports of which I am aware of light-induced sex ratio changes in other species with color vision besides fish, but it is perhaps significant that human folklore, at lease in the western world, associates pink with girl babies and blue with little boys, and humans are among the few mammals with color vision.

This raises 2 rather leading questions. First, might artificial lights account in any way for the allegedly "chance" births of all male or all female offspring into certain families? Might a housewife's preference for pinkish lights in her bedroom conceiveably tip the balance in favor of girl babies? Or might some innate tendency to produce females not perhaps manifest at the conscious level in a preference for a pinkish ambiance? And might this preference not still further heighten the probability of female births? The second question relates to the significance of these curious color effects in the natural order. What useful purpose do they serve in promoting, say, the survival of the species? It is certainly difficult to imagine just what this might be. Or are they in some say related at an even more fundamental level to those strangely disparate building blocks of the universe, the electron and the proton? This is not an idle question, since electrons produce a blue-violet glow in a high voltage corona discharge while protons glow red. And is it entirely coincidental that the sperm is small in size compared to the ovum as is the electron compared to the proton?

One way of assessing the importance of visual stimulation to the chemistry of the body is to study the blind, and the available evidence points to certain curious abnormalities of growth and function resulting from blindness. These have been described in 3 separate studies carried out in Germany on a total of 95 blind subjects of whom 81 were either blind at birth or became blind in early childhood and the remaining subjects became blind after the age of 15 (38, 39, 40). These studies agree on the occurrence of at least four abnormalities in subjects blind from birth or infancy, while one investigator reports that such deviations are less pronounced, or absent, in subjects who retain some capacity to see light, particularly if they became blind after the age of 15 (38).

All subjects showed a disturbance of fluid metabolism as shown by the Volhard test which measures urine output and concentration at regular intervals after the intake of a standard amount of water. Blind subjects in all 3 studies voided less during the day and more than twice as much during the night as normal controls. As there was no evidence of kidney or circulatory disease, this suggested that the antidiuretic hormone produced by the posterior pituitary gland was being secreted at a greater rate than normal during the day as a result of the absence of light stimuli. Similar findings have been reported by other investigators in measurements on blind subjects who maintained their normal activity (41). It is interesting to note that brief flashes of light at short intervals have resulted in increased urine output over a 3 hour period of albino rats (42). This was found to coincide with a decreased content of antidiuretic hormone in the posterior pituitaries of the irradiated animals. In the absence of light less urine was secreted during the period of the test and the posterior pituitaries showed an increased content of antidiuretic hormone, more also presumably being secreted into the bloodstream in the absence of light.

The second abnormality common to subjects blinded early in life was a modified blood sugar metabolism. When 2 standard doses of glucose were given 90 minutes apart and blood sugar measured every 30 minutes for 3 to 5 hours (the Staub-Traugott test), it was cnsistently found that the curves relating blood sugar values to the time when measured showed 2 distinct peaks of equal height, only the first of which is present in normal controls.

A third abnormality was an altered response to insulin. Blind subjects showed a prolonged depression in blood sugar values after being given 0.2 units of insulin per kilogram of body weight. In Fuchs' study (38) the 10 subjects tested showed an abnormal early rebound with a second subsequent depression.

Finally, all 3 studies showed in blind subjects a decreased cross–sectional area of the Sella Turcica on lateral X-ray of the skull. The Sella Turcica is the bony cavity in which lies the pituitary gland and its size correlates roughly with that of the gland which it contains. Fuchs, in addition, claims to have found a correlaton between the average cross-sectional area of the Sella Turcica and the age at which the subject was blinded. In 10 subjects totally blind before the age of 6 years the average was 61 square millimeters. In 10 subjects blind from early childhood but retaining some ability to distinguish light from darkness, the average was 68 square millimeters, and in 10 individuals blind from the age of 15 or later, with some remaining light-distinguishing ability, the average was 90 square millimeters, which is within the normal range for the age group examined (38).

While the authors of these studies are inclined to view the findings on the Stella Turcica as evidence for pituitary underdevelopment and hypofunction, it should be kept in mind that such measurements are not generally accepted as providing accurate estimates of the true size of the gland or of its functional state (43). However, the reported differences in skull structure between blind and normal subjects may be significant per se. It has also been reported that in a study of 326 blind girls the onset of menstruation occurred up to 1 year earlier, paradoxically, than in a comparable group of girls with normal vision (44).

Perhaps the best single piece of research on human responses to color stimuli is the work of Robert Gerard, an American psychologist. In 1958 he reported (45) that "red", "blue", and "white" light stimuli carefully equated for apparent brightness produced consistent bodily and emotional responses in 24 normal adult males. The following variables were measured: 1) brain wave patterns, 2) respiratory movements, 3) electrical activity of the heart, 4) frequency of eyeblinks, 5) blood pressure, 6) palmar skin conductance (a measure of autonomic arousal based on reaction of the sweat glands in the palms of the hands). In all physiological measures except heart rate there was significantly more arousal with "red" than with "blue" illumination. Intermediate levels were obtained with "white" light. Brain wave tracings showed less arousal during "blue" illumination, although all the stimuli were equal in apparent brightness. The subjective responses paralleled the physiological data. All the subjects reported a feeling of greater over-all well being, greater relaxation and calm, more pleasant ideation, and less hostility and anxiety during "blue" than during the other stimuli. Under "red" illumination there was clearly more tension and anxiety, excitement and arousal, including sexual arousal.

These findings are reminiscent of the animal data we have reviewed and also suggest that certain scattered cultural observations may have a common physiological basis. One need only think of the traditional association between the color red and erotic passion: valentines and red roses, the Scarlet Letter of the Puritans, the "red light district", "painting the town red" and so on. The familiar expression "I saw red" is usually used by a person describing an episode charged with hostility and terminating in aggression. It is worth noting the interesting triad of erotic arousal, aggressiveness, and anxiety which are elicited by red light. It has long been held by psychoanalyst that there are aggressive and even sadistic components in the sexual impulse and that anxiety may have many of its roots in this complex of forces and associated guilt feelings (46).

Ott has reported an interesting anecdote about the apparent influence of pink fluorescent lamps on human behavior. Several years ago the staff of a St. Petersburg, Florida, radio station replaced the white fluorescent lamps in the control rooms with F-40PK pink tubes in an effort to brighten the surroundings. About 2 months later personal relations had deteriorated to a noticeable degree: poor performance on the air. Two employees abruptly submitted their resignations without any known reason for leaving other than dissatisfaction with themselves and their co-workers. At that point one of the staff said that if the pink tubes were not removed he would "go out of his mind". They were promptly replaced with the original white tubes. Within a week a dramatic change occurred; tempers ceased to flare, congeniality and cooperativeness began to reappear, the resignations were withdrawn, and performance on the air improved noticeably, with mistakes at a minimum (47).

There is yet another way in which we respond to color which is poorly understood and may well have a demonstrable physiological basis. This is the designation of colors as "warm" and "cool", a universal attribution of temperature properties of visible light with no foundation whatsoever in purely physical act. A thermometer placed in various parts of the sun's spectrum will show no difference in temperature of the visible colors. Only in the infrared portion of the spectrum will the temperature rise. In subjective experience, however, there is little doubt that red, orange, and yellow are, indeed, "warmer" and that blue, indigo and violet are "cooler" than their complementary opposites or white. Green is sometimes referred to as a "cool" color, although when speaking of light, as opposed to complex mixtures of pigments, it is more accurate to designate green as the neutral point in the spectrum around which the other colors may be arranged in "warm" and "cool" groups. This agrees rather well with the way in which the visual apparatus responds to color stimuli in terms of complementary pairs. Each spectral color except green has a single complementary spectral color which when mixed with it produces the impression of white for the normal person. "Red" is complementary to "blue-green", "orange" to "sky blue", "yellow" to "indigo blue' and "yellow–green" to "violet". True "green", the wavelength band between 492 and 560 millimicrons does not have a complement in the color spectrum. Its complement is the color "purple" which must be synthesized by mixing spectral "red" and spectral "violet" (48, 49). These are, curiously enough, "warm" and "cool" colors and their combination is neutral in this respect, as is green. The natural spectral complementary pairs, therefore, may be thought of as balanced about green, the neutral center point.

There is a remarkable lack of precise experimental data as to how colors give rise to temperature responses. The most common belief is that their responses are due to some association between sources of heat and "warm" colors. It might be argued that the reddish-yellow flames of burning leaves and wood may have impressed this association upon the human mind from the earliest times. However, anyone who has experimented with fire knows that the hotter a flame is made the "bluer" it becomes. The changing seasons would not give rise to such an association either, since the yearly pageant of nature the blue-green mantle of plant life is spread over the earth during the warm months. With cold weather comes the "warm" colors of autumn. Sunlight, a major source of warmth, is certainly rich in red, orange and yellowlight, but even richer blue-green and blue, with peak energy in this last part of the spectrum (50). The sun is, in fact, a "blue" star. Although the apparent color of the sun's disc varies greatly depending on its position in the sky, being redder near the horizon, nevertheless maximum heat radiated to the observer and maximum "blue-whiteness" occur together when the sun is directly overhead. Such paradoxes hardly make the associational theory of "warm" and "cool" colors very attractive, although they do not disprove it.

What of a physiological theory? Definitive evidence is still lacking, but the theory is simple enough and fits well with data on human autonomic responses which have been cited earlier. The essence of the theory is as follows; the two great divisions of the autonomic nervous system in man are selectively sensitive to color stimuli - the Sympathetic to the blue-violet and the Parasympathetic to the red-yellow fractions of the spectrum. Blue, for example, could cause a reaction of the sympathetic nerves sufficient to result in slight constriction of the small blood vessels in the skin as well as in other viscera. This, in turn, would result in a diminished flow of blood to the skin and therefore of heat from the interior of the body. Since the temperature-sensitive nerve endings of the body are almost entirely in the skin, the net result of exposure to blue would be a slight sensation - perhaps only semi-consciously perceived - of lowered skin temperature. The converse would occur upon stimulation of the Parasympathetic nerves by red, with a resulting dilation of skin blood vessels and a slight sensation of skin warmth.

The foregoing ideas together with the work of Gerard and the animal data suggest certain therapeutic possibilities which can hardly have escaped the alert reader. A review of the history of so-called "color therapy", however, reveals a decidedly muddled state of affairs dating back about 100 years, with a long succession of advocates ranging from ingenious experimenters to fraudulent quacks (51). There has been a most regrettable lack of systematic, imaginative scientific inquiry into this province of photobiology, indeed almost a tendency to shy away from it lest the investigator be branded a charlatan. Such attitudes have no rational place in the scientific world. They serve only to hinder the growth of insight and competence and deter not only the investigator but also those who control funds needed to carry out research.

One of the problems which have beset the unwary in experimenting with the spectrum is the necessity in most cases of relying on glass or other types of filters which absorb unwanted energies and transmit a certain percentage of the desired color. Unfortunately there are no perfect filters. To isolate colors of true spectral purity at effective power levels require either a large prism or diffraction grating and associated optics, expensive equipment not readily available. Filters usually transmit to some degree more than one of the spectral colors, although on visual inspection this may not be obvious. This might be only a minor problem if all that mattered to the physiological response were the apparent color perceived consciously in the visual cortex of the brain. In fact, however, these responses are demonstrably due to the unconscious reactions of the autonomic nerves, and these exhibit a very significant difference in their reactions to what the retina of the eye receives from the outer world compared to the reactions of the visual cortex.

The neurons of the visual cortex do not report passively what the eye "sees". They edit, censor, and otherwise process the retinal messages to a very considerable degree. This is most striking in the case of hysterical blindness, a condition in which the eye and the brain are intact physically, but the brain apparently blocks the conscious awareness of what the eye transmits. The opposite happens in the case of the "blind spot" in each of our eyes. This is the small patch of the retina which lacks light sensitive cells because the optic nerve comes to the surface of the retina at that point. The result is a "hole" in the visual field where we see nothing. At a distance of seven feet this hole is about 8 inches in apparent diameter and this increases with increasing distance until when we look at the sky it covers a region about 11 times the size of the moon. Although the eye literally sees nothing over this area none of us is ever conscious of emptiness or blackness because the visual cortex of the brain "fills in" with whatever happens to be in the immediate vicinity. The blind spot surrounded by newsprint will seem to be filled in with newsprint, surrounded by trees it will seem to be filled in with trees, surrounded by red satin it will seem to be filled in with red satin (51).

When confronted with a mixture of colored lights transmitted in varying degrees through a color filter the visual cortex processes the impulses coming from the retina in such a way as to increase the relative importance of the more intense wavelengths and to suppress its awareness of the less intense ones. This serves the purpose of cutting down the distracting clutter of less important stimuli to attend to those of the highest priority. It has the drawback, however, of sacrificing awareness of components in the total energy input which are nonetheless effective in producing responses in the unconscious nervous system and the tissues which it enervates. In some cases this dissociation between what the retina sees, what the brain perceives, and what the autonomic nerves respond to produces strange results. A number of subjects have been described in the Russian literature who could not - consciously - distinguish red from green but nevertheless showed normal unconscious differential muscular reactions and occular electrical sensitivities to "red" and "green" lights, earning these subjects the title of "cortical achromats" (52, 53). These differential responses to red and green lights of equal brightness are thought to be due to selective responses of the autonomic nerves to these stimuli, although the visual cortex is for some reason unresponsive (54).

In short, if one looks at light filtered through what appears to be, say, a blue filter, but, which actually transmits to the eyes significant amounts of other wavelengths, the actual nervous response will be "diluted" in ways that may prove very difficult to analyze or duplicate in confirming experiments unless the identical filters and the identical light sources are used under the identical conditions. Nor are filters the only problem. Light sources vary greatly in the relative amounts of the visible colors which they emit and these proportions change as the light sources age with continued use. The eye itself is by no means uniformly sensitive to all colors, being much more so to yellow than to red or violet. These considerations may help to explain the confusion in some of the therapeutic work involving visible light.

Despite these strictures it should be emphasized that the controlled use of light and color does offer real possibilities for transforming human life as opposed to simply prettifying it. Consider, for example, the population "explosion". It has been suggested that merely installing electric lights in underdeveloped areas may prove to be effective in curbing excessive birthrates, if the experience of one South American village is any criterion (55), the birthrate having allegedly dropped there after electric lights were installed. The reason suggested is that the villagers found other diversions for evening hours besides the obvious one, but there may be other factors at work such as the total amount and color distribution of the light reaching their retinas. Conceivably the birthrate might be even more effectively limited by making the light bulbs of glass which cuts down the percentage of wavelengths which stimulate sexual functions and increases the percentage of those which inhibit it. Research on this problem might prove enormously rewarding.

Light may prove to have an unusually effective role in family planning. In a paper with the challenging title "On the Possibility of a Perfect Rhythm Method of Birth Control by Periodic Light Stimulation" Dr. Edmond Dewan has reported encouraging preliminary success in controlling the length of irregular menstrual cycles and in triggering ovulation on schedule by the simple expedient of burning a light bulb all night on certain days of the month. The method is simplicity itself: a 100 watt bulb supplying indirect light is kept on in the bedroom for the entire night of the 14th, 15th, 16th, and 17th days of the menstrual cycle, day 1 being the first day of menstrual flow (56). Continuing research has confirmed Dr. Dewan's preliminary findings and clinical trials on a larger scale are in progress in collaboration with Dr. John Rock (57). Here, too, there is an urgent need to determine what role color plays in this important effect.

As an example of how useful a tool the control of color might eventually become in understanding human physiology and in controlling the environment to human benefit, I would like to mention the suggestive association between the following 4 ostensibly unrelated items: 1) the color red, 2) the response of the human nervous system to pulses of light, 3) the seizures of epileptics, and 4) sexual intercourse.

It is now known that many epileptics can be caused to have convulsions by simple expedient of flashing a bright light in their eyes at a rate of the order of 2 to 20 pulses per second. Epileptics have been known to induce convulsions in themselves by simply staring at a bright light or the sun and moving the outstretched fingers of one hand rapidly back and forth in front of their eyes, or by blinking (58). Indeed, watching television or other flickering lights has induced in some individuals the first convulsions of their lives. Experiment has shown that red is the most efficient of all colors in inducing such convulsions and it has been reported to be 10 times as effective as green or blue (59). This observation may have a bearing on the theory of the epileptic personality. While there is disagreement over the psychological factors in idiopathic Grand Mal eplilepsy, most observers are said to agree on the frequent occurrence of certain character traits, among them "explosive impulsivity" and "egocentricity" (60). Some authors emphasize the factors of aggressive impulses and repressed homosexuality, and Wilhelm Reich concluded that the epileptic convulsions represents extra-genital orgasm (61), although orgasm may actually occur during epileptic seizures occasionally.

We have previously noted the association of red with erotic arousal, hostility and anxiety. Kinsey, summarizing data from a number of sources, emphasizes the numerous common physiological elements in the "sexual syndrome", anger, fear, and epilepsy (62). Among the data which he cites is the work of an Argentinian neurologist, Dr. Abraham Mosovich, is of special interest. Mosovich has obtained brain records from healthy normal couples during sexual intercourse. The recording obtained at the moment of orgasm bear a striking resemblance to the abnormal "spike-and-dome" pattern of Grand Mal epileptics! (63). In view of these facts one might well wonder what could be the therapeutic effects in epileptics of systematic avoidance of "warm" color stimuli in the "cool" part of the spectrum by means of suitably tinted eyeglasses, color therapy, and control of the visual environment. In at least one case of so-called "photogenic" epilepsy this has, in fact, been done. In this case the individual had suffered 10 to 12 major convulsions per year for 21 years. Simply wearing eyeglasses which filtered out much of the red part of the spectrum completely eliminated the seizures (59).

Conversely, it would appear quite feasible to use red light in activating unconscious, deeply buried memories and complexes relating to sex, hostility, anxiety, and guilt and help to bring these above to the threshold of consciousness where they can be dealt with by the conscious awareness. I have not seen any reports of such a use of light, but it is certainly consistent with what is known and might greatly improve the efficiency of the psychoanalytic process which tends to be prolonged, expensive and not infrequently unproductive. One cannot help wondering also what careful investigation into the contents of the unconscious which "resonate", as it were, to orange, yellow, green, blue, indigo, and violet, might not uncover. Our nervous systems hardly insist on perceiving visible electromagnetic waves in these categories without good reasons. Although the "red light district" of our unconscious seems for the most part rather gamey, if not downright awful, tapping the stream of consciousness at higher frequencies may reveal refreshing waters of which we know not and after which we thirst unknowingly. Was not the rainbow to the writers of the Old Testament the sign of the covenant between man and God?

Man is still very much a mystery and in order to grow in knowledge of ourselves we need to shed, literally, all the light we can upon the dark interior of our being. Bold imaginative, systematic research is needed to do this - and the financial support without which imagination cannot obtain a grip upon the material world . If such support can be found it may be safely predicted that the future of this work will be bright - and colorful.

Francis Woidrich, M.D.

Copyright, 1979, by the author. All rights reserved.

Section II
Warning: Man–Made Dangers

UNION OF CONCERNED SCIENTISTS

Dear Fellow Citizen:

This is to advise you of the serious risk you and other Americans face from nuclear radiation accidents.

This isn't a call to hysteria. It's a sober warning from a group of university physicists, engineers, biologists, chemists, medical doctors and others who have volunteered their time for the last five years to work with the Union of Concerned Scientists to study the hazards involved in the U.S. nuclear power program.

It's a plea for you to examine the facts about nuclear power plants, and to join with us to help bring these nuclear dangers under control while there is still time. These are the facts:

A typical nuclear power plant contained an amount of radioactive material equal to the radioactive fallout from thousands of Hiroshima-size weapons. The fear is not that these plants will explode like an atomic bomb. But much of this radioactive material is gaseous and could easily be carried by the wind for many miles if accidently released. An it can be accidentally released.

One accident — from one plant — could kill as many as 45,000 people, cause $17 billion in property damage and contaminate an area the size of Pennsylvania. In the next 25 years, the nuclear industry wishes to construct 1000 such plants.

The basic safety system in nuclear plants designed to prevent such accidents known as the Emergency Core Cooling System (ECCS) - has never actually been tested under realistic accident conditions. And when it was tested on small-scale laboratory models, this system consistently failed to function properly.

The history of the 63 nuclear plants now operating in the United States shows many malfunctions of major equipment, operator errors, and design defects, as well as continuing evidence of shoddy construction practices such as poor welding, upside-down installation of critical components, etc.

No safe way has yet been demonstrated to dispose of the millions of gallons of lethal nuclear wastes. These radioactive wastes, created when spent fuel is removed from the reactors, are among the most dangerous cancer-causing substances known to man. Radioactive wastes remain harmful for centuries - a grim legacy from present nuclear plants to future generatons.

Present safeguards are inadequate to prevent plutonium (a by-product of commercial reactors that can be used in making atomic bombs) from being hijacked by terrorists or others who wish to sabotage or blackmail the United States government.

The nuclear industry looks forward to ever—increasing sales of reactors abroad. Industry pressure to start the move toward plutonium as a fuel enhances present fears that the reactors are the stepping stones for nuclear weapons. If unchecked, the proliferation of nuclear weapons will make the world an increasingly dangerous place.

What is equally shocking is that for years, the American people have been kept totally unaware of these dangers. The Federal government and the nuclear industry repeatedly suppressed key technical data about the perils of nuclear reactors, while giving the public continuous promises about nuclear power as a miraculous new energy source.

It was the Union of Concerned Scientists that pressured the Federal government's Atomic Energy Commission into revealing the truth about nuclear reactor hazards. This private publicly supported group is doing what the Federal government should have been doing all along: regulating nuclear power. Indeed, two present members of the UCS staff resigned from the Federal government's nuclear safety program in order to help UCS do what they thought the government had hired them to do. Ralph Nader called UCS's work on nuclear power "a public service which will go down in history".

As you read about some of what the Union of Concerned Scientists has achieved in its dedicated work to protect the public from nuclear dangers, bear in mind that UCS is an organiztion that exists only because concerned people enable it to carry on its efforts through their financial support.

UCS was the first independent group of scientists to carry out a major review of the safety of nuclear plants. The deficiencies they uncovered played a key role in arousing national concern about nuclear power.

UCS exposed the government's efforts to suppress data on nuclear plant hazards and its failure to enforce strict safety standards at U.S. nuclear power plants.

UCS forced the Atomic Energy Commission to hold a massive rule—making hearing at which — for the first time — Atomic Energy Commission nuclear safety experts could be questioned under oath about key elements of federal nuclear policy. The 20—month hearing disclosed a wide range of suppressed safety issues.

UCS prepared the most comprehensive technical review of the Atomic Energy Commission's official "Reactor Safety Study".

UCS aids investigatory committees, foreign governments, state governments, and other decision—makers in their work on nuclear power issues.

UCS takes necessary legal action to compel basic changes in the government's nuclear power policies, and to make known to the public governmental data on nuclear power hazards.

UCS has extensively studied the alternatives to nuclear power. These studies have shown how conservation can greatly reduce future energy needs and how energy sources such as solar power can begin to make significant contributions to our energy supplies.

The men and women in the Union of Concerned Scientists have been joined by thousands of scientists across the U.S. — including pioneers in nuclear science and leading figures in every branch of American science — in urging a drastic reduction in new nuclear power plant construction starts until adequate safety can be assured. These scientists once shared, along with many Americans, the dream that nuclear energy might become a fine new energy source for mankind. But UCS now believes that the nuclear industry has failed to control properly the awesome hazards which could arise with this unique technology. Particularly unsettling have been recent serious accidents in a number of nuclear plants — ominous warnings for the future. After the $150 million fire at the Brown's Ferry Nuclear Station in Alabama in 1975, one official said that a nuclear catastophe was averted "by sheer luck".

BY SHEER LUCK!!! — HOW LUCKY WILL WE BE NEXT TIME??

Must we wait to see the country suffer a major nuclear power plant accident before we take action? An accident, for example, in which virtually all the children living up to 50 miles downwind of the plant could get thyroid cancer? Aren't the present warning signs of nuclear dangers clear enough?

Our nation should be deeply involved in steps to minimize the chances of nuclear catastrophe, not multiplying them. Yet the nuclear industry has laid plans to increase the number of nuclear plants in the United States to between 500 and 1,000 in the next 25 years!

If those plans are carried out, by the year 1999 there will be large clusters of nuclear plants near Boston, New York, Chicago, Des Moines, Miami, San Francisco, Seattle, Los Angeles and St. Louis — to name just a few of the cities whose inhabitants will be living with the threat of nuclear radiation accidents.

Something must be done to curb the country's poorly controlled nuclear power program — and that something has to done NOW, before any real damage is done.

Acting alone, as private citizens, there is little any of us can do to bring a halt to further nuclear power plant construction until basic nuclear safety problems can be resolved. But by acting in unison with others, by joining forces, by uniting behind the organization that has spearheaded the movement for nuclear safety, you can have a very strong influence on this country's nuclear policies.

The federal government plans to spend billions of dollars to promote the expansion of the nuclear power program. To counter this, the Union of Concerned Scientists needs support from people who are concerned about the nuclear issue, and who want to do something to stop the spread of nuclear plants throughout the land, until safety can be assured. To continue our technical research on nuclear power problems...to continue our public advocacy projects...to continue our work to bring the truth about nuclear power to the public through the news media...to continue our efforts to get the truth to the government decision—makers...to continue our court actions to bring about change in nuclear power policies..to continue our efforts to seek out the best way to solve this nation's energy problems.

We need help from you. Just $15 is all it takes for you to become a sponsor of the Union of Concerned Scientists.

But — even if you can't become a UCS sponsor, we would like to know your views on the nuclear issue. Do you agree that the United States should cut back on its nuclear power program? Has this letter helped to enlighten you about what's wrong with nuclear power? Would you like to see this country embark on an energy program involving conservation, solar energy, and improved use of fossil fuels?

If you do choose to become a sponsor of the Union of Concerned Scientist by sending a donation, please accept our heartfelt thanks and our assurance that your tax deductible donation will be put to work immediately in efforts to ensure that the many and serious problems of nuclear power are controlled.

Sincerely,
Daniel F. Ford, Executive Director, Union of Concerned Scientists

---

RADIATION

Prehistoric mans first and foremost concern was self preservation. Because he had little defense against outside threats, he lived in constant fear of death. As man developed and civilized himself, he became more and more secure by eliminating the threats to his existence and taking protective measures. There became more time for progressive thought and creative pursuits. Today, he has developed his technology to the point where it has become a monster which will destroy him. Again he is running from the pursuers of his own creation. Mankind has evidently come far, but gone nowhere.

By tampering with nature's elements, scientists and technologists have produced high-level radiation through the violent unnatural clashing of atoms under intense heat and pressure. In doing this, he has sadly misused his place as planet caretaker. Any violation of Nature's plan always results in a heavy penalty. Having lost sight of our role in nature, by striving for powers beyond our comprehension and control, we have permanently threatened our chances for survival. Atomic weaponry, nuclear power stations, nuclear testing, x-rays and other forms of this malignant pollution, hover like dark clouds over all living beings. Had we remained a simple species, we could live innocently with the rest of creation. This not being the case however, we must take preventive measures to maintain our desired degree of health.

Most of us don't consider radiation a threat because we can't see, hear, or feel it existing and harming us. Just the fact that it is not detectible through our senses is proof of its alienation in the environment. Solar radiation, is, of course, natural, as we can feel it on our skin and can see it with our eyes. Its effects on us are beneficial, not destructive; however even too much sun radiation can result in burning our skin if we are not used to the exposure.

We must all begin to take radiation seriously; just because we don't notice it, doesn't mean it's not there. Radio waves are constantly traveling through the air around us and we don't notice them either. The effects of radiation upon nature are irreversible. It destroys, mutates living matter, and obstructs normal life processes, and in our bodies can lodge in the cells creating cancerous diseases.

We can't allow the abuse of life to continue by those immoral and ignorant persons of wealth and power. The trees, oceans, rivers, pure air and sunlight sustain us, and were meant to remain pure sources of that sustenance. These precious entities are now ignored by modern men who are driven by greed and the lust for possessions. We must never lose sight of our origin, for in realizing it, we realize who and what we are on the earth.

In daily living we are exposed to many radiation sources. To minimize the effect on us physically, we should take in food which helps to counteract its destructive forces. A diet rich in chlorophyll is the number one precautionary measure. Experiments reveal that greens reduce the hazardous effects of radiation. Sprouted seeds (alfalfa, particularly) are an excellent source of chlorophyll, especially when exposed to sunlight on the third or fourth day of sprouting; this causes the developing leaves to turn a rich green. Wheatgrass is perhaps the most powerful and concentrated source. Beginning with wheat seed or 'berry', the wheat is soaked, sprouted, then grown in trays or outdoor garden space. The resulting growth looks much like thick lawn grass and tastes very sweet. It can be added to salad, chewed on alone or juiced. Wheatgrass juice therapy (as practiced at Hippocrates Health Institute in Boston) has been dramatically successful in treatment of many so-called 'terminal' illnesses, by bathing the body with internal sunshine.

Iodine is important too in minimizing radiation's effects. Seaweed, rich in iodine, helps the body discharge radioactive waste. Sea salt is another good source. Bee pollen is just now being recognized as a strong heath restorer. It contains all known amino acids and helps bolster the body's natural resistance to radiation and other disease. To obtain the pollen, there is exploitation of the bees, so it is up to you whether or not you wish to support that. Raw honey also represents the theft of the bee's necessary substance, but if you choose to use it, it is a very pure source of nutrients.

Miso, fermented soybean paste, has an alkalizing effect on the blood and is an easily digestible vegetable product. Tamari soy sauce is a liquid miso, so to speak. In Japan, these ancient foods are diet staples and have been known to be powerful radiation resistors.

Clay is an element in nature which was formed from earth, air and water. These energies are capable of restoring vitality and they unite to create a strong healing force. When exposed to the sun, clay draws impurities out by absorbing them. It attracts foreign particles, which is any disease-producing material and waste from the cells--radiation definitely falls in that category. So if a teaspoon of clay is taken daily in a cup of tea or any liquid, we can trust clay to use its natural food stores. Pierre Cattier's French green clay is best for internal use.

It is becoming increasingly necessary to take these preventive measures, as each day more radioactivity is cast into the environment. Nature is doing her best to cope with radiation and all other pollutants, and we must do the same. Protect yourselves and eat mostly a raw food diet, rich in solar force. Another wise consideration would be to live in higher elevations where radiation is less likely to be concentrated. Naturally, remote regions are best. Radiation travels horizontally with the air currents, so try not to be down wind of a radiation source, nuclear power plant, etc. Grow your own food to be sure of its quality as chemical additives only hasten the slow poisoning in modern living habits. Or let nature provide for you completely by eating fruit in a place untouched by modern agricultural methods. Take as much solar radiation as you need; unlike the atomic variety, it loves your body.

In conclusion, the feasibility of nuclear waste materials leaking into the environment is becoming more obvious to those who investigate the facts. The results of which may in our lifetime and the lifetime of our offspring, produce a horror show of defects and diseases never before imagined.

The motives of those men who would risk the potential poisoning of their families and the very environment which they themselves inhabit, must be seriously questioned.

Burk Schmidke and Ann Wadsworth

WHAT YOU SHOULD KNOW ABOUT THE HAZARDS OF NUCLEAR POWER

A Call to Proceed with Caution

The commercial nuclear power plant program planned for the next 25 years in this country represents a serious threat to your health and safety and to the health and safety of the American people. Yet, despite the hazards, despite the growing danger of sabotage from terrorists, depite the unresolved problem of disposing of lethal nuclear wastes safely, you are asked to accept this program as necessary to solve this nation's energy problems.

The Wall Street Journal labeled these nuclear plants "atomic lemons", pointing out that "their unreliability is becoming one of their most dependable features". Yet, you are asked to accept the program as the mainstay of the nation's future electric power supply.

The MITRE Corporation, a Virginia think tank, warns that nuclear materials in the hands of a terrorist group "would give it a power of blackmail over the world at large and the U.S. in particular without precedent in history". (Between 1969 and 1975, ninety–nine threats of violence were directed against commercial nuclear facilities). Yet, you are asked to accept the program as safe.

Insurance companies have refused to provide the public with full coverage against nuclear accidents because the risk is too great. Yet, you are asked to accept the program as safe.

Consumer advocate Ralph Nader warns "...there is no practical solution for protecting our generation, much less our children's and grandchildren's, from the immense accumulation of lethal wastes that are inevitable in the nuclear power industry". Yet, you are asked to accept the program as safe.

According to a report by the Atomic Energy Commissions's Regulatory Staff, U.S. nuclear plants are "besieged" by serious safety problems arising from faulty design and construction. Yet, you are asked to accept the program as safe.

This is to enlighten you about how electricity is generated through nuclear power so that you might understand more precisely why the problems involved are so threatening.

This is also to advise you that there is an important step you can take to help control the nuclear risks. That step is your becoming a sponsor of the Union of Concerned Scientists, the organization dedicated to preventing such a disaster.

"The technologists claim that if everything works according to their blueprints, atomic energy will be a safe and a very attractive solution to the energy needs of the world. This may be correct. However, the real issue is whether their blueprints will work in the real world and not only a 'technological paradise'." (Hannes Alfven, Nobel Laureate in Physics).

"The NRC (Nuclear Regulatory Commission), under pressure from the industry, has allowed serious compromises with safety to creep into the design, construction and operation of U.S. nuclear plants. As a result, the country has no present|way of knowing how safe or unsafe its nuclear program is". (From "Reader's Digest" article, "The Burning Question of Brown Ferry". James Nathan Miller).

What is a Nuclear Reactor?

The heart of a nuclear power plant is an array of long, thin rods filled with pellets of uranium fuel. As uranium atoms are split within these fuel elements, energy is produced to heat water circulating through the reactor. This heated water produces steam which is carried to a turbine–generator, which spins to produce electricity.

If a pipe breaks which carries water to the fuel, emergency cooling water needs to reach the fuel WITHIN 60 SECONDS to prevent over–heating, melting and release of radiation from the massive fuel "core" of the power plant. An emergency core cooling system (ECCS) has been designed to prevent such a catastrophe. If this backup coding system fails to work effectively, the reactor core would overheat and the stage is set for major radiation release into the environment in which radioactive material in gaseous form could be carried by the wind to nearby cities.

Additional Survival Information

During nuclear disaster or polar shifts or any major ionospheric disturbance, shelter must be taken from the fallout or cosmic radiation for three days or often longer. Indoor central rooms away from outer walls and windows are most available, but not as safe as basements, bunkers, public shelter areas, caves, sewers, etc., where three to four feet of earth, stone, concrete, or heavy metal are before the outside air and sky. Radioactive elimination applications: chelated minerals, especially zinc and magnesium, algin, alginates (sodium, etc.), sea plants, plantain, (both internally and packed on skin), aloe vera, chlorophyll, vitamin A,B,C, and E, sprouts, wheat grass, pectin, lecithin, vegetable gums, other binders and emulsifiers, and clay or mud as skin packs left to dry (i.e. while in sun) and then rinsed off, carob powder, potassium iodide, crushed grasses, onion, or greens. Clay, sea water, and many other homeopathic sources (silica, etc.) may be taken internally. All these are as important as food stockpiles (which probably should be geared for 80–90% raw food diets). Solar stills for water and tight fitting wool clothing or beekeeper's suits will protect the skin and metabolism...face masks, filters, negative ionizers, nostril filters, camphor oil vapor to clean bronchials.

Jupiter and Uranus will align in March 1983, with the meridian of Uranus' axis conjuncting with earth and sun soon after. This means that gravitational pulls will be accentuated on the earth, especially in October, when the orbit of the earth continues to wind inward again. Theoretically, a shaking then of the rotational speed of the earth or a conjuction of Uranus' meridian within 15 degrees of a sensitive area on our planet can result in quakes. Signs of worldwide disturbance are major quakes concurrently in the Mediterranean and South Pacific areas, or the major reactivation of Mt. Vesuvius or Mt. Pelee. Edgar Cayce says the morality of a community can temper and sometimes postpone or prevent disasters.

With cancer or contamination of fallout to the body, sprouts, raw foods, prayer, fasting, and celery, carrots, lettuce, beets, or greens daily (to prevent infection or lymph failure) are necessary for two to seven years, and aren't so bad in normal life! Herbs, massage, manipulations, and special naturopathic applications help the sensibilties. Peace be with you.

Drew Allen Harris, Sepulveda, Ca.

GREEN GRASS NEWCLEAR POWER

This is a single blade of grass within the green grass infinity (affinity) group for Seabrook occupation and others and direct action/civil disobedience against nuclear power and weapons industry. We share with others the vision of transforming unconsciousness and manipulative forces causing disease, oppression, and virtual elimination of all life as we know it on the planet into light pouring onto the earth through growing and providing living food on site as grasses and sprouts; through natural and simple healing, through theatre..channeling the spirits messages in song...opening the hearts and minds of people.

Seabrook occupation. October 6th, 1979, New Hampshire. Standing in full moon, centre camp, hands in pockets, shoulders creeping tighter in the cold...breathe deep, let go and flow in feelings of humor and horror. Comrades within various affinity groups shouting commands, "secret" names and numbers like a scrimmage count down, running close to the earth out of sight of "aerial field enemy attacks" in voices high pitched, hysterical and authoritative. Feel as though I have just walked through a time tunnel...knowing not whether past or future. Feel no affinity whatsoever with these frames of the movie, yet know deep within my heart I am suppose to be here now, playing my part. Someone please give me my lines. I feel a stranger in a strange land. Are these my people playing war with war toys; two apparent sides, —one of smiles, tears, laughter, singing and fears, wirecutters, gas masks, back packs and a vision of life and light; the other of sober grim—faced national guard, state troopers, guns with long points, little guns in belly belts, helmeted, bullet proofed male bodies—only, viscious barking dogs, an arsenal

including mace, gas, water hoses, clubs for beating people, silent, black phallic cylinders shaking in my face and seconds later I am wretching evil from the pit of my guts, puking war games silently by the fence, then breathing in the universe of love singing the lines to "Both Sides Now". "And do not think that just because the true Hopi people have been told by the Great Spirit never to take up arms that we will not fight, even die, for what we know to be the right way of life. The true Hopi people know how to fight with truth and positive force in the light of the great mystery. Do it peacefully...do it loving fully...do it peacefully...do it nonviolently".

The news media called it a failure. We occupy a place in consciousness in mind and heart, the failure may be knowing the truth and choosing to stay at home, watching us on t.v.

We want to save the earth mother from devastation and destruction, she is our home and mother. We are her children. So many people are deeply committed to the well−being of the earth world, yet scared of the politics of the spirit: unconscious of the body/spirit world within, the sacred temple connected to the universal force, the force which makes us breathe each breath and takes the last one whenever. Most, if not all of us know some place within that alcohol, tobacco, drugs, chemicals, sprayed/poisoned foods, sugar, salt, white flour, flesh and cooked/dead food are not life enhancing, spirit sprouting, yet we pollute our inner world with these and negative thoughts and reasons why we still need these trips. Silently at first, the horror dawns in our awareness, then begins to tug for our attention. We push it away knowing truth and the right way of life, yet everywhere we turn it seems we meet sweet sleep/seduction and escape the pain of dealing with our bullshit thinking: tommorrow will be a better time to change ourselves significantly. Let us set up infinity/affinity groups to help one another in our transition from death to life, in our painfull transition embracing the spirit in politics, inspire devotional hearts burning with love and divine light within us all.

To live in truth is to clean up all the garbage inside and out. The cleaner these environments, the more one piece of garbage sticks out for attention and won't leave us alone until we deal with it. Sometimes we are asked to be in the front line, other times supportive in the spiritual warfare happening now. That means aligning ourselves in strength/commitment/love pointedness, doing all we know is necessary to stop nuclear technology. I say spiritual warfare because today the war is different. We've fought in many wars, globally, nationally, racially, religiously, socially, economically, politically, personally. Throughout them all our focus has been "change   their behavior, change their attitude". The sickening feeling deep within is "there are no winners in war, only losers". We cannot change others; we can change ourselves. We live the dawn of life's creation! When we change from the inside out, the world out there becomes a part of us; the flow from inner to outer is one wave of light followed by another in the ocean of love...and the nuclear power plants are among the last to go, since we've put them so far outside ourselves stead of creating newclear power within our pineal glands. The divine plan was/is to create newclear power plants/atomic reactors within our own beings generating energy to keep us warm or cool, full of light and able to move through space in an instant to dematerialize and materialze. We saw enough of the vision to understand atomic reactors, abandoning our body sensitivity to this power spot within our heads without full vision we built unclear/nuclear power plants outside our bodies on the Earth

Mother! Now, unclear power/technology may yet serve us in the last hours pushing us desperately and deeply within to create newclear power. And the light generated within will fullfill the spirits plan for "Inlightened" power plants, each one of us. Every sacred blade of chlorophyll green grass and sunlight sprout is a symbol of these newclear plants as well as our medicine for cleansing and purification of the deepest cells of body/tissue, mind/thought and spirit/heart. When we are clean and clear (newclear) there will be no unclear power/weapons technology on the planet.

We can do it in the twinkling of an eye: lets do it now and for the first time all will have won – become ONE. Eat green and we'll become green light and air planets.

Inspiration   Inspirecreation   Inspireaction

From the Universe

THE MARGIN OF LIFE

It's thin, very very thin, and for a lot of people around the world there is no margin. In 10 to 20 years of continuation of the present ecological idiocy, time will erase the margin for all of us.

A measure of the time left to us is given by a table taken from the book "Soils" by Donahue, Shickluna and Robertson, 3rd ed., 1971, Prentice–Hall. It purports to give the total NPK, Calcuim (Ca), and Magnesium (Mg) content of soils in representative states in relation to annual precipitation. Moon soil was also included. The original table as from "Atlas of American Agriculture", C.F. Marbut, USDA, 1935. Apparently USDA has been too busy promoting chemical company products since 1935 to bother with an old–fashioned idea like Marbut was working on.

To this table the writer has added the same elements for silicate rocks, glacial gravel, sea salt, and Hamaker's ten acres. The collection of figures provides a basis for understanding what is happening to our soils.

The silicate rocks come up as intrusions into the mountain ranges. The glaciers and erosion level the mountains mixing these new materials with the sedimentary (old ocean floor) rocks which comprise most of the land area. Originally all of the land was of the analysis of the silicate rocks, but life developing in the oceans segregated such minerals as calcium and magnesium to form the limestones, dolomitic limestone, phosphate rock, etc. In this way the compositon of the top of the earth's crust has evolved to approximately that of the glacial gravel with almost four times as much Calcium as in the silicate rocks. The magnesium being more active than the Calcium has not increased proportionately. But note that the sea salt is high in Magnesium. Thus the microorganisms have available more than is apparent from a rock or soil analysis. Iodine is obtained almost solely from the sea spray carried in the clouds, Therefore it is extremely important that we add sea salts to inland agricultural lands.

It is the total balance of elements available to microorganisms which is critical to maximum quality and maxiumum production of foods.

The moon soil has Calcium intermediate in quantity to the silicate rocks and glacial gravel, and it has magnesium at a higher percentage than either. The high values of Calcium and Magnesium are a strong indicator that the lunar landing site was once an ocean with living things capable of concentrating the Calcium and Magnesium of the silicate rocks. The sediments which would have contained nitrogen–bearing organic matter were probably washed into the cracks in the ocean floor into which the oceans flowed to fill the voids forming under the crust as the tectonic system failed and cooled down. A great deal of that water must have recycled as steam from the lunar crust forming clouds and falling as rain to erase this evidence of life.

The 1935 figures show that all of the soils had just about used up their minerals. One percent of the top 8 inches (1000 tons per acre) is 10 tons per acre. Arizona at the top of the list had only 14½ tons of calcium per acre in the top 8 iches of soil out of the 130 tons per acre which it had 10,000 years ago. This in spite of the fact that normal rainfall is only 10 inches per year. South Carolina has a 50 inch rainfall only and 1.4 tons left in the top 8 inches.

It was shown in the study "The Human Race is Programmed for Death" that Hamaker's 10 acres with .30% Calcium was just about shot for growing crops. The limestone that was there was probably an accumulation of oversized particles of dolomitic limestone from several applications by a distributor truck. It was also shown that adding limestone and NPK did not prevent Sr, Li, Sn, and Zn from disappearing from the soil to the extent that they were not detected by spectrographic analysis in the amount of 1 ppm (.0001%). The absence of these trace minerals can shut down the growth of microorganisms (and hence plant growth) just as surely as the absences of Calcium and Magnesium. Furthermore, a shortage of such elements will so reduce a plant's resistance to disease and insect attack that a useful crop cannot be produced no matter how much poison is applied.

Most farmers of those 1935 soils with 20" precipitation and above have already found that large tonnages of limestone must be added periodically in order to get a crop. What most of them have not discovered yet is that the trace minerals cannot be replaced by limestone alone. The Michigan Department of Agriculture has discovered the need for adding trace minerals and lists about 10 of them which can be added to sacked fertilizers in specified minimum amounts. So here we go again leaving the whole thing up to the agricultural chemical people. As with NPK we can expect a build-up of toxic amounts of some elements and, as is the case of Hamaker's 10 acres, nothing is done to replace the shortage of lithium, strontium and tin. The Michigan Department of Agriculture did manage to include zinc as one of the 10. They've got 13 unbalanced elements in the sack now and about 79 to go.

The figures for nitrogen are not important as such. One has only to supply the total balance of minerals plus adequate plant residue to supply the carbon needed by microorganisms, and they will get all the nitrogen they need from the air. However, one–twentieth of soil organic matter is nitrogen, and organic matter is a measure of carbon available. Soil organic matter consists primarily of live microorganisms or the cell walls of microorganisms. In either case, it is primarily protein and that means carbon and nitrogen. If the soil is black the organic matter is mostly skins of microorganisms. The addition of the total balance of minerals in sufficient quantity will quickly convert all carbonaceous material to live microorganisms (the food of plants in which case the soil will turn from black to brown to light brown as the soil goes from a shortage of minerals to an excess of minerals.

Note that P and K in most of the soils is not much less than either the silicate rock or the glacial gravel analysis. With regard to the relatively small quantity for P and K in glacial gravel, which is lower than that on all of the soils (except for South Carolina's coastal plain and Hamaker's ten acres) there is a possibility that sedimentary deposits containing phosphorous and potassium (being soft) are quickly ground up and spread over the outwash lands leaving only the phosphate in the underground silicate rocks. How much is really needed? Are these two minerals returned to the soil in nature while Ca and Mg escape to the ocean? Does sea salt maintain the level of P and K (and some trace minerals) better than it maintains the level of Ca and Mg? What has been the effect of selective leaching by the acidic fertilizers on the balance of elements? How many trace elements have been brought into the soil in NPK and Ca-Mg applications? Is the table data accurate in all details?

There are many questions presented in this table which considers only 5 of about 92 elements. But there are also obvious facts which cannot be ignored.

All of the 1935 soils listed contained less than one-tenth the minerals of fresh ground gravel.

The South Carolina soil was already sub-marginal soil abandoned for farming by its original owners. Such land can not feed this nation. Forty-one years later Hamaker's ten acres at 30" rainfall or more is in as bad shape. Most of it will certainly experience a collapse in production with 10 years. When the water-suspendable portion of the rock is stripped of minerals the collapse is inevitable.

Most farmers find that they must add increasing quantities of acidic fertilizers in order to survive. A few, mostly in stronger soils of the plains states, find they still have enough minerals to compete on an organic basis. But even these organic farmers generally add some natural trace minerals mixture. All present techniques are still removing more minerals from the soil than they are putting back. Furthermore, the attempt to substitute bits of human knowledge for nature's almost infinitely complicated system for producing life is resulting in imbalance and omission of components of the world's nutrient supply all of which is generated in the soils.

Our margin of life now consists of what we add to the soil. The only things which demonstrably can greatly increase production and food quality is the finely divided particles of the total mixture of rock in the top layers of the earth's crust. The only adequate, easily available supplies of such material are deposits of loess, such as the Chinese have in abundance, or gravel mixtures which must be ground. In addition, sea salt must be added to agricultural land more than six or eight hundred miles from the ocean. At least a ton of materials per year are required. Most of the world has no mineral delivery system and all nations are in the initial stage of starvation - malnutrition. There will be much misery in the world before we can establish an adequate flow of minerals to our agricultural soils.

The present condition of the soils and the time required to initiate a flow of minerals to the soil insure that much land will drop off dramatically in production before the situation is reversed. Meanwhile the weather, incited to even greater violence by the increasing burden of wind-eroded spent soil, will be doing its best to destroy the weakening topsoils by wind and water erosion.

We get down to the hard question. Is there enough intelligence and courage in the U.S. Congress to do what must be done? Right now the voting record shows that something like half the seats in Congress are occupied by people who think environmental problems are something conjured up by "effete snobs" to hassle the industrial establishment. If we are to have a chance at survival, the voters had better get rid of some of those longtime Congressmen who have demonstrated that their votes are already sold to the big campaign contributors. How they vote on environmental matters is a clear indication of both the intelligence and/or the integrity of Congressmen. The legacy of old statistics left to us by C.F. Marbut along with what we know now makes it crystal clear that we are in a deepening crisis of survival. We can no longer be tolerant of public servants who do not serve the nation's interests.

Corruption of legislative bodies, administrative agencies, the educational establishments, and the mass media by the power of money offered in one form or another has brought this nation to the brink of extinction. Those who have read the articles, "Life or Death — Yours", "The Human Race Is Programmed For Death" and now "The Margin of Life" should recognize the gravity of our present situation. A good many people, however, tend to let others do their thinking for them. Such persons once brain–washed with the idea that chemical agriculture is the "eighth wonder of the world" are quite incapable of conceiving of a time in their lives when the regular flow of food from the farm to their table will cease. Those who take comfort in the establishments' brain–washing in preference to facts should consider some recent evidence that the die–out of the human race has already begun.

In the local newspaper of October 6, 1976, there were two articles. One was about the observation of the Public Health Service to the effect that suicides among teenagers have almost doubled since 1970. During the same period we have been hearing more and more about the shortages of minerals like zinc, chromium, iron, selenium, etc., and some of the specific problems associated with an inadequate supply of them in the diet. Mental problems like depression (the preliminary to suicide) schizophrenia, and aggression have been tied in with mineral shortages or shortages of specific brain or nerve compounds which require minerals either in their compositon or in the production of enzymes required to produce the brain or nerve compound.

Those who write about these mineral shortage problems generally ascribe the shortage to food processing which removes the part of the food which contains the mineral in question. This assumption does not explain the matter because food processing in the last decade was even worse than it is now and the suicide rate already doubled since 1970. Chemical contaminants also affect mental state either by direct action on the brain or nervous system or by lowering the vitality of the whole body. Whether their effect is more or less than in the last decade is anybody's guess. But it is no guess to say that each year's removal of minerals in the crops means less minerals in next year's crops. Every veterinarian in the country worth his salt has found that livestock is suffering from various mineral deficiencies. The livestock eat unprocessed food which is mineral deficient as it comes from the soil.

The second article is an AP dispatch from Boston about a new infant death problem. It's called "failure to thrive". The baby stops eating and stops responding to other people — apparently state of depression. Suicide at the infant level. The baby soon looks like the starving Biafran children. If the baby is taken to a hospital and force fed about twice its normal food requirement, it picks up weight rapidly and recovers a responsiveness to others. It has learned what its parents already know, that the food is so poor in nutrients that you have to overstuff with food in order to get enough essential nutrients for survival. The mothers of the "failure to thrive' infants almost always show stress symptoms.

In this writer's garden, stress occurs in plants only under conditions which interrupt the flow of protoplasm from the micoorganisms in the soil to the plant. Stress from mineral shortage does not occur because all the minerals have been added as ground glacial gravel. However if seed has been sprouted before the ground has warmed up enough so the new crop of microoganisms can accomplish the job of turning last year's frozen and dehydrated microorganisms into new organisms, young sprouts will often show the purple color indictive of phosphate shortage. Other nutrients are also short in the plants because they will not thrive until the ground warms up. Drought causes stress by dehydrating the microorganisms to the extent that the protoplasm is too thick to flow from the microorganism into the plant root. Too much water in the soil sets up a toxic anaerobic conditon. Regardless of the cause of stress the result is always an interruption of the flow of top quality protoplasm from the natural balance of organisms in the soil to the plant. Invariably this means susceptibility of the plant to disease and insect attack.

The summer of 1976 was the driest year ever. A good 3½" soaker came at the end of July and most of the growth occurred in the next 30 days. By that time the sweet corn planted the first of June sprouted only about ¾ of the seed, tassled before it silked and matured before the ground got adequate moisture. The sweet corn yield was a fraction of the 1975 yield. But tomatoes and cabbage with their long growing season produced the best yet. The 11.3 tons of dust put in the ground in '74' and '75' had been loading the soil with microorganisms and when the soil moisture was adequate, the plants responded. Stress symptoms showed a clear relationship to the flow of protoplasm from the soil.. Plants which matured in the very dry weather of June and July did poorly. Radishes wouldn't grow until fall. The stunted corn had earworm and smut problems. Leaf lettuce gave a poor yield and went to seed. The growth varied depending on the extent of development of the soil, i.e. how long I have worked that section of the garden, how much dust has been added, how much peat has been added. It all added up to a very direct relationship between the amount of microorganisms in the soil and the amount of stress symptoms. It seems clear that if the whole garden had been loaded with microorganisms to an 18" depth, there would have been no stress symptoms at all.

American agriculture has done everything possible to destroy the life in the soil. Excessive tillage, an awesome variety of deadly posions, and acidic fertilizers (the wrong ones to support soil life) have reduced the margin of life in the soil and consequently on top of the soil. The stress symptoms seen in the crops are clearly reflected in the problems of malnutrition which afflict the American people.

We have run the gamut of nutritional deficiency diseases, and now it has come down to infant suicide — loss of the will to live. Perhaps it is just as well because the lead time required to correct our errors on a global scale insures that a baby born today can expect a great deal of misery and perhaps death before the situation improves. The margin of life is very thin.

John D. Hamaker, 112 S. Nelson, Potterville, Michigan 48876

AGRICULTURE AND COMMUNITY

This article is intended to reach those who are coming upon an awareness that our Earth is dying, and who are ready to do what they can to help bring forth the positive energy and action and needed for us to not only survive but to thrive.

Those of us who have understood the vast importance of live food/optimal nutrition to human and planetary health, should now take the next step and understand some things concerning soils and agriculture. The following are proposed as proveable facts:

1) Human health is primarily dependent on high quality live foods adapted to our organisms.

2) Food quality is dependent on soil quality, which essentially means the relative presence or absence of live micro−organisms. These micro−organisms constitute the natural nourishment of plants. De−hydrated and frozen micro−organisms, also, called humus, in conjunction with unused rock particles, make up the soil's bank of fertility.

3) Human health, and that of all life, is dependent on the health and abundance of micro−organism life in the soil. The micros build the initial link in the Chain of Life: they do this by somehow transforming the inanimate (mineral water) to the animate microorganism protoplasm. This means we must see to it that our tiny friends receive an abundant, well balanced, complete natural diet.

4) Virtually every farm soil on Earth is declining in fertility due primarily to − erosion by water and wind, mechanical cultivation, crop exportation, leaching, salinization, and of course the countless toxic genetic chemicals.

5) Only 1% of U.S. farms are considered "organic" farms. The soil on most of these farms are declining also due to all the above mentioned factors excluding the chemical poisons. Therefore our organic produce is declining in quality and prices continue to soar as our farmers are forced to compete in the "food business".

It is clear that our agriculture, along with most of our present ways of living, is not being conducted on a sane, long−term basis of health and stability. In fact, a continuation of our present agricultural practices will virtually insure that we and our children will live in a world of extreme food shortage, uncontrolled social violence, and unimaginable destructive weather. All of these will reinforce the severity of the others. The next few years and decades will call for an unprecedented expression of our intelligence and natural goodness.

Here is some of what we can do if we wish to live on this beautiful Earth enduring health and peace.

First, and foremost, we should join together in truly spiritual, cooperative communities for which there is no blueprint nor authority. The meanings behind the

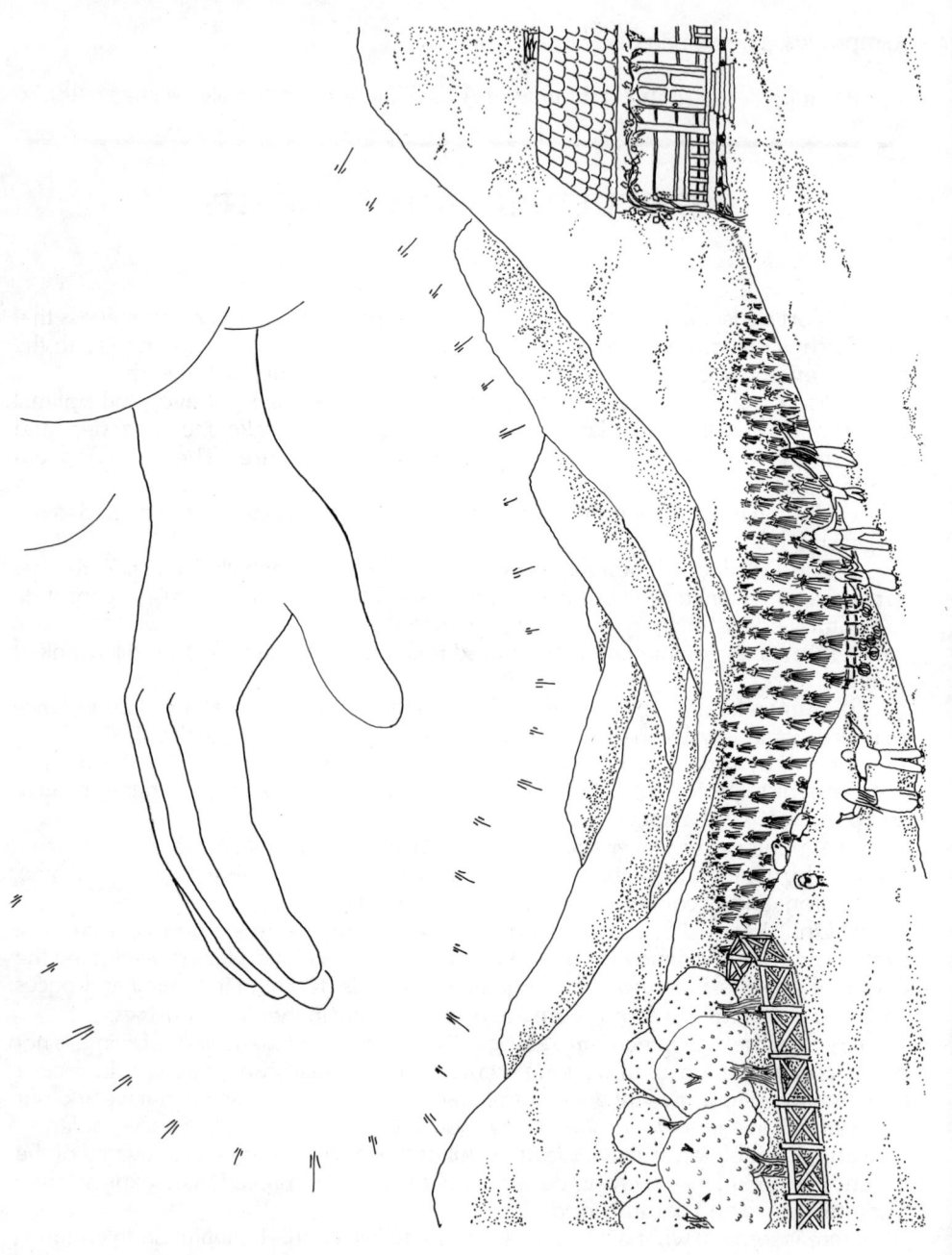

words "Intelligence", "Truth", and "Love" need be the guides.

These communities should try to settle on enough land to grow all their own food, and if possible their own fibers and wood for clothes, shelter, simple furniture, etc. trees can provide us with virtually all our physical needs. Nutritionally, trees give us our most healthful, natural, and delicious foods — ripe fruits and nuts. Trees and tree crops, grown without human cultivation or irrigation, when possible, will give forth their joyful abundance for many years. Meanwhile they shade, fertilize, and hold the soil from eroding; provide oxygen and shelter for human beings and wildlife; help balance and moderate the weather cycles; and teach us the beauty and generosity of a loving nature. When a tree's life ends, it can be gently replaced by another from the community tree nursery. Only the careful propagation and nurturing of our own trees will assure a healthy, stable, and permanent agriculture and communities.

Vegetables, melons, seeds for sprouting and planting, as well as grapes and berries can be grown between the trees if desired, at least until the soil is built up to an extraordinarily fertile state. (Remember, fertility equals live plus dormant micro–organism protoplasm. The plants feed on this protoplasm to build their own protoplasm compounds, and we build our innumerable protoplasm compounds for eating the plants).

Now, how are we as our own farmers to bring about this wonderfully fertile soil? It is basically very simple. We can all learn to be farmers (and gatherers) in a very short time, as can our children. Virtually all we need to do, aside from propagating/planting trees, etc. is to feed the micro–organisms their original diet of rocks (ground to silt or dust size) and a carbon energy source (i.e. crop residue, leaf fall, green manure, etc., as well as our feces to complete the cycles. The feces of those on a natural live food diet is a thoroughly safe and beneficial fertilizer).

When we add this finely ground mixed rock dust to our soils, in conjunction with adequate organic matter, we will be able to approach the photosynthetic limits to plant growth in a few short years. The best rock dust will contain the complete spectrum of minerals found in the top layers of the Earth's crust. Most river gravels and all glacial gravel deposits will prove to be excellent after grinding. This gravel dust is so effective because it provides the soil micro–organisms with all the minerals they require in a highly available form (analagous to chewing our food very well). This creates a population explosion of micros (also earthworms which grind additonal rock particles) which plants grow upon like mad, fruiting prolifically. The micros, when given all the minerals, are able to obtain all the nitrogen they (and therefore the plants) require by breathing in and out of the well–granulated soil. No concentrated nitrogen fertilizers are needed; in fact, they can do much harm. The atmosphere contains 78% nitrogen which the micros will utilize as they need it.

As of this writing (January 1979), the only known sources of gravel dust are the many gravel, and concrete plants which have gravel crushers in operation. What we need from these plants are the smallest size crushed gravel available. The preferred dust size may not be available, but the silt size–gravel crusher screenings–should be. These screenings should be applied in amounts of 5 to 40 tons per acre and more, if possible, it is practically impossible to add too much of a balanced rock mixture such as gravel dusts. Do it soon while access to the gravel, trucks, tractor–spreaders still exists. The more you add, the richer the soil and food from it will be for many years. You needn't do it every year, quite possible only once if a complete recycling program is practiced. We can fertilize the soil for ourselves and for our children. If the actual dust size were available, only 3 to 10 tons per acre would be needed, although to reach the photosynthetic limits more might be necessary. Of course, we must not forget to feed the micros plenty of organic matter also. "And Replenish the Earth".

The authors are working towards bringing together joyfully serious people who are deeply concerned with the Health of Man/Environment, rebuilding our Paradise Earth from the soil up and finding out for themselves what a truly religious life is. We are involved with the setting up of a global network of village communities of people living/demonstrating/teaching an ecological way of life based on Tree Crop agriculture/nutrition optimum health of Man and Nature, and social harmony and cooperation. We are presently working on the task of finding human and financial support for the production of a patented, highly efficient gravel grinder which can be powered by the wind. It grinds rock into dust and would be ideal for farms and communities throughout our planet.

All of our brothers and sisters who are ready to help co−create such communities, won't you please contact us soon to share your feelings and ideas with us? Are you with others of a mutual concern? Do you have suggestions for community sites?

Don Weaver/Mark Chass, 138 Valderflores, Burlingame, Ca. 94010

ENERGY AND CLIMATE

A panel of the National Academy of Sciences has issued a report on energy and climate. Its chairman, Roger Revelle, sums it up by saying that we can use coal (fossil fuels) for 20 or 30 years but that we must move to other fuels in 50 years and stop fossil fuel usage in the year 2050.

This forecast is based on an estimated temperature rise of 5% F. by 2050, and on the opinion that, while this rise in temperature would change in a lot of things, the change in temperature would be tolerable. The rise in temperature would result from the greenhouse effect of carbon dioxide released into the atmosphere from fossil fuels and from a decrease in the world's forests. (Sci. News, July 30, 1977).

If the panel's analysis is accepted, the governments of the world would have the green light to continue their present energy practices for a minimum of 20 and a maximum of 73 years. If this course of action is pursued, it will be the last major mistake which this interglacial chapter of human history will have a chance to make.

It is a truism that nothing happens on this earth without an expenditure of energy to make it happen − including glaciation.

For about 10,000 years a balance of energy has been maintained insuring a temperate climate over most of the earth. It has been maintained because carbon dioxide, coming into the atmosphere from volcanic sources, has been removed by increased biological activity and a corresponding depositon of plant residue in repositories on and in the crust of the earth.

A necessary precondition for maintaining the energy balance is that there be plenty of minerals in the topsoils and in the waters of the world to supply the minerals required for the necessary growth of microorganisms. The microorganisms are required to supply the protoplasm to the plant life which in turn uses up the excess carbon dioxide in the air. (Carbon, in the form of plant residue, is eventually deposited in the earth to maintain the carbon dioxide balance and hence the energy balance). When the soil is demineralized, the microorganisms die out. Without a supply of protoplasm compounds, the plant life sickens, dies, decays, and burns. The carbon dioxide balance is destroyed. Our soils have become demineralized and the forests are diseased, dying, and burning. Their carbon is building up in the atmosphere as carbon dioxide. Furthermore we are releasing additional carbon dioxide from fossil fuels.

The stage is set for glaciation — nature's way of remineralizing the soils by grinding large quantities of rock and distributing it over the earth on violent winds.

The necessary precondition of glaciation is a supply of energy capable of evaporating huge quantities of water from the world's oceans and transporting them to the polar region where it can be precipitated as snow which ultimately builds up into glacial ice sheets. We now have that precondition in the form of excess heat caused by the "greenhouse effect" of the build–up of carbon dioxide in the atmosphere. The carbon dioxide is effective over the area near the equator, but over the polar regions the water vapor condenses into clouds protecting the polar ice from the sun and from the rays reflected back from the carbon dioxide.

For some years now the gently undulating path of the west winds blowing over the Northern Hemisphere has had impressed on it increasingly strong flows of air moving from north to south over the Northern Hemisphere continents and south to north over the oceans during the winter months. In the summer of '77' the pattern persisted over the Pacific well into July. However instead of turning to the southeast over Alaska and flowing down over the continent, the weather satellite pictures showed cloud masses moving around the Arctic Circle to the Eurasian continent where record rainfalls and floods were reported.

In late July the Pacific air stream collapsed over the continent bringing heavy rains and breaking the summer draught. Spring and summer were hotter than usual on the North American continent. Since the Arctic air was drawn down over the Eurasian continent it is a good guess that the weather there was cooler than usual.

With the winter of '77–78' we will see a return to the pattern of strong southwest winds flowing up over Alaska and the Scandinavian countries and descending in a southeasterly direction over the North American and Eurasian continents. The moisture must necessarily be precipitated over the polar regions leaving only dry cold air to descend over the continents. The increased energy at the surface of the earth is presently meeting the criteria for glaciation — the evaporation and transportation of water from the equatorial oceans to the polar regions.

How soon will glaciation occur? The NAS Panel on Energy and Climate provides a clue in the form of a very frightening statistic arrived at by Charles Keeling. (Science, Energy and Climate, Philip H. Abelson). Keeling says that there has been a 13% rise in atmospheric carbon dioxide since the industrial revolution began. The alarming thing is that 5% of the 13% has occurred in the last 15 years. The accelerated rate of increase is far less attributable to the increased use of energy than to an accelerating rate of forest destruction. Forest destuction is an indicator of soil demineralization.

Keeling estimates that the atmospheric carbon dioxide will be 25% above preindustrial revolution levels in the year 2000. This is a very conservative estimate considering the accelerating rate of forest destruction. At one time in the summer of '77' there were forest fires burning in Alaska and in all the states west of the Rockies plus a lot of the forest states east of the Rockies. California lost 10% of its lumber capacity for the next 50 years. That's optimistic because if the soils aren't remineralized and much of the carbon dioxide withdrawn from the air in 50 years, there won't be any lumber in California nor anyone to sell it to.

In 1976 and 1977 there has been a 8½ and 12½% increase in the use of chemical fertilizers. That translates to mean that farmers are having to use more and more acid to dissolve a few more minerals out of the dwindling supply in the soil in order to support enough microorganisms to get another crop at a competitive yield. A very extensive record supports the conclusion that when farmers increase their use of acidic chemicals at such rates, the collapse in production on such soils is only a few years away.

All of these things point to the fact that the NAS Panel's conclusion that fossil fuels can be safely used for 20 to 30 years has no basis in fact.

Some 20 to 25 thousand years ago glaciation began. Unless someone can show that the way the biological and physical factors worked then was fundamentally different than the way they work now, the only rational conclusion must be that we are now in the initial stage of glaciation. Large quantities of water are being transported from the warm ocean waters to the polar regions.

When the ice build—up begins to sink large land masses, the magma under the crust is forced to flow back into the tectonic system and out in volcanic eruptions. The volcanic dust will help the soil dust to cool the surface of the earth widening the temperature differential between the equator and the polar and temperate zones. Winds will increase to hurricane force whipping up soil dust in some areas and dropping torrential rains in other areas to wash away the top soils. The agricultural support of civilization will be destroyed.

Glaciation will occur long before the full temperature drop occurs. The temperature drop can occur only after an extensive ice field is built up and only late in the period of glaciation when some of the carbon dioxide has been removed from the air by new growth on tropical and subtropical soils newly remineralized by glaciers. The mineralization of these soils must occur late because the wind pattern must be compressed toward the equator and the ground rock dust released by the glaciers far to the south in order to bring heavy quantities of dust to the equatorial zone. As the carbon dioxide is reduced by tropical growth, the quantity of water transported to the ice sheet decreases and the rate of melt exceeds the rate of build—up. Then the ice sheet starts reducing in size and portions of the depressed continent again begin to take up magma under the crust. The reduced flow of magma into the tectonic system decreases the volcanic dust and carbon dioxide emisson which decreases cooling of the land mass and the transportation of water to the polar regions. The biological control system can then rapidly reassert control of the energy balance in the atmosphere.

A major temperature drop is not needed for glaciation — it only needs a different way of handling the total energy supply from the sun. The excess accumulation of heat at the equator is used to carry water and heat to the poles where the heat transfer to space is more efficient than at the equator. The heat is dumped to space and the frozen water falls on the center of the continent. Part of the earth gets warmer and part of it gets colder. Thus Alaska, in the path of the wind off the South Pacific, was not glaciated last time and it is warmer than usual now. It is therefore foolish to wait for a major temperature drop worldwide before worrying about glaciation.

In view of the rapidity with which the biological system for maintaining the delicate energy balance is being destroyed, it would be foolish indeed to think that we have any chance of survival unless we start now on a massive campaign in conjunction with all other governments to remineralize the soil and stop adding fossil fuels carbon to the atmosphere. Only by so doing can we expect to produce the soil and plant life necessary to withdraw the carbon dioxide from the atmosphere and restore the energy balance. Any other course is suicidal. The present international energy policy is writing "finis" to this interglacial chapter of human history.

As the writer has shown in previous articles, the average mixture of rocks in the top strata of the earth's crust provides the proper balance of elements. Glacial gravel and most river gravels are generally suitable. These should be ground to 90% passing 200 mesh. At this fineness as little as three tons per acre over all of the land which now has any growth on it may be sufficient to stabilize forest deterioration, but for near maximum growth twenty tons per acre are required. The more dust we can get on the soil, the more growth we will get. However plant residue carbon is needed to balance with the minerals as required for the growth of microorganisms, and there is no point in putting large amounts of dust on soil without adequate carbon (do not burn crop residues!). Excessive dust turns soil to sand color. Excessive carbon turns soil black. The two are balanced by maintaining a brown soil as observed at the end of the growing season.

Needless to say, we must replace fossil fuel energy with biomass and other forms of solar energy just as fast as we can.

We are technically capable of doing the job of establishing and maintaining suitable levels of minerals in the soil. The question of whether the time required to establish biological control of the energy balance exceeds the time it will take for irreversible glaciation to take control is an open question. (In this writer's opinion our chance of survival is decreasing with every day of procrastination).

John D. Hamaker, 112 S. Nelson, Potterville, Michigan 48876, November 27, 1976

THE DANGERS OF ALUMINUM

May this letter to my many friends be one of joy to you and to your friends and all people with whom you come in contact. Over the years since I was four years old, and mostly during the past 22 years of my bonus life, the many people working with me, and I, have learned so much about ALUMINUM and its deadly dangers and the method of changing it into other elements. I just could not wait longer to pass this information on to you, so that you, too, may benefit from the things learned, and be thankful to your Creator that He has let us understand this.

When I was just a little girl, my mother read an article in the Golden Age Magazine, now the "Awake!", and in my youth before I was able to read, I can just remember my parents talking about the article and to my young mind it went something like this: "If you want to die of cancer all through your body, just keep eating food cooked in aluminum cooking utensils. If you cannot get to the cemetery quickly enough by doing this, perhaps you can check into some hospital where they feed you food cooked in aluminum. And if this still does not do it quite fast enough to suit you, you can, for a goodly sum of money, convince someone to cut you up in little pieces, in order to rush your trip".

I remember the impact that this had on our family. My father had been having acute indigestion, and migraine headaches, especially in the spring of the year. Both he and my mother had nasal catarrah to the point that they were "blowing" a great deal of the time. They had just "sold the fatted calf" so that my mother could buy a beautiful set of aluminum cooking utensils. But when she read this article, it changed our lives. She immediately took all her nice new pans out into the yard and started to use them to feed and water the chickens. About a month later she said, "What am I doing? We are eating the chickens and we are eating the eggs! We are still getting aluminum!". She felt so guilty about putting them in the trash and perhaps the trash collector would take them home to his family, that she took a hatchet and destroyed them, before throwing them in the river. Later, she wondered if she could have made the fish sick.

My father had no more indigestion or headaches, and neither of them had any more problems with nasal catarrah. All of my growing up years, they were not bothered with any of these problems and maintained wonderful health for their family. We did not know a family doctor, as one was only needed when my mother had a baby — sometimes. We were taken to the dentist only to have our baby teeth pulled. They were such strong, good teeth that our parents could not get them out! You must know that we raised almost all the food that we had to eat, and the water we had to drink was just run through a filter to take out sticks, etc. Our water came from Randell Lake near Danison, Texas. In 1956 I was desperately trying to clean enough fast enough to save my life — we were having many problems trying to find poison–free food for me. I was no longer able to take care of a garden during this year of my recovery, and it was a great concern since it was imperative that I have poison–free food, and I was also concerned for my children, especially since the younger daughter had been born with leukemia, and it had been only two years since she was freed from it. We realized the dire importance of nourishing food and water, but either of these was difficult to come by.

It was in May of this year, after I had completely given my life over to my God, that all of sudden I knew what was wrong with our food supply, earthwide, I knew what had happened with the chemicalization of food and water, but most of all, I knew how to overcome it. I knew how to raise healthy food by overcoming the chemicals in the soil and returning it to a natural balance.

It was in July of that year I discovered what has now become the little Spring Life Polarity Plus Pillows. The story of this discovery is all explained in another part of the literature. It was on September 23, 1956 that my body cured itself, God forgave me for my stupidity, and I have not been ill for a moment since. He has given me a bonus life and He has shown me what to do with it. This is the day that I was set free!

.Sometime in 1961, while working with polarization of gardens, we discovered something else about aluminum. That is, when a pipe of this material was used in the garden or orchard, when water came out the other end, this water would contain aluminum and would cause bugs to try to eat the garden down. This was without fail, every time an aluminum pipe was used, there would be myriads of scavenger insects trying to eat the food prematurely, and we recognized this as one of Creation's Laws. If scavengers where there before the harvest had been completed, then the food was truly not fit for humans to eat, and the bugs were trying to fullfill their function and return the plant to the soil. We had only the cotton covered Pillows at that time, but we used some of the mixture in the initial polarization of the garden. We discovered that when we put the mixture in a bucket and walked slowly down the aluminum pipe on the way to the garden that then when water came out of the other end of the pipe it did not contain aluminum, and bugs would not try to eat the garden down. This truly shocked us into recognition that something had happened to the aluminum. We knew that it had been changed to something else because it no longer attracted negative rays, death rays, as aluminum must. But we did not know how to check to see what it had become. Then we realized that aluminum phosphate fertilizer has been used just about every place that food is grown commercially. Could this be the reason for the war on bugs??

In all nature, like attracts like. Things attracting negative radiation, also attract the negative forces of nature. Many years ago I asked a lot of people all over the country to watch for every tornado report and if they reported the destruction of a trailer park or other large amounts of aluminum, (and it seemed they all DID) and if they EVER found that a tornado had first destroyed one such large amount of aluminum and then continued on to destroy other things before being spent, would they please pick up the phone and call me collect, and I did not care where in the world they would be at the time, and they could talk all day if they wanted to, but I wanted them to tell me all about it. I never did get one of those 'collect' calls, but I did get a host of front pages from newspapers all over the country. Many of them will be the entire front pages, and some of them are even in color, showing the devastation of trail parks during a tornado. One little girl, 14 years old, was pictured in the paper and was on television, when she said that she had been 'watching that cloud' over Emporia, Kansas, and it was 'way up high'. Then it came down 'just like a bomb!' It destroyed 95 of 105 trailers and tore the aluminum awning off the adjoining shopping center. But she said it was 'just like a bomb!' We all know that only an atomic bomb continues on. This tornado did NOT.

There is so much in the news about the tremendous amount of research that is going on to try to find out why tornados seem to strike in the suburbs of towns and cities, and it used to be that they were more prevalent in the country where we heard of a barn now and then being destroyed. But now they are striking in the more densely populated areas. Why the change?? Could it be aluminum? The farm land

When we first went to Molokai in 1968, several of us went to see a man who could help us with getting land. While we were talking, while sitting out under a big mango tree in the front yard, he mentioned that he had that beautiful tree but it had never had any fruit. The little mangoes would all fall off while small and green. Also, his avocado never had any fruit because the same thing happened. I told him that if he would take all the juck out from under his trees, and be certain that he had no aluminum there, including the chairs on which we were sitting, that he should see a big difference in his trees. Then we moved to Molokai. The next year when I returned from a teaching trip here on the mainland, this man was working for us. One morning I was carrying the survey equipment up to the end of the 40 acres and he came running up behind me and said, "Ethel! Let me carry that for you. Let me just work with you because I want to learn all I can about what you are doing. I have something out in the car for you". He went over to his car and brought out a sack of avocados. He said, "You were gone during the mango season, and I could not have any for you, but believe me, those trees have done nothing but produce since I did what you told me to do!"

When bomb testing takes place, a LOT of radioactive aluminum is spewed into the atmosphere, and the clouds pass over us with this dangerous waste. But you say, "I have not eaten food in aluminum. I have no aluminum." But from the foregoing, you must realize that there is absolutely no way you can avoid aluminum. We are working with radiations, and we have found that when you are even close to aluminum, within a 45 degree angle to be exact, you are being affected by the aluminum. How does it affect you? We have found that it affects the entire body, but the body trying to get rid of it and trying desperately to protect you and your life, will cause much of the aluminum to remain in the alimentary tract, where it forms a thick, hardened, tarlike mucous lining on the walls. Then all food that you eat and all water that you drink must go through this first before it is picked up by the blood. Several years ago I was reading were Surgeons, during an operation any place in the body, were running into black in the connective tissue and they did not know what it was or where it came from. They just knew that it certainly did not belong there! Could it be that this 'lining' is also finally working through the lining of the alimentary canal and is getting into other parts of the body?

In 1969 we found how to check to see what aluminum had become after polarization. But we were running a Foundation and were trying to keep a farm going. It takes a lot of time and work to check against all 92 atoms and find out which it had become and we just did not have the time to do it. We knew that some place along the line we would find it, but we had no idea how many of the atoms we would have to check. Then Mr. Richey, the scientist working with me for the last ten years of his life, found a book written by the French scientist, Fritz Kahn, an article that interested him very much and he came to show it to me. He said, "Look! This scientist has found out what happens to aluminum when subjected to helium. Lets check these two changes and see if he is correct. Perhaps we will just have to check 2 instead of 92!"

On page 108, I believe it was, in the book "Design of the Universe" there was a picture that appeared to be a photo taken of a painting. It showed some circles with atoms in the center. Up at the top it had an arrow pointing to the top circle and a caption which said that when a helium atom came in contact with an aluminum atom,

THE NEW AGE KNOWLEDGE /143

that the helium atom caused the aluminum atom to collect two free electrons from the atmosphere to join in the nucleus. Since aluminum appears on the Periodic Table of the Elements as No. 13, meaning that it has 13 protons in the nucleus, since the two free electrons have been added, it changes the element to phosphorus which is No. 15. Then, because of the instability of phosphorus since it has been made imbalanced and caused to wobble in its oscillation pattern, that exactly 14 days later one of the free electrons would dislodge and would rejoin the atmosphere, but the other one remained in the nucleus and stabilized the atom as silicon, No. 14, which is inert.

When we checked after polarization, this is exactly what happened. The aluminum would be changed to phosphorus and exactly 14 days later it would automatically convert to silicon. It was in 1974 that we discovered some errors in the Periodic Table of Elements. We were so reluctant to make these errors known, thinking that it would be almost impossible for them to be incorrect. Then we realized that no one has ever seen an atom, and it would not be hard to make a mistake. So we quit believing scientific things are correct until we prove that they are. And try as we did, we could not make aluminum fit into No. 13! We found that aluminum is No. 79 and even then it is not bauxite aluminum as we know it. No. 79 is Bentonite, Fullers Earth, which is natural aluminum, and is the only thing known that will remove aluminum from the system. Bauxite aluminum had no place at all on the Periodic Table of the Elements, and I believe that it is the most dangerous thing we have in the environment, even more dangerous than Strontium 90. This information along with other changes that we found, was put into a copyrighted article in early 1975.

We also found that polarization changes Strontium 90 back to its original Strontium 38, and No. 38 is not radioactive. Indeed it is one of the elements that are necessary in our bodies, and is a very important one.

For more than 20 years I have lived in camp trailers, all silicon. In Hawaii our students lived in four silicon campers and two other buildings made of natural materials. No runny noses, no loss of energy, no tantrums.

Do you know that you cannot live under a dome of clear glass? Nothing can? Do you know why? Life energy cannot penetrate clear glass, and it would be like trying to live in a vacuum. Aluminum is a definite attractor of negative rays. Luckily, these negative rays do not penetrate the aluminum or inside the aluminum house they would die quickly, instead of slowly because the Life rays are not coming through at all. Then, when one turns on the TV - the broadcaster of negative rays, (also much of the interior of the TV is aluminum) these come out into the energyless interior and the aluminum picks them up and re-broadcasts them. It would sort of be like living inside the TV set, wouldn't it?

On the Monterey Peninsula, in 1975, there were 196 trailer villages. Aluminum - negative energy. Nature's weapon, we have found, can be in the form of tornados, hurricanes, earthquakes, tidal waves and other such weapons of destruction. All these weapons are highly serious negative forces that are leashed against areas of predominant negative attraction. We all know that tornadoes and hurricanes in the Northern Hemisphere go in a counter-clockwise direction - opposite of Life. But did you realize that so do tidal waves and earthquakes, including the explosion that precedes the earthquake? We found that all these forces of nature are used to break the negative vacuum and restore the equilibrium all over the planet. People unknowingly build targets, and we believe that aluminum is the Bull's Eye.

Another of Nature's weapons, we have proved to be, is BUGS! BUGS! BUGS! at the wrong season of the year. In a healthy area, bugs of a scavenger nature will not be evident until after the harvest at which time they are supposed to be there to help to get the excess plant matter back into the soil. If they are there during the productive season, it is because the plant or food that it produces is not fit for us to eat anyway. They are truly our friends, put here for our protection, and mankind has surely given them a big job to do!

A doctor in Sherman, Texas, has been doing much testing using kineosiology, or muscle testing. He has one of his assistants tear off a sheet of aluminum foil and hold it over a person's head. Immediately their energy is almost non-existent. No muscle can overcome the stress. Then he lays one of the large steel pillows on the floor with the label facing the person. Immediately the energy level is at its peak! The aluminum foil is still there, but it is not aluminum anymore. We have also found that two of the small steel pillows can be used with one on each side of the person, with the labels facing each other and labels turned upright. I have found that many doctors all over the country are using this method of testing and proving the energy that is existent. We do not make therapeutic claims of any nature for the pillows, but dentists and other doctors of the healing arts are finding out much in ways of increasing the energy flow.

Several years ago I was working with a retired Doctor in helping to straighten out the problems he had with his garden. When I went back the next year, he was picking his apples off his one tree. He had all the baskets that he could get together beneath the tree and I looked down and exclaimed, "Doctor! What are you doing with that aluminum pot?" He replied, "Why, I am picking my apples." I told him that I would get some of my instruments out of the car and I would prove to him that every apple in the pot was poisoned with aluminum whether or not it had touched the sides or bottom of the large pot. After proving this to him, he was nonplussed. Then I told him that every apple still on the tree that was in a 45 degree angle of the aluminum pot was also poisoned with the aluminum. When I proved this to him, and proved that the other apples on the same tree were not poisoned with the aluminum, he was speechless. Then we took the poisoned apples and placed them on the Pillow for 2½ minutes. They were no longer containing aluminum.

After so much information on the danger of aluminum, do you still wonder why so many people all over the world are polarizing every trailer in their Park? At this time I am trying to get some help. I would like for a comparison to be run between these parks and others in the same area of the same sizes. It would be good to check such things as the ratio of divorces, deaths of elderly people with a list of the immediate causes, incidence of colds in children and adults, and other types of bronchial disturbances. We are also trying to get together information on the incidence of eye problems, including cataracts.

I even notice that some caskets and vaults are aluminum. Ironic, isn't it?

Many car motors are aluminum. With this attractor of such high negative energy always going ahead of one, could this also be a cause of accidents? I had three cars with aluminum motors and would not get in them to drive home until I had polarized the motors and then the entire car!

THE NEW AGE KNOWLEDGE

In Honolulu I went out to see one of my friends, a beekeeper. For years he had sold honey and was one of the leaders in the Honolulu Health Club which had been active for about 30 years. Two of our students went with me, and he showed us how to rob the bees and how to extract the honey. He wore no gloves or helmet, and neither did we. Some of the hives were long overdue and were brimming over. Then he took me over to one hive where he said that he could not get the bees to stay and in fact the first ones that went into it died. We were getting hives from him, but this one he certainly would not suggest that we take. It was one that he had ordered from a catalogue for apiaries. He took off the lid to show us, and the frames inside which are usually made of wood, were all Aluminum! We polarized the hive for him so that until he could haul it to the dump, it would no longer harm his mango tree above it.

A lot of people have asked me what I do when I move into a new house. First of all I find out if there is aluminum under the shingles of the roof or if there is any insultation covered with aluminum in the attic. If there is, then I have someone climb onto the roof and lay the Pillow on it for about five minutes, and then go to another section of the roof and do the same thing, just in case the sheets of aluminum would not be touching each other and there could be something between the sheets to stop the traveling of the rays. If there is insulation wrapped in aluminum foil, then it is good to carry or push the Pillow ahead of one, so that at one time it is directly over each section of the foil. Then I come into the house and open all the doors and windows and touch the aluminum screens and frames, first outside the house and then inside. Next I walk all over the house, first near the walls, and then into the center of the room, carrying one of the Pillows with me. Vacaville adds aluminum fluoride to our water. It smells so bad that it permeates the room at all times. In the bathroom the faucet of the sink is flat and I keep a Pillow there all the time. In the shower, I have to hang one in a cotton sock so that it will stay in place. In the kitchen, I polarized every drop that I take out of the line, and make certain that the pH is 6.5, which is perfect water. I also polarize water in the washing machine to purify it and make it soft. My clothes get cleaner.

Every airplane that I have been on, and this has been many as I have flown more than a million miles, is truly permanently polarized. I would not think of going into that negative vacuum-like vehicle without first taking care that the life energy can come into it. How do I do this? I carry the Pillow in my hand as I go through the doorway. The if I eat something while on the plane, it, too, can be polarized, and I have no indigestion. Also no jet lag, or any other kind of 'lag'. I also like to think that it is not as apt to have lightening knock the tail off. We know that it is only God that can protect us, but He has surely given us a way to help protect ourselves, too. Many of my friends were insisting that I fly down to San Diego last month when I had to go there on business, but I would not hear of it. I said I was going to drive and take a vacation all the way there and all the way back. If I had flown, I would have been on the plane that crashed as that is the one plane that goes from Sacramento to San Diego to arrive there in time to conduct business that day.

When I mentioned this to my daughters, one of them said, "Mother, you know that Jehovah has been protecting you all your life, and He certainly protected you now, but even if you had been on the plane, He could have protected you there also and maybe it would not have crashed just then." I told her that her faith was outstanding, and just to continue on with that faith!

There is nothing 'absolute' in the Universe except God and His Law. So we know that even when we have found out much, we have found out only a fraction of what there is to be known about any subject. We are continuing our research and wish to thank those many people who are helping us in it, and extend the invitation to anyone who is also searching for Truth. We are living in serious times, and the imbalance in Nature is overwhelming. We are continually thankful that God has let us find a way to overcome at least part of it. We know that there are probably other scientists in the world who would wish to disagree with us and this is their right. But the information that we have gleaned over these many years is factual and I have explained it to the best of my ability. Please always remember that we welcome other ideas and want our ideas to be accepted only after you have proven them to be true.

Take care, now, and keep happy, knowing that God is in full charge of the affairs of men, and the situations in the world today are certainly not going by unnoticed. When we see the problems existing today we can only repeat, "Father, let your Kingdom come. Let Your Will be done on Earth as it is in Heaven", and it is only then that all living will have peace and tranquility.

Love and Blessings,
Ethel Starbard, Ministry of Dietetic Law, Box 825, Vacaville, Ca. 95688, December 1978

SUCCESS?

I speak with great sadness of what I see happening to this beautiful island and its peoples. For many years I lived in the California desert area, known to many as Palm Springs. As little as thirty years ago my Indian brothers lived on and owned this land. They lived simply and close to nature. Progress to them meant growing old in health and happiness. Many tribes valued the healing waters in this remote mainland area; but alas, the rich developers discovered it and decided it could be capitalized on, as a recreation and vacation area for the city people who would come to escape the cities they built, lived and worked in. Success?

The Indians were convinced to sell their lands with the promise of a "brighter future for their children" – jobs, education, a higher standard of living and so on. Slowly they sold out and development crept in. At the start there were jobs for the Indians as dishwashers, bus boys, bar maids, cashiers – laborers, all for money and the promises of what they could have with it. But there came a time, after many years, that the number and power of these pro–development peoples became great. They hired their own kind – the Indians were no longer needed or employed.

The Indian was now lost, having forgotten how to hunt, fish, farm – the ways of nature. He had forsaken the ways of nature for the ways of progress, of materialism, of cars, cokes, twinkies, stereos, t.v., and aspirin – for the headaches.

So now they all live in cities such as Los Angeles, work in factories or live on welfare and will never afford a vacation to Palm Springs, their homeland, or live there as they once did close to nature since the land cost too much to buy back.

Progress is conquest, to enslave people's time, energy and land and develop it towards materialistic, monetary gain is a poor measure of "success". Working 9–5 indoors, as dishwashers, waitresses, store clerks, rent a car agents, etc. is really not much to look forward to in life.

No, life is the sun, moon, ocean, trees, balmy breezes of clean air, and farming and the health and happiness that can't be bought.

Do not sell yourselves out. Measure the values of success carefully.

Mahalo,
Joshua Rainbow, The Garden Island

EARTH AND THE U.F.O. PHENOMENON

Reality is energy. A reality of energy is consciousness. The reality of all things is a network of consciousness of the Infinite. Therefore, because Earthman perceives all things in a finite manner, we shall attempt to raise Earth's level of awareness to greater levels of comprehension and acceptance of the Law of the Infinite.

U.F.O's and their inhabitants are nothing more than consciousness of light rays functioning on levels of higher vibrations which surpass the speed of light. Planetary Beings have, through necessity, thrust their vibrations into Earthman's reality, not for conquest, but to guide their total vibration toward an expanded reality of responsibility toward, and the preservation of, Planet Earth.

In past generations when mankind recognized his dependency upon the earth, technological growth was directed toward a balanced earth–human relationship. There was no need for Galactic supervision, so Planetary Craft sightings were relatively rare. As technology advanced to the stage of atom splitting and began channeling this knowledge toward the destruction of life, Earth's finite intelligence became a threat to the Natural Law of the Magnetospheres and Ionospheres of other Galaxies. A clarification of this would be the analogy of vibrational disruptions created by dropping a pebble into a pond. Though the surface ripples diminsh in one's sight, the energy force continues outward to the farthest shore and back, disturbing the serenity of all things from plant and animal life to particles of electrons within the pond. However, the rippling effect does not stop at the shore but continues outward to affect the earth and the atmospheric light rays beyond the earth. The mere dropping of a pebble, a violent thought or act affects the consciousness of all things, but these imbalances can be fairly well neutralized within the Ionosphere. Emanations of Nuclear Radiation can not be. Planetary Law is now manifesting itself within Earthman's realm of perception to teach the urgency for greater awareness of one's actions.

Sightings of Planet Beings and Space Vehicles, actual contact and telepathic thought communications are common occurrences in Earth's reality today. Each time a Space Flight is launched, an Inter–Galactic Craft follows this capsule of belching, toxic gasses, in hopes that Earth's Scientific Field will recognize the need for outmoding the volatile fuel mixtures now being used. Anti—gravitational propulsion, utilizing atmospheric and ground energies, which enables vehicles the ability of surpassing the speed of light, is being offered to enhance Earth's technological growth. Methods and formulas for achieving this feat are being mentally projected to many Earth Humans to counteract the dangers Earthman has created for Galactic Life. Earth Science, however, continues to turn a deaf ear to new ideas being perfected.

Because the symbol of status seems to be the ultimate goal, Earth Beings destroy the Earth's potential, which sustains him, his fellowman and even his own, unique, creative abilities in order to attain recognition by a select few. This deadly game has increased alarmingly within the last thirty—five years. The Oil Cartel is now frightened that a more adequate means of propulsion would leave them financially devastated. The career politician is frightened that superior, less manipulative, Planetary Beings would jeopardize their political stranglehold. The career Military Staff are intent upon disintegrating all Space Craft. The Scientific Field is frightened that their obsolete conclusions on energy theories might come toppling down around them— — —each holding fast to the finite ideas of success, while the rest of mankind feels the strands of the web tightening around his reality.

Earth is being monitored continually. When a Space Craft is sighted, the News Media is fed the bizarre reactions of Governmental Heads and projects its own commercial reality: "MAN CAPTURED BY U.F.O", "SPACE CRAFT LANDING IN DESERT", "ANIMAL MUTILATIONS", "ARE WE BEING INVADED BY SPACE CREATURES?". There is no denial of the truths of these occurances, but exception is taken to the fear being projected by the News Media to a world yet unable to function beyond panic. Need you be reminded that not one Earth Human has been injured in this exchange, except by his own psyche, or by one recklessly dashing forward into the force field surrounding the craft. Indeed, animal mutilations have taken place, but this has been done in the interest of Earthman. The blood, tongue and vital organs of grass eating animals are removed and examined aboard Space Vehicles to determine the levels of radiation absorbed by them. This method produces a fairly accurate estimate of damage already incurred from radiation within humans, through their consumption of contaminated vegetation. The degree of pollutant absorbtion shall confirm the time span given by other Planets, before more drastic steps shall be taken toward the preservation of Earth.

Fear, anger and panic are readily generated by Earth Beings. They show very little self dicipline and a pronounced lack of control over the nerve centers of the brain. Their emotions seem directed toward frustration, which leads to limited foresight and poor judgement. The advent of Nuclear Weapons, coupled with this tendency toward spontaneous hysteria, has brought Planet Earth under close scrutiny by all Galaxies. A concerted effort by Inter—Galactic Planets is being made to halt further violations of the Natural Law of the Universes and to prevent an annihilation of the Earth, by raising Earthman's consciousness. This procedure has already taken affect and is being accomplished by enlightening those upon the Earth who have calmed their vibrations to the point where they can receive telepathic messages.

Planet Beings have penetrated the consciousness of Earth, not for control, but to enhance the life style upon the Earth. Earth Beings have, for the most part, heaviness of body because low vibrational rates of energy produce a density of matter. Higher vibrational rates expand the conscious perception of light rays, from which all matter is composed. As this transpires, an increase in the agility of movement, within all energy patterns, becomes a functional process which blends with the Law of the Infinite. By accelerating the vibrational rate, one no longer chooses to manifest fear. A merger then may be achieved which will allow the consciousnesses of all Beings, in all Galaxies, to create an atmosphere of harmonious exchange.

Marjorie Buckley Turcotte

Part IV

NEW PATHWAYS TO HEALTH

The Coming Age will be an era of hitherto thought impossible states of physical health and well-being. A truely marvelous wholistic paradigm is becoming increasingly prevalent and is replacing the current system of health based on disease, suppression of symptoms and eventual physical degeneration and death. The new wholistic approach, with its all-encompassing emphasis on the triune nature of people — who are body, mind, and spirit — holds forth promise in the healing of existent physical diseases, the prevention of occurrence of disorders, the regenerating of the human race to its state of primordial perfection, and the increasing of longevity many-fold.

The following pages includes articles, essays and letters which touch on all the diverse aspects of wholistic health. From new theoretical approaches to health, to the effects of mind power and positive thought on physical well-being, from the usage of herbs to a delineation of the more esoteric unknown cleansing practices of Hatha Yoga — all seek to establish a new age of total health where each ad every aspect of a person's nature — his or her physical mental and emotional components — flourish in Joy and Love.

Section I
The Wholistic Paradigm

VIKTORAS KULVINSKAS:
Planetary Healer

Viktoras Kulvinskas is a scientist, humanist and explorer in the realms of human potential. He is revolutionizing the concepts of nutrition and vitality in this phase of human evolution on the Earth. Though his own process of life – experimentation he is developing some of the most dramatic scientific/spiritual breakthroughs of our time: health and attunement, wholistic diet and universal truth, rejuvenation of the self and of the planet. His magical discoveries focus on the sprouting seed which is literally, the basis of all Life and symbolically, the historic source of all growth. People are already now, for Viktoras' explorations with sprouts and health, especially at this time when many still consume "health" foods that are filled with processed starches, fats and dairy products that continue to clog the system and make the body a harbinger of disease.

Everyone appreciates the value of good health; it effects the physical, mental and spiritual strength of every organism. It is the key to the joy and peace we seek. In this present world of inflation, escalating prices, anxieties and shortages, Viktoras Kulvinskas is an extraordinary pioneer who offers a simple, organic, rejuvenating diet that costs $61.00 per year. Add your current food and medical cost to see what kind of savings are involved and then wonder about the kind of planet we could have. Imagine a life – span of several hundred years in perfect health, in perfect attunement with the laws of nature.

Viktoras, through his life and through his writings, offers an exciting journey into health. He gently puts forth guides to the consciousness of food consumption: the choice between eating live food or dead food. Raw fruits and vegetables, especially sprouts that can be grown anywhere and in any season, provide the highest possible nutritional value, both physically and spiritually and Viktoras, as a scientist and humanist provides constant verification. He describes the process this way:

> "The kind of diet we emphasize has to be considered rejuvenating because it has the capacity to rebuild the body to its youthful state,

maintain it, and increase all the other laws of life that are worked with such as physical activity, positive attitudes...These will start developing on their own if you allow it because as your energy increases, that is, as your body becomes more alkaline, you have more voltage potential for all those cellular activities both on the physical level as well as being receptive to the more subtle forms of vibration. I found that ESP just started operating on its own, communication with others, ability to project thoughts and the ability to actually hear in your head, sounds and things that people were communicating. This was just happening. They had been blocked out before because of so much static in the organism. The nerves were all in a state of misfiring, or else not being able to send the messages across because of weak energy."

The essentials of human nutrition, material and spiritual, are expressed in Viktoras' most comprehensive book, "Survival into the 21st Century: Planetary Healers' Manual". It is a panorama of the New Age, written simply and lovingly and offers, as he states in his Introduction, "...alternatives, not unqualified ultimatums. To remove the confusion from dietary philosophies I have examined Kosher, vegetarian, macrobiotic, sproutarian, fruitarian, aquarian and breatharian paths in the light of scientific documentation and spiritual qualifications." It is a Healer's Manual suitable for every home, evolving and regenerative in itself. It can be read in sequence for cummulative information, or by flipping back and forth like a reference book. There are three main areas of fucus: first, a section on basic nutrition and food combining gives extensive information about sprouting, wheatgrass therapy and fasting; secondly, he explains the many forms of natural healing such as iridology, zone therapy and massage; and third, he offers a full range of New Age Resources, an extensive compilation of information sources throughout many countries. "Survival into the 21st Century" is revolutionary in style, dramatic in concept, yet always loving and healing in intent. For example, Viktoras explains how to live longer and healthier by eating less; how fasting and wheatgrass therapy can prevent disease; how proper diet can reduce a woman's menstrual period to a flow of twenty minutes; how all the nutrients needed for survival are provided for us by the land on which we live, wherever it is on the planet. The illustrations in the book are by Jean White who provides extremely imaginative and delightful visualizations of our evolving future heritage. She captures the dimensions of the expanded consciousness, the awakening potential of the human soul.

Viktoras' other books are shorter, more compact. "Sprout for the Love of Every Body" contains specific data and research compiled and presented in a scientific format. There is increasing demand for this information, as he explains in his Preface:

"The Sprouts Are Coming! No, the sprouts are already here. Once there were relatively unknown outside of health food circles. Now sprouts can be found virtually everywhere. They are used by catering services, airlines, hospitals, old age homes, schools, steakhouse salad bars, etc. They are sold everywhere...I have seen alfalfa sprouts, mung bean sprouts and cress sprouts proudly displayed in stores that had not sold them previously because of a lack of public demand."

In the practical area of food preparation, "Love Your Body" contains live food recipes, a wide variety of sumptuous formulas for salads, sauces, soups, main dishes, and desserts, all made from simple fruits, seeds and vegetables. All food combinations are designed for maximum flavor and easy digestions, allowing the system a freedom on the mental plane from a food/physical overload. Some of the treats included are "apple ambrosia", "autumn symphony", "festivity red sauce". The book provides a "complete organic diet on 8¢ or less per day. Viktoras' writings span the gamet of information and technique, providing comprehensive manuals not only for nutrition but also for human growth and development. As a scientist, he is objective. Only occasionally does his personality emerge as a beacon of inquisitive energy. He describes his first experiences with nutrition in the Preface of "Sprout for the Love of Everybody". There is a photo essay in "Survival" which dramatizes his courageous experimentation with his own diet and lifestyle (vegetarian, fruitarian, sproutarian). He has studied extensively at the Harvard Medical Library and co-directed the Hippocrates Health Institute in Boston with Dr. Ann Wigmore where thousands of people have experienced rejuvenated health through organic diets of "sprouts, green juices, fermented seed milks, baby greens, vegetables, sea vegetables and seasonal fruits". Viktoras' early motivations parallel the dilemma many feel when groping for nutritional information.

"When I dropped out of the computer field, I went into a Health Food store and was overwhelmed by so many contradictory positions taken by the authorities as well as by other individuals, especially when they start viewing not only the body, but the mind. I just thought that I wanted to offer my services to bring cohesion, order, or at least a perspective with which one could view a lot of these things so that one doesn't feel all that contradictory, that it's just a matter of spectrum, from one side of the energy spectrum to the other and each one has its virtues. Eating meat has its virtues from the point of view that if you eat it, you are able quicker to be brought to an awareness of a lot of things about the laws of nature, the way the body works, and extreme forms because of the high energy vibes in your adrenal system incorporated from that animal that was in a state of fear. You experience this so that you'll never want to go back to it. Living in that other range where you're doing nothing is, again, a place that teaches you the need for activity. The Bagavad Gita says even God, Himself, works...That's a good indication...the path is one of participating in Life which means participating in activity."

Not only by his words, but also by his lifestyle Viktoras is constantly guiding and teaching. As a means of correlating all the inquiries he receives from all over the planet, he most recently published "The New Age Directory", a compendium of healthful resources around the planet, a project begun in "Survival into the 21st Century". For example, it includes: Holistic Health Centers and Resorts, Spiritual and New Age Centers, Healing and Lifestyle Directories and Libraries, Community

Living Centers, Vegetarian Resources and Organizations. He publishes continual updates on this information.

But Viktoras himself is a resource. He shares his own energies, in spite of the time it takes from his research, by doing lecture tours, speaking to all varieties of audiences. He does workshops in Harlem, teaches among Native Indian peoples, travels to remote outposts in Ecuador, fascinates delinquent adolescents who never before have had an attention span of three hours except during one of his lectures. Viktoras explains by saying: "It's a matter of reaching the heart of the people, talking their language, accepting them for wherever they are; it doesn't matter what they're doing, but accepting their humanity - going from there as to what they can do for themselves and not going too extreme because with each group I modulate to their needs...I'm a pretty patient person so I don't expect anything miraculous out of anybody, including myself".

The demands on Viktoras' time and energy are increasing; so too are the communities of people growing and thriving on live food energy. He gives two unique examples:

> "One prison in Georgia, there are right now about 30 raw foodists and I also have communication with people on chain gangs who are just living on grasses and weeds because the other foods are just junk and what I very strongly stress with these folks is that they don't make themselves known because the guards and the warden can become abusive. They have established pretty good rapport in (one particular) jail because the guy who runs it is a minister and he is very impressed by their inspirationaly thinking and their awareness of the Bible. So that's what turned them on. They couldn't believe that all those folks were just eating raw foods...It's something you can do even in a limited, restricted environment.
>
> There is a little old lady I've been communicating with for quite a few years who is in a convalescent home. She drives the nurses and doctors crazy because she won't eat any of their food and when they force her she gets sick. She's been treating a lot of people there with zone therapy, they're getting well, and the nurses are coming for treatment from her. One of them, who had three Caesarian births, was told by the lady: "You don't have to have the fourth by Caesarian; here's what I want you to eat..." The nurse followed her advice and had a completely natural childbirth without need of Caesarian."

As for the future, Viktoras intends to continue researching, speaking, publishing. Now he draws to him authors and great thinkers who ban together in search of a better planet on all levels, physical, mental and spiritual. He remains a channel, a funnel of information and resources, and a pioneer, a visionary working on a healthier path into the future. His work now includes the planning of tropical raw food communities in the Virgin Islands, Ecuador, Belise, St. Croix, Costa Rica.

Viktoras Kulvinskas is a tribute to the loving process that is transforming the planet by beginning with the basic energy source, the body, and treating it as the

Viktoras Kulvinskas, author, lecturer and healer

spiritual temple it is. He lives the philosophy of dedication to service, to love, to non-attachment. His vision is one of "Survival into the 21st Century"; his work is making that happen now. His life speaks like his words:

> "But as significant as our gains are, we should all realize that this is only the beginning. We have just begun to use the light within, and I know that we shall never lose sight of the light. The light will help us learn things that we didn't know existed. (Preface, "Sprout for the Love of Everybody")

Dear Viktoras,

Thank you. Thank you for sharing a newness, an extraordinary awakening.

For abundance: I realize the power of a tiny seedling and its ability to give me all the strength and nourishment I need on this planet.

For energy: Your works and your self have transformed the bodies and spirits of anyone ready to listen.

For love: You have given your life to teach, to travel, to write in order that all humanity might have the opportunity for the growth you have experienced, for the depth you envision.

"We are living in an age where eating lots of raw foods is essential. Cooking destroys many of the vitamins, all of the enzymes, chelated minerals, nucleic acids and chlorophyll. The heat disorganizes the protein structure, leading to deficiency of some of the essential amino acids. The lack of complete protein in the diet contributes to premature aging. If the diet is at least 80% raw this does not occur. Researchers all over the world are showing that the body is self healing when it is nourished on living foods and fresh juices". (Viktoras Kulvinskas, Preface, "Light Eating for Survival" by Marcia Acciardo).

I met Viktoras' spirit many years before we sat and talked in the grass on his farm in Connecticut. Here is the magical story:

After teaching school for 10 years, I became a nomad with no particular goal other than to seek Enlightenment and felt that the best place was (of course) California. An archetypal quest. After a year of pursuing a photography career without success, I decided to sell everything and head for South America. But before leaving, a friend gave me Viktoras' book, "Survival into the 21st Century: Planetary Healers' Manual". Wow! The depth, the expansion, the potential of this inspired work made me grateful, congratulating myself, that my journey to California was verified. Yes, California was the birthplace of revolutionary thought and revolutionaries. But when I looked at the back page of the book...oh no...it said: "Omangod Press, Wethersfield, Connecticut". This was the town where I had spent my childhood.

Viktoras lives on an "energy center" in Connecticut, a small farm in the northern part of the state which is alive with spiritual pioneers and healers, all welcoming both new residents and tourists like me with loving warmth.

The day I arrived to speak with Viktoras about writing this article, his home was bursting with people. Two friends arrived from Florida to continue discussions of tropical raw food communities; author, faster and marathon runner, Chris Young was planning articles for Viktoras' new book; 3 lively film producers from New York were spending the weekend arranging "New Age" materials; and still Viktoras, with peaceful eyes flashing with infinity, took time to sit by the garden and talk to me.

"The earth is a paradise, and it will be realized when we stop abusing nature, the mother of paradise. Earth is the base of mother nature and earth is part of our being. The first step toward achieving paradise is to till, plant and grow the earth that lies within. From castles of light shall the light go forth." (Viktoras Kulvinskas)

Lynn Farrell

SYNERGETIC MEDICINE

Introduction

Everyone is aware that as time passes diseases, especially of the degenerative kind, have been proliferating. As there can be no effect without a cause, it is evident to the reasoning mind that this phenomenon must owe its existence to something (probably more than one thing) having gone wrong in the conception and development of modern methods for dealing with the problems of health. Since we cannot allow this tragic state of affairs to continue we should summon enough intellectual courage and take a very fundamental and very thorough look at the theories and practices of the health sciences vis−a−vis the laws governing life processes, and, with respect for truth and love for our fellow beings, do what is indicated to arrest and reverse this sad decay. To know which of the commonly employed therapeutic procedures are in tune with and which are against the body's own laws it is first necessary for us to be familiar with these laws.

Motivation by personal tragedies resulting from modern medical treatment, and convinced about the validity of the foregoing observations, the present writer launched himself, more than a decade ago, upon a research for the laws governing life processes.

A New Science Is Born

The attempt to discover the inexorable laws of biological systems was quite successful. These laws have now been systematized in the form of a new science which gives a rational framework to the hitherto empirical life sciences, like biology, agriculture, nutrition, et cetera.

The predominantly empirico-analytical approach used by the life sciences has severe drawbacks, most of the time so severe that it becomes more of a curse than the blessing it is capable of being. This is because the pursuit of truth, by its very nature, is not merely an analytical exercise - it is partly analytical and partly synthetic. All creative acts are the result of synthetic mental processes. Where truth and beauty are concerned it is synthesis that shines. An analogy will be useful in clarifying some of these ideas.

A 'jigsaw puzzle' is a game in which the child attempts to fit together scores of small interlocking wooden pieces (each representing one small part of a picture) so that when the game is completed a picture results. Anyone who wants to try this must have a prior idea of the whole picture, without which success is difficult or impossible. This illustrates the great but rarely accepted truth that even an exhaustive knowledge of the parts cannot lead to an understanding of the whole, that empirical data cannot be put to proper use when deprived of the guidance that only a rational framework can supply. It is no wonder then that empirical scientists are piling up mountains of facts, but are nowhere closer to understanding the principles of natural systems. Teihard de Chardin, the noted scientist-philosopher and Jesuit priest correctly observed that "analysis, (the) admirable and powerful tool for dissecting the real leaves us with terms that become ever less intelligible and more impoverished". Any discipline that relies solely on the analytical method ends up being so improverished that it becomes useless, nay, indeed dangerous.

The new science which provides the rational—synthetic complement to the life science is therefore a potent tool in man's attempt to understand natural phenomena. Buckminster Fuller, the renowned scientist—philosopher mathematician—architect said that "discovering nature's principles is the key to making man a success in the universe". The new science is a systematization of these very principles. It is quite possible to progress without transgressing the laws of nature, and such progress alone will enable man to solve the very many riddles that confront his over—taxed mental and material resources — problems such as cancer, mental retardation, heart diseses, inadequate production of food et cetera. These cannot be provided with lasting satisfactory solutions by orthodox methods, notwithstanding pious hopes and very many oft—heard pronouncements to the contrary. True, empirical sciences have been solving problem after problem, but these do not stay solved for long, in the sense that new and worse ones arise in their wake! Our new science shows why this is so.

One of the most spectacular failures of empirical science is that of the misguided war against malaria. If the principles of the new science were known 20 years ago, this failure could have been predicted. It took empirical science 20 long, painful years to realize its impotence to exterminate the lowly anopheles! How many millions of dollars, what incalculable human energy and sinful damage to the environment could have been saved if only a rational approach were used.

Synergy

Since all natural systems, including the human body, have been evolving over thousands of years it is clear that every organ present and every biochemical reaction that is allowed to take place in them have a raison d'etre, and any modification of the structure or arbitrary interference with the biochemistry of these systems cannot but result in upsetting their orderly working, thereby compromising the natural characteristics with which such a long evolutionary development has endowed them. Measures to correct imbalances (diseases) in living systems, therefore, should be such that they do not oppose their innate qualities nor stymie their own efforts to restore balance (self−regulation is one of the chief characteristics of biosystems).

One of the most important qualities of systems, living or non-living, is that of synergy. It is defined as the quality which causes the whole to differ in its characteristics from those of its constituent parts. It may also be defined as the degree of unity among the parts of sub-systems needed to restrict the activities of each of them, qualitatively and quantitatively, in order to give rise to and maintain the viability and identity of the whole. From this it follows that complex systems must possess a greater degree of synergy than simple ones for them to function as stable entities. An analogy will be useful. A club (system) consisting of 100 members (sub−systems) needs more unity (synergy) among its members if it were to hold together (maintain systemal viability) than one having a membership of just 10. In the former case each member has to act in harmony with 99 others, which naturally calls for a greater sense of responsibility and unity on the part of everyone whereas the members of a small club would be able to hold together with less of these qualities.

Synergetic Interference And Its Dangers

It has already been mentioned that arbitrary structural and biochemical modifications of a system would tend to upset its natural equilibrium. Let us study an analogy to get the picture clear. The airplane has five control surfaces, each of which has to be deflected in a particular direction and to a certain degree to achieve any of the maneuvers it is capable. Since it is humanly impossible to manipulate all of them simultaneously by individual actuators for each, a coordinated control stick is provided by means of which the control surfaces may be deflected, each in the right manner and degree to elicit any desired response from the aircraft. The pilot does not think in terms of the individual ailerons, elevators and rudder and their movements at any given moment. His mind anticipates and registers only the banking, ascending and descending movements of the whole machine. In other words, the aircraft acts synergetically, the pilot thinks synthetically. This is so because the plane is built that way, and it would be impossible, useless and, in truth, dangerous for the pilot to think in any other way. The pilot's mind has been trained to understand the aircraft in its unity (i.e. as a machine with certain responses to given stimuli) and not in the diverse functions of its component systems. The minds of physicians, unfortunately for mankind, are not trained to think in terms of the body in its magnificent unity. Their ministrations improve the function of the parts and compromise the health of the whole.

If just five sub-systems cannot be individually manipulated to achieve a desired reaction from a crude system such as the airplane, by what strange reasoning is it possible for us to conclude that an immensely complex system like the human body may be beneficially influenced by meddling with its scores of sub-systems, each capable of hundreds of responses? A sick man is a sick man, not a malfunctioning kidney, a cirrhosed liver or a cancerous lung.

From the foregoing observations and arguments it is clear that therapeutic measures should be designed to work within the laws (such as synergy) operating in natural systems. It is also clear that some sort of input (analogous to the pilot's actuation of the 'joy stick') is necessary. The two requirements, therefore, for the synergetic treatment of ailments are (1) a corpus of knowledge dealing with the behaviour of biological systems, and (2) an agent, not tissue-specific, which the body can absorb and utilize to favourably influence all its sub-systems synergetically.

The first, our new science, is already existent. The present writer is trying to establish conclusively that the natural curative agent he has discovered satisfies the second.

The Problem Of Cancer

Applying the principles of the new science to the knotty problem of cancer the present writer was able to pinpoint the ultimate causative factor. What is of far greater import for the welfare of mankind was the discovery that the ultimate reaction at the cellular level in all degenerative diseases is the same of very similar. Basically, this degenerative reaction is the amount of the curative agent, named Alpha Factor or AF, going below a certain level. A research project to study how to reverse this reaction in each disease is of utmost importance and of great urgency.

It should be noted here that in cases of spontaneous remission of cancer the curative agent involved is none other than AF, and it is through a synergetic process that adequate AF is made available to the affected cells. A more natural, easy to employ and synergetic agent is hard to imagine and impossible to find.

Anti-Cancer Vaccine: No Solution to Cancer

Dr. Alexis Carrel, the Nobel Prize winning medical researcher wrote: "Medicine is far from having decreased human sufferings as much as it endeavours to make us believe. Indeed, the number of deaths from infectious diseases has greatly diminished. But we still must die, and we die in a much larger proportion from degenerative diseases...diseases have not been mastered. They have simply changed in nature. This change comes undoubtedly from the elimination of infections." There has never been a dearth of opinions, and most of them are fanciful products of the mind. Is this statement by Dr. Carrel one such? For one thing, he was not the type of man noted for making scientifically untenable statements. A study of natural systems shows that Dr. Carrel's conclusion is wholly tenable. The following facts should prove helpful in understanding why asynergetic suppression of one disease leads to the creation of another.

a) All actions contrary to the body's natural tendencies and synergetic operation are AF-depleting.
b) Forced excitation of the immunological reaction is asynergetic.
c) AF-depletion proceeds in a selective manner according to the law that the most vital sub-system is most protected and the least vital the least. (Let us call this the Law of Proportionate Protection.) Because of this characteristic of biological systems more AF drains out of certain parts than from others in an AF-depleting situation.

d) The cells in the AF-starved area suffer the degenerative reaction, and a disease develops in that locality.
(In cancer, if AF-depletion is halted, not only will the cancer not metastasize, but will actually regress. It is continued AF-depletion that causes metastasis.
e) Eliminating the disease thus developed by other than synergetic means blocks the working of the Law of Proportionate Protection, which results in the forced irrigations by AF of that very part the system chose to starve in the interests of systemal viability.
f) The outcome is that a more vital part of the system suffers the degenerative reaction and a more serious or more deep-seated disease arises.

The infectious diseases are relatively superficial and less dangerous to systemal viability than the degenerative ones, as the new science shows. Therefore elimination of the former by anti-natural procedures cannot but lead to the development of the latter. Dr. Carrel was not just right when he made the above statement, but brilliant, as he always was.

The best solution that empirical science can hope to offer is the anti-cancer vaccine. However, this will be just like any other solution that orthodox science has always been coming up with - the type that creates worse trouble than the one it is intended to cure.

Conclusion

The time has come for us to take a very fundamental look at reality and change our thought patterns and the actions that they give rise to if change is indicated. Those of us who prefer to hang on to outmoded theories and pet opinions have no right to pretend that, and continue to act as if we are really concerned about the welfare of our fellow beings. We will succeed only in advertising ourselves as weaklings without intellectual courage and gutless slaves to habit were we to plead that hundreds of years of tradition could not be discarded and that due to our training we would continue to venerate empirico—analytical methods to the exclusion of superior modes of activity of the human mind. If a few hundred years' distorted thinking is so sacred to us, what strange logic would permit us to imagine that living systems used to nature's laws for millenia are going to change their wonted behavior to please us. Nature never bows her regal head before puny mortals. Let us, therefore, be smart enough to join the winning side!

Benedict Arul

THE FIVE POINTS
LIVING IN THE ECONOMY WITHOUT BEING DESTROYED

The five points describe the areas in which man must reason to protect himself while he is in an economic system. As long as he is of life he is subject to the cosmic laws. Even when he believes he is protected by the economy the cosmic law has already anticipated his death, for being part of society is his death warrant.

One can see that all that has been created of an economics has returned to the earth, while all that is of nature has remained. For everything that is created nature has an antidote to return the thing to its natural formation. There is no escape from the cosmic law but to understand it and to take the proper precautions.

The five points will keep man in harmony with the cosmic law. It protects him physically until such time that he is able to withdraw from society, or it prevents some of the suffering he would experience in an economy.

It also enables him to function economically, to provide himself with the material goods that he needs to fulfill his anxieties. It covers both this role in society and in nature, it is a formula that covers both truths.

1. Health

Man must have health.

You are designed physically to eat fruit, the embryonic food, and as long as you provide your body with this fuel you are able to replenish your cell structure with new cells and to combat any germ in your body.

You should train yourself to disregard the idea of cooked food, so that by the time you would begin to age you are able to satisfy yourself with a completely raw diet.

Raw fruit, raw nuts, all roots and vegetables which contain seeds and berries are suitable for the human system. Leaves of any type are not correct, for they require several stomachs to digest.

Water is the best liquid because it is pure. Water is designed to clean out the body and any other liquid introduces particles which interfere with this cleaning.

The milk of the mother is the only milk designed for the human. After he develops the molecular structure the body changes and he is no long in need of milk. If the mother cannot feed the child from her own breasts the correct substitute is fruit crushed to the consistency of applesauce.

2. Love Yourself

Man must love himself. He must realize that he exists here to express himself physically. When he does so his mind and body are in harmony. It is not thought that is reality in this dimension, but action. When the mind and body are in harmony through action then man expresses the love for himself, the understanding o himself.

He must realize that he is the supreme force, that there is no concept greater than he is, no concept that is worth the sacrifice of his body. He must at all times protect his body from whatever force would injure him.

He should see that eternal life is not gained by any action other then the action that develops and secures him physically. For when we are speaking of eternal life we are speaking of life in this dimension, life in a full area of consciousness. Of course all people live eternally, but their life changes from one thing to another. Eternal life is within this body.

He must realize that the economics is destructive to him if he does not understand it. The economics should only be a stepping stone, and he should use it without conscience or guilt until he becomes secured enough to leave the society and go on to the next area of reasoning.

3. The Alter Ego (or The Other Self)

Man must have an Alter Ego. There are two statements which portray this reality, one by Shakespeare:

"All the world is a stage, and we are only players," and "Never let your right hand know what your left hand is doing."

The Alter Ego is the self which exists to the society, and which portrays those things which will protect him from the particular society which he is in. It is the self which obeys the laws of the economy.

For instance, let us say that a man is hungry but he has no money. Should he go out and rob a store so he can buy some groceries? No, because then he will be confined to an institution. He has to go about getting the money through an accepted form, not because he will be punished by the cosmic law, which has no regard for these things, but because he will be punished or even killed by the society.

He must never take the economics to heart, nor let it affect him emotionally!

It does not matter what the society thinks of him, as long as he knows who he is. He must see that the economics is only to secure himself financially and has no ultimate meaning, whereas he himself can have an ultimate meaning.

4. The Third Eye

Man must have a third eye. This is the ability to see himself and his environment objectively, from the top view. He inherits the third eye when he becomes more developed in the area of reasoning.

With the third eye he is able to reason beyond the thing which would affect him. He has this ability when he is able to watch the movements of his own body.

With the third eye working for him he cannot make a mistake, because he is able to direct himself. If he sees himself getting into a dangerous situation he can either withdraw or take the right course of action.

The third eye enables him to become emotional only when he wants to be emotional. Nothing can affect him unless he allows it to do so. This would prevent him from becoming depressed because he could laugh at the things that would sadden him. He would see that he can make himself feel any way that he wants to feel. He can turn his emotions on and off at will.

You must become your own audience. This enables you to know when to be persistent and when to stop. Then you are the greatest salesman.

5. Sex

Man must know sex.

Sex gives the meaning, the glamour and the incentive for all activities. Sex vitalizes all things, and must be used in the natural way to enhance all activities.

He can reach an understanding of sex not by seeing it vicariously but by experiencing it. He must not allow any force to inhibit this experience. He may consider that the sex act is fully appreciated only when one is in harmony with the partner of the opposite sex.

Sex should never become a perversion or a vulgarity by deviating from the natural expression. If one must use it in an economy he must realize that the economic expression is not the truth but a means to an end. In his personal life he still has to cultivate the truth of it.

THE STORY OF CREATION?

Many times the thinking seeker asks what it is that he or she feels itself to be. The pioneers into truth think of the many theories of origin, physically, mentally and spiritually. They may read, study a course of occultism, metaphysics, yoga, religion, philosophy, astrology, etc. or they may practice the teaching of knowledge, and not indulge in mere intellectual pursuit. They may just think of the various theories, or they may meditate or "pray".

Truth is ever tacit, and her stillness entertains not in the least the channel, medium, instrument, method or technique of reaching its unfoldment from the state in which one exists.

For it is in the stillness that Light comes — in that control of mind from which one thinks attachment to the things of sense. When one detaches and frees the reality of self from the illusions and dream states caused by attachment he becomes aware of the true conscious "I", an entity above nature. It is an intelligence, but the body and body mind are not, being aware of their functions only.

So it matters not what one reads or studies as Truth, relative to the goal, which is self awareness within. The essential object is to attain this illumination.

There must be true Sons of God who did not enter into the animal entanglement, the true Adam who took the straight and narrow way of attainment as intended, in whom the division of Adam and Eve were balanced as one, without creating the need by the same eternal Law of Life for offspring is issue of lower expressions sacrificed into occupying lower forms suitable to this degeneration. It follows therefore that in this failure of the renegade entities of the Sons of God to continue their progression after the whole (God) divided for expression, and showing lack of control to balance the Adam and Eve test of sex balance, resulted in Man's gradual degeneration to mortal beings, and many into animals bodies which gives the basis of our legends. Entities took possessions of animal forms already occupied, and the condition resulted in the battle of the animal nature and the intruder (Spiritual man versus animal).

So today we have peoples of the earth living and acting as animals, and yet here and there we have noble humans and the rare teachers who come now and then to Earth when conditions permit to shed some Light for the return of the original state from which one then progresses as was intended from the beginning. "In the beginning was the word". (St. John's Gospel).

It is now imperative for man, the conscious being, to conquer and rule his animal body machine which expresses as feeling dominant in the female and desire in the male, working through nerves and blood respectively. We can do this only when we first realize the true conscious "I" distinct from the body–mind and the body – an animal automaton and product of nature.

It is only in this awareness of true self that you can interpret and know correctly the story of creation – how and why you came into the dream the run of humanity calls reality. Unless the teaching leads to this awareness it is either useless, or more likely – dangerous, and creates more Karma before success.

The dividing of the way led man into the entanglements of a varied creation thru the elements of nature. In blind pursuit to find the way of the return thru mineral, plant and animal kingdoms, a dropout was created, a lost panorama of entities (Sons of God) caught up in the currents and forces of the earth unable to free themselves.

From this basic description one can imagine the varied ideas, theories and legends concerning the mixture of God's Sons with that primal, preparatory emanations and expressions of nature – creating animal–human combinations through self improvement. A fascinating romance, surpassing any romantic novel dealing with the petty pursuits of man in his attachment to sensations created by food, money, power, fame, mixed in with what is the basis of the dilemma – sex division in all deviations and forms. For thru the dual divisions and expressions of sex in the in's and out's of things, left and right, male and female in various aspects including the true hermaprodite in the unbalanced center – false civilizations, based on conquest, and the dual temporal things – fashions, split political governments, and all the panorama of the vast cineramic world of dream, the temporal, changing, fluctuating conditions and states of creation manifested. Yet most of humanity does not recognize it as the illusion.

SYSTEMOLOGY

Untruth, falsehood, wrong values, distorted thinking, these and other evils gnaw at the vitals of the human race. During the course of history, great men and women arose and sought to teach us the love and pursuit of truth, for only truth possesses the power to set us free. These wise counsels have largely gone unheeded and the malaise that afflicts homo nonsapiens is fast becoming an incurable epidemic.

In the field of science, as in almost all fields, outright falsehood and half truths are having a field day. Science is admired with religious fervor by most of us. Science is intrinsically good because pursuit of truth is intrinsically good. But distorted science is every bit a vile as distorted anything. How can we distinguish truthful and useful science from the phony variety? By what standards can we separate good science from bad science? How can we distinguish useful science from science that is largely meant to satisfy private curiosity at public expense?

The answer is clear - by truth's own standards, by reality's own standards, by nature's own standards. Evidently we need to study nature's working in the way nature meant it to be studies, i.e. holistically, and develop a body of knowledge, a whole new science, whose principles and methodology would serve us in our truth seeking endeavor. Such a science is now existent and is called Systemology.

Systemology studies living organisms (and everything else) viewed as whole systems for, in nature, everything lives and acts as wholes. Systemology studies the common law that govern the actions and interactions of all systems. These systemal movements are related to the exchange of energy and information, both basic and vital to their survival.

Systemology is a new science. Its worth is only beginning to be appreciated. Many will fight it. History of science has repeatedly demonstrated that new developments, especially if they are revolutionary, draw pseudoscientific ire. Just one example: The learned professors of the French Academy of Sciences threw out Edison's representative and one of his first phonographs with the "scientific" opinion that wax could not talk.

The more we realize that our scientific endeavor has led us astray, the more we will percieve the need for systemology's holistic approach in the pursuit of truth. The following words of eminent thinkers (many of them great scientists), it is hoped, will alert us to the undeniable fact that all is not well with science. The realization of a problem is the beginning of its solution.

Buckminster Fuller: "In contradistinction to the esteem in which world society holds them, scientists are the most confused and irresponsible human beings alive...if our lives are left to their care we will all soon be dead".

(Confusion and irresponsibility stem from ignorance of nature's functioning. A little knowledge is a dangerous thing wrote Shakespeare. A great mass of unconnected data is equally dangerous. Systemology is a synthesis which shows the scientist and layman which actions receive natural sanction and are life protecting and which do not and are life damaging.)

Rene Dubois: "This book should have been written in anger. I should be expressing in the strongest possible terms...my indignation at the failure of the scientific community to organize a systematic effort against the desecration of life and nature". ("So Human an Animal").

Science as constituted at present, that is, based on the very defective fragmentation paradigm has a built in tendency to desecrate life and nature. Don't we know that a tree falls the way it leans? Systemology's holistic paradigm is oriented towards reverence for life and nature.

Karl Popper: "In my view the 'normal' scientist...is a person one ought to be sorry for...The 'normal' scientist...has been taught badly". ("Criticism and Growth of Knowledge").

Systemology has been invented so that the future need not see "normal" scientists popping all over the surface of this planet, so that future scientists are taught to use their full mental capabilities.

G.N.M. Tyrell: "The major part of the scientific world does not wish to examine the evidence, but endeavors only to evade and escape it. It is not animated by a scientific desire to know the truth but is in the grip of a psychological urge to disallow what is distressingly familiar". (quoted in "Future Science").

Systemology demonstrates to the scientist that when his love for truth is weak, that is, when he is unfaithful to his vocation, then the Law of Contrary Response induces the psychological urge to run away from truth.

Morris Goran: "According to Catholic philosopher Jacques Maritain, science set off the "deadly disease" of the "denial of eternal truth and absolute values". ("Science and Anti–Science").

Systemology establishes the inviolability of eternal truth and absolute values.

Alexis Carrel: "There is not a shadow of doubt that mechanical, physical and chemical sciences are incapable of giving us intelligence, moral discipline, health, nervous equilibrium, security and peace...

"Medicine has been paralyzed by the narrowness of its doctrines...". ("Man the Unknown").

Deficiencies of present day sciences and paralysis of medicine will not bedevil the human race if systemology is accorded its rightful place.

Plato: "The cure of many diseases are unknown to physicians...because they are ignorant of the whole which ought to be studied also; for the part can never be well unless the whole is well". ("Charmides").

Systemology shows that the part can be well only when the whole is well. It is capable of providing a holistic solution to every human problem.

Gregory Bateson: "Medicine ends up...as a total science whose structure is essentially that of a bag of tricks. Within this science there is extraordinary little knowledge...of the body as a...self corrective system.

"Cannon wrote a book on "The Wisdom of the Body", but nobody has written a book on the wisdom of medical science, because wisdom is precisely the thing it lacks". ("Steps to an Ecology of Mind").

Systemology studies, deals with and applies Divine Wisdom reflected in nature. It is not a collection of malignantly proliferating data but wisdom that the human race sorely needs. Wisdom is precisely the thing systemology offers

Mahdi Tavassoli: "The triumph of modern medicine appears unrelated to improvement in the world's health, which is retrogressing, while "spectaculars" in medical science appear at an even quickening pace..."

"What are we doing wrong if these diseases persist despite our efforts? How is it that the world's health fluctuates independent of our efforts? The answer is distressingly simple. The medical community is not ethically or professionally equipped to solve pressing and soluble health problems..." (Journal of American Medical Association 230:1527, 1974)

To a Systemologist what you are doing wrong is distressingly evident. You are applying to whole systemal manipulation the knowledge gained for studying subsystemal performance. When you do this you get an effect that is favorable immediately but you don't produce a solution that is favorable forever. Since Systemology shows, among a whole lot of other things, how to produce long lasting solutions to disease problems, it is the best thing that could happen to the medical profession and to the world's peoples.

J. Bryant: "In our effort to limit the destructiveness of these diseases, we seem to be mired down in a mud we do not understand. One can almost sense that the health profession, with all its weapons of modern medical technology, is being mocked. It is possible, even likely, that the medical tools we are using are not the right ones." (Health and the Developing World)

When you understand how living systems function, you would quickly become certain that the medical tools you are using are not the right ones. Systemology is that science which shows how living organisms operate.

Nobel laurete Alexis Carrel, in his celebrated book "Man the Unknown" actually prophesied about Systemology: "In bringing to light our true nature, or potentialities, and the way to actualize them, this science will give us the explanation of our physiological weakening, and of our moral and intellectual diseases. We have no other means of learning the inexorable rules of our organic and spiritual activities, of distinguishing the prohibited from the lawful, or realizing that we are not free to modify, according to our fancy, our environment and ourselves. Since the natural conditions of existence have been destroyed by modern civilization, the science of man has become the most necessary of all sciences." Not only does Systemology nearly fit Carrel's description, many of his own conclusions stand validated by its principles.

Carrel also foresaw the opposition that the new science would face, and warned that the dogmas which men of science had come to accept over several hundred years would not be given up easily since such a change would shake the empirical science to their foundations. Not only Carrel's warning and the history of science convince me of the certainty of a vicious attack, the study of living systems shows me the mechanism that is involved in the phenomenon. In Systemology it is called the Law of Contrary Response.

When a system is given a stimulus designed to induce a change in its characteristics this law, operating in the system, so disposes its reactions as to produce a response that not just neutralizes the effect of the stimulus, but swings it a bit in the opposite direction (in a perfect system the opposite swing would be absent, and the principle involved is called the Law of Stability); the net result is that the system successfully resists a change in its behavior and even takes up a position diametrically opposed to the sought change. An example is the lowering of blood sugar level consequent to the intake of sugar. Another one is seen in child behavior: when asked not to do a certain thing the child makes it a point to do that very thing, and does it with considerable relish.

The present character of science is heavily overlaid with the philosophy of compartmentalization of knowledge, laboratory experiments, specialization and analysis; in short, the fragmentation philosophy. Systemology, on the contrary, is heavily holistic, is in favor of direct observation of natural phenomena, advocates few and purposeful laboratory experiments carefully designed to mimic natural conditions, suggests specialization only after the thorough grasp of systemal dynamics, permits analysis only combined with synthesis. As can be seen there is almost direct paradigmatic antagonism between these two approaches so that the Law of Contrary Response tyrannizing over minds not consummately committed to the pursuit of truth will produce an explosion of opposition to Systemology.

There is also another law which operates concomitantly and it is the Law of Evolutive Action. Whenever an ongoing beneficial stimulus is applied to a system, the system produces a harmful response that is short lived followed by a beneficial one that is enduring. In our case, if Systemologists persevere the vicious attacks will die down and the superior holistic principles of this superior science will begin to animate the minds of every genuine seeker of truth.

Benedict V. Arul, Washington, D.C., August 1978

THE SPIRIT OF HEALTH

"The body therefore is to be presented to God as a living and acceptable sacrifice." (Rm 12:1) "It belongs to the Lord, as the Lord belongs to the body." (Co. 6:13) Eighty percent of Americans now living wouldn't pass Federal inspection for slaughter as cattle do. Surely our bodies aren't acceptable sacrifice when corrupted with pollution of media, food and environment.

Religion and Hygiene must encompass each other because our Spirit needs its body to serve God and our body needs its Spirit to endure life's trials and truly enjoy its pleasures. Religion is an anchor in the sea of life and health. It is the axis upon which all life revolves. God created nature, nature didn't create God. Therefore God doesn't need nature but nature needs God to give it life. Our creator is the source of all life.

The hygienic approach and any approach, unless it is intimately bound to the love of its creator, will never attain health of body. We are Spirit and Flesh. See what the Desert Fathers did — they prayed and fasted. Praying to cleanse Spirit and fasting to cleanse body. Look at the lives of the Saints — they prayed and fasted. St. Francis continually prayed and fasted. I always enter a fast from prayer and the deeper the prayer the stronger the fast and the longer I fast the deeper the prayer. Jesus is the supreme example of prayer, fasting and health. The Great Commandment "You shall love the Lord, your God, with your whole heart, mind and soul and love your neighbor as yourself". In seeking spiritual perfection we will attain physical health. One cannot love the creator without loving His creation (our bodies and the universal beauty of nature). Nature has a very healing effect upon man — the gentle breeze, and rustling leaves, warm sun, birds singing.

Love is the essential food in total health. Notice the great commandment. We cannot love God without loving His children, we cannot love His children, without loving ourselves, and we cannot love our total self unless we love our bodies. As hygienists we know that emotionally upset people poorly digest food. Again we see the Spirit and flesh engaged in building the total person. Religion and physical health determines mental health. Both are essential for it.

Our bodies are sacred temples of the spirit and necessary to be effective instruments in building a kingdom of peace on earth. To abuse our temple is a direct insult to the creator. I felt a deep sense of joy while reading Arthur D. Andrews' "Health is Salvation and Salvation is Health" because he is presenting both elements as essential to health. Religion was the natural starting point of my living a fuller life, but I believe hygiene can activate the same end. For total health they must merge. The quality of that merge will determine the quality of our servanthood to God and mankind, and the quality of health.

In "That Man Is You" the author speaks of Christ: "Give me some water", He asked the Samaritan woman but added, "If only you knew the water I can give you — real water, living water, water that will quench your thirst forever". "He noted that bread was tasty, nourishing and beneficial and declared, "I am the true bread that sustains life".

We need to feed our Spirits and our bodies with the food of life. Before nutritional consultation, I try to start with a prayer, if the person is open to it, and most of the time the healing takes place during prayer which may last an hour because many people are spiritually sick which in many cases is the cause of their physical illness. Author's Note: It is in no way my intention to promote a specific denominational belief. I speak as a Franciscan (Catholic) and hygienist. My intention is only to promote religion and nutrition as the essential elements in attaining health. One cannot separate religion from any thing or person without suffering the ill effects of doing so. I am pleased to see an openness to religion in the American Natural Hygiene Society. It is an openness to a more vibrant health that only God can give.

St. Augustine sums up my approach to the whole matter when he says: "Love and do what you will."

Brother Ronald Pickarski, O.F.M., C.W.C.

Section II
Positive Mind and Well—Being

MESSAGE FROM "I AM"

Dear Ones, I am passing this letter on with the understanding that there is really nothing (no—thing) to fear. It is my view that, by knowing what to expect we can be most effective channels in working with this energy and transforming it for the highest good of all concerned. Know with great certainty that the Plan of Love and Light is working out in total perfection through you and me and other light workers.

An opportunity is given to us this fall when the economy collapses (unless we dissolve those plans before then) for us as light workers to step into positions of leadership. These times more than ever, our connection with our inner guidance, our higher self will be extremely important. Listen to yourself (your SELF) in these times for the part you are to play in the up and coming drama. Know that spirit is guiding and protecting you no matter what the outer appearance of things may be.

The following are a couple of methods which you may or may not find useful in dealing with the events as they come up. Use the shield to prevent any thoughts from the world mind from entering into the guidance you are receiving. Use the OM circle to dissolve the negative thought forms and plans of those who would attempt to control us. Beam Light and Love to them through the OM, or whatever method you know and use on your own path.

It's time for us to shine as the Masters that we are! It's time to BE THE LIGHT!

In Truth, Love and Service,
I AM

The OM Circle

Sit in a circle with a group of friends on the ground or floor. The more perfectly round your circle is... the more power it will have. So take time to make it perfect.

Connect the energy by holding hands — left palm up, right palm down.
Speak and think positive things as you sit in a circle.
Don't point your feet toward the center. Sit cross—legged or Japanese style.
If you need to move, walk around the outside, not through the center.
If you need to cough or hiccup, turn away from the center and cover your mouth.
Create a clear space, use signs to let others know not to disturb you.

Anything that is in the center of the circle is felt by all the beings around it. Whatever you aim toward the center of the circle goes out to the focal point and to all the beings taking part in the ceremony. For example, we sit cross—legged in the circle so our feet point away from the center. This is because earth comes from the bottom of our feet, which is a lower vibration than OM.

One way to use the power of the circle is just sit, hold hands together, left palm up and right palm down. Close your eyes and focus on the love and peace of simply being together.

You can use the power of the circle to transmit energy through OM—ing.
1) Pick a focal point, for example: There is total peace on planet Earth now and forever.
2) Write the focal point down and place it in the center of the circle.
3) Everyone sits in a perfect circle with eyes closed.
4) One person says, "Focus", everyone repeats the focal point out loud.
5) Begin OM—ing long on the O, short on the M. Keep a steady harmonic tone, repeating the focal point internally.
6) If you feel resistance, a force that feels like it's pushing against you, or discomfort say out loud, "Intensify". Everyone can OM louder and strenghten their focus.
7) OM until you get to a place that feels clear inside. For example 20—30 minutes.
8) Remain totally silent and still when the OM—ing stops.
9) Offer the focal point up to God.
10) Take the paper out of the center and break the circle to signify the completion of the cycle.

The power of the circle can also be used for spiritual healing and upliftment. Have someone who is clear sit in the very center. Beings on the outside of the circle can close their eyes and use the OM to send loving, healing energy to the being in the center. Because the being in the center is in a clear space, the energy and love of the OM will be felt by everyone.

The Protective Shield

As brothers and sisters, working together to create peace and harmony on this planet, we have found it very helpful to put a protective, high energy shield of white light around us. This protective shield prevents us from being hassled or upset by negativity. And we all know how important that is. The shield will enable you to "maintain" and stay clear. Believe me, in the coming times you will be glad that you know it. I have spent a lot of time hitch—hiking around the country, with and without the Protective Shield. When I learned this method and began using it during my travels, I really noticed a big difference. Any negativity or weird vibes that I encountered just seemed to bounce off. I could feel my own space, my own inner peace, the entire time. It really works!

To create the shield for yourself, complete the following, simple meditation:

1) Sit in a relaxed, comfortable position with your eyes closed, in a place where you will not be disturbed. It is important in creating a strong shield to be relaxed and undistracted.

2) An excellent way to relax is to start at your feet. Feel all parts of your feet relax, unwind, and let go. Continue up your body with your calves, knees, thighs, hips, etc., feeling each part of your body relaxing, until your whole body feels relaxed and quiet. Also, allow any thought in your mind to drift on by. Just don't give them any energy.

3) Now, visualize a ball of sparkling, white light forming about one inch above your head. As you meditate on it, see it become brighter and brighter. When it is completed, affirm: I am protected! Amen!

4) Next, visualize a round, three inch shaft of the same sparkling, white light moving out from the lower side of the ball of light through your head, to your throat area.

5) There, see a second ball of the same sparkling white light, growing brighter and brighter to fill your throat and head, up to your eyebrows. When it is completed, affirm: I am protected! Amen!

6) Visualize the three inch shaft of light continuing down through your body to the heart area where a third ball of this same sparkling white light forms, expanding to fill you chest from the back to the front. Again, when it is completed, repeat the affirmation: I am protected! Amen!

7) Now, the shaft of sparkling, white light moves down to the area of the abdomen (third chakra) where the fourth ball of light grows and radiates. When it is complete, repeat the same affirmation.

8) The shaft of white light continues on down to the genital area. Visualize another radiant ball of light growing to fill the pelvis area. When complete, repeat the same affirmation.

9) Finally, the shaft of sparkling light thrusts down to your feet where the last ball of light forms. Repeat the same affirmation.

10) Now, from the ball of light at your feet visualize a fountain of the same light in liquid form, rising up the shaft through the center of your body and passing through each of the balls of light along the shaft.

11) When the stream of sparkling, liquid light reaches the ball of light over the top of your head, visualize the light rushing out the top of this ball and falling down on you in a shower of radiant, protective light.

12) Feel the shower of sparkling light falling down all over your body, painting it, and filling the entire space around your body with white, protective love—light.

13) When you feel that your space is completely filled with radiant light, finish your protective shield with the following affirmation:

"I AM TOTALLY SURROUNDED BY THE BRILLIANT, SPARKLING

ALL–PROTECTIVE WHITE LOVE–LIGHT OF THE ONE GOD".
Repeat this affirmation over and over again with total focus and intention. Visualize strongly the powerful white light of God totally surrounding you.

When you sense that the protective shield is complete, sit quietly and feel the strength and powerful glow of your new radiant shield. You are totally protected!

PSYCHIC HEALING

Dear Viktoras'

I am healed! I was operated on by a psychic surgeon from Israel named Yuda Gallazan... I saw him take blood clots out of peoples hearts, I saw him remove cataracts from eyes. All is done with a plain exacto type knife. No pain, no bleeding and the wound closes as soon as he finishes working.

When he first opened my leg up the ligament was partly healed already, which means that the psychic Yolanda Betegh from Ramanca (here in New York now) has joined ends together. Yuda confirmed this and it was my privilege to introduce these two healers to each other. (Yolanda teaches para–psychology at the United Nations.)

I have kept and extensive diary of the entire incident and it is my purpose to write a book about this experience.

My deepest thanks for your encouragement. If it were not for you putting me on the right path, I never could have reached these people.

Sidney Filson, April 4, 1978

RAINBOWS TO THE RESCUE

Of all life forms
space is by far the
most accommodating

Every closed system exists within a larger open one. No matter how large a closed system becomes -- it's still a mere baby within a larger womb. Closed systems remain alive and healthy only to the degree that they continue to serve the larger open system that is everpresent.

Such is the case with our physical selves in opening to other people. And such is the case with our planet in opening up to our solar system. If we become overly self-centered -- we become centers of congestion in the free flow of life. By allowing fear, guilt or disappointment to shrivel or overcoat our life energy we feed evolutionary inertia.

To breathe with increasing life -- the energy we wish to receive requires an increasingly clear way in and out of us. Co-operation clears confusion. By taking fruitful energy in - and returning it with interest -- life is lightened up. In and out, up and down, total circulation is the texture of good health. To make opening and closing our aura and physical bodies a dance is the ongoing universal massage.

Section III
Nutrition and Health

HEALTH INSURANCE

Health is something that everyone thinks of as valuable, that everyone wants to have. A few people even put some effort into maintaining their health, but I think that most trust their good luck and pay their health insurance, hoping they don't get sick and trusting that the doctor will give a pill to make it better if they do.

However, health or lack of it is not due to chance, but nearly entirely dependent on our voluntary, controllable actions. It seems to me that our best health insurance, barring accidents, is to learn the simple principles by which the body operates, and with these in mind do those things that make us healthy, not sick.

The human mechanism has three processes vital to its function. These are 1) intake of supplies and raw materials; eating, drinking and breathing; 2) useful work or activity 3) elimination of wastes. Thus the body functions much like my sign business, which must 1) obtain supplies and raw materials 2) produce a useful product 3) be kept clean, floor swept and trash removed.

So for good health we must guide our voluntary actions so that the body may 1) receive good quality raw materials, that is, food, water and air, 2) perform useful, healthful activity, and 3) thoroughly eliminate its wastes. This last point is extremely vital, and rarely considered. Most people have no idea what is needed to allow the body to get rid of, and avoid accumulating, wastes, poisons, obstructions to their health; they have no idea what quantities of wastes they constantly are carrying, causing poisoning stench as in bad breath, irritating to produce nervousness and depression, reducing vitality, producing colds, flu and more serious diseases. The thorough elimination of the body's wastes, and the elimination of habits that allow them to accumulate, is absolutely vital in order to enjoy the real true good health that most of the people never know a single day of their lives, owing to the pervading ignorance as to what really is and what must be done to have proper health. What are the requirements? In light of our 3 points, they are:

(1) Proper food. An unbelievable amount of suffering, mental and emotional as well as physical, I would say at least 99 %, is due to wrong food. Proper food for

humans is raw vegetarian food. Not meat, not milk, nothing processed or cooked but simple and naturally, those fruits and vegetables that are edible and enjoyable without artificial preparation, cooking and refining and other forms of monkeying—around—with. Nature gives us what we need, and when we scorn these things and insist on trying to "improve" them with cooking and other forms of monkeying around, we inevitably harm ourselves in most cases we don't kill ourselves or become outright sick, but go through life with less energy, less sharpness of mind, much less exhiliration, than we are entitled to.

2) We are not like the meat—eating animals, with fangs, claws, short intestines and high concentration of hydrochloric acid in the stomach. Milk is for infants not for adult creatures. Cooking is the great madness, the most destructive thing the human race has ever done to itself. It is the source of the disturbance of mind and emotions leading to hatred and war. How can this extreme heat, burning and baking, improve the quality of the delicate balance of complex organic materials in the food? It cannot; it simply destroys many vital, lifegiving qualities; some such as enzymes, scientists have discovered and I feel certain there are many others they have not been able to discover at present. The proof of the thing is in the practical result, and someone who has lived a couple of years on a raw—food diet will know the enormous difference in vitality, energy, sharpness and unity of thinking, the increase in patience and concentration and desire to do usefull work that enhances the quality of everyone's life. Thus proper food also leads to improvement on point number 2.

3) The common diet of cooked food, junk food, processed food, creates enormous accumulation of rotting organic waste throughout the body, releasing stench and poisons that make life sometimes very unpleasant. The body was never evolved to handle these concoctions, cooked foods and unnatural chemicals. Eating them confuses the stomach and intestines, slows down their work, produces indigestion and constipation. With growing constipation more and more wastes are accumulated, and these are the foundation of disease, of depression. Get rid of them and your vitality and mood will soar. How to get rid of them? Eat only natural raw foods, fruits and vegetables. These the body is equipped to handle efficiently; there wil be no indigestion, constipation or further accumulation of waste. The body can devote more energy to removing existing accumulations that previously was taken up trying to deal with the fresh pile of garbage dumped in the stomach three times daily or even more. This step alone will give superb health after a number of months or a couple of years, depending on the individual and how advanced the deterioration of his health is. For even better health, a more perfect cleansing, we can do fasting which, giving the body a rest from all digestive work, enables it to employ its energies as much as possible in the thorough elimination of all wastes and poisons. For an analogy, if I have no production work in my business one day, I can spend the time to thoroughly clean out the shop. Far from being dangerous, intelligently carried out, fasting is the greatest aid to improving health.

These are the principles of good health. If we guide ourselves by them I think we will never have to be sick or feel down—in—the—mouth until the day we die.

If one changes all at once from a bad diet to a good diet, there is quite likely to be a severe reaction in the form of loss of weight, weakness, cold, coughing, headache, toothache; there may be reactions on the skin too. These reactions should not be feared; they are the visible symptoms and signs that the body is making use of the opportunity to powerfully expel its wastes. A head cold, for instance, is the visible sign that the body is expelling an accumulation of wastes through the nose and throat. But if a person has not thoroughly studied the subject to understand what will happen, he may become alarmed and think his health is becoming rapidly worse. This is definitely not the case, as once the greatest portion of the wastes are removed he will regain weight and feel better than ever; all the weakness and "disease" symptoms will disappear.

But because of these cleansing reactions which may appear to be cause for fear or alarm or giving up the most natural and healthful of diets, I do not intend this article as anything more than a thought-provoker, a stimulus to further study on the part of those people who find some good sense and inspiration in the ideas presented here.. There are a number of authors whose writings I think will prove most interesting and valuable. I will name a few: Arnold Ehret, Paul Bragg, Herbert Shelton, Johanna Brandt, David A. Phillips, and John H. Tobe. There are several others also whose work I think extremely high of, but these I have named seem to have their books most readily available at the health food stores.

Also I have written this as advertising for my own booklet. It is called "Fruitarianism, Diet for A Happier Little Planet"; available at the health food store or by mail from me, it costs $1.00.

I do not claim to have discovered or invented the ideas presented here; I have read them, tested them on myself, and proven them on myself to my complete delight and satisfaction. Best wishes to all readers; I hope this paper will help somebody to more health and happiness.

Sincerely,
Joe Alexander, The Gregory Center, 515 West Spring Street, Fayetteville, Arkansas 72701

VEGETARIANISM

Francis Bacon said: "No pleasure is comparable to standing upon a vantage ground of truth — a hill not to be commanded, where the air is always clear and serene — and see the error and wanderings and mist and tempest in the vale below".

In the field of nutrition, vegetarianism is the door to the truth. Vegetarianism is positive in nature with emphasis on a healthier diet. It does mean eliminating the negative or health destroying foods such as flesh foods, refined and synthetic foods. The human digestive track wasn't designed to digest flesh foods, the human liver wasn't designed to eliminate uric acid from flesh foods, dairy products are acid forming and congest our bodies, alcohol in any form destroys the liver tissue and brain cells, refined foods lose much of their nutrients in the refining process and synthetic foods are foreign to our bodies' metabolism and create chemical havoc internally and sometimes externally. In short, when we eat dead foods (flesh, refined foods and synthetic) we are eating death and will eventually die much faster from it.

I will cite a few examples. Hydrogenated vegetable based fats have to be changed to a fat substance the human body can use. What does our bodies change it to? A saturated fat. Hyrdogenated peanut butter and margarine are harder on our bodies than saturated fats because our bodies have to expend extra energy to change the fat to saturated sustance and later (margarine) it also has synthetic chemicals to deal with.

Much of the fiber in fruits and vegetables passes virtually undigested through the digestive track. It is fiber to keep the intestine and colon clean and waste moving. Fiber fills us up quickly so we don't over eat. It is a natural regulator of nutrient intake. We would have to eat four apples to receive the sugar (38 grams) in a regular serving of soft drink. Fiber regulates the influx of carbohydrates (sugar) into the blood stream so the pancreas doesn't over react. The list of reasons, cases and medical evidence is almost infinite.

Vegetarianism is a positive approach to nutrition. There are many food elements such as coffee, refined white sugar, synthetic foods, etc. that are suppressive on human metabolism as flesh foods are. If I discontinue the use of meat and continue to eat these products I am still destroying my body. Just before giving a lecture to a home economics class on vegetarianism, one of the young ladies said "I want to be a vegetarianism but continue to eat ice cream..." The lecture opened her mind to the positive area of veganism.

An important factor to remember, and I speak from my personal experience, is that our bodies begin to lose their cravings for junk foods when we begin to eat healthier foods. An old universal absolute - good overcomes evil - also applies to nutrition. The positive approach says "eat the healthy foods and your body will lose its cravings for junk foods. In most cases the person will continue to eat junk foods but his use of them will diminish as he increases his use of natural foods.

As a little boy and through high school I was a consumer of meat and potatoes. I easily consumed a whole pizza, a skillet full of ground beef, or a dozen eggs at one sitting. While playing football and doing heavy manual work I was able to burn off the energy, but after the summer of 1968 I weighed about 190 pounds. I became weight conscious and lost 55 pounds by fasting and eating more vegetables and less meat because meat was high in calories. Not being properly schooled in nutrition, I went back up to 160 pounds but I ate less meat and more vegetables. I was a heavy eater of refined foods which are calorie concentrated and vitamin deficient, but these began taking second place to vegetables. In 1970, when I came to St. Paschal's as a Novice (the formal beginning of my life as a Franciscan Brother) I was a heavy consumer of vegetables. I usually ate meat once a day at the evening meal and it was a generous 8 ounce portion. The portion eventually dwindled to about 4 ounces while I ate more vegetables. Refined foods were losing their place in my diet.

When I was about 6 months old I had a severe case of bronchial pneumonia and a mild relapse when I was in the fourth grade. I have always suffered from bronchial congestion and excessive mucus. It was usually bad during the winter so I associated it with weather, but when it started up during the summer I was concerned. Something was wrong. Then Dr. Wesserman, at a International Association of Cancer Victims and Friends chapter meeting said: "Excessive protein can be the cause of mucus congestion." The next day I was a vegetarian (approximately Feb. 15, 1976). I ate fish thinking it was part of a vegetable diet until October 1976 when I became a lacto-ovo vegetarian. The reason being mucus congestion started up every time I ate fish. Later studies proved it to be a wise decision. In May of 1977, after studying Arnold Ehret's book on "The Mucousless Diet" I gave up dairy products and later nutritional studies affirmed the move to pure vegism. I also experienced mucous congestion while eating dairy products but didn't relate it to dairy products until reading Ehret's book. Receiving the proper amount of protein has never been a problem with me. It has always been normal in my body and a recent blood analysis revealed my blood chemistry to be in nearly perfect balance (protein, minerals, and vitamins, etc.).

I never had difficulty giving up these foods because I wasn't eating an enormous amount of them. They just faded by the wayside. I never formally gave up refined and synthetic foods - they just disappeared from my diet because my body lost its cravings for them when I began eating natural foods.

Vegetarianism has many social and moral implications. The food crises need not be. Written on an Egyptian tomb in about the year 3000 B.C. was: "Man lives on one fourth the food he eats and the doctors on the other three fourths". The body efficiency rate is 18% to 22%. By that is meant that 18–22% of the food we eat is used to build the body. The other 78–82% is used by the body to digest and transport food to the vital body tissues. If we eat meat, which is difficult to digest, the efficiency rate drops plus we are not receiving the best form of protein. Hormones to fatten animals, uric acid, and excessive cholesterol (saturated fats) aren't found in vegetable proteins. So the body efficiency rate drops even more. Perhaps now it is 8–12%. If we eat junk foods devoid of most nutritional elements, our body efficiency rate may enter into the Negative Factor, meaning that our bodies are actually expending more energy to rid itself of the foreign elements than it is taking in. The result is, we eat more food of less nutritional value. Why not reverse that the vegetarian way.

to fatten a steer for slaughter. Of that about one million pounds of fat are trimmed off slaughtered steers annually resulting in 5 to 6 million pounds of grain needlessly wasted. There is a social injustice when Americans consume and waste so much food annually while other parts of the world are in a famine state.

A moral matter that I firmly and deeply believe in is the "Right to Life". I believe all life has the right to live from its moment of conception to its natural death. This pertains to animals as well as humans. God is the Author of all life and to destroy life is to insult its author. Animals have feelings and a desire to live and reflect their Author's glory back to Him.

St. Paul exhorts us to: "Offer our bodies as living sacrifices to God, pure and acceptable". Who could offer a friend a rotten banana to eat? But that seems to be the trend with our bodies. Chronic illnesses are on the rampage. True, diet isn't the only factor. Stress, environment, harmony with nature and our spirituality are extremely necessary also. But nutrition is one of the major categories along with our spirituality and environment. A balanced wholistic approach is necessary. A vegetarian diet is a pure diet complementing body hygiene.

A vegetarian diet is also a healing diet. My personal view is that all healing is charismatic. Jesus is the healer either directly by overstepping nature to perform a miracle or indirectly by letting nature heal itself. God created nature and sickness is the result of man's regression from nature both spiritually and physically. The Bible refers to it as sin. During Christ's life on earth sickness was considered sin. Obedience to God must flow from obedience to his laws of spirit and nature. Vegetarianism is in complete accord with natural laws and is thus a healing and body building way of life. I implement vegetarianism in the natural hygienic approach which is primarily raw foods and properly combined. A vegy diet is also a poor man's diet. Vegetables, in general, are less expensive than flesh foods. Dollar for dollar a vegetarian receives more for his dollar. Poor people need not think money is the answer to good nutrition. Good nutrition calls for knowledge of self, the foods we ingest and of God as our loving Father (Faith).

The wholistic approach calls for fasting as a means of body cleansing and mind and spirit cleansing. It isn't purely a physical approach. The desert fathers fasted and prayed. When I pray I can fast and when I fast I enter into a deeper form of prayer. Body energy, especially in the brains, is exerted on prayer. Paul Bragg refers to body care in fasting, etc. as a "Physical Morality". His book "The Miracle of Fasting" started me on the fasting program. Vegetarianism should include fasting. Prayer is essential to all life.

Love is essential to sustain life. A great deal of compulsive eating seems to occur when there is stress and nervous tension. Impulsive eating can also be the result of the burning of nervous energy. Love is healing to the spirit and body. Christ healed with love and usually forgave their sins (transgressions against nature) first and then physical healing. Ever see a mother kiss her child's "ouch" and see the child's smile at the healing. They are really healed. Love is a food for life and essential to total health. Young couples in love or newly married seem to eat less and still maintain their weight and health. After the first fervor of love wears off, they return to their natural diet. In general the Saints were in perpetual love with God and fasted and ate very little. St. Francis of Assisi was a man of prayer, fasting and penance. He lived in harmony with nature and considered himself one of them. To the degree that the food of spirit and body are fulfilled — that will be our degree of health.

Science has opened man's mind to the beauty and marvels of creation — that is good. But in that man is trying to rule creation and side—step the laws of nature — it is disaster. Ivan Illich in "Medical Nemesis" states that doctor created diseases or medical introgencies are on the rampage. Drugs, etc. are the cause of these diseases. He said only one factor is worse than these diseases — poor nutrition. We eat poorly, become sick and run to a doctor to suppress the disease, not cure it. The medical world has a place in our world today, but it can't effectively deal with chronic illnesses unless it gets to the cause. In treating the cause the symptom will disappear.

I feel my role as an executive chef is to deal with a real cause of disease which is poor nutrition. The word chef in French means chief. Americans refer to chef as chief of a kitchen. He could be a chef of a hamburger stand but that isn't what we mean. That is why the American Culinary Federation has started a certification program for chefs. A student starts out as certified apprentice, then certified cook, certified working chef, certified executive chef and finally certified master chef. His certification is proof of his knowledge of the trade. I am lacking a few experience credits of becoming an Executive Chef. I am a certified Working Chef.

But chef and culinary artist have two different meanings. A chef can operate a kitchen, set up menus and prepare gourmet food but miss the essence of culinary art which is nutrition. We should be eating to sustain life, not sever it. I believe a professional culinary artist must have a comprehensive knowledge of nutrition and how it is applied to food preparation and a balanced hygienic meal. I believe that if everyone understood basic nutrition they would easily become vegetarians. A chef in many ways can be a doctor of preventive medicine. In China the chief function of a doctor is to prevent, not cure disease.

My efforts are directed at promoting Vegism on the professional level. Vegism is the first positive step on the road to health. I can see the professional awareness of the food industry. Americans are becoming more nutrition conscious and if the food service industry is going to survive it will have to cater to their demands. Alcoholic consumption is dropping and people are turning to fruit and health drinks according to a recent survey by a Florida Lime Co. Meat consumption is down due to high cost and the cholesterol and nutrition issue, HEW's Joseph Califano spoke out against smoking with no uncertainty that it causes damage to the body. Health foods are on the upswing. In the November 1978 issue of "Cooking for profit" there is a whole section devoted to merchandising vegetables.

Chefs are also becoming nutrition conscious. Alain Senderends, the newest three star chef in his L'Archestrate restaurant in Paris, says "When people sit down, they are eating life. Our food must give them the life force". He isn't a vegetarian but his philosophy is correct. Simone Beck, considered by many the epitome of French cuisine asked "Why do we try to change the taste of things as they are already?" She uses many simple herbal seasonings, has raw vegetable trays (Provence style) and dips. Paul Bucose has a new book called "Paul Bucose's French Cooking" which is a lighter cuisine with less sauces. Michal Guererd, a three star French chef, practices the slim cuisine by thickening sauces with pureed vegetables. It is the only three star restaurant where one can sit down to a diet or regular gourmet French dinner in France.

On the home front there are many health food restaurants (some vegetarian). The Seventh Day Adventists have one in Chicago and Wheaton, Illinois. The Chapman sisters have a Calorie Counter restaurant which caters to vegetarians and flesh food eaters. Even in my home town of Petoskey, Michigan, there is the "Grain Train" restaurant. The population of Petoskey is about 15,000 and the vegetarian restaurant is doing good business.

I am working with the chef of products development for McDonalds Corporation to develop a vegetarian sandwich. He is coming to my kitchen to test the different creations I am preparing. I know the type of product he is looking for as a professional and I know what vegetarians are looking for. Each side will have to compromise to some degree. McDonalds are also seriously considering the salad bar.

Restaurants are utilizing salad bars on their menus for healthier menus and because patrons like to create their special delights. When eating out I often patronize the Ponderosa and Victoria Station salad bars, receiving a complete full course meal at minimum costs. From my experience, steak houses tend to have good salad bars that are inexpensive.

America's interest in nutrition has created a new kind of farmer — the sprout farmer. It has created some more nutritious conscious cooks. I see my role in the culinary arts as one of helping chefs on the professional level to be more nutrition conscious. To help them develop their culinary expertise in Pure Vegetarian cuisine is also another service I offer. That is why I write for the "Culinary Review" a magazine for professional chefs on vegism. America's eating habits, like everything else, is constantly changing, and the trend now is to a more nutritious health food diet of which vegetarianism plays a prominent role. Nutritious health food is the first step toward vegism. Being a vegy, I can relay what pure vegetarians are looking for to chefs and help prepare special nutritious vegy dishes. Some day there will be many certified executive vegetarian chefs and flesh eating will be considered an odd form of cuisine. To date I am the only certified professional working chef. I have proved that it is possible to prepare flesh foods without eating them and many other restricted foods.

Even though I do prepare flesh foods for my community, I implement a lot of nutrition in my cuisine. I serve a minimal amount of fried food, fortify sauce with lecithin, add wheat germ and bran to many of my dishes, use plenty of herbs in seasoning, use a wide variety of vegetables properly prepared, and I use soy bean and bran, etc., in ground beef. I have developed many ways to implement good nutrition to people who don't really value it. I don't push vegism. My example is my best asset. One brother said "I like meat but because you prepare such a wide variety of vegetables so well, I tend to eat less meat". Our province lost 16 brothers and priest of which several were in their forties and fifties (one accident) from heart attacks, etc. I have thirteen elderly brothers and priests, some with heart conditions, but I haven't lost a one in the last three years. Nutrition works with the Grace of God and Love.

I have won several culinary awards. In 1976 I won one first and third at the NRA Culinary Salon in Chicago's McCormick Place. In 1978 I won three firsts, two seconds and one third at Hollebs Sell Fest Culinary Salon.

I worked in my parents' restaurant when I was twelve years old into high school and I came back after my first year at the Seminary in Quincy, Illinois. I worked in the kitchen in Quincy, cooking with a full crew for 150 seminarians and when I came to St. Paschal's I became Soux Chef (second in charge of kitchen). In September 1971, I started school at Chicago's Washburne Trade School for chefs where I graduated at the top of my class. From there I was sent to St. Paschal's as Executive Chef. I have also worked at such places as the Chicago Yacht Club, Medina Country Club, Butterfield Country Club, the Standard Building and a few others. I do everything from ice carving to fancy salads, desserts, hot food preparation, etc.

In 1975, I graduated from a meat cutting course only to turn vegetarian. I still do cut meat even though I wish I didn't have to in order to keep my food costs down but also to keep a better control of the meal served.

I guest lecture on vegetarianism and nutrition and occasionally prepare vegetarian dinners. Presently I am studying for my degree as a Nutritional Consultant and Irodologist. I will graduate from the course in May of 1979. I have already begun a practice as a Nutritional Consultant and Iridologist. By reading the iris I can tell the condition of body tissue and recommend herbs, vitamins, minerals and foods that will help rebuild the tissue.

Our Nutritional Consultants are forming a non-profit organization to build a nucleus from which to learn and share our experiences as N-C's.

Attending the culinary olympics is a goal I am still striving for to promote vegetarianism. I will enter in the pastry category with many vegetarian pastries using no dairy products. I will even attempt to use raw foods in my pastries. The Escoffier pure vegetarian dinner is a second goal to promote vegetarianism. I would like to work with poor people in their nutrition program either in America, Missions or hospitals. The sky is the limit.

La Dean Griffin sums up my attitude towards promoting health and vegetarianism when she says in "No Side Effects" "If it were possible — and it can be if we try — we must learn to turn off those things we cannot solve and pass them onto a higher intelligence than our own — solve the things we can, and cheerfully and patiently wait".

Brother Ronald Pickarski, O.F.M., C.W.C.

FOREVER HIGH

For centuries man has sought the "Godhead" and for just as long he has been involved in trying to get "high". There are many reasons people seek to get high, most being enjoyable (to span time and space in altered states of consciousness, increase perceptions, feel at one with the universe, be free of the burdens of our everyday material existence, to be happy and become more "aware" of what life is really all about). This instinctual urge to be high seems to be programmed into our genetics. Perhaps as God's highest creation, we are intended to experience the joy of being "high" as a permanent way of life, never having to come down out of the clouds. Wouldn't it be blissful to remain high forever instead of having to resort to our usual methods of temporarily escaping reality. Aha, a clue! Escape reality? No, we are really escaping the unreality we live with and things which lower our consciousness level. By taking our drugs we hope to rise from the depths and ease the burdens of a society geared to living against laws of God and nature.

What do God and nature have to do with the high we seek? By achieving the high with drugs we are indirectly obtaining what is meant to be our natural state of being, high forever. The effects of our drugs are temporary and we are soon down again unless we do more herb to get up again. A continuous battle of ups and downs. Wouldn't it be nice to end this struggle and just stay up there? Is there a way to obtain this supreme high forever, never to come down again?

Yes, brothers and sisters, there is a way!

The first and most important step on this trip is to take time to think carefully about what you will soon read. It will be expressed in simple basics, which should make the truth of the matter quite apparent. Once inspired, it will be up to each of us to spend more time investigating the truth from the many sources available in other books, magazines and living examples.

How many of us have ever stopped to consider how drugs work on the mind and body to bring about the desired result, the high? This would involve knowing some simple biochemistry (a heavy word). If we took the time to read a few books on the subject, it comes to light that the active principles causing the drug high are known as the "dangerous alkalies". The alkali is what causes the high. So what in the hell is that? Let us see.

All elements known by man are classified in the "periodic table of elements" which we are all familiar with. These elements have either an acid or alkali reation, one being opposite of the other, as positive or negative, heat and cold, etc. When an acid and alkali combine, they neutralize each other, and the product is called a base, or salt; such as Sodium (Na) being combined with Chlorine (Cl) is Sodium Chloride (NaCl) or common table salt. By combining different alkalis and acids we obtain many different neutral bases with different physical and electrical potentials. Aha!

All the elements have capacity to carry an electrical charge peculiar to itself and varying in context in combination with other elements. Batteries are a good example. There is an electric current in our bodies (living batteries) in every cell (we are familiar with the yin and yang concepts and manipulations of the current by accupuncture).

This electricity is the "spark of life" and conversely can also be the cause of death if not regulated (too much or too little both result in cessation of life). The different elements in the cells and their different electrical charges will determine the polarity and electrical capacity of each cell. Since the body as a whole is composed of all these cells, the "polarity and electrical capacity of the whole body is determined by the types of elements contained in the cells".

How do these various elements get into our cells and body? Obviously by what we breathe, drink, eat, smoke, shoot—up, and snort. This is the key. What we are putting into our bodies is either acid, alkali or base (neutral) and this in turn determines the polarity (direction) and capacity (strength) of current (life) in the body. The alkaline elements direct this energy to the head or higher chakras, or physical stimulation. Are you a "head" person or a "body" person or perhaps "centered" in perfect balance and harmony? Isn't that what most of us are seeking, being centered, masters of our destiny or perhaps we really don't give a s———. If you don't give a s——— about your future or what "life" is really all about, then don't read on. What follows is for the select few who are "seeking the truth" and questioning the mysteries of life to obtain a longer, happier one.

Did it ever occur to us educated people who know so much of the workings and maintenance of such things as cars, t.v.'s, stereos, sewing machines, bicycles, etc., that most of us have very little knowledge on the workings and maintenance of our own bodies. Truly a marvelous invention but one of the most abused and used, without thought of consequences, until it breaks down, some faster than others, ultimately ending in the total "low" death. So let's learn a little preventive maintenance and get real high and healthy doing it. Here's how to do it: all it takes is patience and faith,..too little known virtues in existence in this day and age.

A healthy body must maintain a balance of many things. One of the most important is the acid—alkali balance or ratio. The proper balance being 80% alkali to 20% acid approximately, again depending on many variables (temperature, lighting, humidity, etc.) but relatively stable, otherwise imbalance occurs, disease and ultimately death. Keep in mind how we receive elements into our bodies as stated previously, by what we breathe, drink, eat, smoke, shoot–up, snort or even absorb through the skin.

Now if the acid elements increase too much, a condition doctors call "acidosis" occurs which is the root of most pain and disease in people. If the acid state persists and increases (how?) the result is death, an O.D. of acid toxins. The opposite condition being a rare one, is known as "alkalosis" in which the body is too alkaline, as is the case with extreme drug users (all of our drugs and hallucinogenics being alkaloid derivatives of herbs of the plant kingdom). Death in an alkalosis state is usually painless as we see is the opposite of the acid conditon, which also is usually accompanied by heat and fever. The alkaloid person is often physically numb (how many of us have experienced this with our "high"?). We can observe this in the effects of novacaine. The alkaloid person is also cold rather than in a feverish state. But again, too much alkalinity can cause us to O.D., perhaps painlessly, but unfortunately quite permanently.

Do you hear any bells ringing yet? If not, here it comes! We all wish to be high, happy, and healthy. We temporarily get there by taking an alkaloid drug which results in the munchies usually, so we eat or drink, we come back down to earth. Why? The food that most of us eat is acid forming and keeps us in an "acidosis" state of being, of being low. Should we be satisfied to be temporarily high at the expense of having to use only our known drug highs when we could be "forever high"?

From birth until death we eat and drink food stuffs which ultimately have a biochemical, electrical effect within us. To stay high and healthy (which should make us happy too) we should maintain a higher degree of alkalinity (80%) than acid (20%). How can we expect to do this if we eat 90% acid forming foods, as most of us do in this society, geared to profit on meat and t.v. dinners. Outside of religion the food industry is the largest most profitable industry in the world. The only foods that are alkaline forming are fruits and vegetables. All other foodstuffs (meat, fish, fowl, nuts, seeds, beans, grains, some dairy products) upon digestion form acid elements in our bodies. In turn an acidosis state is created, we hurt, feel bad, depressed, tense, frustrated, sick of living and must get "high" to cope with all the bull s—— we see and feel about us. But why temporarily?

Has it yet occured that our drugs, narcotics, pain killers all contain powerful alkaloids, elements taken from simple plants (vegetables) which when put into the acid saturated body will neutralize the excess acid causing the problem (such as headache pain, acid, neutralized by aspirin) which is caused by an intake of too much acid foodstuffs basically. Once the acid conditon is neutralized by the alkaloid, the salt can be passed out of the body in various ways (sweat) and the body will assume a higher ratio of alkalinity, whether drug induced or food induced. If it is drug induced we are high for a time (we may get the munchies and the battle begins as we are inclined to eat acid forming food and on we go). If our alkalinity is increased through food it takes longer to get off, but if we adhere to a little discipline we could stay high forever. We can expand our minds and free our bodies of negative conditions simply by remaining in an alkaloid state. The way is simple enough for those who will have faith and can be strong enough to be different in their convictions.

those who will have faith and can be strong enough to be different in their convictions.

The answer is Diet -- Fruits and Vegetables. Simple. By eating only fruits and green leaf vegetables and herbs (including grass, hash, cocaine, peyote, opium derivatives, tobacco, etc. as needed for boosters) and cutting out as much as possible acid foods, we can change our polarity and raise our "kundalini" (serpent power) from the lower chakras to the higher, safely, and permanently. The danger of getting high is usually too much too fast. This danger is minimized as it will perhaps take a few weeks (depending on the condition of each individual) for the high to start to come on. If you persevere, the high will last forever. It no longer is temporary, but a new way of life we are born into, which is our God given heritage to be healthy, happy and high. So lets take what is ours rightfully.

Five years ago, living as an unhealthy ganja freak, with deep scientific back-ground, the simplicity of the fruit "trip" seemed almost too incredible to believe. After reading a little more material on it, the truth of it knocked me on my behind. What sense it made, so simple yet so complex. So I jumped right into the fruit trip and found experience to be the best teacher. What harm would there be to experience a simple dietary change in relation to much more harmful experiences I'd gone through. There was no harm, only bliss. The effects were felt within one week in my case. Within one year I felt no need for grass or tobacco (nicotine is an alkaloid) which I'd depended on for seven years to keep me up.

By that time my diet was supplying me with the proper amount of alkalinity to maintain the high and new found health that I experienced. After one more year I had to cut down my vegetable eating as I got to tripping out on them, as I used to with drugs. All vegetables and herbs are extremely one sided alkaline and are basically to be used as medicine during the transition (from one diet to another) to return the over-acid body back to perfect balance. At that point one can live on fruit alone, as it is balanced foodstuff (if grown properly) containing a proper ratio of alkalis and acids which will not imbalance a good body chemistry. At this stage one is centered and quite in tune with the universe as well as local environment. The heavier the stone you get on salad greens, the closer you are to being centered and able to live on fruits alone, which is known as fruitarianism or being forever high.

I sincerely recommend that anyone interested in attempting this transition or making radical changes in diet, to read a few other books on the subject. Much has been left unsaid in this article, which is written as an attempt to stimulate awareness of little known truth. We pursue the subject to familiarize ourselves with other principles involved and to establish a base of faith and trust in what we are doing — if we attempt the forever high.

Shalom.

R.I.S.E., Rainbow Island Sanctuary for Evolution, Lihue, Kauai, Hawaii 96766

NEVER SICK

My Ecuadorean neighbors often make a significant remark, - - "Johnny is never sick; he lives on a strict dietary discipline", as a consequence of noting that everyone else at some time is taking their turn at the sick bed with pains or other bodily disorder. At present, one is dying of cancer, another is with digestive disturbances, another awaiting operation for appendicitis, another years with heart trouble, many with colds taking shots, etc. The sad thing about all this is that the physicians and medical science do not know the cause of the ills they are treating. The Ecuadoreans are slightly more susceptible and dying thus at an earlier average age, and because all medical progress is tied up in the need of catering to costly chemical and drug interests, rather than non−commercialized home remedies available to all, they refuse to consider anything that takes money out of doctoring. They employ drugs in a futile attempt to relieve pain and interfere with the curative process by forcing the symptoms in one part of the body to take on different avenues of elimination or accumulate toxins for a future more serious or fatal ailment. In fact if a person simply employs the simple natural remedy of the elimination of the cause, purifying the blood by not eating so much or not at all in the manner animals remedy their pains, the believers of medical science shout "suicide". Rather than wait a few days till the toxins can be eliminated by such curative diseases as the common cold, childhood diseases, etc., people run to their M.D. who gives them a shot or a pill that does away with what they have, even if it gives them more bothersome rashes or other side effects, beside preventing the elimination of toxins that gradually accumulate in the deap−seated diseases that no M.D. can cure. They don't want to pay the price for their health transgressions immediately, so they accept the rapidly−accumulating interest−rate on serious sickness and early death.

Wouldn't it be wonderful to be "never sick", - -walking like an immortal among mortals, and materially in body feeling you "never die"! There is a new way of life by which you can be "never sick" beside heal most any type of illness if you are not well in the first place. Naturally it is the oldest science, having inspired men thru the ages, and the most logical and easiest provided you are not a bound slave to man's ugly civilization. We have named it "Vitarianism", signifying the cult of life-ennoblement or Life−Conservation, and thus specifically a dietetic science of chastity. All your other sciences have looked upon life thru the values or chemical attributes that can be given things when dead. Thus, what man needs for life is falsely determined by a chemical analysis of man's dead remains, and the life−propensity of food is imagined to be found in sufficient corresponding dead chemicals found therein. But even the nutritionists are beginning to see the fallacy, since the most "well−fed' peoples are the most problematically diseased today, really starved of the elements that give life, in spite of being on diets full of protein, carbohydrates, fats, minerals and even vitamins. However from observing those around me with access to an abundant variety in diet, and of my own living on a healthy farm diet according to medical standards consisting of plenty of animal porteins, home−baked bread, pastries, etc. beside fresh and canned unsprayed fruit and vegetables in extraordinary abundance, - -I noted just as great an occurrence of disease as when vitamins, minerals and other medically—lauded factors were missing. Vitamins may have once meant "life elements" in name but today vitamins are made synthetically, absolutely life—less, and are said to be preserved in sterilized or cooked food. As Morris Fishbein, M.D., says, — — "A vitamin is a vitamin whether it comes from a pill or a cabbage", since modern medical science thinks it can manufacture "life elements" out of dead chemicals, concentrating them hundreds of times greater than found in nature and thus pretending to give us "life" in a pill or shot far beyond the power of the Creator of all. Yet the M.D.s die faster than we do!

For 40 years scientists have known the sole custodians of life force in all organisms to be Enzymes. Of course, vitamins are the essential parts (or co—enzymes) of many enzymes, like a blade of a tool opening up a passage so the enzyme can do its work. But you have no enzymes manufactured in a chemists laboratory, although pretense of concentrating them in natural food has already been made which may not be accurately proven.

Sickness and old age are due to food enzyme deficiency. Youth is the plentitude of this carrier of life force, enzymes. One may ask, why should the enzymes in the body decrease when they are present in all that live? Enzymes have the unique property of being destroyed by temperatures over 120 degrees F., meaning that all food that has been processed by low—heat, pasteurized, boiled, baked, roasted, fried or in any way cooked or heat—treated in its preparation. Enzymes are the life factor in foods that can make other substances change without changing themselves, thus being responsible for the digesting and dividing into small molecules proteins, fats, starches, maltose, sucrose, lactose, and cellulose. However, when one is on a diet of cooked food, or even slightly heated as in pasteurization, the food enzymes have been destroyed, and the inherent body enzymes are used up, expended to digest the heat—treated foods. In spite of the body's wonderful restorative powers, eventually the dead enzyme—less food will so abuse the body's enzyme storage as to leave it lifeless. This is the most satisfactory explanation of the "live—food philosophy" that "life begets life", in that the life elements or enzymes reinforce or restore the life elements of the body used up in the digestion of food and other metabolic processes. When there are no food enzymes on hand in the case of cooked food, the body's enzymes are used up in a constant drain on the body's vitality, bringing on eventual sickness, old age and death. Many have noted the heavy sapped—vitality effect one gets from cooked grains, meat, vegetables, etc. which lacking life—elements are indigestible and unassimilable except by sacrifice to the body's own integrity. Since the enzymes, like vitamins, can be used up or become aged and thus are eliminated in urine and feces, the greater the amount of cooked food consumed, the greater the drain of body enzymes and hence the faster aging of body and greater propensity to disease. Fat or corpulent people not only die faster because of the clogging waste matter swelling their cell—structure, but their greater dead—food—intake takes more of their vitality or inherent enzymes to digest.

In Vitarianism we have taught the "raw" or rather "live—food" diet, excepting in our transition diet allowing 80% live foods hoping it will provide a sufficient plentitude of vitamins and enzymes to digest and assimilate the 20% cooked food. But frankly rather than trying to "fool myself and everyone else as well", one does not sprout life into cooked food no matter how much live food is eaten! Cooked food is dead food always. The transition diet is only a means to get back to true natural values, and not the end in itself, no matter how often its inventor abuses its use for convenience or human weakness. For healing and to never get sick, nothing less than the full quota of enzymes is advised, – – that is, all live foods as soon as possible. Now this sounds like the warned about "Raw–food fanaticism" that M.D.s find popular favor in condemning, but let us examine the facts.

Looking at nutrition from the vista of Enzymology, each food by nature is given the corresponding or necessary enzymes for its digestion and assimilation. Each food has characteristic enzymes so that one cannot expect to substitute protein–digesting enzymes to digest starches, or calcium–accompanying enzymes to assimilate iron, etc.

For instance science is amazed to note that primitive Eskimos, eating raw muscle meat containing an enzyme called "cathepsin" or a protease capable of digesting protein are unknown to have tooth decay, show sugar or albumen in the urine, high blood pressure or arthritis, etc., while the civilized Eskimos on cooked foods are exceedingly diseased with such troubles and short lived. Also pineapple (with Bromelin) and papaya (with its Papain) are known to contain protein–digesting enzymes employed by chefs to tenderize or digest meat, and in nature cure serve to digest excess mucous and albumen existing as pathological waste from past lack of life–elements. Huckleberries and blueberries have the enzyme "neomyrtillin" figuring in the digestion of starches, as utilized in preparation of corn–flour pudding with raw sugar and these berries or certain other fruits with such enzymes by the Indians of the Andes. Although a store banana may be a hard indigestible yellow fruit, if one waits till warmth ripens it to a soft texture or aids the changing of starches to sugars thru the action of enzymes by mashing or liquifying the fruit sometime before eating it, we witness the presence of the life characteristics known as enzymes. The average person thinks cooking changes starches to a more digestible form, and although there is a momentary reaction in bursting the cells with heat, the complete metabolism–favoring enzymes of the starches are destroyed, giving a drain constantly to body enzymes or burdening the body with waste. The corn and barley eating Indian of the Andes, the rice eating Japanese, etc. are characteristically corpulent but short, and the greater lack of live food in grain eaters shows with a pathological laziness or greater effort needed by them to overcome their metabolic burdens. Enzymes change starch to sugar naturally in the ripening of fruit picked green by time or the bruising provided in transportation, while in grains and legumes this is done by sprouting, seeds by nature not intending to expend themselves in their dormant stage and thus being lacking in life–elements to favor digestion or assimilation till they grow. The lack of available enzymes in dormant grains can be seen when green feed gives away in northern winters, horses developing stiffness leading to death by the change to the dry feed of oats, etc. (something that unwittingly happens to grain–eating humans too) filling their organisms with calcareous life–less mineral deposits without the needed enzyme–life for its beneficial use.

Enzymes are living proteins, – – "wonderful spark–plugs of every single chemical process we live by", as medicine calls them, but they are not just any protein as they prefer to conclude so they need not recommend raw food saying we shall get enzymes from proteins forgetting that enzymes would have to do the changing and give life. The gross concentrated proteins are our worst dietetical enemy while these life–carrying enzyme proteins of less concentration but of greater metabolic efficiency are our best health–aids. This we witness in the affirmations of experienced physicians who like Emerson Hartman in "Professional Secrets" says: "So enormous quantities of excess proteins in the American and other civilized diets is basically responsible for the enormous increase in cancer...especially is this true of cooked proteins: people who eat everything raw never have cancer". The enzymes of living protein protect us from the most serious diseases.

Our first concern should not be whether our food contains minerals, protein, fats or carboyhdrates, but rather if it has enzymes that will make the other elements of any use to us, and prevent these other food factors from sapping the life–elements of our body in attempting their digestion. Fruit, the true food intended for man is alive with enzymes, the sugar directly assimilable by the blood and needs very little mineral or protein matter since the enzymes provide for greater assimilabiity than concentrated proteins and minerals which instead burden the body. The more natural a food is, the better it is for you. In a sense the modern craze for fruit and vegetable juices has disadvantages, because the crushing and destroying of plant cells liberates enzymes that destroy the vitamins such as ascorbic acid, and contain only a fractional part of the nutrients of the original vegetables which are lost in the residue, beside eliminate the bulk that can help satisfy the appetite and furnish the roughage to aid intestinal functions. While this is true in the long–term way of diet, for therapeutical purposes in a tired and abused body we may note that raw vegetable juices require no digestion in the stomach, like fruits being directly assimilable into the blood because of their enzymes, besides these striking properties in sunlight energy absent in cooked foods even if they contain many more useless calories of heat energy. Juices can heal.

Enzymes are the life of everything. Without enzymes we would die instantly. We cannot expect life from that which is dead, so really we do not live by eating cooked dead food, but rather we die gradually and eventually from it. Nor does anyone manufacture life into something that has it not, such as when one theorizes that eating plenty of raw enzyme containing food, some enzymes will give life to the dead elements of the cooked food part of the diet. Even of specific concentrates of enzymes we must say they contain known substances. Live natural foods contain all known as well as yet unknown properties necessary for healthy Life–Conservation in our bodies. "People who eat natural foods never eat too much", said the great raw food physician Dr. Bircher Benner. The more live foods we eat the more life–elements (enzymes) we get, while the more dead foods we eat the greater the dead or lifeless burden that will take life–elements away from our body cells to try to digest that life–less matter. As we have indicated, the fruits and vegetables highest in water but lacking in the accepted food elements (fats, protein, starch, etc.), are the greater life–giving foods, usually being high in enzymes and disease resisting factors.

Not only does excessive temperature destroy enzymes, but also excess acidity, just like acidosis can destroy any living organism. Those who have only known fruitarianism as the eating of nuts beside fruit, may not welcome the information that even on strictly fruit and nuts in my California experiments of 1938, I began suffering a burning acidity in the stomach and urine, with an accompanying weakness, while when eliminating acid–forming nuts, all went well. Not only do cooked and acid—forming raw seeds use up enzymes in digestion, but their excess acidity in itself can destroy enzymes thus. Dr. Geo. W. Crile said: "There is no natural death. All death from all so—called natural causes are merely the end point of progressive acid saturation". One can usually judge the health by the purity of the urine which is optimum on a juicy fruit diet. Most of the concentrated percentage of protein of the ordinary diet goes to produce excess acidity in the body tearing down the body rather than being "body—building proteins", while the enzymes are true living cell components, constructors and conservers...the real life factor although hardly registering in the protein percentage of food—tables. More confusing to science is the fact that although their action is more specific than that of ordinary catalysis, simple chemical theory is incapable of predicting the effect of changes in enzyme concentration or substrate. We have to study as the nearest thing like unto life itself, the link with the invisible intelligence that directs life and the material substance that it enlivens.

In our publication "Eternal Youth Life" (founded 1946) and in "Vitarianism" we have indicated that if man lived on a strict juicy fruit diet (and other factors favorable, God—willing), he would have no reason to die physically as the legend of Paradise would assure us, and possibly when man had enough of schooling on earth (a few centuries perhaps as the pre—deluvian man) he would ascend to heaven without dying like Enoch.

Professor J. Lovewisdom, "Eternal Youth Life", Vilcabamba, Loja, Equador

---

WHEATGRASS AGAINST DISEASE
A GREAT HOPE FOR AILING HUMANITY

A virtual epidemic of chronic degenerative disease is afflicting our nation: from cancer to heart disease; from arthritis to schizophrenia; from diabetes to the common cold. These diseases, and so many more, increasingly subjugate a people attuned more to affording sickness than enjoying the natural state of health which is our birthright. The statistics for cancer, for example, are starkly and devastatingly illustrative of the extent to which our well—being is threatened:

"Last year over 405,000 Americans died from cancer."
"Almost 56 million Americans now living will eventually have cancer."
"In 1980, about 708,000 people were diagnosed as having cancer."
"Cancer kills more children age three to fourteen than any other disease."
"The overall incidence of cancer has increased between 5% and 10% since 1970."
(Excerpted from "Cancer Facts and Figures: 1980," The American Cancer Society, Inc., 777 Third Ave., New York, NY 10017.)

A meaningless litany of mere statistics? The real costs of cancer, in terms of human fear, hopelessness and death which have left no family unscathed, suggest

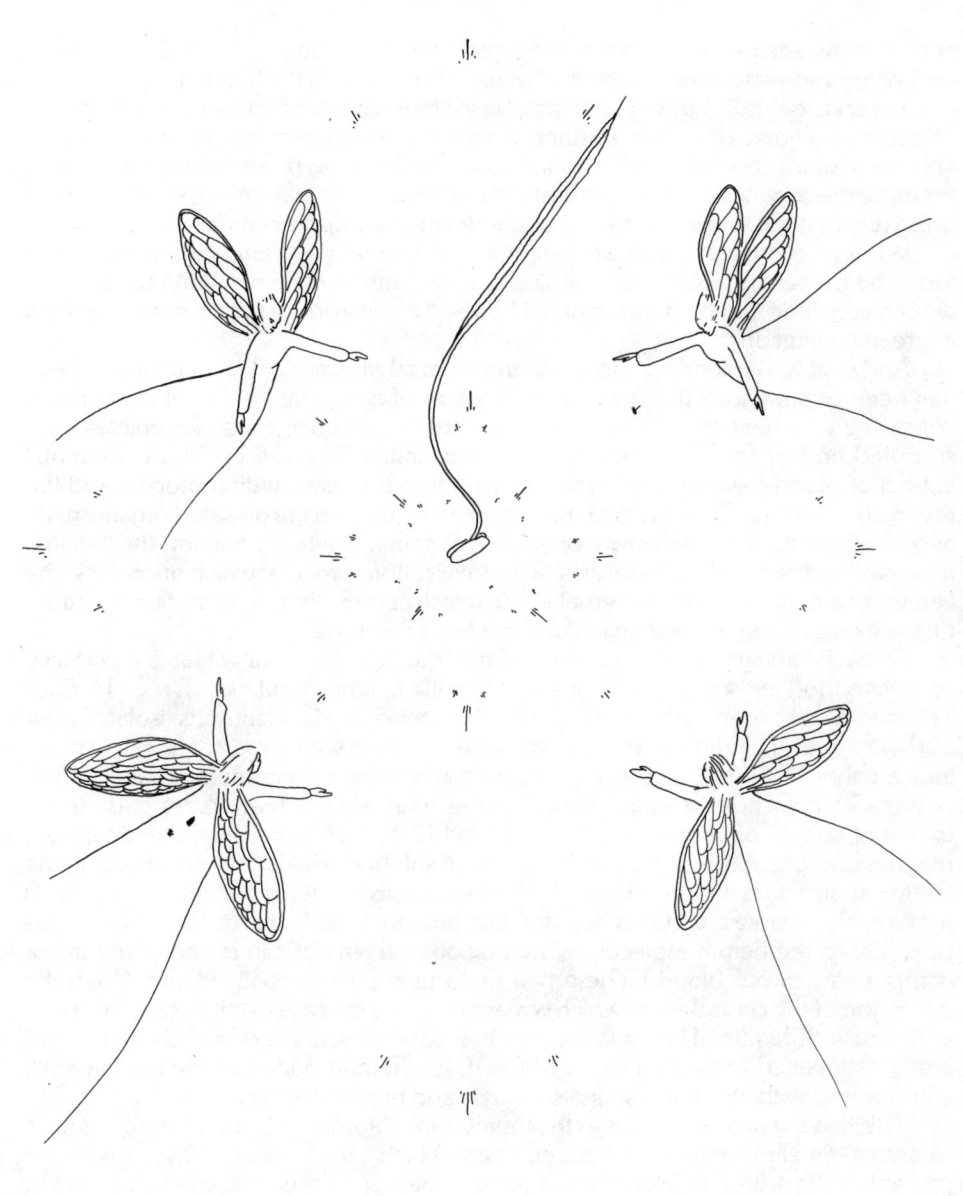

not. For decades now, as mortality rates have constantly risen and millions of Americans have succumbed, medical science has offered little hope of reprieve.

Yet consider this: human strength pales when compared to that of an elephant, rhinoceros, a horse or a steer. Further, whereas man suffers from over 250 diseases, animals in nature are susceptible to only a few. Science has produced no explanation for these discrepancies other than that these animals are herbivorous, subsisting on a living diet of grass and leafy greens, unaltered in any way by people.

Western culture, in contrast, tampers with and radically alters the nature of its foods by processing, cooking, chemicalizing and otherwise devitalizing them. Thus we can conclude that humanity would likewise benefit from an unprocessed diet high in green vegatation.

And so it is. Astounding success in the reversal of chronic degenerative diseases has been experienced through the application of a vegetarian diet of living foods consisting of wheat grass juice, immature greens, sprouts, fruits, vegetables, and sprouted and/or fermented seeds, nuts, and grains. The use of 70% chlorophyll extract of seven day old wheat grass is central to the rejuvenation process and the reversal of disease. The effects of this wheat grass juice on the diseased organism are two–fold: first, it provides an optimal nutritional environment for the healing process; and second, it catalyzes a detoxification process which increases the elimination of accumulated internal waste which causes disease by autointoxication. Let us examine more closely each of these two processes.

Scientific analysis has demonstrated that grass grown from wheat is a perfectly complete food in itself, capable of sustaining life in a healthful way. Dr. G. H. Earp Thomas, a soil expert at the Bloomfield Laboratories in Massachusetts, isolated over 100 elements, including all the known minerals, from wheat grass. His calculations indicate that 15 pounds of fresh wheat grass is equivalent in nutritional value to 350 pounds of the choicest vegetables. Studies have shown that wheat grass in an excellent source of vitamins A, B, C, E, and K, as well as calcium, chlorine, iron, magnesium, phosphorus, potassium, sodium, sulphur, cobalt, and zinc. Further, the chemical structure of the chlorophyll molecule in wheat grass reveals that it is remarkably adapted to utilization by the human blood stream, by virtue of its similarity to the hemin molecule of hemoglobin. (Hemoglobin is one of the major components of our blood.) These two molecules are essentially identical with the exception of the central atom which is magnesium in the case of chlorophyll and iron in the case of hemin. Thus, we can see that within the context of this optimal and easily assimilated and utilized nourishment, the human body has the fundamental components with which to eliminate disease and regenerate itself.

This healing process occurs as the therapeutic chlorophyll in the wheat grass juice catalyzes the elimination of the stored toxins which cause disease. These toxins are present in the ailing organism in the form of hardened mucous, crystallized acids, fatty deposits, calcifications, and solidified, decaying fecal matter. As these toxins are eliminated, the body is cleansed and brought back to its natural state of health. Wheat grass juice also has a very high enzyme content which helps to dissolve tumors. Imagine the astonished rejoicing of persons labeled "terminal" who watch visible tumors disintegrate and disappear before their very eyes!

Recent experiments performed at the M. D. Anderson Hospital Tumor Research

Institute in Houston, Texas, have demonstrated that the chlorophyll extracted from seven day old wheat sprouts inhibits mutagenic activity in vitro. Apparently, the inhibitory effect of the wheat grass juice occurs as the chlorophyll interferes with the functioning of enzymes which activate carcinogens. In separate experiences at the Linus Pauling Institute of Science and Medicine in California, rats induced with squamous cell carcinoma exhibited an astonishing two–fold decrease in malignant growths when fed a sole diet of wheat grass, vegetables, fruits, and seeds. Indeed, this potent nutritive and healing grass offers great hope when all attempts by more conventional means appear to be stymied.

You can follow these simple instructions to avail yourself of this healing food.
1. Obtain organically grown wheat berries at your local health food store or food co–op.
2. Soak one cup wheat berries for 16 – 24 hours.
3. Pour off water and let berries sprout for 16 – 24 hours.
4. Mix peat moss and top soil in a fifty–fifty proportion, adding water so that there is sufficient moisture so that water can be squeezed out by hand. The mixture should have the consistency of a wet sponge, with no puddles.
5. Spread ½ inch wet earth on a cafeteria tray, bakers tray or a cardboard box cut to one inch height and lined with plastic.
6. Spread sprouted seeds on earth, each seed touching another, but without seeds on top of each other.
7. Cover with an opaque plastic sheet.
8. Remove plastic when sprouts are 1 inch high and place in light. Water as necessary. Cut and use when grass is 7 to 9 inches in height.

Uses:

1. Chew, suck in juice, dispose of pulp.
2. Extract juice with manual or electric wheat grass juicer. Drink alone or mixed with water or vegetable juice. Initially, take no more than one ounce at a time as the wheat grass juice can cause nausea and/or dizziness as it begins the detoxification of poisons in the body. Gradually increase amount to 4 to 8 ounces daily. Always drink on an empty stomach!
3. Wheat grass juice is best used in conjunction with a living vegetarian diet of at least 80% raw sprouts, vegetables, fruits, seeds and nuts. To improve health and assist in the elimination of disease, it is best to avoid all animal products, sugar, salt, refined flour products, processed foods, food preservatives and additives, tobacco, alcohol, and caffeine. Use only whole foods, preferably in an uncooked state.

It is axiomatic that disease cannot exist in a well nourished and internally clean body. Our physical bodies are holy temples of light wherein dwells the Spirit of Love. By eating nature's living foods we are purified of all vestiges of disease and become concomitantly more attuned to the Universal Energy which is God and love. Truly, herein lies the key to the elevation of humanity and the alleviation of great suffering. Through the healing power inherent in the grasses and living foods, we can attain once again to pristine godliness and the perfect health which is our birthright.

Richard G. Tasca, Jr., Woodstock Valley, Connecticut, March, 1981

WHEATGRASS – THE CURE ALL?

Recently, an American physician conducted month-long health camps in Bombay and Delhi where a number of patients underwent this therapy. Yashodhara Delmia met some of them to find out how far they have been helped by the treatment.

Nothing helps a patient suffering from chronic illness more than the discovery of a new cure. Or so, at least, he believes.

When month-long camps for wheat grass therapy were held in Bombay and Delhi a couple of months ago, the treatment was hailed as the answer for all incurable ailments. And Dr. Ann Wigmore, its main exponent in America, who supervised the camps helped set up a permanent hospital in Bombay. She is once again in the city at present.

But, with the initial euphoria over, the time comes for a long, sober look at the treatment: just how much does it really help? Most of the 70-odd patients at the Bombay camp have found some measure of relief. A 45-year old lady suffering from rheumatoid arthritis, for instance, found that the pain had decreased.

I joined the camp after having tried everything else. You see, I suddenly developed pain and swelling in the joints two years ago. Allopathic treatment only made it worse and it became impossible to walk. Homeopathy was better but it didn't cure me. I tried nature cure at the Urlikanchan hospital (near Pune) for some time. There I was given a partial raw diet with some boiled or lightly cooked food. Mentally I felt better but the pain in the joint muscles increased.

At the camp I used to feel very weak in the beginning because of the lack of food. Also the massaging had not begun since it was yet to be organized. I think it was towards the last week that my health improved and I could walk. The pain also decreased.

But it is too early to really say something about the treatment. It is a slow process and I can only know after six months. I only know that I have improved enough to want to continue on with it.

While this is more or less the reaction of the other participants, the treatment when examined is more revealing. The same lady said: "We began the morning with a glass of rejuvelac, which is the fermented water of the wheat germ. It is supposed to be very rich in enzymes and therefore helps in digesting food. Then I was given an enema with plain water, followed by another enema with wheat grass juice. This helps to cleanse the system of poisonous substances, particularly since wheatgrass is a good antiseptic. The others were later asked to do yogic exercises. Since I am arthritic, I was massaged.

We were given light and nourishing food to eat. It had to be raw because Dr. Wigmore believes that any food which is cooked destroys its nourishment.

In fact, the major part of the therapy consists of eating raw food and it is this which is criticized by an established naturopath in Bombay. "We can't eat uncooked potatoes, they have to be slightly cooked. Again alfalfa (lucerne) seeds are wonderful raw but the sprouts of methi, moong and wheat, which are staple foods in the therapy, have to be cooked slightly".

"The body", according to him, "requires some warmth". I agree that we overcook and use too many spices, but we need not go to the other extreme. Then again, a raw food diet, he feels, should not be imposed suddenly as there were withdrawal symptoms like dizziness, vomiting and nausea. It had to be done gradually.

It votaries, however, insist that everything must be eaten raw, including potatoes. "There are ways by which potatoes can be eaten uncooked. They can be soaked in water and made soft and then chopped finely. In any case, potatoes are not so essential as greens and sprouts for the diet".

As for dizzy spells, they feel that this happens only in the beginning. The body gets completely accustomed to it after some time. "If you have had decadent food for so many years, how can you suddenly get used to good food? It is like an alcoholic being asked to take coconut water".

They take their cue from Dr. Wigmore who says that cooked food destroys 80 per cent of the essential vitamins, minerals and enzymes. True, it retains proteins, carbohydrates and starches but since these are isolated from other natural elements the body isn't able to absorb them. As a result, there are excessive deposits in the body which cannot be eliminated. This is similar to the imbalance in vitamin pills which are artificially separated from other natural elements and cannot be assimilated by the body.

Dr. Wigmore is also vehemently against meat eating, since it gives rise to harmful waste products like uric acid and other toxins which the body cannot eliminate. In fact, she suggests a link between meat eating and cancer. "Uncivilized tribes living on a vegetarian diet are not afflicted with cancer. Yet when these tribesmen eat civilized food like meat, eggs and milk, cancer develops," she writes.

Hunger for cooked food, she says, is not real hunger since the body is never satisfied. When raw food is eaten, the body requires only one third its normal requirement.

But the base of her diet continues to be wheat grass which acts as a catalyst in the absorption of food. She contends that the grass grown from wheat soaked in water for 24 hours contains a high percentage of chlorophyll, which is best food for the body. It bears a close resemblance to hemoglobin, the red pigment in blood and can therefore be quickly absorbed by the blood stream providing valuable nutrients. It is also an effective blood cleanser.

Underlying Dr. Wigmore's treatment is a wholly different way from the allopathy way of looking at disease. What is important is not that the body gets infected by germs. These exist in the body in great numbers since birth. But the system also can combat these germs and this capability has to be reinforced by the right food and proper elimination of waste matter.

She is also against modern drug therapy which is not only indiscriminately and aggressively used but also suppresses the illness rather than cures it. This in turn leads to the disease becoming chronic or worse still, to drug-caused illness.

"But wheat grass therapy is not God's manna," a surgeon in a Bombay hospital declares. As a form of wholesome food which provides nutrition for the body it is valid. But to claim that it has wonderful, magical properties is another thing. "There have been many such movements in the past — psychic healing, the "miracle chapati" — which have supposedly found a cure for everything. But unless there is documented evidence, we cannot accept it."

"Modern medicine", he says, "can only accept new discoveries which are backed by years of proven successes. It has to, for instance, undergo the double blind test. Two parallel groups of a sizeable number of patients should be administered wheat grass and some other recognized system of medicine. The result of these should be tested over a sufficiently long time. All new drugs in the market have to undergo this test. How then can we accept something which has not been scientifically tested though there may be individual successes?"

And yet the results at the wheat grass hospital in south Bombay reveal more than the odd success. The hospital has ten indoor patients and facilities for consultations. It provides treatment for tuberculosis, cancer and other chronic ailments. Most of the patients I spoke to seemed to have benefitted. Twenty-three-year-old Tejrai Jain, an asthma patient who had been there for four days, for instance, felt a definite improvement and intended to continue. An owner of a small shop for raw materials, he has had asthma for seven years and had to discontinue his studies.

"I tried allopathic treatment. The doctor gave me medicine which I took for one year. The day I didn't take it there would be breathing trouble. When I started getting a rash on the skin, I decided to give it up".

"I finally came to the clinic in the middle of an attack. It was difficult to climb the steps because of my breathing. They told me to lie down but I could only sit holding my head.

"They gave me rejuvelac to drink. Then they gave me an enema. The whole day they kept giving me raw food to eat and juices. In addition, they made me lie down in a tub filled with water and gently massaged my stomach. This known as a hip bath. They also tied wet and hot bandages around me. In the afternoon they tied a thick cloth on my chest for warmth.

"In the beginning I didn't feel much difference. But now the attack has gone completely and I don't think it will come back if I continue with this".

MEDICINAL USE OF ONIONS

Mother Nature has provided us with an abundance of medicinal plants for our use in the establishment and maintenance of healthy bodies. However, many of the simplest, yet most effective of these plants are too often overlooked in our search for the more exotic, impressive sounding herbs. Many times a would-be-herbalist is left powerless to treat a problem because the herb store is closed, when indeed, right in the food pantry or refrigerator are plants that would heal the malady quite effectively. Things like cabbage, carrots, potatoes, and onions are lying there unused while the disease goes untreated.

I would like to take the ordinary onion and show you some of the many ways it can serve you. First of all, let's look at the onion from a nutritional point of view. Onions are fairly high in minerals containing potassium, calcium, iodine, magnesium, sodium, copper and a high amount of organic silica. Also, there are varying amounts of vitamins A, C, B1, B2, B3, B6, folic acid, pantothentic acid, and biotin, plus a small amount of protein and large amounts of natural sugars. So, nutritionally speaking onions are well worth utilizing and to many of us are indespensible as a flavoring agent in our meals.

However, the onion is much more than just a food. It is a very powerful healing herb which is a specific in the prevention and treatment of infectious diseases and wounds, and is also quite effective in the treatment of many chronic degenerative diseases.

Before getting into the actual administration of this healing plant, it is first of all important to understand it from a pharmacological standpoint, where we can get a feel for how it works. So lets take a look at...

    Allium Cepa
    Family: Liliaceae (Lilac)
    Part Used: Bulb
    Action: Rubefacient, expectorant, diuretic, antiseptic
    Constituents: Strong concentration of sulferated volatile oils, mucilage, phosphoric acid, acetic acid and citrate of lime.

The main chemical factor we are concerned with here is the volatile oil which is of the allyl sulfide type $(C3H5)2S$. Sulfur has been used for hundreds of years to fight infections and as a blood purifier. Its use has taken the form of sulfur and molasses "spring tonics" in folk medicine, sulfa drugs in allopathic medicine, as sublimated sulfur in homeopathic medicine, and as the Schuseeler Biochemic Cell Salts, Calc Sulph, Kali Sulph and Natr Sulph.

What we have in the onion is a volatile oil which is concentrated in a highly volatile and penetrating form of sulphur. Sulfurate's volatile oils are also found in garlic, horseradish, and the mustards. These volatile oils are most effectively absorbed into the body through eating or drinking of the fresh juice or herbal tincture, but the oils are also able to be very effectively absorbed through the skin. Just by covering the soles of the feet with a paste made from onions, the volatile sulfur is able to penetrate and disperse throughout the whole body very rapidly to manifest its disinfectant and detoxifying properties. Within minutes, varying amounts of the volatile oils will appear in such places as the saliva and membranes of the bronchials and lungs, the stomach and intestines, the kidneys and bladder, and the uterus and vagina, and traces will begin to appear in the urine and perspiration. The basic action of volatile oils is one of stimulation. In the tissue with which it comes into contact there is increased blood flow resulting in warming and redness of the area. This increased activity causes oxygen and nutrients to enter the tissue, move waste products and toxins to leave, plus there is an increased migration of germ fighting white blood cells to the area. All of this collectively increases the body's ability to resist infection and enhances its healing processes.

Some of the more specific manifestations of these actions would be increased expectoration of viscous phlegm from the lungs and bronchials, increased urine flow, stimulation of appetite and enhanced digestion and blood circulation.

Another aspect of onions' healing qualities is its high content of mucilage. This is best utilized by lightly heating the onion for a brief period. This creates a soft slimy—like mucilage which is very soothing to irritated tissues of the body. It is this soothing quality, along with the antiseptic action of the sulferated volatile oils, which makes onions one of the most effective and yet very simple cough and bronchitis remedies we have in nature.

Still another important healing aspect of onions are Gartwitch Rays which were discovered in Russia. These are organic radiations which were discovered to emanate from onions, garlic, and ginseng. They are believed to stimulate vital processes in living cells and to somehow protect the body from harmful radiations. Perhaps the old use of garlic as protection from "evil spirits" is not so superstitious after all.

Now let's see how we can put the onion to work for us through the preparation and administration of some simple home remedies.

Onion Cough Syrup

Chop into cubes a large strong onion. Place this in a small bowl or wide mouth jar and pour honey over the onion pieces until they are fully covered. Cover this tightly so the volatile oils cannot escape and place in a low-heated oven (about 200 deg.) for about 15 minutes. As alternatives you can use a double boiler or place the onion and honey mixture inside a black box and place the box in the hot sun all day. After heating, press out the onion pulp through a fine strainer, and the resulting honey/onion juice mixture is your cough syrup. To this you can add the juice of half a lemon or a tablespoon of raw apple cider vinegar, and teaspoon of licorice root powder. The dose for small children is one teaspoon and for larger kids and adults one tablespoon. Take as often as needed.

Onion Poultice

This preparation can be applied over the upper chest area for bronchitis and heavy bronchial catarrh and coughs. Also, it is effecive when used over the kidney areas in cases of suppressed urine and other kidney problems where the action of onions is indicated.

Take about 5 to 10 onions - chop them up finely.   Add to this an equal amount in volume of rye or corn meal. Now, make a paste of all this by adding apple cider vinegar and stirring all together. Put this mixture into a pan and gently simmer for about 10 minutes. Stir constantly and work towards a final product that will have the consistency of very thick oatmeal. Ideally, the poultice should spread easily and yet it should not be runny. You may have to add more   vinegar or meal while heating in order to get it right. When the poultice is finished cooking, spread it onto flannel or muslin cloth; cover this with another cloth to make an onion poultice sandwich and apply the wetter side of the sandwich to the area to be treated. To protect the area from blistering, massage a good amount of olive oil into the skin just before applying the poultice. Once the poultice is applied, cover this all with a thick insulating cloth so that the heat does not escape. Remember, it is important that the poultice be used hot but do not burn the person. The poultice can be kept on until it cools or overnite. If there is a real need for vigorous action, then a fresh poultice can be prepared as soon as the old poultice cools down. This can be kept up for about an hour. Here again, it is important not to burn the person and to keep an eye out for volatile oil blistering, which can take place on sensitive skins. When the treatment is over, wash the area well with 50/50 mixture of water and vinegar, and then massage some warm olive oil into the area. Then put the person to rest. Do not go into the cold directly after such a treatment.

Onion Juice Antiseptic

Roast an onion until it is a bit soft, then squeeze out its juice through cotton cloth and add to this an equal amount of honey. This mixture is great to drop into the eyes and is useful in eye infections or tired eyes.

Onion Ear Poultice

This is one of the oldest folk remedies there is for ear—ache and ear infections. Take an onion and bake it until it is soft. Then cut it into half, and place the flat side of each half over each ear (treat both ears even though only one is troubled). Then, cover each onion with several layers of cotton and bind the whole together with cotton bindings. Also, a stocking cap or a cap with ear muffs work great to hold the onions in place. Leave on for two hours or overnite. Also, a couple of drops of fresh raw onion juice can be dropped into each ear two times per day.

Poisonous Bite Remedy

Various types of onion poultices, or just plain pulped onion by itself, have been used for snake, scorpion, and dog bites and for insect stings. This is especially effective when used with plantain leaves. The first plantain leaves can be juiced or pounded into the onion mixture and applied to the area. Also, just rubbing an onion slice over insect stings will usually bring relief from itching and smarting.

Epidemics and Plagues

Eat plenty of raw onions and garlic and horseradish. Wear garlic cloves around the neck. Suck on garlic cloves and/or ginger pieces. This may sound a bit weird to some, but the Gartwitch Rays will help to protect you from evil spirits and germs. Also, saucers with onion slices can be placed around the rooms of persons sick with infectious contagious diseases to purify the air. The onion slices should be thrown away each day and fresh ones put out.

Miscellaneous Uses

Burning urine and bladder stones; Upset stomach and colic: Boil one ounce of fresh onion in 16 ounces of water until it has evaporated down to 8 ounces. Strain well and drink the mixture when it is cooled. Best taken on an empty stomach.

It is important to remember that health or disease is a manifestation of our mental, physical and spiritual lifestyles and our relationship with the environment around us. One single treatment with an onion poultice is not going to cure anyone of a bronchial infection. It is not quite that simple. However, within the context of a full holistic healing program "miracles" can and have happened. The above information is only meant to give you a few tools out of the many that are needed in the treatment of disease. A little bit of knowledge can be a dangerous thing, but we have to start somewhere. Don't expect miracles to happen − help them to happen. Actually, the best way to use onions is to make them a regular addition to your diet and thereby strengthen the body's resistance to disease. Some people may feel that onion and garlic and the like are too stimulating or tamasic and refuse them. I would say "great" −IF you live in a totally unpolluted environment away from poisoned air and man−made radiations, and have a fully purified body. BUT, who does? Also, there are those who eat too large amounts of things like onions, garlic and cayenne, as if they are trying to prove their macho strength. Here, they are only irritating and overstimulating the body and doing more harm than good. Find what amounts are right for you. I do feel that we need a good amount of onions, horseradish, garlic and cayenne on a regular basis if we are living in a polluted environment, and also to prepare us for the hard times to come. So, don't worry about the offended noses of the uninitiated. Stink and be healthy.

Ed Smith, Herbalist, P. O. Box 116, Williams, Oregon 97544

THE RAW FOODS DIET AND WEIGHT LOSS

Every human being who has been living on the conventional diet of so−called civilization, has in his blood and tissues an enormous amount of foreign matter consisting of uric acid, lactic acid, toxins, and mineral deposits in the cells and tissues, that have entered the body with the impure air we breathe, with the impure water we drink, with the drugs we have taken, and with the food we have eaten.

This waste matter rises to great proportions. Even in those persons who, though not suffering any physical discomfort for the time being, believe themselves to be healthy and sound. But cases of sudden death of persons who just a few days before had been examined by doctors of life insurance companies and pronounced sane and healthy, and allowed life insurance policies − (the sudden death of fat and healthy looking people) proves that though a person may look fat and healthy, he may have deposited in and between the cells of his body an enormous amount of poisonous waste, averaging from ten pounds in thin persons to fifty pounds or more in those who are excessively overweight. Let those who look fat and healthy, but who have been living on the conventional diet, begin to fast and they will be surprised to see the enormous quantities of mucus that Nature begins at once to eliminate through the mucus membranes.

Let me say at the beginning, that the loss of weight is more apparent than real. Or in other words, what you are losing is largely the poisonous waste and filth which has been the cause of your troubles.

Now let me explain what happens in your body when you go on a natural, raw food diet: First, you greatly reduce or entirely discontinue the intake of sodium chloride, or common salt. Everybody who has been eating cooked food, well seasoned with salt, has in his cells and tissues, as much as two to four ounces of inorganic sodium chloride. Now, physiology teaches us that the normal physiological salt solution in the blood and other fluids of the body is at about seven to nine per thousand. By using this ratio, we see that for every ounce of salt which we have ingested and is retained in our bodies, we must have about 112 ounces of water or seven pounds, to keep this inorganic salt at a normal physiological solution. So you see, that supposing that even if you have retained in your body tissues only from one to two ounces of salt, you shall have from six to fourteen pounds of water to maintain this inorganic sodium chloride in solution.

Now, what happens when you begin to live on unfired fruits and vegetables? It is this: The excess of inorganic sodium chloride is eliminated, together with the water that was keeping it in solution.

So you see, you have lost six to twelve pounds of your body weight without necessarily having lost any of your healthy tissue. I have experimentally increased my weight six or eight pounds in one week, simply through eating cooked food seasoned with salt, but as soon as I resumed the raw food diet, I lost this abnormal weight in two days.

Nature, when given natural food, starts her purifying process by eliminating the poisons which are in a state of solution in the fluids of the body, such as sodium chloride and other acids, which have been neutralized by the alkaline salts. You can observe the elimination of these poisons through the kidneys, by examining the urine after you have gone on a natural diet. You will find it very cloudy, and leaving a whitish sediment when left for a few hours.

It is usual for people who begin to live on uncooked food, to feel a great improvement at first, but a few weeks afterward, the elimination starts, and different symptoms arise. Nature seems to be regaining power, increasing the alkaline reserves of the body, and when she is prepared, there comes a healing crisis. Nature, having now at hand the necessary solvent, begins to dissolve the accumulated, hardened waste and filth, and carrying it by means of the blood stream, to the depurating organs to be expelled from the body. While a person is undergoing one of these healing crises, he may feel very sick and think that his old pains are coming back. He may feel discouraged and be willing to give up the only process of cure which, if continued, will restore his health, return his youth, and prolong his life many years.

If given the proper materials, nature will build a new body for you under the operation of the Law of Change. But she has to overcome the same difficulties which you would have to overcome if you were to renew your old home.

Let us suppose that you have an old house that is in a dilapidated condition; the walls are cracked, full of holes; the ceiling is cracked and the plaster has fallen down in many places; the joists and laths are decayed and ready to crumble. You call a carpenter and a plasterer, but before they can replace the decayed joists, laths, etc., and renew the plaster, they have to tear down the rotten wood, remove the loose plaster, and take the rubbish away. Under these circumstances, your old house will look much worse than before they began to renovate it. But you know that these bad features are only temporary. Soon the working men shall have replaced the decayed wood with new wood, the plasterers shall have finished the ceilings, and after the walls have been painted and all the rubbish removed, your house will look like new.

This is what nature is doing in your body. She is tearing down the half dead tissue, dissolving calcareous deposits that were hardening your arteries, stiffening your tissues, wrinkling your skin, thus making you old, and carrying all this dislodged waste to the eliminating organs to be thrown out of the body.

But just as the carpenter can not build a lasting house if given decayed wood, or the plasterer perfect ceilings if given slaked, or dead, instead of quick, or live lime, just so nature can not renew your body and make it immune to disease if you give her the carcasses or corpses of long dead animals as the material to rebuild you body with. But if, instead of this stupendous stupidity, you are one of the elect, one of the illuminated ones, and so supply your body with the fruit of the 'tree of life', which was the fruit of primitive man, the food that enabled him to see the rising sun for hundreds of years, the food to which his organs were adapted from the beginning, and are still adapted today — if you supply Mother Nature with the fruit of the 'tree of life', then she will rebuild for you, a sound and healthy body, resistant to disease, and capable of retaining youth and will prolong the life-span far beyond the century mark.

Now, paraphrasing from the words of Christ, let me say: He who supplies his body with decaying building material, shall be likened unto a foolish man that built his house upon the sand; and the rain descended and floods came, and the winds blew and beat upon the house; and it fell; and great was the fall of it.

But those who are supplying their bodies with the fruit from the 'tree of life' and eat it pure and undestroyed by fire, I will liken unto the man who built his house upon a rock — the rock of truth and natural living: And the rain descended, and the floods came, and the wind blew, and beat upon the house; and it fell not; for it was founded upon a rock.

There is no reason why we should be frightened because we lose weight during an unfired food diet. In the first place, we are losing poisonous filth, and diseased and decaying tissue. Even though we did not lose it through the eating of natural living food, we would lose it eventually through any of the many febrile diseases, like influenza, typhoid fever, pneumonia, etc., provided that we did not develop before this, a bad case of hardening of the arteries and die suddenly through the rupture of a blood vessel in the delicate tissues of the brain, or perhaps of heart failure. However, thinness, unless it comes from some diseased condition, means long life.

Those of you who have been living on uncooked food for sometime, may have noticed that as you lose weight, you are gaining in strength and health. If you are not, then you are not living properly or something is wrong with your digestive machinery, and it needs a rest.

When the weather is cold and one has not the proper amount of animal heat, one ought not to introduce into his stomach one to three pounds of cold, fresh fruits and vegetables at a temperature of 60 degrees or less, and thus chill his blood and delay the digestion of his food for two or three hours, or until the blood has heated his food to a temperature of 98 degrees. Therefore, in cold weather, it is advantageous to heat your food and eat it hot. Do this, and you will see and notice a great difference.

Let me recapitulate the most important points:

1. We have seen that the immediate cause of disease consists of retained poisonous waste matter in the form acids and toxins deposited in the cells and tissues of the body.
2. We have seen that as soon as the intake of these poisons is discontinued and nature is given the proper material — in the form of fresh, uncooked fruits and vegetables — she begins at once to purify the body, and the process of disolving and eliminating this morbid waste matter is established.
3. We have also seen that the weight lost is mostly water which was keeping in solution, the sodium chloride, and other toxins.
4. We have seen that the loss of weight is absolutely indispensable in the process of renewing and regenerating the diseased tissue.
5. We have seen that strength and endurance should increase continously, unless you are fasting or undergoing a healing crisis.
6. We have seen that thin people are the ones that live longest and the ones whom epidemics (like influenza) spare.
7. Finally, we have seen that through proper food, eaten as nature meant every living creature to eat it, (uncooked) and through other factors of vital importance, the body can be regenerated, youth restored and retained and the life−span prolonged far beyond 100 years.

You should not be discouraged if sometimes you do not feel well during these healing crises. Remember that as the sun shines brighter after the storm, just so you will feel new invigoration after those periods of lassitude. But persevere to the end, for he who perseveres to the end shall get rid of his pains and be compensated with happiness and long life. Continue to the end, for it is the only way to health.

Whatever happens do not give up, for, after the healing crisis is over, you will experience new delights. I know this because I have lived it. Even after we have regained health, we can still keep improving — ever surpassing our present state of health. I have surpassed many difficulties. I am still surpassing my present state of health every day. What I have done others have done before me. These very things you can do yourself. It is possible to regenerate the body and push back the hands of the clock of Father Time. For it is not the rising and setting of the sun, or the revolutions of the Earth (which we call days and years) that makes our body grow old. It is the waste products accumulated in the tissues that hardens them and makes them stiff and old. Let us get rid of these old deposits at any cost and we will attain such a high degree of happiness that we never before thought that it could exist.

Theophilo De La Torre

RAW FOODIST MISTAKES
(AND OTHER NEW AGE BLUNDERS)

This section is sympathetically dedicated to all those who have ever given a skin-brush treatment to a friend with poison ivy, and to those who have left the evils of civilization behind in search of a new life as a fruitarian in Antarctica.

In the almost three years that I have been a raw foodist, I made many mistakes. Mistakes which could have been avoided if someone wiser and more experienced than myself had but shown me the way. Alas, it was my destiny to go it alone. I learned the hard way. Like the time I mixed potato and watermelon juice together. After a quart of that, my stomach ached horribly. At the time, I thought it was just a cleansing reaction. And the time I ran the 600-yard dash while holding a 16 oz wheatgrass juice implant. That was a hard lesson, too. I guess I just never took the time to sit down and read up on these things. Experience was my teacher. Slowly, I learned the ins and outs of being a raw foodist.

I can sit back and laugh about it now. I remember when I used to think Aloe Vera was just a "hip" salutation -- a cheap imitation of Gary Grant greeting Vera Miles. Every time I greeted the cashier at the food coop, she'd put this gooey cactus in my grocery bag.

What I'm trying to say is that these mistakes can be avoided if pointed out ahead of time. And so I've compiled a short list of pitfalls to watch out for -- so you'll know beforehand if you're headed towards making a Raw Foodist Mistake or other New Age Blunder, such as:

1. Having a full stomach and gas, and going to a chiropractor.
2. When pausing from hitch-hiking cross country, eating a 20 lb. watermelon then catching a long distance ride.
3. Choosing a career in football.
4. Doing yoga with a table on your back immediately after eating five pounds of dried avocados.
5. Trying to dry avocados.
6. Going to an iridologist with sunglasses on.
7. Drinking cherry juice for the runs.
8. Starting an uplifting "Om" chant with your friends in a public library.
9. Eating 12 ginseng roots right before bedtime.
10. Doing an enema with ice water.
11. Going on a word fast while serving on jury duty.
12. Breaking a forty day water fast with guacamoli and dried bananas.
13. Wearing skis to a foot reflexology session.
14. Delivering a speech on "The Benefits of Eating Raw Foods" at a meeting of the American Cattlemen's Association.
15. Tie-dyeing your father's favorite business suit with beet juice (because you thought he'd like it).
16. Eating three-week old seed cheese.
17. Thinking a Healing Festival is a place where you get your shoes

repaired.
18. Trying to become a breatharian in New York City.
19. Sitting down to a nice, big raw Lobelia salad.
20. Squeezing that unripe avocado 203 times a day, until it's finally bruised enough to eat.

Michael Cooper, Dulzura, California

COLDS FOR HEALTH

All of us are familiar with the symptoms of the common cold. Among these are sneezing, runny nose, and stuffed−up head, often accompanied by a fever. Generally, this is what is known as a "head cold". Then there is the other variety, the sore throat, the cough, the aching lungs. This type may also be accompanied by a fever. This is known as the "chest cold". They exist all over the world, affect all races, classes and are present in every climate. Colds are usually not very serious, but they are very expensive. In the United States alone, it is estimated that colds cost up to five billion dollars annually including loss of efficiency and loss of time from work by people suffering from the common cold.

There are many reasons given for the cause of the common cold. The following are some of the common misconceptions: colds are an infection caused by germs, parasites and viruses; colds are caused by extreme changes in the temperature. The phrase "catching a cold" indicates that people believe they can give one another colds. Mental shocks are frequently followed by colds. Pollution is also frequently blamed for being a contributor to colds. There are some logical basis for these theories. The germ theory can be supported by the fact that colds seem to go through families. Extreme temperature changes may cause the contraction of the nasal mucosa and cracks in the nasal mucosa enables the bacteria to enter the organism. However, there isn't a common germ, virus, or bacteria for the common cold. All of these theories deal with superficial explanations of symptoms and not the origin.

There is a common denominator: colds are the result of excess mucous built up within the lungs and lymphatic system. Mucous is a natural, clear, viscous secretion found in the gonads, intestines and respiratory tract. It protects the tissues from irritation by strong acids and/or bases. Muco−proteins react with the acid or base, coagulating its mucous into white dense secretions which are absorbed into the lymphatic system. When observing a non−congestive diet, the small amount of secretions generated is easily broken down into simple components and recycled or excreted. However, when the body's resistance has been lowered by a high stress life style and diet is badly chosen, it results in a daily build up of mucus. In this toxic state, the body will be affectd by such things as drafts, extreme temperature changes, polluted air, exposure to germs, viruses and bacteria. The toxic condition is the result of incomplete metabolism of inappropriately chosen food in the intestines. Overeating of natural food can also predispose the body to be affected by colds because this brings on indigestion and constipation. **Improper** eating is another contributing factor. Examples of this are: too much of any one food such as proteins, sugar, dairy products, starches and concentrated foods; an acid condition in the stomach which can come from concentrated intake of protein, fat and/or starch, from bad food combinations such as starch and protein, starch and acid such as bakery products mixed with citrus, tomato or vinegar in the same meal; processed foods; fluids taken with a meal (especially milk, which hydrochloric acid in the stomach curds in large balls that can take one to three days to digest). Excess protein, especially of diary origin, will leave a residue in the prostate and gonads, as well as in the respiratory tract thereby predisposing one to a painful **menstrual discharge.**

An easy way to demonstrate the relationship of diet and colds is to stay away from all dairy products for three weeks, then have some cheese or a glass of milk. Within minutes all the symptoms of a cold will develop — congested chest, catarrah in the throat, sinus aches, etc...Most people are unable to tolerate a limited amount of such foods, once they have lowered their vitality.

When a build up of mucous reaches a high level where it can interfere with life processes, then a 'cold' can result. When exposed to stressful situations, cold weather or overwork, the body constricts. After the removal of the stress, some lung cavities of the body become shut off from circulation due to failure of the glued up capillaries to return back to former condition. To open them up, the body's intelligence builds up a fever (to cause expansion and return normal circulation). At the same time, leukocyte level goes up tremendously. With their high enzyme concentration mucus can be dissolved. Studies show that blood and urine enzyme level goes up many times during fever. There are some germs (we always have some in our body) in these isolated capillary cavities that start to multiply rapidly at the rate of one multiplication every twelve minutes. Every twenty-four hours 2,000 million new germs will be produced from a single original germ.

Furthermore, with the fever, leukocytes and phyagocytes are able to reach into these areas to attack and destroy the germs by way of enzyme action. The mucous is eaten up by them until it is a liquid secretion which can be discharged through our eliminative organs, specifically the lungs by means of phlegm and cough. Also the urine becomes dark yellow, defecation frequent and loose and the skin — offensive in smell and sweaty.

Colds should be thought of as a cleansing process instead of disease or illoness. Disease never develops if during colds everything is done to encourage elimination. Unfortunately, this is not so for most people. Cold remedies fill the shelves of our drug stores, supermarkets and medicine cabinets. The supply and variety seem endless. In seeking relief from the uncomfortable symptoms of the common cold Americans spend one quarter of a billion dollars a year. This figure applies to only the over-the-counter medications which include pills, nose drops, sprays, cough syrups, cough suppressants, cough expectorants, etc... Antihistamines are often used in addition to these medications. Their primary function is to shrink the mucous membranes of the nose and sinuses. All this does is temporarily dry up the nasal secretions. Added to the long list of medications is the old stand-by, the aspirin. At the onset of a cold, most people take two aspirins routinely every four hours. After all, "it's what doctors recommend the most", as we often hear on television commercials. Aspirins have an analgesic effect and they do relieve the pain symptoms. But this relief is slight and temporary. Then, there are the prescription drugs which can only be ordered by physicians. These are prescribed for the more severe colds. New developments in pharmacology have brought us anti-biotics. One of these is penicillin, considered by many a "miracle drug" for the treatment of colds or the flu. It is a powerful agent and can fight many infections. Today, it is prescribed indiscriminately for colds and infections of the respiratory tract. Now, the body not only has the cold to contend with, but it must rid itself of the drug. Penicillin can become very toxic for some people. They may develop a sensitivity to it and are never able to use it again. Penicillin allergy may vary from mild skin rashes, to sudden death from anaphylactic shock. There are hundreds of documented cases of deaths attributed to penicillin injections. Here, the treatment is worse than the disease, yet antibiotics are a big-business today. The laboratory assembly lines continue to produce and market these dangerous drugs in ever increasing volume.

In brief, medical science has not found a cure for the common cold. The relief from "colds" comes from either enervating the body and suppressing this cleansing process leading to long term build up of waste, or letting the cold work itself through until the toxins are eliminated from the body. At such time, the cold symptoms will subside. This will be as spontaneous as the onset of the cold.

Once one has acquired a cold there are several measures that can be taken to encourage elimination. The body must be allowed to get rid of its impurities without outside interference. Natural treatment is always the most effective way to avoid complications. The proper treatment is to cleanse the system. When a cold appears, give a laxative and wash out the colon with a warm water enema. Repeat until the alimentary canal is free from waste.

To speed up detoxification, all ingestion of food should be stopped until the cold is gone. The mechanics of elimination and cure of cold can be stopped by eating solid food in excessive amounts. This will lead to further burdening of the system and mucous build up. As the years advance this mucous build up is the basis of many degenerative diseases. Drinking warm water, vegetable broth and/or diluted fruit juices is desirable. Hot baths will increase perspiration and bring blood to the skin. This is helpful in getting rid of poisons through the pores. There are some people who find it helpful to engage in exercises, such as walking or working to increase perspiration. For most people, though, bed rest with plenty of fresh air seems beneficial. Massages of the entire spine as well as soles of the feet increase circulation and help return the blood to normalcy. Following these simple yet effective measures, recovery should occur within two or three days.

In order to avoid clogging up our body with mucous and wastes, there are simple dietary measures we can follow. There are some foods that contribute to poisoning our bodies and should be avoided. We should avoid refined white flour products (these are poor food), sugar products, ice cream, cakes, cookies, pies, and candies. Wheatgerm is absent in white flour, and neither are the vitamins and organic mineral salts present. Fried foods should definitely be avoided since they are not digestible and generate a high level of mucous. Keep away from jellies, jams and preserves because they produce abnormal fermentation. They also leave excessive amounts of gas in the stomach and this helps generate mucous. Also, these foods do not contain vitamins.

Eating meat or excessive vegetarian protein foods results in formation of large amounts of digestive acids which induce abnormal amounts of mucus. Uric acid particularly is very damaging; this builds up and crystallizes and is one of the main causes for rheumatism. The person who consumes a lot of meat lacks power and endurance and suffers from lowered resistance, which predisposes the body to colds.

The most important foods to avoid in order to prevent colds are the dairy products. The biggest culprit among these is cow's milk. Cow's milk is food for its offspring, the calf. It contains the nutrients necessary for the growth and development of that animal. It is rich in protein and calcium. This enables the calf to grow to such tremendous size. The calcium content is three times that of human milk. It also contains excessive amounts of glucose which just turns to fat. Glucose is stored in the liver and builds up in the body tissue. The protein in cow's milk is called caseinogen. This is a sticky substance that remains in various parts of the body. This eventually causes blockage in the kidneys, the bladder, and the skin. Cow's milk is responsible for many problems, among them asthma, arthritis, obesity and the common cold. Milk is the most mucous producing food in the daily diet of Americans. It is the cause of colds, flu, bronchial troubles, sinus problems, arthritis, asthma and hayfever. It takes a tremendous amount of effort for the human body to metabolize cow's milk. As a result, milk is the cause of the mucous ailments that affect so many. Cow's milk was never intended for human consumption but for animal consumption. Avoid also tobacco, caffeine and alcohol.

There are many foods which will help us maintain good health and enable us to avoid having colds. A diet rich in B−complex vitamins, such as sprouted grains and beans, greens, seed yogurt as well as the traditional wheatgerm and yeast. Bread should be made with whole wheat flour because it contains vitamin E. Cereals should contain whole wheat and whole grains. Sweets can be obtained from fruits, honey, maple sugar. These are high in vitamin C. Make sure the fruits are fresh and not canned. Dried or evaporated fruits are an excellent substitute when fresh fruits are not available. By eating fruits in abundance, we can prevent colds. Fruits contain acid and they are the best internal systemic cleansers known. Potatoes should be boiled in their skins. Have plenty of fresh vegetables cooked in very little water so there is nothing left to drain. Cover the pot in order to retain the vitamins. Vegetables should be cooked for a short period of time to prevent excessive nutrient loss. Green and yellow vegetables are abundant in vitamin A. Raw vegetables and salad vegetables are the most desirable. One will never get a cold when eating raw foods only. All other vegetarian foods can lead to cold if the body is enervated. The raw foods normalize the bowels with their high roughage and help purify the bloodstream. With this diet, the body will obtain what it needs to avoid getting colds.

Fasting is a natural way of ridding the body of excess toxins, wastes and diseased tissue. It purifies the bloodstream. Nature heals through fasting and this is considered a miracle cure by many. All animals fast when they are sick, and chidren instinctively know this. However, Americans are preoccupied with food and we keep eating while sick which further complicates matters. We have to unlearn our bad habits.

The first thing to do before a fast is to empty the intestinal tract. At bedtime take a familiar herbal laxative (Shaklee or Dr. Christopher's L.B. are excellent) in the evening at retirement. This will empty the content of the stomach, small intestine and part of colon. After morning bowel movement, take a few warm enemas. With this preparation, a liquid diet will be a pleasure. Total fasting means no food whatsoever.

Take plenty of liquids during the fast––distilled water, diluted subacid fruit juices and/or fresh vegetable broths, melon juice, or herbal teas (peppermint, wild cherry, bayberry bark with yarrow, ginseng, ginger––no honey or sweeteners) are good. Try to use only a few mixtures for any one day. Drink distilled water or herb teas in between the juices. Try to get as much rest as possible during an extended fast and also plenty of fresh air. You will feel miserable during the fast as long as the wastes are still in your bloodstream. Once the wastes are gone, you will feel fine.

The best preventive medicine is a weekly fast to maintain good health. This can be either a twenty–four hour or thirty–six hour fast. This does not need to interfere with one's normal activities. At the end of such a fast, the foods should be raw vegetables. A day later, you may include one or two cooked non–starchy vegetables. After a couple of days, you may resume your normal diet. However, it is not advisable to eat three meals a day in between fasts. To maintain a healthy body, one or two meals a day is sufficient. Over–eating is the greatest cause of all diseases.

Fear and worry also lower the body's resistance. This makes the body susceptible to colds as well as to a variety of other diseases. Medical science is now doing a great deal of research to determine the affects that stress has on disease. Stress has been linked directly to causing colds and all psychosomatic disorders, and there may be a link between stress and cancer. So a good preventive measure to maintain general good health is to learn to think peaceful and positive thoughts by toning the ego needs and concentrating ones life on selfless service emanating from a loving heart.

Viktoras Kulvinskas, February, 1979

ARTHRITIS

Modern medicine still cannot give a specific cause for one of the oldest degenerative diseases causing extreme suffering and pain for more than 25 million Americans. The disease is called arthritis.

The term arthritis refers specifically to inflammation of the joints and can differentiate into 100 various forms. But the disease can easily be reduced into two catagories: 1) overacidity of the body, causing bone structure to alter and dissolve and 2) mucus and calcium deposits that settle in joints, resulting in dislocation of bone structures. Most arthritic conditions are a blend of these two extremes.

At one time, we were told that arthritis was a natural disorder resulting from the aging process. The theory was then revised to claim that the mysterious ailment actually seemed to be a "degenerative disease" generally plaguing older people, but with possible origins buried somewhere in youth. Today, the medical profession appears to be as confused as ever in its understanding of arthritis. But most doctors agree that disease is not limited to those in semescense, nor is age necessarily the major determining factor.

In fact, nearly 200,000 American children suffer from arthritis! John Baun, M.D. (U Rocklin) reported that more children are affected by arthritis today than were stricken by paralytic polio during any 10 year period before the polio vaccine. And arthritis is increasing in epidemic proportions. The late President Johnson, in a special message to Congress, quoted World Health Organization figures when he said, "12 million people suffer from arthritis...three out of 100 children suffer from some form of paralysis or orthopedic impairment".

So it is wonderful indeed to discover researchers who are identifying contributing factors in the widespread, painful loss or build–up of calcium. Researchers like Professor Nanna Svartx, Head of the King Gustav V Research Institute in Stockholm, who after thirty years of study, identified the cause of rheumatoid arthritis as a germ found in milk. Professor Svartz said, " Tests conducted on people suffering from rheumatoid arthritis have revealed the presence of milk bacteria in eighty percent of the cases". The Professor declared the germ was found in milk from America, Canada, and six European countries.

In 1973, Americans gulped down 735 billion pounds of pasteurized milk. But still teeth are becoming collector's items and the majority of people wear partial or full dentures. According to Dr. Albanes, Director of Nutrition, Bruke Rehabilitation Center, NYC, calcium imbalance is showing up as osteoporosis. But even though correlation of milk and arthritis is conclusive, the germ is not the causative factor. The germ exists only because of appropriate mucus fed from a dead food diet.

Dr. Francis Pottenger, Jr. studied the effects of cooked food and milk on the development of arthritis. He concluded that pasteurized milk and milk products increase blood cholesterol and cause atherosclerosis or hardening of the arteries. Pottenger said, "Male cats fed on metabolized Vitamin D milk (from cattle fed irradiated yeast) and raw meat showed osseous disturbances very like those on pasteurized milk. Young males did not live beyond the second month and adult males died within ten months. The most noticeable fact was that there is a tendency for the calcium phosphorus ratio to become unbalanced, approaching 2.5 to 1 as compared with normal of 2 to 1. The cats fed pasteurized milk as their principal item of diet, and raw meat as a partial diet, showed lessened reproductive efficiency and some skeletal changes. The most marked deficiency occurred in cats fed sweetened condensed milk". No such problems occured with cats fed a raw food diet.

Pasteurized milk also produces pyorrhea in cats and imperfect development of rats incisors. According to Dr. Pottenger, poor quality or heat treated milk caused osteoporosis and certain types of arthritis in cats and rats.

Dr. Allison G. Lane, D.D.S. in 1947 reported, "The relation of the tooth to the jaw, the dento–alveolar articulation, is similar to other joints of the body, having all the elements of other articulations, even including minute movement. Therefore, disturbances in this joint relationship may be interpretable as arthritic manifestations. Supporting this concept is the fact that chronic degenerative arthritis (hypertrophic) frequently shows typical changes of this character in the dentoalveolar articulation". Studies have shown that certain dietary faults are constant in cases of paradentosis and dental caries; frequently the two conditions are active in the same person.

Patients displaying active paradentosis show an intake of phosphorus exceeding the desired one and one–half ratio to calcium. Such excesses may appear as 1:18, in severe cases of vertical atrophy. Rarely is the phosphorous found to exceed the recommended 1.5 grams daily. The important diagnostic factor lies in the calcium-phosphorus ratio.

Some analyses will show both the calcium–phosphorus imbalance and the acid–base imbalance, and if the latter is caused by acid–ash, refined grain and sugar products in the diet, we may be confident that both dental diseases are active. In every high protein, high fat diet, with no refined carbohydrates, active dental cavities are not found. Symptoms, if any, appear in the dental–alveolar articulation. The patient experiences a sensation of looseness in one or more teeth and may note stiffness or soreness in other joints.

Rice, like all other grains, is rich in phytic acid, which traps a large amount of alkaline minerals making them unavailable for body use. The ratio of rice is 1:15, the mineral content is acid and the protein content greatly exceeds breast milk, fruit or vegetables. If such a food plays a central role in the diet, the result can be dental problems. Mango, as well as other fruits and vegetables, have a 1:13 ratio which leaves the body in a much more favorable mineral balance.

The work of Dr. R. Wulzen and co–workers made a very significant contribution to our knowledge of the destruction of an anti–stiffness factor present in unheated milk and cream. The loss of this element produces abnormal deposition of calcium in many organs and parts. They further isolated the anti–stiffness factor in plant juices.

In 1949, Ross, Van Quagtenkenk and Whulzen discovered a compound that alleviated the stiffness induced in guinea pigs on certain experimental diets. The compound was produced from cane grass juice.

At the University of Oregon, Dr. Whulzen fed guinea pigs on fat free milk diets. The animals developed joints so stiff they could not bend down to eat, and unless hand–fed, starved. The animals were fed leaves of raw chard and kale: stiff joint conditions, even the severe ones, were reversed.

Researchers further discovered that guinea pigs reared on stiffness producing diets finally became deaf. These studies, cited by Wulzen, revealed that the auditory ossicles were often deformed and sometimes embedded in hard white amorphous masses (mucus of casein origin) having the appearance of sugar candy concretation.

Harris and Whulzen described the following anatomical changes in guinea pigs reared on the stiffness–inducing diet: a peculiar type of arteriosclerosis, necrosis and calcification of the skeletal muscle and myocardium; deposition of calcium salts in the smooth muscle of the gastrointestinal tract, in kidneys and liver and development of abcesses adjacent to bones and joints that frequently became calcified.

The anti–stiff joint factor in foods was named the Whulzen factor which was later developed into a fat–soluble vitamin called stigmasterol.

Nutritionist, Betty Morales said, "It is well recognized that people consuming fresh raw vegetable juices, and a large percent of their total food intake in the form of raw vegetables, especially green leaves and root vegetables, often experience blessed relief from stiff joints, and other miseries. Without identifying the exact nutritional factor to be credited; which isn't necessary, because nutrients work together, it appears that what is now called stigmasterol plays an important part in relieving painful joints".

The Royal Society of Medicine of Great Britian made the following observation about bone disorders: "Weakness of abdominal muscles causes accumulation of feces in the pelvic colon, which renders evacuation of contents more and more difficult. Prominence of bones: rheumatic pains simulating sciatica and lumbago;

various muscular pains; muscular rheumatism; arthritis deformities; arthritis, acute and chronic".

The subject of alimentary toxemia was also discussed by the Royal Society of Medicine. The following is a list of poisons of alimentary intestinal toxemia; indol, skarol, phenol, cresol, indican, ammonia, sulphuretted hydrogen, histidine, indican, urrobilin, methylmercaptan, tetramerphy–lendiamin, pentamethy, lendiamine, putrescin, cacaverin, neurin, cholin, muscarine, byturic acid, bera–imidazolethy–lamine, methylgandinine, ptomarrophine, botulin, tyramine, agamatine, sepsin, tryptophane, idolethylamine and sulpherroglobine. One or several of these poisons are constantly bathing the delicate body cells and setting up charges that eventually cause serious disease.

Throughout our lives, we build up inorganic sedimentary deposits in tissues, blood and lymph vessels and eliminative organs of the body. There's a mountain in the water you drink. In your lifetime, you can consume approximately 450 pounds of inorganic minerals from some tap and well water. This sediment could settle in your vital organs like it did in grandma's teakettle, causing all kinds of trouble. Distilled water is the only answer to remove all impurities. At birth a baby is about 75% water; by the time the infant is 30 years old, the percentage of water in the body is about 55%. The water was displaced by the accumulation of precipitated minerals.

According to government figures, over fifty percent of tap water fails to meet minimum standards. The purification process for tap water introduces 20 to 60 new chemicals into your drink. Sodium fluoride (rat poison) acts as an enzyme inhibitor, causing or intensifying alergies, kidney–liver–thyroid–bone damage, or affecting the newborn and causing mottling of teeth. Chlorine (bleach) destroys cells and prematurely ages the body. Additives and pollutants in water are one of the causes of toxemia.

The "pure" water from spring, lake, river, well or running stream is one of the major factors in producing the cemented joints of arthritis, gall and kidney stones and hardening of the arteries and the brain. It is physiologically impossible for your body to assimilate inorganic minerals in building healthy tissues and blood. Calcium carbonate (lime) and other minerals will cement your body. Were it not for the activity of the eliminative organs, most people, by the age of forty, would accumulate enough cement in their bodies to become statues.

Distilled water, although preferable to other water, has a slight tendency to leech calcium and other nutrients from teeth, bones and cells. To prevent leeching, expose water to sunlight for several hours, and/or use colored drinking glasses. Or soak dried or fresh fruit (or vegetables) or crushed grass overnight, to introduce nutrients into dead distilled water and convert it to live juice. Such water will help flush out accumulated poisons from the bloodstream and cells.

When buying distilled water, be sure that it does not come in plastic bottles...the plastic gives a plastic taste and do not buy chemically distilled water; find a source that used stainless steel and glass distilled apparatus. Get a complete analysis of the water, whatever the source. Most companies are happy to provide this information. Tap water is completely unnatural and is necessitated only by a concentrated acid–forming diet. Natural foods like fresh fruits and vegetables contain at least 90% energy–charged tasty fluid. That's all the water that our bodies really need.

Dr. Ann Wigmore of Hippocrates Health Institute said, "I went through the experience at the age of fifty where I was almost hopelessly crippled with disease and was ready for the heap. At that time I had to find the cause. My problem was a great liking for cheese, coffee and sweets. Today I am arthritis free but if I eat only a small bit of cheese I can feel its clogging effect. Folks that like dairy products will have arthritis, gallstones, asthma, constipation or skin problems".

If you do suffer from rheumatic arthritis Dr. Wigmore suggests that you do not waste time with treatment — — it can be very painful and dangerous. Try "Nature's Way" to help the body free itself from the wastes. Eat only living food, organically grown, and use manipulation and heat therapy. Remember that it takes time to eliminate arthritis, especially when the deposits are collected in the joints. Apply moist heat to the affected area and relax. Especially important is a good daily enema followed by a chlorophyll implant.

Dr. F.M. Pottenger suggests that eating raw food is the only answer for curing arthritis. And Dr. Donald Gerber at the New York Rheumatism Foundation stated, "Rheumatoid arthritis could be the result of faulty protein metabolism...a low protein diet might alleviate the problem". Drs. Leven and Butin of the Central Scientific Institution of Nutrition, Moscow, recommends a diet entirely composed of raw vegetables for a short period in the treatment of arthritis.

Raw cherry juice was successfully used to treat an arthritic conditon known as gout. An excess of uric acid in the body is a main symptom of gout. Dr. Ludwig W. Blau treated a dozen people by giving them freshly squeezed cherry juice as well as raw, uncooked cherries. He said, "no attacks of the gouty arthritis occured on a non–restricted diet in all twelve cases, as a result of eating (the equivalent in juice form) about one–half pound of fresh cherries per day". Dr. Blau also reported that he obtained the best results from sour, black, Royal Anne and fresh Black Bing cherries. Enzymes in the cherries appear to have some influence in relieving the pain of arthritis.

Similar studies on guinea pigs were reported in the annual Review of Biochemistry in 1944: "Guinea pigs fed raw milk with an addition of skim milk powder, copper and iron salts, carotene, and orange juice, grew well and showed no abnormalities at autopsy. When pasturized whole milk was used, deficiency symptoms began to appear, wrist stiffness being the first sign. The substitution of skim milk for whole milk intensified the deficiency which was characterized by great emaciation and weakness before death...At the autopsy the muscles were found to be extremely atrophied, and closely packed fine lines of calcification ran parallel to the muscle fibers. Calcification also occurred in other parts of the body. When cod liver oil replaced carotene in the diet, paralysis quickly developed. The feeding of raw cream cured the wrist stiffness".

A British medical journal reported: "Probably pasteurization's worst offense is that it makes insoluble the major part of the calcium contained in raw milk. This frequently leads to rickets, bad teeth, and nervous troubles, for sufficient calcium content is vital to children; and with the loss of phosphorus, also associated with calcium, bone and brain formation suffer serious setbacks".

A study conducted in 1955 showed that rats died when they were forced to sustain on a diet of heated milk (even below the pasteurization point). Rats fed only raw milk survived and were healthy. In this experiment, researchers were testing to see if a essential amino acid, Lysine, was damaged by heat. The tests concluded that little damage was done to Lysine, but it was of no nutritional value because it could not be assimilated by the rats. The physiological unavailability of Lysine was caused by the almost total destruction of the enzyme in milk.

The underlying cause of arthritis may be overacidity of the body due to toxemia or to long periods of stress. Overacidity causes dissolution of bone calcium. This calcium, plus ingested inorganic minerals, are carried by the bloodstream and deposited in areas of poor circulation.

Mucus from processed bakery and pasteurized dairy products (wheat gluten and milk casein used to manufacture some of the most potent water-resistant glues) deposit on blood vessel walls and tissues thereby clogging blood vessels which causes a decrease in blood velocity.

Cooking or heating converts organic materials in plants into inorganic minerals. Since inorganic minerals are highly insoluble, they enter the bloodstream in unassimilable form and tend to deposit in areas of slow blood velocity (highly congested tissues).

Organic sodium has the property of increasing the solubility of inorganic calcium. Some of the best sources of organic sodium are lemon, grapefruit, spinach, celery and dandelion. Carrots and wheatgrass make excellent juices. Wheatgrass juice will produce quick minimization of pain. Try to consume at least one quart of juice daily. Extraneous calcium and other minerals will be filtered out of the body by the kidney and excreted in the urine.

In his sanitorium in Switzerland, Dr. Bircher–Benner, M.D., claims to have had great success with the raw food diet in cases of arthritis, diabetes, asthma and ulcers. Dorothy C. Hare, M.D. has also described successful experiments in treating arthritis with raw foods.

To become and remain free from arthritis, processed foods must be eliminated from the diet. At the initial phase of regeneration there may be periods of increased pain and stiffness and/or its appearance in new areas due to circulation in an increased amount of minerals released by the dietary regime. Many arthritics have reported freedom from pain after following the live food and juice diet for only a few weeks.

Since over–mineralization is evident in most forms of arthritis, eliminating inorganic minerals from drinking and cooking water is essential. Drink four ounces of distilled water every hour to assist the body in dissolving the extraneous minerals. For a one week duration, a juice fast followed by daily enemas must be undertaken. Follow this regime by a two week period of a mucus-lean diet of raw and lightly steamed vegetables.

During the days of your fast, the following juices should be consumed: 16 ounces of grapefruit, 10 ounces of carrot, 6 ounces of spinach, 16 ounces of celery, 9 ounces of carrot, 7 ounces of celery, 10 ounces of carrot, 3 ounces of beet and 3 ounces of cucumber. The juices most recommended are ones from greens, potatoes, fresh, non–starchy 6–8 day old sprouts (no lentil, mung, chick or soy sprouts), celery, carrots and red beets, but all greens are extremely beneficial. The juices should be taken at intervals of at least one hour between servings. You may drink herbal teas on alternate hours, but use only distilled water. The teas of slippery elm, comfrey, alfalfa, parsley, cayenne, and burdock are most recommended.

For your diet to be most beneficial, add one tablespoon to one ounce or more of grass juice depending on your tolerance to all the juices. A fantastic green juice can be made from non starchy sprouts, indoor greens, sweet vegetables. One of the most exciting raw food programs is structured in the book "Light Eating for Survival", by Marcia Acciardo. Ms. Acciardo stressed healthy, healing foods that are also tasty.

During your juice fast, it is extremely important to take a daily enema preferably in the morning after your normal bowel movement. The enemas can be followed by retention enemas of grass juice, or other green juices, as well as herbal teas such as alum root, red rasberry or white oak bark.

While fasting for three to seven days, allow yourself plenty of rest and be sure that there is someone who can look after you if you need help. At least twice a day take hot and cold showers to increase your blood circulation. Also, sweat baths are very important. Drink a cup of pleurisy or yarrow tea and then take a good sweat bath. If you have difficulty eliminating, massage and zone therapy can be helpful.

Follow the juice with a light diet of raw and steamed vegetables. In several weeks, repeat the juice fast. Throughout your entire regime, remember that it is very important for dissolving calcium to have an abundance of sunlight. (Sunlight supplies Vitamin D and keeps calcium in solution). Also keep your skin in good condition by brushing and taking daily air baths.

For quick elimination of pain from arthritis, apply a poultice of crushed wheatgrass to the affected area, the pain will generally be alleviated in several hours.

Viktoras Kulvinskas, March, 1979

WHAT'S THERE TO EAT?

The food supply has been shut off, the markets are bare, it is in the heat of a dry summer, and there is no water for gardens. No wheat grass seeds are available — the rats ate them all. What are you going to eat?? Roots, leaves, wild berries and seeds? Which ones are edible? What water is safe for drinking?
Answer: Use the B.R.T.
What is the B.R.T.?
The B.R.T. is short for the 'Brain Response Test'. It is a simple and highly accurate test of any and all nutrition going into your body through your mouth, skin, ears, or eyes. By careful analysis when testing one specific muscle—nerve grouping, you can determine whether what you are eating will make you healthy or sick. Your brain knows if the food, the root, the leaf, or the water is good for you as an individual.

Even if the above emergency situation never arises, you can use the B.R.T. in your everyday life to determine which foods are best for you, which foods will harm you, and which foods will actually help you to be healthier and happier!

How can you use the B.R.T. to do all of this? Follow directions carefully — and try! In order to obtain accurate results, accurate methodology is important.

Imperative! Rules of Conduct!

a. If possible, dress in white or brown cotton (including underclothing). Black is acceptable, although not as good.
b. Test in a room of very light colors: again, white is best. Avoid fluorescent lights and do not look at bright colors. Testing outside in natural surroundings is also good.
c. Avoid noises. Music or distracting people can influence testing.
d. Absolutely no food or gum in the mouth (unless you are testing that food).
e. No tight—fitting synthetic garments. Remove all metal jewelry, including large metal buckles, metal—rimmed eye glasses, rings, etc. No high heels. For the sake of educational interests, you can test with the harmful clothing on and then off — show your friends the difference. (Note that if one refuses to help oneself, by not wearing the harmful objects, test with them on).
f. Deodorants, perfumes, and powders are usually harmful — it is best to take a good shower before being tested.
g. The emotional and physical health of the testor should be good.
h. Always take into consideration any structural weakness or injury.
i. Your friend must always face straight ahead with the face and eyes while being tested.
j. If your friend is too weak, too old, too young, or for any other reason cannot be using their arm effectively, use a surrogate. (See "How to Take Care of Yourselves Naturally", or "Which Vitamin?")
k. Meditate for twenty seconds on being mild in all your ways.

Always think positive, mild, loving and be neutral as to what you are testing!

Testing Procedures for the Brain Response Test

The procedures are given for testing your friend's left arm. The right arm must also be tested.

Both you and your friend stand with your feet firmly placed about one foot apart. Face each other's left shoulder, not squarely at each other.

Your left palm is placed firmly on your friend's right shoulder in order to stabilize it and provide a good circuit. His right arm is at present hanging free.

No finger tips are pointing at or touching any part of either of your bodies. No fist or curled fingers; all hands are open and flat. Your friend's left wrist will be fully flexed whenever testing.

Your friend's left arm is carefully aligned. First raise it straight out to the side, palm down. Next bring it forward 30 degrees and down 30 degrees. Keep the arm straight. This is the "Brain Response Test Position" (BRT).

Place your right palm on the top center of your friend's left wrist. (Wet your palm for better electrical conduction.) Keep your friend's flexed wrist cupped in your palm.

Press gently on your friend's wrist while he resists. You are not trying to overpower each other, nor to pull muscles. Be gentle. Practice testing, resisting several times until you work as a team.

Resist with exactly the same effort each time. Do not vary your resistance nor your pressure!

Practice — say 'Hold' and press down firmly, gently, and smoothly for one second, with just enough pressure to move the arm 3/4". You will note that his arm will instantly respond and 'lock' in position (if he is in a reasonably healthy condition). With most people this pressure will be from ten to twenty pounds. This is an art — use keen perception! Test many times. Do not hold the arm in this position too long because your friend will tire easily. If his arm is very weak in this position, massage for thirty seconds, one inch under his navel, and both of you roll your heads around in a large circle — ten times clockwise and ten times counter–clockwise, slowly. If his arm is still weak, check for foods, colors, or clothing that is harmful, or after–shave lotion, deodorants, etc. A vigorous rolling of the shoulders is also advantageous sometimes.

While both remaining in this position, take your right hand and with all your fingers pointing straight at your friend, pass your hand from the groin to the chin. Then place your hand gently again on the left wrist and retest. Do this smoothly, gracefully and quickly (approximately 3–4 seconds for the entire swing). The purpose of this is to temporarily over–strengthen the stato–acoustic cranial nerve (Central Vessel in acupressure terminology). This is the procedure for the 'Overstrong BRT Test.'

Again, while both of you are remaining in this BRT position, take your right hand and with all of your fingers pointing straight at your friend, pass your hand from the chin to the groin. Then place your hand gently again on the left wrist and retest. This will test to see if the arm will weaken correctly. If the arm does not weaken during this test, the throat plexus (chakra) is out of balance.

If your friend weakens during the overstrong test, or does not weaken for the throat plexus (chakra) test, have him roll his head as described earlier and think about being mild for thirty seconds. Always recheck to be sure of the correction. If you are unable to make proper correction, use a surrogate or try testing some other day. A competent Biokinesiologist may be able to aid you in understanding your problem.

After being sure that you are 'working' in the clear (i.e. the arm responds strong, strong, weak in the three–step test), you are ready to proceed in testing foods. Place the foods and food supplements very near so that you do not need to change positions in order to reach the item to be tested.

You must carefully prepare foods and food supplements before testing. All foods must be clean, and presented in the form in which you eat them. No banana peels, uncooked rice, or unsprouted seeds. All food supplements and most foods should be put into clean plastic bags (baggies are preferred) when testing on the cheek or the navel. One food per bag: use small quantities. All liquids can be carefully sealed in two such bags.

Your friend will now place the food or food supplement in any of three locations:

1. In the mouth (if this is chosen, then carefully wash out the mouth with clean, nondistilled, nonchlorinated water in between each test).

2. On the cheek near the upper wisdom teeth (the location of the parotid gland).

3. On the navel.

Each of these locations has a high degree of sensitivity to all types of nutrition. This is not true of any other point on the body, according to our years of research.

When holding nutrition on points two or three, your friend must use only the fingers to hold the nutrition to himself — not the palm, nor the fingertips. Scrupulous care must be exercised that the fingers do not point towards any part of the body. Hold the nutrition on the body for ten seconds before testing.

You now proceed with the BRT. Do the basic BRT test (step 1). Does your friend's arm respond just as strong? Weaker? Or much stronger? If very slightly weaker, the brain is responding that this nutrition is harmful. It is causing an imbalance in the body. Remember that authorities are often paid to make their statements. The brain has your best welfare at heart. Your built—in computer is highly accurate. If strong, do the Overstrong test. If the arm is now weak, the nutrition is also harmful. Last of all, do the Throat Plexus Test. If it weakens, all is well. If you desire to throw a slight emotional test at the same time, ask audibly, 'Do you have a problem?' just before each test. This will occasionally weaken the arm if the nutrition is poor. Always repeat the test on both arms!

It is very important to recheck whenever in doubt. Practice! Practice! Practice! You will notice that most food supplements will fail when using the BRT and Overstrong tests with both arms. This is why so many people do not feel better even though taking vitamins or herbs. There is a difference in quality! Test to be sure! Your health and your service to your creator can be at stake.

Points to Remember

1. Always press with the same pressure.
2. Always resist with exactly the same pressure.
3. Always follow through with the pressure. (If the arm goes down, press it all the way down.)
4. Try to isolate the arm muscle that you are resisting with — do not incorporate additional muscles.
5. If testing is not working — check the 'throat plexus' mentioned earlier — or you may be resisting with too much force. It is not a battle of force, but a sensitive difference that you are looking for.
6. Have you properly isolated yourselves as to color, odors, clothing, noise, etc.?
7. Deviation from the prescribed testing procedures can lead you to wrong answers.
8. Asking questions of the near or distant future is misusing our wonderfully created brain—body responses.
9. Exercise loving kindness towards all those that you are working with — be patient.
   From dire emergency to everyday living, use the BRT for a healthier happier life!

The Biokinesiology Institute, John and Margaret Barton, 6157 Coleman Creek Road, Medford, Oregon 97501

OIL FOR PEOPLE

One of the major issues confronting our society is oil. Oil prices, oil supply, oil conservation are all headline issues almost on a daily basis. Yet the emphasis on the thick black gook used to run machines surprises me when there is little concern for the oil we use to run our bodies. Proper oiling and lubrication is vital to proper functioning and performance of the human physiological machine too! As is the case with petroleum products, there are many grades of edible oils, with corresponding benefits or detriments. The truth is that most Americans are certain to properly oil their cars and machines but have not been able to extend that sense of proper maintenance to their physiological machines.

The human body uses oil for lubrication too. The oils we ingest fall into two basic categories; polyunsaturates or hydrogenated fats. The polyunsaturate is the quality oil. Polyunsaturates have "open spaces" in their chemical structures which enable them to link up with nutrients and transport the nutrients to the cells. The hydrogenated oils, originally had that same chemical openness (if from a vegetable source) to transport, but adding hydrogen to the oil (hence hydrogenization) fills up these spaces. Hydrogenated oil is stable, uniform in color and smell but not a good lubricant. Would you mix a little cement in with your motor oil?

Oils, aside from lubrication, can be a source of important nutrients. According to Adele Davis (294) there are three essential fatty acids (EFA) found principally in oils or oil sources. Top on the body's priority list is linoleic acid. The three best sources of linoleic acid are safflower oil, sesame seeds and sunflower seeds (eat the seeds and get the oil at the same time). Linoleic acid and the other EFA are required to produce lecithin. Lecithin should be produced by the body! Lecithin should not have to be taken in whole from outside sources. Polyunsaturate oils with EFA unaltered will cut down on the cholesterol level in the body. Cholesterol is caused by unbroken fats in the body. You either clean your carborator with a good oil that assists lecithin production or else you clog your tubes with bad oil and then try to find a source of lecithin to clean out. Additionally, experiments in animals deficient in EFA have resulted in poor growth patterns, skin diseases and shortened life spans (291). While other studies have linked development of brain tissues with a need for long–chain polyunsaturate oils.

In its original stage, vegetable oil is polyunsaturated not hydrogenized. Before processing the oil it is rich in nutrients. Hydrogenizing and refining the oils is not a necessity. It is a process born of mother money and mother marketability rathar than mother love.

Today oil is produced chiefly in three ways: cold or hydrolic press, expeller press or solvent extraction. The most common method used is solvent extractions. It is the quicker method, highest yielding method and the cheapest method which results in fat profits. However, profit and health do not always serve the same master. In the solvent process, the oil bearing material is ground, steamed and then mixed with a solvent (usually Naptha type petroleum product) which dissolves out the oil from its source, leaving a dry residue. The solvent is then separated from the oil. Completely?

No. The end products has traces of the solvent left in it. So you and your car enjoy some of the same foods like Hexone and Heptane or other Naptha compounds. You and your car can share lunches, that's cute, a real love story. Except you are suscepible to cancer while who ever heard of a cancer of the tail pipe.

Expeller pressing is not too bad. Here the oil source might be cooked and a rotating screw inside a cylinder is used to press out the oil. The friction in this process produces temperatures between 200–250 degrees unless nitrogen is used as the coolant; in this case the temperature is usually around 140–150 degrees. This amount of heat does damage to Vitamin E, A and EFA. Expeller pressed oils can be labeled cold press, even though the process produces heat.

Cold press should refer to simple hydraulic pressing. No heat, just pressure. True cold pressed oils are the only premium oils. They are rich in Vitamin E, A and EFA. An oil labeled "virgin press" or "hydraulic press" is the only true cold press unaltered oil.

Another fate that awaits oil is the refining process. Manufacturers try to give the consumer a totally clear, uniformly colored, bland oil. Refining the oil for the obviously refined consumer eliminates the unneeded extravagance of chlorophyll, lecithin, phosphorous compounds, Vitamin E, A and those awful essential fatty acids. However extraneous these materials are to the consumer, they are nature's way of preventing rancidity in her oil. So, now the manufacturer must add preservatives to his refined oil or else sell rancid oil. But how can you tell rancid oil from non–rancid oil if it all tastes, smells and looks the same? "Ha, ha" smiles the efficiency expert at the big oil producing plant. The ability to sell bad oil reduces company losses. So, let the buyer beware. On the other hand, unrefined oil that has turned rancid will almost knock you out if you taste even one drop.

Mother nature's original, unheated, unrefined oil is really the only oil you should run in your engine. Unless you plan to undergo engine overhaul, develop clogged fuel lines or leave cholesterol deposits in your carborator — use only the best. Take it from the pros who aren't trying to slip one by you. Using cold pressed premium oil not only cuts down on engine wear but actually provides some of the basics for longer life. You can even cut out the middle men. Go right to the source — mother nature with her long line of natural oil sources like olives, sunflower seeds, sesame seeds, avocados, etc. Happy motoring to all.

THE MENSTRUAL MYTH
IS MENSTRUATION NECESSARY TO HEALTH AND FERTILITY?

The human race is at the threshold of regaining the sense of balance and harmony that has been our destiny. Love is the key to the universe and is the threshold of understanding we must achieve to put our lives and planet back into balance. The way in which we define and act out love is changing. Sex as intimate emotional expression and as an agent of the creative force within is being reevaluated. Reproduction, sexual energy and the cycles of nature that relate to the primal life energy, give rise to new human potentials.

Menstruation is one of the most misunderstood cycles that exist today. It has not always existed. It does not exist in all modern societies. It has a definite negative effect on all women and is not necessary for ovulation, i.e. fertility. My research shows a significant decrease in the presence of the menstrual cycle in women following diets of live foods and "natural" lifestyles. I feel that a "natural foods" diet (live foods) is a part of our heritage, and that as we seek to regain the harmony and balance of our predecessors, we must put into our bodies the raw materials as given by God.

Likewise, ovulation is a physiological process influenced by zodiacal and dietary factors; it is not a monthly biological necessity for women. We have found that by altering the influences of different factors, one can change the frequency of ovulation. (Ovulation seems to slow down, until it follows the cycle of the sun instead of the cycle of the moon.) Even in normal circumstances, ovulation does not occur on a monthly basis. It is common knowledge that many healthy women have months of menstruation without ovulation. This could not happen if there was a direct relationship between menstruation and ovulation. In addition, Menarche, which is the first phase of the menstrual cycle, generally occurs without ovulation for the initial two-year period of menstruation. The theory linking regular menstruation with the female's ability to conceive is further broken by the cases of women who have become pregnant while lactating. The concept that conception is not dependent on menstruation is a blow to current thinking and is a profound blessing to the gentle souls seeking to reach their divine potential.

MS Magazine has expressed concern as to the necessity and value of menstruation to women. The magazine published a report stating, "The fact remains that 2 out of 3 women would do away with menstruation, if it could be done safely." Many women consider menstruation a biological liability and believe that men are in a superior position because they have a more advantageous biological makeup. The desire to be free from menstruation and presumably menopause, might be interpreted as a progressive step toward liberation and an instance in which women are exercising control over their bodies."

Further research on this topic by Dr. Raymond Bernard ("Physiological Enigma of Women") states that, "Throughout nature, the biological superiority of the female is evident. Only the civilized female seems to be inferior physically to the male. This condition is brought about largely by the debilitating effect of the menstrual hemorrhage."

Because of more natural living, low protein diet and seasonal sexual practices, menses is less of a problem to the uncivilized woman.

Among many of the primitive races and in technologically undeveloped countries, females work side by side with males; many employers have shown preference for female laborers because of their superior endurance and strength.

In the United States, in spite of the menstrual and social handicap, female longevity exceeds that of the male; a larger proportion of females reach the century mark. Hardening of blood vessels and high blood pressure are more common among men than women. There are fewer miscarriages and stillbirths of females than males; the female brain has a finer texture and more complex organization, and, relative to body weight, is 25 percent heavier than that of the male; her thyroid gland, which has three lobes, is larger than the two-lobed one of the male.

During childhood, female physical size and performance in school exceeds that of the male. This phenomenon is well known to school teachers. With the onset of menstruation and the great loss of essential body fluids, the rapid development of the female is bought to a premature slowdown.

Loss of calcium, which is so essential to develop bone and muscle and to stabilize the nervous system, results in slowdown in skeletal growth. Loss of iodine, lecithin and vitamin E has a detrimental effect on brain development. Loss of hormones, which are more concentrated in menstrual discharge than in the bloodstream, speeds the aging process. Many females are anemic because the monthly hemorrhage causes a reduction of hemoglobin, the oxygen carrier. This has a significant effect on further brain development and nerve activity. Were it not for menstrual losses, the initial superiority of the female would persist in all later stages of physical development.

Historically, menstruation appeared in females after the family unit had migrated to a cooler climate and/or adopted an unnatural diet and increased sexual activity. The development of the family in an unnatural environment involved many hardships. Males very readily used the services of females to do the most unpleasant, monotonous, physically strenuous tasks, while they engaged in the arts of hunting, philosophy, war and religion. The female was the first slave of the male. Often a man kept a large flock of slave wives to perform all necessary chores.

Organized religion, with its male-dominated priesthood, has sucessfully convinced woman that she must have committed some "basic sin" (Gen. 3:6) for which she must enslave herself to the male: "Thy desire shall be to thy husband, and he shall rule over Thee"(Gen. 3:16). Centuries of inculcation of this dogma have helped to make the female subservient to the dictates of the male.

Through false medical and religious teachings on menstruation, the male-dominated society has managed to keep woman in a slave-like position by insuring her persistent weakness through biological ignorance. Men have claimed mental superiority because of a seeming deficiency in production of great works in philosophy, art or science by the female.

There were times in history when women were not suppressed, and had equal cultural, educational and economic opportunity to achieve their potential. There are instances recorded where pagan women achieved high excellence and superiority over males.

The Pythagorean school produced at least fifteen historically outstanding women. The last was Hypatia of Alexandria, who was murdered by a band of fanatic monks led by the jealous Cyrus, archbishop of Alexandria. The great Greek philosopher, Socrates, had studied under Aspasia, the young female Delphic Oracle. Ammian and Diodorus comment that the women of ancient Gaul were stronger than the males and fought the Romans. Strobo mentions that Gallic women were taller than men. Skeletal remains proved them to be seven feet tall.

Havelock Ellis remarks that all outstanding women in history were relatively free from menstruation. They either menstruated slightly or not at all as was the case with Joan of Arc, proven by medical records during her trial for witchcraft. The well–known ninety–year–old Frenchwoman, Ninon de L'Enclos, who continued to look like a young woman to the end, freed herself from menstruation through a special diet. Wallace states: "Some females of robust constitution and right fiber are called viragoes. These, from constitution, menstruate sparingly or not at all."

In our culture many pathological states are considered natural just because they are normal and prevalent. For example, it is "natural" to die from heart attack; doctors predict that by the year 2000 one of the most "natural" causes of death will be cancer. Actuarial reports state that to be at least 20 percent underweight increases health and longevity; however, doctors and friends consider slim vegetarians sickly because they are not "normal" in weight.

During menses it is considered normal to bleed, suffer nausea, and edema and to have headaches, cramps and back pain and depression. These problems, however, seem to exist only in sickly females and domesticated or civilized animals and are non–existent in healthy primitives or wild animals.

A physiological evaluation of menstruation is helpful in understanding how it occurs, how it can be alleviated and how fertility is not affected by lack of menstruation. The menstrual flow actually begins at the end of the menstrual cycle. This cycle develops over a period of approximately 28 days and it represents the body's preparation for conception. We mistakenly name this fertility cycle menstrual, but menstruation is really only the visible blood flow.

In the fertility cycle, estrogen and the growing follicle cause the endometrium (the mucous membrane lining the inner surface of the uterus) to thicken and form glands and arterioles for transporting nutrients. This endometrium continues to grow until release of the egg, which coincides with a secretion of progesterone. At this time, the endometrium lining stops expanding and begins to secrete blood and nutrients. The growing follicle, which ruptures when the egg is released, produces estrogen and progesterone in smaller amounts; consequently, this hormone level decreases steadily. If the egg is not fertilized, all or almost all hormone production stops. The sudden shutoff of these hormones produces a spastic reaction in the blood vessels of the endometrium, causing the arterioles to burst, followed by a restricted blood flow to the endometrium. Up to 70 percent of the damaged endometrium tissue is expelled along with some blood, mucous and toxins in a period of 2 – 15 days. The remaining 30 percent is reabsorbed. The healthier the woman, the smaller the amount of blood loss.

In our studies, two factors seem to be of importance in development of menstruation: first, overall level of obstructive extraneous mucus generated by the diet leading to menstrual necrosis; and second, the level of unheated whole nutritional factors, especially bioflavonoids, which build strong non–fragile capillaries as well as strong bodies. We will now consider the factors individually and how they apply to different diets.

In a state of health, or "live–food" nutrition, the arterioles which exist as a part of the endometrium lining are not spiral and congested. This is one of the key factors in understanding why these arterioles are not damaged when the hormone cessation initiates contractions and spasms in the blood vessels of the endometrium. The endometrium lining continues to be alive, facilitating almost total reabsorption. As a result, there is small or no discharge of tissue, blood, etc. However, if the arterioles are clogged, the body's ability to reabsorb them is going to be hindered. The needed enzymes shut off from their source of blood and oxygen will not be able to reach the extremities, thereby causing cells to die.

The second factor we are considering is the connection between nutrition and the overall fragility of capillaries, specifically as it relates to menstruation. The need for bioflavonoids in the blood-clotting process is becoming common knowledge. Documentation exists relating the need for chlorophyll, Vitamin C and Vitamin P to maintain proper capillary strength. This finding sets the stage for using Vitamin P and C for menstrual relief, which has in fact occurred, with excellent results

The effect of fluctuations in hormone levels on capillary strength has been tested in relation to total capillary strength throughout the body. The test showed a drop in capillary strength in the arms of "healthy" women within two days of ovulation. Continuing the same experiment, estrogen was fed to these women intravenously and capillary strength increased to normal within 2 − 24 hours. Furthermore, it was shown that administration of Vitamin C and P reduced the menstrual flow by 67 percent, indicating the improvement of capillary strength. The same study makes a connection between a woman inadvertently consuming a large amount of ripe tomatoes (high source of Vitamin C and P) and her suddenly experiencing a drastic lessening of menstrual discharge. As a follow up, I contacted Dr. A. Clemetson, a researcher at the Department of Obstetrics and Gynecology at the University of Saskatchewan in Canada, and received this reply:

Dear Mr. Kulvinskas:

It was interesting to speak to you on the telephone today and to know that you have discovered that many women develop a complete absence of menstrual periods while they are taking vegetarian reducing diets.

As I told you on the phone, I know that this is true and it is a most fascinating situation, as they do appear to be in excellent health. Some of them develop orange colored palms to their hands, perhaps due to carotene, but I know of no evidence that carotene is the cause of the cessation of menses.

I suspect that this effect may be different from the effect I was observing in Canada in women I was treating for heavy periods with vitamin C and bioflavonoids, as they continue to have periods but very light ones, as described in my articles entitled "Capillary Strength and the Menstrual Cycle" and also in "Capillary Strength of Women with Menorrhagia" which I enclose.

I spent five years at the University of California studying bioflavonoids in an attempt to elucidate this problem, and this work is summarized in the article entitled "Plant Polyphenols as Antioxidants for Ascorbic Acid" and also in the French and Italian articles which I enclose.

I do believe that I solved the bioflavonoid problem, as many flavonoids are antioxidants for ascorbic acid, but much more work is needed to study other effects of diet on the menstrual periods, as this is probably a very complex problem. Plant estrogens and proestrogens may well affect the menstrual periods and many other substances could also be involved. The effect you describe, namely secondary amenorrhea or complete cessation of menses, has been seen in many reducing vegetarian diets and it will require a great deal of research work to sort it out.

Thank you for your interest in my work.

Yours sincerely,
C. Alan B. Clemetson, MD.

Dr. Clemetson has developed a theory of menstruation based on 10 years of research. His position is detailed in a paper published by the "Annals of the New York Academy of Science" (1962).

> We know that several of the bioflavonoids are estrogenic, and evidence has been produced to show that the estrogens are in a sense bioflavonoidal in that they increase the strength of fragile capillaries. It seems likely that the integrity of the capillaries is normally maintained by ascorbic acid and the bioflavonoids, but that the estrogens when present may compete with the bioflavonoids. Then, when the estrogen level falls or the estrogens are metabolized, the capillaries are left without support and become fragile until such time as the bioflavonoids can return to take their place in the capillary wall. The work of Markee (1940) showed that regression of the endometrium commenced five days before menstruation.
>
> If estrogens temporarily replace the bioflavonoids in the capillary wall and continue to preserve the integrity of the capillaries until they are withdrawn, this would explain why a drop in the estrogen level caused bleeding but a persistently low or a persistently high estrogen level does not cause bleeding.

During the stage of endometrium construction, estrogen is utilized as a replacement for bioflavonoids. As the estrogen secretion level drops off during the premenstrual period, the body tries to maintain a critical level of estrogen in the blood by withdrawing it from the capillaries of the endometrium (as well as other regions of the body, as shown by Dr. Clemetson in studies of capillary strength). This leads to capillary fragility, rupture and blood leakage. Endometrial cells undergo necrosis and shock, and menstrual flow occurs.

In a woman on a raw vegetarian diet — which is usually very rich in Vitamin C and P — the estrogen never needs to substitute for bioflavonoids in the capillary construction of the endometrium. When the cyclic reabsorption is instigated it is done systematically and in a non—hemorrhaging manner just as it was in the earlier creation of the endometrium.

The dietary element in menstruation gets further emphasis from nutritional studies showing that over 70 percent of American women are Vitamin C deficient; the percentage of bioflavonoid deficient women is even higher. This study is a strong statement showing the shortcomings of the societal — not individual — approach to nutrition.

To arrive at a better appreciation of the human female, we will examine reproduction in the mammals.

Undomesticated animals do not menstruate, but have periodic mating seasons, known as heat, rut or estrus, which usually occur several times a year, generally in spring and autumn. In the normal state, during ovulation, the genital organs of females of lower animals are slightly congested and are moistened with mucus.

However, after the non-menstruating animal is domesticated, the estrus becomes transformed into a bloody flow, manifesting as the menstrual hemorrhage. This results from an unnatural diet and artificial living conditions. This occurs with the cow, donkey, mare, bear, pig, cat, rabbit, dog and monkey. Monkeys menstruate five times a year. This has very little to do with fertility, since they rut only twice. The cow has a discharge, sometimes quite bloody, every three weeks; yet it ruts only once a year.

Dr. Rhodes, professor of obstetrics at the University of London, discusses the difference between menstruation and estrus:

> The lining of the uterus is the endometrium, which is under the control of the hormones of the ovary. Since these are produced in waxing and waning cycles the endometrium waxes and wanes in time with the hormone secretions from the ovary. This is true for all mammals, but only in the primates is the phenomenon of menstruation seen. This is the periodic shedding of the endometrium from the uterus, which is seen as a bloody discharge from the vaginal orifice...the physiological significance of menstruation is not known...
>
> In the lower animals estrus occurs in regular cycles depending on the species and its environment. The vaginal bleeding which is seen in the animals at estrus is not comparable to menstruation, as bleeding is associated with ovulation in the estrus cycle; but the vaginal bleeding of menstruation occurs only after the death of the corpus luteum approximatley fourteen days after ovulation.

Menstrual bleeding in Old World monkeys is associated with congestion in the arterioles located in the uterus lining. New World monkeys (Cebus, Ateles, etc.) have periodic cycles of bleeding, microscopic in nature and associated with minimal tissue loss. Goodman, Wislocki and Kaiser have pointed out that there are no coiled arterioles in these forms. Dr. Rhodes writes: "The spiral arterioles are the key to the phenomenon of menstruation for they have been observed to contract and relax in the few days before the menstrual flow. During contraction the endometrium blanches and during relaxation becomes congested. This observation was made by Markee...constriction of the arterioles is intense and so probably leads to anoxia...the vessels break too and this is responsible for the bleeding." (126)

The spiral arterioles are equivalent to varicosities in veins, which result from ingesting mucus-forming processed foods. The Old World monkeys have ready access to this diet from their civilized cousins; whereas, the New World monkeys have to be satisfied with bananas. Gilman and Gilbert (202) showed that menstruation is not natural for the Old World monkey. They observed that when female baboons were fed on a vegetables only diet, menstruation cycles ceased.

There are many cases where menstrual flow has stopped due to a highly toxic diet. The body is weakened to a point where it loses its ability to carry out the monthly cleansing process. As toxins continue to build up, unless there is a change in life-style, the female will develop some chronic disorders.

With cessation of menstruation during pregnancy, a toxic woman experiences many new discomforts when she is forced to hold onto her poisons. Morning sickness, edema, vomiting, dizziness and rapid breathing are some of the visible symptoms. Toxins are excreted via channels other than the uterus, but pain and illness result when these organs are already overtaxed.

When a woman never menstruates, it may be due to some malformation, such as an imperfectly formed hymen, atresia of the vagina or imperfect development of the vagina, uterus or ovaries. It may be due to a general disturbance in the quality and quantity of nutrients as well as to disorders of the endocrine system, including ovarian tumors.

Temporary cessation of the menstrual cycle may occur with a change in routine or in climate, a long journey (especially to ocean or mountains), change of residence from country to city or vice versa, extraordinary joy, grief, anxiety or exciting work, exams and study, entering a new occupation, financial troubles, a love affair, difficulty in home life, and/or obesity.

When the female starts to improve in health due to improved nutrition, if the disorder is not a structural one, she will start to menstruate, quite often profusely. As the months progress, menses will become painless. If the female is healthy enough, menses will cease. This time it will be to her benefit.

"and it ceased to be with Sarah after the manner of women...For Sarah conceived, and bore Abraham a son in his old age." (Genesis 18:11 and 21:2). Most physicians dogmatically believe that it is impossible for a non-menstruating woman to conceive. Sarah was amenorrheic (non-menstruating) and she conceived. Most women who visit doctors for infertility are amenorrheic. This of course should not imply that menstruation is essential for fertility. When physiological factors have been excluded, the doctor looks for malnutrition. Yet we find in undeveloped countries a situation of chronic protein-caloric malnutrition as well as rapid population growth.

The following studies show that, "Severe general under-nutrition may produce amenorrhea (cessation of menstruation) and infertility." In Rotterdam during the period of gross malnutrition from December 1944 to May 1945, fifty percent of the women had amenorrhea and the weekly conception rate fell from a prewar figure of 206 to 93." However, the difference in fertility could have been due to war and the absence of men. Millis, in another study, found no evidence of reduced fertility in Singapore during a period of general under-nutrition in 1947.

Whitacre and Barrera state: "During war and in other situations where starvation conditions existed, amenorrhea is common."

Hommberg found that before the war, out of 1356 patients observed, only nine percent of the cases were amenorrhea. In 1917 there was a rise to five percent and in 1918 to nine percent. German physicians attributed this to "defective nutrition, underfeeding, physical starvation, exposure to cold and wet, and enforced celibacy."

Rubner, in his report on under-nutrition in Germany during the World War blockade, stated that on reduced rations, (31 gm. protein), a cessation of menstruation occurred with many women. Strickel found that during 1917, cases of amenorrhea were seven times more frequent at Charite Frauenklinic, Berlin than before the war.

The conclusion one can draw from these two studies is that general under−nutrition does not necessarily lead to infertility. As a matter of fact, a diet adequate in vitamins, minerals and sunshine, though low in protein, fat and carbohydrates, can provide all nutrients needed for the birth of healthy children. The Hunzas, Georgians and Ecuadorians who eat a diet low in protein, but otherwise adequate, have been around for thousands of years and show no loss in fertility. Their daily dietary intake is 1500 calories and 35 grams of vegetable protein.

> On the Faroe Islands it is said that the women are entirely free from menstruation. Among the Samoyedes, Mantegezza says that menstruation is so slight that some travellers have denied its existence there. Among the native women of Tierra del Fuego, menstruation is said to be absent except in rare instances. According to Velpeau, the women of Greenland menstruate scantily two or three times a year.

Dr. Alexis Haig writes on his experience with humans: "Excessive loss at the period has been greatly influenced by the patient going on a uric acid free diet. A remarkable and very interesting point with regard to one or two of the cases was the tendency for the flow at a period to be missed out all together. These last cases have since married and had children without any trouble. Can it be that by living on a more natural diet woman would have her periods correspond then with those of other mammals (which are bloodless)."

Dr. Israel, M.D. writes that in his practice he has run into some cases where the females do not menstruate but do conceive. He writes: "It is absent in the few women who never menstruate but nevertheless bear children and show on repeated biopsies, cyclic endometrial changes identical with those of menstruating women."

Dr. George White, M.D., who practiced for 50 years in Los Angeles, showed in his book, "The Emancipation of Women or Regulating the Duration of Menses", that menstruation is not necessary for fertility.

> I waited until I had 'naturized' practically all the women in public life and waited years to see the offspring of the third generation because I would publish my findings of facts from which to formulate my conclusions. One of the strangest facts in this 'naturizing' of women is that those women who have been 'naturized' keep the matter secret and rarely tell other women. They often send their daughters to me, for me to tell them how to 'naturize' themselves as their mothers and grandmothers have been 'naturized' by me. Of course, superstition is back of all this secrecy."

He used a totally vegetarian diet to bring about the desirable results. The book contains many examples like the following:

> Single woman, 23 years of age. Flowed bright blood five or six days

of each month. Had such severe cramps that she could not hold her position as stenographer. Treated her three months, three days each month. Then once a month for three months. Her periods changed to half a day mucous flow with not blood at all. She was able to resume her work and did so for two or three years. She married and has had three daughters. Each of them had a mucous flow for about half a day each month and are in perfect health. One is married and had a healthy baby girl.

I think that the negative effect of menstruation on a woman's emotional state is clear to everyone. Just the turmoil endured monthly is sufficient reason to try to look for alternative solutions. In addition to the emotional effect is the physiological damage. It has been estimated that to replace the losses of menstruation during a lifetime, a woman has to synthesize tissue up to 100 percent of her body weight. Nutrients lost include lecithin, calcium phosphate, sodium chloride, alkaline lactates, sodium bicarbonate, potassium chloride, cholesterol, albumin, mucin, Vitamin A and E and amino acids.

It is this periodic depletion of hormones (six times higher in menstrual blood than in regular blood) that leads to menopause. Menstruation is truly a disabling phenomenon and a product of our societal dieting pattern.

Today there is widespread research linking the onslaught of heart attacks, high blood pressure, cancer, etc., with diets containing excessive amounts of protein. As I've shown in my books, high protein intake is a trademark of modern society. And I've documented the success in fighting disease using diets with small amounts of predigested vegetarian protein.

There is a strong association between the high protein diet and menstruation. Dr. Bieler, M.D., Dr. George Starr, M.D. and Dr. Schroyer, M.D., all write of cases where a change from a high protein (meat) diet to natural food reduced the menstruation considerably or to the point of non–significance. The strength of the menstrual myth is the mistaken link between high protein needed for health and menstruation as a basis for fertility.

Research as documented by Dr. Israel, M.D., indicates a similar cyclic production of endometrial tissue in all women, including those who do not menstruate yet still give birth to children. Dr. Alexis Haig sums up his observations on child bearing women who don't menstruate with a question that is the basis for this article. 'Can it be that by living on a more natural diet woman would have periods corresponding with those of other mammals (which are bloodless)?'

In conclusion, as long as the diet provides a complete protein (see 'Survival Into the 21st Century') and is high in life factors such as vitamins, organic minerals and enzymes, the female has adequate amounts of nutrients for reproduction and also for longevity. She will be gifted with health, spirituality and mental powers.

The hypothesis expressed relating improved diet with slowing or stopping menstrual flow, while controversial, has too much potential benefit to be discarded or overlooked. If you are a woman this article gives you a basis to better your life. Research can always be disputed, no matter who the investigator. You can improve your life through diet, and possibly free yourself from the ills of menstruation.

The following letters are a few of the many I have received which relate dietary changes to cessation of menstruation:

Dear Vik,

I was a complete vegetarian by the time I was 15 (I'm now 18). My periods began to come less frequently (about once every three months) and then stopped altogether by about two years ago. My parents were really worried about this but I felt better than ever so I wasn't too concerned. Mom took me to a gynecologist who did blood tests, etc., and said I was 'amazingly healthy'. But he said he could put me on the pill and get me started again! No thanks!

I was getting around to thinking that, since I was feeling so great and not menstruating, perhaps menstruation was a symptom of a 'disease,' rather than the old 'normal, natural process.'

I got to thinking that on my natural diet, I'd 'de–domesticated' myself and my body was behaving accordingly. So I tried an experiment about nine months ago. I ate dairy foods for a few days to see the effect. Sure enough, I got two periods after that. Since then, I've become increasingly confident that not menstruating is natural, and that diet is the key. Eat fresh fruit, raw vegetables and sprouts, some nuts and seeds, and very little cooked food except for some grains in winter occasionally.

Anyway, thanks for the book. It's inspiring and reassuring.

T.T., Montana

Dear Viktoras,

What a wonderful gift I received on my 35th birthday, August 7th — a copy of 'Survival Into the 21st Century.' I spent my birthday on the beach poring over the contents in a great frenzy to take in as much of it as possible! I was a patient of Dr. Bieler's until his death almost a year ago, so you can imagine my joy in finding you speaking of toxemia, the detoxification regimens, and all the principles I either learned from Dr. Bieler or have come to find out about by myself. And the book has answered so many questions I have had about my remaining health and detoxification problems — problems I had come to believe were just never going to get solved. Anyway, your book has given me a new jolt of confidence to continue with my own purification process and a renewal of enthusiasm over the directions I am following. One initial diversion though. The greatest value of your book for me personally was its lifting of my concern and sometimes worry about the cessation of my menstrual periods after a year on my Bieler diet. After a few months on the initial detoxification diet Dr. Bieler set down for me, all usual symptoms accompanying menstruation (tender breasts, fatigue, nervousness, abdominal discomfort, and heavy bleeding) stopped. Then my periods came every other month, every 56 days exactly. This happened for six months. Then my last period — in January 1975. I haven't menstruated since. Nothing I read, nor anyone I spoke to, had any answer. Dr. Bieler said simply that my body now 'had more important things to do' and seemed to indicate that the menstrual function would return when my glands rebalanced themselves. My good friend Rob, a young doctor just beginning to practice nutritional medicine here in California (I'll tell you more about him later) was convinced the amenorrhea was nutritionally based, and gave me supplements guaranteed to work within four months. Nothing happened. That's where I stood when I got your book — and what a relief. I've thrown out those awful supplements and now know I will never menstruate again, and that there's nothing wrong with me. My husband is quite intrigued, and even amused, over this whole turn of events...

Dr. Bieler put me on a diet: Milkshake (raw milk, cooked fruit, and raw egg yolk) for breakfast; milk and a piece of bread and vegetable soup for lunch; and a huge salad and cooked vegetables for dinner; diluted fruit juices in between meals. No salt. I continued on this diet for a year and had one crisis after another after another after another. In a year's time, I had lost 25 pounds, felt great and most of the frequent crises had stopped. We began adding raw fruit, occasional meat, cooked eggs and some starchy vegetables, but I eliminated the bread. I still craved it and felt it better not to have any. We experimented, but I still had constipation, intestinal autointoxication episodes, of terrible severity I might add — and I had no idea what was causing them.

On my own, when Dr. Bieler was ill and dying I stopped my milk, and of course, did much better. I made other changes, but just couldn't solve the intestinal problems. Since your book, I have learned much about my own intestinal functioning. No more eggs and now at last no more intestinal putrefication. I have added much more fruit which always fermented in that horrid mess in the colon, but no more. And I've eliminated cooked vegetables for lunch consisting usually of sprouts, cabbage, celery and whatever else I have (zucchini, onions, cucumber, cauliflower, or broccoli) and a raw salad with olive oil, lettuces, chard, beet greens, and some raw vegetables for dinner preceeded by 8 oz. glass of carrot juice. The quantity is the smallest in servings I've ever had, and I seldom even get very hungry anymore, so I'm ready to begin cutting down even further.

My bowel elimination is gradually improving, which is the last problem I have to contend with. I'm having fuller and more regular bowel movements (usually one a day, and for many days at a time, two per day). I fast regularly, as I can, am working on regular exercises to improve abdominal muscles, and daily do deep breathing.

J.C., California

'I am currently writing a booklet on natural approaches to dealing with dysmennorhea and the premenstrual syndrome.

I know of numerous women who have stopped menstruating while attending meditation courses. Many of the women who cease to have their period on any regular basis afterwards also seem to have the common denominator of being on a raw–food diet. A number of women have reported menstruating twice a year only, suggesting to me an estrus cycle instead of a menstrual cycle.'

A realistic person does not reject certain possibilities just because they are contrary to existing beliefs or cultural phenomena. What is unbelievable for us today may well be taken for granted by our children.

In the future, it is my intention to publish studies which validate further the concept that menstruation is not necessary for fertility and which help the cause of women seeking their divine nature — which in turn will further stimulate the coming Age of Light to planet Earth.

Viktoras Kulvinskas

THE IMPORTANCE OF NUTRITION IN EYE DEVELOPMENT AND VISION FUNCTION

It has been the privilege of this investigator to enjoy the excitement of several discoveries in the past two years relating to the effects of chromium deficiency and calcium mishandling on vision. (1–11) Especially, it is important to note the value of live, whole foods and wheat grass therapies in the prevention of these effects.

Late in 1978 I tabulated and evaluated data from the first 120 consecutive nutrition workups in my optometric files in a double–masked paradigm. Four laboratories scored the mineral content of nape–of–neck hair specimens (biopsies) using optical emission spectroscopy and atomic absorption spectroscopy in automated procedures, and the labs provided computer–calculated inventories of dietary intake. Independently, I had completed standard optometric measurements of eye refracting power without prior knowledge of the lab. results, and I compared these findings as recorded for a period of two years or more to note whether the eye power was increasing or decreasing.

Myopia––otherwise called "nearsightedness", is a state of development of the eyes such that the myopic person can see more clearly with his or her eyes for close distances rather than at or beyond 20 feet (6 meters). What I found is that myopic (nearsighted) persons tend to eat differently than other persons and are chemically different than persons who are not nearsighted. As a class, myopic persons are markedly deficient in the trace mineral, chromium. It is as if low chromium levels define the onset of nearsightedness, until and unless the condition reverses. Other persons may have low chromium, but virtually all myopes who are still vulnerable to myopic increase have low chromium in nape hair.

Why might deficiency of chromium be related to development of nearsightedness? In a study I completed on February 23, 1980, I was able to establish that there is a highly significant correlation of elevation of pressure inside the eye [intraocular pressure – "IOP" – which normally maintains the shape and optical characteristics of the eye] with deficiency of chromium as measured in nape hair. In other words, persons deficient in chromium tend to suffer elevated pressure (IOP) within their eyes and this elevated IOP tends to elongate or stretch the eyeball so that light rays focus in from off the retina, resulting in myopia or nearsightedness. But is this elevation of pressure perverse, or is it response to a human need?

A study I completed in September of 1980 revealed that chromium is absolutely essential for accommodation. [Accommodation is the process by which we engage the ciliary muscle inside the eye to increase the bulginess or convexity of the lens, light rays from nearer objects can be brought to focus on the retina, instead of inadequately converging as if to focus first behind the retina. If our eyes focus well for distance vision, we need accommodative change in focus to see clearly at near distances of, for example, 10 to 20 inches from our eyes].

We are not so well prepared by evolution for daily, repeated, sustained closework accomodation which first hit the masses with the coming of the industrial revolution. Whether we think of it or not, the ciliary muscles which we use inside our eyes to sustain closework focus are probably the only muscles we may use in our bodies for hours of continuous work that were almost never used for continuous work before the last half–dozen generations.

Why is chromium important to accomodation? Probably, it is important in its role as a cofactor potentiating insulin at insulin–receptor sites in the capillaries which supply the ciliary muscles inside the eyes. The insulin then permits glucose utilization and energy exchange. This role of chromium has been demonstrated in other body tissues, but had never been demonstrated in the eye. My theory is that when chromium reserves are inadequate in the body, some ciliary muscle fibers will yet have the needed chromium at related insulin receptor sites, but when these become fatigued, other muscle fibers will not have sufficient associated chromium to take over − hence the effort to sustain accomodation results in accommodative fatigue, and whole–muscle accommodation utilizing all the fibers of all the divisions cannot be achieved even for short periods of time.

As of this writing, all the experimental evidence appears to confirm my theory.

The chromium deficiency mostly becomes a problem, in terms of contributing to accommodative (near–focusing) fatigue, when accommodation is stimulated for long periods of time, as in studying for hours before an exam, or in working overtime at a deskwork job, especially with figures. If the near–focusing musculature is under daily, repeated, long–sustained hours of demand or stimulation, the organism seems to balk and say, "There's got to be a better way!" as it invokes the surrogate or substitute mechanism of elevating the intraocular pressure − as if a servomechanism to reduce the need for so strong or so continuous accommodation, by elongating the eyeball. Modest elevation of IOP occurs with long sustained accomodative stimulus even when chromium seems to be in adequate supply.

My February 23, 1980 study showed that IOP elevation is aggravated when tissue chromium levels are depressed, even when accomodative stimulus is minimal.

How do tissue chromium levels become depleted? Chromium is not consumed in the process of potentiating insulin at insuline–receptor sites. But it is depleted when we eat refined substances that once were rich in chromium until after refining–substances such as sucrose (table sugar). (12–14) It is as if Nature knew that the chromium had to be there for utilization of the sugar − or as if the sugar were only there to entice us to consume the chromium!

Elevated IOP does not in itself cause the eyeball to elongate. Thomas Stuart—Black Kelly (15) has described myopia as a "scleral–expansion glaucoma" in which the sclera [the white of the eye] expands in response to elevated IOP, as contrasted to what we generally call "glaucoma" − the situation in which the sclera does not expand as the pressure elevates, resulting in damage to local circulation and neural elements.

In rapidly progressing myopia the sclera is too distensible. My data shows that the sclera apparently becomes distensbile when there is calcium mishandling and especially when, at the same time, calcium is being shunted to bones for growth, as in youths 7 to 18 years of age.

What causes the calcium mishandling? Well, it really isn't "mishandling" − since the body knows what it is doing. I found that the "calcium mishandling" could be equated with a calciuretic (16, 17) effect; calcium was spilling into the urine and also apparently into hair tissue. This I found associated with excessive consumption of cooked protein. It was not the case that nearsighted people intrinsically consume more protein than normal-sighted people, but only that they consume more when their nearsightedness is increasing. The average ratio of protein (as adjusted for age and weight) was more than triple the RDA for myopes who remained stable.

High protein foods are equipped by Nature with the greatest concentrations of vitamin B6 – until they are cooked. The B6 is not totally destroyed by the cooking, but apparently enough is made bio-unavailable that the body has to steal from tissue reserves to utilize fully the protein. Instead, with deaminization we get a build up of urea nitrogen in the bloodstream from this excessive intake of cooked protein. When the high levels of urea nitrogen are detected in Henle's loops in the kidneys, the parathyroid marshalls calcium from all over the body to chelate with the poisonous urea and pull it into the urine – and presumably into hair. So the excessive protein causes some toxicity and much waste, while mustering calcium out of important tissues like the sclera of the eye where it was, as I see it, complexed with collagen. [The evidence is that there is an extremely low rate of collagen turnover in the sclera, but a high rate of change in calcium complexing with the collagen].

Just as myopes are defined by a tight standard deviation around their low tissue-chromium values, only emmetropes [normal-sighted persons] are defined by tight standard deviations around the normal mean calcium handling levels from calcium in hair.

At special risk for increasing in myopia are kids who consume a high percentage of their high-calcium foods in chocolated combinations, such as chocolate milk. The chocolate contains oxalates which prevent full calcium utilization by the body--enough to make a serious difference clinically in the statistics for myopia development.

Preventive Measures

Preventive measures include:
(a) use of convex reading glasses by persons who still retain excellent distance vision, so as to protect from the unnatural stresses of daily, repeated, sustained closework focussing (accommodation) [enabling sustained closework as if the closework were not so close or as if it were not so sustained];
(b) use by/myopes/of high-segment bifocals or weaker lenses for closework than those that give best distance vision acuity (usually 0.75 to 1.25 diopters weaker) to protect from the unnatural stresses of daily, sustained closework eye focusing;
(c) improvement of lighting so as to reduce the accommodative stress--and improvement of desk and seat height--and provision for sloped reading surface so that reading distance will not be too short, so the reader may back away while keeping the frontal plane of the head parallel to the reading surface;
(d) programmed rest periods for refocussing to distance;
(e) accommodative-flexibility vision therapy exercise;
(f) vision therapy to build fusional ranges and resistance to accommodative stress;
(g) avoidance of refined and processed foods;
(h) avoidance of excessive cooked protein; and
(i) the magic weapon – the Kulvinskas Survival Diet! (26-28)

Why is the Kulvinskas Survival Diet so phenomenal? I have found it especially useful for lowering IOP. The probable reason: The sprouted grains and even Essene bread are excellent sources of amino−acid chelated trivalent chromium (assuming the organically grown grains are not grown on depleted soils). Wheatgrass juice is a superb source of both chelated chromium and vanadium. Vanadium is adjacent in the periodic table and has similar properties to chromium. Bernard Becker (18) believes Vanadium lowers IOP by inhibiting the (Na + K) ATPase pump.

My February 23, 1980 study is the first that I know of to compare habitual daily dietary intake of ascorbic acid against IOP in unmedicated persons. The study demonstrated that the all−too−common diets of cooked meat and cooked starches (hamburgers with french fries) with virtually no fresh fruit and no salads are hazardous to eye health [over a period of years] and especially become injurious to smokers and persons exposed to self−pollution and environmental pollution. The study revealed that average New Jersey suburbanites ingesting only the USRDA for ascorbic acid (60 mg in 1980) had insufficient ascorbic acid to protect against scary elevation of IOP−−levels about which most optometrists and ophthalmologists would express concern. (If these New Jersey suburbanites were fasting on a lean, efficient Kulvinskas−style diet, and/or if they were engaged in aerobic physical activity, this habitually low level of vitamin C ingestion would not likely be a problem). On the other hand, I found that the physiological effectiveness of ascorbic acid or ascorbate in the regulation of IOP is proportional to the logarithm of the amount ingested. If we wish to double the physiological effectiveness of 100 mg ingested (=10 to the 2nd power, log=4), we would need 10,000 mg (=10 to the 4th power, log=4). On the other hand, we don't need to scoff at 100 mg − since 100 mg in food has fully ½ the effectiveness of 10,000 mg!

My study also revealed that we don't need so much vitamin C if our carbohydrate intake is in complex form (not refined), such that it includes the chromium and nutrients that normally reside in the carbohydrate (CHO). On the other hand, if our CHOs are refined, so that they become deficient in chromium, then we need more vitamin C when we load up on deficit−inducing depleted foods and when our digestive system can no longer adequately cope with this overload.

The Key: Living, Whole Foods.

Ten years ago, when I became a fruitarian/vegetarian, I noted my "natural−hygiene movement" friends were the healthiest group of people I had met age−for−age. But I considered their raw−food−only regimen as unnecessarily extreme. In recent years I have come to realize that the simplest key to prevention and reversal of cataract and learning disabilities in many persons and a host of vision problems and discoordinations is a diet of 90 to 100% raw foods.

First, what is cataract? Cataract is a condition in which the crystalline lens inside the eye loses transparency − particially at first − and totally in a mature cataract. (The crystalline lens is behind the colored part of the eye [the iris] and behind the plane of the pupil).

As to cataract, since 1977, breakthrough procedures in veterinary medicine using a common enzyme, super−oxide dismutase (SOD), injected into the front chamber of canine eyes, are completely restoring functional vision within an average of 48 hours to eyes that had been completely blind with hypermature cataract. (19–25).

The SOD enzyme can be adequately produced in our bodies as long as we have the adequate building blocks, including copper, zinc and manganese, and as long as we are not overstressed by internal and external pollutants against which it is rallied. SOD is ubiquitous; it is present in all forms of life from microbe to human, and in all foods––as long as they are FRESH and RAW. But how many older people eat fresh, raw foods these days?

Although the enzyme is broken down in the gut, ingestion of fresh SOD, whether in enterically coated tablets or even in fresh, raw foods, produces statistically significant clinical improvement that would not have occurred without the introduction of either the SOD or the raw foods.

It is now routine – – albeit slow––to reverse even quite severe, mature cataract [but not yet hypermature cataract in humans]. And the armementarium has grown. The natural enzymes catalase and glutathione peroxidase (GSH–Px) are also useful in preventing and reversing cataracts.

Super–oxide dismutase (SOD) especially is valuable in protecting the integrity of the peripheral epithelial layers of the crystalline lens of the eye, particularly at the equator of the lens, so as to prevent disruption of normal transport of nutrients into the lens and exchange of metabolites from the lens. SOD prevents photo–oxidative insult to the lens by catalyzing the super–oxide radicals into hydrogen peroxide (H_2O_2). Catalase protects the lens from the H_2O_2 and protects the SOD from the H_2O_2, catalyzing $2H_2O_2$ into $2H_2O + O_2$ for aqueous peroxides, while GSH–Px accomplishes this for liquid peroxides. In order to manufacture SOD, the body needs copper and zinc for the type of SOD found in the blood, and manganese for the SOD found within body cells. GSH–Px (glutathione peroxidase) requires selenium as the co–factor. Deficiencies in these trace minerals can reduce our ability to fight off cataractous changes. Heavy metal toxicities divert these protective enzymes from their anti–cataract functions.

Ascorbate in the aqueous solution in the front (anterior) chamber of the eye––the solution which bathes the surface of the crystalline lens–– also scavenges the superoxide radical. Animal studies have demonstrated that the concentration of ascorbate in the aqueous is dependent on the proportion of bioflavinoid (vitamin P) intake. When ascorbic acid is ingested without the rest of the naturaly occurring vitamin C complex it is less effective in cataract reversal than when the digestive system has the entire C complex (19, 23).

Other useful antioxidants in cataract prevention/reversal include vitamin E, especially in the mixed tocopherol form––as richly provided in wheat sprouts and in wheatgrass juice. One midwest ophthalmologist and several medical nutritionists, since 1979 and 1980, have been using SOD combined with dimethyl sulfoxide (DMSO)––a "tree juice" derivative––to reverse cataract.

The amino acids, Lysine (as in legumes and raw milk) and tryptophan (as in nuts and seeds and raw milk) in the raw state have been recommended for their value in preventing cataract. The are extremely heat labile. Consequently, heat–died milk and pasteurized milk are not good sources of lysine and tryptophan.

Surgery for the forms of cataract that are nutritionally induced can always be considered as a quick but irreversible remedy with many advantages, but some disadvantages. For most patients who undergo cataract surgery, the result is quick restoration of central vision and economic productivity. But some do not adapt well to the strange postsurgical word of aphakic lenses with unreal magnification of the central portion of the visual field and distorted peripheral vision and the jack–in–the–box surprise phenomenon between center and periphery, unless success can be obtained with contact lenses or intraocular implants. (Implants until recently have been thought of as "intraocular time bombs").

Except for cataract caused by trauma or radiation, cataract is not solely a clinical manifestation of an eye problem, but is also an indicator of systemic disturbance. Removing the cataract may aid vision, but it also removes the indicator and does not correct the systemic problem.

I do recommend to any person with suspicion of cataract to consult a surgically disinterested eye and vision care practitioner, probably an optometrist or a research–oriented ophthalmologist or optometrist at a research–oriented university clinic, so as to measure the changes in any cataract and also so as to have a handle on how well the person is doing in managing his/her nutrition and his/her exercise program. Many medical nutritionists have learned clinically that the key to excellent eye health and excellent vision performance is in the exclusive use of raw, fresh, living food [just as the naturopaths have been proclaiming for many generations]. Fresh, tree–ripened unchemicalized fruits, fresh sprouts and fresh wheatgrass juice are invaluable ingredients in this regimen.

Ben Lane, O.D., F.A.A.O., F.C.O.V.D., F.I.C.A.N., F.A.A.S., 16 North Beverwyck Road, Lake Hiawatha, New Jersey 07034

BIRTH CONTROL: A LOOK AT NATURE

"Neither do we know how some animals know instinctively what to eat and in what proportions, to stay alive and healthy. We do know that human beings are born with some positive instincts in this respect, but that these are quickly extinguished by environment and training". (1)

One view of the future foretells an end to natural childbirth for women. Children will be the products of maternal or cloning machines. Author Shulamith Firestone believes women don't like bearing children and would prefer to be relieved of the burden.

It would be a shame if artificial childbearing were instituted for all, rather than as a possible alternative for some. To some women, childbearing is an act of natural sacrifice, in the sense of a sacred offering.

If childbirth is taken out of the hands of mothers, the issue of birth control would no longer be a problem. Women could be sterilized at birth, and perhaps men could be too, if the new method of creating offspring was through cloning. Before this 1984 or this 1994, what does nature teach us about birth control?

Looking at nature, we find that birth control is not a problem with animals. Even with domesticated animals, it is possible to see examples of this. A male and female dog, for example, don't mate frequently during each day that the female is in heat. I observed one mating a day, at the most, with my male and female dog. My male dog was not overwhelmed by a passion he could not control. I could separate the two if necessary. On their own, they related to each other most of the time in their usual ways: jostling, playing, washing each other.
observed one mating a day, at the most, with my male and female dog. My male dog was not overwhelmed by a passion he could not control. I could separate the two if necessary. On their own, they related to each other most of the time in their usual ways: Jostling, playing, washing each other.

Rather than inbuilt control, this is an example of inbuilt response. Response and control are different. Control is a part of an authoritarian concept of order. Implied in responding is a sense of unfoldment and a sensitivity to the needs of the life process. Sometimes, for example, animals will use spacing as a means of population control in over populated areas. It was found that African elephants in high density areas did not breed until the age of twenty and then bred at twelve year intervals (2). If animals have been able to responsively reproduce or not reproduce their numbers, why haven't human beings, for the most part, been able to do the same?

There are, in fact, over 500 plants with contraceptive properties in the natural world. This is only an estimate. There are probably double that amount and more. Opponents of most forms of birth control have not considered what the natural world may have to teach us as an expression of a creative intelligence higher than our own. Plants with contraceptive properties would seem to contradict the idea that there is something unnatural about controlling or limiting the numbers of births.

Looking at the broad number of plants with contraceptive properties, one is amazed by the tremendous variety and also by the inclusion of some in the daily diet of many people today. I am thinking, in particular, of papaya, pineapple and tomatoes. Tomatoes were once called love apples and considered poisonous — perhaps through some awareness of their contraceptive properties.

In nature, there is a fine line between substances in plants that are contraceptive in effect and those that function as abortants. Those that function as abortants are potentially any that bring on menstruation. As we shall see later on, many plants with contraceptive properties prevent the formation of an endometrium, thereby diminishing menstruation.

Although most of the plants that will be described as a result of this research as having contraceptive properties do not fall into the catagory of foods that most people eat today, many are common weeds and herbs. Examples of common weeds are wild asparagus and wild ginger root.

It is possible that our human ancestors consumed plants that they instinctively knew would prevent conception or would aid it, in harmony with natural life cycles, seasonal variations, population demands and availability of plant vegetation. One of the reasons mating was seasonal, and still is, could well be the presence of plants with contraceptive properties in the animals' diets. Since plants are seasonal themselves, this could have contributed to seasonal mating.

All animals, with very few exceptions, consume some form of plant life. It is stated by zoologists that the consumption of leaves on the part of some largely flesh eating animals might be for vitamins rather than other food content. But the majority of animals are omnivores. It is possible that the eating of leaves and other plant parts was for contraceptive purposes and still is. There is one vitamin that is known to have contraceptive properties. This is Vitamin B−17, Laetrile, found in the seed of the papaya pit and a well known contraceptive among the Indians of the southern hemisphere.

For the aid of those who may wish to perform experiments, it is difficult to evaluate changes in mating patterns among most wild animals in captivity. Although most species mate seasonally, in captivity some animals don't mate at all. Environmental conditions such as overcrowding are attributed as reasons. At any rate, it seems evident that it would be difficult to study changes of diet in settings in which there is hardly a population sample available.

Laboratory animals, however, present another picture. Most laboratory animals such as the rabbit, rat and guinea pig invariably become nonseasonal producers of offspring. This is true of breeds that are ordinarily seasonal producers. Since there is much documentation that the diet of laboratory animals is significantly changed from their diet in nature, experiments could be tried in which all known plant matter of any one species was given in a natural form to the animals. These groups and control groups could be studied to see which bred more and which less.

It is known that new world monkeys mate non−seasonally under conditions of captivity. Yet many of these new world monkeys mate seasonally when in their natural state. Their diets in captivity similarly exclude more peripheral foods of plant origin which they would consume in their natural environments. These monkeys could provide another experimental group.

Most of our knowledge concerning plants with contraceptive properties has been learned from the so-called "primitive" peoples such as the American Indians, Latin American Indians and the Eastern Indians. At the time that contraceptive research in plants began, there was much hope expressed on the part of author Aolmeiro de LaForet in Latin America that the substitution of contraceptive plant substances for existing forms of birth control would be a step forward in the area of contraceptive research (3). From his observations, there were plants that contained substance that prevented conception in ways in which birth control pills did not. These plant substances were not estrogenic in nature but did exert control over the pituitary gland.

Estrogen causes the uterine lining (endometium) to proliferate (to grow thicken, and form glands that will secrete embryo-nourishing substances). The lining is proliferative until the egg is released. Then the amount of estrogen begins to diminish. Usually, fertilization takes place within twenty-four hours of the time the egg is released from the follicle. This would be the time of estrus in the animal.

The reason why it is preferable to have non estrogenic substances is that an excess of estrogen in the body causes hepatomas (cancer growths of the liver) and carcinomas of the uterus. De LaForet concluded that if these plants were tested and it was discovered that they did not have negative side effects, nobody would mind replacing the old products with them. At the same time he discussed the problem of having pilot studies done in clinics because of the prejudice towards having plant substances used for birth control measures (4).

The prejudice towards utilizing natural substances of the earth emerges. The value of plants as contraceptives has been reported by peoples we call primitive. On looking at these peoples beyond our cultural difference, we find they are usually people that are living a more natural life than we are. Unfortunately, the bias continues even though at least one major manufacturer has used the mexican yam as a basis for a birth control pill. Even with this manufacturer, the plant is not used in a natural form but is transformed to the point where its untilization becomes incidental:

> "...The Mexican yam or the root of the barbasco plant has been utilized and is still utilized to a limited extent in the manufacture of oral contraceptives. It should be emphasized, however, that the constituents of the root are not incorporated in oral contraceptives. The basic component of the root which is important in the manufacture of oral contraceptives is a substance known as diosegenin. This substance is not now nor has it ever in the past been used as a component of oral contraceptives. *Diosgenin is simply a starting material which is transformed by many chemicals and biological properties and it is these other compounds, a progestin and an estrogne, which are the basic components of the oral contraceptive. In the case of Enovid, the estrogen is mestranol and the progestin is norethynodrel. These two compounds are not present in the mexican yam or in any other plant source. Norethynodrel and mestranol can also be obtained by chemical transformation of other plant sterols or animals steros and even by total synthesis. The same considerations apply to the estrogens and progestins present in the other currently available oral contraceptives". (5)

The way that the substance from the mexican yam is used is ironic. It is the very fact that plants seemed to have contraceptive properties that did not function like estrogens that made them valuable alternatives to begin with. It may be necessary to utilize the plant organically or wholely in a way that maintains its original composition and balance for full effectiveness and elimination of side effects. There have always been natural methods for drying herbs but there are also technological means that do not destroy the natural content of a product. The old pharmaceutical companies that used to utilize herbs, particularly in the state of North Carolina, are examples of "natural technology." Shakely Corporation is a modern example. This company manufactures vegetarian vitamin pils without distorting the original composition of the substances being utilized. Companies like Shakley could pioneer the way for natural contraception from plant substances. They could make a welcome contribution to the area of birth control.

It is hard to realize that within this present century, respected doctors addressed the North Carolina Pharmeceutical Association and proudly asserted that North Carolina had more herbs that any other state of the Union. In fact, the Associatin consulted with the Department of Agriculture in Washington D.C. in regard to the farming of medicinal plants.

Two authors who have unburied this tradition of plant respect are Henry de Laszlo and Paul S. Henshaw who wrote the following in "Science", May 7, 1954 (vol. 119, p. 626)

> "As work goes forward on other approaches, it may be profitable to consider the information acquired by ancient and more remote peoples concerning the use of herbs and various plant materials for fertility control purposes... Information from such sources is to some extent held in question by modern investigators who often dismiss the accounts as superstitions or 'old wives tales.' Confidence in such sources of information may be strengthened, however, by recognizing examples of valuable drugs recently isolated from plants used by primitive peoples for generations."

Henshaw and DeLaszlo particularly expressed hope for one plant, Lithospermum Ruderale, which had shown virtually no side effects in all the studies that had been done at the time the article was written. Ruderale means nemishaw or stoneseed. In Orange County, North Carolina, where this is being written, a related plant, Lithospermum Arvense (whose common name is corn gromwell) grows wild in abundance. This plant is designated by Henshaw and DeLaszlo as reported to have contraceptive properties.

Some of the plants reported to have contraceptive properties have also been included in books on edible weeds. It is interesting to note that among those plants which contain some edible parts and some poisonous parts, there is no overlapping. In other words, the same parts of the plant to be avoided for plant contraception are to be avoided for eating. Wild ginger root, milkweed, wild asparagus and dogbane are plants reported to have contraceptive properties that are also listed in books on edible weeds. A list of plants that have been experimented with for their contraceptive properties or have been reported to have them, will conclude this discussion.

There were two highlights in my research I found particularly interesting. Nicotine taken in large quantities can cause sterility in women (not a recommendation to resume smoking cigarettes if one has quit). There have been speculations as to why the infamous George Sand never got pregnant after the birth of her two children within her marriage, in spite of her many subsequent lovers. After Madame Sand left her home and moved with her two children to Paris, she became a chain smoker of cigarettes as well as cigars. This may be the answer to that mystery. Secondly as the table that concludes this discussion will show, there are plants whose contraceptive properties are spermicidal in effect. Nature seems to have "plans with its plants for both men and women.

Pilot Studies in Plant Contraceptives

There is little point in researching plant contraceptives if plant substances are to be transformed into estrogens and chemically prepared as today's market product with its well known side effects.

There are methods for preparing plant substances in natural form — one such method follows at the end of this discussion. Pioneering corporations have been mentioned. They can inform us of their techniques.

Pilot studies could be conducted in traditional medical or alternative healing centers using plant substances in natural form either through natural or "primitive" technology. Volunteers for these studies would risk less than they do at present in studies in which some form of estrogen is utilized. Women who are married and who want children but who are delaying childbirth for a number of years, might make good volunteers for these studies. Men could also volunteer in these studies with plant substance known to have contraceptive properties particular to men. Finding new and sage birth control measures would be a service not only to women, who risk their health with current birth control devices, but also to a world concerned with population control. Plant dosages could be experimented with, starting with minimal doses. Plants have already been experimented with and there should be no lack of antidotes for the dosages involved. With adequate supervision, however, there should be no risk to the people or animals involved in these studies.

Collecting, Drying and Preserving Plants

The following is reprinted from "American Vegetable Practice" by Morris Mattson, Vegetable Materia Medica, Vol. I Boston, 1841, Daniel & Hale, Publishers.

Roots should be collected in the spring before the sap rises, or in the autumn after it descends. They are to be freed from dirt, deprived of their decayed or useless parts, and dried in the sun, or in a warm, airy room. Artificial heat, varying from 60 to 100 degrees, may be employed, if necessary. If roots are large or juicey, they should be split, or cut into slices, before attempting to dry them. If the bark of the root only is wanted, it should be peeled off, or separated in some convenient manner, and the woody fiber thrown away. Annual roots should be collected just before the flowers appear, and biennial roots, either in the summer of the first years, or in the spring of the second. After the roots are dried, they should be packed in drawers, covered boxes, or barrels, where they will not be exposed to the damp. It should be born in mind, that they lose their strength, if ground or pulverized a long time before required for use.

Barks are collected in the spring and autumn, and if requisite, deprived of their outside coat, as in the elm and poplar. The bark of young trees is generally the best. After it is detached, it should be dried in the same way as roots, using the precautions to keep it out of the rain, and not expose it to a damp atmosphere.

Herbs should be gathered in clear weather, when there is no dew or moisture upon them, and spread thinly upon the floor of a chamber or loft, where there is a free circulation of air. In the process of drying, they should be frequently turned.

Herbs are generally in the greatest perfection just before or during the flowering period. If dried in the open air, they should not be left exposed to the rain, or dew, as this would be likely to change their color, and impair their virtues. If the atmosphere continues damp for any length of time, they may be dried with a gentle heat from a fire or stove; after this, they are usually put into boxes, or cannisters, and excluded from the air. Plants which are exceedingly volatile, should be preserved in well stopped jars. Sumach berries and other medicines which are in danger from worms, or insects, require to be kept in covered glasses.

Leaves are mostly collected when they are full grown. They are to be dried and preserved in the same manner as herbs. Those that are thick and juicy may be exposed to an artificial heat, gradually raised to 100 degrees of Fahrenheit.

Flowers are to be collected in clear, dry weather, just before, or immediately after, they have bloomed. They require to be dried in the shade, and in as short a time as possible, that they may retain their odor and color.

Seeds are gathered when they are fully ripe, separated from the chaff or dirt, and deposited in a clean, dry place, secure from worms and insects.

Families in the country may sometimes find it convenient to prepare their own medicines, and with this view they should be supplied with a mortar, break, and pestle, to reduce the different articles to powder. My friend Dr. A.C. Logan, has adopted a simple and well contrived plan, for this purpose. He has a mortar weighing about thirty pounds, covered with a hood, which is fastened below the rim of the mortar with two or three moveable wooden pins. He then employs an iron break, weighing five pounds, and inserted into a handle three feet and a half long, which enables him to reduce the toughest roots and barks to a tolerable fine powder, in a very short time. The break is worked up and down through a hole in the centre of the hood. Its face is rounding, three inches and a half in diameter, and cut into teeth with a file from the centre to the circumference, in the form of a star. The process of pulverizing is completed by an iron pestle, weighing nine pounds, which is similar to the break, excepting that the face is smooth

Contraceptive Plants

The following is a selected list of plants reported to contain substances that affect human reproduction. If not otherwise mentioned, plants are from the DeLaszlo study.

Devil's Cotton (A. Augusta) — Found: Hindi & Bengali—India. Use: Fresh extract of petroleum either from root—bark is an emmenagogue, acts as an anti—implantation, abortifacient agent.
Poppy Anemone (A. Coronaria L.) — Use: Menses inducing and with abortive properties.
Star Amemone (A. Hortensis L.) — Use: Menses inducing and with abortive properties.
Yarrow (Achillea Mille) — Found: N. Europe. Use: Powdered plant mixed with normal diet (25—50% cone) to suppress estrus; hot infusion used.
Achyrathes Aspera Found: India. Use: Benzene extract from air dried stem bark; oral antifertility agent, abortifacient effect.
Sweet Flag (Acorus Calemus) — Use: Menses inducing and abortive; thrives best in moist soil; prop. spring, autumn by division.
Aeschynomene Indica Found: India. Use: Saponins from whole plant — spermicidal
Onion (Allium Cepa L.) — Use: Menses inducer (& abortive).
Garlic (Allium Sativum L.) — Use: Menses inducer (& abortive)
Pineapple (Anahas Comosus L.) — Found: Malaya. Use: Unripe pineapple juice taken raw, sometimes salt added.
Beardgrass (Andropogon Schoenanthus L.) — Found: Old World Tropics. Use: Oil producing grass; menses inducing and abortive.
Androsace Septentrionalis Found: Siberia, Russia. Use: Tranquilizing and contraceptive effects; also used for angina, epilepsy & gonorrhea; tincture.
Fennel; Dill (Anethum Segetum) — Use: Menses inducing & abortive properties
Anisomales Malabarica Linn. Found: India. Use: Plant without roots for saponins, spermicidal
Dogbane (Apocynum Androsaemifolium) — Found: N. America. Use: Roots boiled with water and liquid drunk once a week
Indian Turnip (Arisaema Triphyllum L.) — Found: N. America (Hopi). Use: Decoction of powdered, dried root 1 tsp. in ½ glass cold water strained and drunk prevents conception for 1 year; two tbs hot infusion renders permanent sterility.
Birthwort (Aristolochia Clematitis L.) — Found: Hungary. Use: Seed parts used to prevent fertility and menstrual pain.
Climbing Ylang Ylang (Artabotrys Odoratissimus) — Found: India. Use: "Leaves...afford protection against conception when adminisered **orally** with the onset of Oestrus." Was found safe & effect of long duration.
Wormwood (Artemisia Absinthium) — Use: Menses inducing & abortive properties.
Wild Ginger (Arum Canadense) — Found: N. America. Use: Root and rhyzone boiled slowly in a little water for a long period; decoction drunk by women.
Milkweed (Asclepias Hallii) — Found: N. America/Colorado (Navaho). Use: Infusion of plant drunk after childbirth.
Petitscochons (Asclepias Syriaca) — Found: Canada/Quebec. Use: Handful of roots and rhizomes dried and powdered, infused for 20 minutes in part of water and drunk to produce temporary sterility.
Asparagus (Asparagus Officinalis L.) — Found: S. Europe. Use: Fresh or dried berry decoction drunk as contraceptive; fruit or plant infusion drunk to induce menstruation.
Black Spleenwort (Asplenium Adiantumnigrum L.) — Found: India/Himalayas.

Use: Considered in Yunani system of medicine to produce sterility in woman.
Avocado   Found: N. America/southern & southwestern U.S.A., Central America, and South America. Use: Decoction of sprouts, shoots, buds in absence of menstruation; abortive properties attributed; In Cienfugos, Cuba, they used a concoction of three cogollos, shoots of plant, of avocado as an abortant. In Camaguey leaves used for same purpose.
"Twisted Medicine"   (Babia Dissecta) − Found: N. America (Navaho). Use: Infusion of roots boiled 30 minutes, drunk by women during menstruation; said to be used by both sexes.
Begonia   (Begonia Balmisiana) − Found: C. America. Use: Promotes Menstruation.
Butea Monospermia   Found: India. Use: Taken with Ghee & honey; spermicidal jelly; petroleum ether extract when administered from day one to day ten of pregnancy at the dose level of 250 mg/kg prevented pregnancy in two out of six animals.
Nanche   (Byrsoniam Crassifolia) − Found: C. America (Oaxaca). Use: Bark, leaves, and fruit used to expel placenta; roots used by Indians of Oaxaca to produce expulsion
Posion Arum   (Byladium Seguinum Vent.) − Found: S. America (Indian). Use: "Heard of plants used by Indian women to render temporary or permanent sterlity; on two occasions evidently Araceae"; stops spermatogenesis and follicle growth in rats
Cactus   Found: North America, South America and Central America.
Argerarger   (Callicarpa sp.) − Found: Torres Straits. Use: Young leaves well chewed until women's bodies are saturated with the juice swallowed; causes permanent sterility.
Marsh Marigold   (Caltha Palustris) − Found: India. Use: Whole plant (saponins) spermicidal; menses inducing and abortive actions.
Birtentaschelkraut   (Capsella Bursapastoris L.) − Found: N. Europe. Use: Powdered plant mixed with normal diet (25%−50% cone) to inhibit the estrus cycle; hot infusion used as emmenagogue.
Thistle   (Cnicus Benedictus) − Found: N. America (Quinault Indians). Use: Brewed and taken as tea.
Indian Paint Brush   (Castilleja Linariae Folia) − Found: N. America (Hopi). Use: "A decoction of this plant was sometimes used as it dried up the menstrual flow."
Squaw Root   (Caulophyllum Thalictrodides) − Found: N. America (Chippewa). Use: Strong decoction of 5−30g. powdered root taken to expedite parturition and menstruation.
Weisser Gansefuss   (Chenopodium Album L.) − Found: Hungary. Use: Powdered plant mixed with normal diet (25%−50% cone) found to suppress estrus cycle.
Spotted Cowbane   (Cicuta Maculata) − Found: America (Cherokee). Use: Women chew and swallow roots on 4 consecutive days to produce permanent sterility.
Cinnamon   (Cinnomum Cassia) − Use: Menses inducing and abortive properties.
Clerodendrum Serratum L.   Found: India. Use: Plant without root, saponins, spermicidal effect.
Green Coconut   (Cocos Nucifera L.) − Found: Pacific Isles. Use: Milk used; "too much may be injurious." People in Java afraid to drink milk of coconut (ripe or

unripe) because it is believed to diminish libido or fertility.

Os Segi (Cordia Quarensis Gurke) – Found: Africa (Masai). Use: Pieces of root chewed by girls.

Cuminum Cyminum Found: India. Use: In test with rats, alcoholic extract from seeds – 100% anti–fertility effect at dose of 150 mg/kg; air dried powdered plant material – subject to soxhlet extraction with petroleum ether (60%–80% C.), 95% alcohol & distilled water. Extracts evaporated to dryness under reduced pressure & different dosage forms prepared by suspension in gum acacia.

Phala Kantaka (Daemia Extensa) – Found: India. Use: Leaves used in the preparation of a purgative medicinal oil for amenorrhea and dysmenorrhea.

Balibagan (Dalbergia Terruginae) – Found: West Indies. Use: Decoction of wood of stem or root used as emmenagogue and in doses to induce expulsion of fetus.

Carrot (Dacus Carota L.) – Use: Menses inducing & abortive properties.

Dimeria Gracilis ¶ Found: India. Use: Whole plant, saponins, spermicidal effect.

Tjarri (Dioscorea Sativa L.) – Found: Cape York, Australia (Kawadji). Use: Generally eaten raw, some times roasted; taken in early morning on empty stomache, after which women lies down and does not drink throughout the day.

Barronwort (Epimedium Alpinum L.) – Found: N. Europe. Use: Finely ground leaves; 5 drams taken in wine after menstruation prevents conception for 5 days; root causes sterility.

Antelope Sage (Eriogonum Jamesii) – Found: N. America/Arizona (Navaho). Use: Root boiled for 30 minutes and 1 cupful drunk by woman during menstruation to prevent conception; used by both sexes.

Xtokabal (Eupatorium Odoratum) – Found: C. America (Zapotec). Use: Root used; plant consecrated to goddess of pregnancy and childbirth.

Ficus Carica L. Found: Menses inducing & abortive properties.

Deer's tongue (Frasera Speciosa) – Found: N. America/Nevada (Shoshone). Use: "...a half cupful taken once in a while" as a contraceptive.

W. Fruticosa Found: India. Use: Aqueous extract and alcoholic extract (after removal of petroleum ether & chloroform extractives) of the flowers showed 90–100% abortifacient effect.

Ruprechtskraut (Geranium Robertianum L.) – Found: C. Europe. Use: To stop excessive hemorrhage at menstruation.

Cotton Root Gossypium Herbaceum L.) – Found: S. America. Use: Greoles give a decoction of plant root for contraceptive; also give seeds to mothers to increase lactation.

Gysophila Cerastioides Found: India. Use: Whole plant, saponins, spermicidal effect.

Ivy (Hedera Helix L.) – Found: Mediterranean. Use: The finely pulverized berries drunk after purification; dose of 1 dram causes sterility.

Christmas Rose (Helleborus Niger L.) – Found: Europe. Use: Solid extract of root, 3–5 grains, taken to induce expulsion of the fetus.

Hyptis Suaveolens Found: India. Use: Leaves 100% antifertility at a dose of 125 mg/kg.

Ipil Ipil (Leucaena Glauca Benth) – Found: W. Indies & C.A. Use: Decoction

of root and bark used.
Win (Licuala Sp.) — Found: Solomon Isles (Buka). Use: Outer part of root chewed and swallowed by both sexes.
Lily (Lilium Candidum L.) — Use: Menses inducing and abortive properties.
Gromwell (Lithospermum Arvense) — Found: C. Europe. Use: Powdered plant mixed with normal diet (25%–50% cone) and used to suppress the estrus cycle.
Nemishaw or Stoneseed (Lithospermum Ruderale) — Found: N. America/ Nevada (Shoshone). Use: Cold water infusion of roots taken daily for 6 months insures sterility.
Hassen (Lomatophllum Reflexum) — Found: Africa/Madagascar. Use: One or two budding flowers eaten is powerful emmenagogue.
Asam (Lygodium dichotomum) — Found: Solomon Isles (Buka). Use: Root chewed with betel and some of mixture swallowed.
Haholon (Mallotus Sp.) — Found: Oceania (Buka). Use: Scrapings from root chewed with betel mixture and swallowed.
Horehound (Marrubium Vulgare L.) — Use: Mensés inducing & abortive properties.
Balm Melissa Officinalis L.) — Use: Menses inducing & abortive properties.
Pennyroyal (Menthu Pulegium L.) — Use: Contraceptive & abortant properties.
Zoapatle (Montanoa Tomentosa) — Found: C. America (Zapotec). Use: For difficult parturition and postpartum uterine hemorrhages.
Oil of Basil (Ocimum Basilicum L.) — Use: Menses inducing & abortive properties.
Wine from Carrots (Oinos Daukites) — Use: Menses inducing & abortive properties.
Marjoram (Origanum Majorana L.) — Found: Germany. Use: Taken as a tea during menstruation.
American Mistletoe (Phoradendron Flavescens) — Found: California (Indians of Mendocino County). Use: Tea made from leaves.
Spitzwegerich (Plantago Lanceolata L.) — Found: C. Europe. Use: Powdered plant mixed with normal diet (25–50% cone) suppresses estrus.
Water Pepper (Polygonum Hydropiper) — Found: C. Europe. Use: Liquid extract of powdered plant used.
White Poplar (Populus Alba L.) — Found: Mediteranean. Use: Popular superstition that the bark taken with the kidney of the mule causes sterility.
Pueraria Mirifica Found: Thailand. Use: Estrogenic substanced called mirestrol — small clinical trials successful. Twining herbs or shrubs, often climbing, grown for ornament.
Pterolobium Indicum Found: India/Old World Tropics. Use: Plant without root, saponins, spermicidal effect.
Radish (Rhaphanus Radicula L.) — Use: Menses inducing and abortive properties.
Rosemary (Osmarinus Officinalis) — Found: C. America (Opata). Use: Tea made of rosemary and the "ocean artemisia" for fertility control.
Rue (Ruta Graveolens L.) — Found: Europe and S. America. Use: Hot decoction of plant, 1 oz. to 1 pt of water, allowed to stand for 8 hr. and then drunk to promote menstruation; larger doses induce fetal expulsion.

Raintree (Samnea Saman) — Found: India. Use: Saponins from plant without root, spermicidal effect.
Garden Burnet (Sanguisorba Officinalis) — Found: C. Europe. Use: Powdered plant mixed with normal diet (of mice).
Soapberry Tree (Sapindus Mukorosii) — Found: India. Use: Saponins from fruit, spermicidal effect.
Savory (Satureja Capitata L.) — Use: Menses inducing & abortive properties.
Schlefflera Capitata Found: India. Use: Saponins from plant without root, spermicidal effect.
Pavak or Agui Tree (Semecarpus Anacardium) — Found: India (Hindu). Use: Roots cooked in sour rice water and taken for 3 days at end of menstruation produces sterility.
False Solomon Seal (Smilacina Stellata L.) — Found: Nevada (Indians). Use: Root infusion regulates menstrual disorders; conception prevented by tea of leaves, ½ cup daily for 1 week.
Terminalia Belerica Found: India. Use: Saponins from fruit, spermicidal activity.
Fenugreek (Trigonella Foenumgraecum) — Found: India. Use: Saponins from seed, spermicidal activity.
Wuzawuza (Urena Lobata L.) — Found: New Ireland. Use: Leaves chewed and juice swallowed.
White Hellebore (Veratrum Album L.) — Use: Menses inducing & abortive properties.
Black Haw (Viburnum Prunifolium) — Found: Italy. Use: Relieves dysmenorrhea and controls fertility; hot decoction taken 4 or 5 days before menstrual period.
Monchpfeffer (Vitex Agnus–Castus L.) — Found: C. Europe. Use: Sterility increased with increasing doses; retardation of estrus observed in female rats.
Parparau (Vitex Negundo L.) — Found: Solomon Isles (Buka). Use: Root scrapings chewed with betel mixture and swallowed.

JoanNewman

Copyright 1981, by Joan Newman. All rights reserved. Reproduction in whole or part by any means is permissible only with the prior written consent of the author.

Section IV
Internal Hygiene

FASTING, CHLOROPHYLL & COLOR

Whether it is the light or the warmth from the sun that is most needed can at times be quite confusing. A tomato plant of course depends upon sunlight for growth, but a tomato can ripen in a dark room when warm. This much is certain: those regions which are warmest also receive the most direct light. Of all plants, trees gather the most light; of all fruits from trees, tropical fruits are the "lightest". Except for the severest of hypolglycemics, the exceptions who prove the rule (for the exceptions which proves the rule that there is an exception to every rule is that there are no exceptions to this rule), we would all do well to increase the fruits in our diets and particularly those from the tropics. Of all fruits the mango is just about the sweetest, the papaya the most soothing, and the avocado probably the most nutritious. Arctic Eskimos can survive almost solely on fish: on the other hand, desert nomads can live for years on figs, dates, and St. John's bread alone. Continents control continence.

Fruits contain the greatest concentration of sun energy in the least amount of space. Indeed we need the least exertion of our own energy to assimilate that plant matter: a fruit typically takes less than an hour to digest, a fruit juice twenty minutes. This is opposed to four hours for fresh or unsoaked nut. (A soaked nut, requiring an hour, become more like a fruit. And the opposite is true: a dried fruit becomes more like a nut and requires nearly four hours. So we soak nuts and dried fruits before eating). When fasting the foods to eat just before and just after are fruits. This is the classic form of the sonata, as in a Beethoven quartet: 'ACA'. They are the foods nearest to nothing just as fruit juices are the liquids nearest to water. In fact, a far more gradual transition occurs when surrounding the days of fasting and of fruit juice with fruits. Here we hear, if we have the ear, the particular "andante" movement in Op. 132 as a prayer of holy thanksgiving for recovery from a near–fatal illness: "ABCBA". Clearly traveling fast is best accompanied in priority and posteriority by eating light.

Long–life fasters, those who have tried various techniques on themselves as well as read various experiences of contemporaries and of forefathers, generally agree fruit is best with which to break a fast. A few say vegetables, one is so hard–pressed as to say vegetable oil, but no one says flesh. As though eating flesh, or cake, or pizza or french fries, were not bad enough, what is worse is eating them as the last thing preceeding or the first thing following a fast. An alternate line of reasoning defends such a technique by beginning fasting precisely because flesh, or cake, or pizza, or french fries has been eaten. This forgets all else and employs fasting solely for its cleansing effects. This is indeed why fruits best break fasts; what flush through the body with the greatest of ease are melons, plums, grapes, and the blackest cherries. Flesh however will clog the flow like mortar in the hole of a dam. Meanwhile the waters grow more and more polluted as the mortar dries to a consistency and substance of the concrete walls. Actually, undigested flesh need not dry to become something close to the walls of the intestines; frankfurters or any prepared cold cuts already are the intestinal walls of another animal.

Fasting's metaphor to the human body might be: turning it upside—down and inside—out. What goes inside—out are the toxins, and upside—down are the intestines. Though nothing is eaten, much waste comes out. The average person walks around with five pounds of feces, from even a healthy diet; not only will a first fast of at least three days be the most effective means of discarding it, but if one then fasts fairly regularly that five pounds will be permanently lost. Imagine hanging upside—down: a piece of flesh which hardly differs from one's own esophagus is more likely to cause one to choke than a piece of fruit. Yet when hanging upside—down, why would anyone what to eat? The point is that although eating fruit is less an effort than eating flesh, eating nothing is the least of all efforts. Nothing is easier than not doing something; difficult is beginning again to do the thing which for so long went undone. Thus the first fast is the most troublesome and even painful because of what comes out (Ehret warns carnivores to proceed with great caution: one's own toxins are already too much; the stampede of animal toxins as well is enough to kill the carnivore), just as the first day of eating after any fast can be catastrophic precisely because of what does not come out. Fasting is easy, breaking the fast is hard. No effort is necessary to eat nothing, but after breaking the fast more effort is needed to eat little than to eat a lot. The easiest and worst thing to do is gorge oneself, like a Tantalus maddened by hunger.

A modified form of fasting is fruit juice fasting, whereby no central days of total abstinence occur but only the precautionary days of juice which would otherwise surround the days of water. Some eat whole fruits and call that fasting. The implications are obvious. Every argument defending carnivorism can be extended to periodic cannibalism in much the same manner that any proposition favoring vegetarianism extends to periodic fasting, as do those favoring fasting extend to vegetarianism. Vegetarians who eat especially, but not necessarily only, large quantities of fruit hardly need to fast yet when they fast the task of breaking it is all the easier. Less toxins are excreted because less were eaten: the opposite of flesh is fruit.

A famous comedian once fasted on fresh fruit juices for months. That was fine and good. But when he said he was doing it for political reasons and the rest of the nation looked on with awe, what appeared as self—sacrifice was almost an act but anyway the best thing for himself at that time, for whatever politics or protests. What must be emphasized is that it was at that time and that time only the best thing for himself and himself only. As with eating, much concerning not eating must be found out for oneself. Who would not rather experience life for themselves than read the exegeses and conjectures of a hundred philosophers and a hundred-thousand professors of philosophy? Indeed, through finding out about fasting for oneself, one will find a lot out about oneself.

When one eats, the body directs its energies to digestion, to overcome food to make it become oneself. Fruits of all foods offer the least resistance, but fasts offer no resistance whatsoever. When one fasts, the energies can instead be directed to making oneself become more oneself. One looks into the mirror and does not recognize the face, one thinks and does not recognize the thoughts, one speaks and does not recognize the voice. One becomes someone other than normally known, someone otherwise hidden deep within. But one is not transformed, nor is the old self forgotten; rather, one's conception of the old self is forgotten; one all of a sudden sees and hears as for the first time. The stupor of the first fast is difficult, but compensated by the vigor of the first days after the first fasts. Some might confuse this with banging one's head against a wall: it feels so good when one stops. This laziness of logic is conceived in simplicity and excused only by stupidity. Actually if fasting is to be compared to banging one's head against a wall, it is because after the fast a hole has been made in the wall through which one sees a new view and indeed conceives a new vision.

Now our question is: "How to fast?" Techniques vary. Some call eating only apples a fast, others drinking only apple juice, some say to drink any fresh fruit juice, others to drink herb teas with some honey and lemon; some clarify fasting as drinking only water and specify spring water because distilled water drains the body of minerals, others say to drink distilled water precisely because those minerals are the inorganic deposits for which the body has no use; some recommend fasting until the tongue clears, others until hunger reappears; some assert the necessity of enemas, others condemn them except in the extremest of cases. It is easy to see the science of not eating is as confusing as of eating. One can ignore it all and choose never to fast, though this is like developing an aversion to drinking water because of an inability to swim. This much might be construed: the reader would be as wise to ignore those books which advise how and when not to eat but not how and what to eat as to ignore the opposite, those which discuss food but not fasting from food.

One reason the American urban population is so frenetic is that its diet of fried foods, white foods, and flesh foods, and indeed fried white flesh foods, is particularly high in phosphorus which disturbs the balance of calcium and magnesium, in turn causing nervousness: mineral imbalance is but a step toward mental imbalance. Another reason is that it rarely sees green so 'loses its cool' and 'sees red': red opposes green on the color wheel. The substance found outside the body most nearly identical to the hemoglobin inside is − chlorophyll. They differ chemically only where iron is found in hemoglobin, magnesium constitutes chlorophyll; and they differ chromatically in that blood is red while plants are green. Although complementary colors equally oppose the effects of each other, a good cure for anemia is nevertheless chlorophyll.

Those who see green least have a greater cause for eating it. The best greens are the sprouts and grasses easily grown indoors in even cramped quarters of a city apartment. These are the cleanest, freshest, and indeed the greenest of any vegetables urbanists can hope to obtain: outdoor park city victory gardens are full of lead which leads to no goal they would wish to go, and of fall—out though the only war waged is against insects.

It is one thing to do what is best, quite another what is worst. The worst thing for city folks to do is eat red meat since their bodies are red enough yet they have no green in sight to balance. The more red meat eaten, the more are green vegetables needed to match. Hence bottomless salad bowls frequently accompany mistaken main courses at steak houses. The carnivores who can get along eating flesh — for people can get along eating almost anything, else humanity long ago would have perished in the ice age — are farmers and woodsmen who not only live among green but kill their own red. Just as painting masters mix their own paints, carnivores should spill their own blood if they endeavor to view a clear picture of reality. Those who ignore mineral balance, color harmonies, and moral imperatives should forewarn others. For instance, they should affix on their cars the bumper sticker: "Warning, I Breakfast on Animals". Thus others will know to steer (sic) clear.

Everyone, not just the carnivore, of course benefits from chlorophyll. Some get by (again that great 'get by' — a peccable alternative to 'good—bye') eating few greens so long as they eat fewer reds and instead all the other colors between. This is rather near to fruitarianism, the antonym of carnivorism: a fruit generally ripens from green to red, while no—nitrate red flesh putrefies to green. (The only truly green fruit is the avocado which is nutritionally more like vegetables and digestible more like a nut). Food—combination and protein—complement charts could probably be drawn according to color alone. In fact a whole healing discipline already exists based on eating food by its color. But older than chromotherapy is healing by fasting, whose science consists of consuming no color: clear water and invisible air both are colorless. Pure water is even more important during fasting than otherwise, and those who fast in cities should do so on weekends when industrial factories are closed. Those who desire a "little something" more than water might indulge with clear fruit juices or herb teas since these are translucent as opposed to opaque.

The interaction of color relates to fasting in yet far stranger ways whose mention might cause average eaters and readers to twist in their stools. But eaters and readers must realize that "Fast" is a palliative euphemism for "Feces". When a painter mixes all the colors of the palette, no matter how intense the yellow, or deep the blue, or bright the red, it all comes out a dull brown. The same for eating: no matter how green the spinach, or red the raspberry, or yellow the lemon, or orange the orange, or even white the flour or the sugar, it too all comes out a dull brown. Were the fasting process merely material, nothing would come out where nothing was put in; quite the contrary, color has as much to do with not eating as with eating; bowels still will move, but instead of the brown color from mixing everything, the absence of food shows the absence of color: black.

Done in conjunction with the raw vegetarian diet, fasting is perhaps superfluous. "How are you?" you ask a friend. A colloquial answer often is: "Not too healthy". Not that anyone can ever be 'too' healthy, the vegetarian should be happy being healthy enough. Lumberjacks catch neither Chestnut nor Dutch Elm Disease, and farmers are immune to the blights to which their crops succumb; but many illnesses in the chicken coop are contagious to their keepers - a tubercular cow transmits her bacteria through raw milk, and trichinosis is communicable to anyone who brings home the bacon. The lower along the twisted chain of life from which one eats, the less incidence of disease is received from that food. Fasting extends these ends so far down the line that one is below it, escapes it, and transcends it. Furthermore what already is caught can more easily be dispelled. From nothing comes nothing, said King Lear.

The scale of eaten animal life to eater human death, already calculated in an earlier chapter, comes out to one day more of animal–eating equal one day less of human–living. Such a system of subtraction carries no place for addition; that is the measure where fasting makes its mark. Every day fasted is as much as an extra day of life, for as far as concerns the body metabolism a day of rest from the toils of digestion is a day not lived. Thus the person who fasts a day a week should live eighty years, not just seventy. Proof of this need not be sought in any library stack, livery stable, or infirmary operating table; all one need do is listen to the beat of one's own heart. The pulse rate lowers with each day of fasting as happens to animals in hibernation. Clues become keys, keys become knowledge — so long as one has found the door of disquisition along with the keys. The pulse is the clue, the body is the key, health is the door, and long life is the knowledge.

Ignoring length of life, time is saved another way by length of day. If daily meals are reduced from thrice to twice, more is eaten at each meal but less time is eaten away preparing and cleaning after them. If eating is similarly reduced to two of every three days, a third more will be eaten at every meal if one is eating two–thirds as often. Twice as much time is needed to prepare a salad twice than a twice larger salad once, and likewise to eat it, clean it and digest it. While a good cause to fast is to gain time, a silly reason is to lose weight. A day gained is more important than two pound's lost, and more enduring. Indeed it is better to fast not to lose one's body but to lose one's mind — for that never is regained.

The bible warns that he who does not fast cannot enter the kingdom of heaven. In other words one way among many ways of achieving eternal life is through fasting. (Hogwash!) It has been 'only' long life, not eternal life, about which we here have spoken. Eve's temptation of the apple is a parable of gluttony, a sin from which other sins and other little Adams and little Eves sprout and stem. Noah should have fasted for those forty days and nights while floating upon the sea of wrath, but instead turned the ark into a cupboard and brought food along for everybody. This meant food for lambs, lambs for lions, and fodder and lambs for Noah. Though never connecting it with his dereliction of duty, only with Noah does the Bible mention human carnivorism.

Many new fasting books with calligraphic titles and psychedelic covers apppeared in the late seventies whose one synonym for the subject was 'weight–loss'. These books, written by and for average carnivores, were sold more in regular bookshops than in health food stores; they appeared almost overnight as a fad and disappeared as quickly as a fashion. The reader whose concerns are nutritional and not merely cosmetic must be vigilant to discern the quick from the dead. The serious books on fasting have been available for years and all along were sold only in health food stores. Like figs and dates, they are sweeter aged than fresh. The three best books thus are not coincidentally but absolutely essentially part of a larger system of diet and living. The first, Arnold Ehret's "Mucusless Diet Healing System" (in print since 1922), should be read before the first fast; the second is Paul

Bragg's "The Miracle of Fasting", best read during the fast; "Fasting for the Renewal of Life" by Herbert Shelton is the third which serves as a reference for any developments, usually good but sometimes bad, during and after the fast. Their emphasis is upon fasting as part of a sane system of eating, vegetarian at that; they chiefly concern sustenance, not just abstinence.

All the books, good and bad, whether written for health of readers or wealth of writers, need not be read to discover their differences. A glance is enough; you can tell a health book by its cover: the meritorious serious fasting books display photographs of their authors whose 'pictures of health' promote their fasting programs and their accompanying vegetarianism. The meretricious fake fasting books dare not show their authors: they have too much to hide. The most notorious of these is Dr. Linn, shown aiming a fat finger at an unknown target like Moses pointing at the promised land into which he is forbidden entry. This appears the common case of almost all health books written by doctors of traditional allopathic medicine. One who looks neurotic writes a book on overcoming nervousness, another who is growing bald writes on healthy hair, a third who chain smokes writes on physical fitness. True too for pill nutritionists: well known is the vitamin therapist who died of cancer. Traditional medicine is opposed enough to traditional nutrition, but fasting and vegetarianism contradict them both. Meanwhile all health services and nutritional advice contrary to allopathic medicine must be administered accompanied by an obligatory caveat, hardly endured and hopefully ignored.

Whatever nutritionists claim in good intention about the needs of this vitamin from flesh or that mineral from milk, vegetarians contradict not by claiming anything but by simple living in good health. Those who without pills or potions thrive their whole long lives with just one − quarter of the supposedly essential food groups − the fruits and vegetables, and even the fruits or vegetables − prove by living example the superfluity of scientific nutrition and the phony−baloney of pharmacology. Yet it is better for such heretics of health to keep their peace, and their peas. From the canned food and t.v. dinners of factories, not farms, to the canned laughter of televison, and from the platitudes of presidents to the white−sugar placebos which doctors (witch−doctors?) themselves would never take, ours has become a society where falsehood cons the conscience while truth goes unheeded, an organic carrot held out to a blind donkey.

It hardly occurs to the polluted and deluded to fast. This is perhaps expected. If many had this notion, no delusion would exist: what the deluded most need is what they least believe. Meanwhile they settle for pills, symbols and substitutes for what they seek. No pill has ever cured any disease; nor has fasting cured any disease; the body cures its disease; fasting lulls the body to cure itself the way a mother lulls her child to sleep to rest itself; a pill lures the body the way a piece of cheese lures a rat into a trap; thus as many people die from their pills as from their ills. That someone ill stands a good chance of regaining health from just a week fast is perhaps only half as amazing as that after a fast someone already healthy will feel even healthier. Furthermore, the person who eats judiciously and fasts regularly can actually survive for several weeks without food and feel better during those weeks than before. Why? The Greek gods dined on only ambrosia and nectar, but Nietzsche reminds us in "Beyond Good and Evil" ("Epigrams and Interludes", No. 141) that our abdomens are the reason we cannot easily take ourselves for gods. With every mouthful we remind ourselves of our mortality. For the cast–iron pot we give up an iron stomach, and end up with a pot belly. Humanity, bulbous–bellied but still its eyes bigger than its stomach, will never return to grace with its gods by saying grace at any dinner table. Fruit alone will not even help; the apple was the problem in the first place.

Courage is nevertheless necessary to defend against the philosophies and religions of absolute asceticism which would induce us to eliminate ourselves from the ranks of the living; but this does not mean that gluttons who are obese as much from self–confidence as from over–consumption endure more than those who, despairing over existence, have yielded to self–effacement. Rather, they have never fed themselves any food for thought because their minds always are occupied by thoughts of food. Mystics have seen god, or anyway have seen the light, usually only when fasting. Food was the last thing on their minds. This no one can understand who has not fasted for more than three days, nor frequently. The fasts of Western religions usually last only one day, as in Judaism, or only during the day, as in Islam. This is just long enough to begin to feel hunger; otherwise, by the second day or certainly the third all hunger disappears. In fact healthful eaters and frequent fasters never experience hunger; hunger itself is a sign of ill health, a nudge in the ribs to remind sufferers of lives gone wrong. Eventually a forgotten meal or first day of a fast causes only a funny feeling in the throat. But try telling this to people on the first day of the first fast! Initiates will need more than just assurances; they will need faith. As for seeing gods, instead they will see only a lot of mucus, feces, and even vomit: one must venture through the bottom of life before aspiring to reach the top.

Before the leap of faith is needed the sweep of faith: the sweep of the intestines, not just the intentions. It is the sweep more than the leap which loosens the mental strait-jacket in which even the most rational wrap themselves. Almost like Baron Munchhausen with no foothold anywhere but who takes himself by the hair and lifts himself into the air, those who have long ago taken the sweep elevate themselves higher and higher, because lighter as they rise, they see all things beneath them grow smaller and smaller while they hover in the air in an ascetic satisfaction of foodless toxicless bliss. Yet the firm ground of reality remains always beneath their feet. Following the sweep comes the leap: after the intestines are cleared of waste those who maintain a whole or mostly raw diet will no longer need food in gross amounts specified by government officials, bureaucrats notorious for waste in all they do. The heavy meat and sugar-sweet diet of complicated cookery and simplistic food combining (which simply combines everything) necessitates ridiculous recommendations for numberless nutrients merely to cut through the almost impenetrable digestive system, stuck with muck.

The case of B–12 illustrates precisely the point. Researchers recommend about 5 micrograms for the typical consumer of the average American diet of lots of fat and lots of protein from lots of flesh and lots of milk, as well as lots of nothing from lots of white food. But they are blind guides leading a blind tribe. Flesh and milk are the most often cited sources of the vitamins and yet the most saturated of all sources of fat: deficiencies develop in laboratory animals fed normal amounts of B–12 but also high amounts of fat. Similarly high animal protein diets deplete the vitamin, and diets dominated by white foods double the B–12 required by baboons. (These are insights already adduced by vegetarians, but it took the sufferings of thousands of animals to knock this into the skulls of scientists, numbed and defiled by death. One need be neither a plumber of pipes nor a prober of the pulsars to realize that grease clogs drains). Humans who only eat whole plant foods need no more than 0.05 micrograms: 100 times less the amount of carnivores. And humans who fast, drink no alcohol, smoke no tobacco, and eat only whole raw plant foods produce all the vitamins they need themselves. $B-12$, or not $B-12$: that is the question.

Until one fasts, all reasoning concerning it supports opinion but does not prove it. Its merits will remain hard to defend and difficult to understand. Once one has indeed put the horse of experience in front of the cart of rationality and has taken the sweep, excessive needs of nutrients are not the only things eliminated. Just as the desire for food disappears after the first day of a fast, other desires disappear after other days. For instance, after about three days one might walk past the store window in which is displayed that new coat eyed so enviously for weeks but which today no longer is wanted. Certainly by the fifth day all sexual impulses for moonlight liaisons eclipse into evanescence and become moonlight sonatas. Gandhi rarely could discuss fasting without bringing in the subject of celibacy. Wooing and eating and drinking are pleasures, but only of the body; denying sex and food and drink are also pleasures — of the soul.

Desires are passed behind not just during fasts, but if regularly conducted between fasts as well. If one had not already done so, vegetarianism will surely be embraced by the faster. While Moses fasted for forty days and forty nights ("forty nights' is seemingly redundantly added to the Jewish Bible's 'forty days' to differentiate from what is practiced by Muslims who fast for forty days but not for forty nights) atop Mt. Sinai his people were worshipping a calf, which lucky for the calf was made of gold instead of flesh and blood. Moses, not very happy about the whole idea, realized that his generation was not ready for a new life. So for forty years he led them in the desert until they grew new bodies; only with that would they be prepared for their new lives. Their wandering was a sort of fast to prepare their steps into a new land.

The carnivore wishing to convert to vegetarianism, the vegetarian to veganism, the vegan to raw foods, all would more assuredly confront their transitions if they fasted in between each of their steps. This way the fasts would detoxify them over a period of days instead of the change in diet doing so over months, and no one could mistakenly attribute the sickness from cleansing instead to the new vegetarian diet. If we ignore all bad news, we will cease to be given it. Those who complain of tiredness and headache within or soon after the first month of vegetarianism place the blame on doing without flesh food rather than having done with it for so long. Such sychophants to sickness are impatient: willing to try everything once, they rarely try anything twice. Unwilling to endure, they go back to flesh foods. But house — cleaning must precede house — moving. It is easier to dump wasteful baggage which should never have accumulated in the first place than to pack it along to the second place. Old habits are as much embedded in the mind as old feces in the intestines. Many people accept both as part of a normal life. But what kind of life is that? It is the life of the old man who carried a chair wherever he went so that whenever he tired he could sit on it. He felt grateful for the chair yet never realized carrying the chair was what made him so tired.

At least a full year is necessary for initiates to judge a diet's difference for that is how long the very last old cell will live before replaced anew; if the first month is sustained then one's abstinence is bound to last. Fasting will facilitate graceful transitions in life not just bodily but spiritually. Gandhi grew so intensely in his later life that he fasted as many days as he ate; when he ate he limited his menu to five items a day, and never ate after sunset or before sunrise. His mind was elsewhere than on food, or perhaps just on everything at once: not just on what grows under the sun but with what glows above it.

Nevertheless, a stage along life's way can be reached when fasting no longer is necessary. Toxins are produced in the body simply by its being, yet these are no more than the healthy body is capable of expelling; what are too much are those toxins from impure foods eaten by a consequently unhealthy body. A few years of periodic fasting should rid the body of its old load, and a raw vegetarian diet should prohibit it from acquiring any new one. Indeed after such years fasting could become difficult to do though it previously was easy: This is a sign that the body is clean. A negative proof of this are sick people who never voluntariy fast but automatically lose appetite despite the tea and chicken soup in which they are drowned, and the aspirin and anitbiotics by which they are inundated. So those who constantly and easily fast need to do so until they reach the last stage where though they still wish to do so it no longer is easy nor therefore as constant, and so is severed like an umbilical tie. Only those parents are successful who have raised their children to the age when they as parents are no longer needed.

We all need green. It is a metaphysical, if not medical fact that no color renders rest so immediately to its viewer. Chlorophyll is green, thus leaves are green, thus forests are green. Where climates are coldest, where winters are whitest, trees' leaves stay green year—round. While nowhere else than out to pasture is better for a busy businessman to relax his tired summer soul, the more active weekend vacationers usually head for the hills for skiiing, the snow, and seeing the cedars. Suburbanites grow green gardens as hobbies, and even city dwellers cultivate house plants by their soot—stained windows to compensate for what they do not see outside. In New York City the dollar sign of affluence is a penthouse upon whose roof is installed not a swimming pool, nor a tennis court, but an aerial arboretum. The less fortunate tenant might settle for a Fifth Avenue apartment looking out onto Central Park. But a woodsman whose home is made of the very trees surrounding his cabin needs no windows.

All things considered, a remaining question is: "Why does not everyone fast?" This also brings to question: "Why is not everyone a vegetarian?" We will unfortunately disregard the first, leave until later the answer to the second, and here be content with having addressed ourselves to a third: "Why does not every vegetarian fast?" An objection has been raised that fasting is an extreme form of carnivorism, a self—cannibalism. Shame on vegetarians for doubting such a useful tool when they should be denigrating the like of Frank Purdue, Oscar Meyer, and Colonel Sanders! While they worry over losing a few pounds of feces, Frank Purdue is busy devising ways to pluck and freeze his chickens live!

Once upon a time a city supermarket Daniel Boone meant to kill a chicken but instead of the head he chopped off his own head. Since he was as hungry as the chicken was hasty, he quickly reasoned that if he could eat pig's knuckles he might as well eat his knuckles; so instead of a ham sandwich he made a hand sandwich, like Harpo Marx spreading mustard not on the hot dog but on the hot dog vendor, biting into his hand between two slices of bread. Recalling his mother's recipe for fried chicken handed down from generation to generation in his old Kentucky home, the next day he dipped the leftover in batter, shook the hand in bread crumbs, and fried it in chicken fat. Chicken-Fried Kentuckian.

Mark Mathew Braunstein, New York, New York

DISCOVERING FASTING

When I sit down to write, it seems hard to know where to begin because all the events of my life fit into the pattern, intermingled in the experiences and interpretations which make up composite reality to me.

In the ancient biblical records one may read about a man who was born blind and how he received his sight by a miracle. When the crowd inquired about his healing he could not answer all of their questions, but he said: "This I know, once I was blind and now I see."

Like that man, I can not answer all the questions about my healing, but I can say: "This I know, once I was sick and now I am well."

To keep me alive, my beloved husband, Howard took me either South or West for many years to avoid the coldest months of the Maine winters.

Medical science had done its best but still I remained in poor health. I became a seeker after truth and the truth has led me, step by step, towards ever increasing better health.

It's slow progress but each time something was learned which helped me, if only a little bit, it was a joy. I wanted everyone I met to know that one small healing fact and what it had done for me, in order that others might obtain benefit, also. When I shared my new found knowledge, almost invariably I came away with more helpful information. This may be one of the key requirements for healing: the desire to share knowledge - and whatever else necessary - to help another suffering person obtain relief.

When my granddaughter, Roberta was about fourteen years of age she selected a gift for me. It was a small plaque which reads:

> It is good to be a seeker
> But sooner or later you have to
> Be a finder
> And then it is well
> To give what you have found
> A gift into the world
> For whoever will accept it.

(Jonathan Livingston Seagull)

At times of discouragement her gift would be a comfort to me. Sooner or later--Yes. The seeker must find, and then comes the enjoyment of giving freely the victorious revelations gleaned during the quest of the seeker.

Events That Led To The First Fast

We were in Homestead, Florida the winter of 1957. A member of the church which I was attending at the time, (while making a study of their doctrine) asked me if I would please go to the jail and visit a young woman named Catherine. She was an alcoholic and had been arrested for drunkenness. I agreed to do so.

It was my first time inside of a jail. That was the new jail so it was clean, but the designer had perhaps forgotten that people were to be housed therein. The policeman opened the cell door and placed a chair in the small space at the foot of the two bunk beds which nearly filled the cell.

There were two women, one sitting on each lower bunk, facing each other. Their hands could easily have touched the other person's knees. At the farther end of the cell was a barred window and a few feet beyond the window was a block wall. That was the only view.

The policeman closed the door and the lock was turned. I sat down, holding my Bible in my lap. After I said hello, both women began to cry. I felt like weeping and said; "Oh! I wish I could help you". They both responded that I already had because I had come to see them.

One said she had been locked up sixteen weeks and not one of her relatives or acquaintances had come to speak with her. Catherine appeared to be a gentle person and she was pretty in a way, but her face was marked by the ravages of alcoholism. There they were, condemned to just lie on the beds or sit on the edges of them looking at each other. There was nothing to read, nothing to do. They felt so hopeless and I felt so helpless about their situation.

When the policeman said time was up I asked if he would permit me to visit the colored cell. There were six woman there and three bunk beds. They also appreciated my coming.

A week or so later the church in which my husband, two of our daughters and myself had our membership, held it's Missionary Society meeting. Many winter visitors belonged to that church. Diamonds and furs were customary among those who attended there.

The chairwoman announced that the work for the coming year was to be planned. She asked who had any suggestions. I arose at once and told them of my experience in the jail and my plan for helping women who had been arrested.

Two of the women from the church should go to the jail and do visitation at regular intervales. Our Missionary Society should provide Bibles and other good reading material. The police should cooperate and notify us when each woman was to be released. Some church members could take her home, see that she had proper clothing to wear to church and bring her to the church service the following Sunday, if possible. I loved my idea!

When I had finished, there was a long silence. Then, looking about among the women before her and past me as if I did not exist, the chairwoman cleared her throat and asked: "Does anyone have any suggestions?"

I was stunned and sat down immediately. It was my first rebuff in a church. At home I said to my husband; "Howard, I just graduated from the Missionary Society". I considered that it was past time when we should do our missionary work right here at home.

When reading the Bible one day I came upon some instructions in the book of Matthew that I must have read hundreds of times before but they had never registered in my mind. There they were, plainly listed in Chapter 25, verses 31, 46 where a description of the final judgement is given. These are the five specific things Jesus said His followers must do.

1. Feed the poor.
2. Clothe the destitute.
3. Entertain strangers.
4. Visit the sick.
5. Go to the prison. (or local jail).

Forty five years I had been a Christian and never been inside a prison. How have I missed these important instructions? Why had I not been taught to do those five vital things?

It may have been a couple of weeks after my visit to the jail when, one evening a strange car arrived in our yard and several sailors brought Catherine to the door, leading and half supporting her. What a sight she was, standing there, hugging her whiskey bottle! I had never in my life seen anyone in such a condition. Her face was red and swollen and her pleading eyes questioned me. I held out my arms and she staggered into them with a moan.

The sailors told me they had picked her up off the street several days before, to save her from being arrested. She had been so inebriated that she had not been able to tell them her name or where she lived. She had remained in a state of delirium but in her ramblings they had caught the name, "Mrs. Pease".

It came time for them to return to their ship which was harbored at Key West. They did not know what to do with her so they looked in the telephone directory, located a Mrs. Pease and brought her to our address.

The young men were not completely sober themselves. I walked with them to their car and, aloud, I said a prayer thanking God for men who had so great a compassion for a fellow human being, and asked special protection for them as they traveled. Then I returned to Catherine, whom I had led to the bedroom before bidding farewell to the sailors.

There she lay, thrashing and moaning. I sat on the edge of the bed beside her and began to pray. She would say a few words of prayer and sometimes she would plead in song; "Just a closer walk with Thee Oh! Lord..Let it be...let it be".

I played some spiritual songs on the record player. She was steadily growing worse. She screamed that snakes were crawling on her and she begged for help from God and from me. Never again after that night did a (so—called) joke about pink elephants seem funny to me, for she would crawl into the corner of the bed in terror, covinced that pink elephants were coming to stomp on her.

Finally, from sheer exhaustion, she went to sleep. I walked into the living room and, if I recall correctly, these are the exact words I said to my husband. "Howard, I don't know what I have seen but I know I have seen Hell, and I shall never rest until I find out what can make a person suffer like that".

Catherine stayed with us for many days and thus I learned my first lessons in alcoholism.

One day a tall, very thin young man came from across the tracks. He said he had heard that I was helping Catherine and he wished I would help him also. I was so sure that Catherine and I would find the answer to the alcoholism that I readily agreed.

Fred and his wife lived in a shack that leaked and had only rough boards for siding. They were being charged an outrageous price for rent, which embittered him. His wife worked as a nurse's aid to support them.

When Fred was able, he came over to our place but if not, I went to their shack to see how he was getting along during the hours his wife worked.

One day there was trouble between Fred and his landlady over the excessive rent. He grew more drunk and then he decided to kill her. A great tragedy was averted by my appearing on the scene, for eventually I was able to reach through to his mind. But the potential for murder remained and something had to be done at once.

Howard and I had an apartment that we had left vacant because we were in litigation with the former tenants. To allow another occupant in would have a damaging effect on the law suit, but the emergency required immediate action, so we moved their old mattress and the two chairs they owned into the apartment and abandoned the law suit.

Fred's behavior held startling surprises. One day I went to the apartment with a lovely plate of food and started to pass it to him. With a roar and great violence he knocked the plate into the air and the food went all over the walls and even on the ceiling. After that display he was weak and repenant. I got him more food which he ate with gratitude for he had been hungary. So why had he thrown the food? The only answer seemed to be that he was insane.

Another time I came in and he rushed at me, fists in the air. Just as he was about to hit me a peculiar thing happened. It looked as if he were fighting to prevent himself from hitting me. He forced himself to take two steps backwards and turn a little to the left. His fist then went crashing through the large window of the door instead of hitting me directly in the face. I often wondered about why he stepped back after a forward rush to hit me. It was very puzzling, and it was years before I found a satisfactory answer.

Fred became so sick that he would beat his head against the cement wall. His wife and I had a small padded quilt and we would hurry and put it between him and the wall when he had those head pounding spells. It seemed as if we were in a nightmare.

We appealed for help from the police, the medical profession and several government agencies. We were directed to an alcoholic center in Miami, but Fred was raving crazy by then and it was unsafe for us to take him. The police would not escort us. When we finally made the trip Fred tried to jump out of the car into the moving city traffic several times.

At last we arrived with great relief, but that relief turned to fear as we watched Fred being manhandled by two attendants. I took extra care that the receptionist understood they were to phone me when Fred was released so we could come for him.

A few days afterwards, during the aftermath of a hurricane, in walked Fred, drenched and exausted. He had been released and sent out into the storm. Later we heard that one of the attendants had been hitting an elderly patient so Fred had gotten out of bed and beaten the attendant severely. We were told that a nurse watched and said that was good, for it was time someone gave the bully a thrashing. It was not hard to figure why they wanted Fred out of their institution as speedily as possible.

So we were again caring for Fred. He was trying desperately to stop drinking.

One afternoon I went to the apartment to check on him. There he lay on the mattress. He was unconscious and his body was all twisted out of shape. I could not rouse him and his face had the color of death. It looked as if time was running out for Fred.

I had heard of cases where alcoholics were thrown in jail and had died for want of alcohol which their systems needed to survive the shock of withdrawal.

From personal experience with Fred I had learned that a very small amount of good whiskey would relieve his shaking after he had been drinking an excessive amount of the cheap, chemicalized wine. I had purchased a bottle of whiskey which I kept at our house for dire emergencies.

Rushing home I grabbed the whiskey bottle and ran back. Fred's jaws were set and had to be forced apart so I could administer the whiskey with a teaspoon.

Eventually his body began to jerk and he moaned. Slowly he came back to consciousness. The color of his face improved and finally he spoke to me. It was like watching a dead man return to life. I believe Fred was very close to death and that the whiskey saved his life.

Some years later, when Mr. Pease and I had opened our home as an alcoholic mission, one church group accused me of having a devil's mission because I allowed alcoholics to come to the altar bringing their whiskey bottles, if necessary. I tried to explain and told them that when I found out why Fred had lived because of the whiskey, then would be the time to decide whether or not alcoholics should be stopped from carrying their whiskey bottles to the altar. The church people could not understand, and they even had prayer meetings, asking God to drive us out of the town of Farmington. They did not realize that such prayers are evil, and in the category of black magic. They were practicing witchcraft and did not know it.

Here are some of the words of a song they used to sing. "Just as I am without one plea, save that Thy blood was shed for me...Just as I am, Thou wilt receive, will welcome, pardon, cleanse, relieve; because Thy promise I believe. Oh lamb of God, I come! I come!".

They could not have understood the true meaning of the words they were singing, it seemed to me.

One night Fred was especially bad off and I stayed with him and his wife until about two o'clock in the morning. Then I literally staggered home and to bed, but was too tired to sleep. I reached for the Bible and a strange thing happened. It was as if some power controlled my hands and opened the Bible for me. My eyes were riveted on the passage to which my left thumb was pointed. Matthew, Chapter 17, Verse 21. "This kind cometh out only by prayer and fasting".

I was startled for it appeared that the passage was a message for me to fast. Never having known anyone who fasted, belonged to a church that recommended fasting or read hardly anything about the practice, I was at a loss.

It did not seem logical for me to stop eating when there was so much worked to do and so much energy was being expended on Fred's behalf. Then I had an idea. Telling God that I wanted to obey Him but did not understand the directive, I asked Him to take away my appetite for whatever period He wanted me to fast and make me hungry when I was to eat again.

For four days and a half I was not hungry. After that I ate and found that my sense of taste had improved and the food tasted unusually delicious. It seemed impossible, but I felt better and was far less tired than when the fast began although the work had continued on schedule.

My first fast led me to wonder why, in all the years of religious training and my years of sickness, no one had recommended fasting to me.

My conclusion was that fasting was wonderful for the person who fasted. However, there was no visible evidence that Fred was better and the fast had been to benefit him, or so I had thought. It was time to find facts on the subject.

A systematic study of scriptures regarding fasting revealed that there are at least seventy-seven places in the Bible where some information regarding it is given.

Thus, my first fast led to new information.

Then it was spring and time to return to Maine and prepare for planting of the crops. Fred and his wife went North in the car with Howard and our daughter Sandra. Gram Pease, my mother-in-law and I were to follow soon.

I promised Catherine that as soon as the mystery of alcoholism was solved I would return to her. Years later, when it seemed as if enough information had been found so that she might be helped by it, I went back to Florida. Dear, sweet Catherine had died.

Mrs. Gladys Pease, 13 Franklin Avenue, Farmington, Maine

TWO GREAT MEN

Dear sweet, little Jewish Princess: It was joy to have you with us for Thanksgiving dinner. It has occured to me that you may wonder why I am fasting during these holidays. It is my pleasure to write you the message that came into my mind this forenoon.

Centuries ago there was a Jewish man who had great love and pity for suffering humanity. In his zeal to protect a man from persecution he killed another man. Then he had to run away to save himself.

For many years he must have been a very lonely person. He became sure that there was one supreme God and that when he prayed and meditated that supreme being communicated with him.

Finally the man became a great leader of the Jewish people. They were an unruly group of many thousands and the problems of leadership were great. In search of more knowledge from God the man went into the mountains where he prayed and fasted.

The record of those events has been passed down through the ages. In that record it states that the man fasted – without food or water – for forty days and forty nights.

During this period of amazing dedication he received Ten Commandments, which he believed were given to him by the supreme God. In brief those Ten Commandments are as follows:
1. Have no other Gods before Me.
2. Do not make any likeness of anything that is in the heaven above; or that is in the earth beneath; or that is in the water that is under the earth. Thou shall not bow down to them or serve them.
3. Do not take the name of the Lord, thy God in vain.
4. Remember the Sabbath day to keep it holy.
5. Honor your parents.
6. Do not kill.
7. Do not commit adultery.
8. Do not steal.
9. Do not lie.
10. Do not covet things that belong to others.

The stringency of these rules were so advanced beyond the former requirements that it was extremely difficult, if not impossible, for even the most devout individuals to obey the commandments to the letter. However, by diligently attempting to do so, they found that their lives became happier and their bodies became healthier. They recognized that these revelations were given for the protection of God's people. This strengthened their faith and belief that there was one supreme God and that He cared for their wellbeing.

Among the many written records that were left for posterity one finds that, in succeeding generations, some of the holiest Jews received supernatural messages pertaining to the future. Repeatedly it was promised that, when the time was right, a great personage would be sent to earth. This one would have the anointing of Almightly God and He would bring the final spiritual truth to the world. That truth would end sin, sorrow, and sickness. Even death would be no more.

In time the general population came to believe that the Messiah, who would save them from their sins, would come. He would be called Emmanuel, (which means, God with us) and his body would never see corruption. He would have eternal physical life and the final enemy, death, would have been overcome. So generation after generation watched and waited, not knowing exactly what to expect but living in hope of fulfillment of the promise.

It was almost 2000 years ago, in the land of Judaea, that a certain child was born. Wise men came from far to the East asking, "Where is he that is born, King of the Jews?"

Apparently these men had received by psychic message that the Anointed One, so long promised, had been born. So strong had been their teaching, so close their communion with the world of spirit that they arose in confidence and started out to find this child, born of a Jewish woman.

They were nearly two years reaching their destination. Spiritual phenomena verified to them that here, in a humble carpenter's home, was the One whom God had selected to bring to the world the final revelation which would alleviate suffering and eradicate death.

These wise men believed that here was the child who, in years to come, would deliver to mankind the truth which would set them free. They accepted him as the Messiah and, in reverence, presented to him their gifts of gold, frankincense and myrrh.   In the record one may read that the child grew in stature and in wisdom. When he was about twelve years old he went with his parents and a large group of people to a distant city to worship in the great temple. After the worship services were over the multitude started back home. When evening came the child's parents realized that their son was not among the assemblage and they returned to the city sorrowing and seeking him.

He was finally located in the temple where he was sitting with the learned men of the synogogue, listening and asking such penetrating questions that the great scholars were amazed. When his parents wanted to know why he had brought all this trouble upon them he replied, "Know ye not that I must be about my Father's business?" It seems that already this boy recognized the urgency of time regarding God's work.

As a young man he became a spiritual leader. According to the ancient records, some of which are supposed to have been penned by eyewitnesses, many miracles took place as he went about his ministry. One may read that the blind received their sight, the lame walked, the demon possessed became free and sane, those with diseases were healed and upon occassion the dead were brought back to life.

The great crowds that followed him observed the miracles and were awed by them. Some believed him to be a great prophet, a teacher sent from God. Some considered him to be the Son of God.

He called himself the Son of Man and the Son of God. When he was criticized he replied, "Is it not written in your law; I said, Ye are Gods? If he called them Gods to whom the word of God came, and the scriptures can not be broken; Say ye to him whom the Father hath sanctified and sent into the world; Thou blasphemest; because I said; I am the Son of God?"

He urged the people to believe him and learn the spiritual principles which had been revealed to him. He tried to explain that the miracles were the natural result of the operation of spiritual laws. Whenever those laws were observed properly miracles would take place. He taught them, saying: "He that believeth in me, the works that I do shall he do also; and greater works that these shall he do, because I go to my Father." But the people could not understand.

He was called, King of the Jews. When he replied, "My Kingdom is not of this world" they were bewildered. They had anticipated a king who should wear a crown of gold and jewels. Few had any conception of a spiritual kingship.

There were unbelievers and scoffers, as well as political bureaucrats who opposed this popular young man. Most dangerous of all were the spiritual leaders who watched and feared him, and who planned his destruction.

So he became a controversial figure and thus he remains to this day.

The young man went into the desert to be alone with God. The report states that he prayed and fasted forty days and forty nights. There is no mention as to whether he drank water or not but it is likely that he followed the same spiritual principle when he was fasting as did his predecessor during his experience on the mountain.

Let us take time now to consider these two men.

The man on the mountain, during his long fast, received the Ten Commandments.

What did the second man learn during his equally long fast in the desert?

What was so strange about the doctrine which he preached with such authority and demonstrated so remarkably?

A part of what he preached was new and different, but he made it very clear that the truth he brought was based on the former revelations from God, on the foundation of the spiritual concepts which the Jewish people had known for centuries.

Today millions of people believe that the Ten Commandments were given by God. If one accepts the message received on the mountain as authentic it appears logical for such individuals to look carefully at the life and teachings of the second man who is being considered. Could it be that he, also was in communication with God?

Should we not study his doctrine and research it diligently? For this new doctrine will determine for all time the question regarding the divinity of the man who said: "I am the Son of God."

There are in print many loose translations and paraphrases of the ancient Hebrew records. Some of them differ dangerously from the literal translation which was made by collaboration of seventy eminent Hebrew scholars, in the year 1611.

From that preferred translation one may read that the man made the following remark about fasting. "But the day will come when the bridegroom (speaking of himself) shall be taken from them (his followers) and then shall they fast in those days."

That is one of several passages which indicate that fasting is a requirement, when seeking spiritual truth. One might ask, "Why should they fast?" There are over seventy-five references to fasting in the few records which were compiled into one book. They give many reasons for fasting, such as when praying for healing of some suffering individual or petitioning God regarding other important issues.

The man said of evil spirits and demons; "This kind cometh out only by fasting and prayer."

There are statements in the record which indicate that both physical and spiritual changes must take place if one is to find the truth of God. Fasting cleanses the body of poisons, and that should be born in mind when considering passages which refer to physical changes.

The man said: "Verily, verily, I say unto thee, except a man be born of water and the Spirit he can not enter into the Kindgom of God. Marvel not that I say unto thee' Ye must be born again."

What can be the meaning of this passage? What does "born of water" mean? Does that reference to "water" pertain to what is termed "living water" in the two passages quoted below?

The man was at a well when a woman came to draw water. He said to her, "If thou knewest the gift of God and who it is that sayeth to thee, Give me to drink, thou wouldst have asked of him and he would have given thee living water. Whosoever drinks of the water of that well would thirst again; but whosoever drinketh of the water that I shall give him shall never thirst; but the water that I shall give him shall be in him a well of water, springing up into eternal life."

Again he spoke. "If any man thirst let him come unto me, and drink. He that believeth in me, as the scripture hath said, 'Out of his belly shall flow rivers of living water.'"

Man is admonished to cleanse the body, which is called the Temple of the Living God. Could it be that the body would function differently if it were free from the spiritual pollution of sin and the physical poisons that are within?

Having fasted extensively and received much healing, I have come to believe that the body would produce a fluid which would cleanse and heal continually if man were in the right positon towards God.

To the best of my ability I follow the teachings of the two great men of whom I have written. Evidence leads me to conclude that both men walked with God. The old doctrine and the newer one belong together for the ultimate glory of mankind.

Farewell for now.

Mrs. Gladys Pease, 13 Franklin Avenue, Farmington, Maine

CONSTIPATION AND OXYGENATED INTESTINAL IRRIGATION

Intestinal irrigation refers to the infusion of aqueous substances into the large intestine, generally through the anus. These, i.e. enemas, were first recorded in 1500 B.C. in the Ebers Papyrus, an ancient Egyption document dealing with the practice of medicine. Hippocrates (4th and 5th century, B.C.), Galen (2nd century A.D.) and Pare (16th century A.D.) advocated the use of enema therapy. Pare was the first to describe a total intestinal irrigation. This is quite different from an enema. The latter generally flushes the end of the colon, while a total irrigation will cleanse the entire colon, rectum to cecum. Waddington (1940) states that "there is no resemblance one to the other, except that both procedures begin by the injection of fluid into the rectum and sigmoid."

An intestinal irrigation is initially a diagnostic procedure which subsequently becomes a therapeutic measure of great value for the relief of a variety of syndromes. An irrigation should enable the therapist to study and diagnose several closely related phenomena of the normal and abnormal intestinal canal. We should expect to determine the presence of such intestinal conditions as: the amount, consistency, and color of intestinal mucus; the size, concentration, and approximate location of fecal impactions; and the shape, density, and color of feces.

The cecum and ascending colon are responsible for a large amount of water absorption. Bacteria and their toxins, present in high numbers in this region, can also be absorbed. Therefore, to obtain the full benefit of an irrigation, the entire bowel should be cleansed. For this purpose a total intestinal irrigation, not an enema, is chosen.

Waddington (1940) accuses medical prejudice for the lack of acceptance of intestinal irrigation as a therapeutic measure. Those who condemn irrigation usually lack knowledge of, or experience with the process. Its backers have had personal experience of its benefits. The administration of irrigations by untrained personnel has often resulted in detrimental effects on the patient. These instances have greatly discredited the therapy. Snyder et. al. (1933), after administering over 16,000 irrigations without incident, states that the literature depicting the dangers of intestinal irrigation is based on theory, not fact.

Intestinal hydrotherapy is part of a treatment plan, resulting in tubular, tissue and cellular drainage via the anus, portal system, and lymphatic system, a reduction of intestinal toxins prevents their build up in the portal and lympatic vessels. This relieves stress on the liver as well. A condition of intestinal toxemia can be improved through drainage, restoration of normal mechanical and cellular function, improvement of lymphatic and capillary function, and through relief of the liver from its toxic load (Wiltsie, 1938). Dietary changes, rest, physical therapy and vaccines may also be included in the overall treatment.

This therapy is not intended to be a cure-all, but is a valuable procedure for a wide variety of conditions of ill health. Intestinal malfunctions are precursors of many illnesses. The restoration of intestinal elimination, too often ignored, is an important preliminary course to the restoration of health. An inefficient colon is not always the cause of sickness, but it is believed to accentuate and prolong any and all diseased conditions of the human body (Waddington, 1940).

The effects of intestinal hydrotherapy are many. They include:

1) A feeling of well-being which hastens the removal of bowel contents (mucus, gas, bacteria, parasites, undigested food particles, glandular and cellular debris, bacterial toxins, etc.)

2) Abdominal massage administered during an irrigation breaks up fecal impactions, moves water around impactions, breaks up the solidified crust on the inner surface of the colon, stimulates peristalsis, and helps return the colon to its normal shape. The latter removes pressure on other organs as well (liver, gall bladder, stomach, heart, etc.).

3) Oxygen infusion aids in the healing of sores and wounds. European investigators have found that oxygen injected into the colon was more effective than the inhalation of large quantities of the gas (Waddington, 1940); oxygen also irritates, kills or incapacitates anaerobic bacteria and parasites. A sufficient supply of oxygen to the nervous tissue is a must. This is enhanced through intestinal lavage. Patients generally exhibit a state of reduced nervousness and irritability following a series of intestinal irrigations.

4) Water is absorbed through intestinal capillaries during an irrigation. This dilutes toxins in the blood and increases the rate of kidney involvement in detoxification.

5) Hot water supplies heat to the body, relaxes intestinal muscles, and softens the fecal crust in the colon.

6) Cold water helps to bring down fever, helps to shrink swollen and edematious tissue, stimulates peristalsis, and it is thought to contract the colon cells forcing toxins from them. Temperature fluctuation, in general, irritates intestinal parasites. They reside there because they have adapted to 98.8F., not 80, 85, 105 or 109 degrees Fahrenheit.

7) A large amount of weight loss may also be attributed to intestinal hydrotherapy. Intestinal stasis can be responsible for the accumulation of large amounts of fecal matter as well as allowing the body wastes to build up at the cellular level.

SATKARMASADANA
PART I

When Viktoras called me from Connecticut one evening last April and asked me if I would write a series of articles on Shatkriya (Body Purification Techniques of Hatha Yoga and Ayurvenda), I immediately said yes, in spite of the fact that I don't claim yet to be a yogi much less a "guru". My qualifications for being so presumptuous to write articles on the subject are experience and practice. Although I had practiced Asanas before, I didn't begin serious Shatkriya Sadhana until 1966, beginning with Uddiyana and ordinary enemas. In a matter of a few weeks I was doing Nauli, Lauliki, and Basti. In the last 13 years I have been able to perfect about 80 different body purification techniques to the point where I can now talk about them (Kriyas, associated Asanas and other preliminary preparatory techniques such as Bandhas and Mudras). Some techniques I do not talk about. It's not that they are secret, but talking about a thing before one has done it dissipates the motivating energy necessary to accomplish that very thing (the first important admonishment given to Theos Bernard (1) by his guru).

It is a great pleasure for me to describe techniques of traditional Hatha Yoga. I learned what I know by first conducting a thorough literature search to collect information, by studying the ancient translations, by experimenting and applying the information, by visiting various health yogis in India who checkedc me out on my techniques and showed me those techniques which aren't in the books, and by practice, practice, practice.

Before I get into the subject of Shatkriya, it is important that I clear up some misconceptions prevalent among American Sadhas. Hatha Yoga and Patanjali Yoga are not the same (2), (11). Asana and Pranayama are common to both, but for different reasons. In Patanjali Yoga, Asana and Pranayama are used to release tension and quiet the mind for meditation so that the desired autosuggestions can be programmed into our consciousness. In Hatha Yoga, Asanas are used to recondition the glandular and nervous systems, and to prepare for Mudra, while Pranayama is used to selectively charge certain autonomic nerve ganglions (plexuses) with prana (atmospheric ionization energy). Yogis who have practiced both types of yoga (1) claim that the results of Patanjali Yoga are subjective and strictly mental and are the results of autosuggestion, self–hypnosis; the programming of the mind by meditation into believing that "we are one", "God is love", etc. Hatha Yoga, on the other hand, produces definite, observable, objective, psycho–physiological effects. Being of scientific inclination, I have chosen that path for myself: the objective path without devotion, worship, dogma, ritual, guru bhakti, chanting, or religious belief. I believe that the way to God is through science (4) namely discovering and obeying the laws of nature or the universe.

The first two out of the eight steps in Patanjali Yoga are Yama and Niyama (observances and restraints) such as non–violence, non–stealing, celibacy, purity, austerity, contentment, etc. In technical Hatha Yoga, Yama and Niyama are replaced by Shatkriya (3) the purification techniques. If the body is clean from mucous, protein metabolites, or other nerve stimulants such virtues as non–violence, celibacy, consideration of other people, etc., appear by themselves, they don't have to be "observed" or "obeyed". People who have purified themselves don't have to "restrain" themselves from murder or rape (9); such thoughts and desires simply do not arise if the bloodstream and nervous system have been cleaned. In Patanjali Yoga, Shatkriya is not even mentioned as one of the eight steps. In Hatha Yoga, Shatkriya is prescribed daily during sadhana until results are attained, and thereafter to maintain superior health. Before the nervous energy can be safely directed to the chakras through Pranayama and Mudra, it is necessary that the nadis or tubes (blood vessels, lymphatic vessels, nerves, alimentary canal, lungs, and other channels) be purified by Shatkriya; hence Shatkriya is the first step of Hatha Yoga. Self–realization or a subjective feeling of one–ness with God does not make one a yogi. I have experienced the feeling several times as a result of applying various techniques (by the way, although very awe–inspiring, it is not always pleasant or blissful) yet I do not call myself a yogi; for example I still do not have voluntary control over my entire autonomic nervous system like a true yogi does (and I have never experienced sensations or any apperception of light or mandalas along my spine). I have no siddhi, and I am not in perpetual effortless awareness of one–ness with God (Sahaja Avastha).

My reasons for agreeing to write these articles are several. Perhaps the foremost is the fact that in the English language there is no single one book on the subject of Yogic Purification which gives such important details as only one who has actually done the techniques would know. It is sadly amusing to see so many books in English supposedly on Hatha Yoga, where the Author is shown smugly demonstrating Asanas, but when we come to the sections on Kriyas and Mudras (if they are included at all) we find outright plagiarism; usually from Hatha Pradipika, Gheranda Samhita, or Siva Samhita. I have been able to discover only two sources of credible information. The first one is a book which all serious sadhus must read called "Hatha Yoga" by Theos Bernard (1), perhaps the only non–Indian to ever completely master the Traditional Hatha Yoga, including all the Kriyas and Mudras. There must have been others but they didn't write any books on the subject, at least not in English. My second source of information, by far the most comprehensive, are the publications of the Kaivalyadhama, specifically, their quartly journal "Yoga Mimamsa" begun in 1924, plus their books "Yogic Therapy" and the "Satkarmasangrahah". When I was beginning my sadhana years ago what wouldn't I have given for a book describing in detail the techniques which I am now about to describe in my articles. I pray that my articles will be of help to other such serious sadhus.

Another reason for the articles is that I know of no–one in this country who knows these techniques much less teaches them. Once in a while you might find someone who has done two or three of the six esoteric Kriyas (Neti, Khauti, Nauli, Basti, Kapolabhati and Tratak); yet in all my searching for the guru I have not met any other American who has ever swallowed a dhauti, for example. The "gurus" who come here from India are not much better when it comes to Kriya or Mudra.

For that reason, I am very happy that the directors of the Kaivalyadhama College of Yoga in Lonavala have given me their permission to organize a local branch of the college here in California. Hopefully, soon, we will be able to bring a real yogi from Lonavala to fill the needs of serious American sadhus.

I will begin to describe, in this issue, the various yogic purification techniques in the same order in which I do them every morning for reasons explained. Tradition prescribes a glass of water drunk through the nose (ushahpan, nasapan) immediately upon awakening. However I prefer another similar technique (nasadanti, to be described later) which I do after neti kriya; this is so as not to wash the impurities from my sinuses, accumulated during sleep, into my stomach.

So, to begin, my first act upon arising is to defecate. If I don't have the urge to defecate then I do all my Kriyas as usual but only up to (and not including) Basti, the yogic washing of the colon. If we suck water into the colon with fecal matter still present, the water will facilitate the re—absorption of the impurities from the colon.

One time when I had been fasting for several days, I did Basti but didn't get all the water out; the resultant re-absorption of poisons brought on such serious auto-intoxication that I vomited for 8 days continuously day and night every 20 minutes or so, forced to drink gallons of distilled water and retching until I thought I would die. I had several such cleansing crises. So please be certain bowels are empty before doing Basti. Fecal matter will have no bad smell if no concentrated protein, starches or dead (cooked) food is eaten. Foods requiring digestion (instead of direct assimilation) will always produce toxic, offensive, metabolism by-products.

After defecating, I brush my teeth; for this I use Vajradanti, an Ayurvedic herbal tooth paste if we are to believe the label. Next, I scrape my tongue with a tongue scraper (Fig. 1). Those who do it for the first time will be surprised at the amount of yellow-brown sticky stuff which can collect on the superior surface of the tongue overnight. The entire tongue must be scraped many times, repeatedly, before it is clean, fresh and pink.

Next, I do two wonderful techniques described in the Satkarmasangrahah. The first of these, called Madhyacakri calls for rubbing the root of the tongue with the fingers. For a long time I thought that the virtue of this Kriya was to clean the tongue; however, through persistent practice I discovered that rubbing the root of the tongue stimulates a strong spasmodic vomiting reflex (retching action) which squeezes out mucus and impurities from the aesophagus, trachea, stomach, sinuses, and even makes the eyes water copiously. The second technique called Urdhvacakri consists of rubbing the soft palate with the thumb. If this is continued, a different spasmotic shuddering reflex whose purpose I don't yet completely understand is stimulated, liberating large amounts of mucous from the throat and sinuses. All this is accompanied by lots of Sthivana (spitting) and Kasanam (coughing). A third technique called Adascakri is used to stimulate the defecating reflex (spasmotic contractions of the colon used to forcefully eject fecal matter. It will be described when we come to colon purification techniques in a later article).

The next technique in my routine is Sutra Neti (6) using rubber catheter tubes

(Fig.2). It is done exactly the way it looks: a thin rubber urethral catheter is inserted into the nose, and pulled out through the mouth from behind the palate. I succeeded upon my first attempt. In the beginning there is discomfort and some stimulating of the vomiting reflex because of the catheters tickling the throat, but these sensations diminish with time until they disappear altogether. Two catheters are inserted simultaneously, one in each nostril, and are pulled back and forth several times through the sinuses. The old traditional method used waxed threads and strings, and I must really confess that they gave better friction to the nasal passages, but were more difficult to keep. The waxed ends kept getting undone. I had a collection of these at one time before I settled for the more convenient rubber catheters.

The next technique that I do at this point is Khechari Mudra; it consists of putting the tongue into the sinus cavity behind the palate.   Before this can be done, the frenum holding the tongue to the floor of the mouth must be cut away. Since Khechari is not a Kriya but a Mudra I will not dwell on it here. I may describe the various traditions and my experiences with this Mudra in some future article if there is sufficient interest in the subject. I mention it here only because I do this technique at this point in my routine, namely after Sutra Neti. When the tongue is put inside the head, the sinus cavity almost immediately fills up with fluid.

The next technique that I do is Netrikarana, passing a string into one nostril and pulling it out through the other (See Fig. 4). The Satkarmasangrahah mentions it but doesn't tell how it's done. One way to do it is told in Yoga Mimamsa (6): you wax both ends of a string, insert one end into each nostril, and pull both ends out through the mouth from behind the palate. Next you tie the ends together in a small knot and

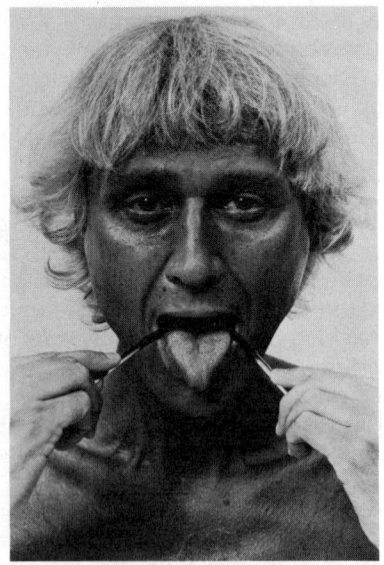

Figure 1

Figure 2

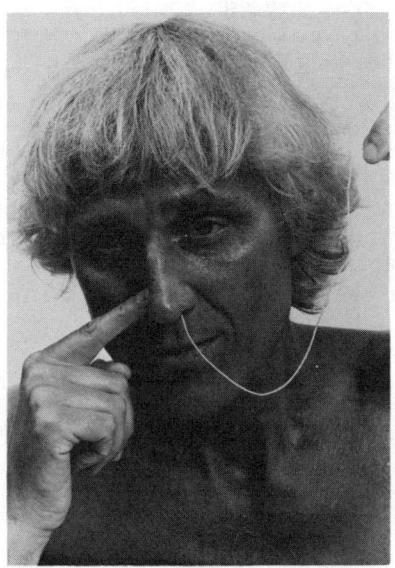

Figure 4

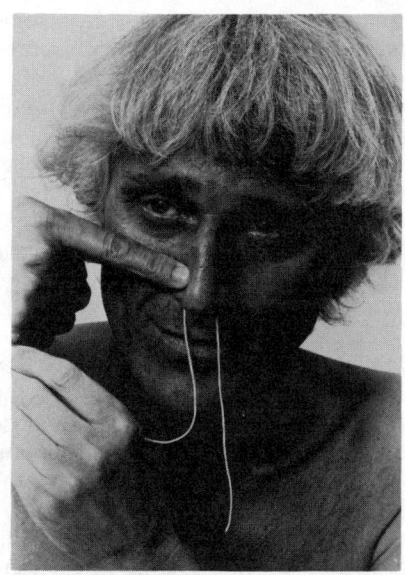

Figure 5

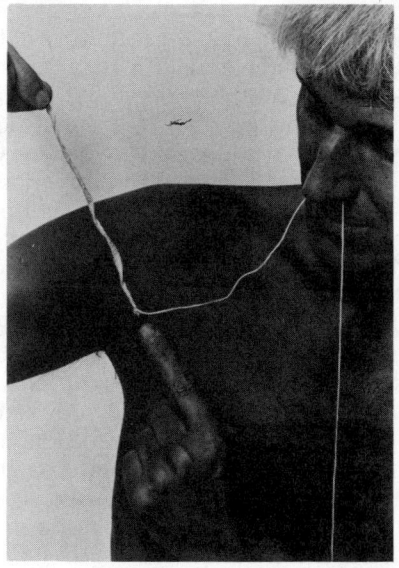

Figure 6

bring the knot around until it comes out through the nose, then you untie the knot, and pull the string back and forth several times to clean behind the septum bone. I have never done it this way; I use a different method. I take some very thin and strong white string and inhale the string through one nostril, using powerful, short snorts while keeping the other nostril closed (Fig. 5). When I feel the string under the soft palate, then I close the nostril with the string going in, and exhale using powerful snorts through the other nostril (Fig. 6). Sometimes it takes a little maneuvering to get the right length of string under the palate, but very soon the string reappears out the other nostril, blown out by the snorting exhalations. Then I tie a thicker string to one of the ends of the thin string using a very small knot (Fig. 7) and carefully pull the thick string in one nostril and out the other. It's the thick string that does the cleaning.

The next three techniques require a hypertonic saline solution, which means that the concentration of salt is greater than in the blood. Such solutions are used for all nasal washes, for the intestinal tract purge called Varisara (Shankhapraksalana) to be described in the future, and by some people for stomach washes. A hypertonic saline solution will draw impurities from the system through dialysis by mobilizing the body's water to dilute the poisonous salt, but if you make the concentration to salt too high, approaching saturation, that also is not good; such a high concentration of salt will irritate the tissues and produce irritation and pain. I use about one heaping teaspoon of Kosher salt (large crystal variety) per pint of warm water which is about right. Sadhus who do a nasal wash for the first time with hypertonic saline solution are surprised to find that the stinging discomfort always experienced when water enters the sinuses, like when swimming in a pool, is absent. If the concentration of the salt in the solution is less than in the blood (hypotonic), the salt will be absorbed into the body from the solution. This we don't want; drinking glass after glass of hypotonic saline solution, as in the technique of Shankapraksalana, could cause salt poisoning and bloating. That is why in nasal and stomach washes, etc., where saline solution is specified, it must be hypertonic. In stomach washes (Kunjala, Gajakarani) you end up absorbing some salt in any case, for that reason I have abandoned using salt for my stomach washing and use distilled water instead. Now that we know about how to prepare the salt solution I can describe the next three techniques.

Jala Neti consists of inserting the spout of a neti–cup (or teapot with a small spout) into one nostril, tilting the head and letting the water flow out through the other nostril (Fig. 8). Then repeat through the other nostril.

Next, some water is sucked in through the nose and expelled through the mouth, this is called Vyutkrama Kapalabhati. After this, I do a technique which for me was the most difficult to learn of all the netis. It is called Sitkrama Kapalabhati. Water is taken into the mouth, the head bent forward, and the water pushed backward by the tongue. Then the soft palate is relaxed and the water is pushed out through the nose (Fig. 9) by blowing out while the tongue pushes up toward the palate. No description is adequate for this technique. You just practice every day until you coordinate the various actions and sort of develop it by feel. Once mastered, however, we can send streams of water out through the nose like an elephant, Matangini Mudra (10). At this point I do a technique which I have never heard of before and which may conceivably be my own modest contribution to the art of shatkriya. If I hold my nose while attempting Sitkrama Kapalabhati, the water enters the eustachian tubes to wash out the inner ear. However before you attempt to drive water into your

NEW PATHWAYS TO HEALTH /279

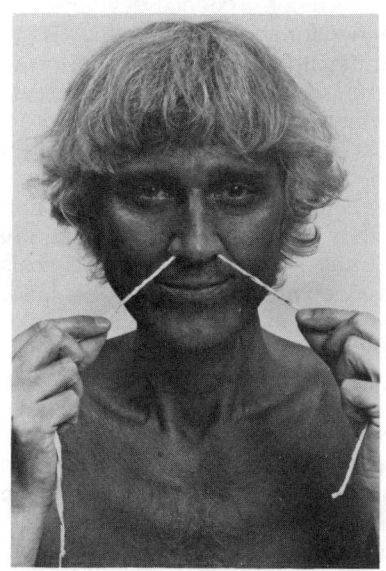

Figure 7

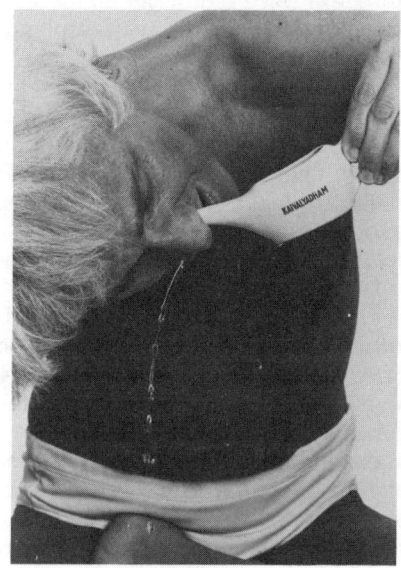

Figure 8

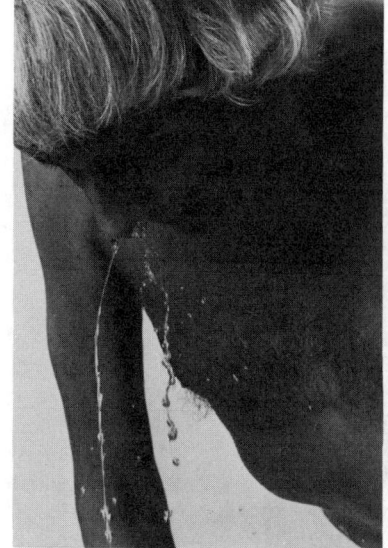

Figure 9

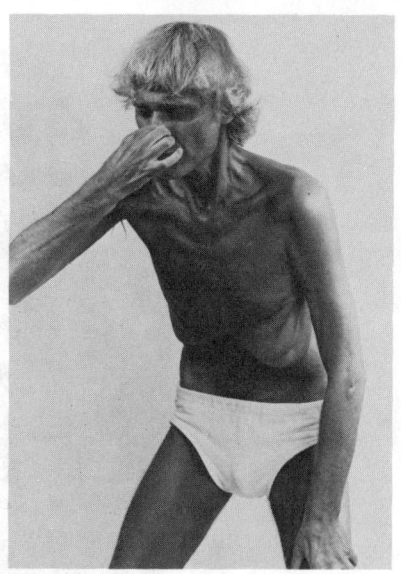

Figure 10

eustachian tubes you had better know how to get it out. While developing this technique, I once didn't get all the water out and as a consequence developed an infection of the inner ear, with resulting loss of hearing for about three weeks. To get the water out of the inner ear I pinch my nose shut with my fingers and perform a powerful Uddiyana (Fig. 10), this creates a powerful vacuum in the entire pharynx and you can feel and hear the water sucked out from the eustachian tubes. A note of warning: a very powerful Uddiyana and probably Nauli can harm the heart if the heart is not first strenghtened through Pranayama, running, mountain climbing, etc. Sometimes I feel a slight pain in the region of the heart during powerful Uddiyana. One other observation that I have made, is that during a powerful Sitkrama Kapalabhati I often experience strange smells. I suspect that I am mechanically stimulating the nerve filaments in the olfactory sinuses. The remaining saline solution I use for Gandusa (gargling) and Kavalagraha, holding a mouthful of saline solution (or other Ayurvedic pepartion) and vigorously rubbing the gums.

The next technique is one called Nasadanti by the Satkarmasangraha. Distilled water is drunk through the nose until the stomach is full then vomited out through the mouth (Fig. 11). I do it a little different. I drink only three pints to prevent stomach from distending too much; also if stomach is completely filled with water we cannot swish the water around to wash all the parts of the stomach. Also I drink only one pint through the nose, to which a few drops of wheatgrass juice has been added, half a pint through each nostril, plus two more through the mouth. I don't want to get into stomach washes at this time since it is an extensive subject, gone into in the next article. The notable fact about nasadanti is that we don't use saline solution in this technique but distilled water, and when it goes into the sinuses it will sting. In the

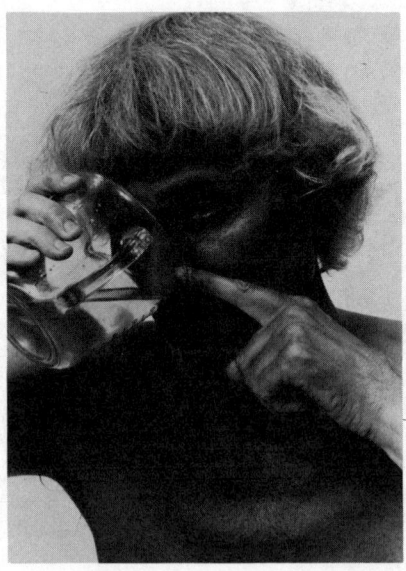

Figure 11

beginning while drinking water through the nose, we keep gasping for air. This feeling of shortness of breath has nothing to do with lack of oxygen or actual rise in carbon dioxide concentration, but is a reflex action caused by water in the sinuses. I suspect that the traditional value of this exercise was to train to subdue the autonomic suffocation reflex for purposes of prolonging Kumbhaka during pranayama. After five months of daily practice I could comfortably drink one pint of water through the nose while holding my breath without discomfort. For removing the remaining water from the sinuses which may be remaining after these exercises, we do a powerful Uddiyana with nostrils pinched closed as described above. This is repeated several times with tilting (swinging) of the head forwards and backwards. Unbelieveable amounts of water keep draining out from the head. When the water finally stops coming out, we clear the nose and sinuses by doing several rounds of Vayu Kapalabhati, short snorts of abdominal breathing, with emphasis on the exhalations, repeated at about two or three a second. Both Uddiyana and Vayu Kapalabhati are described at length in Yoga Mimamsa, Volume I, pages 1–6, and Volume IV, No.2, pages 69–87, respectively. They are described also in "Yogic Therapy" (reference 2); in "Asanas" and "Pranayama" by Kuvalayananda, (7), (8) and Theos Bernard (1), better than I could describe them in a short space. They are not difficult techniques in fact it takes longer to try to describe them in detail in a book than to simply demonstrate them. Once shown, they are easily picked up by the student.

With the exception of techniques for eyes and ears which I do not normally do every day as part of my routine, the above techniques cover most of the cleansing methods that one can do to one's head. There are other techniques such as Simba, Mudra, Jihva Vanda, Brahmamudra, and Khechari which can be done to the head but they are not strictly speaking cleansing processes with which we are here concerned.

Up to now I have described 17 techniques for cleansing the mouth, head, and sinuses in the order that I do them every day. The next article will continue with the other half of Nasadanti (how the water which was drunk through the nose is vomited out again by Kunjala, Gajakarani, and Danda Dhauti) also the preparatory techniques for Gajakarani (Udgarakarma and Manibandha) plus Viparitakarani, Agnisara, and Vastra Dhauti. After that, in following articles I will describe colon purification (Nauli, Basti, Asvini Mudra, Lauliki) followed by several versions of the purge (Shankhapraksalana) for the entire digestive system (alimentary canal) and finally Vajroli Kriya, a technique for washing the bladder which is also a preliminary preparatory technique for Vajroli Mudra (an esoteric technique for resorption of seminal fluid to arrest the physical aging process). See (9) for scientific basis of Brahmacharya; also Yoga Mimamsa, Volume III, No.2, pp. 138–145.

Mat Rosmarynowski, Los Angeles, California

SATKARMASADANA
PART II

In the previous article I last described a process called Nasadanti where water is drunk through the nose. I drink one pint through the nose and two more through the mouth. Right after drinking the third pint, I quickly assume Viparitakarani (Fig. 1) and quickly perform Agnisara about ten times. Agnisara is described in Yoga Minamsa (1). It consists of alternately pulling in the stomach toward the spine and pushing it out, with emphasis on protrusion (2). This shakes the water all around the stomach. After this I jump up quickly to a standing position; we must do Viparitakarani and Agnisara quickly and return to upright position quickly because if we remain in the Viparitakarani position, the water will run out from the inverted stomach through the pyloric valve into the duodenum and into the intestines. This we don't want. This water is used for washing the nose and stomach and is to be expelled. We don't want to assimilate all the impurities into the intestines. (Viparitakarani is the first position to be used for the technique for Shankapraksalana, where we drink glass after glass of water and perform certain asanas to propel the water from mouth to anus until it comes out clear).

After standing back up I lean over the toilet and perform Gajakarani (3). For many years I did not know how to do Gajakarani until I was shown the correct method at the Kaivalyadhama. Gajakarani is the controlled Yogic vomiting without the fingers in the throat. After drinking the water you take a deep breath, bend forward at the waist, contract the muscles of the stomach pushing in and upwards (this is called Manibandha (4)), and then perform a belching type action (5) with the throat sphincters. After a few months of practice I can almost get the water to flow out in an even stream (Fig.2) by continuing the pressure and the belching action. I get about a pint or a pint and half of water out of my stomach in this way saving the rest for Dandadhauti, the next technique. You can taste the sour acid coming out with the water when you do Gajakarani in the morning.

Before you master the technique of Gajakarani (controlled Yogic vomiting), you have to use the fingers to tickle the throat to get the vomiting started. This is this preliminary easier technique of Kunjala. Those who have difficulty doing Kunjala must resort to using salted (hypertonic) water in the beginning. This emetic solution irritates the stomach lining and insures a good strong retching reflex; however, because some salt (a strong poison) is always absorbed in the stomach anyway, I recommend giving up the salt solution as soon as the technique is well established in one's Sadhana. I hate the poisonous effects of salt so much that I never used it, consequently it took me longer to master the stomach washes. Kunjala really gets more mucous out than Gajakarani by stimulating the spasmodic retching reflex (described in detail below for Dandadhauti), but Gajakarani gets the water out quicker like turning a hot water bottle upside—down.

Another similar technique is used in Ayurveda to expel food from the stomach after eating. It is called Vamana (or Baghi in Northern India). Vamana is done by vomiting out the food within a certain time after eating, whereas Gajakarani and

Kunjala are done in the morning on an empty stomach with water only. To do Vamana, we must wait at least 2½ hours after eating and no longer than four hours. Then we drink water, shake the stomach, and vomit out the contents, repeating the process if necessary to get everything out. If the technique is performed between 2½ to 4 hours after eating, it is claimed that we will absorb all of the nourishment from the food, but that the bulk requiring digestion is eliminated, and the body doesn't have to work hard expending energy to digest the rest of the bulk. Tradition prescribes a mixture of rice and milk or rice and mung beans cooked together to be eaten after Vamana. Since I eat no dead (cooked) food or grains of any kind, I have not followed this advice and seem to be none the worse as a result. Unless one is a heavy protein eater whose stomach is constantly secreting hydrochloric acid, there is probably no harm in having a glass of carrot or wheat juice after Vamana. That is what I do when I do it which is not very often. I don't do Vamana every day; it is not part of my daily purification routine, rather it is a therapeutic Ayurvedic technique employed for curing diabetes, ulcers, and other digestive complaints.

So, to get back to my routine: after getting half of the water out with Gajakarani or Kunjala, the rest of the water I get out of my stomach by using the wonderful technique of Danda Dhauti.

Danda Dhauti (6): you get a tube about 36 inches long, rubber or plastic; start with a small outside diameter (o.d.) of about 5/16 inch, then after a few weeks go to a ½ inch or ⅝ inch tube. This is because the throat must get accustomed to swallowing the Danda Dhauti. Around the end that you swallow you cut several holes in the side of the tube (Fig. 3) so that if the open end should be blocked by pressing against the stomach wall, the water can still flow through the other holes. When using the Danda, at first you chew the end of the tube for a few seconds to fool the body into thinking food is coming; this relaxes the throat sphincters. Later you just stick the end of the tube into the throat as far as it will go, and go through swallowing motions. As soon as the end of the tube passes through the throat sphincters, the rest of the tube can be pushed down into the stomach without the swallowing motions if you wet it first. After this, the truck is bent at the waist and the stomach pushed in and up with a tightening of the stomach and abdominal muscles (4); the water will rush out through the tube (Fig. 4). This removes the water and sourness from the stomach.

The real benefits of Danda Dhauti however, are more complex. If we move the Danda in and out many times through a distance of a few inches, and at the same time put the other hand deep inside the mouth at the root of the tongue, we stimulate a powerful retching reflex. This not only pushes the water out from the stomach, but causes enormous amounts of mucous to be expelled. The spasmodic contractions caused by the retching reflex put pressure on the lymphatic ducts, resulting in a copious flow of mucous from the sinus cavity, the trachea, esophagus, salivary glands, and tear ducts, so much that vision becomes clouded with tears. By repeating the process until the water in the stomach is gone, we at the same time flush an enormous amount of mucous from our body, aided by blowing the nose, coughing and spitting. If the process of pushing the Danda in and out is continued over a sufficient period of time, we begin to see yellow bile come out through the tube. This is not because the Danda has penetrated into the duodenum through the pyloric valve, but because the continued pushing of the Danda against the stomach walls causes the pyloric valve to open, and we can wash the stale bile out through the

284/ **LIFE IN THE 21ST CENTURY**

Figure 1

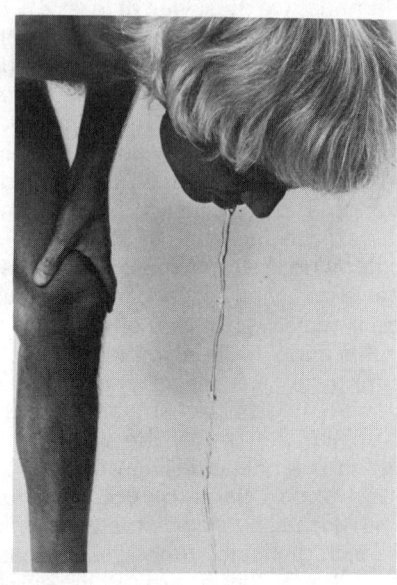

Figure 2

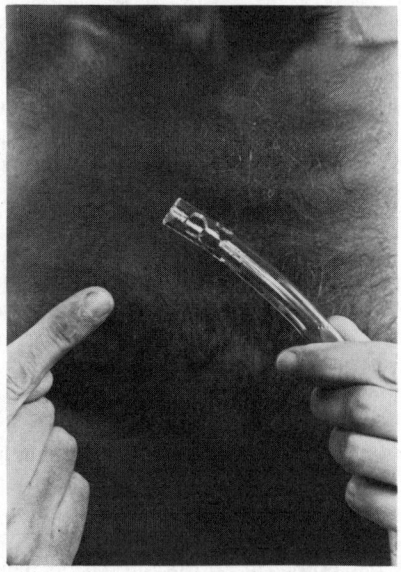

Figure 3

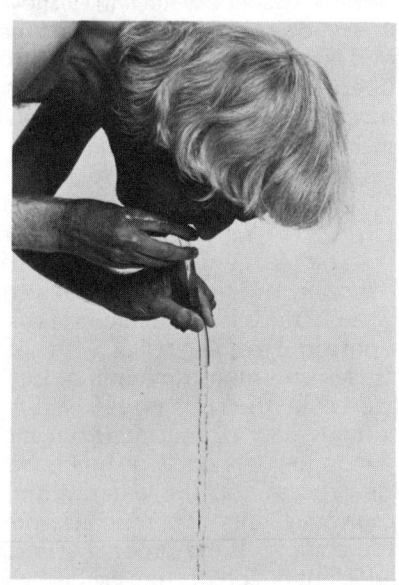

Figure 4

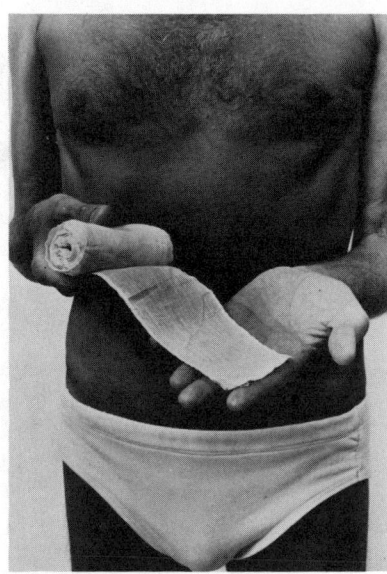 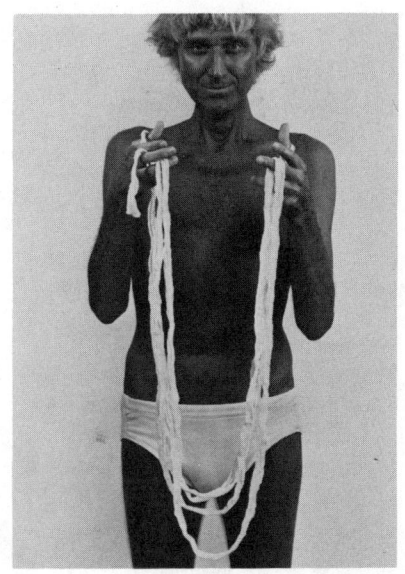

Figure 5   Figure 6

stomach. In my routine, after drinking three pints of water as described in the previous article (see Nasadanti) I usually expell one pint using Gajakarani (this is practice to control the throat sphincters for Plavini Pranayama) then I expel the rest with Danda Dhauti. Kunjala I usually use only to get Gajakarani started if it doesn't start by itself sometimes.

The next technique that I do after this is called Vastra Dhauti (7) or simply Dhauti, swallowing the cloth to cleanse the stomach. The cloth itself is called the Dhauti. It is a piece of thin white muslin 3 inches wide and 23 feet long, with finely stitched lengthwise edges and ends so that we have no loose threads to become enmeshed in the soft uvula (7). The Dhauti is shown roled up in Fig.5 and unrolled in Fig.6. You must use muslin cloth. Linen is too stiff and rough and will scratch the delicate linings of the stomach and esophagus. Do not use gauze. The threads will come loose from the edges and cause serious entanglement. Before swallowing, the Dhauti is examined and arranged so that the folds and knots are removed; this will enable the Dhauti to be swalowed and pulled out without entangling. The Dhauti is then saturated with water and gently squeezed out. If too dry, it will absorb the saliva and become difficult to swallow. If too wet, the saliva and throat mucous will be diluted also causing insufficient slipping and consequent difficulty in swallowing. What I do is pour some distilled water (about ⅓ pint) into a one pint measuring cup, then I put the unrolled Dhauti in it after arranging the consecutive folds for easy unfolding. Then I take one end, fold it double lengthwise two times (Fig.7) and place the ends at the back of my throat. A couple attempts at swallowing and the Dhauti is on its way down

286/ **LIFE IN THE 21ST CENTURY**

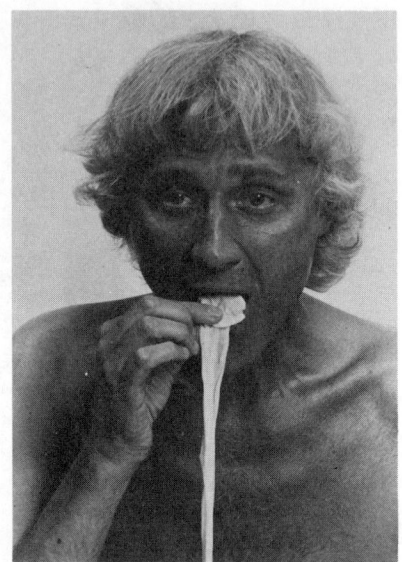

Figure 7

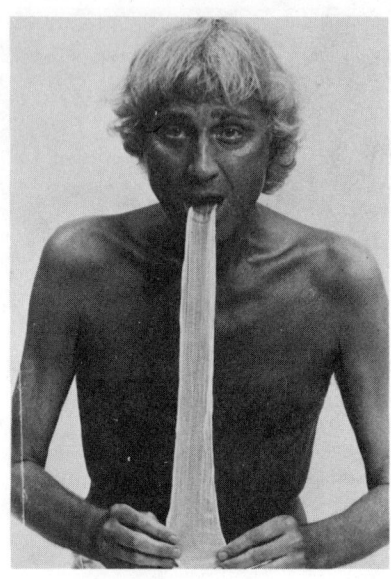

Figure 8

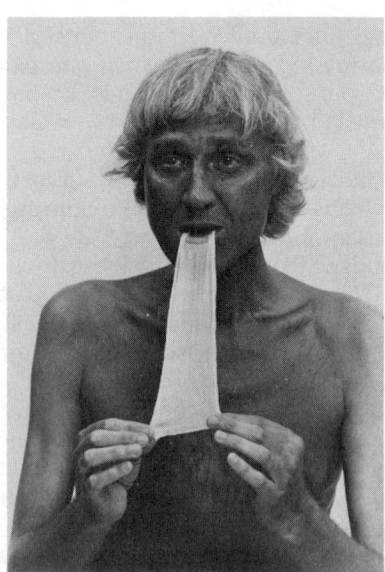

Figure 9

into the stomach. As I keep pulling the Dhauti from the cup I squeeze any excess water by lightly squeezing down along the cloth. This in my experience provides the correct moisture for the process. I continue the swallowing action (Fig.8) until the entire Dhauti has been swallowed except for a few inches (Fig.9). It took me a long time to learn to swallow the Dhauti. In the beginning I always did it too fast and I would vomit out the Dhauti after swallowing only about ⅓ of it. To help overcome this compulsion to regurgitate the Dhauti, I was told to do first Kunjala and Danda Dhauti so as to deaden or depress the vomiting reflex. After following this advice I succeeded in swallowing the entire Dhauti on my second attempt. One observation I made is that along with the Dhauti one swallows large quantities of air; this must be carefully expelled periodically by belching or else nausea will come. When nausea comes, one must stop the swallowing, sitting quietly without motion. After a minute the nausea will pass and one can continue swallowing; otherwise, the Dhauti will be vomited out before it can be swallowed in its entirety. After a few weeks of practice I could swallow the entire Dhauti in about 4 minutes. After the Dhauti is in the stomach we can perform Uddiyana, Nauli, and Agnisara; these are traditionally practiced to massage the stomach by gently rubbing its walls with the cloth. Have no fear of entangling the cloth; the cloth is so thin that with the slime it picks up thee is no danger of being unable to pull it back out. In all of my experience I have never had a Dhauti stuck down in my stomach and unable to pull it out. As a matter of fact, a few times when pulling it out, the whole Dhauti came out in one big glob. Yu must leave several inches unswallowed so that you can pull it out when the time comes. If however you should accidentlly swallow the entire cloth, then drink a large glass of some strong saturated salt solution. This emetic will immediately cause the Dhauti to be vomited out. The Dhauti should not remain in the stomach for longer than 20 or 25 minutes. Otherwise there is the chance that the Dhauti will pass through the phlorus into the duodenum. This is dangerous because of the possibility of injuring the pyloric sphincter. At the Kaivalyadhama Research Laboratory they have conducted experiments where the Dhauti was allowed to pass into the duodenum and jejenum (see X-rays of Barium soaked (8) Dhauti experiments). However, this is not standard procedure and is not to be recommended. I myself have observed a few times that upon withdrawing the Dhauti, the end which went in first was yellow with bile for a length of several inches. This was after I swallowed the Dhauti and walked around for about 10 minutes, which I sometimes do. Did the Dhauti go down into my duodenum or did bile some into my stomach through the pylorus? I don't know.

When we withdraw the Dhauti we find an enourmous amount of mucous clinging to the cloth. A thin, light Dhauti, scarcely wet, goes down into the stomach but when it comes back out it is a heavy glob of slim loaded with mucous. We are amazed how much slime comes out with the Dhauti, especially if before swallowing the Dhauti we had performed Kunjala and Danda Dhauti which already had brought up very large amounts of mucous. After withdrawing the Dhauti, we wash it many items with soap and water, repeating until all the slime is gone, and then we hang it up to dry, preferably in the sun to sterilize it by ultraviolet radiation. Tradition requires the Dhauti to be sterilized by boiling before every use; this precaution I have never obeyed. I keep it clean and in a clean place without rodents and insects, which was the main traditional reason for the injuction.

A body nourished by living food and cleansed daily by Shatkriya has no need to worry about pathogenic bacteria (10), (11). Two exceptions from my experience are Dysentery (an amoeba not a bacterium) and Malaria (a parasite). The former can be cured by certain Yogic processes (9), the latter by Pranayama (9).

The next article will continue with techniques for colon purification.

Mat Rosmarynowski, Los Angeles, California

SATKARMASADANA
PART III

Uddiyana is illustrated in Fig. 1. For more detail see references (1), (2), (3), (4). In the old tradition (5) Uddiyana was considered to be mastered when the practitioner reached 1500 rounds per day. Uddiyana puts pressure upon the heart, so people with weak hearts should not attempt to perform powerful or prolonged Uddiyana until the heart has been strengthened (1), (2). Also there is a difference between Uddiyana and Uddiyana Bandha which is an entirely different technique used in Pranayama and is done with the lungs full, see reference (6) for detail.

Tradition says that after Uddiyana has been mastered we can start working on Nauli. In my own case I must confess that I never mastered Uddiyana to the extent of performing 1500 rounds per day. I personally found Uddiyana so easy that I went ahead and began to practice Nauli simultaneously. This was back in 1966. I never kept records or timed myself, but I would guess it took me two to three weeks of sadhana (practice) before Nauli began to appear. I would take an ordinary enema (gravity fed, rubber tube and all) and try to do Uddiyana and Nauli while the water was going in: as colon began to fill with water these techniques became more and more difficult to perform. After evacuation I would practice some more. Uddiyana and Nauli are illustrated in Fig (1) & (2).

Nauli is done as follows: Take the same standing stance as for Uddiyana, hands on knees, etc., exhale deeply, do Uddiyana and then try to push the rectus abdominalis muscles forward so that they stand out like a pillar from the rib cage down to the pubic bone, (Fig.2), this is called Nauli Madhayama or Central Nauli. This is easier said than done. However through practice I was able to feel out my rectus abdominalis and get them to stand out from the concave abdomen. The fact that I was able to do this technique from instruction in a book, Ref. (5), (7), without personal instruction from any guru shows that it is not that difficult or mysterious, all you need is practice. The importance of this technique is that it creates a low pressure (see Madhavadasa Vacuum Volume I of Yoga Mimansa), in the lower and transverse colon and bladder, enabling the practitioner to suck water into the colon and bladder (Vajroli Mudra to be described in detail in a future article, and Basti which I shall describe later on in this article). To get an idea of the magnitude of the sub−atmospheric pressure created in the colon (8) after about two months of practice, consider the following: for Uddiyana, up to 40mm Hg., for Central Nauli, up to 86mm Hg., for Left Nauli, up to 60mm Hg., and for Right Nauli, up to 55mm Hg.

NEW PATHWAYS TO HEALTH

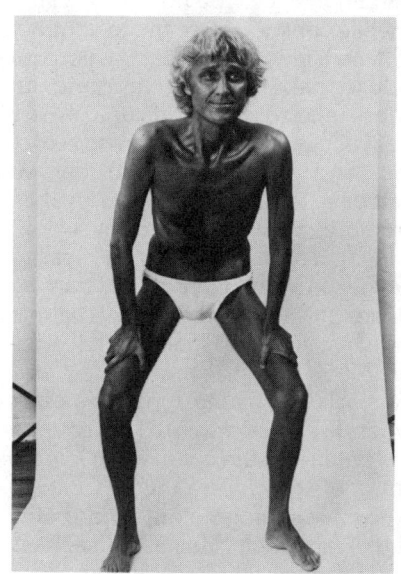

Figure 1

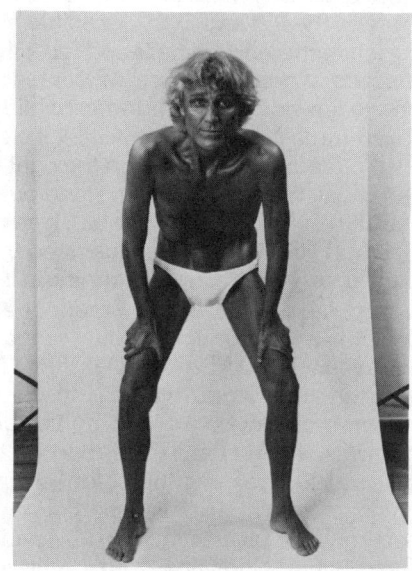

Figure 2

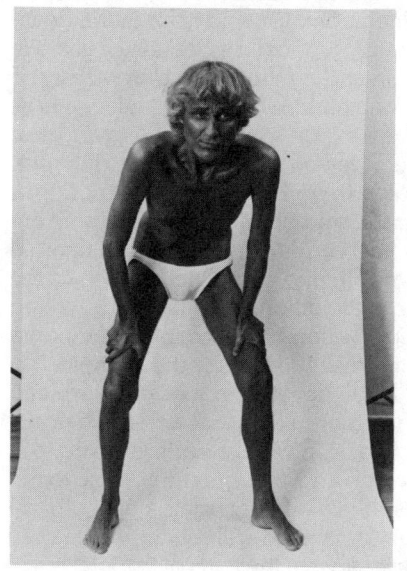

Figure 3

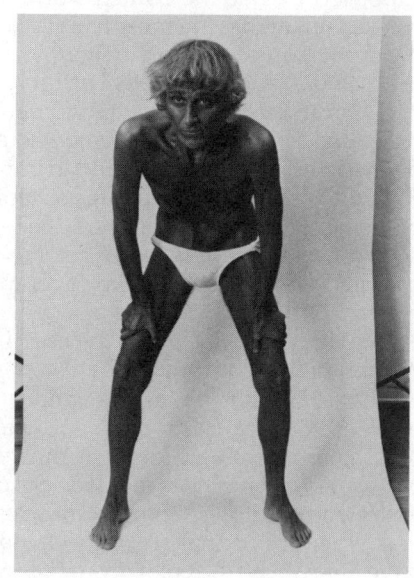

Figure 4

While Nauli Madhayama is fairly easy to learn, the next three variations are a little more difficult. While standing bent down in the standing stance, you now bend a little more to the left and twist just a little bit to the left while consciously trying to contract the left rectus abdominalis and relax the right one. After a few days of practice you will succeed in getting the feel of it and you will be able to make the left rectus stand out on the left side of the abdomen while the right one is relaxed as in Uddiyana. This is called Vima Nauli (or Left Nauli); it creates a partial vacuum in the descending colon. If we put our weight more on the right leg and bend—and—twist a little to the right, we can cause the right rectus to stand out while the left one is kept relaxed. This is called Dakshina Nauli (or Right Nauli), it creates a lowered pressure in the ascending colon. Left and Right Nauli are illustrated in Fig. 3 and Fig. 4. The next technique is called Lauliki or Naulicalana (churning). It consists of the previous techniques, namely Uddiyana, plus the above—mentioned three varieties of Nauli performed in a certain order so as to produce a rolling or rotating motion. If we perform Nauli Madhayama, Vama Nauli, Uddiyana, Dakshina Nauli, Nauli Madhayama, Vama Nauli, etc., etc.,...in that order, we will observe a counter clockwise rolling type of motion (counter clockwise as seen by the performer when he looks down). This counter clockwise rolling Lauliki is supposed to move the contents of the colon (the water to be used for washing the colon) from the rectum and sigmoid, up the descending colon, across the transverse colon, and down the ascending colon towards the cecum. If we reverse the sequence and perform Uddiyana, Left Nauli, Central Nauli, Right Nauli, Uddiyana, Left Nauli, etc., etc.,...we produce a rolling motion which appears clockwise to the performer as he looks down. This clockwise Lauliki is supposed to take the contents of the colon up from the cecum, up the ascending colon, then across the transverse colon to the spleenic flexure, and from there, down the descending colon to the sigmoid. Note that I said "supposed to"; after 12 years of practicing these techniques I still have trouble persuading the water to traverse the circuit from rectum to cecum and back again out the rectum by using Lauliki only as described above. Never having had any real Yoga expert to show me how, I have been forced to experiment and to improvise. Every person's colon is a little different. The relative lengths of the three sections of the colon (plus the sigmoid), the positions of the hepatic bend and spleenic flexure, and the size and position of the sigmoid are different in different persons. For me personally, the bends and folds of the sigmoid present the greatest difficulty of obstruction to smooth and complete passage of the water. For that reason I use a sequence which is a little different from that described above for Lauliki, including the use of the inverted positions (Sirshasana and Viparita Karani) during some of the Lauliki phases so as to erase the folds of the sigmoid.

Once Uddiyana plus the various aspects of Nauli have been mastered, we can proceed to learn Basti, the Yogic washing of the colon. Note that besides being a preliminary technique for Basti, the technique of Nauli is a very valuable technique in its own right. It provides massage not only to the colon and its contents, but also to the entire complex of abdominal muscles (those responsible for peristalsis plus others) and other abdominal organs, helping to dislodge impacted fecal matter which may have been lining the colon from many years back; caught in the folds of the intestines, gradually decaying, slowly poisoning the organism, causing constipation, ulcers, tumors, etc. For detailed description of the unspeakable horrors that go on inside the colon, everyone should read Kuvalayananda's series of articles on "Cecal

Constipation" in Yoga Mimansa, see references (9), (10). When reading the above articles remember that Kuvalayananda speaks about the colons of typical Indians who are vegetarians. The worst thing that an Indian might eat would be unsprouted grains (starch—protein combinations such as chapatis), cooked starches and dairy products, all of which produce mucous and a starchy glue to line the alimentary canal and clog up the capillaries so that the necessary nutrients and oxygen cannot reach the cells (11), (12). If that is the case, then just imagine how frightfully worse off is the colon of the typical American, the overfed omnivarian who devours at one single meal great quantities of proteins of various kinds, cooked starches, sugars, sour acid condiments, fats, salts, preservatives, artifical flavorings and coloring, emulsifiers, fillers, all washed down with alcohol plus caffeine (to stop production of enzymes necessary to digest the rest of the junk). Is it any wonder then, that one out of every four Americans is dying from cancer while the rest succumb to other degenerative diseases (11); very few Americans die from infectious diseases as compared with degenerative diseases. Programmed from childhood by well—meaning and loving but ignorant parents and a profit oriented society, the average American will fight for his right to eat s... and to die from cancer on the operating table while his family weeps and moans. It is truly amazing how the people of a country as advanced technologically and as wealthy and creative as Americans can be so blind as not to associate cause and effect; namely the eating of corpses, both animal and vegetable (cooked vegetables) with the epidemic rise of degenerative diseases in this country.

Besides childhood programming which teaches us to like dead unwholesome food (and is extremely difficult to break in later years), a large part of the blame rests with the conspiracy of the general foods syndicate, a coalition of major "prepared" food manufacturers, to keep information about nutrition out of public media (newspapers, television, etc.). They get wealthy selling us junk food so that we can get sick from degenerative diseases and doctors get wealthy suppressing the symptoms with their selection of drugs.

To those few readers who have broken through this programming sufficiently to at least investigate the truth of what I am saying, I would advise to stop eating meat and devitalized food, go on a series of gradually longer and longer fasts, and by all means learn to wash out the colon (cesspool of the body). They will be amazed and pleased by the results. It is regrettable that some of the older, conservative people (who still cling to the customs, manners, traditions and taboos of their parents and grandparents) tend to view colon washing (plus other Kriyas as well, such as vomiting, spitting, nose cleaning, etc.) with upturned noses and an affected disgust. To them, an enema bag is something to be hidden from sight when guests come to the house because it is "disgusting". Besides having a beneficial effect upon the colon, Nauli has one more purpose of which many yogis are perhaps not aware. Theos Bernard in his book (13) mentions how his Guru told him that by continuing daily prolonged Nauli for a year, the Kundalini Shakti can be raised. This aspect of Nauli I haven't verified and Dr. Bernard confesses that he hadn't either (13), but the important point that he was trying to make was that to really awaken and raise the Kundalini (nerve energy) Hatha Yoga Asanas, Satkarma, pranayama, Bandha and Mudra are required, and that no amount of ceremony, guru worship, fancied love, selfess service, chanting/praying, or wishful thinking can actually awaken this nerve energy or bring it under control. All such methods are strictly mental and subjective.

They may bring a sort of happiness to some types of mentalities. It is one thing to make yourself "believe" that you are God through prolonged daily autosuggestion and to feel happy as a result. It is quite another thing to actually become a part of God with the accompanying Godlike Omniscience and Omnipotence or to approach Godhood as close as possible considering the limitations of our minds and bodies.

Now that you know how to do Nauli, you are ready for the next step, namely Basti. A couple of important points should be mentioned here first which I have never seen in any books n Satkarma. First of all you do Basti in order to wash out or rinse out the colon after it has been emptied through the morning defecation upon awakening. You never perform Basti while the colon is still full of fecal matter. To do so invites disaster; the water will dissolve the fecal matter so that the poisons which were waiting to be expelled are re−absorbed through the walls of the colon. This can cause severe poisoning, especially if the subject has been fasting and his fecal matter is composed not of undigested remains of food but from poisons released from the deep body tissues during the fast.

The second point that I should mention is that one should not do Basti, even after defecating, if the body is in a dehydrated condition, otherwise the body will thirstily absorb water from the colon together with the poisons from any fecal mater which may remain in the colon after defecation (some impurities always remain in the folds of the large intestine), in which case poisoning will also result through re−absorption. Maybe not as serious as in the first case but a poisoning nevertheless; therefore before doing basti I will drink a pint of water. The exception to this case is when I intend to do Vijroli after Basti on that day, in which case I drink no water. I found through experience that a pint of water (473cc) in the stomach will reduce the vaccum that I can pull with my bladder by a half; from about 9 mm Hg. to about 40 mm Hg. Apparently the stomach as well as the entire alimentary canal must be completely empty in order to secure a powerful Nauli and consequently a good vacuum in the bladder.

The technique of Basti is very simple. After defecating, a Basti tube is inserted into the anus, the subject squats in a river (traditional) up to his chest or navel and performs a powerful Nauli Madhayama. This is held as long as possible while the water rushes into the colon. When the breath can no longer be held out, the subject puts his finger over the protruding end of the Basti tube so that the water will not escape, he takes a breath, rests a while, then empties his lungs again, performing another powerful round of Nauli, releasing his finger from the open end of the Basti tube so that more water can flow in. This process is repeated until a sufficient amount of water has been sucked into the colon. The subject then removes the tube from the anus so that the water cannot escape. He then stands up and performs Lauliki; 40 times counter clockwise to bring the water up the descending colon across the transverse colon and down the ascending colon to the cecum. At this point I personally like to do Agnisara about 40 times; it is my idea; I have never seen it recommended in any of the traditonal writings on Hatha Yoga. I do it in order to shake the contents of the colon around and to make sure that the impurities are well mixed with the water before I let the water out, so that more of them will be carried out by the water. After this I do Lauliki again 40 times but this time in a clockwise direction; this is supposed to bring the water and impurities up and around from the cecum back to the sigmoid and rectum. The subject then squats down and expels the contents by defecating and periodically doing more clockwise Lauliki alternating until the colon has been emptied. The entire procedure may be repeated two or more times until the water comes out clean and clear. If you have trouble conducting the water through the colon because of blockage at the spleenic fold or the folds of the sigmoid, you might try going into an inverted position and perform a sort of pumping action by altenating Nauli Madhayama with Uddiyana several times (adding Agnisara if you like). If you are able to do left and right Nauli in an inverted position you might want to try that also (I personally have never been able to do Left and Right Nauli while in Sirshasana or in Viparita Karani). Also I discovered that it helps to bring the water up the decending colon if I alternate between Left Nauli and Uddiyana many times and then finish off with counter clockwise Lauliki. There is probably a sequence of techniques to pull the water in all the way into the cecum and back out again easily and quickly but I haven't yet met anyone who knows how. I am reproducing at this point a couple of charts from the first volume of Yoga Mimansa (no longer available). The first chart shows the position of the various parts of the colon during Uddiyana, Central Nauli, Left Nauli, and Right Nauli. The second chart shows the distribution of the contents of the colon during Uddiyana, Central Nauli, and Right Nauli. The information on these two charts was gathered from the results of hundreds of experiments and x−rays, using a radiographically opaque barium solution in place of water. I understand that the brave souls who posed for these hundreds of x−ray radiographs have suffered severe radiation burns of the spine as a result of these experiments. We must be grateful to these pioneers and scientists who risked their lives and sanity so that we could have accurate scientific information about the process of Hatha Yoga. I hope and pray that the publication of these reports which I am writing will start debates, controversies and experimentation; and that the real yogis who are real experts at some of these advanced techniques (Kriyas and Mudras) will come out of hiding and begin publishing their experiences and results, and sharing their knowledge with others. Yoga is a Science not a Religion. It is a science for the development and perfection of the body, the mind, and for the awakening of the spiritual centers in the brain through psycho−physiological techniques, so that Man's relation to God may be actually experienced.

A word here about Basti tubes. I found that the traditional wooden Basti tube (about 16cm. long with an inside diameter of about 8mm.) is difficult to use. Because of the small bore, the flow rate is very low and it takes a long time to fill the colon to capacity. Poiseuille's law states that for a pure liquid (such as water) and non-turbulent flow, the flow rate is proportional to the fourth power of the radium (or diameter) of the inside radius of the tube (18). Thus doubling the radium will increase the flow rate by 16 times! A Basti tube with a small radius has the disadvantage that we must hold a powerful Nauli for a very long time while the water slowly seeps through the thin tube. This may be all right for a beginner trying to develop a powerful Nauli. However, for ease of cleansing the colon through Basti it is a decided disadvantage, forcing the sadhu to repeat several rounds of Nauli, closing the end of the tube with his finger between each round.

With this in mind, I made for myself a Basti tube of plastic (lucite) which has an opening of 16 mm. in diameter and a wall thickness of about ⅛ of an inch. See Fig. 5. The resulting outside diameter of ⅞ of an inch still allows the tube to be comfortably inserted into the anus. Now when I insert this plastic Basti tube into my rectum and

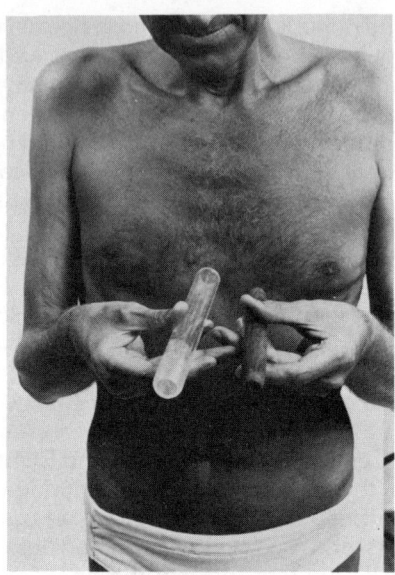

Figure 5

squat down over a one pint measuring glass cup (putting the other end of the tube into the cup so that it touches the bottom of the cup) and perform a powerful Nauli Madhayama, I can observe the level of the water in the cup going down very rapidly and the entire contents of the cup (one pint, which is equivalent to 473 cc or almost half a liter) is sucked— in about 5 seconds or less. Needless to say I can do this in one round of Nauli.

Nowadays, people don't go down to the river any more to do Basti or any other Kriyas like in the old days. Today you do it in your own bathroom. This presents a multitude of problems as contrasted with the old traditional techniques.

If you try to do Basti in your bath-tub, especially in the beginning before you have developed the necessary strength and control, you will find that some of the water which you have drawn in will escape back out; you have to use a finger over the other end of the tube to close it off between successive rounds of Nauli Madhayama, or withdraw the tube quickly at the end of each round. In either case some of the water and contents will escape anyway, and before you have finished the process you are sitting in a bathtub full of your own defecation. This is obviously unsatisfactory. Even after mastering Asvini Mudra (voluntary control over the opening and closing of the anal sphincters) at which time you dispense with the Basti tube, I found the bathtub unsatisfactory, because before you can open the anal sphincters you must push and move them in and out several times; the powerful contractions and dilations will allow some of the contents of the rectum to escape into the bathtub as before (with the Basti tube). I solved the problem by a couple of different "tricks". I made my Basti tube about 8 inches long so that after insertion into the rectum it will still stick out for a considerable distance. I squat down in Uttkatasana over a shallow pan, small tub, or my one pint glass measuring cup and insert the smooth (rounded off) end of the plastic Basti tube through my anus deep into the rectum. The other end, of course, goes into the container which is filled with water. Then I suck the water in by performing a powerful Nauli Madhayama. After this I stand up and proceed to do the churning (Lauliki Agnisara) then, Uddiyana, Central Nauli, and Agnisara in an inverted posture, then Lauliki plus left and right Nauli alternating with Central Nauli to conduct the contents of the colon in the desired directions (see the two charts reprinted from Yoga Mimansa). After this I evacuate the contents of my colon into the toilet. The procedure of doing Basti over a pan or cup requires much more control than doing it in the river or bathtub, because if you are squatting in water up to your naval or chest, the height of the water level above the tube opening (at the anus) provides an added pressure to help push the water up the tube. Those familiar with elementary Physics will remember the formula $P=dgh$, where P is the pressure at a depth h below the surface of the liquid, d is the liquid's density and g is the well known acceleration of gravity. Therefore the deeper one sits in the water the greater will be the pressure at the submerged end. Although I have never done Basti in a river, I can imagine how the technique would be greatly facilitated if you are in water up to your chest.

Someday, someone will invent a small one-way valve to put on the end of the Basti tube which will allow the water to flow up but not back down, and which will not introduce turbulence that cuts down the flow rate. When that happens then we will all be able to do Basti in our bathtubs without the drawbacks mentioned above.

The next three techniques are for cleansing of the anal opening and are also preliminary exercises to prepare for Asvini Mudra. The first of these is called Mula Sodhana (13, 14); it consists of cleansing and massaging of the anus by using the middle finger. Traditionally, the root of the Haridra (tumeric) plant was also used. The modern way is to use a finger stall (the finger cut off from a rubber glove) with a little vegetable oil on it. After insertion into the anus, the finger is rotated both ways, clockwise and counter clockwise in order to massage both the internal and external sphincters. I personally have never used these techniques for the purpose of cleaning the anus; I always did them after Basti (when the rectum is already empty and clean) for the purpose of massage only, so that eventually voluntary control over opening and closing of the sphincters is established. The next technique is called Ganesha Kriya; the distinction between Ganesha Kriya and Mula Sodhana is not very clear. Presumably, in Mula Sodhana the desired effect is the massage, for toning up the sphincters and their nerves; whereas in Ganesha Kriya the desired result is the cleansing of the anus and rectum by removing the impurities with one's finger. I have never been forced to resort to this. Such a technique would be indicated in severe cases of pathological constipation in which impurities cannot pass out because of obstruction in the rectum, and thus the hardened material must be removed manually. Such methods are more akin to surgery rather than preventive measures. The next technique is called Adhascakri. I have seen it described in only one place, namely the Satkarmasangrahah (15). From reading the translation one would think that the technique Adhascakri is identical with Genesha kriya (removing the impurities by inserting finger, etc.). However, since the Satkrmasangrahah mentions it along side two other chakras (Urdhvacakri and Madhyacakri) both of which are used to stimulate a nervous reflex (see the first of my articles on throat purification;

Urdhvacakri stimulates a shuddering reflex and causes a copious flow of mucous from under the palate, and Madhyacakri stimulates a vomiting reflex or spasm), therefore I suspected that Adhascakri would do something similar. And indeed my suspicions proved to be true. Inserting a long middle finger as far as it will go, deep into the rectum and massaging the walls of the rectum does indeed stimulate the defecating reflex; a strong spasm of peristaltic contraction is experienced, forcing any remaining impurities from the deeper colon and sigmoid where they may have been remaining hidden. When I was in India, suffering from Dysentery, the inflamed colon was so sensitive that even a very slight pressure of the finger upon the inner walls of the deeper rectum would trigger a powerful, spasmotic defecation reflex. A note of warning: before attempting any one of the last three techniques that I described make absolutely certain that your finger nails have been clipped. Cutting or scratching the delicate inner walls of the rectum could be very painful, and any infection caused thereby could lead to very serious complications.

The next technique is Asvini Mudra; this Mudra requires time and effort. Yoga Mimansa devotes 23 pages to the detailed description and explanation. If readers can get access to Yoga Mimansa, be sure to read this article (16), you will learn a lot of other interesting things besides Asvini Mudra.

Asvini Mudra is considered to be mastered when one can open the two anal sphincters at will, at which time one can dispense with the Basti tube. Because of the construction of the western bathroom facilities and their shortcomings (mentioned above under Basti), I do not use Asvini Mudra for drawing in water (Jala Basti). Instead I use Asvini Mudra for the technique of Vata Basti, (or air Basti); after the colon has been washed with water by doing Jala Basti (Lauliki, etc.), I like to finish off the whole colon purification process with aeration of the entire colon. The technique is as follows: sitting in the Uttkatasana position (a sort of squatting with the buttock resting on the heels and the knees very slightly above the ground), you spread the buttocks with the heels, perform a very powerful Nauli Madhayama and simultaneously relax the anal sphincters. A large amount of air will rush in (into the colon) with a great noise, bringing oxygen to the cells which make up the walls of the colon and rectum. For the past few years, we have been hearing a lot about the miraculous virtues of colonic oxygen therapy for curing a number of diseases of the colon. The tissues of the colon are invariably never exposed to air and oxygen: they, like the walls of a cesspool, are constantly in contact with the offensive poisonous gases resulting from faulty metabolism of improper food mixtures and with the fecal matter containing poisons scheduled for elimination. Is it so miraculous then, that a good washing−out with water followed by a good airing−out can restore health to such a colon? The technique of Vata Basti enables a Yogi to receive all of the benefits of Colon Oxygenation Therapy without the necessity of tubes, valves, oxygen tanks, etc., not to mention the expense of such treatments and the time wasted in going to and from the doctor's office. In the beginning, before I was able to do Asvini Mudra, I used to do Mula−Sodhana, that is, to insert a finger into the anus and move in a circular motion, massaging and spreading the sphincters. When the sphincters became relaxed, the finger was removed, a powerful Nauli Madhayama was performed, and air rushed into the colon.

After control over the sphincters is established, we do not need to use finger to open and loosen the tightness of the sphincters. Nowadays, I do Vata Basti in the ordinary sitting position on the toilet as follows: After evacuating the water remaining from Jala Basta (water Basti), I move the circular muscles (sphincters) of the anus in the out several times, alternately contracting and relaxing the sphincters, then I perform a very powerful Central Nauli and simultaneously relax the sphincters. If the Nauli is sufficiently powerful, air will be sucked into the colon by the negative pressure (Madhavadasa Vacuum). I have found that the sphincters will open easier if I concentrate the relaxation not exactly upon the sphincters but on a point slightly forward of the anus, namely the perineum. Although I have been using Asvini Mudra for a few years now, there are still days when the stubborn sphincters simply just refuse to open up, requiring the intervention of the finger. It is good to finish the whole colon purification process with Vata Basti; the air which has been sucked in can be left inside the colon for as long as comfortable. When I do it, I pull in as much air as I can, then let out only enough so as not to feel bloated or uncomfortable; the rest I allow to remain in the colon and become absorbed into the tissues of the walls of the colon. One other interesting observation that I made at the time that I was suffering from Dysentery: because of the Dysentery, the sphincters became so very relaxed due to the constant defecation and inflamed walls of the colon, to the extent that Asvini Mudra became extremely easy to do at that time, requiring only a very weak Nauli. In fact, the sphincters would open by themselves when I didn't want them to open every time that I came to Nauli Madhayama during the cycle of Lauliki (described above) and it required a conscious effort to keep them closed.

One last observation that I made in this connection related to colon purification: tradition prescribes Mayurasana, (see volume I of Yoga Mimansa or reference (17) in the Bibliography) to be performed after Jala Basti in order to completely eliminate any water remaining in the colon. Having personally had some trouble in this respect (evacuating all of the remaining water after Jala Basti), I tried Mayurasana for shorter and longer periods, but for me, this didn't seem to help. When we bring a real yogi from India I will ask him why. Is it because I am not doing Mayurasana properly or is it some peculiarity of my own colon?

Mat Rosmarynowski, Los Angeles, California

THE CURATIVE CRISIS

One of the most important reasons for the writing of this treatise is to warn the reader about what I will call a curative crisis. This crisis will appear as soon as a natural detoxification program is started by which the body is cleansed of toxic materials through the employment and use of natural means. This is to say that unpleasant symptoms shall appear shortly after or during the cure. These symptoms should not be a reason for alarm since they will disappear shortly after, and as we shall see later on, represent a natural and logical process.

It is possible that during the first days of the cure one shall experience, for a short time, symptoms of diseases and conditions previously treated artificially by the employment of medications such as aspirins, drugs, injections, etc. In other words, by the use of poisonous remedies. These symptoms shall appear for a while only to disappear later, after natural treatment. The explanation for this phenomenon is that drugs, injections and other artificial treatments do NOT really cure but only stop symptoms of diseases, meanwhile poisoning and weaking one's blood as well as diminishing natural resistance within the organism.

Only the employment of natural treatments is effective in reaching the roots of one's problems and the true cause of illness and diseases while expelling all toxic materials causing damage to the body and promoting truly natural health. You shall understand that such a powerful healing and cleansing action, occuring within the organism, will logically bring about brief but transitory uncomfortable symptoms. It is this aspect of the recuperative process which we have called "curative crisis". It is precisely the signal indicating that the processes of healing and purification have started. It also signals that the organism had been previously treated anti−naturally.

In order to obtain definitive success one must be patient and persistent, one must sacrifice: most desired things are difficult to attain, but one learns that persistence results in success and fullfillment. This is particularly so in the case of one's health. It seems that one can only reassure the value of health when it is gone. Many persons have told me: "I will pay any price, just tell me the remedy." But there isn't a magical formula. There isn't an instant cure or drug. Healing occurs in the same manner in which a disease develops from a mild into a chronic ailment − very gradually. One must retrace those steps in reverse.

It is known that chronic ailments are not painful at that stage. Pain is a signal from the nervous system and/or from the brain and will not be felt whenever there is a toxic blockage on the system. Now during treatment and as soon as the natural process of elimination of toxic substances from the central nervous system begins, old aches will reappear briefly for a few days. Commonly, healing of the body occurs from the feet to the head or inversely to the manner in which the organ degenerated. Ailments previously suffered, such as ulcers, infections, skin conditions, mouth infections, tumors, sores, etc., will march in reverse through our organism.

In many instances, the patient will re−experience the flavor of medicines taken previously. In some other instances, the patient re−experiences the smell of pharmaceutical products, this along with nausea and vomiting, indicating that the body is cleansing and freeing itself of foreign matters possibly accumulated internally over a period of many years.

You should understand that such a process of purification shall bring about unpleasant symptoms, such as the ones described. To that effect we offer this writing, in order to inform and warn you. DO NOT give up. Many individuals become scared and are taken to hospitals when they experience symptoms such as weakness, nausea, dizziness, pain, or diarrhea − there they are bombarded with drugs, thus stopping the normal curative process. As symptoms are stopped, so are the natural reserves of one's organs which fight fiercely to expell its enemy. The organism loses its battle and one has to wait for another opportunity which may never come. This is how many persons begin a natural treatment program, become scared and discontinue the treatment, thus denying their body its right to the natural and fair process of recuperation previously started. Some persons complain to us that they had not suffered headaches for years and that now their headaches are back. We tell those individuals to be thankful because their bodies are recuperating! Wait a few days and they will enjoy the results. Other persons loose their long-standing aches and ailments. But every organism is different and must go through its unique purification process. The symptoms are tolerable for some people, while for some other persons it may be difficult. Some organisms require rest for a few days, in these cases one should stay in bed in a well ventilated room, bathe two or three times per day using clean towels after each bath; change clothes after each bath. In addition one should only eat and drink raw fruits and vegetables. One should also read books on natural medicine, this in order to strengthen the intellect as well as to gain the mental energy needed to make correct decisions.

If we put nature to the test, we will see the evidence clearly. It is natural to be cautious and to "test" those things which make us doubt. We believe that 4 weeks in a well-balanced vegetarian diet will convince even the most incredulous. Let's take meats and other toxic foods away from our usual diet and substitute for these healthy and nutritious foods. We will see that within hours or days (depending upon the nature of the organism) the "curative crisis" will appear. In other words, we strengthen the organism and immediately following it starts cleansing itself. Simply stated, if we give it the right instruments and raw materials, it will provide its own maintainence.

Notice what I emphasize in the previous concept. This is the foundation of naturism. The human organism is so marvelously designed as to not only fight disease for itself, but also to provide its own maintainence, given the opportunity to do so.

What are the "means"? Simply stated — natural feeding.

In order to develop our bodies' resistence to disease, it is necessary to provide it with a balance of the basic nutritional elements.

If you compare our vegetarian nutritional recommendations with the recommendations of traditonal nutritionists you shall see a big difference in terms of the concept of a balanced diet and the above statement may appear conflictive to you.

The vegetarian knows that there is not a healthier and happier way to live than through his lifestyle: nutrition is harmony with the natural laws.

Enemas

Place one liter of warm water inside of an enema bag. For insertion, patient should be lying on his back, his or her hip slightly lifted by means of a small pillow, legs should be separated and slightly bent at the knees.

Insert enema into rectum and lift bag as much as possible, this will facilitate the flow of liquid into the rectum. In order to soften fecal matter and aid to ease its elimination, hold liquid inside of body for a while. Massage stomach region gently rubbing the area from the appendix (right side) to the descending colon area (left side) in a clock-wise circular motion.

For herbal enemas, boil 8-10 grams (2 teaspoons) of desired plants in two liters of water for three minutes. Let liquid cool and proceed as indicated above.

It is convenient to use a second enema once the contents of the first enema have been eliminated from the body. This second enema will help eliminate fecal matter softened from the first intestinal wash.

Important: For children, use only 75 cc of liquid for each year of age.

EVIDENCE FOR INTESTINAL TOXEMIA
AN INESCAPABLE CLINICAL PHENOMENON

Introduction

This paper will focus on the concept of intoxication of intestinal origin. The subject is of wide-ranging clinical importance and should be emphasized. As will be made clear, intestinal toxemia is frequently found as either a basic cause of or contributing factor to many clinical phenomena. In 1933, Dr. Anthony Bassler, a professor of Gastroenterology in Fordham University Medical College and New York Polyclinic Medical College, and consulting gastroenterologist of Christs Polyclinic and Peoples Hospitals in New York stated, after 25-year study of over 5000 cases, that: "Every physician should realize that the intestinal toxemias are the most important primary and contributing causes of many disorders and diseases of the human body" (1). Dr. H.H. Boeker, in 1928, went so far as to say, "it is now universally conceded that autointoxication is the underlying cause of an exceptionally large group of symptom complexes" (2).

Intestinal toxemia is a process resulting from a certain type of diet or from intestinal obstruction. Various toxic chemicals are produced in the lumen by bacteria. These toxins are absorbed into the bloodstream either as a result of a pathological or a non-pathological state of the mucosa. Some of the toxins escape the detoxifying action of the liver because of pathological, functional (cannot act upon all of the toxin present), or physiological (normally does not act upon this toxin) liver insufficiency. These chemical poisons then enter the general circulation and exert deleterious effects before being excreted by the kidneys. The result of the intoxication is to produce a pathological change in the tissues, or to aggravate a previously existing condition. Each of these steps will be considered.

A thorough review of the literature was undertaken in the preparation of this paper. "Index Medicus," from the years 1879 to 1978, was checked under multiple listings; many medical texts were perused to finds leads to articles; the "Citation Index" was also checked. The result of this search was to find that almost no clinically-oriented articles have been written in the English language about intestinal toxemia since the late 1950s. In fact, few papers have been published since 1940 which directly address this subject. It is for this reason that most of the clinically-oriented papers reviewed in this paper are dated from before 1940.

The reader may wonder why the theory of intestinal toxemia has not been discussed in recent times, and is not well known today. The fact is that a change in opinion over the years, not based on any new scientific research, has led to the abandoning of this idea by the medical profession. It is important to emphasize that this has not resulted from new scientific research proving the error of the theory of intestinal toxemia. It is well known that certain ideas fall into and out of favor as the years pass, regardless of their validity, which has been the present case. An analogy may be drawn from the theory of chiropractic which, despite its great clinical usefulness, has been repeatedly "discovered" then abandoned or forgotten since ancient times; D. D. Palmer was the most recent individual to revive this old healing practice and bring it to our attention.

Some of the articles cited in this paper were written over 50 years ago. Quite naturally, a question may arise in the reader's mind as to whether or not such research could be reliable, having been done so many years ago. The answer to this is unequivocally affirmative. Portions of this paper as well as a great wealth of scientific information available today were uncovered many years ago, and are still valid. Modern textbooks in microbiology and biochemistry discuss many of the facts presented in this paper as true information; one text in each area is cited herein to demonstrate this point. Although scientific technology was not as sophisticated in the 1920's, the scientific intellect was equally keen; many important discoveries were made and theories confirmed. It is most important to emphasize that older research and clinical observations are not necessarily invalid because of age.

The writer is well aware of the fact that current opinion in the medical world does not agree with the conclusions reached in this paper. However, the theory of intestinal toxemia as presented is scientifically and clinically sound; this ultimately is the main concern of an objective scientist. Opinion should be based on solid scientific research, and it is the purpose of this paper to aid in the formation of a scientifically—based opinion.

Effect of Diet

The experiments of Herter and Kendall (3), performed in 1909 at the Rockefeller Institute for Medical Research, were among the first to prove a definite connection between the nature of the diet and the type of bacterial flora found in the intestine. In experiments on cats (chosen because of their biological similarity to man), it was proven that the intake of a high protein diet resulted in dominance of a strongly proteolyzing putrefactive type of flora (note: the term putrefaction refers to "decomposition of proteins by anaerobic organisms" (4)); also that conversion to a high carbohydrate/low protein diet resulted in dominance of a non—putrefactive type of flora. Fecal samples were cultured after a change in diet, and concentrations of endproducts of bacterial metabolism were measured in the urine to determine the type and character of the flora. The change in flora resulting from the change in diet was the same regardless of the animal type. The products of the putrefactive flora included indole and skatole (from tryptophan), phenol (from tyrosine), and hydrogen sulfide from the products of protein breakdown. Of importance to health care professionals is the following observation seen after a change in diet from high protein to high carbohydrate: "Clinically, the most striking feature of the change in diet [in monkeys] is an improvement in spirits and activity which may safely be construed as showing a markedly improved sense of bodily and psychological well being." (5) The results of these experiments were confirmed by other investigators of that same period. (6, 7, 8, 9) Many recent experiments have shown the presence of products in the urine of the putrefactive flora following ingestion of a high protein diet. (141, 142, 143, 144, 145, 146, 147, 148) Other experiments have shown that ingestion of fermentable carbohydrates such as glucose, fructose or lactose results in delay of or complete inhibition of the putrefactive process. (141, 148, 149) Inhibition of the putrefactive process is reflected by decreased urinary output of putrefactive products.

Intestinal Obstruction

Obstruction in the intestine causes toxemia only in a small percentage of cases. However, it is far more likely to be rapidly fatal than toxemia resulting from diet. The main reason for considering obstruction is derived from the insight gained into the study of intestinal toxemia.

Obstruction in laboratory animals is produced by the surgical formation of a closed intestinal loop. The loop is washed to exlude the secretions of the stomach, liver, and pancreas, along with the products of food digestion. The result has been the same in all experiments; the bacteria multiply greatly, the proteolytic bacteria overgrow all others and produce toxic chemicals, the toxins are absorbed, and the animals become sick and die. (10, 11, 12, 13, 14, 150) The toxins produced include histamine, (15) which is normally present but may be in a greater concentration, and various protein decomposition products. (16)

The toxins produced in the closed intestinal loop have been removed and injected into healthy animals with a reaction "more intense but similar to that developing a closed–loop" animal. (17, 18) Of importance is the fact that injection into the portal vein "gives a reaction similar to intravenous injection" (19) indicating that "the liver plays no essential role as a protective agent against this poison." (20)

These toxins have been produced by putrefactive bacteria which are normally present but have multiplied greatly and overgrown all other bacteria in the obstructed intestine. Therefore, it is within the realm of hypothesis that some amount of toxin is produced and absorbed in the case of intestinal stasis with a high intake of protein but without total obstruction.

It is important to emphasize again that intestinal obstruction similar to that observed in animals with surgical closure of an intestinal loop is rarely seen in man; such complete obstruction is certainly not the basic cause of intestinal toxemia, in most cases. However, insight into the process of intestinal toxemia probably can be gained by the consideration of such an extreme case; therefore, this consideration has been included. When researchers feed lab animals ten times the amount of saccharine a human being would ever consume in the same time period, identical logic is used. This logic is accepted by the scientific community. It is well recognized that much information can be gained from experiments with animals, using extreme conditions.

Nature and Action of Chemicals Produced by Proteolytic Bacteria

To date, the exact nature of all such chemicals has never been completely identified. Unfortunately, along with the development of instrumentation sophisticated enough to yield a complete answer to this question, there has been a simultaneous loss of interest in the subject of intestinal toxemia. However, much information is available from various research studies.

The reader should bear in mind a basic tenet of modern pathology which is too often forgotten today. This tenet states that inflammation is a response of the body to tissue injury, and that this response serves to protect the body from the injurious agent. (151) Many times it is thought that the basic problem in a tissue involves inflammation, as if such a state existed in a vacuum. That would not be possible. Inflammation is the response of the body to local injury and attention should be paid to removal of the injurious agent, a truly protective response, rather than to suppressing the inflammation.

Some ammonia is formed by bacteria in the intestine, mainly from urea and digestive products of proteins (21); ammonia is also formed, as is well known, by the liver and kidneys. In liver disease such as cirrhosis, or in disease of portal circulation, "abnormal elevations in the level of ammonia in peripheral blood may occur and these are accompanied by corresponding but lesser elevations of ammonia in the cerebrospinal fluid." (22) Many studies show that this increased concentration of ammonia causes severe neurological symptoms resembling hepatic coma such as mental disturbances, characteristic tremor, and altered EEG pattern. (23, 24, 25, 26) A low protein diet minimized these symptoms. (23, 24, 26)

This reflects modern medical opinion as well. Harrison's "Principles of Internal Medicine" states that "both hepatic coma and the chronic form of hepato−cerebral disease are characterized by hyperammonemia, which is probably important in their pathogenesis. Ammonium is derived from the bacterial action on intestinal proteins and normally is converted to urea in the liver. (152) Confusion, drowsiness, or other signs of impending hepatic coma should be treated by prompt decrease in protein intake to levels of 20 to 30 grams daily or less." (153) In regards to treatment for hepatic coma: "Reducing the protein intake, cleansing the colon of blood, suppressing the bacterial action on protein in the intestinal tract with neomycin or kanamycin, and administering the acidifying agent lactulose, all of which lower the NH_3 levels in the blood, have been found to restore many of these patients to a relatively normal state." And, "Although the biochemical mechanism is not fully understood, the most plausible hypothesis is that the levels of blood NH_3 are elevated because the diseased or bypassed liver fails to convert it to urea; the high serum NH_3 causes elevated NH_3 levels in the brain which interfere with its metabolism in some obscure way." (154) Ammonia may even be involved with the malignant transformation of cells. (27)

Clostridium perfringen enterotoxin has also been found. (28) This is well known to be highly poisonous. (29)

Indole is formed from tryptophan by proteolytic bacteria, (30) and is known to be toxic from results of experiments on animals, (31) and man. (32) It is also known that certain metabolites of tryptophan can cause bladder tumors. (33, 34) With normal liver function, most, if not all indole is detoxified by the process of conjugation. In the case of sickness, this may or may not occur. A high protein, low carbohydrate diet results in increased excretion of conjugated indole, called indican, (7, 35, 141, 146, 147, 148) as compared with a low protein, high carbohydrate diet. The amount of indican in the urine has been widely used as a measure of intestinal putrefaction.

However, indican determination used by itself is not reliable. For diagnostic purposes, it is interesting to know that combined determination of phenol and indican in the urine has proved to be highly valuable in the detection of the stagnant loop syndrome. (145) Stagnant loop syndrome is defined as bacterial overgrowth in the small intestine, vitamin B12 malabsorption, and steatorrhea, all of which improved by treatment with antibiotics. (155) This syndrome is believed to be present if the levels in the urine of both phenol and indican are abnormally elevated. Tabaqchali cautions, however, that since his experiment utilized only 51 patients, this observation of diagnostic reliability needs confirmation in a larger series. (145)

Phenol (carbolic acid) is formed from tyrosine in the process of putrefaction. (30, 142, 143, 156) It is so extremely poisonous that it is used as an antimicrobial agent. It is both a local corrosive and systemic poison which can cause necrosis of gastrointestinal mucosa, renal and hepatic cells. (36) Phenol is absorbed into the body, and most of it is excreted in a free form — not conjugated and, therefore, not detoxified. (37, 38) As is the case with indole, the concentration of phenol in the urine is increased with a high protein diet. (39, 40, 157, 158)

Skatole is formed from bacterial action on tryptophan. (30, 159) It is regarded as a "toxic substance causing depression of the circulation and of the central nervous system," (32,41) and is found in increased concentration in the intestine following a high protein intake. (42) Skatole, "when in excess in the circulating blood through failure of conjugation by the liver," imparts a foul odor to the breath. (43) Skatole and indole are partially responsible for the characteristic odor of feces. (44) Skatole antagonizes acetylcholine and potassium (160) in smooth muscle preparations. Pseudomonas migula has recently been identified as a bacteria capable of converting tryptophan to skatole. (161) Following formation, skatole is converted into 6−hydroxyskatole by the cells of the gut wall, and possibly by other host tissues. (162) 6−hydroxyskatole damages lipid−absorbing cells, the hemoglobin within red blood cells, and hemoglobin found free within the body. (162) This destructive action probably accounts for the presence of metabolites of skatole in the urine of many patients suffering from the malabsorption syndrome and certain anemias. (162, 164)

Hydrogen sulfide gas is another byproduct of protein decomposition. (43) In comparable concentrations it is "as toxic as cyanide and interferes with the cytochrome system." (45) It is obvious that this gas can irritate the mucosa; this brings about congestion and makes the mucosa more permeable to intestinal contents because of the presence of gas in solution. It may be responsible for "neurocirculatory myasthenic symptoms, for poisoning by this gas will cause: weakness, nausea, clammy skin, rapid pulse and cyanosis." (43)

Neurine is formed from sphingomyelin by anaerobic bacteria. This compound is toxic to animals. (46, 47)

Aminoethyl mercaptan is formed from bacterial decomposition of the amino acid cysteine. It has a "profound hypotensive effect." (48)

Putrescine and cadavarine, formed from putrefaction of tryptophan, can lower blood pressure. Tryptamine, from the same source, raises blood pressure after an initial depression. (49)

Histamine is the last important decomposition product of tryptophan that is well known. (15, 49, 50) Poisoning with this compound can produce "headache, head congestion, nervous depression, cardiac arrythemia, fall of blood pressure, nausea, and collapse." (32)

Tyramine is a putrefactive product of tyrosine. It is structurally similar to epinephrine and can raise the blood pressure. (49, 50)

It should be mentioned that some current writers hypothesize that putrefactive endproducts "irritate the receptor nerve−endings, thereby bombarding the associated spinal cord segments with afferent impulses, which result in muscular response and subluxations in the lower thoracic and upper lumbar areas, as well as predisposing to sacroiliac subluxation." Furthermore, "noxious materials in the bloodstream circulate to the central nervous system and... increase its irritability to afferent stimuli leading to increased hypertonicity of muscles and greater likelihood of subluxation." (51) We, therefore, may not have only the circulatory but also the nervous system mediating the effects of toxins to all the cells of the body.

Many other chemicals, too numerous to consider in detail, have been found to be formed in the intestine from bacterial putrefaction. These include guanidine, (52, 53) and many others. (54, 55) Besides the known substances, many chemicals of unknown character may be produced. Some of these chemicals may be toxic to a degree; of the toxins, some may be completely detoxified by the liver but others not at all. Other substances may be only partially rendered harmless. As is obvious, the subject of the chemistry of intestinal toxemia is highly complex and only partially understood. However, as will be seen, the situation from a clinical perspective is much clearer.

Intestinal Stasis

Delayed intestinal motility of the small and large intestines will now be discussed. Sir W. Arbuthnot Lane, MS, was one of the most knowledgeable men to work in this field. Being a surgeon, and having a penchant for surgical treatment of intestinal toxemia, he observed first hand the pathological state of the intestines of many sick people. His therapy, as might be suspected, was to remove the diseased section of the bowel; this was successful in providing temporary relief to the patient. However, as will be seen later, other treatments exist which are as successful but are non—traumatic and do not involve the use of drugs or surgery.

Lane defined chronic intestinal stasis as an abnormal delay in the transmission of the intestinal contents through some portion or portions of the gastro—intestinal tract, which delay may be accompanied by constipation or by a daily or even more frequent action of the bowels." (56) He further states that any such delay facilitates multiplication of organisms and the subsequent development of toxemia in the bloodstream. This leads to a "progressive degenerative changes in every tissue and a very definite and unmistakable series of symptoms." (56) It was mentioned in the discussion on intestinal obstruction that bacteria multiply greatly, with the proteolytic—putrefactive bacteria overgrowing all others. Is it not reasonable to consider that some of the features of chronic intestinal stasis are of the same kind but not as severe as those encountered in total obstruction?

Other physicians concur that delay (stasis) may be accompanied by one or more movements of the bowels per day. (57, 58, 59) This is of great clinical importance. It removes the foundation to the widely held belief that daily movements of the bowel are conducive to health.

Concerning clinical evidence, the following is worthy of mention. In a clinical study of 50 cases of intestinal toxemia, Dr. H. J. Bartle found constipation in 72 percent, and delayed intestinal motility in 60 percent. (60) Dr. Satterlee found constipation in 84 percent of his cases of intestinal toxemia (61); in 1916, this doctor was attending physician to Fordham Hospital, Chief of Clinic for Gastroenterological

Diseases, University and Bellevue Hospital Medical College, New York.

Consideration of the chemical aspect of intestinal stasis is also worth of note. In this regard, Drs. Underhill and Simpson of the department of Experimental Medicine, Yale University School of Medicine, state the following: "the effect of even mild constipation overshadows the effect of diet on the excretion of phenol and indican. Constipation causes a large increase in the excretion of these substances." (62)

In conclusion, it may be said that many physicians believed that delayed motility provides the foundation for building the condition of intestinal toxemia. (7, 63, 64, 65, 66, 67)

Distension

Distension of the intestine has been attributed by some to be the cause of the symptoms of intestinal toxemia. (68) In experiments performed by Dr. Alvarez or the Mayo Clinic, it was shown that pressure upon the rectum by sterile gauze could produce symptoms of intoxication. (69) There is no doubt that the effect of mechanical distension of the intestine is irritation to the nervous system, which is of no small importance. However, the presented evidence shows that mechanical irritation is indeed accompanied by chemical irritation. "Because it has been shown that constipation headache can occur in persons whose spinal cords have been cut, we know that this headache is not caused by nervous impulses from the colon. Therefore, it possibly results from absorbed toxic products or from changes in the circulatory system." (70)

Distension in obstruction of the intestine results in "more or less splanchnic congestion" (71) resulting in "interference with its [the mucosa] normal circulation." (72) This may result in functional or anatomic injury to the mucosa, allowing absorption of toxins to take place faster than the liver can detoxify them. Distension could lead to a "hemorrhagic and frequently necrotic condition of mucosa with a consequently hastened absorption of poisonous substances." (73)

As can be clearly seen, distension is a condition which the clinician will wish to reduce. Treatment will be discussed later.

Absorption

Absorption of toxins may occur through an intact gastrointestinal mucosa. (74, 141) For example, a recent study has shown that indole and skatole can be rapidly absorbed at any level of the small or large intestine. In this experiment, medical students with normal health and patients in the hospital with no symptoms of gastrointestinal tract disease were used as subjects. (141) Many other writers feel that an inflammation of the mucosa is necessary before absorption will occur. Such inflammations of the rectosigmoid colon are described as "common." (75) Of 50 cases of intestinal toxemia examined by another physician, 80 percent had lower colon inflammation, and 62 percent had inflammation of the duodenum. (76) Others have reported general inflammation of the intestinal wall. (77, 78) Inflammation of the terminal ileum or appendix will "elicit intense enterointestinal reflexes resulting in severe inhibition of gastrointestinal motility; as a result, functional obstruction often occurs in the small bowel." (79) Of interest is a description of the changes in the colon wall observed during the autopsy of insane patients residing at New Jersey State Hospital. Seen were large areas of destruction of mucosa plus atony and atrophy of smooth muscle. (80)

It is well known that mucosal injury may result in death from septicemia. Here it is stated that mucosal inflammation alters permeability, thereby allowing absorption of bacterial toxins which cause pathological changes in tissues. It is obvious that in septicemia, the bacteria produce metabolic toxins throughout the body. Many scientists believe these toxins are the cause of death in this type of situation.

Detoxification

Detoxification is primarily the responsibility of the liver. Though this subject has already been covered to a certain extent, a few additional remarks are necessary.

Detoxification is primarily the responsibility of the liver because the blood flowing from the stomach and intestines is "not returned directly from these organs to the heart, but is conveyed by the portal vein to the liver." (81) Once the portal vein has transported the blood to the liver, "this vein divides like an artery and ultimately ends in capillary—like vessels [sinusoids]." (81) From these sinusoids, substances absorbed from the intestines become exposed to liver parenchymal cells. These cells, hepatocytes, act upon such substances in many ways.

Ideally, hepatocytes will detoxify any poisons present and thereby protect the body. The important point here, however, is that toxins upon which the liver can act and detoxify, may be present in too great a quantity for complete liver action. As Dr. Bartle says, the liver must be compared to other organs; "they can do just so much work and no more. In the case of the liver it is always carrying an unusual burden in chronic intoxication states, and naturally the breaking point must now and then be reached. This comes with an acute outburst of intoxicating symptoms..." (82) With mucosal injury especially, "absorption of toxic substances may take place faster than the liver can detoxicate them and toxemia and death ensue." (73) Many authors concur in this viewpoint. (56, 77) Of course, there are poisons against which "liver plays no essential role as a protective agent." (71) Phenol and skatole are examples of poisons which for the most part, escape liver action. (141, 142, 143, 144, 145, 163)

Symptoms

Information on symptoms arising primarily from intestinal toxemia could fill volumes. Not only have books been written, (84) but literally thousands of articles in many languages have been published in the scientific literature on this topic. Obviously, an exhaustive discussion here is an impossibility.

No claim should be made that every symptom described in the following paragraphs arises from intestinal toxemia. However, by examination of the following, one must note that such toxemia is at the root of more problems than commonly imagined; it is at the root of many conditions more often than might be suspected.

Generally, intestinal toxemia manifests as one or more of the following: fatigue, nervousness, gastro–intestinal conditions, impaired nutrition, skin manifestations, endocrine disturbances, neurocirculatory abnormalities and headaches. (43) Arthritis, sciatica and low back pain; allergy, asthma; eye, ear, nose and throat disease; cardiac irregularities; pathological changes in the breasts; all these conditions have responded to therapy directed at a toxemic state in the intestine, and the evidence for this follows. You will note that therapy is described only generally as being aimed at relieving the toxemic state of the intestine. To be more specific in each instance is impossible in this paper. Treatments mentioned will be representative of that which has been used by many doctors, not including surgery and drugs.

    A.   Allergy: Dr. William Lintz, MD, successfully treated 472 patients suffering from "gastrointestinal allergy, a condition of hypersensitivity of the digestive tract," by eliminating the following allergens from the gastrointestinal tract: "bacteria and their toxins, foods and their split products." (85) The most frequent symptoms were endocrine gland disturbances of many types such as hypothyroidism, pituitary malfunction, etc.; heart disease; hypertension, and many others. (86)

    B.   Asthma: Dr. Allan Eustis, MD, instructor at Tulane University of Medicine in 1912, reports that 121 cases of bronchial asthma were relieved by eliminating the intestinal toxemia universally present. (87) Dr. D. Rochester, MD, of the University of Buffalo School of Medicine in 1906, states that it is his conclusion, after 23 years of observation, that toxemia of gastrointestinal tract origin is the underlying cause of asthma. He says, "I believe the results of treatment justify my position." (88)

    C.   Arthritis: Dr. Anthony Bassler treated 44 arthritic patients by relieving intestinal toxemia, and observed "marked improvement in 21, moderate in 19, none in four." With the addition of physical therapy, all but nine cases showed more marked improvement. (89) Twenty years later, Dr. Bassler said a similar handling of 300 additional cases "has not modified my opinion a particle." (90) Sir W. Arbuthnot Lane, MS, FRCS (surgeon), believed that arthritis could not develop in the absence of intestinal toxemia, and says there is clinical and x–ray evidence of stasis in such patients. Furthermore, he states that, "the symptoms disappear and the patients recover sometimes with startling rapidity when the condition of stasis has been effectually dealt with." (91) Others confirm the connection between intestinal toxemia and arthritis. (92)

    D.   Cardiac arrhythmias: Guyton (93) states that "toxic conditions of the heart" can cause arrhythmias. Dr. Bassler reports 100 percent success in eliminating such heart irregularities in 43 patients treated by reducing intestinal toxemia. (94) Dr. Bainbridge, MD, stated that "intestinal toxemia is common among the causative factors of so–called functional heart disease. (95) Dr. D. J. Barry in 1916, professor of Physiology, Queens College, Cork, England, stated that: "There seems little doubt that substances having a deleterious action on the heart musculature and nerves are formed both in the small and large intestine, even under apparently normal circumstances." (96)

    Toxemia is further implicated in high blood pressure. Dr. Hovel states that "toxemia due to intestinal sepsis is a common cause of increased blood pressure." (97)

    E.   Ear, nose, and throat problems: The experience of three doctors is neatly summed up by Dr. J. A. Stucky, MD. (98) "In several hundreds of cases of diseases of the nasal accessory sinuses, middle and internal ear,...I have found unmistakable and marked evidence of toxemia of intestinal origin as evidenced by excessive indican in the urine, and when the condition causing this was removed there was marked amelioration or entire relief of the disease."(99, 100)

F. Eclampsia: R. C. Brown, MB, MS, FRCS, an obstetrical surgeon in England in 1930, linked intestinal toxemia and eclampsia.

G. Eye problems: Dr. C. W. Hawley, MD, treated many cases of eye strain and disease with success once again by relieving intestinal toxemia. (101)

H. Thyroid gland disease: Dr. W. S. Reveno, MD, theoretically links exophthalmic goiter to "a toxic process in the intestinal tract." (102) He cites animal studies as evidence. Echoing this view is Dr. A. Eustis, MD, who cites case histories of patients who found complete relief from exophthalmic goiter as a result of eliminating intestinal toxemia. (103) Sir W. A. Lane reports a connection between intestinal toxemia and "several changes in the thyroid" such as "adenomatous growths." (104)

I. Nervous system: Many disorders of the nervous system are involved. Dr. Carl Von Noorden, MD, professor of the First Medical Clinic, Vienna, Austria, in 1913, described a condition of diffuse sensory polyneuritis with pronounced vagal irritation, treated with positive results by relieving intestinal toxemia. He and his assistant extracted a "poisonous substance from the feces, which in animal experiments produced quite similar symptoms." (105) This substance was found to be formed by a "bacterium of the paratyphus group." (106)

Dr. C. A. Herter, MD, in 1892, lecturer on Anatomy and Pathology of the Nervous System, New York Polyclinic, linked intestinal putrefaction to epilepsy in 31 patients. He based this on a successful treatment using drugs to control bacterial activity of the intestine. (107) Agreeing with his conclusion are other doctors. (108, 109)

Drs. Satterlee and Eldridge, in a paper read to the annual session of the American Medical Association in 1917, reported experience with 518 cases of "mental symptoms" including "mental sluggishness, dullness and stupidity; loss of concentration and/or memory; mental incoordination, irritability, lack of confidence, excessive and useless worry, exaggerated introspection, hypochondriasis and phobias, depression and melancholy, obsessions and delusions, hallucinations, suicidal tendencies, delirium, and stupor." (110) Their success in eliminating these symptoms by surgically relieving intestinal toxemia is truly remarkable in the light of today's commonly-held beliefs. In the discussion following the presentation of the doctors' paper, other physicians stated that they shared in this experience. (111)

Of considerable interest is a recent paper entitled, "Biochemical Aspects of Indole Metabolism in Normal and Schizophrenic Subjects" by Herbert Sprince. (163) In this highly sophisticated paper, 11 independent laboratories are noted to have found at least five times more 6-hydroxyskatole in the urine of schizophrenics than in that of normal subjects. Such universal agreement, Sprince says, is highly significant since this is an area where conflict, not agreement, is the rule. (163) It will be remembered that 6-hydroxyskatole arises primarily from skatole in the intestine and that skatole arises from the action of putrefactive bacteria on tryptophan, an essential amino acid.

J. Senility: The following should be mentioned: "Auto-intoxication from intestinal stasis or from constipation due to lessened peristaltic activity, undoubtedly plays a contributing part in the process of senescence." (113)

K. Low back pain and sciatica: Dr. R. B. Osgood, MD, cites six cases of patients suffering from these conditions. A few had also received chiropractic manipulative care with no improvement.   In these cases, the cause was a toxic state of the intestine; the pain completely left upon elimination of the toxemia, and returned upon return of toxemia because of dietary errors. His references point to other physicians who had the same experience. (114)

In this regard, Dr. Von Noorden found "pains especially frequent which corresponded to the ordinary sciatic or intercostal neuralgia." (115) The reader would be well advised to review the facts on irritation to the nerves of the low back area during a toxemic state of the intestine.

L. Dermatoses: Dr. Hans J. Schwartz, MD, in a statistical analysis of 900 patients suffering from acne, eczema, and many other skin conditions, concluded that "intestinal toxemia is an important etiologic factor in the production of many dermatoses, especially those of the inflammatory type." (126) Dr. J. F. Burgess, MB, lecturer in Dermatology, McGill University, associate dermatologist, Montreal General Hospital, reports the results of studying 109 cases of eczema. He states that "on the basis of clinical observations and sensitivity tests against various amino acids and ptomaine bases, eczema is probably caused by intestinal toxemia." (117) Others concur. (118, 119)

M. Breast pathology: Changes in the breast resulting from intestinal toxemia have been described by many doctors. The views of three can be summarized as such (120): the breasts undergo degenerative changes, manifested in the first instance as induration, to be followed by inflammatory and cystic degeneration, and possibly, lastly, by cancerous infection." (95, 121)

N. Cancer: There is no claim that intestinal toxemia is the cause of cancer. However, some physicians believe that "even the beginning of malignant disease of various organs comes within the wide range of intestinal stasis." (92) Sir W. A. Lane recorded his feeling of being "exceedingly impressed by the sequence of cancer and intestinal stasis." (122)

In light of the clonal selection theory of chemical carcinogenesis which states that "all chemical carcinogens will display...a greater toxicity for normal tissue cells than for the cells of a tumor derived therefrom by treatment with that carcinogen," (123) it can be speculated that toxins of intestinal origin may initiate malignant transformations. The malignant cell would be more resistant to the toxic effects than would a normal cell, according to this theory.

Treatment

In the treatment of intestinal toxemia various measures have been used. These include surgical removal of inflamed, ulcerated, or infected intestine (sometimes including the entire colon); autogenous vaccines to kill the bacteria responsible for the production of the toxins; colonics and/or laxatives for obvious reasons; diet therapy, and exercise. Different doctors have used various combinations of these therapeutic measures; some have put great emphasis on surgery, while others none at all. Many have put emphasis on the use of vaccines to some degree. Some recommend colonics and/or laxatives; others literally condemn their use. Almost all have used some type of diet therapy, and exercise has often been recommended.

The author's conception of an ideal therapy will now be described. It is an amalgam of the ideas of the many clinicians cited in this paper, but with the addition of a few basic holistic concepts in the light of the axiom, "Physician, do no harm."

First, if vaccines and surgery can be avoided by the use of other less traumatic and less side-effect-producing therapies which are at least equally efficacious, then vaccines and surgery should not be used. This does not mean that drug and surgical therapies are never needed in the treatment of intestinal toxemia; however, these therapies are almost never needed.

Second, any therapeutic measure which provides only the relief of symptoms is inferior to a measure that removes the cause of the symptoms; symptomatic relief is only temporary, whereas, the removal of the cause leads to permanent relief. These concepts are probably self−evident and surely constitute common sense. Surely no chiropractic physician would argue with this general overview of treatment.

Since a majority of physicians have found success in the use of diet therapy and exercise, these measures will be emphasized. Diet therapy is non−traumatic, does not produce side−effects, and removes the cause of the toxemia. It allows for a complete cure to take place which lasts as long as the diet is followed. Dr. Satterlee stated that "diet and proper emptying of the bowels has always been the recognized treatment." (124)

Treatment can be summarized by the following: "Patients must be taught how to eat, how to live, how to work and how to play. It must be impressed on them that health will not return through the simple act alone of taking medicine from a bottle. If they can be made to see that a general cleaning-up process is to be inaugurated, and that it is their duty to keep things cleaned up as treatment progresses, and after it is ended, and that the whole management of their trouble is really founded on very ordinary principles, then, with great interest, they usually cooperate quite heartily with their physician." (125)

If the reader will refer to the effect of diet on putrefaction, he will see that animal experiments indicate the benefit of a low protein, high carbohydrate diet. This concept is universally agreed upon by the physicians noted in this paper. How much protein should be consumed? The controversy over this issue is great. However, since "protein in an average food intake of 2,500 calories is about 94 grams per day" (126) and the recommended daily allowance is 50−60 grams for adults, it is obvious that an immediate decrease in intake by almost 50 percent can be safely accomplished. In light of studies on minimum protein requirements, we may even consider as sufficient intakes of 15−25 grams per day of high quality protein. (127) Obviously, with this intake of protein, other food components are to be relied upon to supply energy needs.

The remainder of the diet should contain a minimal amount of fat, with carbohydrates supplying the bulk of the energy need. It has been shown that fats, especially heated fats, intensify the process of intestinal toxemia. (128) The dietary carbohydrates should not be the refined or starchy form. The more easily digested and more highly nutritious types are preferred. Therefore, after the intestine has healed, fruits and vegetables should be used to provide the greatest amount of the carbohydrate intake, and thus the caloric requirement. These foods have the additional benefit of being rich in the vitamins and minerals.

Intake of certain specific items should be either greatly reduced or eliminated. These include sugar, (129) as implied above; salt, alcohol, condiments, tobacco (130), tea, coffee, pastry, fried foods, and "any article of food which is known to disagree." (88)

Eating the correct amount of food is an essential feature of the proper diet. Dr. Stucky, MD, says that "all forms of food, when eaten in greater quantities than the digestive fluids can digest, are capable of forming putrefactive poisons which are deleterious to the human organism. I have, therefore, insisted that all my patients should eat small meals in which the protein foods should form a very small proportion." (131) Dr. Rochester, MD, says "the amount of food should be limited to a minimum compatible with maintenance of health and weight."(88) Echoing this is Dr. Synnott: "Patients do better and feel better when the caloric intake in their diet is curtailed."

In the acute stage, no food at all is recommended. "Feeding bulky foods causes further distension of the colon, an added burden is put upon its weakened walls, the damaged bowel musculature is taxed beyond the power to respond, the delayed motility and stasis are increased, the gastroptosis and enteroptosis are aggravated, the expected increase in peristalsis does not occur, but on the contrary there is more pronounced paresis of the already atonic, overworked and disabled bowel." (132) Dr. Bartle concurs in this view. (130)

Instead of feeding, fasting is recommended. "Fasting is a perfectly sound method of diminishing toxins if combined with copious draughts of water." (133) Fasting has been shown to reduce the phenols to a low level. (134) It has also been shown to increase by one to two days to over two weeks the life span in dogs with duodenal obstruction; the dogs were forced to fast for four days prior to surgical creation of the obstruction. (135) In a 76 kilogram man, "intestinal putrefaction as measured by the output of urinary indican was markedly decreased during the fasting interval" of seven days. (136) Fasting will rest the overworked intestine and allow the physiological process of inflammation to proceed onward to the process of repair. One need not worry about starvation in these cases, since the patients already are suffering from excess food intake.

The administration of Lactobacillus   Acidophilus culture and lactose is said by some to be of great value; but others claim that they are useless. It is interesting to note that the entire basis for the idea that yogurt and its bacteria are beneficial to health is based on the theory of intestinal toxemia. The idea is that the "good bacteria" (Lactobacillus) will displace the "bad", namely the putrefactive proteolytic type. This therapy seems to have some value, at least in a percentage of cases. However, in light of its having dubious value in some doctors' opinion, this therapy should not be relied upon.

The topic of colonic irrigations is surrounded by much argument and controversy. There are some who claim that the colonics have great therapeutic value, (137, 138) and as might be suspected, others avoid its use and decry   its value. (139) Dr. Von Noorden states that such treatments "only hide the pathological condition of the intestine. Instead of helping, they only retard the definite cure. They are justified and advantageous only in acute disease." (105) Dr. Bassler says that colonics "relieve the toxemia by clearing the large bowel for a few days but do nothing to control the bacteriology or the chemistry . . . since the locality for most of the toxic process is in the small intestine. Kept up long enough, they do more harm than good." (140)

Surrounding the subject of exercise there is no controversy, just ignorance or advocacy. Of those in favor, Dr. Bassler presents an average view. "Physical exercise, especially in the open, is valuable to keep back the assault of toxins on body tissues. This is accomplished by increasing the conjugating ability by calling forth higher degrees of protoplasmic activity, higher oxidation and increased circulation." (57) But the clinician should be wary, since increased circulation may carry toxins to previously unexposed tissues, thereby multiplying the symptoms. As is usual in the health care profession, prudent clinical judgement is in order.

If the outlined program is followed, both the doctor and patient will be satisfied with the results.

Discussion

Toxemia and subsequent pathology may result from absorption of certain chemicals formed by bacteria action on amino acids. Pathology is classically defined as abnormal function. The sources mentioned in the section on symptoms reveal that there is a clinical, clearly observable relationship between intestinal toxemia and abnormal cellular function. These studies report thousands of cases of people suffering from various ills who became well after clearing up their intestinal toxemia. For example, eczema is a pathological change; it healed time and again when the source of irritation, intestinal toxemia, was removed. The author is aware that this is a controversial idea today. But, nonetheless, it is certainly conceivable that, for example, the following sequence could occur: high protein diet results in phenol (corrosive poison) production; phenol enters circulation causing local pathology. Evidence has been presented that a high protein diet causes proliferation of proteolytic bacteria; it is well known that such proteolytic bacteria produce phenol from the amino acid tyrosine, and that phenol can kill cells; papers have been reviewed that prove that the majority of absorbed phenol is not conjugated by the liver, and therefore not detoxified; and many papers have been reviewed which relate pathology to the presence of intestinal toxemia in a statistically significant way.

For example, when previously discussing dermatoses: 1017 patients were examined and treated. In a clinical discussion, it is highly relevant and important that many sick people become well when their intestinal toxemia is cleared up. On the other hand, medical opinion states that the etiology of such diseases as Crohn's, Whipple's, ulcerative colitis, and many others is unknown (idiopathic). But the irritation that causes the primary inflammation in these afflictions must come from somewhere, or the entire science of pathology is in error. It has been proposed in this paper that the products of intestinal putrefaction are a significant source of such irritation.

Alan Immerman, B.S., Lombard, Illinois. The American Chiropractic Association Journal of Chiropractic: Volume 13, S-25, April, 1979

Part V

NEW AGE CHILDREN: THE FUTURE HOPE

In any age Children hold within their innocent, pure beings the promise of future hopes, the possibility of future perfection, the potential for the realization of all which is at present imperfect or in some way lacking. And so it is today. Those souls choosing to incarnate at this time bring with them the potentiality for the fruition of the visions and the dreams for the New Age.

Much unexplored territory is at present being charted. New natural methods of child birth are being widely practiced, novel infant and child feeding practices are being established, and unorthodox approaches to child rearing and family living are gaining acceptance as they prove themselves successful. The following selections elucidate in some way these tendencies which, as a whole, have this goal: the birth of the New Age Child, the Child of the Universe, the Child of Love.

Section I
Child Birth in the New Age

BEYOND MIDWIVES, MACROBIOTICS AND THE PHYSICAL REALM

This is the story of my pregnancy and the birth of a Universal child.

I am writing this to share and reach out to those new age Mothers and Fathers, Brothers and Sisters, who wish to be the main energy channels during the birth journey of their child. Also for those who realize the need for proper prenatal care and preparation for this Life giving moment. This preparation being Yoga exercises, deep breathing and meditation techniques. But most of all a diet consisting of at least 80% raw foods (Fresh Fruits and Vegetables, their juices, nuts and seeds).

I attribute my healthy pregnancy and painless childbirth mainly, to my diet. I suffered no common pregnancy problems, i.e. morning sickness, toxemia, swollen ankles, etc. My labor was short and easy allowing Mark, our child, and me to enjoy this beautiful experience to the fullest.

In the beginning of my pregnancy I felt my body cleansing, mentally, physically and spiritually, signifying nature's way of preparing the environment for the fetus to grow. I found myself eating only fruits for the first two or three weeks. That's all that looked good and felt good inside of me. I was thrilled to be so in tune to what was going on. Besides being very careful of my diet I realized the need to continue my Yoga and Meditation. This morning's routine was extended to drinking a jar of Raspberry Leaf Sun tea.

Since it was the middle of Spring, the Sun was hot and the beach sparkled as it met the ocean. This practically being my second home, my body became a golden brown.

During the day my diet consisted of frest fruits and juices. Mango's, papayas, tangelos, cherries and peaches were all at the peak of the season. I felt very thankful to have such sweet nectars build my little one's body and soul. In the evening our dinner usually consisted of a salad of sprouts, greens and a variety of fresh vegetables, with nuts or seed sauce. I tried to drink at least a pint of fresh carrot or green juice daily. This diet and this way of eating ensured me of all that I needed to

build and give birth to a healthy baby. A child born under these conditions is sure to aid mankind in no other way but the best; the Love he will give, there's none truer; the Life he will lead and help others to lead, there's no better.

As the fourth month rolled around, I could feel life kicking and moving around inside. I started doing a special set of exercises for pregnant ladies.

We had been buying and reading all the books on childbirth we could find. I was already aware of the different methods (Lamaze, Bradley, AFCAH). We studied them deeper, putting together our own method along the way. We visited a few local groups which offered classes and birthing assistants. I also talked with a few of the midwives in town.

We had always planned and wanted very much to do the birth by ourselves, in our home, with just the assistance of our family. The midwives I talked with were very negative. Instead of offering the needed information they only warned me of all that could go wrong during the birth. They treated me like many Doctors treat them. We received frowns from all directions.

We studied and tried to learn as much as possible. We knew we had it in us to do it on our own. We realized the risks and we were willing to accept whatever might happen. We knew with proper preparation there would be no problems and all

Valerie Williams in final blissful months of pregnancy

would go well. So we looked forward to this holy time, very joyously.

By the seventh month I had gained ten pounds. Before what seemed like a little cantelope inside, had grown to be a watermelon. We were communicating all the time now. God was in me and I was in God.

As nine months arrived we cleared our minds, freed our spirits and made things ready. Nine months and two days after he was conceived, Mundy Nia slid into the world, into the delicate hands of his father. We needed no other assistants, as we were prepared, but most of all in tune to ourselves, our child, and what was happening; Life was giving Life!

Labor was strong and sweet. It grew stronger as I took my last walk around the house. I felt my bones open wide as Mundy slid down the birth canal in his amnionic sack. I was still standing as my mother helped to support me. His little head crowned, his skull bones overlapping 4 ways, a deep purple. He looked like a flower blooming, (I saw in a mirror). His head came down, a quick minute to clear his face of what little there was to clear. He turned as the rest of his body slid out with a swish. He was all clean with a dab of blood on his head. He had no mucous. His cord was a soft blue and he weighed 6½ lbs. I placed him gently on my stomach. As he sucked my nipple, I expelled the placenta. Now all that had been inside me, was outside. What filled me now was External Bliss!

Valerie and Mundy Williams

The eyes of his Grandmother, Uncle Victor and a close friend, welcomed him with streams of Love and pure energy.

As he drinks my sweet creamy milk, I pray that each drop be filled with pearls of wisdom. Everyday Mundy opens new horizons for us. Together we learn, Live and grow! I cannot over−stress the importance of a Raw Foods Regimen, if you wish to have a truly healthy, happy pregnancy, childbirth and baby. I plan to feed Mundy solely raw foods after he nurses for as long as he likes. The results: your child will be the light; the star that shines. He will walk the earth in peace and Love, inspiring these in the hearts of all he meets.

May the innocence that surrounds these children be the innocence where love need not be spoken, only lived!

This article is a small part of a book I am in the midst of writing, which will have more information and details on this important topic.

I also want to add that I am not against midwives. I wish to be one someday myself. Just make sure you make them a part of your family. It's possible, as we're all brothers and sisters.

From one great family to all the others!

Valerie Williams, Cincinnatti, Ohio

HEALTHY MOTHER: HEALTHY BABY

Long before I conceived Beth, my third child, I knew this baby would be different. Almost 15 years had passed since my last child had been born (I was forty at the conception of baby number three), and much had happened in our lives.

Perhaps the most relevant change was our desire to become vegetarians, because with our new diet came an awareness of the importance of good nutrition as a part of better health. Once we dropped meat from the menu, I felt obligated to ensure my family's nutritional needs through quality non−meat sources. By reading, studying, attending lectures, we generally refined our diet to include more raw foods than cooked.

By the time I became pregnant in the summer of 1978, I knew my diet was crucial to the baby's health. (I also believe your husband's diet is almost as crucial; Roger and I ate very much alike). I ate a great deal of fresh fruits and vegetables, including sprouts; juices and whole grains; and nuts and seeds. I ate almost no dairy because I had learned that it was mucus forming, although sometimes I gave in to my love of yogurt and once in a while fear of "where do you get your protein" questions. Occasionally I binged or cheated and ate a pizza or something sinfully sweet, but for the most part I really ate a good, whole foods diet.

While I was pregnant I also exercised. In addition to the breathing patterns learned at La Maze classes, I continued to ride my bike until snow fell, and resumed this favorite sport in the Spring after the weather was again suitable for bicycling. We had a long, lovely Fall in 1978, so I was able to bike until December, and started again at the end of March. During those non−bicycling months I practiced my yoga to music. I had first learned hatha yoga in the early 1970's from Michael Volin, a yoga instructor who was 70 at the time of these classs. (His classes probably put us on the first rung of conscious awareness about vegetarianism, good health, spirituality, control of the body, etc.).

By the time Beth was due, I felt physically and mentally ready for the "labor" ahead. My midwife came to our home as soon as my pains were regular. She sat with me and my family during the early morning hours of easy labor. My good friend Lois had also asked to be present at the birth, and she came with flowers and candles. With the sun coming across the horizon I started hard labor, and at 9:01 a.m., with the love and strength of my children, my husband, my midwife and friend Lois, I gave birth to a beautiful 7½ pound baby girl. She was strong and alert from the start, and nursed like a barracuda!

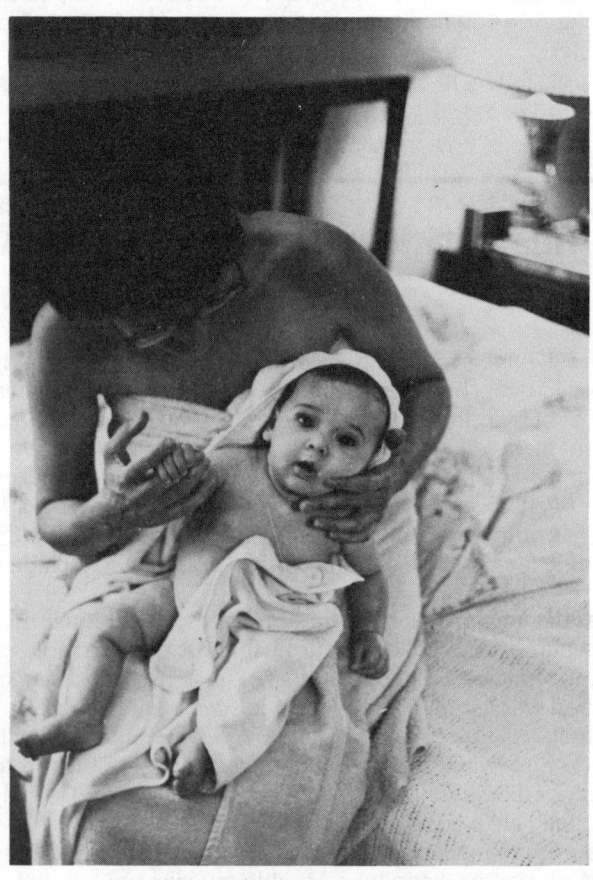

Ellen Sue and Beth Spivack after a massage

NEW AGE CHILDREN: THE FUTURE HOPE

I knew my recovery period would be hastened if I ate only raw food. I had spent one week with Viktoras Kulvinskas and Marcia Acciardo in July 1977, traveling across the country in a van to attend the Rainbow Family Gathering in New Mexico. During that time I ate only raw foods or fasted, and my feelings of energy and well–being were fantastic. These same feelings could be reproduced now, during this postpartum period. I ate lots of fresh fruits and vegetables, juices and seeds, and sure enough, by the end of two weeks I felt strong, and by the time Beth was one month old, I was able to resume all my activities on a gradual basis, including my bike riding. For a 40 plus lady, that's not so bad; especially because I remember feeling terribly tired with both my other pregnancies and births. I could not believe the difference with Beth, despite the fact I was 15 years older, and over–the–hill by many people's standards.

Naturally, I plan to breastfeed Beth until she weans herself. I do not plan to introduce solid foods until she has some teeth to chew it with (see Shelton's "Hygienic Care of Children"), and will probably start with asparagus in the Spring when this cleansing food is available fresh. My long–term program for Beth as a "natural baby" is tentative because I am new at this kind of mothering. My other children were born in a hospital with medicated births, were not breastfed (except for three months I nursed my daughter Eileen because of milk allergies), were given solids at an early age followed by other allergies, were vaccinated, and in general had the typical illnesses and health problems experienced by their peers. (I thought this was normal!)

I hope to keep Beth happy and healthy through natural means – no antibiotics, no foreign vaccines, no routine shots, etc. – and will have to refer often to the appropriate literature gleaned in the last year or so concerning child care. (I have already started an herbal medicine chest for common childhood illnesses). When I attend lectures and workshops on holistic health methods, I plan to "pick the brains" of the speakers to help me in our quest for a wholly, healthy child. My husband and children are behind me all the way, but well–meaning friends and family often undermine what little confidence I have built. I only know that with each day that Beth grows stronger and healthier and happier, I am doing the right thing. In my heart I feel God will help me know when I have stepped too far in the other direction. Modern medicine has much to offer in terms of first aid and diagnosis, and I would be foolish to disregard it altogether. Luckily, too, I have a family physician who respects my ideas.

For those of you who feel that having a healthy baby with as little interference from modern medicine as possible, let me say that it can be done. You and your husband can cleanse your bodies to prepare for conception and pregnancy. Read as much as you can on pregnancy, birth, and child care. Join La Leche League and La Maze classes. Have pure and loving thoughts. Pray for guidance in time of doubt and distress. A healthy baby is the sum total of all these activities. Happy, healthy parents make happy, healthy babies. Doesn't your baby deserve a good start in life? You can give it that start by taking care of your body, so it will take care of you during pregnancy, birth, and the postpartum period. Your baby is a precious responsibility, and there is greater joy when it is happy and healthy. Be a joyful, healthy mother and have a happy, healthy baby.

AUTHORS NOTE: If you would like to know more about Beth's care, you can read about her in my series "Bringing Up Beth" which started with the December 1979 issue of Well–Being Magazine.

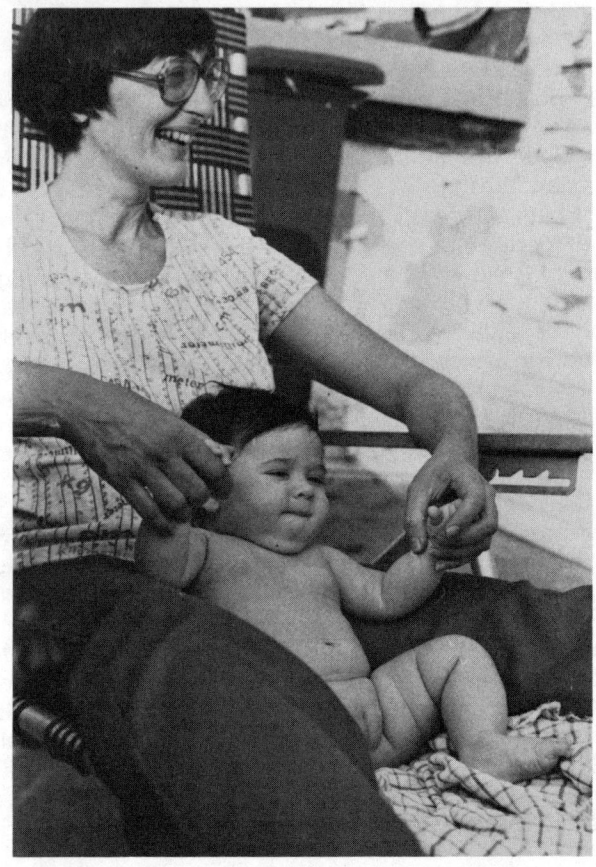

Ellen Sue Spivak, 606 Market Street, Lewisburg, Pennsylvania, 17837

A CHILD'S SONG TO A MOTHER'S HEART

I awoke to the magnificent weavings of the Grand Design. And as my inner eye searched the warm, rhythmic home that was now my own, brilliant blues and soft quiet violets pulsated to my heart. And I could feel. Yes, I could feel the passive hands of my mother sweep across the protective sheath of her womb. Her hands were like searchlights probing the innermost realms of my home, and I was showered with crystalline stars and perfect snowflake patterns that fell dreamily from her palms. The hum of her soul in harmony with mine created a song that only mother and child could know, and it is a song I shall never forget.

I was suckled by the cool blue mists that flowed through my mother's womb, and I knew that she was my source and river of life. I had listened to her calling to me for oh, so long. She had filled the sky with her prayers beckoning for me to enter her carefully prepared home. My mother's desire was to be with child and to fill a heart with her own, and each day I heard her novena of love and moved a step closer to my home.

My journey had been from afar. For I had traveled through seas of stars and over the crests of time to answer my mother's call. And as I lay in the twilight of her womb, nourished by the whispers of her love, I knew that a Child's Song to a Mother's heart had just begun.

As I bathed in my mother's silent gaze, I could see the dreams she had of my life to come. In one of her dreams I was a maker of sails. A sailmaker of ships, yes, but more than that; a sailmaker of dreams. My sails were seamless and of the purest white, and as I flew with the evening winds, my course soared upon the starlight seas, and with her immaculate vision spun about me, she impressed upon my heart the mark of individuality.

Resting in the rainbow world of her womb, I could see the etchings of eternity that lay inscribed upon her shell pink dome. How often I recall she would hold her hands over my chambered world to protect and give comfort to my soul. And in the stillness of a moment she would whisper to my heart and say, "O my child, are you safe? No harm shall come your way".

Each night as I prepared to return to the realms above, I could feel my mother weaving her song of love about my form to protect my soul until the morn. As the melodies of the evening came spinning through my world, I would take flight to the skies and return to the starry classrooms beyond. For in these moments I would close my eyes and be swayed in the heartsong of a mother's love, till I found myself soaring past the archways of my home, traveling on golden threads to the sun. I journeyed to the world many call dreams, but it is a world I knew, where greater understanding resides.

This night as I entered the silent movements of the sun, I communed with the hearts of those who awaited to enter the world of form. For this was the world where all souls abide, and we were held together in a web of light in the invisible world where only children take flight. Here, there was great rejoicing as each child entered a mother's home to be received with love. A candle was lit and placed on a beautiful throne waiting the day the child would return to its heavenly home. And it was here that I learned how many are turned back at the doorway to time, unable to complete their journey from the sun. For their candle was never lit, and their opportunity to bring love into the world never tried, and this was the tragedy of the Grand Design. "How Little", we thought 'must be known of us and our world. How much is to be learned!' Often I could hear the cries of those who were taken from their home, and I silently prayed I would never be left alone. For I knew that within the souls of children lay courses charted carefully to the sun, and that each must have a chance to live and to overcome. This is where the hope of the world lies; in the silent gaze of a child's eyes.

My journey took me past the seas where souls were deftly woven in time, and this evening I touched the secrets of the Grand Design. And as I gazed into the ageless seas of the sun, I saw my past experiences and my struggle to overcome. I saw how each soul is like an author in his own world of time, and how each moment is like a chapter awaiting to be impressed upon the Grand Design. This night, as I penned the final line, I vowed this journey would be my last into time. So much I learned in this world cannot be told, for only with my life can it ever unfold.

With the rising of the dawn as the sun of the east burst to be the morn, angels beckoned for me to return. Spirals from my Mother's heart swirled about mine, and I slowly descended into the realms of time, chanting this cherished rhyme, 'Mother I am coming home for I have traveled afar, and now does the time draw nigh for my soul to become a star'.

I spent hours within her heart, forming mine, and soon, like a crystal tumbling through a river to the seas, my sails began to yearn for the morning's breeze. I knew that I had a role to play in the world of time and that with my birth there would be a sign. Not a day would pass that I would not review my life to come, and I knew the test would be overcome. I smiled secretly as the faces of those I was to meet flashed quickly past my mind, and I knew that this was the one great test; to remember the dream after the memory is set to rest.

Each day I prepared for my journey into the world of form, and one day I knew it was my time to be born. Tiny explosions began to ripple through my world and the warm currents of my home rushed to the outer seas, and I could hear my mother whispering so quietly, 'Thank you my love, thank you, for all the love you have brought to me'. As my mother began to breath deeply, great spirals of light swirled about my form, and like a galaxy spinning outward, I was ready to be born. And with each breath I moved closer to the outer seas, I could hear the endless lovesong of a mother's heart to me 'O child, be free, be free!' And as my mother's hands rested upon her womb she whispered quietly, 'I am always with thee'. As a Child's Song to a Mother's Heart filled eternity, I replied 'Yes my mother, yes, I shall be free, I shall be free!'.

My wing-like sails filled with the morning breeze and all about me crashed the roaring seas, and outward I rushed to hands that anxiously awaited me. Like fog rolling through a sail tipped eve, my memories began to fade, and my designs were put to rest in the world where souls were made. And as I sailed through the canal to open seas, no longer could I recall the dream. A great darkness overcame my form, "Alone", I cried, "why was I to be born?"

Yet in that moment my heart leapt to my mother's side and her arms enfolded me in love, and in the cool blue mists of a mother's song, my soul took course and aligned with the star above. My sails unfurled and were at rest this day, for before me I knew a great destiny lay.

James R. Vollbracht

WHITE LIGHT BIRTHING

Hello Viktoras, It was wonderful seeing you again, I wished our visit was longer as we would love to spend the day with you! At least, I was able to give you that hug that I've been waiting to give ya! (I was the lady that came up after the lecture at Raychel's with the "Raw Food Baby"). I wanted to say how much you and Ann Wigmore helped us in changing our lives! My husband and I were suffering in bodies that were well on their way to degenerative diseases. We have been raw foodists for 2 years. After being on a transitional diet for a couple of years before that. We have had some healing crisis, let me tell ya! Still bringing up poisons, getting into the lymphs and major vessels for myself; it has been rough! I've been overweight ever since I was 5 years old — I am now 30. I've gone thru healing crisis in my lungs, opening up a catarrh lesion, heart, (had a major valve disturbance), brain area, cleansing, (low grade malignancy in my ovaries and fallopian tube, manifestations in genital area, deteriorated lower spine, I passed 2 gallstones — really heavy duty cleansing. In irises I had third layer degeneration in my pelvic area, big black gaping holes. My irises were dark brown with black holes all over. Now my irises are turning blue and light yellowish brown. I am sure you looked into my eyes and saw where I was at.

    We never could afford going to Hippocrates or a Naturopath so we did our healing by gathering all the information ourselves. Bernard Jensen's book on iridology became my study book until I knew what I was looking at. Your "Survival" bible! We clearly understand what causes dis–ease and inherent weakness can virtually be erased thru proper diet and living habit. We lived on a side of a mountain in Tum Tum, Washington, for most of the time we were kicked back healing ourselves. Went to Hawaii for a few months to bask in the warmth, then back to San Diego. Gregg's Mama was dying of cancer in her spine, (started in her uterus) and we came home to help her. We tried to get her to see the right way to heal herself but our attempts were ridiculed by other family members and M.D. doctors. The time she was drinking wheatgrass juice and raw food diet, her tumor was shrinking and she was feeling better. She had too much chemo–therapy and within the year she died. We lived with her, watching her waste away to a skeleton. It was so painful for her as she died in agony! (She was 52 years old). Now we are coping with another dilemma as my madre is failing with emphyzema . She has changed her diet considerably — but still eats animal (chicken & fish) and dead foods. Every time she does, she gets sick and fills up with mucous. Her lifestyle is still the same, resentment and hatred is still in her heart. My sister and I have tried on numerous occasions to get her to go to Hippocrates, but she won't! It won't be too long before she goes and completes her cycle. My grand mother passed on in April with a massive heart attack — another cope with dealth!

    Inspite of all this stress we were high as we had a White Light Birthing! Our baby–son Matthew was born on a bright morning in our living room on November 7th, 1978. It was my 3rd child and my first experience having it at home. A beautiful experience it was! My labor was only 3 hours. It went very smoothly, I was able to relax and breathe out my son. We took a birthing class with a Kundalini Yogi who was also my coach. What a beautiful bonding we had: my husband and I, my 8 year old son Jason and our new little creature, fell in Love.

We have a movie film of the birth. Wheatgrass pulp was used for my hemorrhoids as my butt—hole looked inside—out. Wheatgrass juice cut with water was used as an eye wash for the baby. No episiotomy, or tears and my uterus firmed up within minutes. A glass of green juice (12 oz.) was given to me right afterwards for energy, no postpartum bleeding. Everything went back into place just fine. I drank Raspberry and Comfrey tea my whole pregnancy — firmed up my uterus nicely. Did Yoga asanas, went for long walks, did squats too. Five years ago I had a handful of M.D.'s tell me how I would never be able to have any more children because of all the degeneration and scar tissue! Little do they know! Yes, it sure is amazing, and a miraculous feeling to be healthier at 30 than I was at 20 years.

I had nobody that could help me after I had the baby except my son and husband. They went to work and school the next day and I was up and around doing for myself. I felt fine, no after birth pains to speak of. I was amazed how firmed and flat my tummy went. My kagel was number 10 a week after birth.

My husband and I did our own pre—natal exams, as I was getting so much harrassment from M.D.'s. I gained only 14 pounds during my gestation and because of my diet they didn't think I was getting enough protein! Ha! Raw foods brought nutrients not calories, I kept telling them. Every month I went to an M.D. They kept taking a hemoglobin test, I got tired of defending myself, so I stopped going and did the examinations myself. Checked blood pressure, urine, too, and listened to fetal heart beat. The book Spiritual Midwifery was a good guide book for us. Our baby weighed 7 lbs. 4 ozs., 19½ inches long, beautiful, so firm and well developed. His aura was so bright, he had a beautiful glow all around him that lit up the room! He took to the breast right away. I started giving him rejuvelac in between feedings and he loved it.

He is almost 3 months old, sitting up from a semi—laying position, pulls himself up, firming up his spine. I was glad to hear from you that his heart and lung areas were strong as I thought he had picked up a weakness and was worried!

My 8 year old son's eyes are changing color from brown to blue. They are green with more blue coming through. I have a 10 year old daughter that couldn't overcome her stomach and went to live with her dad and started eating meat and processed foods again. She gained about 25 pounds and got allergies back again, all I can do is pray for her, as she is against all that we do. My husband has cleared a lot of mucous lesions from his lung area. His eyes are blue already, but had a good amount of drug settlement (suppressing asthma) deeper into his lungs.

Right now, we are going thru a trip with our emotions and nerves! We stopped drinking alcohol a year ago, but smoke pot occasionally. Use it more for a calming effect than to get stoned. We are trying to overcome it as it is our last addiction to give up. Sometimes I feel bad about smoking it, but it has helped with the pain I've had; I do a lot of pranayama exercises afterwards.

We find ourselves alone in our task for good health. Our family is just beginning to listen to us, our old friends don't bother to come over any more, which is O.K. by me because of the karma they carry.

I wish I wouldn't have to send Jason to public school as he gets bored with the crap they teach him. Someday it will happen for us to be with loving folks who believe the same as us! I find it hard coping with all that goes on here! We live close to the ocean now, and it is real satisfying for me to be at peace.

We have acquired a beautiful friendship with a couple who were struggling also. Brought them to your lecture and re−inforced our beliefs and vibrations! A good feeling to hear them talk about all they are experiencing. We do have a handful of people who come by every now and then for advice and teas, even after they have partied too much. Someday it will happen for them I suppose. They will relate to what we have said when they find themselves flat on their backs SICK!

Well Viktoras, we are still searching for more information, everything costs so much money it makes it hard on us as our income is low. I wished I could save enough money for one of your extensive workshops.

You are with us in our thoughts and someday maybe we can sit with you on a more personal basis.

I hope you will be back again. Do you stay at Hippocrates when you come? Maybe we could meet with you somewhere else − would love for you to come to Imperial Beach. We do have a great need to talk with you without a crowd of people around.

Are there any books on suppressed illnesses? Wheatgrass pulp and coconut oil is good for diaper rashes (I just found out).
Love is all around us and I feel it!

Namaskar,
Linda, Gregg, Jason & Mathew Carver, 131 Carnation, Imperial Beach, Ca. 92032

Section II
Positive Childrearing

A SIGNIFICANT RIPPLE IN THE SEA OF LIFE

There is no malice in truth. Only within the realm of patronizing deceit lie the seeds of despair.

A small child's world consists of color, sound, movement and vibrations. They delight in a twirling leaf, and falling rain and can remain absorbed for hours creating their universe in the sand. Their life is suspended in a timeless zone of make believe. Therefore, if we insist they join our reality before they choose to seek it for themselves, they shall have great difficulty adjusting in either world. The healthy seed sprouts in its own time. So too, the healthy child.

Truth is inborn within a small child and he speaks it with shining innocence. It is we adults who cannot accept this gift, but insist that truth be stilled. Little Johnny might say "Aunt Marion, you're fat." The parents are mortified and Aunt Marion, indignant. Yet this statement, in the child's mind, may be a lovely compliment. Maybe Johnny likes broad, comfortable laps to crawl into, but because of truth, he is reprimanded. "That was a naughty thing to say to Aunt Marion. You mustn't tell people they are fat." The point is made and absorbed by the child. The next time Johnny meets an obese person, and because he is so eager to please, he goes out of his way to announce, "You're not fat lady." An embarrassed hush falls over the room. Johnny is confused when reprimanded again, because he did exactly as he was told.

Let this marvelous gift for truth be encouraged, not stifled. With greater insight into a child's world of joyous honesty, perhaps we may relearn the almost forgotten freedom of laughter, which comes so naturally in early childhood. The Biblical quote, "And a little child shall lead them," may be our key to everlasting happiness.

Perhaps by merely understanding our own responses and reactions, we shall resolve our own plight and minimize the world's frustrations as well. We can, each, become a significant ripple in the sea of life, if we so choose.

"Mommy! Mommy, a bird just talked to me," the child bubbles excitedly.

"Johnny, you're tracking mud on my rug," mother yells angrily. A lifetime of her stifled anger spills over into Johnny's life, as she adds, "Stop telling those awful lies." The moment is lost. What could have been a close communication, resulted in a confrontation.

Small children are extremely open and co-operative. They offer us their pure love, in the hopes it shall be returned. They are also the world's greatest imitators. They revel in sweeping the floor, just like Mommy, or cleaning the garage, just like Daddy. They delight in working to please us, but instead of our reacting with a measure of appreciation we, •because of our inner tensions, are all too quick to criticize. We, unwittingly, heap multitudinous guilts upon the confused child, because he spilled a little water on the floor, in the process of trying to wash his own glass, just like Mommy does. Small wonder that by the time the child reaches six years of age, he refuses to participate in any chores, unless forced. We label his attitude laziness, but is it?

What begins as the child's giving process, backfires. As a result of continuous rebuffs, he stifles his hurts; burying each one in the darkest recesses of the brain. Momentarily gone, but not forgotten. The child quickly assimilates a series of guilt feelings he cannot comprehend. At too early an age, he finds himself not only trying to struggle with his own guilt, but also enmeshed in the parent's traumatic, emotional stress with their own accumulated guilts, as well; a problem he cannot psychologically handle.

When the child's minor, compounded hurts and rejections surface again, they shall be tinged with violence, anti-socalism and a deep seated dislike for self. This feeling is closely followed by the need to absolve self, by blaming another. Authoritative figures, whether they be parents, the educational system, or the political system, all become his mental targets.

This is not written to absolve the grown child for his contemptible behavior, nor to create even greater guilts within parents. We all make mistakes and react, at times, in a way that is not in the best interest of all concerned. I offer these alternatives, in the hope that one day these words may bring the worlds of children and adults into closer harmony, by broadening insight for all who love.

Responsibility for self means simply controlling one's own responses toward others. When this eventually becomes a way of life, you will be amazed at your calmness when Johnny runs in to tell you of the bird that talks to him. Quietly, you shall say, "take your shoes off Johnny, they are messy". As the child, eagerly, complies, you can say, "Thank you. Now tell Mommy all about the bird". This is an extremely far reaching approach, in that, this single act of concern for his world, helps Johnny determine his eventual response to our world. You have taken responsiblity for suppressing anger, while protecting the rug. What is of greater importance, you have allowed Johnny to take responsibility for himself, by becoming aware of the mess he is creating. Relaxed, you can both enjoy his story of the bird and the honor in being given the opportunity of sharing in the wonderous world of imagery all children possess. Understanding his world shall enhance your own imagery and who knows, perhaps one day a bird will whisper in your, more receptive, ear. After the story, you offer Johnny the opportunity of helping you clean the rug, and you will be astonished at how enthusiastically he responds.

If this example sounds like a Utopian Fairy Tale, which can not, or does not exist

in your world of reality, then why not consider changing your reality?

People often waste their precious life's energy forces by generating either defensive anger or despondent self pity, thus reducing themselves to victims of society's whims. This shall continue, in an ever consuming process, until each begins to take responsibility for himself.

The victim consumes the chemical additives society chooses to add to the produce; chemicals which leave the nerves raw and the blood pressure high. The victim then consumes tranquilizers to placate the taut, nervous system, becoming steadily drained of these vital life forces, until illness ensues. There are alternatives to this dismal life style, but it takes one's own efforts to seek them.

Good nutrition heals the body. Meditation heals the mind; an unbeatable combination.

Meditation simply means designating a portion of each day to you and your growth process. It can be ten minutes, a half hour, or whatever you, not the family, feel you need. This is devoted to enhancing your imagery. Everyone daydreams so you can consider meditation a form of daydream with a purpose. This self discipline stills the brain, eases body tensions and allows one's vibrations to become attuned to the Universal Energies, for greater knowledge and understanding.

As the parent's tensions diminish, little Johnny's path shall become more joyful. Instead of becoming another victim, he shall become an important contributor to the new age of awareness.

Meditation creates the balance of the mind, but what about the chemical additives society adds to the foods, which create an imbalance within the body structure? It's simple. Grow your own food supply, in your own apartment, for far less than the cost of canned beans and the Ricky Dinky Binkys you now buy for Johnny's treats. He and his body will one day thank you for it.

When nutrition and meditation working in unison within a family, Johnny becomes more responsible for his own actions, by becoming significantly brighter and more talented. No longer will he be forced, by society, to become either defensive or aggressive, in order to survive. He shall expand his own life force energies, into more creative channels, which shall ultimately change and enhance his own life style.

Johnny's learning experiences grow, in a positive manner, through his parent's self-education search. He will not allow himself to be victimized by the alcoholic beverage manufacturers, tabacco industries, or narcotics pushers, legal or illegal. If we all become self-actualized, what will big business do then?

When parents choose to change their reality, by taking responsibility for themselves, the little Johnnies of the world will be able to share the story of the bird without fear of reprisal.

Each child who grows without fears or guilt, shall touch our world of tommorrow in a uniquely beautiful manner.

Marjorie Buckley Turcotte

NATURAL MAMA

Hello my fine brother, We are fine, really did enjoy those tapes Viktor! Cleared up a lot of misconceptions. Damn we can clearly see why we were chronically ill, being on a high protein and calcified diet most of our lives!! I have been overweight ever since I was 5 and now I am 30, still overweight but losing every month, I used to weigh 178 before I started a vegetarian diet, now I weigh 143, still losing. Developing muscles, that used to be ladden with fat and waste products. Too much protein and calcium.

Our baby is 8½ months now, walking all over holding on to a table or something. I've noticed how much more alert and active he is, compared to my other two. Top and bottom teeth are in. Still nursing, I chew fruit and sprout salads first then give to him. I was hoping that feeding him was the right thing to do as he acted like he wanted more than breastmilk. I kept watching his irises to see if there was any change, but there wasn't. He eats one meal a day, the rest is breast milk and juices.

He is so happy, rushes out with laughter and screams of joy! His skin glows and his eyes are so blue! I am still writing my book, making it more of a guidebook for the natural mama and baby. I have observed a lot of babies recently, fatty cheeks, fat bodies, not nearly as active as Mathew, I can see why, when I see them eating baby food and cereal and cow milk.

Gregg and I have long talks about our encounters of the day and we both sense the negativity in the air. It is just the start. I know San Diego is going to be a CRAZY place to live 3-4 years from now! Over 1,000 a day are moving here!! The price of living is ridiclous. We are using every penny to survive here. I wished we could find a place to go! I sure don't want to be here after Haley's Comet, the crap that's going to come down! We are aware of it! Have already gotten visions of what it will be like!!!

I hope you are taking it easy and enjoying your new place. You give out tremendous amounts of good energy and information in your travels, that's for sure!

We are on a low income level, thank goodness we are vegetarians and can grow most of our food!! We can't afford to join the Survival Foundation but sure would love to have a copy of a Survival Journal!

My nine year old son's irises are green and turning blue (from olive brown). Pretty good huh? My irises are bluer every day!

Namaskar,
Linda, Gregg, Jason & Mathew Carver, 131 Carnation, Imperial Beach, Ca. 92032

NOTES ON BEARING A CHILD

Diet

First six (6) months of pregnancy lacto−ovo−vegetarian − meat a couple of times − no sickness from pregnancy but head colds, full of mucous. Sometimes in bed for weeks; took tomatoe, garlic, onion, sage, etc.; it helped.

Next two (2) months of pregnancy mostly vegetarian − no mucous. Last month, strict vegetarian, fresh organic fruits, nuts: almonds, seeds − sunflower and pumpkin, no bread, some steamed vegetables − but mainly raw − alfalfa sprouts − mung bean − buckwheat lettuce, sunflower lettuce; comfrey, green drinks − papaya − watermelon − peaches, apricots, figs, dates, raisins, grapes − no butter, oil or peanut butter, etc; no salt except small amount of earth salt; kelp − dulce − Waltkers minerals − avocado − some Essene bread (but an exception).

We don't drink with our meals unless we have dried fruit for breakfast, then we use grape juice.

We eat two (2) meals a day − 6 hours apart with herb tea or fresh water in between, nothing else.

We have no sickness − coughs − Sarah has never had a runny nose (except when sick, described below).

We go to bed early, arise early.

We are Seventh Day Adventists − so God gives us good health.

I have prayed at each step we have taken and God has lead us to the good health we have.

Offspring

Girl, 8 pounds ½ ounce, 19 inches long. Never cried.

Lost two previous babies: (1) July 7th, 1974 in 7th month of pregnancy. Ate regular all American diet. (2) July 6th, 1975, after a couple of weeks. Ate a lacto−ovo−vegetarian diet. Pregnant with Sarah, October, born June 29, 1976 (9 months).

Up to birth Sarah was posterior. She was born posterior.

Sarah was born naturally. Prior to birth I went to "Natural Birth Classes" given by the hospital and free to all patients.

Doctor gave due date as June 30th.

May 18th I was having contractions but no pain, just the sensation of tightening so I was put on a machine to record contractions and stayed overnight at the hospital.

June 29th − all morning weird sensations happening inside − no pain − drank lots of Red Raspberry tea. I had an appointment with the doctor at 3:30. My husband came to get me at 3:30 so we were a little late for the appointment. The doctor said I had lost my water that morning, there was a small tinge of blood and mucous but no pain. Still had weird sensations, a little stronger. Doctor wanted me to go to the hospital to keep an eye on me because of previous births, but after May 18th I wouldn't go. He said the baby would probably be 8 hours or so away, so I talked him into letting me go home. I felt great and continued drinking red raspberry tea. (Up to this time for 5 weeks I had been taking capsules of herbs for easy birth, they contained black cohosh, blue cohosh, etc.; can't remember the rest).

We stayed in town and visited. We arrived home at 5:00. I was now having contractions 2 minutes apart but still up and around, no real discomfort. Then I went into transition, my husband threw a sleeping bag into the back of the truck and I walked to the back of the truck and lay down, he drove to town and I rolled on this huge pillow in back; I was quiet. With my first baby I had hyperventilated so this time I brought a paper bag and did my breathing in the bag. I was feeling great and was starting to push when we arrived at the hospital; it was 5:30. I was put on the Gerney, given a checkup (after they thought I was kidding that I was having a hard time holding back). After a quick checkup they called the doctor and now it was about 5:45. They took me up in an elevator and a doctor quite well known in natural methods was there to help. I sat up and soon after a couple of quick pushes I said Hi to my baby as her head was born. She was smiling; at 5:55 the rest of her was born. She never cried and sucked hard as I fed her. She was healthy, not red or discolored, lots of dark hair and wide eyed; she just stared. She was 8 lbs. ½ oz., 19 in. long. After 24 hours we went home.

NOTE: Sarah was posterior; doctors had never seen a baby born so fast and easy that was posterior. My husband's brother who is an O.B. Gynecologist recommended a C−section because she was posterior!

I nursed Sarah for 3 years and it wasn't until 2½ years that she had any other food besides breast milk. At 2½ because of problems from others I took her for a physical. No signs of rickets, blood disorders, etc.; she (for her age group) was a little under weight and height. She was in the 3% bracket, she toilet trained herself at 20 months. Completely understood everything; happy, yet quiet. Walked at 10 months, not bowlegged (walked like anyone else).

Sarah's diet was fruit at first.

Then some alfalfa sprouts, some avocado and leafy greens, all raw vegetables.

Her diet at 3½ years old is two meals a day 6 hours apart:

Breakfast: Apple, banana, apricot, peach, fig, date, pear, raisins, grapes, etc., organically grown. With slippery elm and fresh grape juice.

Dinner: Variety of sprouts with avocado, kelp or other fermented (yogurt) seed dressing. With ¼ slice of Essene bread, plain, rather an exception than a rule.

We eat the same foods, no nuts; I believe they are too hard for her to digest till she is older, 8 or 9. At 3½ we just went through the procedure again of taking her to a doctor and pediatrician because of others. She had blood tests (twice), urine, feces, etc.; everything is perfect; they couldn't find anything wrong mentally or physically. She wrote her name all over the doctor's pad, which she picked up from watching me write it!

She has been sick 3 or 4 times:

First time from hot springs at 8 months old and I gave her some carrot juice. She was sick for 3 or 4 days. I never gave her anything after that. We gave her lemon, water and garlic to clear the fever and mucous.

Second time: I ate some bread, fresh (yeasty), the only time and got sick and she got sick. She was 2 years old. I gave her garlic and cayenne by the spoonful with water. She never complained. Also slippery elm and ginger.

Third time was from a green banana at 2 years, 4 months. Someone gave her a green banana. Her fever was high, 105 deg. I gave her enemas and slippery elm, golden seal, cayenne and fresh water.

Fourth time: At 2½ years old someone gave Sarah some fruit punch full of sugar and artificial color, preservatives, chemicals, canned, etc.; she was so hyper I knew she had eaten something; two days later her nose was running. The day after that she had a 104 deg. fever. I gave her a tepid bath with ginger and cayenne along with cayenne enema and wrapped her in a cold sheet then plastic then warm blankets and put her feet in quite hot water, as hot as she could stand it, with ginger and cayenne. She had two of these treatments and the fever was broken.

She has been in good health and so have I.

She has been exposed to all of the childhood diseases but has not had them. God looks after us and none of the diseases come near our dwelling!

Also I do not have a menstrual period any more, more like a small amount of clear fluid and when nursing Sarah full time I never used any contraceptives and we had intercourse nearly every day.

A HEALTHY CHILD DESIRES HEALTH

Dear Viktoras, Bless you and thank you for sending this library of material to me on vaccination. I am also much appreciative of the little formula you included as a "body builder". The world around me of McDonald's, Fish and Chips and supersonic everythings weakens my own strong view on occasion in regard to vaccinations for my own child. When people ask I say, "No, she has not had shots." They look at me as though I could just as well be putting a knife through her, hurting her with my ridiculous unfounded views.

It was only yesterday that my friend accompanied me and my daughter to a restaurant to get a salad. My child asked me what she should do if she gets thirsty. My answer was that she would wait till we got home, no water. The friend looked at me and laughed because I was so absurd to live this way. Funny, my daughter looked at the friend and said, "My mommy just wants me to be healthy that's all."

Judyth Douglaston, New York, August 27, 1979

Part VI

PEOPLE LIVING IN THE 21ST CENTURY TODAY

The Coming Age which is upon us holds forth promise for a broad redefinition of human nature, a realization of hitherto thought impossible realities, and an actualization of the as yet unknown potentialities of men and women. Current limitations on the nature and sphere of people's activity will yield to the limitless universal energies which, in establishing people in cosmic origin, will lead to the acknowledgement and fulfillment of latent possibilities.

In the New Age people will travel by astral projection at will, psychic attunement to the universal forces will be normative, perfect health and well-being will be the lot of all, longevity will be increased manyfold, breatharianism will be commonplace, and death, or transition to other realms will occur painlessly and at will.

Already many persons have, in their own lives, whether by divine design or personal accomplishment, expanded the conventional parameters for human activity. The following articles relate their stories. The lives of such are mere harbingers of a future in which limitations have no part and all potentials will be realized as men and women everywhere become vehicles of Divine Love.

Part VI

PEOPLE LIVING IN
THE 21ST CENTURY TODAY

Section I
Breatharianism

AIR AS FOOD?

Nutritionists are probing a protein puzzle among New Guinea highlanders whose diet consists largely of sweet potatoes.

The researchers, led by Dr. E.H. Hipsley of the Nutrition Section of the Commonwealth Department of Health in Canberra, have put forward an interesting hypothesis to explain why the highlanders, with what is considered to be a grossly inadequate intake of protein, manage to remain in good health.

Their hypothesis is based on the theory that the body may be capable of making food directly from the air we breathe.

The diet of the highlanders of New Guinea consists mostly of sweet potatoes supplemented with bananas, cassava and other root vegetables, corn and leafy greens. Pig meats are eaten on ceremonial occasions, but not often.

Compared with European type diets which are based on cereal and meat, the diet of the highlander is very low in protein and fat. But despite this, he is generally of good physique and appears healthy, although there is evidence that his children grow more slowly and he is of smaller stature that his counterpart of European origin.

Measurement of nitrogen in food prior to consumption is a reliable guide to the amount of protein being consumed. Professor H. Oomen, a scientist from Amsterdam and Miss Margaret Carden, Senior Nutritionist with the Commonwealth Department of Health in Canberra compared a group of Port Moresby medical students living on high protein European diets with a group of subsistence farmers in the New Guinea highlands whose diet consists of sweet potato and other starchy foods low in protein.

Excess Nitrogen Produced

They measured the amount of food nitrogen taken in by both groups, and then compared it with the amount of nitrogen excreted. Among the medical students, food nitrogen 'in' equalled the food nitrogen 'out'.

But the puzzling factor was that the highlanders, with their low protein intake, excreted about twice as much nitrogen as could be explained as food nitrogen. Where then, was the excess nitrogen coming from if it had not been consumed as food?

Dr. Hipsley thought that it might come from the atmosphere, even though his view is contrary to articles of faith on this subject which go back 200 years. He and his team began a search for micro-organisms in the intestines which, like micro-organisms of soils, may be able to fix atmospheric nitrogen into useful protein.

He and Dr. F.J. Bergersen of the C.S.I.R.O. say they have now conclusively demonstrated that nitrogen-fixing micro-organisms can be isolated from the intestines of humans, although they make no claim to have shown that the organisms are actually fixing nitrogen on a large scale.

Utilizing Protein

It is the way in which these sweet potato eaters may be able to utilize the low protein of their diet and even supplement this with additional protein, which interests Dr. Hipsley and other researchers who are working with him.

A basic assumption of nitrogen metabolism in the human body has always been that the only way we can get protein nitrogen is through the food we eat. It has always been said that atmospheric nitrogen is just breathed in and out without participating in the process of they body.

It is known that the bacteria in the soil and on the roots of plants fix the nitrogen of the air into compounds which plants can use in making proteins. We get these proteins either by eating the plants, or directly by eating animals which have eaten the plants and converted the plant protein into meat, milk or cheese.

Understanding Diet

The ingredients used by these micro-organisms are atmospheric nitrogen and carbohydrate and it is in the fermentation of carbohydrate that the atmospheric nitrogen is converted into bacterial protein.

It may well be that proof of this mechanism within the human body will lead to a deeper understanding of the relationship between diet and health of New Guineans and similar people.

This data collected by Professor Oomen and Miss Corden indicate that about 16 grams of protein a day more than was previously thought, may be available to New Guineans if in fact this process of protein manufacture is taking place.

Since these people only consume about 16 to 20 grams of protein this means that they may be effectively doubling their protein consumption in this way.

PEOPLE LIVING IN THE 21ST CENTURY /343

THE PHYSIOLOGY OF BREATHING

It has been said by many yogic teachers that the breath is the bridge between the body and the mind. Before people feel that they need to practice a different kind of breathing, they should know why such practice is beneficial.

There are chiefly seven (7) reasons why they should, and thus be fully benefitted in every way. They are: (1) that his blood be purified and recharged, and that his arteries and veins do not become congested or hardened; (2) that his heart action be perfect; (3) that the metabolism of his body be regular; that the brain and all the other cells perform their work properly and not separate and scatter; (4) that the glands function in their due amount of secretion and excretion; (5) that his stomach and the other organs of digestion be normal; (6) that his lungs and other respiratory organs receive their due amount of vitality;   (7) that his cerebro − spinal and sympathetic nervous system (particularly the latter) do not become deranged. All of this depends solely upon man's ability to extract from the air and absorb into his body the required amount of Prana or Vital Force (1).

I have done some research into these bodily functions and discovered for myself why this is so. The research was basically aimed at answering questions such as those above in relation to the function of breathing. There are two states of breathing, one being conscious or contemplative and the other being accomplished by the autonomic system of the body which regulates and rules our breathing. Under normal breathing conditions the signal to take another inhale is dependant upon the amount of CO2 (carbon−dioxide) in the lungs. When the CO2 level falls we breath less until more waste has accumulated. When the CO2 level rises we breath more to expel greater amounts of it. The breath is automatically regulated to meet our oxygen needs during the whole range of activity from heavy physical exertion to thinking, to deep sleep. Yet we can at any moment exercise our will and change the pattern or extent of breathing. We tend, however, to remain unaware of our breath.

The breathing process only rarely becomes conscious e.g. when a person feels jolted or suprised with intense feelings such as fear, joy or pain. To gasp for breath or to experience a sense of breathlessness, is an experience which often accompanies a shock of some kind. Concentration on or awareness of the breath also occurs during the period of physical exertion such as is experienced during heavy manual labor or athletic activity.

Physically the muscle system accomplishes breathing. The primary muscle responsible for respiration is the diaphragm. "A secondary and interrelated muscular system includes the intercostal muscles (external   and internal) and the serratus posterior superior muscle. The secondary muscles are generally used only during sleep or labored breathing as when engaged in physical exertion or when under emotional stress" (2).

The diaphragm is of major interest for me and will be the subject of the next section of this paper. The diaphragm is the floor of the chest cavity (thoracic) and the roof of the abdominal cavity. This lets the lungs expand causing a vacuum in the air sacs (alveoli) which brings the air into the lungs. With exhalation the diaphragm relaxes and curves up into the thorax which results in the squeezing out of some of the residual air. The external thoracic muscles aid in respiration by elevating the ribs. The external throacic muscles also relax during expiration. In general, the exhalation is accompanied by an overall relaxation and release of tension of the body.

The diaphragm attached to the twelfth thoracic vertebra and the lumbar spine at the back, and to the ribs at the sides and in front. It is important in this respect because it has a relationship to an important grouping of muscles which affect the balance, symmetry and the functioning of the entire organism, (the iliopsoas, the quadratus lumborum and the abdominal obliques). These muscles play a vital role in supporting the enormous amount of body weight which falls upon the lumbar spine from above. Where they degenerate a condition of lordosis develops which destroys body economy and alignment and impairs breathing as well. When the integrity of the lumbar spine is disturbed the muscles in the upper back are prevented from functioning freely in the thoracic region. This inhibits the normal lengthening of the rib cavity essential to deep breath and the flow of breath is deprived. Additionally, the crura, the longest fibers of the diaphragm muscle, which act to initiate its downward excursion, are readily interfered with by any unfavorable pressure upon them, such as may be exerted by the lumbar spine when the curve is exaggerated by an unbalanced condition. Thus we see that free action and balance of the skeletal parts is necessary for balanced breathing, and that the musculature of the lumbar and pelvis region is a determining factor here.

This connection then demonstrates the law of interdependence of structural systems and functional systems. The diaphragm finds its connection to the motory system through the pelvis, wherein the relationship between the respiratory, skeletal, and motory systems becomes apparent. (3)

The heart, spleen, liver and stomach all lie within close proximity to this hard working muscle and are aided and affected by its functioning. It has connections with the skeletal system, as previously discussed, as well as the visceral. "Molding"in the diaphragm results in decreased stimulation to the vital organs and impaired functioning of the muscles. A collapsed chest and labored breathing also constricts the diaphragm which decreases the stimulation to the organs and impairs the normal functioning. For example, I will discuss some details of the heart.

Corpulent people generally have weak hearts and are urged to have medical checkups before going on with yogic breathing and other exercises because the discomfort of breathing may cause the person to become fearful. The discomfort will reduce as one works with the exercises. "The heart will be raised and lowered during the more or less energetic breathing movements, (4) via the pericardium. The pericardium is "a double sac that envelops the heart. The outer fibrous layer extends over the large blood vessels and merges with their outer coats; it adheres to the diaphragm and breastbone. The thin inner layer adheres to the heart muscles."(5) This then is the connection to the rythmic movements of the diaphragm. As we right kinds of breathing and exercise various heart problems and diseases "can improve, if not be cured". (6) At this point there can be seen a very interesting connection between coronary disease and the interrelationship the organs have to the breathing process.

Coronary disease may occur in any of the many parts of the heart or in any of the blood vessels of the circulatory system, including the large arteries and the arterioles. It can also affect the kidneys, adrenals, thyroid, or nervous system.(7)

Later on in life, early weakness such as birth defects and childhood infection can be aggravated by emotional tension, physical overwork, cigarette smoking, or use of drugs in which breathing patterns and intake of air are inhibited. As I realized the interconnectedness between the glandular system and emotions, and their link to a person's breathing patterns, I see that the heart is ultimately affected. One of the most common disorders, hypertension can be relieved by relaxation excercises and breathing techniques and other forms of stress release, it is actually oxygen insufficiency which can cause damage to the kidney, brain and the heart itself.

The Dual Cleansing Effects of Breathing

We see then that heart disease is linked to the emotional life, and the emotional life is linked in many respects to the glands (endocrine) these glands system is directly responsive to respiration. Respiration is really the key to body function. The next part of the paper discusses more of the healing qualities of the breath in terms of the function of the diaphragm.

One of the most interesting analogies I found to explain the lungs is to think of them as sponges. Like sponges, they absorbe air and filter special gases. By exhaling, the external function of the lungs is carried out (that is the exchange of gases in the lungs, internal respiration is the exchange of gases in the tissues). Exhalation is the squeezing out of the carbon dioxide which in the analogy is compared to milk. If the sponge is not fully squeezed out the milk becomes sour and stale. So it is with the residual air in the lungs. We have about six liters of air in the lungs; one and one half to two liters are considered residual air. There are also impurities in the air that tend to ferment in the lungs if the residual air is not exchanged and kept clean.

Many people who do not use their lungs fully are not getting good residual air exchange. An example of this is seen with the elderly who are not moved often enough to get good exercise for the lungs. They often get fermentation in the lungs which leads to inflammation then to plurisy or pnbeumonia. When you think of keeping your breathing capascity at its optimum, you want to be able to exchange the residual air. In this respect alone breathing is a cleansing function.

The blood comes to the lungs for nourishment and to exchange the waste materials. The breath introduces oxygen to the system for one purpose which is to metabolize food in digestion. "To prevent premature exhaustion it is essential to eliminate all waste matter smoothly and regularly and, in addition, there must be sufficient alveoli in working order as well as the necessary amount of active red corpuscles."9

The dual action of the diaphragm also helps to clean the body through the gentle stimulaton of the intestines as the breathing diaphragm massages the colon and causes peristalsis to cleanse the intestines. With proper breathing, natural elimination can take place; this process includes the burning off of stored fats in the veins and arteries. Improved cleansing is as important to energizing the body as is taking in air. The inhalation then increases the proper functioning of the exhalation or cleansing action. So the storage of tension is directly linked to respiration, although we think of stress and hypertension as a psychological response. The tension causes one not to breathe and exhale the CO_2 by not fully exhaling. The CO_2 turns to lactic acid and causes dis-ease and stiffness, which in turn, sets off a cyclic reaction, to not exert one's self. Without exercise then the lungs are not activated sufficiently to exchange the air necessary to reduce tension or to stimulate elimination in the intestines. The diaphragm then is a very important muscle in terms of these cleansing processes.

The influence on the abdomen from proper breathing is that the exhalation is accomplished, in part, by gravity (when standing) when laying down the action of the diaphragm is slightly different because the center of gravity is changed. In sitting or standing, the stomach, liver, gall bladder, and the pancreas are being massaged. These organs need to be massaged to function properly. These organs are essential to our getting complete nourishment, and the right kind of nourishment for our daily life and contentment.

I have experienced hypoglycemia and a weak pancreas. I have taken pancreatic enzymes to support its functioning; if that goes on unattended, then depression and loss of memory are experienced as symptoms of hypoglycemia. There is in evidence, a relationship between the hormones and the glandular systems to breathing as well as to the emotional experiences within our lives.

The Nervous System in Breathing

This is a very complex aspect of the breathing process. I will attempt to bring into focus several areas of the body that seem to me to be key points to understand in the process. Some things that need to be discussed at this point are the differences between regular and concentrated breathing practices. In the introduction I mentioned that the autonomic nervous system was the ruler of our breathing patterns in ordinary conditions. In practicing special breathing excercises people must make the effort to control this process consciously, which produces different results. Some of the topics which I researched are the autonomic nervous system and the parts of that system called the sympathetic nerves and para-sympathetic, of which one ganglia was most relevant, the vagus nerve. I have also explored the scientific explaination of the yogic term the "third eye" as it relates to contemplative breathing excercises.

The two centers that might be considered the top and bottom of the breathing mechanism would be the solar plexus and the third eye respectively. "The solar plexus means the 'sun plait', a braid of major nerves" (10). The third eye is that space between the eyes where there exists specific nerves which act as trigger points. These nerves link into the medulla, at the back and above the throat, the air passes into and through the upper sinuses. The pituitary gland is also situated there and is only divided by a thin bond or cartilage. Also part of the third eye is the upper two nerve ganglias of the sympathetic nerves. In the conscious breathing practices, air and prana (life force) is directed into this center and causes a neural stimulation which effects vital organs of the body. So, consciously, the attention is focused on the solar plexus and the third eye which causes warm relaxation and healing as well as an opening of one's intuition. Details of this process will be discussed at another point.

The solar plexus was considered by "Homer to be the seat of the mind and was more important than the head (11). My feeling about this is that this nerve center can be very receptive to vibrations. We usually are aware of these feelings when we experience "fear, disappointment or annoyance which produces a contraction in the solar plexus. The statements like 'I can't stomach it' or 'I feel sick when...' are common statements which identify people's feeling there. Disturbed and nervous people are known to be susceptible to duodenal and other ulcers, intestinal cramps or colitis" (12). In a healthy relaxed person the stimulations can be very useful information received at an intuitive level of consciousness, sometimes. For example, E.S.P is often described as a feeling. With the practice of abdominal breathing many positive results can be recognized, such as greater feelings of alleviation of tensions, and release creating a warm comfortable relaxed state of being.

The autonomic nervous system begins at the top of the spine. Here the breath is controlled by the medulla. "From this center, nerve fibers continue through the phrenic nerve to the diaphragm. Usually we breathe without thinking about it at all, the medulla is then in control. This center is governed by variations in the chemistry of the blood which stimulate the nerves in the medulla and send impulses down the phrenic nerves to the diaphragm" (13).

Also in the area of the third eye is the vagus nerve. This space in the center and back of the eyes is also called the "triple peaks, in Sanskrit Tri–Kuta", because of the three basic nerve centers which are, (1) the medulla, (of which the vagus nerve is a part) and (2) the pituitary gland, and (3) the nerve ganglia that serve the sympathetic nervous system. My interest in this is because in breathing, especially through the nose, all of these centers are stimulated and are absorbing vital energy from the air. (In my own experience with breathing excercises I have a direct experience of the results, and effects of such excercises on my body. I have been therefore, more than excited with my journey through the body and in discovering its mechanisms).

The vagus nerve is of importance because of its connection with vital organs, the heart, bronchial tubes, lungs, stomach and intestines. "The vagus nerve starts in the medula oblongata, just above the spinal cord. The nerve's paired trunks pass downward, one on each side of the neck. The fibers soon branch out (to the organs mentioned above)"(14). The vagus nerve starts at the midbrain, and is in fact part of the sympathetic nervous system. "The vagus nerve and the accelerator nerves act in harmony, though in opposite ways – one speeding up the heart, the other slowing it down" (15). In the same way the para–sympathetic nervous system acts to adjust the control of the vital organs of the body and act as a balance. The "para–sympathetic system brings about constriction of the pupil, slowing the heart rate, and constriction of the bronchial tubes; the most important to remember, this system stimulates peristalsis and increases the quantity and fluidity of secretions. The saliva flows more easily and profusely" (16).

It is the autonomic system which responds to a crisis or other stimulations of emotions. For example: when we are angry, swallowing food is difficult and it remains in the stomach much longer. It is the adrenal glands on top of the kidneys that respond most easily to stress and anxiety. "The stimulation of the adrenal gland, produces hormones, including epinephrine (or adrenaline), that prepares the body to meet emergency situations in many ways. The sympathetic nerves and hormones from the adrenal reinforce each other. Disorders and irregularities are complicated by psychological influences" (17).

It is important to understand that these sensory impulses do not reach our consciousness (generally). However, it is possible to increase our awareness and to plug into these points of stimulation and become more sensitive to these nerves. Yogic masters have not only been able to do that, but they have mastered their bodies to such an extent that they can exert direct influence over these bodily functions. The yogic teachings suggest to the student that greater powers are available through the mastery of the breath.

The third point in the Tri−Kuta is the pituitary gland.

"The pituitary is a small gland about the size of a cherry. It is nearly surrounded by bone except for its area of connection with the brain. The pituitary is located in a saddle like depression just behind the point of optic nerve crossing in the midline (18).

The pituitary gland has two lobes which produce different hormones. 1). Anterior Lobe. Hormones: somatotropic; gonadotropic; thyrotropic; adrenocorticotropic; lactogenic. 2). Posterior Lobe. Hormone functions: stimulate smooth muscle of blood vessel; reabsorption of water; stimulate uterine contraction (19).

We breathe through the nose so that the inhalation or cooling breath touches the trigger points inside the head as just described in detail. With positive thoughts and clear attention on these areas (the third eye and the solar plexus), one can create sensation of well being which will spread to other parts of the body as mentally directed. The exhale or warming breath flows through the forehead and the relaxing sensations can be felt in the solar plexus. I used the cool/warm breath concentration while jogging and found that it provided a meditation that works for me in order to get more distance in my run.

Another way to use the exhale is by consciously relieving contraction of the muscles. In the use of the rebirthing breath the exhale is never forced out, it is always popped out at the top, and is relaxed. A new word for rebirthing may be "the conscious art of abreaction − a contribution to rejuvenation which is one of the aims of many Hatha Yoga students" (20) who practice the art of pranayama or conscious breathing exercises. The word is a German psychology term used in English as a technical term. It entails both breathing techniques and mental process, which is the use of positive thoughts or unlimited ideas.

Linda Bayer

SISTER SUSAN KURUVILLA
STIGMATIST NUN OF SOUTH INDIA

Dear Viktoras, I'm sending you this article because I know you and your readers are interested in breatharianism. Yes, this exalted state of living is within the realm of possibility for all of us, if we can surrender ego and pursue a life of thoughts and acts utterly devoted to the spirit of love.

I am a professional journalist, and made very close scrutiny of Sister Susan during Easter 1978. I am convinced she is an absolute servant of love. If any of your readers would like to write to her, or perhaps make a contribution to her charitable work, her address is:

    Mar Gregorios Ashram
    Sister Susan Kuruvilla
    Mulanthruthy North
    Kandanad P.O. 682305
    Kerala, India

With brotherly wishes and love,
Richard, December 26, 1979

On the coast of the Arabian sea, in the flat green tropical state of Kerala in South India, there exists a unique blending of the spiritual traditions of the East and with the oldest form of the Pentecostal message of Jesus Christ.

Hidden in this isolated region flourishes the ancient ritual of the tiny Syrian Orthodox Church. Consisting of but a few hundred thousand members, who trace the origin of their ministry to St. Thomas the Apostle. the church claims to have been founded in 52 A.D.

In the rural village of Mulanthruthy, as if bearing witness to the spiritual vigor of Thomas' Church, lives Sister Susan Kuruvilla, a fifty–two year old Syrian nun who bears on her body the stigmata of Christ.

As a journalist and student of yoga, I spent most of 1978 in India. When the Easter season drew near, I decided to check first hand the reports I had received about the nun. Specifically, I had heard what seemed to me a miraculous outline of Sister Susan's life. She received the stigmata when she was thirteen, and for the past 27 years had taken neither solid nor liquid food, except for a rare glucose injection. Every Tuesday and Friday the wounds she bears bleed slightly as she reexperiences the death of Christ. During Easter Week, I learned, she relives the entire passion of Christ, culminating on Holy Saturday with her receiving a miraculously materialized "Manna from Heaven" to renew her strength.

Through my own early Catholic upbringing, I knew that stigmatism is an extremely rare phenomenon, and more or less unheard of outside the Roman branch of the church. The word dirives from the Greek word "Stigma", meaning a puncture, mark, or brand.

Stigmatists develop wounds on palms and feet, as well as, often, on the head, back, and sides, corresponding to the biblically described wounds inflicted upon Jesus Christ during His Crucifixion. Only 60 of the 330 stigmatists chronicled by the Roman Catholic Church have been beatified, or declaired saints – among them St. Catherine of Sienna, St. Francis of Assisi, and Saint Veronica Guilani. The Syrian nun thus seemed to represent a truly remarkable case of spiritual power.

So on March 17, 1978, I found myself outside the humid coastal city of Ernakulum, careening by bus through scrub, jungle, green fields, broad sweeps of rice paddy, coconut plantations – the village world of central Kerala, the half–forgotten enclave of oriental Christianity.

I outlined my request: to visit for 10 days and be present with the stigmatist nun through the Easter Passion. "You are welcome here," smiles Matthew the Ashram Secretary. "Consider this your home". Almost immediately a deep voice comes from within, speaking Malayalam. "That is Sister there," he continues. "She said you must consider all of us here as our own family".

Soon the nun herself steps out to greet me warmly. The slight white sari clad figure (she weighs only 80 pounds) framed by the door jam was bouncy, erect and sparkling, appearing younger than her years. I was struck by the high cheekbones, luminous eyes, and the detached air she projected. Handing me a glass of tea and some food, she spoke to me very kindly in English. "I am your sister in Christ, and you are my brother. While you are here you must consider us all the same as your blood kith and kin".

I realize that Sister Susan Kuruvilla is totally unselfconscious about the three inch gash of caked blood on her forehead, or the small cross–shaped incisions, surrounded always by a slight red stain, on each hand. Her suffering for this, the Friday prior to Holy Week, is over; always, it is only a temporary manifestation, seeming to cause no permanent harm. Now her spirit is bubbling over – friendly, intelligent, talkative, curious.

Amazed by such a warm welcome, I fall into the family spirit of Mar Gregorios. Sister Susan is the center of energy, her days kept busy with prayer, correspondence, cooking and serving food, and supervising the 18 ashram residents. Surely, I think to myself, she must eat something to keep up such a pace.

I notice that everyone follows her example of constant work. Carpenters are busy roofing a house, constructed under ashram auspices for a tubercular patient. Women are washing, cooking, gathering firewood; orphan children are keeping crows away from coconut bits drying in the hot sun. Several cattle are being tended, and the ashram's scant acreage is thoroughly husbanded. Two very small tikes walk about purposefully, carrying a large wicker basket between them and picking up all stray leaves which have fallen on the ground during the night.

For the next several days I recuperated from my'journey, participating in garden work and attending the Syrian Orthodox mass on Palm Sunday. Poor neighbors, beggers, the sick, hungry children whose parents can't afford to feed them that day, always people are stopping by for help and comforting. Orthodox priests regularly visit to lead prayers. The tiny nun never seems too busy to counsel, feed, or pray over the sick.

With each passing day, I find Sister Susan's humility and accessibility more heartwarming. In response to my inquiry, the nun allows me to examine the stigmatic

PEOPLE LIVING IN THE 21ST CENTURY

Sister Susan Kuruvilla

wounds. On both hands and feet, they are very pronounced, cross—shaped, the blood coagulated except in her times of pain. The gash across the forehead is the same, giving evidence of the crown of thorns. The wound in her left side is kept tightly bandaged to prevent loss of blood. Non of the punctures has ever become infected.

"Sister, don't you ever eat, or at least drink water?" I ask. "Nothing", she replies, with a radiant and childlike smile. "Isn't it a wonder!"

I asked about her healing powers, and how she came to Mulanthruthy to live such a remote life. "When I first received these wounds, there was no publicity", she answered. "God told me 'You must show your love for me by acts, not words' I lived for a long time in my native place, near Parumala Church, where the tomb of St. Gregorios (the only Syrian saint, aside from Thomas the Apostle) lies. All during those years, I experienced the wounds, the pain and healings. But healings only come to those who have firm faith in God. Those who only claim that faith don't get well".

"All night, during meditation, Christ speaks to me, just as you and I are speaking now. At these times I experienced very deep concentration. In 1973 He told me that as my patron saint had been born in Mulanthuruthy but had died in my birthplace, I should now go live and do Christ's work in his place. He told me that the time had come to start an ashram and orphanage, to feed the poor and help the suffering. So I have begun as directed".

The nun's life, as I piece it together through conversation, reveals a strong pattern of humility and devotion.

She was born in 1927. While still a child, praying in church, she heard a voice saying "Go and mend my broken church. Observe lent, prayer and fasting for 41 days, for I would make you a useful weapon for me". During the evening's prayer, she beheld Christ moving on the crucifix on the wall and heard him ask "Are you willing to follow me whenever I call you to take up my cross?" Affirming her belief and love, she received a sense of spiritual uplifting which has never left her.

After 41 days of fasting, she was overwhelmed by what she calls "grace power" – her voice became deep and resonant, she moved her hands in gestures of priestly ritual, and suggested remedies for people who were ill. Because of these trances, her parents felt she was possessed by epilepsy or hysteria. Her father in particular ridiculed her. With the support of her uncle and her Bishop however, she was encouraged to continue her growth in the life of prayer.

On Good Friday at the age of thirteen while at church she had a severe attack of pain all over her body and received the stigmatic wounds for the first time. They healed after three months, but a similar event recurred for four consecutive years.

During her sixteenth year, she was subjected to spiritual scrutiny and test by the Syrian church hierarchy, and during these meditations the bleeding wounds and regular Tuesday and Friday manifestaions of pain followed by "grace" became permanent.

After undergoing the orders of her church and passing three years in a Catholic convent, the stigmatist became a nun. At the age of 23 she stopped taking food, after praying for respite from this basic human function because "food draws by mind outward to worldly things, and I never liked food greatly, even as a child". The need for sleep also left her at this time, although she lies down during late night hours for 3 hours of meditation, during which she has regular visions and conversations with Christ.

Concerning her apparently miraculous life energies, she says, "I am alive only through the grace of God. I ask his mercy to help endure the pain. For if it is God's will, then I must endure it. But we can suffer to any extent through God".

During her time of pain for half an hour twice each week, she relives a measure of the agony Christ endured at His Crucifixion. Most Christians who meditate upon their beliefs prefer the promises of the Last Supper and Resurrection to reflect upon the genuine suffering Jesus bore.

It is 11:30 a.m., Sister Susan is bathed. The blood upon her forehead, other days caked in a dark coagulate streak, is thickly sticky, obviously fresh. Already groaning, she hobbles to a clean pallet spread before the small chapel's altar; suddenly her entire body goes through a wreching spasm. Loud cries come from her as, surrounded by attendants, she begins thirty minutes of the most incredible suffering I have ever witnessed. The bloody patches upon her feet are large and fresh, as are the scars on the hands. Her throat is choked in pain and she must expectorate constantly. The name "Jesu, Jesu" or "Ishwara" (Sanskrit for Lord) is continually on her lips. The nun's writhing, moans, tears, and anguish require four people to hold her down.

Everyone present is engaged in the repetitive soothing drone of liturgical chanting; several followers are crying softly. Fanning Sister Susan, they massage her twisting limbs and small, tortured body. Jaws tightly clenched, the nun pulls frantically on her fingers.

One prays for it to end, and inevitably, in some form, one enters into a new, entirely heart–opening relationship with Christ. There is a last cry, a gasp, and the nun's body shudders into quietness. Though she is exhausted, a beatific light seems to surround her. She is draped in a cool white cloth, and suddenly conveys a radical sense of peace and repose. There is a sense of high relief, exhausted exhilaration, sadness, thanksgiving, renewal.

Soon the nun opens her tired eyes. Holding the silver cross of the Syrian Church she speaks in a sepulchral, trancelike voice, first in what seems to be Aramaic (the language spoken by Jesus), then in Malayalam. This is the period of grace, when those seeking healing, or Sister Susan's prayerful intercession with Christ, speak to her either publicly or privately.

Later she rests again for a quarter of an hour alone. Then she struggles out to return to her daily round of duties. I ask how she is feeling. "Today I feel a little tired", she admits with a wan smile. Later, she describes the pain she undergoes. "It feels like pin pricks all over the body, but magnified a thousand times".

Yet a scant 15 minutes later, she is stooping, bustling, carrying out huge dishes of rice to each inmate and visitor, and asking what special dish they will take to eat. Her form is erect, there is the familiar bright sparkle in her eye. Seeming totally self–effaced, yet more present than anyone else on the premises, she is relieved, at least for the next 72 hours, of her stigmatic burden.

Good Friday dawned to the sound of chanting. From 11:30 a.m. until "about the third hour", at 2:53 p.m., I witnessed the agony of Christ's death through Sister Susan Kuruvilla, dressed in a wine–colored sari. Very quickly a supernatural–seeming energy possesses her small frame. Otherwise, for one whom

Sister Susan Kuruvilla shows the stigmata of Christ which she bears

this observer never saw eat or drink or sleep during ten consecutive days of intimate contact, there can be no rational explanation for the stigmatist's strength sufficient to bear the obvious wracking pain, which continues without letup for three and one half hours.

Finally it is finished. About fifty devout followers stand or kneel in awe, many sobbing or trembling in sorrow, surely having borne the most excruciating witness to Calvary available in the contemporary world. Sister Susan sinks back silent at last.

On Holy Saturday morning, under the influence of her power of grace, Sister Susan prayed that God's mercy shower down on the assembly of worshippers.

The "manna", when it came, appeared sporadically in small flecks, none of them larger in size than a dime. The flecks came singly and in two's and three's, sprinkling at wide-spaced and random points upon a white veil which had been spread to receive them, but also upon the floor and under the altar table before which Sister Susan prayed.

Seen very clearly in the bright, flourescently-lit room, they could only be described as materializing out of thin air. About half the pieces materialized directly on the floor. Other flecks would drop suddenly out of mid-air, several seeming to materialize directly from the flat silver cross held in the nun's hands.

The flecks came during the nun's final 20 minutes of prayer; at first they appeared semi-transparent, like small flat bits broken from a communion wafer. Gradually they seemed to swell, or push themselves up, forming small crystalized granules, yellow and white in color.

A total of about 21 small pieces of "manna" were finally collected and Sister Susan distributed five or six to those who attend her so devoutly during her times of pain. Flashing her radiant smile, she placed one of the granules upon my tongue. By now it had a rock-candy hardness. Its taste was fresh and sweet, but with an aftertaste more difficult to describe. As the author of Exodus writes (Ch. 16:31): It (manna) was like a small white seed, and tasted like a biscuit made of honey"

As night falls, I try to impose a rational model upon what I have observed. The Roman Catholic Church has always taken a low-key attitude toward reported stigmatics, and the Oxford Dictionary of the Christian Church, while validating the existence of the phenomenon, cautiously denies that the wounds stem from supernatural means. Skeptics have gone so far as to charge stigmatics with self-infliction of the wounds

But a team of New Jersey doctors examined Sister Susan in October 1977 during her only trip to North America. Based on blood samples, x-rays, cardiograms and encephlograms, the three medical men, while attesting to "some slight evidence of bleeding of the stigmata on a Friday, "unanimously' denied the likelihood that the cross-shapped wounds were self-inflicted. Their x-rays showed the nun's stomach to be completely empty. Dr. Eugene Ged of Patterson, N.J., told the "Toronto Star": "We don't think the woman is a sham, but scientifically it doesn't add up. This business of her not eating or drinking really puts us in a dilemma as doctors".

Dr. Samuel Phillip, of Irvinton, N.J. reported that during Sister Susan's three month stay in his household she was never seen to take food of any kind or perform any normal excretory function.

In ten days' close observation, I was unable to disprove these statements. Although I often retired after midnight and awakened to the 5 a.m. noise of kitchen workers, I never saw Sister Susan asleep. On four occasions I woke in the still hours of the night to relieve myself. Each time the slight noise of my opening the door outside brought a quiet inquiry from the meditating nun in the next room.

As the time came for me to leave MarGregorios, I felt caught in paradox. On one hand I was warmed by an intense sharing of Christ's spirit with a group of otherwise foreign people, yet I felt an intimate, even horrifying awareness of what it really means to co–participate in that deepest mystery, the awareness of suffering, which is the very center of Christ's message   I found myself thinking of the stark Presbyterian Sunday services where attendance was mandatory when I was at college, of the more elaborate ritual of Episcopal high mass at Washington's National Cathedral, and of other holy weeks I spent as a boy in the Roman branch of the Catholic Church – each experience purveying a completely different flavor of meaning to Christ's death and resurrection. Not one, I realized, could duplicate the intense and agonizing nearness to Jesus Christ which I experienced in this obscure corner of Christendom at the loving and self–surrendered hands of Sister Susan Kuruvilla.

Section II
Superhumans

Dear Viktoras: We wish you all best wishes on your Holistic Life Seminar in Hawaii, and feel you are doing tremendous work. We are a non-profit organization dedicated to the awakening of the Highest Potential within man, mentally, physically and spiritually. Gene Stanlee has researched and taught for over 40 years. He's 67 his next birthday. He has gone 31 days as a breatharian − no food, water, etc. and many fasts (over 45) on water only, the longest being 2 months. I, his wife, have gone 8 days breatharian (I will be 48 my next birthday) and many fasts, the longest one being 1 month. People come from all over the world to be under my husbands' and our teaching. I recognize him as a true Master of the Now.

Sincerely,
Erin Stanlee

DR. GENE STANLEE

Born in Chicago, Illinois, Gene Stanlee was one of 15 children. At the age of 5 years, he fell down many steps, incurring paralysis of the spine, and was given up for dead. He had lost all movement of his body and his speech. After seeing a strong man perform, he had a new desire to live. At the age of 8 years, he entered a Chicago Playground 3−day Wrestling Tournament. Gene won the tournament after defeating eleven older boys. At the age of 15 years, Gene was claimed to be the World's Strongest and Best Built Boy.

Gene is an outstanding Mechanical Engineer. While in the Navy during World War II, he broke all existing records on strength and endurance. He won the title of "The Navy's Strongest and Best Built Man", and has won nine trophys for outstanding achievements. He wrestled 134 contest matches on 35 islands, and 88 different ships and won them all. He was credited by the U.S. Navy for selling over one million dollars worth of war bonds.

As a wrestler, he toured all over the United States and most of the world, breaking all wrestling attendance records. He sold out Madison Square Garden 18 times, and the Chicago Stadium twice with over 22,500 fans on all occasions. He also sold out a ball park in Caracas, Venezuela, South America, drawing over 70,000 fans, won 18 championship wrestling belts, and 2 jewel studded crowns for being "King of the Mat". Gene owned the most luxurious wrestling costumes in the world, ranging from $300.00 to $2000.00 each — 52 total.

Gene has been featured and has been the subject of more magazine covers than any other wrestler in the world.

Gene is credited to be the only man in the world who defeated five professional heavyweight boxers in a mixed match within three minutes for a $50,000.00 challenge.

Feats of Strength

Gene chinned himself with 150 lb. man hanging to his waist; lifts 215 lbs over head with one arm; can lift 600 lbs. to his waist in the Dead Lift; does a knee bend with 400 lbs. on his back, five repetitions, and does 5 pushups with 185 lbs. on his back. He lifted 350 lbs. with two arms in the Clean and Jerk; does a leg Press 15 times with 1000 lbs.; and is the heaviest man known to do the either arm chin. Gene has wrestled a professional football team and defeated them all in less than 18 minutes. Among his many titles, Gene has won the "Professional Mr. America" (twice), "Pin-up Boy of the Navy", "America's Most Popular Athlete", and "World's Strongest and Best Built Man"; he has been credited with more trophies, gold medals, and plaques than any athlete over the world, (155 total). Gene has collected over one million dollars for various charity organizations, and was highly praised by 3 presidents of the United States for his marvelous cooperation in helping to build our country strong. He has handed out millions of copies of the Declaration of Independence and the Allegiance to the Flag wherever he appeared on his wrestling tours, to foster Americanism.

Gene promoted the largest Beauty Queen Contest in the East coast to find the "Gene Stanlee Beauty Queen" with over 10,000 participants.

Gene was Vice—President of a large California investment firm. He sold over 3 million dollar's worth of Mutual Funds.

Gene has a Ph.D degree as "Doctor of Philosophy in Physical Science". He has written 2 books — "Reversing the Aging Process", and "Health, Wealth, and Happiness on $1.00 a Week on Food" in order to help humanity. Gene is a teacher on the Physical, Mental and Spiritual Laws of Life and also the quickest and shortest way of developing the internal and external organs of the body.

Gene is the Founder and President of the Gene Stanlee Foundation whose purpose is to help man find the truth about his Higher Self so that he can be set free.

REAL LIFE SUPERMAN

Captain Alan Jones of the Marine Corps is a real–life Superman.

There isn't anything I can't achieve if I set my mind to it", he snapped impatiently, wiping away the sweat generated by his daily 15–mile run.

This granite–hard soldier battled his way back from childhood polio to perform feats of physical endurance that stagger the imagination. This summer he did 27,003 nonstop situps, swam 100 miles down the ice–cold, churning Columbia River in Oregon, lifted 75 pounds, half his body weight, over his head 1,602 times, and swam three miles with his hands cuffed and feet shackled towing a 3,200 pound barge! And on November 10, he ran 199 miles nonstop to celebrate the Marine corps' 199th birthday.

"I don't believe in failure", Jones said. "The possible things are those that have been done. The impossible things are those waiting to be done...".

Unlike the tall, husky Superman of comic–book fame, Jones, 27 – stationed in Portland, Oregon, Marine Corps headquarters, is lean, knotty, 5 feet 9 and 147 pounds.

HE EATS ONLY FRESH FRUITS AND VEGETABLES and takes more than 50 vitamin pills every day, plus additives such as kelp and brewer's yeast.

When he was only five years old, Jones contracted polio in both legs and was faced with spending the rest of his life as a cripple. "The doctors told my parents I'd be an invalid for life", he remembered. But his father, a high school athletic director, set up a physical fitness program for him and he slowly recovered normal strength. "But I didn't stop there", said the rugged marine. "I kept on to attain maximum physical condition".

His biggest asset, he says, is mental conditioning. He listens with quiet intensity to motivation experts such as Earl Nightingale and former Olympic pole–vault gold medalist Bob Richards.

"I lie in bed at night listening to tapes of these great men talking", he told the Enquirer. "It stimulates me to greater achievement".

When Jones was lifting the 75–pound barbells 1,602 times, he recalls, "Both my hands were rubbed raw and bleeding. I just had no option but to grit my teeth, shut the pain out of my mind, tell myself I could reach 1,600, and keep going"

Jones collapsed after 1,602, slept for 14 hours straight, and was stiff and sore for 10 days.

Said his commanding officer, Capt. Vince Goewey: "I can confirm the details of his feats to date. He's undoubtedly one of the fittest men alive".

The Guinness Book of World Records is currently investigating Alan Jones' superhuman achievements.

WILEY BROOKS
LIVING ON LIQUIDS

Wiley Brooks does not look much like a typical weight lifter.

Brooks, 44, who is 6 feet tall and weighs 135 pounds, seems out of place among the muscular types in the lifting pit at the Venice Beach Recreation Center. He has pole-thin legs and looks as if he can hardly raise a muscle or two by flexing his arm.

Despite his slight build, Brooks does possess strength, so much that he can lift 965 pounds from a squat rack — two iron poles. When he tried to prove his ability by lifting close to 1,000 pounds recently, he did get the bar off the rack, but the bar snapped in half.

Regulars at the pit weren't very happy with the results. The broken equipment — since replaced — meant there would be one less bar to go around for weight lifting for them that day.

"I was just demonstrating what I could do," he said "The only other guy I've heard of that can lift 10 times his body weight weighs 375 pounds and can barely walk around."

Brooks admitted he does not have a good style in lifting. His technique does not fit any established rule. He has weights put at both ends of the bar; while standing, he lifts the bar, which sits on the rack at almost shoulder level.

"My best lifting weight is 120 pounds," he said. "When I was eating right — about once a week — that was what I weighed and I lifted 1,200 pounds."

Brooks, who lives in Venice, has a simple way to stay slim — he rarely eats solid foods. His diet, when he eats at all, consists of fruit and fruit juices.

Brooks said he discovered the benefits of fruit when he went on a diet and only drank grape juice. "I believed like everyone else in the idea of a balanced diet and the need to eat to stay strong," he said. "But I found that the longer I fasted, the stronger I got."

Lately Brooks, who is a salesman, has been eating other foods like bread, cheese and meat as a research project for a book he is writing on the diet.

"I'm not interested in tryng to save the world. I'm only showing what I have found. The body is ruined by auto-intoxication, overeating and eating the wrong things I only need about seven hours of sleep a week when I'm eating right. I heal faster. I haven't had a cold in years.

"Solid food is like poison; it clouds the blood. With the blood cleansed, more energy flows through the body.

"The only time I eat now is when I go out with friends. I guess you could call me a social eater."

When Brooks breaks training, he feels the effect. "I can't lift weights at all after I eat a cheese omelette."

Part VII

TESTIMONIALS

The following are letters which have come to the desk of Viktoras. Many seek his advice, his counsel, his encouragement as they undertake new ways. In these letters, the joys, the struggles, the triumphs, and the despairs of changing, of being reborn to new life and new Light are detailed. They are reflective of an ever increasing minority of women and men who are everywhere seeking to create a better life in harmony with a better planet. Perhaps you will recognize your self and your own experiences described therein and thereby be encouraged to persist in ways which often seem difficult because they are different. It is out of such persistence that the New Age will be created. It is because of such lives that Love will triumph.

Section I
Transformation

REBIRTH

My dear Viktoras, A couple of months ago I wrote Ann Wigmore a long testimonial interwoven with immeasurable gratitude regarding the fact that "Be Your Own Doctor" salvaged what was left of my life and led me to new ideas and alternatives, none of which have ever failed to show positive results. Then I, by some great grace from God, brought your excellent book, "Survival Into the 21st Century" (Plantary Healers Manual). It is and will be a classic.

I have read every word in it and have applied your revelations of the truth to my life totally. You, dear Viktor, are responsible for my new life. I want to say thank you and my appreciation but feel frustrated – – how on earth does one thank you for saving her life and giving her a second chance to start again in health and love??? Thank you for caring enough, about the ignorant people in the world to have gone to the great effort to write and labor over a literary work that contains everything someone in the dark like me needed to reestablish her life and health. Thank you. Your motivation to write such a book is the depth of your own goodness and love. What a fine soul you are. Your manual is my most loved possession – – it is one of very few objects I would rescue in case of a fire!!

I am a 30 year old woman who had suffered suicidal tendencies and severe depression since age 12 or 13. (I will not give all the background information to you unless you would like it for a "testimonial" purpose in order to help spread the truth. I would be most happy to testify). Not until Ann Wigmore's book did it even occur to me that my lifelong constant extreme constipated years, because my mental health was as poor as it can get before giving up, I did everything in my power to be wise about by physical health. I spent years – 15 lost years – in psychiatric care trying to uncover the mystery of my inability to function and continuous suicidal thoughts. I was given drugs galore – of course, to no avail. I had "attempted suicide" on 3 occasions, years apart.

Finally, I had had enough. I flushed all my drugs down the toilet – told **my psychiatrist good-by,** and out of sheer desperation to find an alternative to ending my life, I walked into a health food store and purchased Ann's book – and applied its principes immediately. This was the beginning of the beginning. Then I bought your book.

I have eaten only raw food since December. No animal products of any kind. No grains or starches. I drink 3–4 ounces of wheatgrass juice a day, one quart of rejuvelac and fermented seed sauce is the only manner I ingest seeds and nuts. I have a Champion juicer which most of my meals revolve around. I have unplugged my stove. I eat fruit, juice vegetables!

I went on a 7–day juice fast in January. I followed your instructions exactly as outlined on page 32 ("Mucus cleared up") of your manual. I lost amounts of black mucus and was in bed most of the time. My complexion is clear and beautiful for the first time in my life. I use no soap on it. I wash my face with wheatgrass juice and distilled water only.

My hair has grown back with color I never knew I had and thickly – like when I was younger. I have had quarter–size bald spots for 5 years. Dermatologists told me it was "Aloepecia Areata" and there is no cure for it. Despite their opinion, they saw fit to inject my scalp with drugs once a week for 1 month until I saw how insane it all was.

My gums have stopped bleeding. My mouth is in excellent shape now. My menstruation cycles have ceased. I have not had a period since February. When I was so unhealthy my periods gave me painful cramps and always further increased my suicidal thoughts and my complexion monthly at this time became worse. My legs ached a lot.

I feel as pure as snow now. I use a smattering of baking soda for deodorant and a little on my toothbrush. There is not one chemical of any size, shape that I ingest or apply topically to my skin and body.

My body has gone through such a transformation. I am delighted that what my family refers to as my "unbreakable self–discipline" is no effort at all. Living as I do and eating God's food in its natural state is pure joy for me. I get up everyday at 4 a.m. and never do I feel tired or pathetic or depressed.

I unplugged my television two months ago and am now trying to find someone to give it to. Whole undiscovered areas of my life are surfacing. I read much.

Also, there is no drainage from my ears at all anymore. There is no discharge from my vagina, either. My eyes on the other hand, secrete much of a mucus–like material as a result from rinsing my eyes with a few drops of wheatgrass juice. My eyes cramp and tear randomly. I have assumed they are trying to detoxify – as my vision has been very poor all my life and until you and Ann came into my life, my vision was even further on its way downhill. It will be interesting to see the prgress – however slow – my eyes and vision make. They are somewhat stronger already.

I've left much out of this letter for you on purpose because of my presumption regarding your busy demanding schedule. I will on the last page plunge into what is most important to me.

Because I am starting a new life for myself, because I am not materialistic; because· I have suffered such agony and isolation in my life, because I know absolutely the quality of life I want and need, because I believe 100% in your principles, because I realize there is nothing without Love and caring, my plans for the future have and are influenced by these past recent months of enlightenment and by the truths outlined in your manual.

The greatest motivation I feel for my future is to somehow, someway involve myself in helping to spread these same principles in your book...a more meaningful life I could not ask for.

Can you give me some clues, direction as to how to accomplish this? Do you suggest I work at Hippocrates Health Institute for a while? I consider myself intelligent and friendly so that I do feel I could be a good vehicle to help get the word out, and educate people about the potential for harmony in their own bodies. Would it be feasible to come back to study with you personally? I am capable of real commitment in this endeavor.

I am serious, sincere, responsible, highly motivated and a hard worker. And since I am in superb health now I have great energy. I despirately need a meaningful outlet for this motivation and energy. One of few directions I feel I can go in is to follow up some suggestions you might be able to make to me. There is such an ocean of unnecessary, avoidable suffering and sickness going on today due to ignorance that I would like to make a contribution in alleviating it. I want to give much in this regard and I would most like to work with individuals who eat, live and feel as I do as I plan to maintain this quality life I now have. I want to give back to life the goodness I have been shown.

Love,
Marcia James, May 23, 1979

RAW FOODS AND BEAUTIFUL FEELINGS

Hello, hello, hello, Viktoras we would love to hear your 24 hour seminar tapes!! Yes, we are estatic that you offered! We get so high whenever we receive a letter from you, we gather all around reading it together. I must say sometimes it takes all of us to figure out your slant! Ha Ha, you have that doctor's scribble don't cha? It means a lot to correspond with you and we appreciate you taking the time to answer. Believe me, you are our guiding brother and we feel very devoted to you.

In your letter you mentioned seeing a lot of acidified folks in your travels — well we sure did go through a time of it for awhile, over—eating and constant nibbling too. We realized pretty quick, the symptoms occured with headache, painful stomach zones and intestines, in hands and feet. Feeling drowsy, unclear head, too full feeling for sure. Overcoming the stomach and old habits is teaching us real good by direct experience and how crappy we feel afterwards — sick. Thank goodness for Marcia's book, helped me a lot to put raw live foods together nicely. To keep my family interested enough, you know? They are doing good, we love the deep connection telepathically that we all have! It's neat, and we are a closer family because of our diet, I know that for sure now. At first as our heads are clearing we didn't know for sure, thought but by chance Gregg, Jase and I just happen to show up at the same place about the same time. Especially Gregg and I, we experience the same type of dreams. Jason is an alert and active 8 year old. Has never had a barber type of hair cut, only trims (he is proud of that) smart kid, blows us away with his awareness! His irises are changing colors, to blue. His growth pattern has doubled every 3 or 4 months an inch or so is noticed.

I am definitely seeing the benefits of our diet paying off as our bodies come alive with beautiful feelings.

We really enjoyed chanting with you. My, you have a beautiful tone to your voice, so strong and deep.

I just wanted to let you know how thrilled we are and excited about wanting to hear your tape. I promise to send it back right afterwards!

Our little baby is so beautiful! Really alert and alive, his body is full of muscle no fatty parts. He sighs with joy all the time, so glad to be here! What a difference I see in him compared to a friend's baby his age who feeds her baby food already! Get's the flu — been sick with fever and diarrhea.

Well I am going to take some pictures of us now, you may have. Keep in mind we looked much different 2 years ago. And 2 years from now we will even be more different. Gregg's hair is hanging there, gotten much thicker, but he was going bald. My hair was thin and brittle, no shine and wouldn't grow much. Now boy, what a difference!

God bless you, my brother of inspirational light. You bring us a lot of knowledge. Thank you again for sharing.

Imperial Beach is a small beach town. No big hotel or condominums yet. Under–development, but beautiful beach land where the whales cruise by migrating and breeding to the warmer waters down south. We are fortunate to live close to the ocean, a nice calmative...doing a lot of meditation and traveling.

We love you,
Lynda, Gregg, Jason & Mathew Carver, Imperial Beach, California, March 1979

WHEATGRASS AND PSYCHIC HEALING

Dear Viktoras:

Without knowing it, you have had a profound influence on my life. It started with Jeremy Gordon being so super kind when the promoters of Diet Expo were hassling me, and ended up with you bringing down a lump on my arm with some chewed wheatgrass. Remember? Well, I certainly never forget.

Jeremy gave me a copy of "Survival", and it became my bible, and I passed my new found knowledge on to my students. Last summer, one of my garbage eating karate students came down with a roaring case of Hepatitis. Poor girl, she was told by the doctors there was nothing to be done except sit and wait for about 6 months and hope her blood count changed. Out she came to Sensei (instructor) Filson with her tale of woe. I was in the country for the summer and, armed with my trusty juicer, assaulted her disease. Needless to say, Ann was fit and ready to work out in ten days. I just pumped her full of every green juice available all day.

Since then, there have been numerable incidents where I have been able to help students and friends with the knowledge I gained from you. I only wish it was easier for people to get your book. I am always telling them to buy it, and the only place in New York City I have found it is the "Health Nuts" store on 2nd Avenue, once in a while the "Good Earth" on 1st and 71st St.

My classes at the 92nd St. "Y", are loaded. Some classes have as many as 100 at a time. So, I am talking to people and they are listening to me. Is there any way we could get your book to more interested athletic types?

Viktoras, I am astounded by the wheels you have started turning when you had me call Dr. Sierra in Puerto Rico and Miryam Ralph. The rest of the story reads like the "begats" in the bible. Dr. Sierra told me to get in touch with a young man named Bruce Gregory who he had just put on a plane to NY. He told me Bruce was a healer and had been out to study magnets with him. Got in touch with Bruce who sent me to a psychic healer named Yolanda Betegh. Ever hear of her? She's a great big Rumanian woman who is reputed to perform healing miracles. I have always been a great skeptic and was totally flabbergasted when she zapped me with her energies! Electric like tingles surged thru my body when I am with her, and seem to center in my injury. She tells me I will be totally healed, (this will be a miracle, as you know my ligament it totally severed) after 10 visits with her. Monday is my 5th. I have called Bruce when in a doubtful mood and he assures me she performs miracles on a steady basis.

A famous plastic surgeon named Jerry Imber gave me a copy of a book, "Arigo: Surgeon of the Rusty Knife", John G. Fuller, author, Crowell, publisher. I had never heard of this Brazilian peasant who cured 300 per day, and operated with scissors or anything he could get his hands on. Never any bleeding or infection or pain. Nothing used during operations and patients felt no pain. What's great is that his miracles are documented and cannot be disputed. From this book, I got a lot of hope.

I was in the pool at the "Y", being assaulted by friendly members who cannot understand why I didn't have traditional surgery, when a man approached me and told me he was operated on by an Israeli surgeon named Yuda Gallazan. He showed me his back where he said the surgeon went in with his fingers, operated, removed the offending problem and closed him up. There was no bleeding, no pain, and all scaring gone in about two weeks. He was in the "Y" pool swimming one hour after the man operated on him. He got me in touch with his wife, she was also operated on by him, and they have set up an appointment for me at the end of the month. They reached him by long distance and he said he didn't know if he could help me, (according to doctors, ligaments should by now be dead beyond repair) but he will see me. Unlike the psychic healer I am seeing, he charges a healthy fee, $250.00 per visit. (Hard to get money now, as injury has stopped my personal appearances which were bringing steady money.) Yolanda told me not to worry about money, just let her heal me.

So, personally I am in a terrible quandary. Almost wish I were a small child, so that a parent would have to decide what was right for me to do. I haven't used Dr. Sierra's magnets because Yolanda told me not to do anything but what she says, and I have committed myself to her treatment. I might as well go all the way.

I am keeping a detailed diary of all these events and people. I will write a book about the whole experience and the new world that has been opened to me.

Meanwhile, dear Miryam Ralph continues to write me words of comfort and call me now and then; "Don't you worry Dear, I have a daughter just your age, and everything's going to be all right". What better medicine could there be?

Much love,
Sidney Filson, New York, New York, March 19, 1978

DOCTOR GOES NATURAL

Dear Viktoras, Thank you for your letter and the information enclosed with it.

You ask what I think of your book?

Dick Gregory says in the introduction 'This book of Viktoras' is seeded...'. Your seeds found in me a receptive soil and, in sprouting, transformed my life. God only knows what will happen as they flower!

I graduated in medicine at Sheffield University, in the industrial north of England about 14 years ago. My background was of the elegantly–termed 'lowest group on the socio–economic scale'. For reasons indefinite still, I decided at the age of 4 or 5 to become a doctor. For a young bookworm the realities of University came harshly. Orthodox scientific education (rather, indoctrination) buried the scant spiritual awareness surviving from school days and so it remained until a few months ago.

Fatherless from an early age, upheavals in family relationships, the strain of study and the impact of sudden freedom on an immature personality produced a stormy University career, a marriage on shaky foundations and a son; eventually I acquired a degree. Not coping with life at all I fled to Australia a year after graduation.

We settled in the island state of Tasmania at Hobart, Australia's southern most capital city. After a few cold wet winters I realized I'd recreated all the problems, their external manifestation was the only thing that had changed. Medicine was a drudge, Tax department and long haired pinkos being blamed for all my troubles. A heavily smoking alcoholic I became national secretary of a strident society of capitalist general practitioners and eventually a founder member of libertarian political party based on Ayn Rand, Von Mises, etc. I knew a lot about economics and politics in those days?! Between times I worked in psychiatry, surgery, did a couple of years in forensic pathology and when the disgust finally got to me "settled" into general practice.

This all took about 10 years, another child added en route. Finally after a worse−than−usual month during which I had polled ignominiously as Senate candidate for our 'Workers Party', had twice smashed up my Lamborghini in drunken madness and repeatedly violently assaulted my wife and children I ran away again, this time alone, to Queensland. Slowly the terrible mess I'd deserted tidied up by my long−suffering ex−wife.

After a time in black suicidal limbo I met a young lady I subsequently married. Very close to nature, she taught me about beauty, peace and love and how to relax. She also introduced me to dope and mushrooms and had the strength to guide me through some terrible experiences into some form of insight and self−control. We ate omnivourously.

I obtained a well paid job as assistant to a long established local g.p, I practiced orthodox medicine, of course, and we settled together. Over the next two years we explored each other and I began to re−read S.F., occultism etc. which had always fascinated me as a boy. We went to an occasional public meeting of the Rosicrucions and other groups, not knowing what we sought and certainly not finding it.

Medicine was more satisfying, I began to look at people instead of symptoms but I knew I wasn't coping with disease, even less with the plethora of new drugs and therapies and the constant veiled threat of the professional bodies to 'Keep up to date'. I began to feel that I wasn't cut out to be a doctor and I blamed my self for lack of discipline in medical school. I never seemed to be able to grasp the fundamental issues.

The week prior to our marriage of March 17 this year we called at a friend's to score our honeymoon supplies. During the course of conversation on bad knees he said "...if you eat meat it rots inside you". For some reason it was like a bomb going off in my head. We argued for hours and he lent me Arnold Ehret's 'Mucusless Diet System'. I read it that night and began modifying my practice of medicine the following morning. That day I read 'Back to Eden' and the die was cast. Every patient thereafter was harangued about diet and disease. These days and following were a flat out black microdot permanent trip and I had no control except on routine levels, my mind seemed to be on its own, unfettered and uncaring of consequence.

We had a beautiful wedding standing beneath the gum trees under a high sun with birds singing our vows and went for a three week honeymoon on a perfect deserted island paradise. It was wonderful, we had immediately stopped all meat, dead and processed foods on that night−some 4 or 5 days previous−it seemed like eons; also, no time at all. We ate fresh fruit and some cooked vegetables that week with one binge on fish and white wine and both vomited and were unwell for days after. We each lost a stone in weight in seven days and my mental response was similar, reflecting profoundly on the inverted knowledge that had I learned from orthodox scientists.

I craved more knowledge — I had a million unanswered questions. We returned home for 2 days so I could visit my bricklayer's labourer friend and learn more. He showed me 'Survival' and said I'd find in it all I needed. I purchased it and 'Be Your Own Doctor' and 2 boxes full of other books from a health food store (I'd never been near one before!) and we scooted back to our new life.

Your book was a book of revelations, a new world.   I really believe that, for some reason, I have been given a second chance in life and that I have finally begun the study of Medicine. The same with life. I shall ever be grateful to you. We returned home and I recommenced work on April 9th. Your lecture here was on April 19th The leaflet advertising your visit hit me like a thunderbolt when we had both undergone such changes in the previous two weeks as a result of reading your book, we had spent many hours discussing your ideas and speculating on what it would be like to talk to you.

I was in a dilemma regarding patients. I didn't know what to do with them, the drugs I had maintained them on for the previous 2 years, what would happen when I altered them and changed their diets. I had a nervous breakdown with every patient but earnestly cajoled each and every one, trying to convert the world back to nature yesterday. The adrenalin was sky high and uncontrollable, I relied heavily on dope to keep my sanity. Patient numbers fell off after only one week, I had allowed my hair to sprout, the local chemists were murmuring about the sudden decrease in my prescriptions. I spoke earnestly to the pharmaceutical travellers about God and disease. Yet deep down, I knew the risks of such intemperate behavior. My employer didn't see me very often and I hoped to have 6 months to consolidate debts and lower material requirements before he woke up and I had to face reality. I was hoping to use that time to find my bearings.

When I appealed for your help at the lecture I'd been back at work for 10 days and was having nightmares about how safely to handle the transition of people from orthodox to natural methods. I felt responsible for a number of near−deaths when I had perhaps precipitately changed invalid's diet etc. and I felt sure I would kill somebody. I had soon searched around and contacted a number of naturopaths, yoga teachers, iridologists and so on for advice and information and had been pretty much disappointed. Each was involved in some personal indulgence and/or approach to disease as sychronous. None of them even looked healthy and most still drank alcohol, smoked and ate animal protein.

From when I read Ehret's book it seemed to me that to successfully preach it, one had to be it. It seemed that I had recognized a truth and then had to live it otherwise admit its falsity. This is why I jumped in feet first and how I reconciled my rash or precipitate behavior. I felt that I was doing everything for the right reasons and therefore should do as much as I possibly could immediately and that everything was then bound to work out correctly in the long run. I still don't know if that's confused rationalization.

I was feeling exuberant and that nothing could touch our magic. A week after your lecture, my employer sacked me. So, with a brand new wife, recent mortgage on house and 2 acres, 2 horses, 2 dogs, 3 cats and no job, life was viewed from a new perspective!

Anyway four weeks later I opened my own practice and have now been running for six weeks. With all the arrangements this is the first time I've had the opportunity to reply. Since we met I have read and studied. I have explored most of the eferences in 'Survival' and now have a more balanced attitude and a glimmering of self confidence in practice.

From 12 stone a week before marriage, I am now 10. Now 36 years old, I have regained the body I was proud of as a teenager but then neglected. I did suffer from a duodenal ulcer, lumbar arthritis, chronic sinus and chest trouble, partial deafness, obesity, heart palpitations, chronic bowel and liver trouble, myopia and astigmatism. (I wonder why Cecily married me!)

My eyesight has improved considerably, symptoms of every other problem have been gone some eight weeks now.

I have matured somewhat in the past twelve weeks. Although calmer and more responsible with my patients and trying gently to work out individual treatments from fundamental principles, I still believe I must push myself far and fast and hard. A sense of urgency for some reason. The new methods are becoming a gossip item in the pensioners' club and your seeds are floating on the breath of old ladies' conversation landing here and there to sprout slowly. They are coming − asking "...Mrs. Smith has too much acid, do you think I might...you put Mrs. Jones on fresh fruit and vegetables and she says she feels wonderful...what about me?" The wonder and truth and beauty of it all is that it works and people feel it, know it and believe it. And you showed me how as I show others.

I'm much older and wiser and sadder. The long hard path of the past few months makes me apprehensive about the years ahead. Caution about my desires, motives and judgement makes me sometimes wonder if I've gone mad and if all the other doctors are right. One day will someone show me, simply, the false premises on which I presently act and then will I have to go through the whole process again in reverse? I don't think I'd have the strength. I also question my real intellectual capacity. I know one's intellect should improve but, if past programming is hard to define, how can one judge if apparent increase in mental ability is such or merely an egotistical delusion. Do I suffer a fundamental lack of insight or is this an unrecognized and prolonged excretion of intellectual forms as part of a healing process. I might add that I've suffered little with physical crises yet. Can one draw a line between better knowledge and arrogance? Between self respect and pride? Is it justifiable objectivity or arrogance that leads me to seek criticism from one with higher standards than myself and do I not find such a person because they are rare or am I merely blind to my deficiencies? Also the writings of Bernard and others have placed a great strain on us. Sexual activity before we married was warm, loving and happy. Now that I accept the evolutionary and individual harmful effects of such activity, how far am I to inflict the attitude upon a loving wife. For myself, or any individual, aceticism is a free and valid choice. But when another person is already within the sphere of influence and activity, can a line be drawn between restriction of freedom and free choice.

I have told you all this as best answer to you question. How else could I describe what I thought of your book. It is brilliant, a guide to all paths, a friend, a comforter. I sent a copy to Professor Julius Sumner Miller, an American teacher of Physics who a show here for school children which is superb. The ABC gave me his address as 16711 Cranbrook Ave., Torrance, California 90504 if you feel it right to contact him.

Have you seen 'Nuclear Evolution – Discovery of the Rainbow Body' by Christopher Hill, University of Trees Press, Ca. 1977? Most Interesting.

Having read George Ohsawa's "Body of Judgement", Zen macrobiotic theory and practice is disappointing. Where is the defect between theory and practice, or is there a flow in the Ying–yang conception of creation?

In Australia there is a need for a small cheap paperback that contains basic anatomy, physiology, nutrition, health and disease, self treatment, etc. much of which could be condensed from your writings. I have a few chapters in my head, if you are of such mind we could perhaps publish a joint venture. There are the usual problems with multiplicity of half baked books in the shops and very confused populace and it is, as I'm sure you know, tedious to handwrite similar lists for each person.

Two years ago I read 'The Master Game' by Robert S. DeRopp. In it he discusses his opinion that psychedelic drugs may be useful because they may give 'a glimpse of the mountain top' also a warning that they might, with repeated use, exhaust or deplete certain inherent abilities such that a 'natural trip' might eventually become impossible. I have experimented heavily with mushrooms, discovering that they were a tool to self analysis and after some horrendous trips, began to experience peace and calm in them such as never experienced before. Also much imagery of color and beauty. Now, some of the time, I feel a similar serenity in ordinary consciousness and frequently experience the same decategorization of thought which allows what I call 'free thinking'. I am in two minds if ever to trip again. In some ways I view the natural psychedelics as medicines for the mind and as a personal rationalization, sincerely believe they were of great benefit to me previously. However, any drug is abused. I 'feel' that a trip might help me solve some problems and also give me a different view of a different mountain. Then again it might be dangerous or, ultimately, restrict potential spiritual development. If you are of mind to comment I would appreciate it. Also I am still relying heavily on smoking for relaxation and the ability to cope with hard times. Yoga exercises, breathing and meditation all help, but presently not enough. Does true tranquility come with time. If the wheel is inexorable and if 'that which has a face, has a back' is true then how does one find happiness en route to the goal. After a good day I relax and think 'well, the greatest success leads to the greatest failure...' and become neurotic and out comes the dope. Then I can accept a concept such as life is a charade, a projection and, death being the beginning and not the end, life doesn't matter. But that doesn't help the next morning when the mortgage is still due and still no money in the bank and I can't break security programming.

Please forgive me for being so demanding. It helps to talk and I believe you understand that which I am expressing poorly and inadequately. I really wonder if smoking just makes me more confused.

Well, my friend, my thoughts are with you and of your work. May you always live in Love and Happiness. Thank you for everything.

Dr. Michael Stanton, M.D., Atlantic Arcade, 2468 Pacific Highway, Mermaid Beach, Queensland 4218, Australia, July 29, 1979

HEALING

Dear Vik, Thanks for answering my letter, as busy as you are, you always take the time to write me back! You are wonderful!

I know someday the Spirit will connect us, and I will be able to talk to you in person. There are so many questions I have to ask about different things. We have been bringing about healing crisis ourselves, can't afford to pay the high price of what some practitioners charge. You have helped us tremendously! Your books and lectures opened our eyes and I use your books as reference for all those who are interested in cleaning out their bodies.

We find ourselves going through a lot of predicaments where we are being challenged! By our friends, loved ones, and medical doctors. Boy, oh boy, negative reactions! And I know only those who have gone through a healing crisis themselves know what it is like.

As you know, we are being tested everyday! We are being faced with death everyday, as members of our families are dying of chronic diseases. The conventional medicine isn't healing them of course, and it is one funeral after another.

We are working for our needs in San Diego, and there is nothing keeping us here and we can leave anytime. My children are 10 and 8 and it kills me to put them into another year of the Public School System crap. They have been going through a healing crisis also, right along with us. Their irises are changing color from Brown to Blue and it's beautiful to see all the repairing and healing going on in their bodies!

We live our lives with Yogic philosophies, and find ourselves wanting to be with the same.

I know you must get a lot of letters like mine asking you the same thing, as you have a great following.

We have lived off of the land, know how to use and put back. We have traveled looking and searching for what is within ourselves. We've gone through our programming, had a few primals and gotten rid of most of our negative emotions.

You will know how truthful we are by our vibrations.

If there is a chance that you can find room for us, we would be overjoyed! We are hard workers, and very devoted to You. Please keep us in mind as our paths are the same I am sure.

We are still healing ourselves, I am opening a closed lesion in my right lung, 7 months pregnant, feeling better everyday. Thank God for iridology! I have been studying on my own and it has been very valuable for me and my family.

I will understand Vik if you aren't into picking up brothers and sisters along the way as some are into bringing karma with them.

We are free to travel at any time, just let us know when you are ready. Because we are!

I finally found a mid-wife that is a Kundalini Yogi that will help coach my man and I to deliver our baby. San Diego is a tough place to get the word out. The consciousness is slowly rising around the country, but it is slow, not too many people are into Raw foods and Sprouts.

Our Love to you Shining Brother, Morning Star and Sunrise, Lynda and Gregg Carver, 131 Carnation, Imperial Beach, California 92032

ALMOST A FRUITARIAN

Dear Viktoras, I received your invitation to the Rainbow Gathering. I won't make it physically this time but perhaps in the future.

I just finished a half of a very good watermelon and am sitting in the San Luis Obispo Park writing this letter. I can hear and see all the things people do to grow themselves. Like BBQ roast pigs and such. That's the way it is and I must flow with it for now.

A good fruit story could be many things but the way I started could be based on growing up with the belief of nothing's impossible if you want it bad enough.

My mother raised 3 kids alone and stressed "Good nutrition" without getting fanatical about it. She never deprived me of anything sweet that I could get by with. I ate lots of candy she couldn't control. We always had fruit and all that and lots of vegetables. But you know most kids stick up their nose at cooked vegies a lot. We did, me mainly.

I had the history of illnesses: rheumatic fever, rheumatoid arthritis, scarlet fever, polio, etc. and never was in school much except the 5th and 6th grade which I didn't miss because I liked it, so I faked a lot the other time I guess. When I went into the Army I was physically disqualified once and given a deferment but got drafted later. I fought to get out and wouldn't go along with the regimentation fearing going to war and being ruled. So after that I realized the battle for freedom and finding who I was had just begun. My dad was the gung ho type so I don't have to tell you what a hard time I had when I saw him. He wanted me to be a "normal" person and play football like him.

After many jobs, starts, ties, jeans, and lifestyles I had always kept one secret and that was that I was differently aware than everyone I had ever met and had a connection with space as long as I can remember. I scored high in space relations in the ninth grade having never read a thing. The teachers were stumped as my score was 98 compared to the average trend of 65 to 75. And that was promotional stuff they taught.

Well, after being stuffed with hamburgers and steak and salad which I had a lot, but never felt the real need for it, I got kind of tired of the same old thing and thought many times of certain foods or maybe a vitamin that could make my body immortal. I never read or heard any body talk about this, it was my feeling. So I worked a job at a toy store department chain to lead me into many experiences not yet presenting a healthy diet but leading me in that direction at a fast pace. I met a fellow who worked with me who joined Jack LaLanne's Health Spa so the sparks started to fly. I worked out to the point of exhaustion to unkey myself from the pressures of work. Time was on my side; things would happen at regular intervals to teach me new feelings about our world. This working out had introduced me again to "Health Foods" and protein drinks which they had at a Bar as you walked in. I had a high protein drink four times a week with a diet of steak and salad and orders of wholewheat toast for breakfast. I usually had Chinese food or a Carl's hamburger for dinner when I did other than Chinese. Being that I eliminated fast due to much steam baths and fast long workouts helped prepare me to take on a tougher feat later on. I never ate breakfast all through Jr. and Sr. High school because I would throw up. I always reacted strangely health wise so it seemed until I met Mr. Kover who owned a little fruit and nut store in Costa Mesa that was after 4 years of 4 to 7 days a week at LaLannes and eating "Health Food" Ha! Ha!

I was in real estate by 1973 and my consciousness was being uncovered at a fast rate. I remember going into Ric's store and understanding without question what he would say to me about the body not needing anything that it does not already have. So I started by eating ¼ lb. mixed nuts and bottles of pasteurized grape juice all day and still occassionally having pizza, but I soon would throw those up too. So it was fruit and nuts to start and lots of dried fruit. Keep in mind that I never heard of a vegetarian before and could go for 1 year on fruit and nuts from Ric's store until I blew it on craving some of that good ol' Natural Food like Avo sandwiches for 1 day a month because after one day I could not live with myself or function on my bicycle. Sweating from cooked bread or anything occured and also weakness and cramps.

So from the start on fruit and nuts I never went through a weak period but did lose 14 pounds in two weeks.

I give credit to my cycling and good feeling when on raw fruits and nuts then. My balance and diet was fun and comfortable. I never worried about not ever getting enough of protein on all that other stuff because I always had the belief that we could live simply without it all somehow. And I knew I found it. Belief wasn't enough because it worked.

In my physical adventures the once sickly kid was all tan and weight increased to an even appearance. I am 5 ft. 7 in. and weigh from 119 to 124 depending on heavy exercise or not.

Juicing diet does not take weight off one now only a pound or less and I did a 17 day juice fast without losing at all. Three ten day orange juicers set me in an unlimited power source on my bicycle. I then was doing 60 miles a day 6 days a week in 1974 with amazing results often beating some of the most experienced riders in my area.

Before I got into cycling I met a fellow who presented me to Arnold Ehret's wonderful book; it was me throughout. I knew it was right for me and so with much family troubles with my mom's cancer and retarded brother I crunched through the diet with no fail after two years. But family pressure from home had me turning into a cashew addict until I almost killed myself with them; I would eat 2 to 5 lbs. a week and more! My friends would tell me I was a cashew drunk and said they will kill you in time at that rate. Well it was bad food or cashews so I moved out and switched to almonds and dates and felt less painful but I soon had cashew withdrawals and blew it on worse stuff like Bronner's chips and stuff from Vegie Restaurants that I never had a chance to experience. So I had to get it out of my system but knew it was wrong to do and bad for my body, but good for my satisfaction it seemed. One week it lasted with much fruit in-between thinking that I could wash the bad away. At least most of it from doing me too much harm. So I improved even more greatly after that and in 1975 was drinking 80 pounds of oranges a week and eating only dates for my bad habits. But 1975 I was 90% Fruitarian and raw salads for 2 months out of the year.

I took four day trips to see if hunger was in my head or stomach and found out it was in my head. I would go to the mountains and not miss food or juice and do with water for the four days. I feel now that if all food disappeared I could do without it all because I would have to and could accept it. I get mad at myself for having an occasional salad of greens but when I eat them I find out that I feel more down until it is out of me. I have been at limits where most people would return to steak only to hold even stronger realizing pure mind and body is more important than ever during stress and hard times.

Fruitarianism is fairly hard yet for me, but my readiness carries me through. After four years, those salads and sprouts still come up during the winter once a week or so. If I were away from all the influence of looking and thinking about the stuff there would be no problem but at least after only 6 years since the start of raw foods I find no desire to ever return to cooked food or even nuts, seeds, dried fruit, except juicy type dates. It's all an addiction. I know from all the days of dandruff, flaking skin, puffy eyes and body. I would even turn a shade lighter after popcorn without oil or an avo sandwich would puff up my belly and give me an awful headache. There is much more to be said of all this but it is simple if you believe you can do it. But if you can't do it then it would seem that a person doesn't believe it or understand it. I have met raw foodists who ate raw meat and tried to balance everything out in protein and vitamins, they soon fail and miss the point of it all. I have never met anyone who didn't realize that the sun is energy and that it is really the universe that plays the title role in delivering power to us. Though anyone with a strong desire could make it on the mucousless raw diet. One fellow I knew did a 40 day orange juice fast after only 6 months on raw fruit and vegetables and looked so good and well proportioned that you could not believe it. I saw him all the time and know that he did it truthfully. He was ready and is a true space brother. I've had many experiences with him that would fill a book.

Another fellow would eat avocados by the truck load a year who called himself a fruitarian, but was so addicted to avo's that he returned to a cooked diet not being able to go further into any spiritual awareness at all. I could never talk to him about anything except fruit, so it got monotonous after two years of keeping my tail in.

In the last year I have seen my past lifetimes being replayed in my mind and thoughts. I know much of how I got here, and in much detail. I felt this at an early age but could never get it together really or understand why I "saw" these past lifetimes. I retraced one of them and came up with a name that I had remembered seeing in a book from the Civil War, so things are steadily growing. I need to do some more cycling to clean out and it doesn't help a lot. I explained this in my way, so I hope this will be of help to somebody. I've done much checking on Ehret and know some dazzling things about him. Later I'll tell you. The winds getting wild now.

Lots of Love,
Mike Moore, P.O. Box 940, Morro Bay, California, 93442

FRUITARIAN ARTIST

Dear Friends, Thank you for your interest. If you have people who want to see or talk to a person who has become a 100% raw foodist, eating fruit and salad vegetables only, with great benefit, all in a cold climate like Toronto, I am happy to be of whatever service I can. Many people seem to have some notion that the healthiest diet will make you less resistant to cold; which is a contradiction from the start, isn't it?

Of course I have dreams of going to a warmer climate but have recently been studying Dr. Lovewisdom's ideas on "Paradise Building" that it is possible and should be done anywhere. I am getting in the last few months a growing desire, an obsession or mania in fact, to leave the city and I will soon. It strikes me that it would definitely be a good service to demonstrate (and hopefully find out for myself) that one can live on home grown fruit and salad all year in a cold climate...so maybe I can manage to bang my head back on straight somehow and stop dreaming of California or other southern USA places that I think I would so much like to go.

The result of raw food diet that intrigues me most is the way my paintings have become fabulously brilliant–colored as I never could paint before so that people who see them like to stare and stare and stare at them and say they have never seen anything like it before. Throughout all history, it seems, every artist has had blood poisoning and has been restricted to how brilliantly he could use color. Have you heard of any other artists experiencing this result?

Best wishes.

Sincerely,
Joe Alexander

FRUITARIANISM IN THE HINTERLAND

"It is impossible to live on a fruit–diet in a northern climate...the winters are too cold!" Sound familiar? It is the same argument I found myself continually confronted with all during my transition and beyond, by virtually everyone I knew. If you are finding yourself haunted by that little sentence, don't despair! Sit back and enjoy – you should find this story interesting.

Currently I'm 21, living in a small town in northern Wisconsin, and am faring fairly well on such a diet, in spite of these winters. During the winter of 75–76, while out west, I began my transition; I was 18. My health had been on the wane for some time owing to having lived on a high—protein, "muscle—building" diet since age 12 and from having become involved with drugs as a consequence.

At the time I had problem acne, falling hair (a lot), more than 2 years of insomnia, and depression, frequently increasing fatigue despite my muscle size, bad breath, body odor and gas to name a few. I had also worn glasses since I was about 9.

At 16 I had decided to give up on the idea of doctors being any help for my then increasing acne and generally slipping health. For 2 years I ran the rounds of herbal teas, vitamins/minerals & mega—vitamin trips, certain raw food diets, mind—over—matter creeds, and even a look into psychology; all with little improvement. Then I came across the fruitarian arguments and idealisms (quite stunning at the time) and after giving it much heavy thought, decided to give it a most determined try. For as long as I live I shall always be quite pleased and happy that I did — the results alone are reward enough.

That is not to say, however, that everything went as smooth as silk and was one big rose garden; indeed far from it, but it was well worth it. I found, in the beginning that I didn't even miss meat, eggs, milk or cheese nor have I ever craved them. I did crave toasted whole—wheat break and Granola—type cereals. I later found this to be typical of transitioners. I also quickly acquired a taste for yogurt (which I had disliked) and for fresh carrot juice. With an acid—saturated body, such as mine was, anybody will find fresh carrot juice to be the "liquid gold" it is sometimes called.

In time I would buy a juicer and be drinking as much as a quart a day (a little much); however, my body eventually no longer required it and hence I stopped "imbibing". Similar to carrot juice, my body would continue to crave grains for my first year. The craving was so strong at times that, after having gone a few days without, I would give in and sometimes scarf down as much as a ½ a loaf at a time. It would be 1½ years before I would no longer desire yogurt and 2 before I would be able to go for extended periods without vegies.

While out West I had found myself going through a series of mini—heart attacks, due to drugs I had previously taken. These attacks were mini in the sense they didn't kill me, but I can assure you they received my undivided attention for their duration, 6 of these I remember distinctly. All occurred before I returned here.

I found pot to increase my blood pressure and so stopped smoking it. I never liked alcohol and so it never was a problem. Once you reach a certain stage on this diet you find there is a kind of continuous—even—keeled high (awareness, if you will) which is the result of an internal balance or "calm". You also learn to be physiologically aware of where your emotions are coming from. A very pleasant feeling.

My teeth also bothered me for sometime. In the very beginning, for a short period, they turned a funny yellow color which no amount of brushing could remove. Later on I found them to be rather loose at times. They strengthened up though and none fell out, even though such had been prophecized by a few I knew.

In the 6 months out West my acne, insomnia, and virtually entire depressed feeling had disappeared. My once continuously oily skin and scalp were now bone dry, owing to sun and diet, with the skin peeling somewhat and the scalp registering a dramatic increase in dandruff production. Hair continued to fall, sometimes in seemingly increasing amounts, but, like others, I reasoned that to be part of the overall cleansing process. Dandruff is still around, but in subdued amounts. To date I have not gone bald and my hair grows well.

After returning, for a period of 6 months, my "wisdom teeth" gums swelled up at almost regular intervals. This was painful enough at times to make closing my mouth difficult. I steadfastly refused to get them pulled inspite of repeated urgings, and in the end they stopped swelling permanently. Very recently I've noticed a few cavities forming there, which is annoying, but I am confident with proper care these will be made to disappear. In part they are caused by food particles becoming stagnant there. At any rate, they don't hurt.

Usually once a day I brush my teeth with a mixture of baking soda and salt with occasional lemon rub–downs. Aside from the cavities my teeth are white and gums healthy.

There are other incidents that have occurred from time to time in the past, now if faced with the same situation again, I would re–do it; for although eliminations can't be considered fun, neither is being sick as a dog.

In this land of frosty–white beards and numb–tipped noses, where I have often risen in the morn to find the air temp. from −15 deg. to −30 deg. F, you can bet that 'longies' come in handy for most of the winter. Still, in view of everything, I feel that the cold affects me less than most. Not only can I go all day without eating and not feel chilled, I am also quite unworried about 'catching a cold' as most are. Often I go out into the icy sub–zero blasts with little more than a shirt on to get the mail, for instance, or simply a breath of fresh air. I just stay out till cold.

My diet consists of bananas, apples, and oranges of which, when things are all going well, I eat one meal a day, consisting of about 4 to 8 pieces. Overeating is the problem most often associated with a diet such as this for 2 reasons. First we have been trained most of our lives to do just that and as a result, old habits die hard. The second reason is that our body cells have been starved for so long, owing to bad diet, that they all call out for food at once and so a person overeats. In time this comes under control, but its not always easy.

I was eating avacadoes for awhile to see if fat was necessary in the diet, but soon grew tired of them. Until recently I was eating dried fruit; most, I have found, like dried figs best. Eventually you lose your taste for this too. If I eat nuts on this diet for any length of time, they will give me bowel problems. I still eat vegies from time to time, whenever I feel they are necessary, however, partly out of idealism, I keep them to a minimum.

To keep bodily functions working properly, one has to learn how much water to drink each day; it will differ with the individual. Too much and the cold affects you; too little and the bowels might not move properly after awhile. Generally the water I drink is either filtered or distilled.

I'm not making claims to perfect health or anything like that, but I do say that if given time, patience, common sense, and a little smarts, it is possible to live on a fruit diet in a northern climate. All in all most of my symptoms have disappeared; I still wear glasses and hope to be rid of them in about a year or so. During my first 2 years I often felt weak or tired and though I'm no Hercules now, I'm not weak either. My muscles are lean, well defined and toned and all without lots of exercise being necessary. I believe I can out run the average person.

If you are contemplating a transition, you should realize that it may become difficult at times and seemingly tax your patience and will power beyond the limit, but if you hang in there you will find the end rewards worth it. In time, living on a fruit and vegetable diet should be snap.

As a final word, about the only bad thing about a fruitarian diet is that you don't often meet someone who eats like you! It would be nice to hear from those of you out there on such a diet, especially those of you living in the near vicinity. Write to the editors of this publication and they will give you my address.

Good Eating and Good Health to You All!

Phil Aldenbrook

AS A TREE GROWS THE SPIRIT UNFOLDS

Dear Viktoras:

I wanted to share some of my more significant and basic feelings of experiences in my life the last several years. Indeed it has been an evolutionary period of my life, in which you have played an instrumental part.

As I sit at the bedside of a wonderful brother in a hospital in Hawaii, it comes to my mind and heart the pains of the past.

This man, unable to function in daily living as most of us know it, was injured severely in an automobile accident one year ago; the result, being bodily damaged beyond repair. Why is he there, unable to speak or walk? Yet in all his pain and loneliness, his one hand squeezes mine, compassionately, responding to love, by giving love. Perhaps he is there to help touch other souls and open us all to giving more thanks...more love.

Reflections of myself, five years ago, following an automobile accident. In a circle bed, for many months, unable to move, staring at one square on the ceiling, metal tongs inserted into my skull to hold the damaged spine in place. So alone, no one there holding my hand. If only I could feel the caring of another.

These months of slow repair and recuperation brought about an amazing healing to the damaged areas, but amazing damage to other areas.

Months of accumulated drugs, no exercise, nutrition-deficient meals, and stressful days of thought, brought me to a healed spinal cord, but weakened the rest of me in almost every imaginable area.

Back on my feet a year later, I began hemorrhaging on and off vaginally for the next year. I became extremely anemic from blood loss, and was experiencing pains in the lower abdomen beyond description. Little did I know that a cancerous growth was causing the uterus to hemorrhage.

My husband Steven, our three children, and I, sold all our posessions and began to search across the country for the answer to this traumatic situation within my body.

Specialists and doctors from all walks of medicine gave their suggestions and methods of treatment. All seemed to offer ideas which did nothing at all to ease the condition. A gynecologist in Oregon even prescribed a hormone injection which, if I had taken it as he directed, would have caused an increase in malignant growth; for that was one side affect of the drug. Needless to say, I refused to follow his advice.

Our family's savings were depleted to nothing. Frustration and weakness was growing daily. I had been reading a book which had fascinated me for a long time.

The "Survival Into The 21st Century" book was telling of the miraculous things which could be done by treating a body with a raw food diet, green chlorophyll juices from wheatgrass, living a life of love, and being one with the God within us all.

A strong feeling told me to contact this man Viktoras Kulvinskas. Through the health institute he co-founded in Boston, I obtained his phone number. Immediately I had Steven call him and share our situation with him, and ask his advice.

From the moment he answered the phone, he gave nothing less than 150% of his love and attention to my problem. He requested, without hesitation, that I come to stay at his home and center, though it was not complete or open to people at the time. Overwhelmed and hopeful, I accepted the invitation and flew there, feeling guided from above.

The next few weeks of my life were emerged in a therapy which was not only going to bring my body toward renewed good health, but turn the tide of my life mentally, emotionally, and spiritually also.

Still hemorrhaging profusely each day, Viktoras immediately began daily doses of green chlorophyll juice from wheatgrass. Within three to four days, the bleeding ceased. The next days to follow brought more green juice and vegetable juice therapy, both orally and implant; with enemas also to get the intestinal tract free of built up toxins which had to be expelled; so did the emotional and mental poisons (which also had been built up and shut in for years) have to surface, be released, and eliminated from my life also.

During this traumatic time emotionally, Viktoras was constantly there with me; supporting, being firm in his advice, yet a more loving soul you could not find. No other work to which he was committed entered the next days.

My need was great. And so the space in his life was geared toward that need, no matter the time, energy, or patience required. Hours I cried, releasing pain from years of stressful events, one after another. Hours this man remained nearby.

And as more and more and more dark poisons were eliminated, the stronger I came to feel each day. The chlorophylrich juices were a rejuvenator to my blood and body cells. So amazing...I would not have believed it, had it not been happening before my eyes, and within this body.

It is now summertime and my children needed to be with me. So, after Viktor's loving invitation, we had the children flown to join me during my healing crisis while Steven remained at our home in Michigan with his work.

The next weeks found the children learning and growing with their bodies, and spirits too. They received ounces of wheatgrass to help their growth and transitioning toward a more raw food diet. They added so much love and simplicity to the surroundings as only children can. Perhaps this was one of the most outstanding sharings to come from these next few weeks.

Through all of Viktoras's years of nutritional expertise, there was something new of love in this life he came to experience. That being the love that can be shared and felt from a truly bonded family. Our family seemed to open that particular door for him, and made the exchange of love and healing so whole, for all involved.

As the most intense crisis of the cleansing passed, the end of summer was nearing. At this point Viktoras again extended his open arms and home center for my husband to join us; as many life changing decisions were in the air for our family.

After many months of frustration and painful days, on all levels, we were, at last, to a point where it seemed time to be in a place on earth to settle in, repair and rebuild all of our bodies and souls; also to share with others the many experiences and lessons we had come through, in hopes that they might be helpful in some way.

I knew that for my body to climb back to renewed health, that ocean and sunshine would be instrumental. As our family (of which Viktoras had become a part) shared ideas of our alternatives, we came to feel that the islands of Hawaii were calling us the strongest at this time.

Viktoras not only had intervened at the last possible moment to reverse my road to ill health, but his teaching and sharing with us of his knowledge and love turned our lives toward carrying out these messages (and more) to all in our path.

He supported our choice to go to Hawaii and it seemed that a permanent life connection had been made between he and I, and also my whole family.

I had an instinctive feeling that the sun and ocean would be ideal to begin our mission to aid others in their life stresses and dis–eases.

During our first few months in Hawaii, it became so clear to me the real need for a place where people on the islands could come to cleanse their bodies, hearts, minds, and lives. To aid others in beginning to experience love and life to its fullest potential was, and is, my primary focus.

We felt the greatest way others could benefit through our experiences was (1) through a center for detoxification, nutritional guidance, and learning in many areas; and (2) writings in book form of our feelings on healing the whole self (projected and expressed through our own life experiences, knowledge, and intuitive natures). These are the goals that my family and I are presently working toward.

Of course, the road to a new body and healthy living is slow, and requires much discipline and patience. The conditions we bring ourselves to, through our attitudes and ways of living and eating, are there from years of wrong–living. Therefore, it can only be overcome by patiently adhering to a healthy plan of daily living for as long as needed, according to our individual situations. Do not be driven to frustration by the difficulty, pains, etc., involved in the rebuilding processes. You will be rewarded 100–fold for your new way of living.

Here I am, living simply and peacefully, continuing my transformation, bodily and spiritually. Hawaiian land for our coming center is within sight now, and my forthcoming book with Steven is near; to relate, in detail and love, the life I am living today, and how I arrived at this most living, magical space in time in my life.

Anyone in need of nutritional guidance, counsel, cleansing, sharing of nature and awareness (amidst waterfalls and sunshine), relaxation, or any services of love which my family will be offering, are welcome to our island home and center...or simply write:

Tree and Family
P.O. Box 1309

Kihei, Maui, Hawaii
96753

Children are more than welcome, as a large part of our activities involve groups of children.

It is still one beautiful wonder to my being, how just a few weeks with this man, Viktoras Kulvinskas, could so dramatically change the outlook of my whole life, inside and out. His total love and faith, and commitment to others, is truly a message which we would all do well to hear. For only through the path of pure love and truth can all aspects of ourselves be healed and whole.

Here I choose to share a moment of feelings and realizations of Steven; shared with me, written to me, of me, and as it now appears in my memoirs:

"My Tree of life"

"Seems my life is making such gigantic thrusts upward in self–growth since spending my life with you. Your warmth, your total, unconditional love you give each moment, is so beautiful, and needed by all

Were it not for the day of unbending truth which you opened my heart to, years ago, my life would not be the joyous experience that it is today. No other being or influence has been so essential to my physical, mental, and spiritual health.

There have been moments when your self–discipline and firmness on the path has seemed so out of sorts to me But today, I've come to see clearly that it has been that discipline and steadfastness which has been my most special teacher in bringing myself to being the whole person that I am. That firmness, yet at the same time your loving softness which is your way, truly is the balance which so many people today must strive to achieve.

Thank you, Tree, for being you; being a friend.   My heart and soul give love to you. You have helped make my life whole, so that I might know all the love and happiness there is to know for us all.

You are one of God's special angels. I am thankful beyond words, each day, for the blessing He has bestowed upon me...

To serve His plan with you...

and simply,...to love.

To me, you are a healing, Tree.

Loving you endlessly,

Steven"

My reason for sharing what I have in this article, is to show how the spiral of love works in healing the body, mind, and spirit. Just as the love and caring from Viktoras opened many needed doors for my health and being...my evolution, toward God's ways of love and caring, then shared with others (as I have shown coming from Steven), is the healing catalyst which can be a never–ending cycle between us all.

Tree

Appendix

FOOTNOTES AND REFERENCES

PART III, SECTION I: THE RESONANT BRAIN

1. Rowan, W., Proc. Boston Soc. Nat. Hist. 38:147–189, 1926.
2. Bissonnette. T. H., J. Exptl. Zool. 58:281–320, 1931.
3. Bissonnette, T. H., Proc. Roy. Soc. London B110:322–336, 1932.
4. Baker, J. R. and Ranson, R. M., Proc. Roy. Soc. London B110:313–322, 1932.
5. Bissonnette, T. H., J. Heredity 27:171–80, 1936.
6. Yeates, N. T. M., J. Agri. Sci. 39:1–43, 1949.
7. Wright, P. L., Anat. Record 100:593–602, 1948.
8. Pearson, O. P. and Enders, R. K., J. Exptl. Zool 95:21–35, 1944.
9. Hammond Jr., J., Vitamins and Hormones XII:190–191, 1954.
10. Kitay, J. I. and Altshule, M.D., "The Pineal Gland," Harvard Univ. Press, 1954.
11. Fiske, V. M. and Greep, R. O., Endocrinol. 64:175–85, 1959.
12. Fiske, V.M. et al., Endocrinol. 66:489–91, 1960.
13. Wurtman, J., Hospital Practice 4:32–37, 1969.
14. Lerner, A. B., Scientific American 205;98–101, July 1961.
15. Hammond Jr., J., Vitamins and Hormones XII:167–169, 1954.
16. Hammond, Jr., J., "Effects of Artificial Lighting in the Reproductive and Pelt Cycles of Mink," Cambridge, 1954.
17. Wolfson, A., Condor 47:95–127, 1945.
18. Bissonnette, T. H., Anat. Record 63:159–168, 1935.
19. Bissonnette, T. H., Endocrinol. 22:92–103, 1938.
20. Bissonnette, T. H., Quart. Rev. Biol. 8:201–208, 1933.
21. Scott, H. M. and Payne, L. F., Poultry Sci. 16:90–96, 1937.
22. Ringoen, A. R., Am. J. Anat.
23. Benoit, J., et al., Compt. Rend. Soc. Biol. 144:1206–1211, 1950.
24. Granit, R., Acta. Physiol. Scand 4:118–124, 1942.
25. Yogo, E., Jap. J. Ob. Gyn. 23:149–159, 1940.
26. Sakaguti, M., Jap. J. Ob. Gyn. 25:91–103, 1942.
27. Yagi, K., Jap. J. Ob. Gyn 25:153–6, 1942.
28. Benoit, J., Compt. Rend. Soc. Biol. 118:669–691, 1935.
29. Benoit, J., Bull. Biol. France et Belg. 71:393–437, 1937.
30. Benoit, J., Compt. Rend. 201:359–62, 1935.
31. Benoit, J., Compt. Rend. Soc. Biol. 120:136–139, 1935.
32. Benoit, J., and Kehl, R. Compt. Rend. Soc. Biol. 131:89–93.
33. Benoit, J., Compt. Rend. Soc..Biol. 127:909–914. 1938.
34. Ott, John N.: "My Ivory Cellar," 20th Century Press, Chicago, 1958.
35. Ott, John N., Ann. N. Y. Acad. of Sci. 117:626–629, 1964.
36. Ott, John N., op. cit. p. 632.
37. Ott, John N., op. cit. p. 632–634.
38. Fuchs, J., Deut. Med. Wschr. 78:1054–56, 1933.

39. Wassner, L., Med. Wschr. 8:530–535, 1954.
40. Hollwich, F., Acta Neurovegetativa 9:330–336, 1954.
41. Lobban, M. C. and Tredre, B., J. Physiol. (London) 170:29P
42. Boyd, E., et al., Endocrinol. 32:27–32, 1943.
43. Shanks, S. C. and Kerley, P., "A Textbook of X–ray Diagnosis," p. 51, Sanders, 1957.
44. Zacharias, L. and Wurtman, R. J., Science 144:1154–55, 1964.
45. Gerard, R., "Differential Effects of Colored Lights on Psychophysiological Functions," Ph. D. Thesis, U. C. L. A., April 1958.
46. Jone, E., "Papers of Psychoanalysis," pp. 297–304, London, 1948.
47. Ott, John N., Optometric Weekly, Sept. 5, 1968.
48. Dawson, H., "The Physiology of the Eye," pp. 83–4, London, 1949.
49. Stevens, S. S., Ed., "Handbook of Experimental Psychology," p. 825, N. Y. 1951
50. Pettit, E., Astrophys. J. 75:185, 1932.
51. Birren, F., "Color Psychology and Color Therapy," University Books, N. Y., 1961.
52. Gurtovoi, G. K., Probl. Fiziol. Opt. 9:90–104, 1950.
53. Shevareva, V. K., Probl. Fiziol. Opt. 9:131–133, 1950.
54. Shevareva, V. K., op. cit., p. 127–130.
55. Medical World News, Feb. 21, 1969, p. 56.
56. Dewan, F., Am. J. Ob. Gyn. 99:1016–19, 1967.
57. Dewan, F., personal communication, March 1969.
58. Robertson, E. G., Brain 77:232–251, 1954.
59. Marshall, C. et al., AMA Arch. Neurol. and Psych. 69:760–765, 1953.
60. Delay, J. et al., "The Rorschach and the Epileptic Personality," p. 32, Logos Press, N. Y., 1958.
61. Reich, W., quoted in Delay, J. et al., op. cit., p. 25.
62. Kinsey, A. C. et al., "Sexual Behavior in the Human Female," pp. 704–707, Saunders, Philadelphia, 1953.
63. Kinsey, A. C. et al., op. cit., pp. 630–632.

PART IV, SECTION III: THE IMPORTANCE OF NUTRITION IN EYE DEVELOPMENT AND VISION FUNCTION.

1. Lane, B. C., "Myopia triggered by sustained accommodation and deficit–inducing diets," Journal of the Optical Society of America, 1979, 69, 1477.
2. Lane, B. C., "Myopia prevention and reversal: New data confirms interaction of accommodative stress and deficit–inducing nutrition." New Dynamics of Preventive Medicine, Vol. 6, Houston, TX: International Academy of Preventive Medicine, 1980.
3. Lane, B. C., "Human myopia related to interaction of sustained accommodation and anomalous concentrations of chromium and calcium," AAAS Abstracts of Papers. Washington, D. C.: American Assn for the Advancement of Science, 1980, p. 153, No. 434.
4. Lane, B. C., "Elevation of Intraocular Pressure with Daily, Sustained Reading and Closework Stimulus to Accommodation." (Master's Thesis, State University of New York, State College of Optometry, N. Y., N. Y., 1973). Ann Arbor, MI; University Microfilms International, 1980, Publication No. 13–14, 525.
6. Lane, B. C., "Chromium and accommodative weakness." Proceedings of the International Society for Eye Research, Vol. 1, 1980, 72.
7. Lane, B.C., "Calcium, chromium, protein, sugar and accommodation in myopia," Documenta Ophthalmologica: Proceedings of the 3rd International Conference on Myopia, 1980. (The Hague, Netherlands) In press.
8. Lane, B. C., "Elevation of intraocular pressure with daily, sustained closework stimulus to accommodation, lowered tissue chromium and dietary deficiency of ascorbic acid (vitamin C)." Documenta Ophthalmologica: Proceedings of the Third International Conference on Myopia, 1980. (The Hague, Netherlands) In press.
9. Lane, B. C., "Elevation of intraocular pressure (IOP) with sustained stimulus to accommodation, lowered tissue chromium and dietary deficiency of ascorbic acid." AAAS Abstracts of Papers. Washington, DC: American Assn for the Advancement of Science, 1981, p. 509.
10. Lane, B. C., "Nutrition and myopia: New data from hair mineral analysis," American Journal of Optometry and Physiological Optics, 1981, 58, in press.
11. Lane, B. C., "Deficit nutriture, accommodative stimulus and ocular hypertension," American Journal of Optometry and Physiological Optics. In press.

12. Hunter, B. T., Some nutritional shortchanging from food processing," Journal of the International Academy of Preventive Medicine, 1977, 4(2), 59–71.
13. Mertz, W., "Effects and metabolism of glucose tolerance factor," In D. M. Hegsted (Ed. Com. Chmn.) Nutrition Reviews' Present Knowledge in Nutrition (4th ed.) New York: The Nutrition Foundation, 1976, 232–240.
14. Schroeder, H. A. "The role of chromium in mammalian nutrition," American Journal of Clinical Nutrition, 1968, 21, 230–244.
15. Kelly, T. Stuart–Black, "Myopia or expansion glaucoma," Documenta Ophthalmologica: Proceedings of the Third International Conference on Myopia, 1980. (The Hague, Netherlands) In press.
16. Linkswiler, H. M., "Calcium," In D. M. Hegsted (Ed. Com. Chmn.), Nutrition Reviews' Present Knowledge in Nutrition. (4th ed.) New York: The Nutrition Foundation, 1976, 232–240.
17. Margen, S., Chu, J.–Y., Kaufman, N. A., & Calloway, D. H., "Studies in calcium metabolism:I, The calciuretic effect of dietary protein," American Journal of Clinical Nutrition, 1974, 27, 584–589.
18. Becker, B., "Vanadate and aqueous humor dynamics," Proctor lecture. Investigative Ophthalmology and Visual Science, 1980, 19(10), 1156–1165.
19. Cobble, R. S., & Lynd, F. T., "Preliminary observations on orgotein treatment of canine cataract," Modern Veterinary Practice, 1977, 58, 1009–1012.
20. Varma, S. D., Ets, T. K., & Richards, R. D., "Protection against superoxide radicals in rat lens," Ophthalmological Research, 1977, 9, 421–431.
21. Bhuyan, K. C., & Bhuyan, D. K., "Superoxide dismutase of the eye: Relative function of superoxide dismutase and catalase in protecting the ocular lense from oxidative damage," Biochimica et Biophysica Acta, 1978, 542, 28–38.
22. Crouch, R., Priest, D. G., & Duke, E. J., "Superoxide disutase activities of bovine ocular tissues," Experimental Eye Research, 1978, 27, 503–509.
23. Lynd, F. T., & McDonald, N., "The treatment of senile cataracts in dogs by the intra–ocular injection of superoxide dismutase," Journal of Veterinary Pharmacology and Therapy, 1978, 1, 85–88.
24. Varma, S. D., Kumar, S., &Richards, R. D., "Protection by ascorbate against superoxide (02) injury to lens,"Investigative Ophthalmology and Visual Science, 1979, 18 (ARVO Supplement), 98.
25. Bhuyan, K. C., Bhuran, D. K., & Podos, S. M., "Hydrogen peroxide and oxygen − free radicals in triggering cataractogenesis," Proceedings of the International Society for Eye Research, Volume I, 1980, 92.
26. Kulvinskas, V., "Survival into the 21st Century," Omangod Press, Woodstock Valley, Ct.
27. Kulvinskas, V., "Love Your Body," Omangod Press, Woodstock Valley, Ct.
28. Kulvinskas, V., "Sprout for the Love of Every Body," Omangod Press, Woodstock Valley, Ct.

PART IV, SECTION IV: SATKARMASADANA PART I

1. "Hatha Yoga," by Theos Bernard. Samuel Weiser, New York.
2. "Yogic Therapy," by Kuvalayananda & Vinekar. Kaivalyadhama, Lonavala. p. 78.
3. "Yoga: The Method of Re–integration," by A. Danielou. University Books, New York. p. 18.
4. Private communication from Dr. M. L. Gharote.
5. "The Satkarmasangrahah," Compiled from ancient manuscripts by Dr. R. G. Harshe. Kaivalyadhama, Lonavala.
6. Yoga Mimamsa, XIV (1, 2), 15–33.
7. "Asanas," by Kuvalayananda. Kaivalyadhama, Lonavala.
8. "Pranayama," by Kuvalayananda. Kaivalyadhama, Lonavala.
9. "Rejuvenation through Dietic Sex Control," by Dr. Raymond Bernard. Essence of Health, P. O. Box 2821, Durban, South Africa.
10. "Gheranda Samhita," Lesson III, p. 89–91.
11. Yoga Mimamsa, XVII (3, 4) 79–80.

PART IV, SECTION IV: SATKARMASADANA PART II

1. Agnisara, by Swami Kuvalayananda. Yoga Mimamsa, Vol. VII, No. 3, pp. 195–199.
2. Private instruction from Dr. M. L. Gharote, Kaivalyadhama.
3. Gajakarani, by Swami Kuvalayananda, Yoga Mimamsa, Vol. XVIII, No. l, pp. 1–13.
4. Manibandha. "the Satkarma Sangrahad." Publ. by the Kaivalyadhama.
5. Private instructions from O. P. Tiwari, Kaivalyadhama.

6. Danda Dhauti, by Dr. M. L. Gharote, Yoga Mimamsa, Vol. XI, No. 3, pp. 39–44.
7. Dhauti, in Yoga Mimamsa Vol. II, No. 3, pp. 168–175.
8. X–Ray Experiments on Dhauti, Vol. II, No. 3, pp. 176–183.
9. "Yogic Therapy" by Srimat Swami Shivananda Saraswati (not to be confused with the person from Rishikesh by the same name). Publ. by Umachal Yogashram, Kamakya, Gauhati–10, Assam, India.
10. "Rational Fasting," by Arnold Ehret. Published by Ehret Literature Publishing Co., Beaumont, California, 92223.
11. "Raw Eating," by A. T. Hovannessian, Place Sanai, 2 Kamkar Ave., Tehran, Iran.

PART IV, SECTION IV: SATKARMASADANA PART III

1. What is Uddiyana? Yoga Mimansa Vol. l, pg. 9–14
2. What is Uddiyana? Yoga Mimansa Vol. XVI, No. l, pg. 1–16
3. Uddiyana. Yoga Mimansa Vol. IV., No. 4, pg. 318–319
4. A note on Uddiyana. Yoga Mimansa Vol. VI, No. 3, pg. 209
5. Hatha Yoga, by Theos Bernard. Published by Samuel Weiser, New York
6. Five Variations of Uddiyana, Yoga Mimansa Vol. XV, No. 2, pg. 25–35
7. Asanas by Kuvalayananda. Published by the Kaivalyandhama, Lonavala, India 410403
8. Pressure Changes in Internal Cavities During Uddiyana and Nauli, Yoga Mimansa Vol. XIII, No. 4, page 19–25
9. Cecal Constipation:
    Yoga Mimansa Vol. I., No. l, pg. 42–47
    Yoga Mimansa Vol. I., No. 2, pg. 114–125
    Yoga Mimansa Vol. I., No. 3, pg. 201–214
    Yoga Mimansa Vol. I., No. 4, pg. 257–262
10. Cecal Constipation:
    Yoga Mimansa Vol. XVI, No. l, pg. 33–40
    Yoga Mimansa Vol. XVI, No. 2, pg. 95–109
    Yoga Mimansa Vol. XVI, No. 3, pg. 201–214
    Yoga Mimansa Vol. XVI, No. 4, pg. 257–262
11. Survival Into the 21st Century, by Kulvinskas, Published by Omangod Press, Woodstock Valley, Ct. 06282
12. Mucusless Diet Healing System, by Arnold Ehret, Published by Ehret LiteraturePublishing Co., Beaumont, Ca. 92223
13. See reference 5.
14. Yogic Therapy by Kuvalayananda & Vinakar, Published by th Kaivalyadhama, see 7
15. Satkarmasangrahah, Published by Kaivalyadhama, see 7
16. Asvini Mudra, Yoga Mimansa Vol. VII, No. 2, pg. 97–107
17. Mayurasana, Yoga Mimansa Vol. XVI, No. 1 & 2, pg. 86
18. Physics for the Health Sciences, by Nave & Nave, Published by W. B. Saunders Co., Philadelphia,

PART IV, SECTION IV: CONSTIPATION AND OXYGENATED INTESTINAL IRRIGATION

1. Snyder, R., C. Trawger, S. Finema and C. Zoll, "Colonic Stasis in Chronic Arthritis," Arch Phys. Ther. 14:610 (1933).
2. Waddington, J., "Scientific Intestinal Irrigation and Ajuvant Therapy," The Bryan Publishers, Chicago. (1940) 309 pp.
3. Witsie, J.   "Chronic Intestinal Toxemia," William Wood & Company, Baltimore (1938) 268 pp.

PART IV, SECTION IV: EVIDENCE FOR INTESTINAL TOXEMIA

1. Bassler, A.: "Intestinal Toxemia", Medical Journal and Record, Vol 136, 1933, p 322.
2. Boeker, H.H.: "Autointoxication", Medical Journal and Record, Vol 128, Sept. 19, 1928, p 293.

3. Herter, C.A. and Kendall, A.I.: "The Influence of Dietary Alterations on the Types of Intestinal Flora", Journal of Biological Chemistry, Vol 7, 1909-10, pp 203-235.
4. Orten, J.M. and Newhaus, O.W.: Human Biochemistry, 9th ed., C.V. Mosby Company, St. Louis, Missouri, 1975, p 469.
5. Herter, op cit, p 216.
6. Cannon, P.R., Dragstedit, L.R., and Dragstedt, C.A.: "Intestinal Obstruction", Journal of Infectious Disease, Vol 27, 1920, pp 139-144.
7. Underhill, F.P. and Simpson, G.E.: "The Effect of Diet on the Excretion of Indican and the Phenols", Journal of Biological Chemistry, Vol. 44, 1920, pp 69-97.
8. Torrey, J.C.: "The Regulation of the Intestinal Flora of Dogs Through Diet", Journal of Medical Research, Vol 39, 1918-19, pp 415-447.
9. Folin, O. and Denis, W.: "The Excretion of Free and Conjugated Phenols and Phenol Derivatives", Journal of Biological Chemistry, Vol 22, 1915, p 309.
10. Gerard, R.W.: "Chemical Studies on Intestinal Intoxication", Journal of Biological Vol 52, 1922, pp 111-124.
11. Cannon, op cit, pp 139-144.
12. Stone, H.B., Bernheim, B.M., and Whipple, G.H.: "Intestinal Obstruction: A Study of the Toxic Factors", Bulletin of The Johns Hopkins Hospital, Vol 23, No 256, 1912, pp 159-165.
13. Gerard, R.W.: "The Lethal Agent in Acute Intestinal Obstruction", Journal of the American Medical Association, Vol 79,.No 19, 1922, pp 1581-1584.
14. Whipple, G.H., Stone, H.B., and Bernheim, B.M.: "Intestinal Obstruction", Journal of Experimental Medicine, Vol 17, 1913, pp 286-307.
15. Gerard, R.W.. "Chemical Studies on Intestinal Intoxication", Journal of Biological Chemistry, Vol 52, 1922, pp 111-124.
16. Gerard, R. W.: "The Lethal Agent in Acute Intestinal Obstruction," Journal of the American Medical Association, Vol 79, No l9, 1922, pp 1581-1584.
17. Stone, H. B., Bernheim, B. M., and Whipple, G. H.: "Intestinal Obstruction: A Study of the Toxic Factors," Bulletin of the Johns Hopkins Hospital, Vol 23, No 256, 1912, pp 159-165.
18. Whipple, G. H., Stone, H. B., and Bernheim, B. M.: "Intestinal Obstruction," Journal of Experimental Medicine, Vol 17, 1913, pp 286-307.
19. Whipple, ibid, p 306.
20. Whipple, ibid, p 305.
21. Wilson, D. R., Ing, T. S., Metcalfe-Gibson, A., and Wrong, O. M.: "In Vivo Dialysis of Faeces as a Method of Stool Analysis. III. The Effect of Intestinal Antibiotics," Journal of Clinical Science, Vol 34, 1968, pp 211-221.
22. McDermott Jr, W. V., Adams, R. D., and Riddell, A. G.: "Ammonia Levels in Blood and Cerebrospinal Fluid," Proceedings of Society of Experimental Biology and Medicine, Vol 88, 1955, p 382.
23. McDermott, W., Adams, R. D.: "Eck-Fistula - A Cause of Episodic Stupor in Humans," Journal of Clinical Investigation, Vol 32, 1953, pp 587-588.
24. Phillips, G. B., Schwartz, R., Gabuzda, G. J., and Davidson, C. S.: "The Syndrome of Impending Hepatic Coma in Patients with Cirrhosis of the Liver Given Certain Nitrogenous Substances," The New England Journal of Medicine, Vol 247, No 7, 1952, pp 239-246.
25. Berger, R. L., Liversage, R. M., Chalmers, T. C., Graham, J. H. McGoldrick, D. M., and Stohlman Jr, F. S.: "Exchange Transfusion in the Treatment of Fulminating Hepatitis," The New England Journal of Medicine, Vol 274, No 9, 1966, pp 497-499.
26. Sherlock, S., Summerskill, W. H. J., White, L. P., Phear, E. A.: "Portal-Systemic Encephalopathy. Neurological Complications of Liver Disease," The Lancet, Vol 2, Sept 4, 1954, pp 453-457.
27. Visek, W. J., Kolodny, G. M., and Gross, P. R.: "Ammonia Effects in Cultures of Normal and Transformed 3T3 Cells," Journal of Cell Physiology, Vol 80, 1972, pp 373-382.
28. Williams, B. W.: "Importance of Toxemia Due to Anaeroibic Organisms in Acute Intestinal Obstruction and Peritonitis." The Lancet, Vol 1, April 30, 1927, pp 907-912.
29. Jawetz, E., Melnick, J. L., Adelberg, E. A.: Review of Medical Microbiology, 12th ed, Lange Medical Publications, Los Altos, California, 1976, pp 189-190.
30. Orten, op cit, p 471.

31. Herter, C. A.: "An Experimental Study of the Toxic Properties of Indol," NY Medical Journal, Vol 68, July 16, 1898, pp 89-93.
32. Korenchevsky, V.: "Autointoxications and Processes of Aging," Texas Rep Biology and Medicine, Vol 12, 1956, p 1016.
33. Bryan, G. T., Brown, R. R., and Price, J. M.: "Incidence of Mouse Bladder Tumors Following Implantation of Paraffin Pellets Containing Certain Tryptophan Metabolites," Cancer Research, Vol 24, 1964, pp 582-585.
34. Kerr, W. K., Barkin, M., Levers, P. E., Woo, S. K-C, and Menczyk, Z.: "The Effect of Cigarette Smoking on Bladder Carcinogens in Man," The Canadian Medical Association Journal, Vol 93, No 1, 1965, pp 1-7.
35. Herter, op cit, pp 203-235.
36. Robbins, S. L.: Pathologic Basis of Disease, 1st ed, W. B. Saunders Company, Philadelphia, 1974, p 520.
37. Folin, op cit, p 320.
38. Dubin, H.: "Physiology of the Phenols," Journal of Biological Chemistry, Vol 26, 1916, p 99.
39. Folin, op. cit, p 317.
40. Underhill, op cit, p 96.
41. Salant, W. and Kleitman, N.: "The Toxicity of Skatol," Journal of Pharmacology and Experimental Therapeutics, Vol 19, 1922, p 313.
42. Herter, op cit, p 215.
43. Bartle, H. J.: "Protein Intoxication," Medical Journal and Record, Vol 128, p 30.
44. Orten, op cit, p 335.
45. Challenger, F. and Walshe, J. M.: "Foeter Hepaticus," The Lancet, Vol 1, 1955, p 1240.
46. Orten, op cit, p 467.
47. Haubold, H. A.: "General Considerations Regarding Self-Intoxication," The NY Medical Journal, Vol 60, Dec 25, 1897, p 857.
48. Orten, op cit, p 468.
49. Orten, ibid, p 472.
50. Baker, C. E.: "The Physiological Effects of Certain Toxic Substances of Gastro-Intestinal Origin," Illinois Medical Journal, Vol 51, April 1927, pp 325-327.
51. Homewood, A. E.: The Neurodynamics of the Vertebral Subluxation, 3rd ed, Valkyrie Press, St Petersburg, Florida, 1977, pp 77-78.
52. Korenchevsky, op cit, p 1815.
53. Major, R. H.: "Relationship Between Certain Products of Metabolism and Arterial Hypertension," Journal of the American Medical Association, Vol 83, No 2, 1924, pp 81-84.
54. Barger, G. and Dale, H. H.: "Chemical Structure and Sympathomimetic Action of Amines," Journal of Physiological Chemistry, Vol 41, 1910-1911, pp 19-59.
55. Korenchevsky, op cit, pp 1006-1036.
56. Lane, W.A.: "Chronic Intestinal Stasis", Journal of Surgery, Gynecology and Obstetrics, Vol 16, 1913, p 600.
57. Bassler, A.: "Chronic Intestinal Toxemia", Medical Record, Vol 145, 1937, p 160.
58. Hertz, A.H.: "Chronic Intestinal Stasis", The British Medical Journal, Vol 1, April 19, 1913, p 817.
59. Binnie, J.F.: "Symptoms of Colonic Intoxication", Journal of American Medical Association, Vol 58, No 26, 1912, p 2011.
60. Bartle, op cit, p 63.
61. Satterlee, G.R.: "Chronic Intestinal Stasis", American Journal of Medical Science, Vol 152, 1916, p 729.
62. Underhill, op cit, p 96.
63. Lane, op cit, pp 600-606.
64. Satterlee, op cit, pp 727-738.
65. Hertz, op cit, pp 817-821.
66. Lucas, C.G.: "Symptomatology of Chronic Intestinal Stasis", Southern Medical Journal, Vol 17, No 9, 1924, pp 659-661.
67. Bartle, op cit, pp 63-66.

68. Tucker, John: "Intestinal Toxemia", Medical Clinics of North America, Vol 19, May 1936, pp 1819–1830.
69. Alverez, W.C.: An Introduction to Gastro–enterology, 4th ed, Paul B. Hoeber, Inc., New York, NY, 1948, p 638.
70. Guyton, A.C.: Textbook of Medical Physiology, 5th ed, W.B. Saunders Company, Philadelphia, 1976, p 674.
71. Whipple, G.H., Stone, H.B., and Bernheim, B.M.: "Intestinal Obstruction", Journal of Experimental Medicine, Vol 17, 1913, p 305.
72. Gerard, R.W.: "The Lethal Agent in Acute Intestinal Obstruction", Journal of the American Medical Association, Vol 79, No 19, 1922, p 1583.
73. Cannon, op cit, p 143.
74. Whipple, G.H., Stone, H.B., and Bernheim, B.M.: "Intestinal Obstruction", Journal of Experimental Medicine, Vol 17, 1913, p 322.
75. Soper, H.W.: "The Mucosa of the Rectum and Sigmoid Colon as a Focus of Infection", Boston Medical and Surgical Journal, Vol 176, No 22, 1917, p 766.
76. Bartle, op cit, p 64.
77. Lucas, op cit, p 660.
78. Woolley, P.G.: "Intestinal Stasis and Intestinal Intoxications: A Critical Review", Journal of Laboratory and Clinical Medicine, Vol 1, 1915–1916, p 50.
79. Guyton, op cit, p 897.
80. Synnott, M.J.: "Intestinal Toxemia, Its Diagnosis and Treatment", Medical Journal and Record, Vol 136, No 11, 1932, p 144.
81. Warwick, R. and Williams, P.L.: Gray's Anatomy, 35th British ed, W.B. Saunders Company, Philadelpha, 1973, p 588.
82. Bartle, op cit, p 387.
83. Haubold, op cit, p 859.
84. Bassler, A: Intestinal Toxemia Biologically Considered, F.A. Davis Company, Philadelphia, 1930.
85. Lintz, W.L.: "Gastrointestinal Allergy", The Review of Gastroenterology, Vol 6, 1939, p 321.
86. Lintz, ibid, pp 320–332.
87. Eustis, A.: "Furthe Evidence in Support of the Toxic Pathogenesis of Bronchial Asthma, Based upon Experimental Research", American Journal of Medical Science, Vol 143, 1912, p 863.
88. Rochester, D.: "The Treatment of Asthma", Journal of the Amercian Medical Association, Vol 47, No 24, 1906, p 1984.
89. Bassler, A.: "The Colon in Connection with Chronic Arthritis (Arthritis Deformans)," American Journal of Medical Science, Vol 160, 1920, p 357.
90. Bassler, A.: "Aging, Arteriosclerosis, and Cardiac Conditions", Medical Record, Vol 153, Jan 1, 1941, p 21.
91. Lane, W.A.: "Consequences and Treatment From a Surgical Point of View," British Medical Journal, Vol 1, March 15, 1913, p 547.
92. Lucas, op cit, p 661.
93. Guyton, op cit, p 213.
94. Bassler, A.: "Coronary Disease and the Intestine", Medicinal Record, Vol 155, April 1, 1942, p 249.
95. Bainbridge, W.S.: "The Constitutional Effect of Prolonged Intestinal Toxemia", Medical Journal and Record, Vol 122, No 8, 1925, p 438.
96. Barry, D.T.: "Intestinal Toxins and the Circulation", The Lancet, Vol 2, July 1, 1916, p 15.
97. Hovell, T.M.: "Gastro–intestinal Sepsis, a Cause of Meniere's Symptoms", Proceedings of the Royal Society of Medicine, Vol 11, No 3, 1918, p 16.
98. Stucky, J.A.: "Intestinal Autointoxication as a Factor in the Causation of Pathologic Conditions of the Ear, Nose and Throat", Journal of the American Medical Association, Vol 53, No 15, 1909, p 1185.
99. Hovell, op cit, pp 15–18.
100. Gatewood, W.L.: "Symptoms of Gastrointestinal Origin in the Ear, Nose and Throat", Archives of Otolaryngology, Vol, 33, 1941, pp 592–598.
101. Hawley, C.W.: "Autointoxication and Eye Diseases", Ophthalmology, Vol 10, No 4, 1914, pp 663–674.

102. Reveno, W.S.: "The Cause of Exophthalmic Goiter", Archives of Internal Medicine, Vol 48, Oct 1931, p 597.
103. Eustis, A.: "Some Interesting Observations on Goiter", New Orleans Medical and Science Journal, Vol 85, June 1933, pp 892–898.
104. Lane, W.A.: "Chronic Intestinal Stasis", Journal of Surgery, Gynecology and Obstetrics, Vol 16, 1913, p 602.
105. Von Noorden, C.: "Intoxication Proceedings From the Intestine, Especially Polyneuritis", Journal of the American Medical Association, Vol 60, No 2, 1913, p 104.
106. Von Noorden, ibid, p 105.
107. Herter, C.A. and Smith, E.E.: "Researchers upon the Etiology of Idiopathic Epilepsy", NY Medical Journal, Vol 56, 1892, pp 208–211, 234–239, 260–266.
108. Satterlee, G.R. and Eldridge, W.W.: "Symptomatology of the Nervous System in Chronic Intestinal Toxemia", Journal of the American Medical Association, Vol 69, No 17, 1917, pp 1414–1418.
109. Haubold, op cit, pp 857–861.
110. Satterlee, op cit, p 1414.
111. Satterlee, ibid, p 1417.
112. Bainbridge, op cit, pp 437–443.
113. Nascher, I.L.: "Lane's Autointoxication Complex and the Manifestations of Senility", NY Medical Journal, Vol 100, No 6, 1914, p 256.
114. Osgood, R.B.: "Etiologic Factors in Certain Cases of So–Called Sciatic Scoliosis", Journal of Bone and Joint Surgery, Vol 9, Oct 1927, pp 667–676.
115. Von Noorden, op cit, p 103.
116. Schwartz, H.J.: "Association of Intestinal Indigestion with Various Dermatoses", Archives of Dermatology and Syphilology, Vol 13, 1926, p 674.
117. Burgess, J.F.: "Endogenous Irritants as Factors in Eczema and in Other Dermatoses", Archives of Dermatology and Syphilology, Vol 16, No 2, 1927, p 139.
118. Galloway, J.: "Cutaneous Indications of Alimentary Toxaemia", British Medical Journal, Vol 1, April 19, 1913, pp 815–817.
119. Bartle, op cit, p 28.
120. Lane, W.A.: "Consequences and Treatment from a Surgical Point of View", British Medical Journal, Vol 1, March 15, 1913, p 547.
121. Lane, W.A.: "Chronic Intestinal Stasis", Journal of Surgery, Gynecology and Obstetrics, Vol 16, 1913, p 601.
122. Bainbridge, op cit, p 443.
123. Prehn, R.T.: "A Clonal Selection Theory of Chemical Carcinogenesis", Journal of National Cancer Institute, Vol 32, No 1, Jan 1964, p 1.
124. Satterlee, G.R.: "Autogenous Colon Vaccines in the Study, Diagnosis and Therapy of Chronic Intestinal Toxemia", Journal of American Medical Association, Vol 67, No 24, 1916, p 1731.
125. Bartle, op cit, p 448.
126. Goodhart, R.S. and Shils, M.E.: Modern Nutrition in Health and Disease, 5th ed, Lea and Febiger, Philadelphia, 1973, p 30.
127. Hegsted, D.M.: "Minimum Protein Requirements of Adults", American Journal of Clinical Nutrition, Vol 21, No 5, May 1968, pp 352–357.
128. Turck, F.B.: "Intestinal Venous Stasis: Diffusion of Bacteria and Other Colloids", Boston Medical and Surgical Journal, Vol 176, No 19, 1917, p 665.
129. Soper, H.W.: "Autointoxication in Chronic Constipation", Journal of the American Medical Assocation, Vol 69, No 18, 1917, p 1512.
130. Bartle, op cit, p 447.
131. Stucky, op cit, p 1186.
132. Synnott, op cit, p 444.
133. Saundby, R.: "Alimentary Toxemia: Its Symptoms and Treatment", British Medical Journal, Vol 1, March 15, 1913, p 545.
134. Dublin, op cit, p 91.
135. Gerard, R.W.: "The Lethal Agent in Acute Intestinal Obstruction", Journal of American Medical Association, Vol 79, No 19, 1922, p 1583.
136. Sherwin, C.P. and Hawk, P.B.: "Fasting Studies: VII. The Putrefaction Processes in the

Intestine of a Man During Fasting and During Subsequent Periods of Low and High Protein Ingestion", Journal of Biological Chemistry, Vol 11, No 3, 1912, p 177.
137. Fitch, W.E.: "Putrefactive Intestinal Toxemia", Medical Journal and Record, Vol 132, Aug 2, 1930, p 186.
138. Bainbridge, op cit, p 440.
139. Soper, H.W.: "Autointoxication in Chronic Constipation", Journal of the Amercian Medical Association, Vol 69, No 18, 1917, p 1512.
140. Bassler, A.: "Chronic Intestinal Toxemia", Medical Record, Vol 145, 1937, p 159.
141. Fordtran, J.S. Scroggie, W.B., and Polter, D.E.: "Colonic absorption to tryptophan metabolites in man", J Lab and Clin Med, Vol 64, 1964, p 125–132.
142. Bakke, O.M.: "Urinary simple phenols in rats fed purified and nonpurified diets", J Nutr, Vol 98, 1969, p 209.
143. Folin, op cit, p 309.
144. Bakke, O.M.: "Urinary simple phenols in rats fed diets containing different amounts of casein and 10% tyrosine", J Nutr, Vol 98, 1969, pp 217–221.
145. Aarbakke, J. and Schjonsby, H.: "Value of urinary simple phenol and indican determinations in the diagnosis of the stagnant loop syndrome", Scand J Gastroent, Vol 11, 1976, pp 409–414.
146. Tomkin, G.H. and Weir, D.G.: Quart J Med, Vol 41, 1972, pp 191–203.
147. Fordtran, et al, op cit.
148. Neale, G., Lambert, R.A., and Gorbach, S.L.: "The production of indole by bacteria in vitro", Gut, Vol 10, 1969, pp 1056–1057.
149. Happold, F.C.: "Tryptophanase–tryptophan reaction", Advances in Enzymology, Vol 10, 1950, p 51.
150. Donaldson, R.M., Jr.: "Malabsorption of Co60–Labeled Cyanocobalamin in Rats with Intestinal Diveticula. I. Evaluation of Possible Mechanisms", Gastroenterology, Vol 43, 1962, p 271.
151. Robbins, op cit, p 55.
152. Thorn, G.W., Adams, R.D., Braunwald, E., Esselbacher, K.J., Petersdorf, R.G.: Harrison's Principles in Internal Medicine, 8th ed, McGraw–Hill Book Co, New York, NY, 1977, p 715.
153. Thorn, ibid, p 1606.
154. Thorn, obid, p 1909.
155. Tabaqchali, S., Scand J Gastroent. 1970 Suppl, Vol 6, pp 139–163.
156. Bakke, O.M., Scand J Gastroent, Vol 4, 1969, pp 603–608.
157. Alam, S.Q., Boctor, A.M., Rogers, Q.R., and Harper, A.E.: "Some effects of amino acids and cortisol on tyrosine toxicity in the rat", J Nutr, Vol 93, 1967, p 317.
158. Bakke, O.M.: "Urinary simple phenols in rats fed diets containing different amounts of casein and 10% tyrosine", J Nutr, Vol 98, 1969, pp 217–221.
159. Horning, E.C., and Dalgliesh, C.E.: "The association of skatole–forming bacteria in the small intestine with the malabsorbtion syndrome and certain anemias", Biochem J, Vol 70, 1958, p 13.
160. Izquierdo, J.A., and Stoppani, A.D.M.: "Inhibition of smooth muscle contractility by indole and some indole compounds", Brit J Pharmacol, Vol 8, 1953, pp 389–394.
161. Proctor, M.H.: "'Bacterial dissimilation of indoleacetic acid: a new route of breakdown of the indole nucleus", Nature, Vol 181, 1858, p 1345.
162. Horning, E.C. and Dalgliesh, C.E.: "The association of skatole–forming bacteria in the small intestine with the malabsorbtion syndrome and certain anemias", Biochemical J, Vol 70, 1958, p 13.
163. Sprince, H.: "Biochemical aspects of indole metabolism in normal and schizophrenic subjects", Annals New York Academy of Sciences, Vol 96, 1962, pp 399–418.
164. Dalgliesch, C.E., Kelly, W., and Horning, E.C.: "Excretion of a sulphatoxy derivative of skatole in pathological states in man", Biochemical J, Vol 70, 1958, p 13.
165. Horning, E.C., Sweeley, C.C., and Kelley, W.: "mammalian hydroxylation in the 6–position of the indole ring", Biochem Biophys Acta, Vol 32, 1959, pp 566–567.

SURVIVAL INTO THE 21ST CENTURY

by
VIKTORAS KULVINSKAS

Introduction by Dick Gregory
Cover by Peter Max
Illustrations by Jean White

includes a complete program of
WHEATGRASS THERAPY

Learn:
— how to transform your body and restore its youth at any age through the vitalizing energies in SPROUTS and GRASSES

— how to heal yourself of the whole spectrum of degenerative diseases — from cancer to arthritis, from heart disease to the common cold — by the use of LIVING FOODS

— how to grow completely organic, nutritious, and delicious salad GREENS, SPROUTS AND GRASSES indoors in only seven days for as little as 20 cents per pound

— how to experience the esoteric realities.— the BLISS of the Universe, the Energy of DIVINE LOVE, as proclaimed by the Ancient Masters, by means of YOGA and MEDITATION

— how to attain the vibrant HEALTH, perpetual YOUTH, and ecstasy of LOVE which are your BIRTHRIGHT.

320 pages, with full color illustrations;
revised and expanded in 1981..................................$12.95

THE NEW AGE DIRECTORY
WHOLISTIC HEALTH GUIDE

by
VIKTORAS KULVINSKAS

— includes over 3700 entries in 45 categories

— each entry is cross—indexed by subject, key word, state, and alphabet for easy reference

— complete listings of vegetarian organizations, cancer cure clinics, holistic M.D.'s, spiritual communities, naturopaths, health resorts, and many more

— the most complete, definitive guide to natural healing and alternative lifestyles available

1981 Edition, 340 pages **$4.95**

---

available from
OMANGOD PRESS P.O. Box 64, Woodstock Valley, Ct. 06282.

Our 52 page catalog, complete with excerpts from and reviews of books, nutritional information, recipes, indoor gardening instructions, and much more, is available for $1 to cover postage and handling costs.